# DATE DUE

| | | | |
|---|---|---|---|
| | | | |
| | | | |
| | | | |
| | | | |
| | | | |
| | | | |
| | | | |
| | | | |
| | | | |
| | | | |
| | | | |
| | | | |
| | | | |
| | | | |
| | | | |
| | | | |
| | | | |

DEMCO 38-296

OPERA BIOGRAPHY SERIES, No. 7

*Series Editors*
Andrew Farkas
William R. Moran

*Frontispiece*: Jussi Björling, Florence, 1943. Photo Schemboche.

# *Jussi*

by

## Anna-Lisa Björling and Andrew Farkas

### Chronology by Harald Henrysson

AMADEUS PRESS
Reinhard G. Pauly, General Editor
*Portland, Oregon*

ISBN 1-57467-010-7

Printed in Singapore

AMADEUS PRESS
(an imprint of Timber Press, Inc.)
The Haseltine Building
133 S.W. Second Avenue, Suite 450
Portland, Oregon 97204, U.S.A.

Library of Congress Cataloging-in-Publication Data

Björling, Anna-Lisa.
    Jussi / by Anna-Lisa Björling and Andrew Farkas; chronology by Harald
Henrysson.
        p.    cm.—(Opera biography series; no. 7)
    Includes bibliographical references (p.    ) and index.
    ISBN 1-57467-010-7
    1. Björling, Jussi, 1911–1960. 2. Tenors (Singers)—Biography. I. Farkas,
Andrew. II. Title. III. Series.
ML420.B6B48    1996
782.1′092—dc20
    [B]                                                                95-50104
                                                                           CIP
                                                                            MN

To my children
and
Jussi's fans

# CONTENTS

Contents

*Photographs follow pages 48, 144, 176, and 336*

# PREFACE

In the years that have passed since Jussi's death in 1960, I have often been asked to write a book about him. Although I never had any writing ambitions, I accepted long ago that I am an inescapable candidate for Jussi's biographer; after all, my life and his intertwined for three decades, both onstage and off, through much happiness and trouble, many joys and sorrows—perhaps more of each than we deserved. For a long while I felt unable to relive the memory of those years. Rather than attempt a book, I thought it wiser to let time heal my great sense of loss.

With the passing years Jussi's many admirers prevailed, and at the urging of my children and grandchildren I wrote a very personal account of my recollections of the life we shared—*Mitt liv med Jussi*, my life with Jussi. The book was well received in Sweden, but it didn't satisfy Jussi's many fans worldwide; it became clear that nothing less than an English-language biography was expected of me, and on a scale much broader than my first attempt. As an eyewitness to Jussi's entire adult career and a partner in the highs and the lows of his private life, I came to realize that to relate the life story of Jussi Björling was more than yielding to his public's interest or curiosity—it was an obligation.

The extensive international research that this book necessitated turned up many forgotten facts and fresh details. They prompted my memory and enabled me to correct some longstanding mistakes and misconceptions about Jussi's life. The passage of time has given us a near-historical perspective about the man and artist. It made it easier for me to be objective about his sterling qualities and human failings, without being boastful of his greatness or ashamed of his shortcomings.

I have treated with complete candor the less savory aspects of Jussi's personality, and the reader may be surprised at times at the blemishes that appear in this biographical portrait. My collaborator, Andrew Farkas, and I agreed that to withhold any information would impair the credibility of our efforts and allow speculation and conjecture, or worse, invite distortion and fabrication about his life. Jussi deserves to be shown as he was: an immensely gifted singer, a conscientious artist, a loving husband and father, and a kind and good man caught up in a lifelong struggle with a disease—alcoholism—that he could contain at times but was unable to conquer.

Although I have told Jussi's story from a first-person vantage point, the narrative is not exclusively mine; rather, this book is the product of a collaboration with my children and Jussi's friends, colleagues, and admirers. The content of each chapter was painstakingly collected, verified, organized, and substantially augmented by Andrew Farkas, who repeatedly read, revised, and edited the manuscript in consultation with my children and me; with Harald Henrysson, the leading expert of the Björling career and curator of the Jussi Björling Museum; and with Bertil Bengtsson, president of the Swedish Jussi Björling Society.

Collectively, we have tried to convey Jussi's innate talent, warm humanity, and inner conflicts. I hope we have succeeded to inspire not only the respect and admiration but the compassion and understanding that Jussi Björling deserves.

Anna-Lisa Björling

# ACKNOWLEDGMENTS

First among the many individuals who so generously volunteered their assistance for this project, I want to express my deep appreciation to every member of Jussi Björling's family. Their kindness, candor, linguistic and research assistance, and unwavering commitment made this biography possible. Their invaluable help, along with the contribution of Jussi's former colleagues and associates, enriched this narrative of his life in many important ways.

Nearly all those whom I approached for information were glad to respond and did so with enthusiasm and reverence for the memory of a great artist. Many wrote letters, some responded by phone or fax, and others granted interviews or received me in their homes. The attitude of most can be summed up in Robert Merrill's reaction to my request for a visit: "For Jussi—anything!"

In addition to those who knew or worked with Jussi Björling, I received extensive help from friends and acquaintances, writers and researchers, librarians and archivists, collectors and music lovers. They helped with source material, translations, interpretation, research, typing, documents, and photographs. Trying to detail at length their courtesy, support, generous devotion of time and effort, and the precise nature of their significant contribution would add several pages to this book. Unable to do so, I want to gratefully recognize the following individuals for their invaluable help: Leif

Acknowledgments

Aare (Stockholm); Barbro Åkesson (Jacksonville, Fla.); Licia Albanese
(New York City); Lorenzo Alvary (New York City); Eduardo Arnosi
(Buenos Aires); William Ashbrook (Terre Haute, Ind.); Rose Bampton
(Bryn Mawr, Pa.); Fedora Barbieri (Florence); Byron Belt (San Francisco);
Bertil Bengtsson (Gothenburg, Sweden); Count Carl Johan Bernadotte
(Båstad, Sweden); Kurt Binar (San Francisco); Anders and Janet Björling
(St. Peter, Minn.); Ann-Charlotte Björling (Stockholm); Lars Björling
(Stockholm); Märta Björling-Kärn (Mora, Sweden); Maestro Bertil Bok-
stedt (Stockholm); Eileen Brady (Jacksonville, Fla.); Ernesto Breviario
(KwaZulu, NATAL); Dr. Bergljot Krohn Bucht (Stockholm); Bruce Bur-
roughs (Los Angeles); Rosanna Grosoli Carteri (Monte Carlo); Schuyler
Chapin (New York City); Boris and Franca Christoff (Milan); Kathleen F.
Cohen (Jacksonville, Fla.); Joseph Colley (Bebington, England); Anselmo
Colzani (Milan); Dr. John Cone (Highlands, N.J.); Dr. Richard Copeman
(London); Irene Dalis (San José, Calif.); Dr. Ronald L. Davis (Dallas); Con-
nie DeCaro (New York City); Dr. Hugh Davidson (New York City); Dr.
James A. Drake (Cocoa Beach, Fla.); Juan Dzazopulos (Santiago); Carl
Edwards (New York City); Maestro Sixten Ehrling (New York City); Len-
nart Ekman (Stockholm); Her Majesty Queen Elizabeth, the Queen Mother
(Clarence House, London); Regina Fiorito (New York City); Andrew Foldi
(Chicago); Gino Francesconi (New York City); Nicolai Gedda (Stockholm);
Barbara R. Geisler (San Francisco); Roger Gross (New York City); Marit
Gruson (New York City); Rina Gigli (Recanati, Italy); Enrique Gilardoni
(Santiago); Cantor Don Goldberg (Merrick, N.Y.); Michael Gray (Alexan-
dria, Va.); Dr. Örjan Grimås (Stockholm); John Gualiani (Milan); Bertil
Hagman (Stockholm); Diane Haskell (Chicago); Hugo Hasslo (Stockholm);
Harald Henrysson (Säter, Sweden); Vicki Hillebrand (Pacific Palisades,
Calif.); Alfred Hubay (New York City); Sture Ingebretzen (Stockholm);
Jane Jackson (London); George Jellinek (New York City); Nathaniel John-
son (New York City); Bosse Kärn, Margareta Kärn, and Kerstin Kärn (Orsa,
Sweden); Thomas G. Kaufman (Boonton, N.J.); Alan Kayes (Water Mill,
N.Y.); Dorothy Kirsten (Pacific Palisades, Calif.); Bruce T. Latimer (Jack-
sonville, Fla.); Cornell MacNeil (Charlottesville, Va.); Ann McIntire (San
Francisco); Robert Merrill (New Rochelle, N.Y.); Kerstin Meyer (Stock-
holm); Anna Moffo (New York City); Richard Mohr (New York City); Wil-
liam R. Moran (La Cañada, Calif.); Barry Morell (Denver, N.Y.); Dr. Robert
Morrison (Hawthorne, Fla.); Danny Newman (Chicago); Birgit Nilsson
(Kristianstad, Sweden); Jarmila Novotná (New York City); Dr. Reinhard G.
Pauly (Portland, Ore.); John Pennino (New York City); Sarah Philips (Jack-
sonville, Fla.); Claudia Pinza (Pittsburgh); Andrew S. Pope (Bowie, MD);
Salvatore Randazzo (New York City); Nell Rankin (New York City); Frank
Ré (New York City); Regina Resnik (New York City); Terry Robinson (Los
Angeles); Bidú Sayão (Lincolnville, Maine); Hjördis Schymberg (Stock-
holm); William Seward (New York City); Cesare Siepi (Atlanta); Paolo Sil-
veri (Rome); Giulietta Simionato (Milan); Erik Smith (Somerset, England);

12

Otniel Sobek (Buenos Aires); Elisabeth Söderström (Stockholm); Harold Sokolsky (Burlington, N.J.); Maestro Sir Georg Solti (London); Risë Stevens (New York City); Mrs. M. Swart (KwaZulu, NATAL); Italo Tajo (Cincinnati); Renata Tebaldi (Milan); Blanche Thebom (San Francisco); Jim Thompson (Greenwich, Conn.); Richard Tibbett (Bishop, Calif.); Giorgio Tozzi (Bloomington, Ind.); Robert Tuggle (New York City); Giuseppe Valdengo (Saint-Vincent, Italy); Astrid Varnay (Munich); Nelly Walter (New York City); Bert Wechsler (New York City); Albert White (New York City); Sallie Wilson (New York City); Sarah Zelzer (Chicago); and Dr. Adrian Zorgniotti (New York City).

Rather than summarize or paraphrase what these individuals had to offer, the original text of an interview, letter, or published reminiscence was allowed to stand whenever it was deemed preferable. Admittedly, a straightforward narrative would have resulted in more even, better flowing prose, but Mrs. Björling and I felt that recasting a singer or conductor's recollections, a critic or reporter's judgment, an opera manager or agent's business correspondence would have diminished the impact and immediacy of their statements. Thus we consciously sacrificed unity of style, allowing Jussi's life story to be told by many voices, and we hope that readers will concur with the validity of this decision. It also bears mentioning that the absence of a discography has been intentional: Harald Henrysson's *A Jussi Björling Phonography*, distributed by Amadeus Press, was prepared as a companion volume to the present work.

The following organizations and institutions also deserve thanks: Drottningholm Theater Archive (Stockholm); Jussi Björling Museum (Borlänge); Metropolitan Opera Archives (New York); Newberry Library (Chicago); Royal Opera Archives and Collections (Stockholm); Royal Opera House, Covent Garden (London); San Francisco Performing Arts Library and Museum; Országos Széchenyi Könyvtár (Budapest); and Thomas G. Carpenter Library, University of North Florida (Jacksonville).

Finally, a special note of thanks is due to Franni Farrell of Amadeus Press. Her excellent sense of style and proportion helped the manuscript achieve a greater unity and flow, and her capable editorial hand, invisible to the reader, improved this book in many ways. I am happy to record my boundless gratitude for her contribution.

In the course of this multi-year project, I faithfully kept track of every contributor. If, by chance, a name or group has been inadvertently omitted, I beg understanding and forgiveness for the oversight.

Andrew Farkas
Jacksonville, Florida

# Da Fine al Capo

It was still dark when I awakened, sensing something was wrong. I looked at the clock on the nightstand; its illuminated dial read almost 4 a.m. The bedroom on the second floor of our summer home was filled with the grayish light of dawn. I could barely see the contours of the furniture, or make out the square outline of the window.

It was 9 September 1960; autumn was approaching, and the nights had grown longer. The radiators had to be turned on at night, and the windows were misted with moisture. Jussi and I usually weren't on Siarö[1] so late in the season, but this year the house was undergoing the remodeling we had so much looked forward to and we wanted to stay as long as possible to oversee the work.

The house in Stockholm's archipelago had been our summer refuge for nearly 20 years. It was the place Jussi loved most—but we were seldom alone there, just the two of us. Our children were always with us, and many visitors and guests from Stockholm or abroad came and went—accompanists, coaches, friends, and acquaintances. My mother, Emy, too joined us for at least part of every summer. Mother and I were as close as any two people could be. After my father's death in 1939, she made it her mission in life to care for our home and our three children during our constant travels. She shared my happiness over Jussi's rapid rise to the top, his many subsequent successes—and my many dark moments of anxiety for him. In times of trial she was my foundation, my rock, my source of strength and security.

She wasn't there that morning. She had returned to Stockholm with our

15

daughter, Ann-Charlotte, now a young lady of 17, who had begun the school term two weeks earlier. Anders, our eldest, was vacationing in Dalarna with his American wife, Janet. And Lars, who was to begin classes at the Stockholm School of Economics, was interning at a bank in Paris. So it was just the two of us, Jussi and I—and Bongo, of course, the little black poodle Jussi had received as a farewell gift six years earlier after his concert tour of South Africa.

I was grateful to be there, both for my sake and for Jussi's, for each day on Siarö allowed us a bit more time to relax and gather strength before the long tour ahead. Jussi needed all the relaxation and rest he could get. His heart had been bothering him, and he routinely took pills from a little box he carried in his pocket. His doctor, who didn't seem to be alarmed by Jussi's increasing shortness of breath, gave him prescriptions and made only vague statements about "palpitations and fibrillations," adding the usual caution to "try to take it easy and avoid stress."

Jussi had been told to lose weight, but a very strict diet a couple of years earlier had only worsened his heart. In May 1959, he finished his traditional annual concert at Skansen with great difficulty; for once, encores were absolutely out of the question. The next warnings came in August, when two episodes of heart fibrillations followed in quick succession. The first hit Jussi at Bromma Airport just before his departure for a concert at Liseberg in Gothenburg. The concert had to be canceled. That time I was able to care for him at home, but 14 days later another episode occurred, this one so serious that Jussi was hospitalized for a week. Soon after, in September, he had an attack of fibrillations during a recording session of *Madama Butterfly* in Rome. The recording had to be delayed a few days until Jussi was able to continue.

I was worried, but Jussi always seemed to bounce back quickly. Besides, his doctor maintained that he wasn't in any danger. But in March 1960, before a performance of *La bohème* at Covent Garden, with the Queen Mother in the royal box, he suffered a mild heart attack. Despite a doctor's warning, Jussi went on and finished the performance. Had I been there, I'd have made every effort to prevent him from singing. But I was in Sweden with my mother, who was very ill, and while I was caring for her, Jussi traveled alone.

Three weeks later, at a recital in Pasadena, California, it happened again. This time I was there, but the discomfort passed relatively quickly and Jussi insisted on singing his program despite my protestations. The five months since, although emotionally and physically draining for Jussi, had passed without incident. I was hoping that his heart had stabilized and that with rest he would regain his strength.

Thinking back, it seems unbelievable that neither Jussi's doctor nor any of us reacted to these warnings with genuine alarm. No one in the family understood—perhaps didn't want to understand—how serious his condition was. We didn't know that Jussi suffered from an enlarged heart, a so-called

16

athlete's heart; this we learned only later. To sing as Jussi sang and to maintain the schedule he did was as physically demanding as running a marathon. Did he know what was happening to him? If he did, he kept it to himself.

Jussi was very close to his younger brother, Gösta; only two years apart, the brothers were like twins and since childhood had called each other *Boren*, Swedish for brother. When Gösta died unexpectedly in 1957, Jussi took it very hard. Some time later we visited his grave in the cemetery of Stora Tuna Church in Dalarna. Jussi, terribly distressed, stood silently for a moment. "Yes, Boren," he said quietly, "I'll follow soon." He looked so sad standing there. He meant what he said.

"You mustn't say that!" I cried. Perhaps I thought unconsciously that something tragic could be prevented merely by our not speaking of it. I pushed it aside, refused to hear it. But now I regret that I didn't insist Jussi tell me what he may have sensed about his illness.

Anders too remembers that his father intimated that he didn't expect to live to an old age. "I don't know how much longer I'll last," Jussi would remark, vowing that once he felt his decline had begun, he'd stop singing. "I probably won't be around by then anyway," he'd add morbidly. "Don't say that, Dad!" Anders would beg him.

But these scattered warnings *had* made us realize that it was time to start limiting his engagements. At 49 years old, Jussi still retained much of the youthful lyrical timbre in his voice, mainly because he had stubbornly resisted singing heavier, more dramatic roles. He never accepted a part not fully within his capabilities, thus sparing himself the criticism that he didn't have the power and range the role required—and preserving the brilliant sparkle of his high notes. But now, having reached the maturity needed to portray them dramatically, the time was right for Otello and Lohengrin, two roles he'd long dreamt of but hadn't felt ready to take on. Having thus crowned his career, he'd cut back on the strenuous tours, take it easier, and maybe even retire for good. Perhaps in a few years; it was too early yet, he still had much to give. Besides, another extensive trip lay before us.

The tour as originally planned would've taken us to South America, South Africa, Japan, and Australia—Jussi's first worldwide tour. Along the way he would've performed at the Metropolitan Opera in New York, followed by several concerts in North America. We wanted very much to see Australia, and Japan was on the way there, but with Jussi's health problems, we asked that the tour be shortened. To our agent's distress, we eliminated both South Africa and South America from the itinerary.

Soon we would return to the city to pack and make arrangements for this long trip, but there was still some time to enjoy the end of Swedish summer at our archipelago paradise. We had celebrated our silver wedding anniversary in June, and during our years together I had learned Jussi was more complex than his fans could imagine. Most of all he was a warm-hearted, spontaneous, and infinitely generous person, deriving a childlike happiness from surprising someone with an unexpected—and often very expensive—

gift. He was cheerful, funny, and had a fine sense of humor. He also had a certain innate shyness not uncommon among Swedes—and in his outlook, thought processes, behavior, manners, and most of all, his loyalties, Jussi was Swedish to the core.

But the private Jussi Björling had another, darker side. He could be introverted to the point of being unreachable; a great loneliness lay deep inside him, no doubt stemming from his childhood and his difficult formative years. He had an inner restlessness that seemed to be woven into the fibers of his character. When it emerged, he tried to drown it with alcohol. Many times it was almost impossible to help him, even to stay with him. Life became so hard that, at times, I reached the edge of despair and even contemplated leaving him. But an existence without Jussi, even in the worst of times, was inconceivable to me. For more than a quarter century my life had revolved around him. We were attached, helplessly and uncontrollably dependent on each other.

The last of our restful days was calm and quiet, with the deep blue waters of the bay glittering in the still-warm sunshine. Jussi was a little tired, yet happy and relaxed as he almost always was at Siarö, helping the carpenters pull nails from the boards they removed from the second story of the house, to be reused later in the remodeling. I was always gratified to see him enjoying himself like that. As I watched him, fighting the nails in the time-hardened boards, I was overwhelmed with an awareness of all he had given me, the life we had shared, the life we believed we'd always be sharing. "Just think what a fine and modern place this is going to be," I said to him, "and all this because of your singing!"

Jussi stopped his work and took my hand. "Yes, of course," he said. "This is where we will grow old together."

After supper, Jussi made his way upstairs. Before going to bed, he telephoned Ann-Charlotte in Stockholm. "Hello, my dear. I'm just calling to say good night to you." Ann-Charlotte was surprised; it wasn't like him.[2] But I wasn't ready for bed yet. I was filled with such enthusiasm about how fresh-looking everything appeared that I wanted to stay awake a little longer, just to walk around and enjoy it. I turned on a lamp and went out on the terrace to see how the lit-up room looked from outside.

Jussi called from the top of the stairs, "Mama, aren't you coming up?" "Yes, I'm coming soon!" I called back. But when I finally crawled into bed, Jussi was already asleep. Bongo stirred in his bedside basket, where he spent every night, and then he too was asleep. It was very quiet—not even a whisper from the evening breeze rustled the birch trees outside our windows.

I don't know what startled me at dawn. I sat up in bed, turned on the light, looked at the clock. Then I glanced at Jussi. My eyes saw something that my mind could neither comprehend nor accept. I didn't let it reach me; as the minutes passed, I wouldn't let it reach me. I refused to accept the unacceptable.

Jussi was dead.

# Chapter 1

# THE BERGS

As a child, I found it unimaginable that some people lived without music. In my parents' home, it would've been unthinkable. My father, John Berg, the parish clerk in the Palace Congregation in Gamla stan, Stockholm's Old Town, was a musician, an oboist in the Royal Opera Orchestra. During the day he rehearsed all his solos and the more difficult passages for the evening's performance. The sound of the oboe in our apartment was inescapable; everything we said and did was to the background music of the oboe. Naturally, the din seemed worst when I was supposed to be studying and longed for quiet, but no matter: Papa was my childhood idol, the best, kindest, and most handsome father anyone could have. Gentle and outgoing, he looked stately with his neatly trimmed mustache, and he always had a gleam in his eye. That gleam, I later realized, was something many women found hard to resist.

My father would himself carve his oboe's two reeds with a watchmaker's accuracy, holding his breath while working on a marble slab at the dining room table. The reeds, Papa said, were the stalks from a tall grass that grew only in southern Spain and Sicily; he kept a ready supply of this important raw material in a large tin box. It took forever to carve the reeds—that much was obvious to me by the look of concentration on my father's face while he worked away with his knife. When he finally finished, he'd tie the two reeds together with a red silk thread, leaving a tiny space between them, and insert them into the oboe to test the results.

I was born on 15 March 1910. After I turned six, Papa used to take me to the Opera whenever a performance appropriate for children was scheduled. Off we went, hand in hand, from our home on Odengatan 33 in Vasastan. Sometimes we took the trolley, but when it wasn't raining or too cold, we walked all the way to the theater. In the midst of World War I, automobile traffic was almost nonexistent. Some of Stockholm's streets were still lined with ornate cast-iron gaslights, which gave off a much softer glow than today's harsh electric lights. Outside the Opera on a misty evening, a golden halo encircled each one. Across the Strömmen channel the quivering lights from the Palace windows were mirrored in the fast-flowing dark water. The whole scene had an enchanting radiance that only increased my anticipation of the wondrous world awaiting me inside.

By the time the clock at St. Jacob's Church struck half past seven, we were usually at the stage door. I trotted behind Papa down the spiral staircase to the orchestra pit, holding his hand as he squeezed his way through the chairs to his place with the woodwind section. Papa looked extremely stylish in his tails, I thought, almost as nice as when he wore the light blue uniform with the brass buttons, epaulets, and striped pants of the Svea Lifeguards Band. Standing on a stool beside him, my nose reached just high enough to see over the ramp to the other side of the orchestra pit. Arne Henriksson, the son of one of the French horn players, about my age, stood next to me. We had to be careful not to be seen above the velvet-covered railing that separated us from the audience. Just a few yards in front of us was the enormous curtain, painted with stiff, imitation velvet folds in crimson and gold. All around the musicians were tuning their instruments, and behind us was the hum of the audience. Then a sudden silence and the customary applause welcoming the conductor.

High above, the enormous crystal chandelier dimmed, the curtain lifted—and Arne and I were transported to a dazzling fairyland. As it was for many other children, my first opera was *Peterchens Mondfahrt* (*Little Peter's Trip to the Moon*), a wonderful drama that has since vanished from the repertoire. It was also my introduction to the sound of a full orchestra, and to me the roar in the pit was deafening. It left us almost staggering by the time intermission came. Papa, immensely proud of his daughter, took me by the hand and led me backstage to greet the singers—or, rather, to show me off to them. Eventually, I saw *Hänsel und Gretel*, *The Värmlanders*, *Der Freischütz*, *Carmen*, and many others. But Puccini's *Madama Butterfly* affected me like no other. Not only did Cio-cio-san's tragic love invariably reduce me to tears but the visual spectacle it afforded was extraordinary— the shimmering kimonos, fluttering fans, and all the silk and glitter on the stage.

When Papa came home after a performance, Mother was often sewing despite the late hour. She made most of my clothes and those of my brother Olle, two years older than I. During the daytime, my maternal grandmother took care of us while my mother worked in her studio.

My mother, Emy Sörman Berg, was a portrait photographer. Our apartment, the studio next door, and my grandparents' apartment were on the same floor. It was a practical arrangement; Mother never needed to worry about Olle and me, and we had both her and Grandma Emma nearby. Grandma was also a working woman; she owned a delicatessen. "Emma Sörman's Homemade Food" stood in large white enamel letters right across the window of her store in Vasastan.

Thanks to my mother's photographic work, we could afford more than what Papa's small income would've allowed us. For a while Mother's business was so successful that she maintained two studios and had to hire an assistant. In addition to wedding pictures and naked babies posed on sheepskins, her largest orders were for small photographs, dozens at a time, to be given away at Christmas to relatives and friends. Before Christmas, Mother had so much to do that Olle and I helped out as soon as we were able.

For a time, it was popular to have a light, tinted background on the photographs. Papa was very artistic—he had studied at Carl Wilhelmson's Art School—and for a while he shared a small studio in Gamla stan with another artist, Justus Bergman, Ingrid Bergman's father, where he did some painting. It was Papa's job to tint the background of Mother's photographs; he would dab the prints with a cotton ball dipped in lead powder to give the picture an ethereal quality.

Mother resembled Princess Ingeborg of Denmark; she was tall and slender with thick, chestnut-brown hair and dreamy, deep-set, heavy-lidded eyes. She was more serious than Papa and seemed more weighed down by everyday worries. She, too, was musical and played the piano well. Olle played the violin, and when I started school, I began taking my first piano lessons. We didn't own a phonograph, but when relatives or Papa's colleagues from the Opera came to visit, our apartment was filled with music.

My grandparents would come over after dinner, and we'd all sit in the living room on the long sofa with the flowered throw, under the painting "Napoleon's Death," idling the evening away with music. A fire burned in the tiled stove, making the twilight seem more dense in contrast. Then Mother lit some candles and sat down at the piano to play a selection, maybe "Evening Bells," which I thought most delightful of all. Afterward, Papa sang in his fine tenor voice, Olle and I sang duets to Mother's accompaniment, and Grandma Emma, who was very religious, read from the Bible. The music must have sounded good because our neighbors would ask us to open the front door during our evening musicales so they could hear us better.

These musical evenings bound our little family into a harmonious whole. We all enjoyed hearing music and making music, but when I was asked to sing a solo for guests, I became abnormally shy. I really wanted to do it very much—it was just that no one was allowed to look at me while I sang. First, Mother and Papa had to blow out the candles, then I'd stand in the doorway between two draperies so that no one could see me. After these preparations I would sing loudly and happily some romantic piece.

Where this terrible shyness came from, I cannot say, for I was surrounded with the security of love and, in fact, was quite spoiled. My parents always provided us with the best they could afford. When the time came for me to begin school, it was a foregone conclusion that I'd attend the finest in all Stockholm: Afzelius Elementary School for Girls on Biblioteksgatan.

Just as I was beginning first grade, Grandma Emma died, a victim of the worldwide "Spanish" influenza epidemic. I remember her terrible suffocating cough, and the knowledge that we could do nothing to help her. Mama took care of her until the end, and it was really a miracle that no one else in the family was infected. It was the memory of my Grandmother's illness and death, my life's first real sorrow, that prompted my desire to become a nurse. I didn't dare think about becoming a doctor because the cost of schooling was beyond our means, but the decision to care for the sick, somehow, remained with me for a long time. If it hadn't been that Papa had other plans for me, in all likelihood I would now be a retired nurse.

Grandmother's passing completely changed our lives, particularly for Mother. In addition to her work as a photographer, she now had to run a postwar household, despite her inexperience with or, truth to tell, disinclination for cooking. She worked from morning to night, ran between the home and the studio, and never seemed to sit down and rest. Then in August 1921, when I was 11 years old, our family increased by one: Olle and I welcomed a little brother, Gösta.

By that time Olle and I had grown very close. We enjoyed each other's company and being older, he looked after me. When we were both young, however, I was the tougher of the pair. If my mother was late picking us up after school, Olle would start crying: "Where is my mother?" Not me; I just sauntered home by myself. As we grew up, if either of us was invited to a party, one wouldn't go without the other.

Papa was frequently absent during this time, and even when he wasn't working at the Opera, Mama sat at home alone many evenings. Papa was a member of several choirs, one of which, The Swedes, a male chorus, occasionally traveled around Europe. He also belonged to several societies and other organizations and had numerous colleagues who would invite him to various functions.

Mama wasn't as enthusiastic as Papa was to go to parties. Even if she'd been able to leave her children, she was too tired in the evenings to go out and have fun. I remember many times seeing her look very sad during these years and understood only later that Mama had to take on all responsibilities for the finances and for everything else concerning the home. It was she who saw that the money coming in was sufficient for our needs. It was her strength that kept the family together. Her burdens became even heavier when we children unfairly compared her serious nature to Papa's generous charm. She was the one who had to say no when a thing cost too much, perhaps something desirable that Papa, happily but thoughtlessly, had placed before our eyes.

In assuring that her children had a secure and peaceful childhood, she only followed an established pattern: what Grandma Emma had done for her family, Mama was doing for ours. And so, eventually, did I for mine.

⁂

My last years in school were carefree, with hardly a worry and something exciting happening nearly all the time. My brother's school, Norra Real, held dances, and classmates threw private parties at their homes. I don't know how many pairs of dancing shoes I wore out.

When I finished school in 1929, I never doubted for one moment what I was going to do with my life: I was determined to become a nurse trainee. In order to defray some of the costs and to pay for my own wardrobe—by this time I loved beautiful clothes and playing the coquette—I took an office job at the Tellus Automobile Company and planned to begin my nurse's training the next fall. I even bought an appropriate blue dress and white apron. Dr. Reuter, our family physician, had kindly promised that I could practice in his office the spring before I entered nursing school.

Then, without warning, Papa vetoed my plans. His daughter wasn't going to be a nurse—she was going to be an opera singer! With such a voice, he decreed, I had no alternative. Though I loved singing, I resisted. In those days it wasn't easy to oppose one's parents, especially for a girl, and my father made a last, strong appeal. "Can't you make me happy by at least trying out at the Academy? If it doesn't work, it doesn't work. But for my sake, would you just try?"

For Papa, I was willing to do almost anything. Only two weeks remained before the entrance auditions, so Papa got in touch straightaway with tenor Torsten Lennartsson, an opera singer who taught solo voice at the Music Academy. "Of course, Anna-Lisa should try out," Lennartsson allowed after he heard me sing some short selections. "She's a natural, but how can you expect me to have her ready to audition in just two weeks?" "Because I have made up my mind about this," my father answered.

*He* most certainly had made up his mind! I, on the other hand, was scared to death, and how I made it through those two weeks I hardly remember. I only know that I vocalized from morning to night, both for Papa and Lennartsson, who rehearsed me in a couple of songs he thought appropriate for the audition. Papa, who sat through every lesson in order to oversee my progress, approved Lennartsson's final choice, "Voi che sapete," Cherubino's aria from *Le nozze di Figaro*. I learned later that Lennartsson, after a few lessons, had phoned Papa to tell him I was particularly good at imitating, so everything was sure to go well. For my part, not for one moment did I believe I would be accepted.

When the day came, much too quickly for me, I was nearly paralyzed with nerves. But before Lennartsson coached me, Papa had let me sing a few songs for his friend, Madame Andrejewa von Skilondz, one of Stockholm's most famous voice teachers; she thought I definitely had talent, and remembering her assessment loosened the worst tension in my throat. As I began the aria, I noticed that one member of the jury, the legendary operetta king Hjalmar Meissner, looked up surprised and observed me thoughtfully. I had no idea how I sounded, and it didn't help that no one in the jury gave an opinion afterward. "Thank you, that's fine," they said. No suggestion was made that I sing anything more than "Voi che sapete." When I slipped by the jury on my way out, I heard Meissner whisper to his neighbor, the director of the Royal Opera, John Forsell: "She's going to sing operetta!"

But on the way home the little flickering flame of hope went out, and I rushed in to Mama, bawling, certain I had appeared ridiculous. "Why did I submit myself to such an ordeal? To make a spectacle of myself?" Mama tried to console me, saying not to worry, it didn't matter. After all, I had fulfilled my father's wishes!

During the unbearable days I awaited the decision, I gradually realized that I *wanted* to be accepted, more than I had wanted anything in my entire life. Intuitively I believed I had a small chance. The day came when the results were to be posted on a white sheet on the green door of the Music Academy, for all passersby to see. I flew there, early in the morning, my heart in my throat. On the door were the names of the lucky few, listed alphabetically. I hardly dared look but finally forced myself. Of the many who had auditioned, only three or four had been admitted, first one name under the letter A, and another under B—Anna-Lisa Berg! From that day on, I no longer thought about becoming a nurse.

※

The Royal Music Academy was built on the premise that the country was rich in young talent, most of them belonging to a socio-economic stratum that found the necessary education and professional training prohibitively expensive. It was the state's obligation, therefore, to underwrite the cost of education and nurture this native talent, and so over the course of four years, we at the Academy received thorough instruction from the very best teachers to prepare us for our careers—at the symbolic cost of $1 each term. Apart from the main subject of solo voice, we had lessons in choral and ensemble singing, stage deportment, harmony, music theory, and music history; lessons from native-speaking teachers in Italian, French, and German; and dance with the well-known Anna Behle. We were required to play at least one instrument, so I took piano lessons from Gottfrid Boon.

The Music Academy had two parallel classes in solo voice. My class was taught by Torsten Lennartsson. The other was ruled with absolute power by the director of the Royal Opera: former lieutenant and Royal Court Singer, baritone John Forsell. Forsell had been a career officer in the Swedish Army. While still in uniform, he had joined the Royal Opera in Stockholm, where he made his debut as Rossini's Figaro on 26 February

1896. Although he became a regular member of the company, he didn't resign his commission until 1901. His career blossomed; from 1903 to 1906 he was a member of the Opera in Copenhagen and made guest appearances in Germany, England, and the United States. He was appointed *Hovsångare* (royal court singer) in 1909; for many years he was the only one to hold this title. He used to boast that a letter addressed only to "The Royal Court Singer, Stockholm," was delivered just as surely as a letter addressed to "His Majesty the King" or "The Archbishop, Uppsala." Like the king and the archbishop, John Forsell was then at the zenith of his field, a fact that nobody doubted, least of all himself.

He made his debut at Covent Garden in 1909 in the title role of *Don Giovanni*, partnered by Emmy Destinn and John McCormack; a busy season at the Metropolitan followed. He had 90 roles in his repertoire, and those he performed at the Met that season indicate his broad range. He sang seven concerts and 29 performances of seven roles: Telramund, Amfortas, the elder Germont, Tonio, Rossini's Figaro, Peter the Great in *Zar und Zimmerman*, and Prince Yeletsky in the American premiere of *Pikovaya Dama* (*Pique Dame*), opposite Emmy Destinn and Leo Slezak. Such versatility notwithstanding, his contract was not renewed. It is unfortunate that he didn't have a chance to perform Don Giovanni, the part that most appealed to his musical taste and his ego. Forsell had perfected his interpretation of Mozart's antihero over 25 years; it was considered by many his finest creation, and his interpretation received international acclaim. No less an authority than Adelina Patti wrote,

> When I hear about poor Forsell having had to come back from America, owing to his failure there, makes me very angry. The artists over there were *simply* jealous of him—and worked very hard to get him away from the camp. . . . Moi, je dis, that he is a *most* excellent artist and the best Don Giovanni I *ever* heard or saw. His pronunciation of the Italian language is quite perfect and distinct, which is a great thing for a singer.[1]

Forsell was appointed director of the Royal Opera in Stockholm in 1924, and concurrently he became a professor at the Music Academy, discharging his duties in both positions with boundless energy. Even in 1930, when at age 62 he was invited to sing Don Giovanni in Salzburg under the baton of Franz Schalk, his voice and gymnast's figure were intact; he was still energetic, vigorous, and in full possession of his renowned magnetism to women. Flinty, gray-brown eyes darted under his bushy brows, matching his temper for fire. Everyone at the school dreaded Forsell's sarcasm; in an instant it could turn the most confident, self-assured student into quivering jelly. Fortunately, I was spared. My self-confidence was not yet what it should've been, thus I was quite happy to have landed in Lennartsson's class.

Because my speaking voice is low, Lennartsson decided I was a mezzo-soprano, while in fact I am a lyric soprano. Not daring to complain, I tried to force my voice down into the low register where he had me sing, straining my vocal cords. Lennartsson must have heard that my voice didn't sound good, but instead of correcting the situation, he became less and less interested in me. One day, I bared my soul in Elsa's Dream from Wagner's *Lohengrin*, and sure I had done my best, I expectantly awaited his praise. But Lennartsson just walked to the window and gazed out at the bay, where the boats were moored together in rows. He then turned around and said nonchalantly to Anita von Hillern-Dunbar, the accompanist, "Oh, Mrs. Dunbar, I believe they have repainted the *King Karl!*"

I was too young to shrug off this discourtesy, and Lennartsson was too old and insensitive to understand why it hurt me. It wasn't the first time nor the last that such an incident occurred, and after a time my courage and love of singing were deeply shaken. It seemed Lennartsson was too jaded, too uninterested—or possibly both—to pay much attention to his pupils. One thing I didn't consider: he may also have been too sick. Not long after this Lennartsson became ill and withdrew from teaching; he died a year or so later, in 1933. He was succeeded at the Academy by the alto Julia Claussen, and with her in charge of my voice everything changed.

The motherly Mrs. Claussen took a real interest in me. She realized that I wasn't a mezzo-soprano at all but a soprano, and she had me sing a completely different repertoire. Almost immediately, I began to improve. She taught me the mechanics of breath control and support; I still remember her pressing her fingers into my diaphragm so hard that I had marks from her nails after a lesson. But that didn't matter. When a teacher shows a genuine interest and strives to bring out the best in you, you are willing to go along with almost anything. Soon, Mrs. Claussen had me sing solo at every student recital given in the Academy's Great Hall, where the students showed the public what they had learned. It gave me much-needed self-confidence; I felt I was finally where I belonged.

Outside of school, I was very much in the innocent swing of Stockholm nightlife, and my loyal brother Olle would come to pick me up in the evenings from what seemed like one continuous round of parties. Whether it was he who took on the role of protector or it was Mama who sent him, I never really knew. In any case, I felt quite secure with him. For the most part, I didn't care to run around in the middle of the night, giving my name at the door and being secretly admitted to the post-party *nachspiel*s at nightclubs like the Atlantic or Grotta Azurra, where the evening traditionally would be capped with early-morning hash and eggs. Not for me; I had to be at my lessons at the Academy early the next morning, and it was my strict obligation to take care of myself.

More and more, I was beginning to discover how much singing meant to me. It practically took over my whole being and began to affect my lifestyle. At first, I was charmed by the superficiality of Stockholm's inner circles, and I liked being courted by the young men in the high-society crowd of the city's fashionable Östermalm. But as soon as I was accepted at the Academy, life became much more serious. Only singing and music mattered, and everything else gradually became irrelevant. Furthermore, in the spring of 1931, something happened that would change my life.

Two brothers were attending the Academy at that time—Olle and Gösta Björling, from Stora Tuna in the province of Dalarna. When the formidable Forsell auditioned the two Björling boys, he exclaimed, "But you're so short!" Olle and Gösta were afraid they'd be rejected by the mighty professor, not for lack of voice but for lack of height. "Oh well," Forsell reasoned, "what can I expect? You're tenors!"

The Björling boys had excellent voices. Gösta was headed for the Opera, and Olle planned to be an oratorio and church singer, since he was very short and somewhat hump-backed, a condition caused by the rickets he'd suffered as a child. The disease, a result of a deficiency of vitamin D, was more common during that time, and its effects precluded a stage career for Olle Björling.

I liked the Björling brothers very much; they were cheerful and fun-loving, and besides, they had the same first names as my own two brothers. We soon had a little gang, which included the sopranos Greta Hallgren and Astrid Carlsson (Lennartsson found Astrid's surname too ordinary, and on his advice she later changed it to Gregert), and the baritone Sigurd Björling (no relation to the Björling brothers). I knew there was a third brother somewhere. He had been accepted to Forsell's class at the Academy in autumn 1928, and he also attended the Opera School.

Our group often practiced scales and sang together at each other's homes. When we weren't singing, we talked about music. None of us could afford to go out; our biggest splurge was to sneak off between lessons to Lenna's Konditori, a pastry shop on Arsenalsgatan. Our entertainments were mostly musical and free: we had student passes to the Opera and to all the concerts at the Academy, where we heard such singers as Marian Anderson, Richard Crooks, Alexander Kipnis, and Richard Tauber. Never in those days did I imagine that I would eventually meet every one of these great artists.

Olle and Gösta lived with their brother Jussi in a four-room apartment at Storgatan 56. Jussi was never around during my first months at the Academy, but his brothers assured me he had a fantastic voice. He had completed the three debut roles that were required for an engagement at the Opera, and he was already a member of that august institution, the goal the rest of us shared. In addition, he had made several recordings and had even sung on the radio!

Olle and Gösta added that their brother was John Forsell's special protégé: it was he who had arranged for a scholarship to help take care of his expenses during his studies. When Jussi began to earn a little money, Forsell helped him get an apartment that included the services of a housekeeper; Forsell's wife, Gurli, had even made curtains for the rooms. What's more, Jussi was one of the exceptionally gifted students who were offered free room and board and daily singing lessons during the summer months at the Forsells' country home. Olle and Gösta were obviously very proud of their brother; he was their hero.

The more I heard about this remarkable but elusive person, the more curious I became. Sometime in the spring of 1931, I stood before the mirror in the hall outside the classrooms putting on my little black hat. It was the beginning of the lunch break, and I was preparing to rush home and eat before the afternoon classes began. Gösta Björling stood nearby speaking with someone; I overheard that person ask, "Who is that girl? Could you introduce me?" Yes, Gösta said, he could do that. But as I understood later, what really mattered wasn't so much that the young man should find out my name, but that I should find out who he was.

"This," Gösta announced proudly, "is my brother, *the opera singer* Jussi Björling." After a little pause to let the words "opera singer" sink in, he added, "And this is Anna-Lisa Berg."

I missed the point entirely—I wasn't one bit impressed with the fine title. Besides, Jussi was just 20 years old, a whole year younger than I. He was a little short, a little plump—exactly like his brothers—but I paid no particular attention to that. I noticed only that he looked so sweet and pleasant, that his blue eyes were kind, that his glance radiated a special warmth.

I couldn't linger and talk; I had to get home for lunch. So we said a quick goodbye, and the brothers went off to get a bite to eat, as planned. During the next few days I didn't think much about the meeting. Jussi Björling was simply not around. By this time he was completely absorbed with his work at the Opera and showed up only when he was to sing at one of the student recitals in the Great Hall, or to say hello to his brothers.

The next time we met was at the Academy Ball. We were glad to see each other, and we had a wonderful time, dancing together most of the evening and getting to know each other a little better. He was very modest and a little bit shy; he didn't have the money to dress stylishly, but his simple suit was neat and clean. We laughed a lot over the funny stories he told me; he was really entertaining company. I don't know if he danced only for my sake, or whether he enjoyed dancing then; in later years he did not. But I was on his arm on the dance floor as the orchestra played its last song, and when I went home that night, I carried with me a new feeling, quite unlike what I felt after an evening spent with the wealthy young men who typically invited me out.

Between 6 and 9 May 1931 the Stockholm Opera gave four guest appearances in Helsinki: two of Mozart's *Don Giovanni* and one each of Nathanael Berg's *Engelbrekt*, in which Jussi sang the role of Bishop Sigge, and *I cavalieri di Ekebù* by Riccardo Zandonai, the latter Jussi's first broadcast of a live performance. The brothers proudly told me that this tour, and specifically the role of Don Ottavio in *Don Giovanni*, was Jussi's first appearance outside of Sweden. When Papa and his oboe came home from the tour, he delivered a little silver pen to me. "I received this from a young tenor named Jussi Björling," he told me. "He said that you are Academy friends and asked me to give it to you." This was my first gift from Jussi, a pleasant surprise. I was glad to know he was thinking of me.

"He is quite round and plump, this Jussi Björling," Papa ventured in passing.

"No, he isn't at all!" I protested.

Papa looked a little surprised at my reaction but made no more comments about Jussi. Of course, I wanted to know more—did he sing well, was he a success in Helsinki—but I asked no questions. I didn't want to seem too curious. But to this day I treasure that little silver pen.

# Chapter 2

✳

# THE BJÖRLINGS

Jussi and I couldn't have had more diverse backgrounds. Jussi came from the country; I was born and raised in the capital. Jussi had already lost both parents, his mother when he was only six. I still had both my parents, and my brothers and mother with me long after I was married. After his mother's death, Jussi and his family were constantly on the move, and as a result he received only a rudimentary education; I grew up in the home where I was born and enjoyed the best standard schooling. His family's fortunes depended on his father's fluctuating engagements and pupils; ours was an average middle-class home with a steady income. Finally, my whole family was Swedish, and part of Jussi's ancestry was Finnish.

Jussi's grandfather, Lars Johan Björling, was born in 1842 in Voxna, Hälsingland. His family had moved there from Norrbärke in Dalarna during the 1700s. A blacksmith by trade, he was blessed with a wonderful voice. He was about 20 years old when he traveled to Fredriksfors ironworks in Finland, where he met and married Henrika Mathilda Lönnqvist, a Finnish woman from Pori, two years his junior. Tall, stately, and deeply religious, she too was gifted with a beautiful singing voice. As Jussi observed in his autobiography, "We are a singing family and have always been one, for at least three generations."[1]

When Lars Johan returned to Sweden, he found a home in Borlänge's Stora Tuna parish with his younger brother Karl Erik Björn, a successful

30

house painter and paint dealer. Lars Johan lived on Magasinsgatan in the Hagalund section of Borlänge until his death in 1909; his widow remained there until her death in 1918. Mathilda (as she was known) enjoyed singing till late in life; she sometimes stood up in church with a "Now I want to sing a song!" and would launch into a hymn—which embarrassed the family no end.[2]

Karl David, Jussi's father, was the fourth of Lars Johan's and Mathilda's six children. He was born in the Harmånger parish of northern Sweden's Hälsingland province on 16 November 1873, a golden year for opera singers that also saw the births of Enrico Caruso, Fedor Chaliapin,[3] Leo Slezak, and many others. Karl David (or David) learned blacksmithing from his father. As a young man, he worked as a toolsmith at AB Separator in Stockholm, but the life didn't satisfy him, and after a while he decided to try his luck in America.

David had inherited a full measure of the family's hallmarks—stubbornness and determination—in equal proportions. His disposition was such that when he decided on something, he usually followed through. He was tough as tangled birch and difficult to deal with when opposed; when he grew angry it was best to keep out of his way. He was unbelievably strong—strong as a bear, a *björn* in Swedish. Indeed Björn had originally been the family's name. Six generations back, in the 18th century, Anders Andersson thought that his name was too common. To distinguish himself from the many other Anders Anderssons (literally, "Anders, son of Anders"), he assumed the name Björn. When his great-great-grandson Lars Johan moved to Finland, he changed the family name to Björling, following his brother's example: Per Samuel Björn had changed his name in 1857.

In 1899, David Björling boarded the steamer *Cameo* from Gothenburg to New York City, ready to fight his way into the new world. And fight is what he did—literally. David had his father's strong physique and large fists, and for a while he supported himself as a boxer. He fell back on his blacksmithing skills as necessary, and later he was hired by a Swedish doctor to care for patients four hours a day, for which service he received food and lodging. The doctor reportedly liked David very much.[4] David must have made good reports of his lot in America because his oldest living brother, Gustaf Leonard, followed him, with his large family in tow, in May 1902.

With his strength, David might have gone far as a pugilist if fate hadn't taken a hand in his fortunes. One evening, in a New York pub, someone urged him to sing. He did, and one of the customers noticed that the young Swede had a compelling tenor voice. The stranger was affiliated with the Metropolitan Opera School and advised him to try out.[5] There is no doubt that David Björling was enrolled as a student at the Opera School, but how long he stayed and what progress he made isn't established. Nonetheless, he must've been encouraged, for when he returned to Sweden two years later, in 1905, he was determined to become a singer.

In Stockholm's music circles he met John Forsell, already a member of the Royal Opera, and took part with him in a concert for King Oscar and Queen Sophia. David's American-trained voice must have been considered a superior instrument: he opened and closed the program. The old king was so impressed that he offered David a stipend, which money enabled the young tenor to spend two years perfecting his skills at the music conservatory in Vienna. Upon his return to Sweden, David tried to make a career as a singer. He had no doubt that he would succeed.

When his father died, David returned to the family home on Magasinsgatan in Borlänge, where his mother lived with his sister Lydia and her husband, Reinhold Lindblad, a cabinetmaker. Johan Jonatan, David's younger brother, also lived in Borlänge. Like all the other children, sister Johanna Mathilda in particular, Johan Jonatan had inherited a talent for music along with a fine voice. But, then, so had most of the Björlings. David's Uncle Carl, like his father, had a remarkable voice. All the men were tenors, and, as those in the family who had heard the singing of two or more generations maintained, they all had an unmistakable timbre, a genetically transmitted Björling sound.

Around 1908 David met Ester Elisabet Sund. She was born on 26 April 1882, in Norr Romme, Stora Tuna, in the province of Dalarna, the fifth of eight children. Her father, Lars Erik Sund, a baker, was born in Norr Romme, and her mother, Betty Lundqvist Sund, in Karlstad in Värmland. Ester, Jussi's mother, was gentle and sweet and had kind, smiling eyes. As a young girl, the *vackra kullan* (beautiful Dalecarlian girl), as she was known, had been crowned the town's May Queen.[6] Trained to be a milliner, she too was very musical and played the piano well; she sang in the Stora Tuna Church choir.

It was in this church that David Björling caught sight of her for the first time. He fell deeply in love, and Ester reciprocated. The romance between the two became quite serious and soon after, Ester became pregnant. Their first child, Karl Johan Olof Björling, called Olle, was born on 2 May 1909. On 19 July 1909, David and Ester married and settled in Norr Romme. Two years later, on 5 February 1911, their second son was born on Magasinsgatan in Borlänge; apparently, Ester was visiting her mother-in-law when she went into labor. The baby was baptized Johan Jonatan, after his uncle, but he was never called by either name. He was still a toddler when his Finnish grandmother began to call him *Jussi-poika* (Jussi boy), the Finnish nickname for Johan. The name stuck, and he was soon called Jussi—or sometimes Josse—by family and friends.[7]

An oddity surrounds Jussi's actual birthdate. All his life, he celebrated his birthday on 2 February, but after his death, the engagement book of the midwife who delivered him came to light. It clearly shows that she assisted at the delivery on 5 February 1911. The entries in the engagement book are chronological, thus the possibility of an after-the-fact entry can safely be ruled out.[8] The discrepancy has a simple explanation: David Björling wasn't interested in formalities. When he left for America, he was registered in

Kungsholm's parish in Stockholm, but from then on he was listed as "without known residence"; in 1903 his name was moved to the book of nonexistent people. He had refused to notify the authorities when he changed residences—a requirement in Sweden—and in the same way, he never bothered to report the birth of his children to the parish where such records were kept. When he was later asked the birthdate of his second son, he must have replied that the child was born in early February, or something to that effect, and the second day of the month seemed early enough for the parish clerk making the entry.

Luckily, Jussi was unaware of the mixup surrounding his birthdate, for numbers and their combinations were very important to him. The figures 11 and 13 had a special significance: 13 was his lucky number, and 11 was the year of his birth. Jussi put so much importance on having been born on the second day of the second month because the two 2s made 22, and 22 divided by 2 is 11! No matter that this made little sense to anyone else; it made sense to him.

A year and a half after Jussi's birth, on 21 September 1912, a third son, Karl Gustaf, was born. Like his brothers, he didn't go by his baptismal name; all his life he was called Gösta. To support his growing family, David Björling traveled around Sweden, gave solo recitals, and even began to give voice lessons. On 25 March 1912 he gave a solo concert with orchestra in Gothenburg, which was reviewed by the well-known Swedish composer Wilhelm Stenhammar:

> At a concert arranged by the Gothenburg Orchestra Association, Mr. David Björling sang an aria from *Tosca*, Canio's monologue from *Pagliacci*, and as an encore "La donna è mobile" from *Rigoletto*. He was applauded repeatedly, in my opinion for good reason. Mr. Björling possesses an unusually fresh and beautiful high tenor voice with a distinctly Nordic timbre, which he treated in a most sympathetic and natural manner, free from artificiality and without the slightest trace of that sentimental tediousness that is regrettably too often inherent in Swedish tenors. The performance of the *Rigoletto* aria especially was characterized by a brilliance that gave a truly Italian impression. Undoubtedly this demonstrates great talents, and I would recommend our opera management to take advantage of them and to support their further development.[9]

Stenhammar's advice must have carried some weight with local music authorities because in the autumn of 1912, David was contracted to sing with Sigrid Trobäck's opera company in Gothenburg. He performed in several standard operas, such as *La fille du régiment* and *Cavalleria rusticana*; a surviving review attests to his success in *La bohème*: "Mr. David Björling's Rodolfo was a real bohemian poet, full of love, sentimental, and [sung] with a beautiful warm voice."[10]

Ester accompanied David on his tours until it became apparent, some years after Gösta's birth, that she was suffering from tuberculosis. In those days, the illness eradicated entire families, and to protect hers from infection, Ester kept her own place setting of dinnerware and silverware wrapped in a towel so that no one used them accidentally. Once Ester forgot to wrap the dishes, which so enraged David that Jussi, although a young child at the time, never forgot the scene. Ester devoted herself to David and her brood while she was able, but for long periods she lived with her parents in Norr Romme or with her mother-in-law on Magasinsgatan, during which times David's brother Johan and his eldest daughter Märta helped to care for the boys and keep house.

David's reputation as a singer began to spread, especially after Stenhammar called him the new Caruso. Following several good reviews, Count Hans von Stedingk, manager of the Royal Opera, invited David to come to Stockholm for an audition. But the prideful David was without the slightest desire to be diplomatic to people who could advance his career; he gave a typical answer: "If you want to hear me, you can come here!" Von Stedingk didn't travel to hear him, but he must have discussed the matter with management. They agreed that it would be sufficient if David performed the traditional three debut roles that the Opera required of all new artists before they were offered a permanent contract. When they notified David of their decision, he declined that invitation as well. He'd already performed several lead roles in theaters around the country and received glowing reviews. To his way of thinking, he was no longer a beginner who had to prove himself in three roles—he *was* an opera singer.

Soon after, during a visit to Stockholm, David met von Stedingk in the street. The count reextended the offer that David sing the obligatory three roles. David refused. "Absolutely not. You know very well how good I am." When von Stedingk persisted, David exploded, "No, I say!" Some exchange of words must've followed, because David took a firm hold of the count, spun him around, and gave him a swift kick in the pants. Not surprisingly, this incredible episode put an end to all possibility of Jussi's father's ever having a first-rank stage career in Sweden. Without a permanent engagement at the Royal Opera and disinclined to emigrate with a sick wife and small children, David could not expect to earn a living as a full-time opera singer. He cut back on his stage appearances as well. It promised to be more rewarding to make a career as a church singer together with his sons.

✳

David discovered very early that his boys had inherited their parents' musicality; both he and Ester exposed their children to music and singing from the cradle onward, in the home and in church, the focal point of musical activities in rural Sweden. He claimed with fatherly pride, and quite possibly without exaggeration, that the boys could sing—in extraordinarily clear voices—before they could talk. David began to teach his small boys to sing along with him; he sang the melody and the boys joined in with their bright boy soprano voices while Ester accompanied them on the piano.

Whether David only transmitted what he had been taught at the Metropolitan and in Vienna or he built on the knowledge imparted to him by his voice teachers cannot be established. The proof that he knew what he was doing rests on this: not only did he not ruin the voices of his young boys but he gave them such a superb foundation in voice production that they were able to keep intact the flawless technique they developed under his tutelage for the rest of their lives.

David, a strict teacher and a severe taskmaster, worked with his sons about an hour every day in lessons and ensemble rehearsals. If the boys made a mistake, he rapped them on their legs with a cane, but it didn't seem to bother them. They loved and respected their father—and knew that his love for them was at least as great as his demands. The boys *always* addressed their father with the formal "you," which the Swedish language, like German and French, distinguishes from the informal.[11] Modern English lacks the distinction, but it's comparable to answering with "Yes, Father" rather than "OK, Dad." Stilted as it may seem, our own children too always used the formal form with us.

By November 1915, the Björling family was living at Nygatan 9 in the Nikolai Congregation in Örebro; Jussi remembered going to school here, although the boys received very little schooling in Sweden otherwise. Gösta made his singing debut when he was only three years old at Örebro's Trinity Church; the small boys usually stood on a bench so that everyone could see them, and during this debut concert, Gösta climbed down from the bench and turned a somersault on the floor to show that his talents weren't limited to singing.[12] Once, when Gösta didn't feel like singing, he unceremoniously pushed his brothers off the bench; had David not disciplined him on the spot there's no telling how it might have ended. One of Jussi's earliest memories was how he, at five years of age, sang in a church, most likely Trinity Church, where his father sang every Wednesday. Jussi couldn't say precisely when their singing travels began, but Örebro was the starting point for David's and the boys' tours in central Sweden.

They must've been an irresistible sight, dressed in authentic folk costumes of gold moleskin pants with red tassels at the knees and small slouch-hats framing their serious, round faces. They took naturally to performing and were quite uninhibited; they even gave concerts in the arbor at their grandmother's on Magasinsgatan, for which Cousin Märta made posters, advising customers of the one-cent admission. A neighbor remembers that when her two-year-old brother died in August 1916, the Björlings were invited to sing at the wake. Gösta was wisely considered too young to be included at such a solemn occasion, so only seven-year-old Olle and five-and-a-half-year-old Jussi stood by the coffin, singing "Children of the Heavenly Father."

Only eight months later, the boys experienced their own sorrow. World War I was in its third year, and a food shortage had struck the countryside. Their mother didn't receive the nutritious food she needed, and her decline accelerated. Moreover, she was pregnant again. On 10 April 1917, Ester's fourth son, Karl David, nicknamed Kalle, was born at the Academic Hospital in Uppsala. But she never held her newborn in her arms; rather than risk exposure to her terminal tuberculosis, the baby was taken from her immediately upon delivery.

The case history prepared by the attending physician of the Clinic of Chest Diseases on 22 March 1917 gives a detailed description of Ester's condition:

> One brother died from tuberculosis, one sister has a milder case of tb. The patient is married and has three healthy children. Pleurisy at age 9. As a child had occasionally recurring cough. When the patient was 14 years old, a physician stated that something was not quite right with her right lung. Thereafter generally coughed during the fall seasons. After first two deliveries, the cough got worse. When the patient was 29 years old, a concentration was diagnosed on her left lung. Still good general condition. After a miscarriage in the fall of 1915, the patient started to feel worse, the cough increased and she often had low fever in the evenings. Stayed up as long as she could. At the end of July [1916] another pregnancy. Thereafter condition worsened. Was admitted to a sanitarium in the beginning of November. The patient says that she has been hoarse for about a month. Three years earlier the patient had been hoarse for three months, but recovered completely.[13]

Ester never left the hospital. Five weeks after this report was prepared, on her 35th birthday, 26 April 1917, she died. David and her three older boys sang at her graveside service in the Stora Tuna churchyard on 30 April.

Jussi was so young when his mother passed away, he had only scant memories of her, but he often talked about his father. In the decade that followed Ester's death, David ruled the household and molded his sons' personalities, the sole source of authority, teacher, and friend. Although David made a conscious effort to give each of his children the same attention, he knew that even among his gifted sons Jussi's voice was exceptional. He once told him: "You're going to be a singer."[14] All his life Jussi was motivated by trying to make his late father proud of him.[15]

※

Ester's death was a great blow for them all. Realizing that the more he was away from home, the less he'd be confronted with the painful memory of his loss, David lived a roving life for the next two years, touring all over Sweden with his three eldest sons; little Kalle, "the tail end" as he was often called, stayed with David's sister Lydia. David approached his brother Johan with an offer as well: if his Märta would come along on their tours and help him out with the older boys, he would teach her to sing. Father and daughter both agreed.

Cousin Märta, only five years older than Olle, was more like a sister than a surrogate mother. Still, for years to come, she made sure her cousins looked nice, mended their clothes, cooked full meals, and prepared quick snacks; she also helped write programs and draw posters. The boys liked her very much and called her "the countess." They confided in her and enlisted her help in coverups when they had some mischief to hide from their father. Once, after a recital, as the audience gathered around the children, Märta heard a lady scream. "When I shook her hand I showed how strong I am," Jussi explained proudly. Little Gösta especially, who missed a mother most, always had his arms around her.[16]

David kept up his end of the bargain: he gave Märta room and board, a small salary, and formal voice lessons. There was nothing pro forma about it; David taught her as thoroughly as he taught his own children. Märta was born with the family's special gifts for musicality and natural voice. All she needed was training, and she found Uncle David a good teacher and his instructions, stressing the importance of breathing and the proper support of the voice, easy to follow: "Don't force! Sing naturally!" he admonished them.[17]

Märta was nine years old when she first heard her Uncle David's voice, singing "Vesti la giubba" in his room at her grandmother's house. She remembers his magnificent stretta from *Trovatore*—well sung, though not as powerful and brilliant as Jussi's in his adult years. In her judgment, David's voice compared favorably with any of the singers then active in Sweden, but he lacked what his son Jussi had, an aura of greatness. Jussi's voice was similar to his father's, but that was not unusual; even Kalle's voice, the only high baritone in the family of tenors, had the Björling coloring.

As a musical group type, David and his sons were completely new to Sweden, whose thriving communities were always interested in music and culture. They performed in churches, with programs that consisted of hymns and folk songs. After the concerts, a collection was taken up in a hat that David passed around. Receipts were good for a while, but by the end of World War I, times were hard—sometimes there wasn't enough money taken in to pay for that night's room. They packed light and often traveled by bicycle. It was a difficult, but not a hand-to-mouth, existence. Between teaching and concertizing David earned a decent living, and he was a good manager of his resources. He could always have returned to the blacksmith trade; he wasn't afraid of hard physical labor. But music was more important to him. He believed in himself and in the special gift of his boys. As long as they earned enough for the necessities, they would be fine.

In the early 1980s, an elderly woman told my son Lasse that when she was a little girl, a man and his three sons rode up to their house one evening on bicycles, looking for lodging. The house was too small, so they were offered the hayloft, which accommodation they gratefully accepted. "The next morning we thought we should invite them in for breakfast," she said. "We had a bit of a guilty conscience for letting them sleep in the hayloft." After the meal the father turned to his sons and said: "Now boys, we are going to thank the nice people for the food!" The boys flew up and stood in a row with their backs straight, and their voices almost raised the roof. Only many years later did this woman realize who their visitors were.

With World War I over, David's thoughts turned beyond the borders of Sweden. Why not return to America? If they worked hard, they could earn a small fortune there, touring the Swedish communities with their program of Swedish hymns and folk songs. David's old steamer trunk came out of storage, and in October 1919, a singing troupe known as the Björling Male Quartet left for New York on the Norwegian steamer *Bergensfjord*. Greta Forsberg, a fellow passenger and Swede, later recalled meeting them on board. She found Olle very precocious; his brothers called him "professor." Gösta, the youngest, was "very sweet with a shy little smile," and "eight-year-old Jussi was chubby, lively, and dangerously impulsive. The father kept a strict regimen of bathing, combing, and finger-nail cleaning. . . . At 8 o'clock every evening, they had to go to bed." The passengers asked David to let his boys sing for them, but he refused: "The boys' voices must be spared." The ship docked in New York on 28 October, and when they gave their first concert on 20 November 1919 in New York's Gustavus Adolphus Church, many of their shipboard acquaintances, including Greta Forsberg, were in attendance.

> First the father sang some songs, . . . then the three small boys stood up and sang. I cannot describe what an impression they made. I just know it was gripping, and their expressions of seriousness and artistic ambition cannot be described. When, at the end, they sang "Sverige" ("Sweden") in harmony, there wasn't a dry eye. During the thunderous applause, they smiled bashfully.[18]

For a time the family lived in a boardinghouse owned by Swedes. David, streetwise from his earlier years in America, watched his boys closely while they were in New York; he was afraid they might be kidnapped. When their new friend Greta Forsberg took them on a walk, she received strict orders never to leave them alone for one second and to hold their hands the whole time—with good reason. Once Jussi pulled the handle on a fire alarm box on Fifth Avenue, thinking it was a postage stamp machine; the shrill alarm halted New York City traffic before David was able to spirit his rascals away.

Soon after their arrival, David read that Enrico Caruso was to sing Canio in *Pagliacci* at a Saturday matinee at the Metropolitan Opera. He stood in line for hours and purchased four expensive tickets for himself and his sons, but on their way to the great event, the boys caught sight of a movie theater on Times Square where a Western starring William S. Hart was showing. They refused to go one step further and for once David gave in. Bill Hart it was. It grieved Jussi his whole life that he missed this chance to hear the singer who eventually became his idol.[19]

During the first leg of their American tour, the Björling Male Quartet spent two weeks in New England, then returned briefly to New York. On their second leg, again of New England, a young Swede, Miss Magnhild Lundquist, traveled with them as their accompanist for two and a half months, in 1920. "The chubby boys attached themselves to me since they were motherless," she recalled. "They called me 'Miss Musician.'. . . Success was a given from the outset when the small Dalecarlian boys dressed in their provincial costumes made their entrance in the Swedish churches. . . . With the Swedish flag and the Star Spangled Banner in their small hands, the little boys conquered the audience from the start." Instead of tickets, the congregations paid them with collections, and the takes were very good. Miss Lundquist noted, "Papa David was somewhat impractical, stubborn as a real Dalecarlian, and hot-tempered too, though it passed quickly. This stubbornness was especially inherited by the middle boy, Jussi." Once she teasingly paused before starting his showpiece, Alfred Berg's "Give Me Angel Wings." Jussi turned to her impatiently: "Let's get on with it!" The audience tittered, and David angrily disciplined his son during the intermission. But Miss Lundquist accepted the blame, "and the episode was forgotten and forgiven. But that evening many more $1 bills found their way to Jussi."[20]

"Miss Musician" further recalled that the boys made half a dozen recordings in Providence, Rhode Island, but here she is mistaken. Harald Henrysson clarifies that Columbia didn't make recordings in Providence; and as they would hardly have sent staff and equipment there "only to record a group which had just been in New York and could easily return to that city, it must be assumed that Mrs. Lundquist-Palmgren's memory about the recording place was wrong."[21] Henrysson concludes that the records were most likely made between 6 and 9 February 1920, meaning Jussi had just turned nine when he made his first records with the acoustical process. He remembered standing on a platform with wheels and singing into a big funnel. When they sang loudly, the wagon—the sound-mixer of that time— was drawn away from the funnel; with the lower tones, it was rolled closer. No solo records were made by any member of the Quartet.

No matter how strict David was, it wasn't easy to control his lively offspring. The boys would ride up and down in the elevators of the high-rise hotels they were gradually able to afford, and they sometimes bribed the operator to let them run the elevator. In Jamestown, New York, with a 70 percent Swedish population, the boys lay atop their hotel's windowsills and shot their BB guns at the umbrellas of unsuspecting people below. Once they sneaked out without permission and got completely lost; they were retrieved only after several hours of search by their anxious, furious father. Every scrape they got themselves into earned them a hard spanking, which helped keep them in check—until the next time.

The troupe continued to Chicago and points north. Wherever they went, the hosts spoiled the youngsters with treats and presents. In Illinois, they visited David's brother Gustaf and other relatives in the area's Swedish settlements: "I remember that we rode bareback on ponies at my uncle's and played and romped around on a couple of farms."[22] Stops in Minnesota included Atwater, Grove City, Oak Park, St. Peter, and Willmar, where, according to one review, the boys "pleased an audience at the Bethel Lutheran Church. It was a remarkable performance these lads put up, all appearing in solos as well as in trios. They sang difficult songs as well as more popular ones with precision, and their child voices blended well. The father, David Björling, rendered a number of selections in the finished manner becoming a professional musician."[23]

Americans were so impressed with the singing Björlings that David was often asked to demonstrate his teaching methods for voice teachers; while in America, David published a bilingual booklet entitled *Hur man skall sjunga* (*How to Sing*).[24] He was the author of the text in both languages, Swedish and English. "I received my training at the Metropolitan Opera School in New York and at the Conservatory of Vienna," he began, "and thus I have come in contact with the world's foremost song artists, and specialists and physicians for the vocal organs, which has been a valuable guidance for my vocal studies, and the unusual vocal endowment of my children proves that my assertions are not misleading."

No one will ever learn to sing from David Björling's booklet, but his elementary presentation is pedagogically correct and shows a good deal of common sense. He stresses the importance of breath control and good posture: "Never allow the chest to sink in when exhaling or when singing. Train yourself and the children to keep the chest high and the back straight." He believed that breathing through the mouth could cause all kinds of ailments and so elaborates at length on the oral hygiene of the mouth and throat, stressing the importance of daily gargling with "one teaspoon of salt in a glass of luke-warm water." He advises short, simple scales for daily exercises, adding, "Never sing a high or low note that you cannot produce with ease; it will come in time by itself." Regarding young voices he admonishes, "Children must not sing *pianissimo* because that contracts the throat and affects the voice. Nor must children sing too loud so that it sounds like screaming, but let them produce a rich and powerful tone with an open throat cavity and chest high and deep breathing, and you will soon obtain results."

His advice about raising children is particularly touching. "Like a growing plant, so develops the child in body and soul," he writes. "Inculcate the good into the child from its very birth. . . . Music and singing are the best things for infants, but must be done with moderation—do not sing or play too loudly or for too long because [their] eardrums cannot tolerate loud sounds or fast tempos." He considers a three-year-old ready to learn to sing. For the development of the child's soul, he also recommends church attendance, "which cultivates the veneration and love of God." Finally,

> Remember that the flowers of the field do not thrive alike, although they are cultivated the same. Likewise it is with man. If you notice a difference in the children's intelligence, do not favor the stronger one so that the

other children notice it, but care for the weaker with love, as you do with a plant that does not thrive—one gives special care to such a plant until it blossoms and grows like the rest.

Keep your children away from the motion pictures where gunplay and hold-ups are shown. The grown-up abhors this and reacts accordingly, but to the child these are heroic deeds which sometimes develop criminal tendencies in its consciousness. In Sweden children are forbidden to see such films. Yet a good film is instructive to see.

The unaffected simplicity of David's writing is the blueprint of the way he raised his own boys, and his work as a singing teacher leaves no doubt as to the efficacy of his method. All three elder Björling brothers could clearly trace their breathing and voice placement to his counsel. Jussi grew up under the vocal tutelage of his father and sang under his daily guidance and supervision for a whole decade. There's no question who taught Jussi Björling to sing.

While they toured America, David tried to educate his sons in nonvocal matters as best as he could but without much result. On the other hand they learned to speak English fluently, which later proved invaluable to Jussi. These were happy days for him and his brothers, and the memory of this first tour, singing their way from city to city, all the way to the West Coast, stayed with them all their lives.

> We sang mostly in churches, and I remember when I sang a little song entitled "Give Me Angel Wings," all the while I was counting the crystals in the chandeliers. It was all mechanical, like an automaton. I'm not sure that's the right way to ask for angel wings, but I think it's the way children act when they perform in public. We sang both in Swedish and English, including many of David's Psalms. I also sang as a solo "Aftonsång" ("Evening Song") by Berg.[25]

Receptions were uniformly enthusiastic. A surviving review, without source or date, shows the impression David and his young sons made:

> The Björling Male Quartet offered us something completely different from what we had anticipated. We expected to hear something angelic, innocent, and untouched in the expression which, up to now, we thought necessarily accompanies childhood. Instead, we heard mature singers with strong voices, masculine breast [i.e., chest] tones, well-rehearsed musical interpretations and feeling, and conviction in the diction.
>
> The three boys stood there, obvious proof of what discipline, serious work, and determination can bring. They aren't just staying in the playhouse on the other side of the ocean. They reverently delivered their program with their hands clasped in front of them.
>
> The best was the young Jussi who sang, "Give Me Angel Wings" by Berg. He had freed himself, through his natural musical instinct, from the forced thick tone which the others were still exhibiting.
>
> Mr. Björling, an opera singer, possessed a strong and fresh tenor voice. He also provided proof of his beautiful musicianship. Mr. Björling

has obviously made an in-depth study of the modern foreign organ compositions as well as the old works from the Netherlands. He is a many-faceted, gifted musician, and not just an opera singer.

From Los Angeles, the Björling Male Quartet returned to the East Coast, where at their hotel in Rochester, New York, Jussi met his first love, Suzanne Gabe, a little Swedish girl. They would sneak off together and kiss. When it came time to leave the city, Jussi refused to go, he would not budge; not even a sound smack across the face from his father had the least effect. "Come along Olle and Gösta," David announced at last. "We're leaving for the station!"

Surely, he thought, Jussi would come dragging after them, but David didn't realize how close a match his son was for him in obstinacy. They left—and still no Jussi. Finally Gösta could take it no longer and returned to the hotel to give his older brother a thrashing. Jussi was stronger but Gösta prevailed, with the extra measure of strength anger provides. Jussi quit Rochester, but little Suzanne left a deep impression on him. "I still remember the address," he wrote decades later. "295 Mage Street, Rochester, New York."[26]

In April 1921, while the Björlings rested up in Manhattan before setting out on another long scheduled tour, David dined at a Swedish restaurant. Perhaps it was the simple meal he was served—pickled herring and crisp Swedish bread—that set off an irresistible longing in him. To calm his homesickness, David decided they should all go aboard the S.S. *Stockholm*, which had just docked, to greet the crew and have some news from home.

It was a grave mistake. Two days later, the 40-concert tour was canceled, and the Björling Male Quartet was heading home.

※

The Björling boys were in high spirits during the passage, roaming the ship dressed in cowboy and Indian outfits. "I became quite good at throwing a lasso," Jussi recalled. "Because we gave concerts on board, the captain recognized me, and when he saw me playing with the lasso, he asked me to catch him with it. So I did, and he was very amused. When he turned to go, I threw the lasso again; it caught his foot and he fell down on the deck." Jussi was terrified and had visions of being thrown in the brig. "But the captain was a real sailor and a good sport. He burst out laughing and thought it was so cleverly done that I was rewarded by being allowed on the bridge to take over the wheel of the ship. Naturally, I convinced myself that I steered the enormous 12,000-ton ship over the Atlantic."[27]

Upon their homecoming, David invited all the family to their hotel for a boisterous celebration. The returning Björlings wore expensive American clothes, and David especially looked the part of a gentleman. They brought presents for everybody. Märta received an antique silver scarf pin with a stone in it—"A real diamond!" Gösta proudly assured her.

With the money he'd saved, David finally bought his first home, in Karlsarvet, a little village across from Leksand on a bay of Lake Siljan. The house afforded a fabulous view of the lake, and in the quiet summer evenings, David would row out on the water, rest on the oars, and sing "Lugn vilar sjön" ("The Water is Still"), his beautiful voice carrying over the silvery surface. Here the boys continued their carefree life. When winter set in, they bobsled down the hill from the house, ending up way out on Siljan's ice, and whereas before their trip to America they had tied barrel staves to their boots, they could now all afford real skis.

But David missed Ester very much, and as time went on, he often drank to numb his sorrow and longing. One evening David and his sons went to visit Ester's parents in Norr Romme. When they reached Stora Tuna's churchyard, David asked the taxi driver to stop. A fiddler from Leksand, Carl Gudmundsson, was traveling with them and witnessed the scene: "The three boys climbed out of the car, stood with their father around [their mother's] grave, and quietly sang 'Still, Oh Still' by Erik Gustaf Geijer. The autumn's first stars shone down from the heavens on the little singing group. It sounded like muffled organ strains floating out over the churchyard. The driver stood there, too. We both cried."[28]

When they resumed their tours, Cousin Märta joined them again, along with an accompanist and a teacher, who tutored the boys a few hours each day. They no longer traveled by bicycle or train but rode in style in a spacious new Chevrolet touring car, another sign of David's newfound affluence. But first David had to learn how to drive; when the boys grew older, they too learned and took turns driving. They returned to Karlsarvet as often as possible and spent every summer there.

Between tours they lived either in Karlsarvet or Örebro, and while touring southern Sweden's country churches, their headquarters was the Hotel du Nord in Ystad. Another favorite spot in the south was the home of David's friend Sven Bosson Zander, in Asarum. The Björlings usually stayed in a hotel in nearby Karlshamn, but a testament to their close association with the town is that a Björling Road now winds through Asarum. Zander and his wife, Emma, had nine children; Jussi was especially fond of their daughter Eva, and for many years he returned to Asarum for visits.

Earnings before the American trip were very modest, but now, boosted by their American credentials, the Quartet attracted a much larger paying audience wherever they went, and the take more than paid the bills. But it was difficult for David to be both mother and father to his sons—especially in later years, when little Kalle would often join them. Märta maintains that when they traveled and performed, David wouldn't drink excessively, that he was *not* an alcoholic. He tried to keep his sons from drinking. When he had a beer or two with his dinner and the boys begged to taste it, he might give them a sip. But usually he would command: "Drink your milk!"

In the summer months, however, when the Björlings were not on tour and Märta returned to her family, David had too much free time. Jussi remembered that between tours his father drank more than he should have. Whenever his increasing dependence on alcohol made it impossible for him to look after the boys, they turned to Hampus Greta, an elderly neighbor who lived alone across the street. If David forgot about meals, she'd give them a glass of milk and sandwiches. She darned their stockings, made sure they bathed regularly, and generally looked after them.

Once, when Jussi sang at the church in Mora, he insisted that I go with him to Karlsarvet to visit Greta. By this time she was a very old woman and almost blind, but she still wove the most beautiful rag rugs. When she understood who her visitor was, she was completely overwhelmed. "Is it really you, Josse? Is it really you?" she repeated over and over, beaming with joy. She was so moved that it took her some time to recover enough to carry on a conversation. I'll never forget it. A short time after our visit, we heard she had died. Jussi and his brothers always spoke of her with gratitude and affection. They never forgot what she had meant to them.

In the five years following their return from America in 1921, the Björling Quartet gave a total of 98 concerts in southern Sweden in 86 different venues—most of them in Skåne and Småland—in addition to some 30 or so performances in Dalarna. Surviving posters, which were printed in quantity, with a blank space for the time and date of the program, are fascinating documents of these recitals. Each featured a large photo of the Quartet, David in street clothes and the boys in Dalecarlian folk costumes. Their programs were typically broken down into groups by performers: the Quartet would begin with "Stilla natt" ("Silent night"), "Stridsbön" by Lindblad, and "Bereden väg för Herren" by David Björling. Then the boys' trio followed with "Svanevits sång" by Geijer and another composition by David, "Jag hör min Frälsares röst." David next sang two solos, Dahl's "Love Song" and Massenet's "Elégie," then the boys continued with an American folk song and "Härliga land" by Nordblom. Next came three solos: Olle sang Stenhammar's "Sverige," Jussi his perennial "Giv mig änglavingar" ("Give Me Angel Wings") by Berg, and Gösta the ballad "Sten Sture" by Svedbom. Finally the Quartet closed the concert with the official national anthem "Du gamla du fria" ("Thou Old, Thou Free").

While touring, the Björlings lived out of suitcases, traveling from one hotel to another. David rehearsed with them and insisted that they practice their instruments, for Olle knew the violin, and Jussi had played the piano for as long as he could remember;[29] when Märta first went to Örebro, she found her five-year-old cousin already sitting on the piano bench, playing little songs. On tour, Jussi would play dance music on the hotel piano, mostly by ear, in his simple, unsophisticated style. When Kalle was old enough to start his vocal training, David taught him too, and when he felt Kalle was ready, the Björling Male Quartet occasionally consisted of the four brothers. The caption of one poster photo identifies the youngest, seven-year-old Kalle, as the one who recently started his singing career; Märta remembers him as a playful boy, hard to control.

The concerts were usually successful, and their press notices were excellent. In 1923, the Västervik newspaper wrote, "Jussi, the middle one, sang beautifully and with much feeling 'Give Me Angel Wings.' It was most beautiful when the three boys sang together as a trio, or as a quartet with Mr. Björling. Such perfection in group singing and such superb phrasing has hardly ever been heard before. Moreover, the voices were so pure that the resulting harmony was captivating." A special day for them all was 6 July 1924; as Jussi tells it, "When I was 13 years old, we boys sang for the king and queen in front of a church in Leksand, and afterward the royal couple spoke to us while holding our hands. The queen sent us her picture with her personally inscribed greetings. That was the first time I sang for King Gustaf—it has happened often since."[30]

In late spring of 1926, while the family was headquartered at the Hotel du Nord, David suddenly took ill. He had suffered for a long time from gastritis, and it was only his strong physique and stronger will that had kept him going. Now he was unable to continue, and Dr. Björklund at the Ystad hospital treated him for three months. The four boys, now 17, 15, 13, and nine, were looked after by the sympathetic hotelier, Miss Hilda Hellberg. But they had to earn some money, so when David was well enough, he held rehearsals and made concert arrangements for them from his sickbed. Olle took his father's place as the group's leader, and they continued to give concerts on their own until David's condition improved.

The poster of their performance in Ystad's Scala movie theater on 26 July 1926—during David's convalescence—shows how their typical program had altered. The concert opened with the familiar "Härliga land," followed by the folk song "Till österland vill jag fara" and Bellman's "Undan ur vägen," all three sung by the trio of boys. Then came Jussi with two solo numbers, "M'apparì" from *Martha* and "Tonerna" by Sjöberg. To fill in for the absent David, their accompanist played three instrumental solos, followed by two numbers each by the boys. Olle sang an aria (probably the "Siciliana") from *Cavalleria rusticana* and Körling's "Vita rosor"; Jussi returned with two more solos: "Lille barn" by Sara Wennerberg Reuter and Leoncavallo's "Mattinata"; and Olle delivered "Ingalill" by Lejdström and his own signature number, "Sverige." Admission was 1 Kronor—half price for children—plus luxury tax. This particular poster carried the advice: "Bring the children to the concert! Awaken the interest in them for singing and music; it is a great benefit for the children and a pleasure for father and mother!"

When David was released from the hospital, they continued to Småland so he could spend the remaining summer days in Tjust, convalescing in part at Västervik's Central Hotel, where his good friend Mr. Gustafsson owned the restaurant. On the evening of 11 August 1926, the little band of four (Kalle didn't join them on this trip) checked into the hotel. A few hours later, David was doubled over with severe stomach pains. Gustafsson gave him opium drops, but it didn't help. Judging from the location and intensity of his pain, David feared it was appendicitis and had Olle call a doctor to get him to a hospital. But the doctor wasn't alarmed at all. "It will pass by morning," he reassured Olle over the telephone.

Neither Olle nor the restaurateur dared to oppose the doctor's authority at first, but by 5 a.m., David's pain was so unbearable that Olle called for an ambulance and had his father taken to the hospital in Västervik, where the hospital personnel treated him for gallstones—another delay. But the correct diagnosis was appendicitis, exactly as David had suspected. The appendix had burst, and David knew that peritonitis from a burst appendix was fatal.

Jussi and his two brothers gathered at their father's bedside. It was then that David, a drinking man all his life, openly admitted to his sons that in recent years he had found it increasingly difficult to control his addiction to alcohol. "Now I want all three of you to promise me, here on my deathbed, that you will never drink a drop of liquor. I don't want you to end up in the same hell as I did." Deeply affected, the boys vowed to do as their father wished.

On 13 August 1926, after two days of agony, David Björling died, leaving his sons completely alone. Kalle had spent most of his young life with his Aunt Lydia in Borlänge, so his sense of loss was less acute, but his three elder brothers had been with their father since they were born, sharing hardships and good times, adventures and successes. David had devoted his life to them. Now the person who meant everything—parent, teacher, provider, protector, and role model—was gone.

What then followed is so macabre that the memory haunted Jussi the rest of his life. The brothers went to the morgue to see their father one last time. When they raised the sheet covering his face, they recoiled in horror. Someone had forced open the corpse's mouth and with inconceivable brutality had broken loose the gold teeth. The face they had known so well since their childhood was completely disfigured by the violence. Shaken and crying, the boys rushed out of the morgue, shattered by the experience. To be left with that image only compounded for them the tragedy of their father's untimely death.

Mr. Gustafsson helped the boys find a coffin and a hearse to carry David's remains to Borlänge. According to his wishes, he was laid to rest under a large birch tree in the cemetery of Stora Tuna Church, in his parents' grave, nearby his beloved Ester.

✳

What were the boys to do now? How were they to support themselves? David had left them some money, but not enough to last. They couldn't live alone in Karlsarvet, and Uncle Johan couldn't take them in; his home wasn't big enough for his children and his nephews too.

Fortunately, David had extracted a promise from his friend Rolf Lundgren to care for his boys should anything ever happen to him. Compassionate and honorable, Lundgren carried out his promise and for the time being let the boys live in his home in Mora. He was the proprietor of a billiard parlor, and the fringe benefit of their stay was that Jussi learned to play billiards. He became quite good at it, and he enjoyed playing it for the rest of his life.

At first, the three brothers continued their concert tours under Olle's direction, but they didn't have their father's organizational skills and the results were disappointing. The worst turnout was in a little Värmland church where not a single person showed up. It appeared that the genius behind their lasting success was David, and they were about to give up when it occurred to them that perhaps they should return to America, where they had been so successful.

Lundgren, himself an amateur singer with a beautiful voice, agreed to join them, and a local hospital manager lent them the 3000 Kronor needed for the journey. They arranged for their passports, purchased their tickets, and hauled the old steamer trunk out of storage once again. Cheered by friends, the four climbed aboard the train for Gothenburg, whence they would sail to New York. But the American consulate in Gothenburg required a deposit of several hundred dollars to guarantee their return ticket. Without the deposit there would be no visas. No one had planned for this large expense, and with heavy hearts they returned to Mora.

The brothers had to find some way to support themselves. Jussi wrote to Hilda Hellberg, and the kindly hotelier found him a position in Ystad as a salesclerk in Hilding Gülisch's lighting fixtures and housewares store. "I cannot say that I particularly enjoyed it," Jussi said of this job. "I was longing to sing, which up to this point had been my whole life. But I will never forget Miss Hilda Hellberg's sacrifices. Our benefactor was like a mother to us boys and did everything to help us. I was the first one to benefit from her warmhearted help."[31]

Jussi was glad to earn some money, but standing behind a counter all day, waiting on customers, had little to motivate him. To relieve the monotony of his life, he joined an athletic club. He soon became quite good at weight lifting, the Roman rings, and arm wrestling, a very popular sport at the time. But he was biding his time and he knew it. Music was his destiny. When a Russian musician who played in the local silent movie theater suggested he get in touch with Professor Salomon Smith, he immediately called on Smith at his home.

Smith was a baritone, a church singer well known in music circles, and apart from his musical pursuits, the town's pharmacist. Their meeting was cordial, and he listened to Jussi's story with interest, especially when he learned that the young man before him was David Björling's son. He and David had met when they sang together for King Oscar and Queen Sophia in Karlskrona, and he was moved to hear that David had died.

"I had the highest regard for your father," he told Jussi. "I once took the liberty of critiquing him, something like 'You force too much! Sing lighter!' His temper flared, and without a moment's hesitation he answered: 'What do you know about it!' That was the greatest rebuff I received during my singing career!" Yes, Salomon Smith did know David.

He then asked Jussi to sing. Jussi chose Peterson-Berger's "Som Stjär-norna på himmelen" ("Like the Stars in the Heavens"). When he finished, Smith remained quiet a few moments. "Well, you certainly have a beautiful voice, and you look just like David. I hold chamber music evenings, and if you stop by, you may sing with my chamber quartet."

But the quartet wasn't meeting regularly, and many days passed while Jussi waited to hear from Smith. Finally, he received an invitation to sing with a visiting quartet from Stockholm. "I had just turned 17, and I was cocky and impertinent. When I was asked what I would like to sing, my sassy answer was: 'You decide!'"[32] He expected to be asked to sing some opera arias, but Giovanni Turricchia asked if he'd favor them with "To-nerna" by Sjöberg.

It was 1928, and with a decade of concertizing behind him, Jussi had a large repertoire. He knew this popular Swedish song and he sang it, leaving the musicians quite impressed. "You certainly have a musical gift, and an extraordinarily beautiful voice!" Turricchia said. Smith, no less impressed, promised to help him. John Forsell was a friend of his, he said, and if he could pique the manager's interest, it would open many doors.

But nothing further happened for three weeks, and Jussi was surprised he didn't break a lamp or two in the store from sheer impatience. When Smith finally sent for him he rushed to the Professor's apartment.

> "Well, young Jussi, I've talked with John on the telephone, and he has promised to receive you! I'm positive you have a brilliant future! But don't be as stubborn as your father. Had his stubbornness not been such a handi-cap for him, he would've been an enormously famous tenor."
>
> I answered: "Yes, Mr. Smith, but to me he's the greatest anyway!"
>
> Smith nodded. "Yes, you're of good stock. If everybody was as hon-est as your father was, this would be a much better world. Good luck, young Jussi, and here is a small contribution toward your trip." Whereby Salomon Smith gave me a nice gratuity.
>
> With his money and my voice I journeyed to find my fortune. Maybe in my suitcase—in spite of Salomon Smith's advice—I also brought along something else: a little bit of my father's stubbornness.[33]

And so with little more than a great deal of self-confidence and high hopes, Jussi boarded the train for Stockholm to meet the legendary opera manager, John Forsell.

Lars Johan and Mathilda Björling, Jussi's grandparents.

JB's birthplace on Magasinsgatan, Borlänge, 1911. L. to r.: His aunt, Lydia Lindblad, with her son Erik and her daughter Rut; his grandmother Mathilda with his eldest brother, Olle. Courtesy Jussi Björling Museum, Borlänge.

Ester Björling.                David Björling.

Three singing youngsters from Dalecarlia, ca. 1916.

Performing with piano accompaniment.

David and his boys.

Front: Olle, Gösta, Jussi; back: Johan, David, and accompanist Oskar Lindberg. Courtesy Märta Björling-Kärn.

Cousin Märta and her four charges.

# Konsert

gives av

## Björling-Kvartetten

i_____dagen den_____kl.____e. m.

Herr Björling med sina tre nationalklädda pojkar: Gösta 8 år, Jussi 10 år, Olle 12 år.

### BJÖRLING-KVARTETTEN

kommer direkt från sin tvååriga turné genom Amerikas Förenta Stater, där den, liksom i Sverige, vunnit sympati och erkännande av såväl publik som kritik för sin goda sång och väl skolade röster.

Tag barnen med till konserten! Väck intresse hos dem för sång och musik; det är barnen till stor nytta, far och mor till glädje.

### PROGRAM

1 a. Stilla natt
b. Stridsbön — Lindblad
c. Bereden väg för Herren — D. Björling

2 a. Svanevits sång — Geijer
b. Jag hör min Frälsares röst — D. Björling

3 a. Toysang — A. Dahl
b. Elegi — Massenet

4 a. Amerika (am. folksången)
b. Härliga land — Nordblom

5. Sverige — W. Stenhammar

6. Giv mig änglavingar — Berg

7. Sten Sture-Balladen — Svedbom

8. _____

Entré_____, barn_____ plus nöjesskatt.

An early poster of the Björling Quartet.

# KONSERT

av

## BJÖRLING-KVARTETTEN

gives i

### Scala Biografen

Torsdagen den 8 juli kl. 8 e. m.

PROGRAM

Tag barnen med till konserten! Väck intresse hos dem för sång och musik; det är barnen till stor nytta, far och mor till glädje!

Björling med sina nationalklädda pojkar, däribland lilla Kalle, den yngsta av bröderna, 7 år gammal, som nyligen börjat sin sångarbana.

**Entré: 1 kr., barn 50 öre, plus nöjesskatt.**

Biljetter säljas i                                   samt överblivna vid ingången.

A later poster of the Björling Quartet, now consisting of Olle, Jussi, Gösta, and Kalle. The penciled date and venue show Ystad, 8 July 1926.

Olle (now shorter than his younger brothers, due to the effects of rickets), Jussi, and Gösta.

The Bergs:
Olle, Emy,
John in full
uniform, and
Anna-Lisa.

Young
Anna-Lisa at
her first
communion.

The birthday boy, 2 February 1927.

Jussi in 1928.

John Forsell, the almighty manager of the Royal Opera, Stockholm, 1938.

Forsell as Don Giovanni, his most celebrated role. Courtesy Richard Copeman.

As Arnoldo in *Guglielmo Tell*, Stockholm, 27 December 1930.

JB as Don Ottavio in *Don Giovanni*, his official debut role.

As Roméo.

Anna-Lisa Berg, Stockholm's Lucia, December 1933.

The Vienna Trio: Barbro Lundquister, Greta Hallgren, and Anna-Lisa Berg, 1934. Photo Riwkin.

On Solliden's stage, Skansen.

Helga Görlin as Rosamund and JB as Martin Skarp in Kurt Atterberg's *Fanal*.

Helga Görlin as Marguerite
and JB as Faust in his
assumption of the role, 1934.

As Luigi in *Il tabarro*, 1934.

Four early roles. Top: Count Almaviva in *Barbiere*, Alfred in *Die Fledermaus*; bottom: Tonio in *La fille du régiment*, Gioacchino in *Rossini in Neapel*.

Hjördis Schymberg and JB, Roméo and Juliette, backstage at the Royal Opera.

As Vasco da Gama in *L'africaine*.

As Belmonte in *Die Entführung aus dem Serail*, a role he sang only four times. Photo Almberg & Preinitz.

Helga Görlin as Minnie and JB as Dick Johnson in *La fanciulla del West*
featured on the cover of the magazine *Svensk Damtidning* following their
assumption of the roles on 29 December 1934.

Jussi and Anna-Lisa at Busstomten's Aquacade the day after their engagement, 16 December 1934.

The wedding dinner party, 3 June 1935. L. to r.: Julia Svedelius, John Berg, Anna-Lisa, Jussi, Emy Berg.

The formal wedding portrait.

4

Foto

Passinnehavarens egenhändiga namnteckning. **Signature du** porteur. Signature of bearer. Unterschrift des Passinhabers.

*Anna-Lisa Björling*

Hustruns egenhändiga namnteckning. Signature de la femme. Signature of the wife. Unterschrift der Frau.

Anna-Lisa's "honeymoon" passport, with her wedding picture glued in by Swedish consulate staff in Berlin.

# Chapter 3

# JOHN FORSELL

Jussi was in Stockholm five days before John Forsell received him in the Royal Opera's office. His patience was nearly gone by the time he entered Forsell's sanctuary—a palatial room filled with oriental rugs, leather chairs, dark mahogany furniture, and an awe-inspiring collection of celebrity portraits.

> Behind the desk in the corner, I was met by a bald pate over a cutaway clad figure, and just beneath the forehead a pair of enormous black eyebrows. He was busy writing and did not look up for a few moments. What continued to make the strongest impression on me was the enormous eyebrows, which his very pale complexion made even more prominent. I would eventually discover that not even the most intense exposure to the sun during the hottest summer days would make him tan.
>
> After I managed to stammer my "Good day!" his face lit up and he looked very friendly. He asked me what I wanted, and I don't remember what I answered except that I wanted to sing, and that I had been singing all my life.
>
> "Oh, really!" he said and laughed. "May I hear a little about all your life!"[1]

So Jussi told his story. Forsell listened sympathetically, and Jussi's fear disappeared. Forsell assured him that he would like to hear him sing—but as to *when* that audition would take place, he said nothing.

While waiting to hear from the Opera, Salomon Smith's generous gift melted away. Jussi had to find some inexpensive lodging and a way to earn a living until something permanent came along. The solution was offered by Emil Lindroth, whom Jussi knew through Rolf Lundgren. Lindroth, a Dalecarlian carpenter who had recently moved to Stockholm's Hagalund district, let Jussi share his room. He also introduced him to Per Hellström, the owner of a small taxi company, who hired Jussi to wash his fleet of four cars. Jussi arose at 3 o'clock every morning to travel to Vanadisplan in time to wash and polish the taxis by 7 o'clock. He received 50 Kronor per car per month, so his monthly income was 200 Kronor, or approximately $40.[2]

To supplement his income, Jussi took on singing engagements in private clubs, at the restaurant Stallmästaregården, and at catered parties. He also auditioned for Nathanael Broman, the music director of the Public Radio Broadcasting Company, with "O sole mio," and apparently "the 17-year-old and completely unknown Dalecarlian really made an impression," for fee cards and printed programs attest that he was invited to join a pianist and a xylophonist in the entertainment program for 9 March 1928.[3] He sang Geehl's "For You Alone," Sjögren's "I drömmen du är mig nära" ("You Are Near in My Dreams"), and "Recondita armonia" from Puccini's *Tosca*. The Radio Orchestra was conducted by Nils Grevillius of the Royal Opera. Jussi was hoping to be paid a dizzying 75 Kronor, about $15, since he had been receiving 50 Kronor at the Stallmästaregården. But when it was over, Nathanael Broman told him he would be receiving only 30 Kronor![4] Jussi's disappointment was so great that for decades he bristled over the incident. He was irritated with Radio Sweden for exploiting a young artist who really needed the money, and he didn't hesitate to say so in print.[5] Nonetheless, his fee card in the Radio Archives shows that he appeared once more, on 20 July 1928, for the same fee. By then his resources were so meager that any income was welcome.

Meanwhile, Jussi waited for Forsell to get in touch with him, but no call to audition came. His patience was beginning to run out. When he read in the newspaper that *Hovsångaren* Martin Öhman, then under contract with the Berlin State Opera, was in Stockholm for a guest appearance, he decided to take matters into his own hands. Never doubting that he had an exceptional voice, Jussi decided to call upon the famous singer at the Strand Hotel.

Öhman was most kind and remembered the visit well: "A plump little youngster came, sang, and conquered me completely. . . . [He sang 'Recondita armonia'] with a natural ease, beautiful tone, and completely correctly. I was surprised. With Leoncavallo's 'Mattinata' the conquest was complete."[6] When Jussi had finished, Öhman exclaimed, "You are only 17 and you have such a B!" In relating his story to the tenor and his wife, singer Isobel Ghasal-Öhman, Jussi mentioned that he had tried to get into the Opera chorus but had been rejected by the chorus director, who didn't think his voice was anything special.[7]

Öhman listened patiently, and in Jussi's presence telephoned Forsell.

Jussi thanked him for his many encouraging words and left in a considerably happier mood. He would've been even more elated had he known that Öhman was impressed enough to call Forsell once more, to tell him that the boy in question had the best Swedish tenor voice of the century.[8]

At long last, Jussi was called for an audition in the Queen's Foyer of the Royal Opera House, accompanied by Tullio Voghera, the Opera's répétiteur. First, Forsell questioned him on music theory and music history; Jussi knew that his knowledge in these areas didn't amount to much. Then Forsell asked Voghera to play a note on the piano, to see if the young man could identify it—he could. But unlike Forsell, Jussi didn't have perfect pitch. When Voghera began to play "M'apparì" from the score Jussi had brought along, Forsell yelled out, "What the hell key is that?"

David wanted his boys' voices to grow naturally into the tenor repertoire. As Jussi told it,

> I hadn't gone through any change of voice, that is to say my voice had just gradually dropped from soprano to a man's voice, and my father had then transposed the music to suit my voice. The aria which I was to sing was a whole note lower than the usual setting, and Forsell picked up on it immediately. I explained what had happened, and he thought my father had been very sensible.[9]

Although Forsell asked for his address and promised to be in touch, Jussi didn't feel he sang especially well that day. Once more, he waited a long time for the call, often wondering if the manager left him in suspense out of pure spite. Forsell didn't exactly have a reputation for kindness, and he could be mean-spirited. He had known David Björling and followed his career at a distance, and he knew that David had never made it to the Opera because of his temper. Perhaps he wanted to test the son, to see whether he was a chip off the old block temperamentally. Jussi, fully aware of his musical gifts, thought that perhaps he had appeared a little too cocky at the audition, and that Forsell was trying to put him in his place. Forsell was unbelievably demanding of his students, especially those of whom he expected much. Doubtless, he expected much of Jussi the first time he heard him sing.

The summer of 1928 passed with Jussi washing taxis, singing at various affairs, and waiting for some sign of life from Forsell. Just before the Music Academy and Royal Opera School entrance auditions, he contacted Jussi. The Academy had four openings that year, one in the solo voice class taught by Forsell himself. Of Jussi's Music Academy audition on 21 August, Forsell noted in his diary: "Remarkably good, a phenomenon, 17 years."[10]

Herbert Sandberg played the piano accompaniment at the audition for the Opera School. Jussi sang Don Ottavio's G-major aria, "Dalla sua pace," from *Don Giovanni*.[11] Of the 13 aspiring vocalists auditioned that day, eight were rejected, three were auditioned again, and two—a soprano and a tenor—were admitted. The 28 August 1928 minutes of the repertoire committee's meeting on admission are interesting. Whereas all other applicants were accorded only a brief phrase or two, they wrote at length of applicant No. 12:

> Mr. Johan Björling: Particularly beautiful tenor, but considered too young for the Opera School. The committee decided to recommend that Mr. B. may receive some scholarship help possibly from the Björn Family Fund in order to preserve this voice for the Royal Theater. It was considered appropriate that B. would study at Borgarskolan [a public school] and would be put under the control of the theater. Born 2.2.1911.

Jussi hadn't deluded himself. His unwavering faith in his voice, in his father's teachings, and in himself had paid off. A singing career was within his reach.

Forsell soon took a personal interest in David Björling's son. He felt that Jussi needed a proper home, an environment where he could advance himself culturally, and so he wrote to Carl and Julia Svedelius, asking them to consider taking in Jussi as a boarder. Carl Svedelius was the principal of North High School with an excellent reputation as a pedagogue; for some years he had taught Prince Vilhelm as well as the future king, Gustaf VI Adolf. His wife, Julia, an educated woman and the author of several books and articles on various social issues, worked at Norrbotten's Industrial School and for the Red Cross. She was a plump woman with graying hair fashioned in a bun at the back of her head, and her wise, clear eyes seemed to look at life with amusement. With no children of their own, the Svedeliuses became quite attached to the students whom they took into their home from time to time.

One autumn morning in 1928 Julia returned from Copenhagen, where she had been gathering illustrations for a book; her husband met her at the train station. "John Forsell called and asked us to board a boy with a most remarkably beautiful voice," he began. "I told him I would ask you if you knew of some appropriate home."

"We'll take him," Julia answered without hesitation.

"But my dear, where are we going to put him?"

"He can have my room!" was her impetuous response.

Julia described this exchange and the subsequent sequence of events in great detail in her book *År och människor* (*Years and People*):

> I ran to the telephone and called the Opera manager, who answered the phone himself. "Excellent! He'll come at once. He's sitting in my office right now."
>
> After 10 minutes, Jussi came. With dusty shoes, greasy hair, short-statured and broad-shouldered, he was not much to look at.[12] Jussi surveyed the surroundings with a quick glance. I immediately took him to my room with a feeling of warm motherliness, because there was something so childlike about the boy.
>
> "Here is where you may stay, little Jussi, and please call us aunt and uncle." I sensed he was shy, and I wanted to help him get started.

"This will be good enough," he answered without letting himself be impressed by the white furniture upholstered in rose satin. He had lived in much finer rooms before, I was soon to find out. "Over there in America, you know." A long and shifting career lay behind this 17-year-old. And he had experiences which were completely foreign to his new "aunt."[13]

The matter of finances remained to be settled. The Svedeliuses were comfortable and prepared to subsidize their protégés to the point of generosity, but they weren't in a position to feed and clothe boarders as a matter of charity. Thus Julia had to reach some agreement with Forsell about the financial assistance the Opera School was willing to give the young voice student. In a letter to Forsell dated 9 September 1928, given here in its entirety, she wrote:

It was a very quick agreement which was entered into, but I want to promise you to do everything I can for the young man. And I know that my husband will be very beneficial. At the agreed-upon price of 300 Kronor per month, a piano will also be included, which will always be well tuned and located in his room, completely at his disposal. If we travel to Dalarna or Saltsjöbaden during Christmas, we will take him along at no extra cost. All laundry and mending of clothes are included. Concert tickets—when free ones aren't available and when it might be beneficial for the young man to join me—will be provided. In addition, I'll eventually be looking for further instructions. I enjoy music enormously, and I'd be delighted if you, Mr. Opera Director, would give me a ticket from time to time. On the 16th of September, at 9:30 for breakfast, he'll arrive with his bag and baggage. I'll then check what needs to be supplemented.[14]

Forsell and his Board found the arrangement acceptable, and Jussi took up residence with the Svedeliuses, an enjoyable arrangement all around. In the warmhearted, kind couple, and especially in Aunt Julia, he found a very close replacement for the parents he'd lost. Uncle Carl became interested in opera, and Aunt Julia deemed it a special treat to have Jussi around. He was unlike other students she'd received in her home, and in many respects unlike anyone else she'd ever met. She enjoyed his fantastic stories as much as she was perplexed by his perpetual motion; her young charge seemed to be always on the go. A good pianist, she accompanied him in Concone's vocalises and simple arias:

His voice carried me far, far away—and I have to admit—we often ended up in a boutique where Jussi had fallen in love with an elegant scarf, or something else "absolutely necessary." He stole my heart with his song and the rent payments with his desires. . . . When we came home from an opera performance to our sandwiches, Jussi would strike up some tenor arias and sing so the whole place resounded. I can't imagine more forgiving neighbors than we had. One woman replied, after I had apologized for disturbing her: "I put on my robe and slippers when I was awakened and went to the next room so that I could hear a little better." When Jussi sang before an open window, a crowd gathered on the street.[15]

As the first year neared its conclusion, it was Julia who approached Forsell about the renewal of the agreement with the Opera. By then she was quite aware of the expenses involved, and on 23 April 1929 she again wrote to Forsell, saying that if he and the Royal Opera Board wished, she and her husband were willing to keep Jussi on "in consideration of a compensation amounting to 325 Kronor per month including a room with a piano, food, pocket money, laundry, lessons in Swedish and German, and clothes." The letter continues:

> The cost for sheet music and medical care, however, ought to be covered by funds which are at the Opera's disposition. This winter we have covered, without asking for reimbursement from the Opera, certain medical expenses, including pumping-out of the stomach, etc., totaling about 80 Kronor. Thanks to prescribed dietary discipline and medication, his health has improved significantly.
>
> It is rather natural that Jussi Björling's clothing costs this last year have been high, as upon his arrival here he owned barely useful shoes, underwear, socks, etc. His wardrobe consisted of one very worn suit and an overcoat, toward which he still owed 50 Kronor. It ought to be possible to significantly reduce his clothing account for next year.... We are awaiting the favor of your reply before June 1.[16]

Forsell replied in the affirmative, and in fact Jussi stayed with the Svedeliuses throughout his Academy years. As he grew older, Aunt Julia's tender care sometimes became too much for him, and his need for freedom drove him to sneak out from time to time. Often she tiptoed into his room to tuck him in at night, but as soon as she padded out, carefully closing the door behind her, Jussi, who was fully clothed under the silk bedspread and only pretending to be asleep, would jump out of bed and slip out on nocturnal adventures with his Academy colleagues.

By the time Jussi and I met he had already moved to an apartment, but he always spoke of Uncle Carl and Aunt Julia with great devotion. The first time I was introduced to Julia Svedelius, she scrutinized me for a moment, then pulled me approvingly to her ample bosom. She saw how highly I regarded Jussi and that was most important to her. I will never forget her words to me: "When Jussi entered our home he filled it with light and music, bringing a whole new atmosphere to our lives." I understood what she meant. I felt exactly the same way.

※

Jussi auditioned for the Opera School's 1929 spring term with "Recondita armonia" from *Tosca*. He wasn't nervous, but his last note was forced and sharp. Forsell raised his enormous eyebrows. "Mr. Björling, did you notice that you ended up too high on the B?" "Yes, I did." "Why—isn't that note high enough?" But, as Jussi observed,

I was accepted in spite of my too-high note. At the Opera School, Set Svanholm and I learned under Forsell's guidance a scene from *The Barber of Seville*. Svanholm sang Figaro and I Count Almaviva, [and] I don't feel I'm exaggerating if I say that we were sensational. There were even some discussions about an engagement, although Forsell earlier had told Julia Svedelius that such a thing was unthinkable within six years. After a year and a half I was close to the goal.[17]

His classmates in the solo class that spring semester of 1929 were Götha Allard, Set Svanholm, and Nini Högstedt, later Mrs. Set Svanholm. On Thursdays, the students from all the solo classes, 15 in all, participated in ensemble lessons. It was during such a lesson that Forsell presented the new pupil to his schoolmates. "Because this was an ensemble lesson, there wasn't much music instruction," Jussi recalled. "Forsell told the other students that I had an exceptional voice, and I sang 'For You Alone' by Geehl, whereupon I was rewarded with a very fine applause from the other students. I can hardly remember having had a more flattering moment."[18]

Despite his reputation as a voice pedagogue, Forsell's singing was old-fashioned, as the recordings he made late in life attest, and his vocal method, which he taught to his students with zealous authority, didn't conform to David Björling's more natural technique. When Jussi went home to Dalarna for a visit, ready to impress his brothers with what he had learned at the Academy, they ridiculed his new, affected way of singing. "Is this what you learned in Stockholm?" Olle asked. "Forget it, Jussi; it doesn't sound good at all."

Jussi let this sink in. It was harsh criticism, but he trusted his brother's ears more than anyone else's—and he knew he was right. During his next lesson in Stockholm, when Forsell corrected him, he shocked his colleagues by interrupting the master: "I must sing *my* way, or not at all!"

Everyone in the class froze, certain that one of Forsell's famous outbursts would follow. But to their surprise, he didn't argue. He must've realized the effectiveness of Jussi's vocal training and understood that Jussi was no ordinary singer. In spite of his intolerant and authoritarian ways, Forsell was broad-minded enough to let Jussi keep to his father's teachings and follow the way he so firmly believed was right for him. It was a wise concession; Forsell didn't ruin a flawlessly produced natural voice, and Jussi maintained his vocal quality till the end of his life. What Forsell did give Jussi in the years ahead was refinement and polish, in good measure, the finishing touches to the singer's art.

The Opera School's mission was to produce successful musicians, and the curriculum was thorough and comprehensive, as Jussi describes in his autobiography:

I had piano lessons from Skarby, studied harmony with Melchers, and learned elocution from Mrs. Anna Simonsson. In music history I had much homework from Tobias Norlind, and I had Bernhard Lilja in music theory. Stage movement was taught by Anna Behle. . . . I lived under the delusion that even during my first music lesson I would begin singing arias, but that didn't happen. I got to vocalize on only one note: aeoieoiaeioaaa. We had to articulate with our mouths, not our throats. This continued for many lessons, and I understood afterward that it was very important I exercise my stiff lips in this way. I studied Concone's vocalises (very beautiful, small compositions) and scales by Panofka.[19]

During these exercises, Jussi contorted his face and wrinkled his brow so much that Forsell told him he looked like a surprised puppy. To correct the bad habit, he had Jussi stick a postage stamp on his forehead.

Eventually Jussi was assigned a number to sing, Josephson's "Longing for Home." He found it rather boring but very good practice, and plod through it over and over again, until, as he expressed it, "I was hoping that Josephson would finally go home so he wouldn't have to long so much." Toward the end of this first term he was given his first opera aria to study, the familiar "Dalla sua pace" from *Don Giovanni*. But it wasn't easy to please Forsell. According to Jussi, he often swore during lessons, sometimes angrily, sometimes sarcastically, sometimes in a friendly way. At times he called his pupils by their first names; when he was very pleased he'd even hug a student. But when he was in what Jussi called a "wart mood," things weren't pleasant. Forsell had a wart on his neck, and when he scratched it, it meant he was very irritated.

When Jussi was asked to audition at the Opera, he sang "Dalla sua pace." Forsell gave Jussi many private lessons at his beautiful home on Torsgatan in preparation.

> The evening before I was at his home for a final rehearsal. Forsell forbade me in very strong terms to sing a note before 5 o'clock the following day, when the audition would take place, and of course I obeyed. But when I was to sing, I felt very hoarse. Forsell had made a mistake: I was used to singing for a few hours every day, and the sudden and unusual rest didn't do me any good. Even so it went quite well, and the board members were rather pleased.[20]

Financially, the first term at the Academy was difficult for Jussi. The stipend and the weekly 10 Kronor spending money wasn't enough, and like any other healthy teenager he was always hungry. It was during this period that he came up with an ingenious plan to get some free food. He and his friend Gösta (Nilsson) Kjellertz would go down to the docks opposite the Strand Hotel and bet with the dockworkers on arm wrestling. "If we can beat you, will you buy us coffee and sandwiches?" As Kjellertz told the story, the seasoned men took one look at the 18-year-old boys and laughed. But their laughter ceased in minutes. Jussi beat every one of them. Other fellows from the neighborhood were called upon to try to defeat him—but none could. For a long time he and Gösta lived royally off the wagers.[21]

Jussi was rapidly becoming "Uncle John" Forsell's favorite. Never, the manager raved to his friends, had he had such an interested, diligent, and grateful pupil, and at the end of the academic term, he invited Jussi to spend the summer at his Villa Gullebo on Stenungsön, a beautiful wooded island about 30 miles north of Gothenburg. This was considered a great privilege, extended only to Forsell's best students from the Opera School. This select group, which included Brita Hertzberg, Einar Beyron, Set Svanholm, Joel Berglund, and Einar Larson, joined John and Gurli Forsell's own five children, Anna, Björn, Jacob, Vidar, and Lolo, and occasional visitors Martin Öhman, Isobel Ghasal-Öhman, and the Scottish tenor Joseph Hislop. The guests never called the place by its geographical name—to them it was Singers' Island. The first summer Jussi shared a small cabin with Forsell's oldest son, Björn, at a boardinghouse near Villa Gullebo; in later years Jussi was the Forsells' houseguest.

Björn Forsell recalled the first time he met Jussi, "a short, humble, pouting, countrified figure with innocent blue eyes and a wonderful lack of nerves. And how he sang, even then! Perhaps more beautifully, more naturally, even more lyrically than he did later when he acquired technique with all its pluses and minuses."[22] Jussi loosened up over the summer and lost some of his shyness. He was cheerful, impulsive, and full of romantic ideas—the library he brought along included books about Tarzan, Captain Horatio Hornblower, and the Scarlet Pimpernel. Little wonder that under the influence of such yarns, one day, with the help of a razor blade, Jussi and Björn Forsell became blood brothers.

During their leisure time at Villa Gullebo, the young people lived a wonderful outdoor life, swimming and sailing; Forsell preferred playing backgammon, baccarat, and bridge with his friend Herman Lindquist, who lived in the neighborhood. But they also worked: the villa's huge attic served as a singing studio, and for the entire summer the students received voice lessons. It didn't cost one penny—but Forsell demanded results! Sometimes Gurli Forsell accompanied them, but most often a very shy young lady played the piano. She was invariably greeted by Forsell with a broad "Good day, Miss Stenberg! And how is this naturally shy child feeling today?" As Jussi wrote:

> Even on his deathbed he greeted her with the same words when she came to visit. Although he was in bad shape from a stroke, he received her, and she tried to cheer him up by saying, "You look much better! Soon we'll be able to gather all your friends around the bed and have a nice time." John Forsell, his old self to the very last day, answered: "Hell, how boring!"[23]

Some have speculated as to how and when Jussi developed his spectacular high notes. According to Björn Forsell, when Jussi first came to the Opera, only his B-flat was secure. It wasn't Forsell, a baritone, who taught him the highest notes of his range—C, C-sharp, and D—it was Joseph Hislop:

> Jussi Björling came to me and asked my advice about some technical problems. . . . I gladly took him on, and the following summer he lived with me

at Brottkärr. To instruct Jussi was like sprinkling water on a blotter—everything was soaked up immediately. He got as much out of one single lesson as an average singer after six months' instruction. . . . His musical taste, his phrasing, and feeling for rhythm reminded me of the violinist Jascha Heifetz' playing.[24]

Björn was present when Hislop gave Jussi his first demonstration on Singers' Island. "This is how you do it. I don't know where you place the sound, just imitate me," he said. Then he tossed off a high C as if it were nothing. Jussi imitated him and Hislop cried out, "Yes, of course! There it is!"[25]

In addition to music instruction, Forsell taught Latin, Swedish, and German to his students, so they'd understand what they were singing. He also insisted they be in good physical condition—he had maintained his erect, military posture and demanded that his students too appear as physical models for other singers—and know how to comport themselves in social settings. Forsell endeavored to turn each young person under his wing into a well-rounded, well-educated individual; he raised a whole generation of singers this way. As Jussi observed, "What he hated most in the world was ignorance."

When Forsell was a young man, a singer didn't command any respect in Sweden. But Forsell loved his profession and wanted it "to be respected and honored beyond the stage."[26] When he discovered a gifted student, he made a strong personal commitment to advance his protégé. For instance, Joel Berglund came from a free-church family, and his parents couldn't think of anything more shocking than their son standing on a stage, singing for money. Forsell went to them and convinced them that Joel's talent must be recognized, that an opera singer's work was at least as honorable as anyone else's.

A gifted administrator, pedagogue, and performer, Forsell was so successful in so many fields that he saw no reason to be humble about his accomplishments. Truth to tell, *braggadocio* fit his persona perfectly: humility would've been out of character. His military background had fixed in his mind the belief that the man in charge was *in charge*, and he consciously promoted his image as all-knowing and all-seeing. Nothing escaped his attention, and Jussi was fond of relating a particular incident to demonstrate the point. One evening around midnight, Jussi was sitting out by the road, talking with a girl, when somebody happened by. Jussi recognized Forsell's dirty old student cap—he was on his way home from a round of baccarat at Lindquist's. Jussi and the girl hid, and Forsell passed them without turning his head. But when he was 50 feet beyond, he stopped, turned round, and called back: "Listen now, Mr. Björling! Remember that God can see you!"[27]

⚹

In 1929 Jussi made his first recordings as a tenor. He cut "For You Alone" and Leoncavallo's "Mattinata" on 4 September 1929 with an orchestra conducted by Hjalmar Meissner; for unknown reasons the records weren't issued, and the matrices were destroyed. One month later, on Forsell's recommendation and after some test recordings, Skandinaviska Grammophon, the Swedish branch of "His Master's Voice," offered Jussi his first contract. The two-year contract, dated 4 October 1929, guaranteed him an annual minimum of 1200 Kronor for 12 sides.

On 18 December 1929, Jussi's recording career under his own name began in earnest. Nils Grevillius presided over the session, the first of countless such collaborations between Nils and Jussi. They began with "Torna a Surriento," followed by two Swedish songs, and ended with Geehl's "For You Alone." The records were intended for the domestic market, and Jussi sang all selections in Swedish. They show a fully developed voice and musicality that would be enviable at any age; for an 18-year-old youngster, they border on the miraculous.

The prospect of hearing his own voice for the first time was very exciting to Jussi. When he went to the company to collect his first record he also received a gramophone. "I took the big parcel in my arms, got into a taxi, and spent the afternoon playing the record again and again. I hope you'll excuse this self-indulgence on the part of a boy who had never before been able to listen to himself from the outside, so to speak. I didn't recognize my voice at all."[28]

The first contract expired and was renewed on better terms, but when an opportunity to cut some discs with Fred Winter and his dance orchestra presented itself, Jussi couldn't afford to let principles stand in the way of increased income. He eventually made 12 forgettable sides of popular ditties, but they weren't the kind of records that met with Forsell's approval. Yes, Jussi needed to earn money, but members of the Royal Opera were not to degrade themselves singing such trash. Forsell informed young Björling (this, or "young Jussi," was his usual form of address), "If you're going to make these records, at the very least you must change your name!"

So Jussi became "Erik Odde" for these records. He made no effort to sound like Jussi Björling—on the contrary, he did his best to create a pop sound. Because only a few copies of these Oddities (pun intended) survived, the records released under the *nom de disque* of Erik Odde are among Jussi's rarest.

Stockholm began to take notice of Björling, and he obtained another radio engagement. On 3 April 1930 he sang four songs and arias from *Rigoletto* and *La fanciulla del West*, finally receiving the fabulous 75 Kronor fee. That summer Jussi was automatically included among the guests on Singers' Island, where under Forsell's guidance he prepared for his first opera season, which started unusually early in 1930. On 21 July 1930 Jussi made his stage debut as the Lamplighter in Puccini's *Manon Lescaut*. He was only 19.

Jussi's first year with the Royal Opera on scholarship was more like an indenture. The 250-Kronor monthly stipend gave the Royal Opera all the rights and the singer all the obligations. If for any reason the stipendiary broke his contract, took employment at another theater, or left the profession, he was obliged to pay 3000 Kronor in damages to the Royal Theater or pay back the stipends if the total exceeded that amount. "When I read it now, my scholarship contract seems like slavery," Jussi thought. "But I was happy and satisfied, and who knows what would have happened to me without this help."[29]

Jussi Björling made his inauspicious debut with a fine cast. Greta Söderman sang Manon, Einar Beyron Des Grieux, and Grevillius conducted. Jussi's role was too brief to inspire nervousness; absent-minded Carl Svedelius missed Jussi's entrance and didn't even notice him. Aunt Julia, on the other hand, was beside herself, sitting on the edge of her seat from the moment the curtain went up.

The long-standing rules of the Opera, which had so rankled David Björling, hadn't changed: every beginner was required to sing three major debut roles before he could be hired. In Jussi's case this minor role as the Lamplighter didn't count; it was merely to afford him a little experience. The same was true for another tiny part some days later, the poet Näktergal in *Bellman* by Ziedner. His real debut was to be Don Ottavio in Mozart's *Don Giovanni*, in a gala performance on 20 August 1930.

It was a role that required some preparation: Jussi never passed up an opportunity to eat, and now, for his Don Ottavio to appear a worthy adversary to the title character, he had to surrender himself to a strict diet, rowing excursions, tennis matches with Gurli Forsell, and fencing lessons with Uncle John. These last were both exercise and stagecraft, to accustom Jussi to handling a rapier. The title role was being taken by the master, of course, and in the first act, when Don Ottavio challenges Don Giovanni to a duel, Forsell wanted Jussi to look like a cavalier with a sword, not a peasant shaking a stick at a dog.

No one thought more of his Don than Forsell himself. One evening, so the story goes, he just couldn't stop admiring his costumed self in his dressing room's full-length mirror. Indeed, the epitome of the Spanish grandee stared back at him from the cheval glass, a true blue blood to the fingertips nestled in his white gloves. On impulse, he sent his dresser upstairs to the boardroom to tell von Stedingk to come to his dressing room. The dresser returned with the message that the Opera Board was in session, Count von Stedingk couldn't come just then. This excuse was too flimsy for Forsell; he ordered the dresser to return and insist that the president of the board come downstairs. Assuming there must be a serious problem for the manager to be so insistent, von Stedingk came.

"What's the matter, Mr. Forsell?" he asked perplexed. The baritone strutted around the room, then stopped and faced him. "I just wanted you to see how a real count should look!"

"I have no memory of being nervous the day of my debut," Jussi said. "The rehearsals had been muggy and sweaty, but when the day came for my first big appearance on the opera stage, I was as cool as a cucumber."[30] This claim wasn't after-the-fact posturing: performing in front of an audience was in Jussi's blood. He was in full control of his vocal resources, physically and technically. He knew his part and had rehearsed it ad nauseam. "That a young debutant doesn't have stage fright is not so difficult to explain," he further mused. "He has nothing to lose and everything to gain. An artist who is already well known struggles against high odds. People expect so much of him, and he doesn't want to disappoint his audience. The greater the fuss over his appearance, the more nervous he becomes."[31]

No, he recalled, "The first time I stood on the stage, my only feeling was acute embarrassment, not on account of the audience but because of those who stood next to me onstage and watched. For every gesture—and the art of opera is closely associated with big gestures—I felt my face redden beneath the makeup. I peeked at the others to see if they laughed, but they did not."[32] Jussi's fear of grand gestures was inborn, and it made him appear somewhat stiff and labored onstage.

His debut performance progressed well. The only mishap occurred when the time came to challenge Don Giovanni. Jussi faced his boss, paralyzed, holding his sword and making no movement. Moments passed, the music moved forward relentlessly. Forsell finally yelled at him so loudly that it was heard clear up in the third balcony. "Get going, damn it!"—and he made an unexpected thrust toward Jussi's stomach. Jussi, a fencing novice despite the summer's lessons, parried the thrust, and the point of the Don's foil flew up, cutting a gash at his eyebrow. With unplanned realism, blood ran down his face, and after the act he had to be bandaged by a doctor.

But that didn't matter. The next morning's reviews were notably kind to the debutant. "Real promising tenor material," wrote Herman Glimstedt in *Aftonbladet*, "and the timbre of the voice bestowed on the character a welcome virility, which this passive stage character completely lacks. . . . For the present it was probably wise, however, not to include the much more demanding B-major aria." It's hard to explain why Forsell decided to shorten the role by cutting "Il mio tesoro." Difficult as the aria is, Jussi could've delivered it.

The revered critic Moses Pergament thought that in the "rather thankless role" of Don Ottavio Jussi displayed "a melodious tenor voice of warm timbre, somewhat baritonal in color, and shows good promise even dramatically."[33] Curt Berg wrote in *Dagens Nyheter*, "As Ottavio, a young singer called Jussi Björling made his debut with a yet immature, but unusually promising voice. . . . He performed his role as the Spanish nobleman with tranquil and natural acting and made a pleasing impression. The diction was very good."

It was no accident that Forsell picked Don Ottavio for young Björling's debut. "Of all the opera styles, Mozart's is the one closest to my heart," wrote Jussi. "My teacher, John Forsell, gave me things to sing that were beneficial both for the throat and the intellect—so it was mostly Mozart. Mozart by no means suits all singers, but if one can sing Mozart well, then I think one can also sing Rossini and Verdi very well."[34]

That autumn, Jussi performed the small role of the Songwriter in several performances of Charpentier's *Louise*. On 6 December he sang his first *Messiah*, with Tullio Voghera conducting, and he repeated Part One on the radio on Christmas Day.

Jussi's second official debut role, Arnoldo in Rossini's *Guglielmo Tell*, followed two days later, on 27 December 1930; Joel Berglund sang the title role. One may wonder why the youthful Jussi Björling was asked, or even allowed, to sing Arnoldo, a role with 19 high Cs and two D-flats. With its impossibly demanding tessitura, Rossini's masterpiece is seldom heard; decades can pass before a suitable tenor emerges. Remember, however, that Rossini composed the role for the exquisite lyric voice of Adolphe Nourrit, not a leather-lunged screamer.[35] The opera was probably performed with many cuts, and while I don't know how many of the Cs and D-flats remained, I'm certain that none of them were transposed. Jussi didn't shout either.

Once again Moses Pergament praised the young singer, saying he strongly believed Björling would become a star among tenors. *Stockholms-Tidningen* found Jussi's acting "stiff and like a beginner's," but *Folkets Dagblad* (30 December 1930) softened this criticism: "He has made strong progress in the development of his beautiful tenor voice—the dramatics will also come eventually; it's said the young man has not yet reached 20 years of age." *Svenska Dagbladet* (30 December 1930) was even more generous: "In this singer, making his debut, our reviewer saw a future star tenor. . . . It sounds like a fairy tale, but this 19-year-old already has 14 years behind him as a singer."

Of Jussi's third debut role, Jonathan in the Stockholm premiere of Carl Nielsen's *Saul and David*, on 13 January 1931, Curt Berg wrote, "[His] performance had merit, but [he] didn't show anything that he hadn't shown before." With each performance, he became more comfortable with stage routine and found it less difficult to act out a part. Having fulfilled the terms of his scholarship, on 19 May 1931 he signed his first "real" opera contract. On 1 July, Jussi Björling became a permanent member of the Royal Opera in Stockholm. The person who appreciated his star pupil's progress most of all was John Forsell. In many ways, he had taken over where David Björling had left off.

# Chapter 4

# THE ASCENT

Four years was the usual length of study at the Music Academy and the Opera School. Jussi finished in only three, ahead of all the other students, and he even received the Academy's highest award, a medal given to students who combined "outstanding musical ability with higher level of training." Jussi often spoke to Aunt Julia about how sorry he was that his brothers hadn't had the same opportunity to further their education. She agreed and intervened with Forsell on the brothers' behalf. They were allowed to audition, and soon both Gösta and Olle were enrolled at the Music Academy.[1]

Gösta had a beautiful voice, albeit smaller than Jussi's, and a very sensitive throat; when he caught a cold it took him a long time to recover. I often sang duets with my classmate Olle, whose voice had a somewhat different timbre, perhaps due to his spinal deformity. But both brothers had a remarkable range and were, like Jussi, thoroughly grounded in their father's vocal technique. The youngest of the brothers, Kalle, whom I met much later, was a late bloomer. A high baritone with a beautiful tone, he had had too few years in which to benefit from his father's teachings.

But Jussi's voice, I recognized almost immediately, was one of a kind, with a color unlike any other. The sound was unforgettable. Many times I've been told by complete strangers that they recognize Jussi's voice at the first note. The timbre was so unique that it couldn't be mistaken for any other except, quite curiously, for one of his brothers. The best qualities of the

Björling genetic imprint for singing had come together in Jussi. He was the lucky one.

Although Jussi had finished his studies, he often returned to his old school. At first I thought he only came to say hello to his brothers but later found out that he was hoping to see me "by accident." For my part, I gradually realized that I was watching for him, and that I would feel a little twinge in my heart if I hadn't seen him for some time. Gösta was very good in harmonic theory, and I asked him to help me occasionally. We would study together at their place on Storgatan, all the while with me hoping that by some coincidence Jussi would show up while I was there. Sometimes he did, and every time we spoke, even for a few moments, I was left feeling happy.

After a while, Jussi and I began to go out together, every now and then at first but gradually more frequently despite our being very busy—Jussi with his work at the Opera, and I with my studies at the Academy. He invited me to restaurants, movies, and concerts; I especially remember us attending a fabulous recital by Marian Anderson—her first appearance in Stockholm. Afterward we'd go to his home and spend the rest of the evening talking, about music, singing, our lives; he had only good things to say about his parents—especially his father. He often spoke of him, with love, affection, and a respect bordering on reverence. Because my own mother was so important to me, I often wondered about Jussi's, but she was just a faint, lovely memory from his early childhood and he mentioned her seldom. When he did, he invariably described her as someone radiant and good-hearted, an angel surrounded by light.

I had dated before, but not seriously. My voice training had come before all else. But the more Jussi and I saw each other, the more I began to discover that this sturdy fellow from Stora Tuna with the phenomenal voice was completely different from the privileged and often spoiled young men I had gone out with before. I realized that I really didn't belong with that crowd; with Jussi I felt at home. Something real and honest in him attracted me, something deeper the others lacked. He had special qualities that, together with his great warmth, made me feel good to be in his company. Despite his happy, good-natured exterior he was a serious young man. His stubborn nature worked wonders for him professionally: it kept him focused.

Now and then, Jussi displayed an unexpected shyness and awkwardness—feelings I knew well myself. As time went by, I suspected that I had something he needed. He may have felt that I understood him, and perhaps my company gave him a sense of security. At that point I wasn't exactly in love with Jussi, I just liked him very, very much. But almost without our noticing it, our friends began to regard us as a couple. Music was our common bond and professional careers our shared goal. My life consisted of study and practice; the days passed routinely enough. But Jussi Björling stood on threshold of an unbelievable career. His rise to the top was about to begin.

※

Jussi's first documented solo recital took place at Stora Tuna Church, on 8 February 1931. He was warmly received but rated little more than an honorable mention from the reviewer. Two hours later, he sang another recital in Domnarvet iron works' union hall in Borlänge, where his father had worked long ago. His most important break came soon after these back-to-back recitals.

"Even if I wasn't around during the beginning of the gramophone, I dare say the gramophone was around during my beginning," Jussi observed.[2] Richard Rydberg, the manager of Copenhagen's Tivoli, happened to hear one of Jussi's early records (HMV X3675); that was all he needed to hire him for a concert at Tivoli. Jussi's explosive success there eventually led to his breakthrough in central Europe and opened the doors to opera houses and concert halls beyond the Continent. The day after the 29 July 1931 concert, Axel Kjerulf's review was headlined in *Politiken*: "Tenor Success at Tivoli!"

> The young Swedish singer, Jussi Björling, was an enormous success with his concert last night. All of a sudden, here comes a 20-year-old Swede from far up in Dalarna, and he sings so your heart melts, sings with a voice fresh and strong, a glowing lyric tenor with the most beautiful timbre, with both softness and power. . . . Seldom has one heard such a beautiful voice—a brilliant tenor of masculine stability and fullness—and at the same time a delightful timbre with a unique, quite enchanting, northern-light shimmer which completely conquered the audience, bursting with applause. . . . There is no doubt that the world lies open to Jussi Björling. He is a world-class singer. A more perfect voice than Jussi Björling's does not exist. Nature has given him everything.[3]

To this point, "very promising" was the phrase usually applied to Jussi's abilities; the somewhat reserved Swedish critics had been reluctant to grant him laurels. To receive such reviews on his first appearance abroad, therefore, was something special indeed! The Danish public remained faithful to him, and after 1931 he was invited back to Tivoli's big hall every year. As a rule, the moment his visits were announced, the box office was stormed and the recitals sold out.

His recognition at home was more gradual, which was probably just as well for his development, both as a singer and as a person; things were happening quickly enough. During those early years Jussi worked intensely at the Opera, alternating between small and large roles as assigned. He was unbelievably diligent and, as someone remarked, swallowed the roles whole. In addition to the parts he had already performed, in 1931 he sang Walther von der Vogelweide in *Tannhäuser* and Tybalt in *Roméo et Juliette*, as well as in Montemezzi's *Notte di Zoraima*, Zandonai's *I cavalieri di Ekebù*, and Berg's *Engelbrekt*.

Forsell's reaction to Jussi's makeup the first time he sang Tybalt was memorable. Makeup man Atos Berg had given Jussi a fierce look to fit the character, "a terrible black beard and enormous, protruding eyebrows." As Jussi admired his appropriately belligerent face in the mirror, his mentor came by and stared at him furiously. "What in hell have you come up with now! Damn it, how you look." He pointed at Jussi's militant eyebrows. "What are those supposed to be? A pair of toilet brushes?"[4]

Jussi sang Tybalt only three times before he gave up the role. A more important assignment was the Norwegian huntsman Erik in *Der fliegende Holländer*, a role that was particularly well suited to his youthful voice.

> The new Erik, Jussi Björling, . . . has evidently learned a few more gestures over the summer. Fortunately, this languishing hunter, like another of this same young artist's roles, Don Ottavio in *Don Giovanni*, is a role in which acting is not of great importance. Especially in the second-act duet with Senta, Mr. Björling's tenor delighted us with seductive timbre and legato, along with good diction.[5]

Jussi's next major role, in Rossini's *Il barbiere di Siviglia*, earned high praise on all accounts. Mezzo-soprano Gertrud Pålson-Wettergren reminisced, "The first time I paid attention to Forsell's tenor discovery was probably in 1931, when he sang Almaviva in *The Barber of Seville*. I remember he sang quite wonderfully, with a sparkling ease for the coloratura and a charming ring in his voice."[6]

The role left the same impression on Gösta Kjellertz. "Above all, he had an incredible coloratura technique, fully comparable to the greatest instrumentalists—violinists or pianists with great technical ability. You heard every note in his scales. . . . Everything sat perfectly for him and he did it with the greatest ease."[7] Moses Pergament was no less pleased and surprised:

> Jussi Björling, whose unusually melodious and warm timbre already has attracted considerable attention, has not demonstrated any obvious dramatic talent until now. But now he surprised [us] with a vivacious and very well-executed portrayal. . . . This interpretation of a new role was good proof of dramatic talent, and the young singer's victory was even more deserved as this time the singing too had brilliance and variety of expression.[8]

*Barbiere* was performed 13 times in 10 months. The curiosity of the casting was the Figaro, sung by future heldentenor Set Svanholm, then a baritone. Jussi and Set eventually sang *Barbiere* together 23 times.

After yet another series of minor roles in *Salome* and *Tristan und Isolde*, in February 1932 Jussi made his first appearance as the Duke of Mantua in Verdi's *Rigoletto*, the first role that was to remain in his repertoire for the rest of his life. Curt Berg thought it rather adventurous "to hand over the role of the Duke of Mantua to Jussi Björling."[9] Another review faulted his "boyish looks and stiff appearance," which failed to convey "the illusion of a Don Juan type. But there was tenorial brio and schmalz in the singing, something which, in this role, matters more than theatrical credibility."[10] Moses

Pergament, on the other hand, found it "a pleasure to listen to the young tenor's phrasing and diction."[11] Right from the beginning, Jussi made his mark, singing the final cadenza of "La donna è mobile" the way Caruso sang it, ending on the high B.

※

Jussi's close relationship with Forsell was not without conflicts. One of them came immediately after Jussi's breakthrough in Copenhagen in 1931. Upon his return, Forsell called him to hear how the concert went. To his surprise, a female voice answered the telephone. When Jussi came on, Forsell demanded to know who she was, adding pointedly "She sounds like a Dane!"

"Well, yes," an embarrassed Jussi confessed. "She's a girl I met in Copenhagen, and she came with me to Stockholm."

"It is inappropriate for an artist of the Royal Opera to have a woman in his room!" shouted Forsell, sounding more than ever the old officer dressing down a subordinate.

"Yes, sir," Jussi managed to squeeze out.

"Come to my office tomorrow!"

When Jussi, crestfallen, walked into Uncle John's office the next day, Forsell barely acknowledged his pet student. Instead, he called one of the clerks: "Mr. Andersson! Bring me the ticket!" Silence. Suspense. Mr. Andersson came in and handed over an envelope. Forsell gave it to Jussi. "Here you are. This is a one-way train ticket to Copenhagen. The Dane leaves today!" That was the end of that. It never occurred to Jussi to oppose Forsell. He was not to be contradicted.

Forsell watched over Jussi's finances as well as his girlfriends. Jussi still accepted engagements at weddings, funerals, and company parties, but the money never seemed to go far enough. Remembering the times when he barely had enough for his daily food, Jussi now enjoyed not only the money he earned but the money he had yet to earn. He bought expensive clothes and began dressing like a dandy; he often treated his brothers at their favorite restaurant, the Tattersall. Money just passed through his hands, and his income disappeared as fast as it came in.

When this had gone on for some time, Jussi was again summoned to Forsell's office. The boss just shook his head, sighed, and announced, "Young Björling, you have debts!" Jussi's innocent blue eyes opened wide in surprise: "Do I?"

He seemed to be unaware of it. Well yes, he occasionally bought things on credit, he owed some money here and there, but that was normal, wasn't it? But Forsell had done his homework and went on to explain how things really were. When he contrasted Jussi's debts with his earnings, Jussi understood that it couldn't continue. So what was he to do? Forsell told him that he had no choice but to place Jussi under the care of a guardian. It was a bitter pill to swallow, but before Jussi could catch his breath and ask who would accept such a mission, Forsell decreed, "I certainly have more than enough to do, but I shall take it on!"

After the initial shock wore off, Jussi was genuinely grateful. When the guardianship ceased, Forsell could demonstrate how well he had handled his commitment: Jussi had a sizable bank account.

�֎

As I began my third term at the Music Academy, I continued to take lessons from Madame Andrejewa von Skilondz. She was born in St. Petersburg in 1882 and began her distinguished career as a member of the city's Mariinsky Theater. In 1910, when Frieda Hempel joined the Metropolitan, Madame von Skilondz took over her repertoire at the Royal Opera House in Berlin. At the outbreak of the war she moved to Stockholm and became a member of the Royal Opera. In 1917 she received the *Litteris et Artibus* medal from the Swedish Academy.

She remained active until 1930 and then began her teaching career at the Music Academy. If, as David Björling had maintained, a teacher's effectiveness can be measured by the achievements of her pupils, Madame was successful indeed. She was responsible for launching the careers of Eva Prytz, Kerstin Meyer, Elisabeth Söderström, and Kim Borg, among others. Her teaching complemented Julia Claussen's very well, and as a soprano her own song and operatic repertoire suited me perfectly; I was fortunate to benefit from her experience and knowledge.

Jussi continued to be busy and in the autumn of 1932, he sang for the first time Wilhelm Meister in Thomas' *Mignon* and Nemorino in Donizetti's *L'elisir d'amore*. It was a period of hard work for Jussi; he had memorized 20 roles in a mere two years. It was amazingly easy for him to learn a new score, but the stagecraft of a role was always more work than the musical aspects.

When it came to singing, he wasn't the least bit shy—he knew exactly how good he was and didn't hesitate to say so if challenged. Johannes Norrby, who sang with Jussi in the St. Jacob's Church choir under the direction of Set Svanholm, once told me,

> One day, when we were rehearsing, Jussi was to sing at the Opera the same evening. He wanted to save his voice and instead of singing with his usual power, he sang at half-voice. Because there were two other tenors in the choir, he thought we would manage. But Set Svanholm noticed immediately that Jussi was holding back. Moreover, he was already angry because Jussi had come late to rehearsal.
>
> "May I ask Jussi Björling to sing with us!" he burst out in an irritated tone.
>
> "No, you may not!" responded Jussi, who thereupon received the abrupt retort: "Then, there is the door!"

68

Jussi didn't hesitate for a moment. He turned, left, and the door slammed behind him. But it soon opened again and Jussi stuck his head in: "Get yourself a better tenor—if you can!" he burst out triumphantly. There was no better tenor, and both Jussi and Svanholm knew it![12]

But they were good friends, and Jussi was often invited to Svanholm's home, where they sometimes passed the time by trying to outsing each other. Before Set made the change to heldentenor, they shared a vast repertoire, and pedestrians often stopped under the windows to hear their splendid voices in duets.

Jussi was only 18 years old when he began at St. Jacob's. Johannes Norrby, later the director of the Stockholm Concert Hall, claimed the Cantate Domine never, before or since, sounded as heavenly as when Jussi was in the choir, and when he first heard Jussi at St. Jacob's, he wondered how such a young boy could sing like that.[13] It is unfortunate that none of Jussi's recordings were made in a church; the acoustics gave an almost unearthly beauty to his voice that elevated the simplest music to a higher plane.

From the first day to the last, 1933 was an extraordinary year for Jussi Björling, ascendent tenor. His hard work of the past two years only seemed to accelerate. On 5 January he sang his first Alfredo in *La traviata* to very good reviews; on 14 January his first Lensky in *Evgeny Onegin*; and on 17 January the minor role of Froh in *Das Rheingold*. On 11 March he added Vladimir in *Knyaz Igor* (*Prince Igor*), and four weeks later Mats in Ture Rangström's *Kronbruden* (*The Crown Bride*). Between these new assignments, he continued to sing his established repertoire.

During the summer Jussi was back on Singers' Island, working on his favorite role, Roméo. "Maybe I love the role so much because John Forsell worked on it with me so carefully."[14] Carefully, yes—but not without his calculated sarcasm. As they rehearsed the closing duet when Roméo feels the poison taking effect, Jussi let loose with an "Ah!" on a high note in full voice, which, according to Björn Forsell, "sounded incredibly beautiful as it echoed over half of Stenungsön." He tells what happened next:

Dad put his head in his hands and said: "Mr. Björling! Mr. Björling!"
"What?" said Jussi.
"Have you ever had a stomachache?" asked Dad.
"Yes."
"Did you sing like this then?"
"No."
"Well, just think, here you are, about to die! It's hurting like hell, so you don't sing like that! It should be a scream, not a beautiful note."
"Yes, of course, sir."[15]

As Jussi began his fourth season at the Opera, my father came home with two tickets to the 22 August performance of Gounod's *Roméo et Juliette*. It was Jussi's debut in the role, and my father said that Jussi specifically asked him to give the tickets to me. Father was playing in the orchestra, so Jussi suggested that perhaps my mother would like to accompany me. Singing his first Roméo was obviously a very meaningful occasion for him, and he wanted me to be present.

It was a glorious evening. Jussi looked very handsome in his red-velvet costume, which showed his athletic legs to best advantage. He had very nice legs and looked good in tights; even after he began to put on weight, he never had a potbelly: his enormous chest and powerful diaphragm simply added up to a large torso with a short waist. At 22, with his cherubic face, he perfectly looked the part of the teenage Roméo. And his singing was heavenly!

The critics were unconditionally impressed. Kurt Atterberg wrote, "The role of Roméo is especially well suited to Björling's disposition, so it was a joy to hear him—and the audience's spontaneous ovations were proof of it. The progress Björling has made indicates that, through continued intensive work, he will be able to liberate himself from the theatrical stiffness which previously has prevented the audience from completely enjoying his song."[16] Moses Pergament found the performance "extraordinarily successful," and he felt that as Roméo, Jussi revealed entirely new aspects of his art:

> In contrast to previous occasions, this evening one was more impressed by his warm, softly modulated *pianissimo* than by his brilliant *forte*. This does not mean that the voice lacked its usual power, but rather that the beauty of the pleasantly surprising, soulfully phrased *piano* singing commanded more attention. The second-act duet—the balcony scene—became a real musical experience not so much for the music as for the interpretation.[17]

Jussi was gratified to receive a review that placed the appeal of his interpretation above the composer's work, but I believe it meant much less to him than his mentor's reaction to his performance, which stage director Ragnar Hyltén-Cavallius later recalled:

> I sat together with Forsell in the manager's box at Jussi's first appearance in this brilliant role. At the end of the second act, when Juliette tosses a rose to Roméo, Jussi sang the beautiful phrases which end the act with such abandon and such harmony, that Forsell with usual dramatic energy squeezed my arm and called out, "Cavallius, did you hear that?" And he rushed down to the stage and wrapped Jussi in his arms.[18]

In Jussi's own words, "Forsell came running into my dressing room after the balcony scene—sobbing, with tears flowing. He was reminded of his dear friend, Arvid Ödmann. Roméo had been one of his great roles."[19] Jussi couldn't ask for greater approval. Ödmann had a bright, gentle tenor voice, and audiences adored him. He sang with the Opera from 1875 until 1911, and his memory was still alive with the public. As a special tribute to his young successor, Ödmann's old, worn-out chair was eventually placed in Jussi's dressing room. The chair followed him throughout his life, and it now stands in the Björling Museum in Borlänge.

On 6 September 1933, Jussi added Haroun in Bizet's *Djamileh*, and on the last day of the month Lyonel in *Martha* to his ever-growing repertoire. Then on 19 October, he sang for the first time Mario Cavaradossi in Puccini's *Tosca*. His body of work throughout the year prompted Moses Pergament to write:

> Nowadays it ought to be rather commonly known that Björling has an extraordinary voice, with dramatically explosive power as well as lyric warmth. It is a true pleasure to listen to this human instrument when, not hampered by the dramatic assignment, it lets its utterly brilliant flow of notes burst forth above the orchestra. One could observe yesterday with great satisfaction that dramatically he mastered the role better than usual. . . . In the later acts one could witness real temperamental outbursts in Björling's acting. It bodes well for the future.[20]

Jussi capped the last two weeks of 1933 with yet two more new roles. He sang his first Tamino in *Die Zauberflöte* on 15 December, and Count Elemer in Richard Strauss' *Arabella* on 30 December. He was praised for both by the critics.

Even a layman can appreciate the immensity of the work involved in the learning, rehearsing, and delivery of such an unusually large number of roles. An overview of the chronology of Jussi's performances shows that in this year alone he added 11 new roles to his repertoire. He sang multiple performances of a total of 20 roles along with a number of recitals and concert performances of Beethoven's *Missa Solemnis* and Handel's *Messiah*. It not only requires physical stamina and vocal endurance for a singer to keep so many works in his active repertoire, it also presumes a flawless technique, sound musicianship, and a prodigious memory, all of which Jussi possessed to excess.

But Jussi thrived on being given the opportunity to perform such a varied repertoire so often, and he gloried in the affection of the audience. Heeding the critics' advice, he tried to make each performance just a little better. As his reviews attest, he was succeeding.

❊

While Jussi was preparing for his first Tamino on 15 December 1933, I was about to become the leading character in a completely different but equally enchanting drama. Each year on 13 December the traditional festival of Santa Lucia takes place. Lucia, in her crown of lighted candles, symbolizes light in the darkness of winter. Cities and villages elect their own Lucia, but to be chosen as Stockholm's Lucia, as I was that year, is an especially high honor.

At the last moment, the very evening before the deadline, I sent my photograph to *Stockholms-Tidningen*, the daily newspaper in charge of the Lucia contest. I noted in my application that I was a student at the Music Academy; if I were elected, I'd be the first singing Lucia in the contest's five-year history. Sometime in November I received a telephone call from the newspaper advising me that several other young women and I had been selected to appear before a jury. I was flattered, but I still had misgivings about the whole thing. The setup seemed too much like a beauty contest; I didn't think I had much chance of winning, and I told the caller so. "Not at all," was the reply. "With your cheerful appearance, you seem to be a very appropriate Lucia-type. So don't worry; everything'll be fine."

I didn't quite know what a "Lucia-type" was, but I thought I owed it to myself to give it a try. After suffering through the interviews with the jury, I became the sixth of 10 finalists. Our pictures were printed in *Stockholms-Tidningen* so readers could vote for their favorite candidate. That the outcome now depended on a popular vote made the contest quite thrilling.

One day in the beginning of December, as I worked on Tosca's aria with Anita von Hillern-Dunbar, a reporter and photographer came to the rehearsal room to congratulate me. I had won the contest, by a comfortable margin, with 11,973 votes. Out of sheer excitement, I choked up with tears and couldn't produce another note.

When the big evening came, in a shiny, white satin gown and a crown that is worn by Stockholm's Lucia to this day, I rode through a wintry city on a gaily decorated float drawn by four strong horses. A parade of floats followed ours. The windows and balconies along the route were crowded with people, and the streets were lined with over 100,000 spectators, stamping their feet to keep warm in the north wind and the 15-degree temperature.

The Lucia festival was held in the evening at Berns Salong, a restaurant with a stage. The guest of honor was Russian author Ivan Bunin, winner of the 1933 Nobel Prize in literature. Governor Torsten Nothin fastened a platinum-set diamond necklace around my neck and placed a sparkling diamond ring on my finger. Then it was my turn to acknowledge the honor; I sang Mimì's aria from *La bohème*. Apart from student recitals at the Music Academy, this was my first public appearance. Fortunately, all went well. In the ensuing days the festivities continued, and I made several guest appearances, visiting hospitals and homes for the elderly and singing in packed churches. It was as thrilling as it was tiring, and I was glad when the hectic days were over.

※

Jussi's career meanwhile was showing no signs of slowing down. In January 1934 he sang Martin Skarp in the world premiere of Kurt Atterberg's *Fanal*. On 6 April, the anniversary of August Strindberg's death, Jussi sang Mats in Rangström's *Kronbruden*, based on Strindberg's eponymous play.

Then on 18 April he sang his first Riccardo in a single performance of Verdi's *Un ballo in maschera*.

During the *Kronbruden* rehearsals, Jussi couldn't find his score, and when it turned up in the Opera's office, Forsell decided to teach him a lesson. On the boss's express orders the score had "disappeared." Albin Rude picks up the story:

> Jussi came to rehearsal and calmly said that he couldn't find his music. "Have you left it at home?" I wondered. "No, I've never taken it home," Jussi answered. "It's been in my dressing room and now it's not there." "Come here and sit by me," I said, "and look at my music, while I play." "I don't think that's necessary," Jussi answered, "I can stand here on the other side of the piano as usual, and we'll see how it goes!" He sang his role completely perfectly, error-free from memory. It was fantastic! Because the part is musically difficult.[21]

Forsell was dumbstruck by this phenomenal display of musical memory. Jussi, for his part, learned a valuable lesson: it was time to start buying his own scores. Most were leatherbound, with his name stamped in gold on the cover. Often he would sign and date the title page, indicating when he bought it. His *Mefistofele* is dated 31 March 1931, *Faust* 1933, *La traviata* 11 January 1936, and *Turandot* 1944.

In the spring and summer of 1934, to supplement our dwindling finances, my Academy classmates Greta Hallgren, Barbro Lundquister, and I formed the Vienna Trio. We sang harmony; Greta and I were sopranos and Barbro a mezzo-soprano. Nathan Görling, another Academy friend, arranged the songs and served as accompanist. We performed at various events, singing everything from opera and operetta selections to popular ditties, and eventually auditioned for Nils Grevillius, who was so enthusiastic that he recommended us to Tivoli in Copenhagen. Later we toured the country, and to our considerable pride, we set a new audience record in Skutskär's Entertainment Park. We were even invited to sing on the radio! What more could three aspiring young singers ask for? To top it all, after hearing us perform at Snäckgärdsbaden, Gertrud Pålson-Wettergren approached me and insisted that I audition for the Opera.

This same spring, Jussi was traveling with *Don Giovanni* and *Fanal*. In July, he returned to Tivoli in Copenhagen. Then Gustaf Nilsson of the amusement park Gröna Lund, Stockholm's own Tivoli, offered him an engagement, and on 29 August 1934, Jussi sang for the first time from Gröna Lund's main stage, the first opera singer to give concerts there. Despite a continuous drizzle the performance was an enormous success, and it was repeated the following day under better atmospheric conditions. "My God, how he sang," the *Stockholms-Tidningen* critic wrote. "Without a doubt, Jussi Björling is the first Swedish tenor who successfully captures the full enchantment of the Italian school. He delighted the audience."[22]

This pair of back-to-back concerts inaugurated yet another tradition: 27

years of annual summer concerts at Gröna Lund. But I jokingly reminded Jussi that as a member of the Vienna Trio, I sang on the stage of Gröna Lund before he did. In the sphere of our musical accomplishments, this remained the only one for which I could claim priority.

Jussi enjoyed singing at open-air concerts. Our generation still possessed the technique necessary to project the voice and sing outdoors without amplification, like the so-called Golden Age singers: Caruso made himself heard even with a full orchestra behind him and gave several open-air concerts in and around New York, allegedly attracting as many as 50,000 listeners. As far as I can remember, Jussi's voice was never amplified in an opera house or indoor concert hall either, yet it was so well projected that it easily filled London's 9000-seat Royal Albert Hall or the giant Shrine Auditorium in Los Angeles. At its purest his voice, especially the *mezza voce* of his youth, was like a silver bell struck by a crystal hammer—the clear, brilliant sound had a sheen and carrying power beyond its innate volume.

When Jussi set his mind to it, he could hold his own against more powerful voices, but on many occasions he simply chose not to strain himself. Hjördis Schymberg recalls: "Jussi never spared himself on the stage. He never held back, but there was one time when we did. It was when Grevillius was so loud with the orchestra that Jussi advised, 'Here we only need to open our mouths. He has no idea if we are singing.'"[23] Many a later conductor, especially in the United States, played so loud and drove an ensemble so hard that it was a waste of effort trying to be heard. Rather than strain his voice and exert himself unnecessarily, Jussi would take his own advice.

Since Gröna Lund hosted many music events, Jussi told Gustaf Nilsson to place an acoustic shell on the stage so that the sound would project better. Nilsson implemented the idea, and Jussi proudly observed, "Since then, such world stars as Richard Crooks, Lawrence Tibbett, Lauritz Melchior, Alexander Kipnis, Richard Tauber, Joseph Hislop, and Martin Öhman have enjoyed the fruits of my suggestion. The audience at these concerts is counted in the tens of thousands, and it is stimulating for a singer to reach so many people at once."[24] Many people for whom the price of admission to the Opera was an unthinkable luxury could see and hear him for a fraction of the cost at Gröna Lund, which pleased Jussi. Nicolai Gedda remembered that during his student days he couldn't afford the opera, but at these outdoor concerts he could hear Jussi and other great singers from around the world.

Outdoor concerts were new for Sweden. Some people felt it was inappropriate for a classical singer to perform among the Ferris wheels and merry-go-rounds of Gröna Lund, but Jussi shrugged it off. He thought that the *where* didn't matter—the important thing was *how* one sang. He loved the atmosphere of these open-air recitals: the people packed together on a light summer evening, the rustle of leaves in the wind, and the cries of seagulls echoing over the water.

No matter the sideshow surroundings, the image Marit Gruson, widow of Göran Gentele, retained of Jussi on the concert platform was that of a dignified man. "He wasn't too short; he had a very wide, broad chest that ran all the way to his belt, thus he looked muscular rather than fat. He had a wonderful smile that reached out to the listeners. He'd come out, bow, grab his lapels with both hands, and start to sing."[25] Jussi also had a special device I was surprised to find how many eyewitnesses remember to this day: when he hit a high note, he would turn his head from his left to right so that everybody in the audience, no matter how vast, would get the full impact of the note, as if it was being sung especially for him or her.

※

In 1934, I entered my last year at the Academy, and Jussi began his fifth season at the Opera. On 25 August, he sang for the first time the title role in *Faust*, a romantic role that soon became one of my favorites. The magic of the music made me melt, and Jussi looked just as good as Faust as he had as Roméo, his other Gounod role. "He brought out everything the role offers in melodic beauty and musical intensity. It was a pleasure to listen to his rare vocal splendor," wrote Moses Pergament.[26] Another critic added,

> I repeat what I predicted in the beginning of the year: this young singer won't be contained within the walls of the Swedish Opera House much longer—sad for us, but a credit for Sweden. His flight will soon lead to the stages on the Continent. From time to time there has been speculation about "Caruso's successor." That time has come again. The new King of Tenors will probably be Swedish. . . . This extraordinary voice is particularly well placed and goes hand in hand with a natural musicality that can never be acquired. No bad habits disturb the impression. Unaffectedness, freshness and a becoming modesty characterize the interpretation. These same qualities disarmingly mark the stage action, although quite naturally there remains a lack of dramatic characterization.[27]

In mid-October Jussi sang his first Rodolfo in Puccini's *La bohème*. "Mimì and Rodolfo had been assigned to Hjördis Schymberg and Jussi Björling, both for the first time," wrote Curt Berg. "The latter sang with brilliant, melodious sound but could have acted with a little more passion."[28] Pergament could "hardly say that the round little figure gave the illusion of a starving poet" and complained that "dramatically, the role wasn't worked through either, partly the fault of the stage director."[29]

A week before his first Rodolfo, Jussi sang Cavaradossi to the Tosca of the wonderful Italian-American soprano Dusolina Giannini. Through my father's connections I received two tickets, but instead of my mother I invited Åke Collett, a young man I'd known for a long time and had dated off and on. Jussi wouldn't find out I thought, and anyway, I had a right to go to the opera with whomever I wanted.

It didn't happen the way I planned, for Einar Larson, Jussi's good friend from Stenungsön, sang Scarpia that evening. He noticed us through the peephole in the curtain, and he was beastly enough to tattle: "Look Jussi,

Anna-Lisa with some strange fellow!" Jussi was furious with me. I felt quite stupid because I really thought he wouldn't find out. He needn't have worried—I wasn't interested in anyone else—but Jussi's mind wouldn't let go of the incident.

On Lucia Day in December, as the previous year's Lucia, I attended the traditional celebration at Berns Salong, accompanied by my parents. Jussi was singing at the Opera that night and was to join us after the performance, but Åke Collett was there and courted me all evening, despite the enraged looks Jussi cast in his direction when he finally arrived. When Åke asked if he could see me home, Jussi's smoldering jealousy ignited. "Anna-Lisa is *my* girl!" he shouted.

It ended with Jussi and me taking a taxi home. My parents followed in another, arriving first. When we walked in, still quite upset, Jussi decided to resolve the matter. We had hardly taken off our coats when he turned to my parents. "All right, look—I love Anna-Lisa. May I ask her to marry me?"

"Dear Jussi, calm down!" Mama said, a little frightened. She wasn't prepared for this sudden turn of events. But Papa was very happy. Jussi and he were colleagues and had known each other for a long time. As for me, I hadn't managed to get in a word. I was *really* surprised. All I could do was scream at him, "Jussi, what are you doing?"

But he couldn't be stopped. He rushed to the telephone and called the newspaper to announce our engagement. With that, it was too late to do anything, even if I'd wanted to. This whole incident sums up Jussi in a nutshell: direct, spontaneous, determined—and stubborn as an ox once his mind was made up.

From the earliest days of our relationship we'd felt a strong sense of belonging to each other. I don't think we ever discussed it, but by this time we both took it nearly for granted that some day we would marry. The awkward incident with Åke Collett was only a catalyst, and Jussi realized that. He never asked me if I wanted to marry him, but it wasn't conceit that reassured him my answer would be yes. The next day we went to Hallberg's, a jewelry store, and bought a ring. We were officially engaged on Saturday, 15 December 1934, and for the first time ever I felt totally happy. The door to life had opened wide.

I wanted to take care of this spirited young man who was orphaned so early in life and never had a real home. All I wanted was to make Jussi happy. Now that I was wearing his ring, I looked forward to a beautiful life together with him. And yet, aware of his impetuosity and his rumored weakness for alcohol, a furtive voice inside me whispered, *What are you getting yourself into?*

# Chapter 5

# Marriage and Family

The day after our engagement, Jussi and I were to sing at Busstomten's Aquacade in the large natatorium of the Stockholm Sports Palace. "We have the pleasure of inviting you to this unique party where the engagement between Sweden's brilliant tenor Jussi Björling, and last year's Lucia, Miss Anna-Lisa Berg, will be celebrated," wrote *Stockholms-Tidningen* (14 December 1934) in its announcement of the event.

> This festive occasion at the Sports Palace provides the first opportunity for the public to honor the newly engaged couple. Of course, all of Stockholm would like to congratulate them. It may appear as if it were planned that this happy young couple would make their first appearance at a charity festival and also sing together. As we all know, the Lucia from 1933 is also a talented singer, who rightfully received a thunderous approval when she sang at last year's Lucia celebration. Music brought the two together, and with their song they will steal our hearts on Sunday [16 December 1934].

Every one of the 2600 seats had been sold. As my attendants and I processed in, "Santa Lucia" was rendered by Jussi "with melting bravura." After a few more features, Jussi and I made our entrance together in what was described as "a festive episode on the Grand Canal." We stepped into a boat fitted up to look like a gondola, I in a Venetian costume, Jussi, as the

Singer From the North, in black tails. With a strong spotlight trained against the pool's green-tiled bottom, the gondola appeared to hover above the water. The Swedish Film Industry Orchestra played, and Jussi sang de Curtis' Barcarola ("Torna a Surriento"), holding my hand the while. During a *forte* our little craft began to shake. "What is it? Don't you feel well?" I whispered to him during the applause.

"No, I feel fine," answered Jussi. "But this is what happens when one really sings!" And he stealthily put my hand on his lower chest so that I could feel how his fantastic diaphragm worked. It was then, I think, that I first understood what remarkable strength went into Jussi's singing and how his entire body functioned as one coordinated system of pump, bellows, and resonator.

Jussi's last new role for 1934 was Dick Johnson in the Swedish premiere of Puccini's *La fanciulla del West*. He repeated the role six more times in January 1935, and on 26 January he added another new role: Belmonte in Mozart's *Die Entführung aus dem Serail*, followed by his first Turiddu in *Cavalleria rusticana* on 14 February and his first Florestan in *Fidelio* on 26 March. With four new roles in as many months, his capacity for work appeared to be unlimited.

When all the commotion that followed the announcement subsided, I calmly grew used to the idea that Jussi and I were actually engaged. We found an apartment at de Geersgatan 14, and set the date, 3 June 1935. My wedding gown, of shiny, white *dûchesse*, was put on order; I was to have a tulle veil, a crown dressed with myrtle leaves, and my favorite flowers, lilies-of-the-valley, for my bouquet. Finally, with a trembling heart, I announced to Julia Claussen that I would be forced to interrupt my studies before the official end of school. "I have to quit now. As you know, I'm marrying Jussi Björling!"

"Is that so?" Mrs. Claussen exclaimed, greatly upset. "Is this the thanks I get? I, who have worked so hard with you and have had such big plans for your future! There'll be no more singing for you, I'll bet!"

I didn't understand. Wasn't I going to sing anymore? I wouldn't stop singing just because I was getting married! But I could no longer concentrate on my studies; wedding plans and thoughts about what lay ahead took precedence over all else, which may explain why my final student recital was a disaster. Jussi had promised to attend, along with some colleagues from the Opera; he wanted them to hear the girl he was going to marry. I had sung my selection, the Waltz Song from Gounod's *Roméo et Juliette*, for Jussi while preparing for the recital, and it went perfectly well. Then came the event, in early May. I was nervous, but considering the stress of the moment I was singing quite well. "It's going all right," I thought.

A moment later, I cracked on the high C.

I was so ashamed, I didn't know what to do. Jussi consoled me with a story about his first performance of *Mignon*, in October 1932. As Wilhelm Meister, he must rescue Mignon from the flames of the burning theater;

Jussi lifted Helga Görlin in his strong arms, and while carrying her through the onstage commotion, he had to sing a high B. Overconfident, he forced it—and cracked completely. An implacable John Forsell stood in the wings, laughing: "That was some yodeling!" Jussi's face burned.

Jussi's exceptional strength failed him on one other occasion, when he lifted Brita Hertzberg as Mimì. Jussi related the incident,

> I've always been strong, so in the last act of *La bohème* I varied the acting of the role of Rodolfo a bit by picking Mimì up in my arms and carrying her to the bed. This particular Mimì was rather plump and, bending over to put her on the bed, I lost my balance and dropped her. The middle slat of the bed crashed and the dying Mimì lay there with feet and head up and the other part on the floor, like a V. A most uncomfortable position to sing and die in. It was very difficult for the rest of us to keep from laughing. We did, frequently turning our backs to the audience.[1]

※

After my recital, Jussi went on tour with the Royal Opera. He appeared in *Don Giovanni*, *I cavalieri di Ekebù*, and *Fanal* at the National Theater in Riga. My father, who was also on the tour, told us that after the last performance some of the singers were presented with medals in a lavish ceremony. Tenor Einar Beyron received one, but Jussi did not—not because he didn't sing well, but because at 24 he was considered too young to be worthy of a medal.

When Jussi realized he'd been passed over, he was infuriated. He stood up and delivered Tonio's aria from *La fille du régiment* with the nine high Cs, then angrily sat down. He felt snubbed, and his lifelong preoccupation with decorations may well have originated from this incident. It was reinforced in later years by Tullio Voghera's stories about Caruso, who had collected a whole chestful of medals from the pre–World War I European monarchs, great and small.

Jussi wanted a collection of his own, and in the end he did. When he'd pinned them all on—and he never missed an opportunity to do so—22 medals dangled across his broad chest. "Perhaps I'm a little vain, but I wonder if a little vanity shouldn't be a part of human nature," he said. "I'm proud of the honors I have received and what's more, I'm not ashamed to say so."[2]

Jussi returned from Riga to a festive Stockholm decked out for the upcoming marriage of Princess Ingrid and Crown Prince Frederik of Denmark. At the end of May, he sang in a gala performance of *Roméo et Juliette* given in celebration of the approaching nuptials. My family belonged to the Palace Church, and since Papa was the parish clerk, the announcement of our wedding was read there immediately after the royal announcement. We were quite pleased, devoted royalists that we both were.

While the royal wedding was taking place in the Storkyrkan, Jussi and I were married in Oscar's Church, the congregation to which Jussi belonged.

Clemens Åfeldt, my confirmation pastor, performed the ceremony, Einar Larson sang, and my younger brother, Gösta, and two girl cousins served as child attendants. The wedding dinner was held at the Strand Hotel's banquet room. We stayed at the hotel that first night, and the next evening we left for our honeymoon in Italy, but not before I gave my first interview as Mrs. Jussi Björling. A journalist from the weekly magazine *Vecko-Journalen* came to our apartment to take pictures of "the Opera's popular 24-year-old tenor" and his new wife.

The trip to Milan and the northern Italian lakes didn't begin well. While we said our goodbyes to family on the train station platform, I left my purse carelessly unattended, on the seat in our compartment. When we reboarded the train, my purse—with my new passport—was gone! Jussi telegraphed the Swedish consulate in Berlin from Trelleborg and asked for their help. This was the first time we realized in what esteem "young Björling" was held by his countrymen. When the train rolled into the Hauptbahnhof in Berlin, an employee from the consulate was waiting to hand over my speedily processed new passport. The consulate didn't have a photo, but quite resourcefully, they clipped my wedding picture from *Vecko-Journalen* and glued it to the passport. I had a lot of fun with that passport until it expired some five years later. "Just married!" the immigration officers would note smilingly, and they would immediately let us pass.

In Milan, we visited Jussi's brother Gösta, who, having completed his studies at the Academy, was studying there with Fernando Carpi, a famous retired singer. When the Maestro heard that Gösta's brother also sang, he asked to hear him—and was astounded. "You have a fantastic voice! You must let me give you lessons!" he declared. Jussi politely declined.

We found the incident amusing, but it wasn't so funny for Gösta, who, although the first to acknowledge Jussi's superior talents, found the constant comparisons to his famous brother unpleasant. He had his own repertoire, leading as well as character roles, but because they were both tenors, he remained in Jussi's shadow. When Gösta was cast with Jussi in *Rigoletto* or *Trovatore*, he sang the comprimario part, although he had the same range as his brother, with brilliant high notes. Luckily, they were fond of each other—so close that they often understood each other without saying a word—and they never became rivals.

From Milan we continued north to Lake Como, where we stayed in a small hotel on the water's edge. The setting was idyllic, the scenery beautiful; we would gladly have stayed for months, but it was impossible: Jussi was booked in Copenhagen starting on 19 June. Much too soon for both of us, we began our journey home via Bellagio and Lugano.

At Jussi's sold-out concerts at Tivoli, I sat for the first time in the audience as the artist's wife. Everyone fussed over the newlyweds, and the newspapers never failed to mention that their favorite singer had just been married. The *Berlingske Tidende* (26 June 1935) quoted my husband thus:

The love one experiences gives both strength and charm to what one sings. Nowadays, I couldn't imagine singing a concert without my Anna-Lisa in the audience—something radiates from her to me—yes, love means everything for a tenor! . . . Before I met Anna-Lisa, I only dreamed of the love I definitely felt would some day come to me, and that was the backdrop to my song. But now I don't need to dream anymore—now it is mine!

*Is there any moment in your life that you'll never forget?*

Yes, I can say exactly. It was when I went to the church on my wedding day and waited for my bride—that was it! When I saw her walk through the church door in the billowing white rush of her veil—yes, I thought one could never experience anything so beautiful in one's life, that one could be a part of something so wonderful!

I was too deeply affected to speak a word and didn't sing a note the whole day. But since that time everything I feel comes through in my singing: pleasure, happiness—it is such a wonderful memory that if I ever met temptation, and came close to doing something stupid, all I need to do is think of that moment to keep me from faltering.

We were so young—so inexperienced—so very happy. I'm sure Jussi meant every word he said.

❈

Upon our return to Stockholm, Jussi left for a short tour. In the beginning of July, we flew to the World's Fair in Brussels, where Jussi joined other Swedish singers in a concert. Afterward, glowing with pride, he received the Knighthood of the Order of Leopold II from Queen Astrid's hand, his very first such recognition; I'm sure he felt that justice was done after what had transpired two months earlier in Riga.

It was wonderful to come back to our own home, six floors up on de Geersgatan. In keeping with 1930s taste, we decorated our apartment with Sveavägs furnishings, birch veneers, crushed velvet upholsteries, heavy candelabra, and velvet draperies. We bought all the furniture at once, all in the same pompous style, with curved legs and lion's feet on practically everything. It may be unfashionable now, but at the time we were immeasurably proud of it.

Among my most cherished memories of our early days together as newlyweds are our late-night talks at the kitchen table, after the evening's performance. I remember the crammed kitchen, long and narrow, with a little table at the window, barely large enough to seat two. Like most singers, Jussi never ate anything before performing, so when we came home we were both ravenous. After we'd eaten, Jussi could finally unwind and relax. It was then, in the quiet of the night, that he would talk about his childhood, his parents, his brothers, his travels. Some of it I knew from our dating, from his brothers, from the interviews he gave and the articles written about him. But during those intimate conversations when we were so close, bit by bit I learned the full details of his difficult childhood and youth. I recognized the single-minded drive that allowed him to reach his goals. I appreciated his accomplishments even more.

As I came to know and understand the many sides of Jussi's personality, I discovered his simplicity was deceptive. He had a great emotional depth he reserved only for those he loved, and in his best moments his good qualities endeared him to family, friends, and fans. He enjoyed his public as a singer, but not as a private person; he valued his privacy and never sought publicity for publicity's sake. He was devoted to his art but resented the trappings that went with it—the functions, receptions, repetitive interviews. Björling was an artist who sang—Jussi was an ordinary man with a life to live.

✳

After we returned from our honeymoon, I didn't feel well. At first I thought it was fatigue, but my mother knew more about life than I and immediately suspected I was pregnant. I wanted to have children, of course—that was my greatest wish—but it hadn't occurred to me that it could happen so soon. Obviously, it could. Our doctor confirmed that our first baby was due at the end of February or early March. Jussi was ecstatic; our firstborn would be a boy, we decided, and he'd be baptized Jussi Anders.

I felt worse with each passing day. I could hardly keep any food down, lost weight, and became apathetic. My condition so deteriorated that I was admitted to Betania Hospital. On the first day there, as I lay in the hospital bed like a limp rag, a nurse opened the door. At her side was Jussi, barely visible behind a gigantic oriental urn filled with dark red roses. Frugality was not in my husband's character—he had simply bought the florist's entire stock of red roses, urn and all. Unfortunately, in my nauseated state I couldn't tolerate the fragrance of roses, and the nurse took the flowers out into the hall. Poor Jussi was crestfallen!

The discomfort persisted, and it was several weeks before I felt well enough to go home. Jussi thought that instead of staying in a stuffy apartment I should spend the summer somewhere by the sea. He rented a couple of rooms for us at Barnekow's pension in Saltsjöbaden and stayed with me until he had to return to Stockholm to begin rehearsals for his sixth season. I passed the days in Saltsjöbaden feeling more and more gloomy. Is this the way my life is going to be from now on? We had made wonderful plans for our future—we would travel the world and give concerts together, perform side by side on the opera stage. Now I was lying here alone, perpetually nauseated.

Jussi did everything in his power to cheer me up. He knew that I loved dogs, and one day after a rehearsal, he and Sigurd Björling came out to the pension with the most adorable little black Scottie. "Here's a little *murre* for you!" Jussi said, putting the dog in my lap. *Murre* is Swedish for chimney sweep, and that became the name of this tiny black ball of fur. Murre turned out to be the best therapy I could have had. At least for the moment he made me forget about myself and kept me from constantly worrying about my condition.

�֍

On 17 August 1935, Jussi assumed for the first time one of his most acclaimed roles, Manrico in Verdi's *Il trovatore*. Kurt Atterberg wrote, "He sang Manrico for the first time Saturday evening with brio, passion and conviction, as if he had known this role long and well. It is also pleasant to see that Björling, alongside his vocal triumphs, is becoming better and better at dramatic interpretation."[3] Another critic only partially agreed with this verdict: "Björling's voice was cleaner and more beautiful than ever—one almost forgot that he forgot to act!"[4] Costumed in stiff, silvery armor, Jussi's movements were anything but fluid. As Curt Berg bluntly put it in *Dagens Nyheter*, "Björling strolled around like a live iron stove."[5]

Jussi returned to Solliden's stage at Skansen on 15 September 1935, sharing the limelight with Helga Görlin and Joel Berglund; he had first appeared there on 10 September 1933. With this latest engagement, a tradition began. All Stockholm looked forward to Jussi's annual concerts, and the capacity audience filled every seat just as they did at his summer concerts at Gröna Lund. These annual concerts were more like family events—with a few thousand friends. The bond between soloist and audience was remarkable.

On 17 September 1935, Forsell, remembering Jussi's comedic talent as the drunken Almaviva, introduced him as Alfred in Johann Strauss' *Die Fledermaus*. Jussi had a lot of fun with the role, and it was a minor sensation. "Jussi Björling was brilliant, vocally as usual of course, but even through his hilarious makeup and his looks. [It was] a tenor parody, which took the audience by storm," commented Kurt Atterberg.[6] "Jussi Björling parodied a tenor, presumably the way only a great tenor can. The makeup was a stroke of genius," wrote another critic.[7]

It was good for him to loosen up, musically speaking, before his next assignment, a truly formidable one for a 24-year-old tenor: the taxing role of Radamès in Verdi's *Aida*. Jussi knew too well what the challenges of the role were—and what the expectations of the audience and the merciless scrutiny of the critics would be. He was nervous at first, and it showed. Remarked one critic,

> Even Jussi Björling, who doesn't normally display too much nerves, forced in the beginning. . . . The role of Radamès provides such rich opportunities to show off the metal [of the voice] that a singer of Björling's caliber does not need to look for them in ["Celeste Aida"], but ought to be able to make it the discrete and exquisite piece it is supposed to be. He showed in the last act that he knows how it should be done.[8]

Moses Pergament was more generous:

> Jussi Björling's interpretation of the role of Radamès was a vocally brilliant performance. In the first act's big aria, however, the brilliance at times appeared at the cost of phrasing: every ascending phrase represented a crescendo up to a *forte*, and that doesn't accord with the mood of the aria. But through the evening Björling showed that he is capable of shaping extraordinarily melodious phrases on the high notes, including a *pianissimo*. Of the acting one can say that although it was somewhat more flexible than usual, it didn't ever overstep the present boundaries of Björling's acting capacity.[9]

On 31 October 1935, he briefly returned to comedy, performing Almaviva to Giuseppe de Luca's Figaro, the great baritone's single guest appearance in Stockholm. But the outstanding event of the opera season was the visit of Fedor Chaliapin. The celebrated Russian was on a Scandinavian tour; in Stockholm he was to sing two performances of *Prince Igor* and one of Gounod's *Faust*, and it fell to Jussi to sing Prince Vladimir in the former and Faust in the latter to Chaliapin's Méphistophélès. Jussi was beside himself with the honor. "Just think," he kept repeating, "to sing with the great Chaliapin!"

Fedor Chaliapin was the quintessential lyric artist, a singer's singer and an actor's actor. But as everyone soon discovered, it was a mixed blessing to have him around. Seemingly bent on living up to his reputation of being difficult and temperamental, he took one look at the *Faust* staging and decided he didn't like it. He thought Marguerite's garden especially looked like a tiny miserable backyard. "I can't sing with this modern scenery! Change it! Don't you have the old sets somewhere? Find them!"[10]

He then walked out of the theater and disappeared. Everyone ran around like proverbial headless chickens, some working at making the changes Chaliapin had demanded, others searching for the basso. He was finally located at Lenna's Konditori, having a grand old time over pastries in the company of some very attractive women. "Mr. Chaliapin," the emissaries begged him, "please come back. We brought out the old sets." "OK," he said, "but why did you do that? The sets were just fine."

He sang first in Borodin's opera, so there was time to resolve the matter of the *Faust* scenery. His *Prince Igor* was a double treat for Stockholm: Chaliapin sang both Prince Galitsky and the Polovetsian Tartar Khan Konchak, since the two characters are never onstage at the same time. Brief as the roles are, he played the dissimilar characters to perfection, his presentations decidedly beyond the skills and talents of all operatic and most dramatic artists. At this late date in his career he had every gesture, every glance of the two parts worked out to the smallest detail, and he gave finely etched, larger-than-life portrayals. His voice, though not what it once had been, was still a formidable instrument handled with the expert skill of a vocal master. Jussi too must have acquitted himself to Chaliapin's satisfaction, because after the performance he presented Jussi with a photo of himself. The inscription read *Bravo pour "Vladimir."*

After a side trip to Oslo, Chaliapin returned to Stockholm for *Faust* on 3 December 1935. When the curtain rose, it was apparent that the great man had been out carousing the night before and was in poor voice. But such a trifle didn't matter; Chaliapin was a frightening Prince of Darkness. When he appeared in Faust's study, he gave such a diabolical howl that poor Brita Hertzberg, the Marguerite that night, standing nearby, almost fainted. Chaliapin's powerful personality dominated the stage in every scene—everyone else seemed to disappear, sometimes literally.

We'd heard about the tricks he'd pull, like bribing the lighting director to keep the spotlight on him. But despite all the stories that had circulated before his arrival, we didn't guess how far Chaliapin was prepared to go to command attention. It didn't help either that on this particular evening Jussi was in exceptionally fine form. In the first scene of the opera, after Faust bargained his soul to regain his youth, Chaliapin moved toward Jussi and with a sweeping gesture covered him completely with the folds of his cape.

Singing at full volume, Chaliapin strode around the stage, holding Faust captive inside the cape. Poor Jussi struggled to surface now and then to sing his half of the closing duet. He couldn't see the conductor or the prompter, and he told me afterward that he almost suffocated. Finally, near the end of the duet, he disentangled himself and made sure that his closing high notes were heard. From that point on, the rejuvenated Faust kept a safe distance between the Devil and himself. Chaliapin gradually overcame his indisposition, his voice improved from act to act, the beyond-capacity audience was delirious, and the curtain fell to thunderous applause.

We didn't realize that the trick with the cape was a feature of Chaliapin's Méphisto. The Italian tenor Giacomo Lauri-Volpi gave the following description in his well-known book, *Voci parallele*:

> When a certain tenor at the Metropolitan complained because [Chaliapin] made him ridiculously disappear by enveloping him in his scarlet cape, Chaliapin replied: "My friend, I am Méphistophélès, you have sold me your dirty little soul, I have given you looks and youth; but now you are mine, you succumb to my will, it annihilates you. I can do with you as I please, understand?" The bird-brained tenor did not understand the comments of the genius, and indignantly complained to Gatti-Casazza. Referring to the incident, the Russian remarked to the author: "Forgive me, but how many of your colleagues so well deserve their reputation as blooming idiots [*la fama d'insigni cretini*]!"[11]

By the time Faust and Méphistophélès were removing their makeup, Chaliapin was in superb humor. It was impossible to hold a grudge against him, and so communicating in English, we invited him to dine with us at the Operakällaren, the famous restaurant in the corner of the Opera proper. He asked if he might bring a guest along. Of course we agreed, and Chaliapin, in an expansive and jovial mood, joined us in the company of a stunning woman.

On or offstage, Chaliapin was a fantastic person; he cast a spell on all around him. I've never met anyone with such a magnetic personality and mesmerizing presence. Over six feet tall and powerfully built (and by this time stout as well), he was a man of immense charm. In a social context he was a perfect gentleman in dress and manners. In the wake of his visit we were left feeling that a powerful force of nature had just moved on. Despite everything, we wouldn't have missed it.

※

On 11 January 1936, Jussi sang his first Canio in Leoncavallo's *Pagliacci*. Although he sang Canio only 20 times in his entire career, it was the role I came to love most. His was a deeply moving interpretation, very human and dramatically overwhelming in the climactic moments. Once more, Jussi surprised the critics. Then less than three weeks later, he introduced another new role, Faust, in Berlioz' *La damnation de Faust*.

The baby was due soon, but Jussi always wanted me out in the audience because he had complete confidence in my judgment. "How was I?" he'd ask me eagerly, sometimes even anxiously, at the first opportunity. When I assured him he was fantastic, as I most often could truthfully say, he breathed a sigh of relief. "If you think so, then I must've been good." At home at the kitchen table, we'd discuss my impressions further. Near the end of a concert, I might actually leave my seat and rush back to his dressing room, knowing Jussi would welcome my assessment of the audience's mood. When I felt that he should replace a predetermined encore with something else, he usually followed my advice. His accompanists were amazed that Björling would decide at the last minute what the encore would be—and many times it was my fault. My instincts were usually right.

No matter how many times Jussi sang a role, I soon noticed that no two performances were alike. Many years later, I met Jascha Heifetz' wife backstage and asked her why she hadn't attended her husband's concert. "Oh, I've heard him so many times!" she answered with a shrug. I was amazed. It never occurred to me to think of Jussi's singing that way. I couldn't hear him enough—and this sentiment lasted until the end. I can say with certainty—and a great deal of satisfaction—that I heard him sing more often than anyone else, a pleasure which I regard as one of the great gifts and privileges of our marriage.

So, I was there on the evening of 1 February for his debut in *La damnation de Faust*, and again on the 3rd. But that night I felt uneasy. All the commotion and stress leading up to the premiere had had its effect. When we came home after the performance, my labor started, weeks earlier than expected. As the pain increased, Jussi became terribly nervous. Neither of us was the least bit prepared for what was about to happen. The time between contractions grew shorter and shorter as I paced around the apartment moaning, pushing against the end of the bed and grabbing the radiators. Jussi called my mother in a panic. "Please come immediately! Anna-Lisa's acting so strangely. She must feel terrible!"

"Has the water broken?" Mama asked.

"Water? What damned water?" Jussi shouted.

We took a taxi to the Allmänna BB Hospital. No rooms were available at first, and I lay in a crowded corridor. My labor was lengthy, and though Jussi wanted to stay with me, I asked him to go home; in the throes of childbirth, I wanted no one but my mother. When it was all over, however, and I was rolled into my room with our little son in my arms, my dear husband was already there. Giddy with pride and happiness, he rushed to the telephone to announce the birth to the newspapers. "A sturdy boy," he told the reporter. "A son," short and sweet, wouldn't suffice. With him everything had to be a little extra.

Flowers from Opera colleagues filled the room to overflowing, and Kurt Atterberg, *Stockholms-Tidningen*'s music critic, and his wife, Margareta, who had seen me in the audience the night before, sent a congratulatory telegram, written in rhyme. Although it loses some of its charm in translation, the message remains clear:

> Bravo Lucia and Jussi
> Lucky the boy is so swell;
> It'll be to his eternal credit
> He didn't arrive while Faust went to Hell.

With the arrival of our firstborn, we were no longer merely man and wife—we were a family. We had a nice home, and Jussi's career was arching ever higher. He was about to sign a new recording contract and would soon make his debut in Prague and Vienna. Our happiness seemed complete.

※

As I've said, even before we were engaged, I'd heard rumors that Jussi had a weakness for alcohol, though I had no clear notion of what these murmurs meant, nor whether they might be true. I pushed aside my vague sense of uncertainty, my lingering suspicions, for during our dating, Jussi made a point of restraining himself in my company. When we were out together at his favorite restaurant, he only drank wine. I heard in a roundabout way that after one of our suppers the headwaiter remarked: "Björling must really be in love—this sure isn't what he normally drinks!" My mother had also heard about Jussi's habits. "I'm worried," she said after our engagement. "I wonder if this is such a good idea."

Plainly, I didn't want to hear what she was trying to say, and even if the rumors were true, surely the trouble would clear up as soon as we married. Naively, I believed that a real home and a happy family life would change everything for Jussi. After a youth spent roaming about from place to place, what he needed was some permanence in his life—a home with a wife who loved him and looked after all his needs. Something about Jussi awakened a strong feeling of tenderness in me. I can only liken it to a silent cry for help and wanted nothing more than to answer it and support him. I wasn't the first woman who thought she could change the man she loved, and not the last to fail.

I soon discovered that there were real grounds for the hearsay; Jussi sometimes drank more than was good for him. Every time it happened, his remorse seemed deep and sincere, and I believed, because I wanted to believe, that each incident was the last. When he sobered up, he returned over and over to the vow he and his brothers had made to their father, never to drink a drop of liquor. "I haven't kept the promise I made to my dying father," Jussi concluded with boundless sorrow, each time. I know that this was the most difficult thing in his life for him; it was his only failure. He was inconsolable, and I comforted and reassured him as best I could.

During our kitchen talks, he spoke about the first time alcohol exerted its grip on him. "It happened when I came to Stockholm," he explained, when he worked for Hellström, washing his taxis. Soon after he started, rooming became a part of his pay, and he stayed with the Hellström family until he moved to the Svedeliuses. The Hellströms were shocked that Jussi didn't drink. When he told them of his oath of abstinence, they just laughed. "Aren't you man enough to drink?" they taunted him. "Do you want to be a sissy for the rest of your life?" Jussi refused as long as he could, but in the end his resistance eroded; for one, he didn't want Linnea Hellström, the boss's daughter, to think he was a teetotalling sissy. He began to drink, and what was just good companionship at first quickly evolved into an addiction. "That's when all the misery began."

He soon discovered that he enjoyed drinking, that alcohol quieted the unsettling restlessness that sometimes overcame him. When the urge to drink was upon him, it drove him out of the house—out and away, at any cost! Since it happened only sporadically at first, I wasn't seriously worried. With just a little willpower he would learn to control his drinking, I thought.

Then during one of our late-night talks, he told me something that was as hard for me to accept as it was for him to say. He confessed that one night, after a long drinking session, he wound up in Linnea's arms. He was 17 years old when on 25 December 1928, Linnea, three years his senior, gave birth to a boy, Rolf. Jussi gave his son his surname. In the years that followed, Linnea and Jussi had drifted apart, and though she hoped Jussi would marry her, he did not.

I didn't know how to react. At that time the attitude toward children born out of wedlock was very different; a shameful silence shrouded such circumstances. It was honest of him to tell me about Rolf and Linnea, and I also found it commendable that unlike many men in similar situations, he'd acknowledged his paternity. But I was terribly upset by the revelation. Inexperienced with life, I didn't know how to cope with the notion that my husband might have divided loyalties, obligations to another woman and another child, and weighing the effect this could have on our marriage nearly drove me to distraction. Jussi assured me that my fears were groundless; he loved his son, but neither Rolf nor Linnea would be a part of our life.

Now that it was out in the open, I was persuaded that indeed there was no reason to worry. But it soon became clear that Jussi had promised more than he could deliver. Linnea complained bitterly to Märta Björling that Jussi had abandoned her to marry me. She saw herself as a victim. Level-headed Cousin Märta tried to make her understand that the clock couldn't be turned back. "Jussi is married, he can have only one wife, and nothing can be done to change that," she said.[12] All the same, Linnea began to telephone our house at night, accusing me of taking Jussi from her. Her claims were absurd; Jussi and I hadn't met till long after they'd parted. As if the phone calls weren't enough, she and Rolf once showed up unexpectedly in Jussi's dressing room after a performance. I felt completely helpless, overwrought by panic. Linnea's intrusions were a threat that not only jeopardized our harmony but might completely destroy the life we had begun to build together.

In the end, Jussi asked his brother Olle to speak with Linnea. He explained the irreversibility of the situation to her; whatever she and Jussi had was a long time ago, and what Jussi and I shared was the present. He reminded her that Rolf was seven years old when Jussi married me. Linnea must have realized that Olle was right, because the telephone calls stopped. A few years later, she married the composer Per Lövquist. I hope they had a happy life together.

# Chapter 6

# An Unknown Young Swedish Singer

In the spring of 1936, Jussi traveled to Vienna. The Viennese first heard Jussi on Austrian radio, on 12 March 1936. He opened the program with "Cielo e mar" from *La Gioconda* and ended with the surefire "Che gelida manina" from *La bohème*. Word of his singing must have spread throughout the city, because his recital at the Konzertverein the next day was sold out. "Jussi Björling, an unknown young Swedish singer, won the critical public with his first notes," wrote the *Österreichische Volkspresse*. Another newspaper praised his attractive voice, adding, "His high register is brilliant; he uses it with skill and care. His phrasing is intelligent, and he has the attractive personality of a child of nature."[1]

With an initial success so unalloyed and complete, he was engaged by the Vienna Staatsoper for a series of guest appearances preceding and during the Wiener Festwochen, the festival weeks in June. By the time he reached Prague for his debut at the National Theater on 17 March, he felt almost uncomfortable with all the advance publicity. This was the first time he felt the pressure of having to live up to high expectations. In Stockholm, or even in Copenhagen and Oslo, there was always a next time. But in cities beyond his own operatic orbit he had only one or very few chances to create a lasting impression.

In *Faust* and *La traviata* Jussi received ovations from the Czech people such as he had yet to experience in his native country, and he was invited back to Prague for a return engagement that was to bracket his performances at the Vienna Staatsoper. The morning after his Prague *Traviata*, Jussi took the train to Denmark for his Copenhagen recital, a wonderful finish for his excursion into central Europe. Now his records circulated abroad, arousing such interest that foreign invitations began to arrive. They never stopped until the end of his life.

In May and June 1936, Jussi returned to Czechoslovakia. In Prague he sang *Aida* and *Il trovatore*, in Brno *La bohème*; moving on to Vienna he made guest appearances in all three operas. The casts were international; his Mimì was the young Greek soprano Margherita Perras, only three years his senior. In the Verdi repertoire his partners were his fellow countrywoman Kerstin Thorborg, Mexican-born German baritone Friedrich Ginrod, and the Hungarians Mária Németh and Alexander Svéd. Before his first appearance, Jussi was approached by a representative of a claque. He refused to pay. His conversational German was nonexistent, so it was Kerstin Thorborg who translated his message: Mr. Björling wasn't interested in buying applause.

Jussi's debut as Manrico at the Vienna Staatsoper took place on 28 May 1936. Every newspaper must have sent a music critic to the performance because in the following days the entire Viennese press carried a critique of the performance. The *Echo* observed, "His voice has a sweet timbre, especially in the highest register—the voice seems predestined for Verdi." The *Neue Freie Presse* pronounced his voice "light and metallic," and declared, "He also knows how to produce a resonant, swelling *piano* in the Italian manner. The stretta ['Di quella pira'] did not fail to please, though one would have welcomed more élan." "A beautiful voice, rich in nuances, . . . good, clear phrasing, an intelligent singer and actor" was the judgment of the *Stunde*.

The critic for the *Neues Wiener Journal* made a special point of Jussi's singing the stretta in B rather than C major and further remarked, "Occasionally this troubadour holds a high note for so long that it would have enraged Toscanini." The *Volkszeitung* noted, "The guest singer was rewarded by applause coming from the public rather than the claque, which was particularly disgusting on this occasion." Of special interest is the *Wiener Neueste Nachrichten*'s comment: "He sang Manrico in Swedish, but the sound was Italian: tender and concentrated. The voice is young, pleasant, lyrical, the high register impressive."

The performances of the "tenor from the north" continued to make news. His Rodolfo prompted the *Tagblatt* to report that he was "a rising star of the first magnitude. Outstanding vocal quality, combined with the right instinct for all that is technical and artistic. . . . His style is noble and highly cultured, yet it doesn't prevent the singer from relishing the brilliant effect of a high C."

"Upon hearing the first notes everyone realizes [that it is] a voice of the highest quality," enthused the critic of the *Echo*, describing his art as "the silver of very attractive lyricism coupled with the gold of virile, dramatic flair." Noting a general agreement that Jussi Björling had "surpassed all famous and ultra-famous Rodolfos whom we have heard recently," the *Neues Wiener Journal* further claimed, "Onstage, Björling is not a tenor but a human being." The reviewer of the *Wiener Tag* was the first to draw a comparison that recurred perennially: "It is a lyrical voice of the first order, worthy of a Gigli."

When Jussi opened the Wiener Festwochen on 7 June 1936 with *Aida*, all reservations were gone. "He sang the romanza without effort, tastefully, as only a young singer endowed with a magnificent voice can" (*Neue Freie Presse*). The critic L. wrote, "The lyrical passages especially are close to perfection. There is a magical tenderness . . . vocal control governs every detail." The *Tagblatt* stated, "This singer, a true artist, doesn't set out to impress with a few sensational high notes; rather he wins over the listener with noble artistry."

The person most impressed with Jussi's Radamès was the conductor, as Jussi himself recalled. "Maestro [Victor] de Sabata was so fascinated by my singing that he wanted me to go immediately to Italy with him, but I had engagements at the Stockholm Opera and couldn't accept his invitation. According to my contract I had only a couple of months' leave, and I was to honor all my foreign commitments during this time."[2] It was true; Jussi received many contract offers, but the restrictions imposed by his contract with the Royal Opera obliged him to turn most down.

On his nights off, as he had from his earliest years, Jussi went to hear other singers perform, as much for musical enjoyment as for the learning experience. When he went backstage to congratulate the soloists of Franz Lehár's latest operetta, *Giuditta*, he developed an instant rapport with Richard Tauber. Jussi wrote,

> During my sojourn in Vienna, I was often with Richard Tauber. Tauber was charming company, and we had a good time together. He noticed my youthful admiration, but his natural manner and self-irony helped me get over my awkwardness. Although I have met many good friends and unpretentious people, very few have been like Tauber. I wonder sometimes if the really great artists ever need to put on airs.[3]

John Forsell and his son Björn had traveled to Vienna to support Jussi in his first performances in one of Europe's great music centers, and Jussi was delighted they were on hand for his triumph. In the *New York Herald Tribune* (5 July 1936), Herbert F. Peyser reported that the Viennese expected just another songbird to pass through the city but were completely taken by what they heard. With his reputation with Austrian audiences secured, Jussi was invited to return next year for a longer period.

With Anders' birth, I hoped that Jussi, for the sake of our family, would curb his drinking. For a while he seemed to, but he soon began to drink with alarming regularity. As if that weren't enough, several months after the baby's birth—I cannot pinpoint the precise moment—our marriage was put to a major test. With gloom and guilt written all over his boyish face, Jussi said he had something to tell me, something of the utmost seriousness. Apprehension gripped me. Although many thoughts flashed through my mind, what I heard next was not one of them.

During the first months of my pregnancy, while I was hospitalized, Jussi visited the Zander family. One thing led to another, and—well—Eva Zander had recently given birth to a baby girl, and the baby was his. Eva wanted to give the child up for adoption, and Jussi was prepared to support the child until we could find adoptive parents for her.

I was shocked and bewildered—and deeply hurt. Sheltered from the darker side of life, I knew that such a thing could happen, but I never imagined it could happen to me. Jussi was remorseful in the extreme and tearfully begged my forgiveness; he deeply regretted causing me such distress and swore it would never happen again.

I don't know what other women might have done in my place. My initial reaction was "This is it! This is the end!"—but ultimately I felt my only choice was to forgive Jussi. Leaving him or asking for a divorce was unthinkable. I loved my husband very much, and I felt that our love was strong enough to survive this crisis.

Jussi went to see his lawyer, Gösta Hansson, and explained the situation. Hansson listened carefully, thought it over, then unexpectedly came up with the perfect solution. "My wife and I cannot have children. If you give me your word that no one will ever know the paternity of this child, we'll adopt her and raise her as our own."

Of course, Jussi agreed on the spot. Adoption papers were drawn up, and the little girl, Birgitta, found loving parents and a wonderful home. Jussi and I faithfully kept our promise, and Kickie, as she was called, never knew who the nice family friend was who visited her daddy on business and brought her presents. But a few years after Gösta and Ebba Hansson died, a family friend told Kickie that she was adopted. She successfully traced her parentage, and through some indiscretion—not hers—it became public knowledge in 1991. If Kickie's father had been a clerk or a bus driver it would've held no interest to anyone, but because he was Jussi Björling, the disclosure created a minor sensation in the Swedish press, finally absolving me of my vow of silence, which I had solemnly kept for over half a century.

Once settled, the matter never came up between us again. Jussi wasn't a saint, nor was he a philanderer by nature, but celebrities and singing artists, tenors in particular, frequently encounter women who explicitly or implicitly offer themselves to the men they idolize. From then on it is no longer a chase but a choice. Perhaps Jussi was again faced with such a choice, such a temptation, but if he ever strayed after this incident, I never knew it.

※

In 1936, we rented a summer house on Sandholmen in Stockholm's archipelago, not far from Ljusterö. There were only two houses on the little island; both belonged to Erik Wirén, an engineer and avid fisherman, who lived in the larger house. Erik initiated Jussi in all the secret ways of pike. Every morning at 4 o'clock he knocked on our window to summon him, and the two would go fishing. On their very first morning out, Jussi reeled in an eight-and-a-half-pound pike and, immediately afterward, a 26-pound monster with sharp teeth and voracious jaws big enough to snap your hand off. Jussi hooked the fish—and was hooked on fishing. Though he never, in all his years as a devoted fisherman, pulled in a pike larger than the one he caught that first morning, from that day on fishing served for Jussi a multiple purpose: it was a sport, it was his favorite form of relaxation, and he loved to eat the fish he caught. A reporter once asked Jussi "What would you like to be if you were not a singer?" and Jussi's answer was "A fisherman."[4]

The record-size pike accompanied him to the city to be shown off at the Opera, where it was immediately purchased by Mr. Ekegårdh, the Operakällaren's restaurateur, netting Jussi more than enough to cover his and Grevillius' luncheon check. Jussi had its head mounted, and to this day, from its place of honor on the wall, opposite the steady silver-framed gaze of Caruso as Radamès, the trophy turns fishy eyes on all who enter Jussi's studio.

The owners of a piano store in town, Valdemar Lundholm and his wife, shared many of our fish dinners that summer, and they became extremely fond of Murre, the little black Scottie Jussi had given me when I was expecting. With baby Anders around, Murre wasn't getting the same attention as before; one day I discovered him standing by Anders' cradle, growling threateningly, and we actually became concerned that the jealous Murre might harm our little boy. Mrs. Lundholm suggested that she and her husband take the neglected pup until Anders grew a little older, ending with this incredible offer: "You may borrow a small upright piano in trade."

We jumped at the solution. Jussi needed a piano to rehearse, but we didn't have one on Sandholmen. A few days later, a superb studio-size piano, precisely what we needed, was delivered to the house. Some years later, when the war began, Mr. Lundholm explained that it had become difficult to import such fine pianos. "So, unfortunately, I must ask to have ours returned."

"Isn't that peculiar," Jussi replied calmly. "Just the other day Anna-Lisa and I were saying how much we missed little Murre. It'll be nice to have him back with us." It was the first and only time I witnessed Jussi resorting to blackmail.

"Keep the darn piano!" Valle Lundholm countered, and the subject was never brought up again. The piano too remains in Jussi's studio.

※

In August 1936, Jussi began his seventh season at the Stockholm Opera. On 5 September he sang his first Lt. Pinkerton in the favorite opera of my childhood, *Madama Butterfly*. Soon after that, he added the role of Tonio in Donizetti's *La fille du régiment*. "Björling managed the role brilliantly—the task involves performing eight high Cs in a row, and that didn't bother him one bit."[5] In addition to his opera performances in Stockholm and around the country, Jussi gave concerts, made recordings, and sang on the radio. It was hard to believe that only six years had passed since his debut.

Jussi, by now the *de facto* premier tenor of the Opera, continued to add new roles while keeping most of his old ones active. With his memory, it was easy for him. In his autobiography, Jussi enumerated the roles he could sing the same evening if he were asked to do so at noon. They were Radamès; Rodolfo in Swedish and Italian; Count Almaviva; Don Ottavio; Alfredo; Lensky; Riccardo in Swedish and Italian; Vladimir Igorevich in *Prince Igor*; Dick Johnson; Martin Skarp in *Fanal*; Faust in Swedish and French; the Lamplighter ("my first little role"); Mats in *Kronbruden*; Nemorino; Pinkerton; Wilhelm Meister; Lyonel; Turiddu; Canio; both Tybalt and Roméo in Swedish and French; the Duke of Mantua in Swedish and Italian; the Merchant from India in *Sadko*; Narraboth; Mario Cavaradossi in Swedish and Italian; Tamino; Manrico in Swedish and Italian; and Arnoldo in *Guglielmo Tell*—an arid list of names until one thinks of the words, music, style, and interpretive nuances these roles represent. When he made this claim he wasn't exaggerating. Jussi's brain could absorb, retain, and recall these parts at will, in toto. Such a musical memory cannot be acquired, it is a special gift.

Jussi's first Scandinavian tour was managed by Sven-Olof Sandberg, a singer at the Royal Opera.[6] When his successes abroad began to attract attention and Björling became a marketable commodity, he was signed by Helmer Enwall, director of Konsertbolaget. "Jussi was called the Swedish Caruso in many countries," Enwall wrote. "When I first became interested in becoming an impresario, it was my ambition to bring Caruso to Sweden. It wasn't possible, but instead I had the great pleasure of launching the Swedish Caruso."[7]

Enwall had the exclusive rights to all Jussi's European engagements, and now agencies from overseas began to express an interest in him. The first among these was Charles Wagner, one of the best known and most successful impresari in America. He was an agent, promoter, and friend to many prominent artists, among them John McCormack, Amelita Galli-Curci, Mary Garden, and Alexander Kipnis.

In his memoirs, Wagner described his 1936 trip to Europe in search of new talent. Of the 75 singers he auditioned in 10 countries, he hired eight.

He read in the *Times* that in Vienna Jussi was hailed as "a singer from the Northland" and recalled his reaction: "Something in that phrase piqued my interest; I cabled for an option, and on this trip flew to Stockholm from London to hear him. His singing of a *Bohème* aria convinced me this was the tenor I sought."[8]

But Wagner had vowed he'd never manage another tenor unless he found one in McCormack's class, and upon his return home he began to have second thoughts. Fearing that perhaps he had been too hasty in engaging a singer on the basis of a single aria, he made a return trip to Stockholm, this time to hear Jussi in a complete performance of *La bohème*. He concluded, "My newfound tenor combined the best values of both Caruso and McCormack."[9]

Jussi had participated in several live radio broadcasts from the Royal Opera. On 15 January 1934, he sang Count Elemer in Richard Strauss' *Arabella*; two weeks later, at 10 o'clock in the morning, he sang with Helga Görlin the third act of *Fanal*. But his most memorable day on Swedish radio was 1 November 1936. He appeared twice that day: the evening's *Il trovatore* was broadcast from the Opera, and earlier in the day he sang Söderman's "Trollsjön" ("Troll Lake") and Sjöberg's "Tonerna." Part of the broadcast was transmitted to NBC in New York.

According to Bo Teddy Ladberg, this was the only time in his experience that Jussi displayed a fit of temper. "Tonerna" ends on a high A-flat, but due to time overrun, the second stanza was eliminated. Ladberg added, "Considering what this transmission must have meant for a 25-year-old singer . . . on the verge of launching an international career, his outburst was completely understandable."[10]

During the autumn, there was talk of Jussi making a guest appearance at Teatro Colón in Buenos Aires, but the long sea voyage and extended engagement would've taken up too much time; the Opera couldn't grant him a leave of absence lasting over two months. Regretfully, he turned the offer down, but on 15 December 1936, he made time for his Paris debut. The Cité Universitaire was dedicating its theater building with a gala concert, and in singing the first act of *La bohème*, Jussi had one of those mishaps opera singers collect through their career. When Jussi, as the poet Rodolfo, tried to open the window to answer his bohemian friends calling to him from the street below, the whole scenery wall fell on top of him!

After several minutes of total confusion, order was restored, the performance continued, and the evening was a great success. Swedish organizer Rolf de Maré, founder of the Swedish Ballet and the Swedish Theater in Paris, had every reason to be satisfied.

※

Jussi launched his 1937 guest appearances in Germany. On 5 February, the day after a *Pagliacci* in Nuremberg, I wrote to my son: "My darling little

Anders! Hope you are well now and that you don't have any fever. Dad sang last night and it went well as usual, enormous success. In an hour we leave for Berlin. Take care of yourself little one and say hello to Mormor [Grandmother] and Nanny Elsa. Hug from Mama and Papa." Writing to a one-year-old toddler was our way of compensating for being separated from him; our postcards and letters were meant for my mother, of course.

Jussi instituted this mode of communication on his first trip to Vienna, corresponding with me through one-month-old Anders. On a postcard he picked up in Berlin, he wrote, "Ask your mother if she has been to the place pictured on the card [Reichstagsgebaude]. Be a good little boy and obey mother, otherwise there will be a little spanking on the bottom when Papa comes home. Greetings to Mama from Papa." It's odd that the idea of spanking ever occurred to Jussi, for in all his life he never struck his children, and in spite of his extraordinary physical strength, he was never in a fight with anyone.

On 6 February, Jussi sang Rodolfo in Berlin, then repeated it on the 8th in Dresden. One critic wrote,

> His youthful, manly grace captivates his listeners before he has sung a single note. He is a convincing actor; his facial expression changes quickly. He would make a fine actor—but he is much more: without a doubt he is one of the most beautiful vocal talents of our time—a time not blessed by much talent. He possesses a large voice that probably is still growing. Yet even today it delivers everything needed for the role of Rodolfo: suppleness, force, brilliance, and a magical, melting sweetness on the high notes.[11]

In another reviewer's opinion, Jussi was "a true Italian tenor, reaching high notes with incredible ease. . . . [His] completely effortless singing [must be] the result of impeccable training. This is particularly evident in his handling of *mezza voce*."[12]

After a day's rest, Jussi sang the Duke of Mantua. His leading lady in both *La bohème* and *Rigoletto* was marvelous soprano Maria Cebotari. Jussi triumphed in the role, bringing to it "an aura of bravado, high spirits—one might say boyish carelessness."[13]

Between 14 February and 22 March Jussi sang a bouquet of his repertoire in Vienna: Rodolfo, Manrico (three performances), Pinkerton, Canio (two performances), Dick Johnson, Faust, Riccardo, and the Duke of Mantua. In his reentry to the Staatsoper, as Rodolfo, Jussi displayed "one of the most beautiful tenor voices to be heard today. He reaches the high C effortlessly, beginning on a most tender *piano*, growing to a radiant *forte*, followed by a *decrescendo*. . . . [Jarmila] Novotná as Mimì was almost his equal."[14]

When Jussi sang the first of three Manricos on 16 February, he felt like a Swedish intruder in the midst of a Hungarian invasion, all forces in their powerful prime: Mária Németh sang Leonora, Rosette Anday was Azucena, and Alexander Svéd Di Luna. But something must've happened to Jussi between the second and third acts, for one critic noted, "The stretta became a victim . . . of a sudden indisposition."[15] It must've passed quickly, because in reviewing Jussi as Pinkerton the very next night, the critic cast all restraint to the wind. "Last night's Butterfly was Jarmila Novotná—poetry personi-fied, a Japanese beauty of unspeakable grace. . . . And Jussi Björling as Pinkerton! He fits that role to perfection—natural, without giving himself airs."[16]

According to one critic, Jussi's success in *Pagliacci* "may have been even greater than that of his Rodolfo." When "Vesti la giubba" and "No, Pagliaccio non son" from this performance were located and released first on LP and then on CD, I marveled anew at the effectiveness and originality of his interpretation; Jussi's rendition of Canio's lament was unquestionably his own, and the recitative in particular, the quiet introspective conclusion, successfully suggests a desperate man talking to his mirror image. As Dick Johnson in *La fanciulla del West*, Jussi was found by the same critic to be "a likeable young man who does not indulge in star affectations. . . . The famous G-flat major aria ['Ch'ella mi creda'] left nothing to be desired."[17]

After wedging a recital between his performances, Jussi sang his second Manrico with a new cast and a new flourish. This time the Swedish Manrico had a Swedish mother in Kerstin Thorborg, Josef Krips had replaced Felix Weingartner in the pit, and for good measure Jussi sang "Di quella pira" with not two but three high Cs.[18] For once it was showmanship, but not without precedent; Joseph Schmidt sang three high Cs in his 1934 recording, creating a sensation. Jussi wanted to give no less to the Viennese in a live performance. The critiques of the 5 March performance made a special ref-erence to the crucial passage: "A short time ago the stretta was marred by his indisposition, but this time the audience was amply rewarded."[19]

*Faust* followed with the phenomenal Ukrainian bass Alexander Kipnis as a marvelous Méphistophélès, but one reviewer complained that the out-ward appearance of Jussi's Faust "made us think that Mephisto subjected him to an all-too-radical rejuvenation."[20] After a repeat of *Pagliacci*, Jussi sang the second Riccardo of his life to a tumultuous reception. "Jussi Björ-ling has become the darling of Vienna opera audiences," the review of the previous evening's *Ballo in maschera* began. "It was his best night." The review also singled out Svéd as Renato, who "nearly equalled the perform-ance of the tenor, whose voice is one of the most beautiful, perhaps *the* most beautiful, to be heard these days in our Opera House."[21]

Jussi wound up the long Vienna engagement with a splendid Duke of Mantua and a third Manrico. He was again called the darling of Vienna audiences, and his popular success can be gauged by the eyewitness account of Otniel Sobek, who well remembers when a throng of autograph seekers mobbed Jussi, pushing him back into the artists' entrance, all the way to the artists' bar inside the theater. The crowd kept growing, and both to avoid being crushed and to have some elbow room, Jussi jumped on top of a table. Thus trapped, he stood signing program after program, for a long, long time.[22]

※

Jussi twice interrupted his appearances in the Austrian capital for his opera and concert debut in Budapest. Anders still treasures the postcard we sent him from that city, on 26 February 1937. "Tomorrow, in the house which you can see on the other side of the card, Dad is singing (*Aida*). Next time you'll be along, because we'll never leave our little boy again."

The Royal Hungarian Opera surrounded Jussi by the best cast at their command for *Aida*. Mária Németh returned from Vienna for the title role, Ella Némethy was Amneris, György Losonczy sang Amonasro, and Mihály Székely Ramfis. The Budapest critics found Jussi's lyric tenor flexible, sonorous, sensuous, and "with a noble ring."[23] "At last a true tenor with the typical, silvery and penetrating sound projected through the entire hall. The tones are well supported; the singer appears to be particularly at ease in the top octave."[24] On 9 March, Jussi demonstrated to the Budapest audience that he was also a competent recitalist. "As a Lieder singer, he is able to recreate the true mood of each song."[25]

A third interruption to the Viennese engagement came on 14 March, when Jussi sang *Aida* in Prague with Zinka Kunc. Neither of them could foresee that Miss Kunc, later Zinka Milanov, and Jussi Björling would be partnered many more times over the years, at the Metropolitan Opera and on records.

※

While we were in central Europe, Jussi's first His Master's Voice Red Seal records were released in Stockholm, a significant event; the records were demonstrated at a reception attended by several special guests. *Nya Dagligt Allehanda* (27 February 1937) reported, "Jussi Björling has entered the star class, the first Swedish singer to enjoy that privilege." The four numbers, recorded in Stockholm on 1 and 3 December 1936, were his first operatic selections sung in the original language. In "Che gelida manina," Jussi mis-pronounced several words, betraying his early incomplete command of the language. Although Jussi delivered his foreign texts flawlessly in the years ahead, because of the immense popularity and countless reissues of this par-ticular record, he earned the critics' recurrent disapproval of his Italian.[26]

Back in Stockholm, Jussi sang Faust, Roméo, Pinkerton, and Radamès at the Opera, and a superb Verdi Requiem with Maestro Fritz Busch, which was broadcast on the radio. On 6 June he took part for the first time in the Swedish Flag Day ceremonies at Skansen; a week later he was back in Paris to participate in two Swedish concerts under the baton of Nils Grevillius. When Jussi sang Hugo Alfvén's "Skogen sover" ("The Forest Sleeps"), the crowd would not stop applauding, celebrating as much the interpreter as the composer, who was in the audience. In the face of such enthusiasm and prompted by Alfvén's presence, Jussi repeated the song, and this time he sang it even better. After the concert, Alfvén said to him, "Thank you, dear Jussi. When you sang 'Skogen sover' the second time, that was the first time I heard it."[27]

As far as I can remember, this was the only time that Jussi sang the same number twice in a concert. Normally Jussi would've considered it artistic bankruptcy to encore in a recital a number he had just sung. He didn't have to resort to such cheap solutions; he had several hundred songs and arias in his repertoire—"my inventory" as he called it—in seven languages, and he was prepared to sing a couple hundred of them at the drop of a hat. "Jussi never sang a song the same way twice," observed Maestro Bertil Bokstedt, Jussi's coach and accompanist in later years. "It was always the feeling of the moment which determined how he interpreted the music."[28]

Hugo Alfvén never forgot that concert in Paris. Years later, he offered Jussi another composition.

> A few days ago I sent to you my latest song: "Saa tag mit Hjerte." It's the most wonderful, heartfelt poem I have ever set to music, so unspeakably tender that I can never read it without getting tears in my eyes.
>
> Naturally my thoughts have gone to you and your interpretation of "Skogen sover"; but I simply have not dared to send my latest song to you, because therein would be a concealed request—would you like to record this song also?—and I don't want to take the risk of receiving a negative answer. But now I feel that I have to take the risk.[29]

※

In August 1937, as he was about to begin his eighth season at the Opera, Jussi confronted a new challenge: he was invited to play the leading role in a motion picture, *Fram för framgång* (*Head for Success*), produced by Svensk Filmindustri. The idea to build a story around Jussi was director-screenwriter Gunnar Skoglund's. It was a simple little plot about a young singer who, after a multitude of contrived complications, finally has a break-through and—surprise!—heads for success.[30] Jussi found moviemaking an amusing if tiresome diversion. The film had five musical numbers, one of them the barcarola, "Di tu se fedele," from *Un ballo in maschera*. Jussi sang both verses as Verdi wrote it, with the leap from high A-flat to middle B. The marvel of that absolutely solid, almost baritonal low note is that it isn't an artificial chest note but a clear extension of the Björling sound.[31]

Helmer Enwall, Jussi's manager, opposed his filming in Sweden. He thought Jussi should wait for the inevitable invitation from Hollywood. Such a film debut would carry more weight, the fee could be 20 or 30 times greater, and with international distribution the exposure would be ines-timably better! It wasn't easy to soothe Forsell's apprehensions either that the filming would interfere with Jussi's obligations at the Opera. It did not; filming began on 14 August and concluded on 10 November 1937. The final scene, an outdoor concert before 20,000 spectators, was filmed at Gröna Lund on 5 September. In between filming, on 14 September 1937 Jussi performed for the last time in his career Don Ottavio, opposite Ezio Pinza's Don Giovanni, and 10 days later he sang the Duke of Mantua with Lawrence Tibbett as Rigoletto. A casual friendship developed between these two guest artists and us.

Right on the heels of the wonderful *Rigoletto* with Larry Tibbett came a failure. In his anthology Bertil Hagman wrote: "Autumn 1937 brought a great fiasco for Björling, though the burden shouldn't be borne by him alone. He essayed another Faust, this time in Boïto's *Mefistofele*, a production that received possibly the most crushing reviews ever given an operatic performance in Stockholm. It was staged only twice [30 September and 3 October] and then quietly withdrawn from the repertoire."[32] Jussi's partners in musical crime were Helga Görlin as Margherita and Leon Björker in the title role.

❋

Jussi's perennial shortcoming was his acting; to pretend to be someone else was contrary to his straightforward, honest nature. He grew up as a concert singer, an artist who entertained his audience with his voice and musicianship, and when he performed in his youth, he was Jussi Björling, a boy from Dalarna. Now he was expected to become someone else: a warrior, a poet, a nobleman, a painter, an Egyptian general. He wasn't extroverted, and he felt terribly self-conscious in makeup and costume. Moreover, he had to overcome a certain amount of inborn shyness. Perhaps subconsciously he felt that in a recital he was exhibiting his voice, while in opera it was himself he put on display. Most of the time Jussi seemed somewhat reserved on the stage—it was the essence of his personality and he couldn't behave otherwise.

He had an intuitive feeling for acting, but the emotions reflected in his face were effective only at short range; they were too subtle to communicate beyond the footlights, and he couldn't project them through posture and movement. He didn't have a stage walk, nor did he vary his stance from role to role. Only with years of experience did he learn to unlock the secrets of assuming another identity; in particular he believed that to express the character's attitude, it was important to position the head correctly.

Essentially, he adhered to Hyltén-Cavallius' teaching of the Signe Hebbes maxim: "Not one step, not one gesture that is not *dramatically necessary!*"[33] In this respect he was decades ahead of his time; he would've fit perfectly in Wieland Wagner's postwar productions in Bayreuth. But this made his acting terribly stiff, and even I must reluctantly admit that he sometimes looked out of place onstage. Clearly, he had to find a way to become Cavaradossi or Radamès, Rodolfo or Faust, allowing Jussi Björling to dissolve in the character.

101

"Some people felt he was awkward on the stage," wrote Hugo Hasslo. *"Sure, sure—he can sing well enough, but he cannot act,* they would say. I do not feel that way. Just the opposite—Jussi never made an unnecessary gesture. He stood still, but he stood well."[34] Stage director Lars Runsten said that when Jussi stood onstage, "he did so with colossal authority."[35] Birgit Nilsson, who worked with Jussi in the last decade of his career, "found him a very good actor. He did not need to use big gestures, screams and sobs to get his message across to the public. As any great master would, he acted with the voice."[36] William Seward expressed the same thing in different words: "If there was no reason for movement, he didn't move. But he was credible onstage and he could be very, very moving. I remember especially a *Manon Lescaut* with Björling and Albanese, with Mitropoulos conducting[37]—their intensity was like electricity. They were breathtaking, it was something unbelievable!"[38]

In addition to his difficulties with stage movement, his greatest worry was his hands. They had short fingers, which Hyltén-Cavallius described as a bunch of plump little sausages.[39] "What should I do with them?" Jussi would ask Forsell unhappily. "Hide them, for God's sake! Put them in your pockets, keep them behind your back, anything! But keep them out of sight." All this gave Jussi quite a complex, which had not improved appreciably with the years.

Sometime in 1937, Gösta Ekman and his wife, Greta, attended one of Jussi's *Faust* performances. Ekman was one of the most prominent, respected actors in Sweden and an acknowledged master of stagecraft. He worked on the stage and in a dozen films, including the first—Swedish—version of *Intermezzo* with Ingrid Bergman, in 1937.

After the performance I went to Jussi's dressing room. Just as I came in, a stage attendant knocked on the door and announced Gösta and Greta Ekman. We were completely taken by surprise and greatly honored by this unexpected visit. After the greetings and general compliments, Ekman came straight to the point. "You have a wonderful voice, Jussi, but what on earth are you doing with your hands?"

"John Forsell says they're big and clumsy," Jussi began.

"What kind of stupidity is that?" Gösta exclaimed. "You have strong, manly hands—you shouldn't be ashamed of them!"

As we watched and listened, Ekman instructed Jussi. How to move onstage, how to walk, turn, and most importantly, how to make a gesture. He ran through a whole range of movements, demonstrating precisely how Jussi should use his hands. Jussi was getting a lesson from one of the great dramatic actors! He absorbed every syllable of Ekman's instructions. It gave me a tiny glimpse of what others had said about Jussi—Forsell, Hislop, Grevillius, Voghera—that teaching him was like sprinkling water on a blotter. He literally soaked up the instruction.

From that day on, his complex vanished; at the very next performance I could see the effects of Ekman's teachings, and several critics noticed the marked difference in his acting. Jussi explained later that to use his hands properly, he needed only to visualize Gösta Ekman's impromptu lesson. Jussi considered meeting him one of the most significant experiences of his career.

But the story didn't end there. Some days later, a package arrived from Ekman. It contained a little silver peacock from India, with ruby eyes and moveable wings. In an accompanying letter, Ekman explained that he was preparing a reading of Hans Christian Andersen's "The Nightingale," which made him think of Jussi. In this fairy tale, a most wondrous nightingale lives in the forest that surrounds the palace of a Chinese emperor. The bird is plain and gray, but its voice is the sweetest thing ever heard; when the emperor listens to it, it brings tears to his eyes. Then one day the emperor receives a mechanical nightingale, covered with diamonds, rubies, and sapphires. It sings just like the real bird, but it has only one song. While it sings, the real nightingale flies away. In time the mechanical bird breaks and no longer produces sound. When the aging emperor cries for music from his deathbed, the real nightingale comes back to him, and his singing restores the emperor to good health.

That story, the plain bird with the exquisitely lovely song, Ekman wrote, reminded him of Jussi, and he was sending us the silver bird as a memento of their first meeting: "Show little Anders how the bird can lift its wings!" It was a thoughtful gesture and an exquisitely crafted gift. Anders marveled at the little bird's moving wings and liked it so much that when he grew older, Jussi gave it to him. To this day, Anders has it in his home.

# Chapter 7

# AMERICA AND THE
# METROPOLITAN

Jussi's request for a leave of absence from the Royal Opera was granted without objection, and his first American engagement, an eight-week concert tour, began in November 1937. The only thing that was terribly difficult for me was to leave Anders for such a long time. My mother promised to take care of him, so as far as his safety was concerned, I had no reason to be anxious.

Helmer Enwall, who with his wife, Thérèse, was along on the trip, combined the tour with additional appearances en route. "The first time you go to New York, you must have your own manager with you!" he insisted, a transparent excuse for an exciting trip to the New World. After all, the 12-stop American tour was under Charles Wagner's management.

Our first stop was Copenhagen, where as soon as the recital was announced, every ticket sold within two hours. On the night of 12 November 1937 Jussi sang his heart out for his faithful Danish audience. In the judgment of *Politiken*, "Björling and Gigli are the world's greatest tenors. A more perfect voice than Björling's does not exist. Providence has given him everything; every note is immaculate, marked by purity, clarity, transparency, and beauty."[1] Jussi relished the warm reception, but more significantly, sustaining the long program reassured him that his voice was back to normal: before we left, he had had pharyngitis, but now he was ready to face the British public for the first time.[2]

When "shy, stocky, blonde Jussi Björling" walked the gangplank to set foot in England for his London debut, reported Phyllis Davies, he was aware that he had, in his own words, "embarked on the first 50 steps of the most important part of my career."[3] His words were prophetic. For the remainder of his life he sang more often overseas than on the Continent.

Ivor Newton accompanied Jussi in his debut recital in Queen's Hall. It began with Mozart, Don Ottavio's two arias from *Don Giovanni* and one aria from *Die Zauberflöte*. Then came "Ingemisco" from Verdi's Requiem, four songs by Schubert, and "Che gelida manina" from *La bohème*. The Swedish songs in the second half of the program, all new to English audiences, were especially well received. "Una furtiva lagrima" from *L'elisir d'amore* finished the scheduled program. As the London correspondent for *Dagens Nyheter* wrote, "the applause and shouts of bravo thundered for several minutes," and Jussi was kept on the platform and obliged to sing four encores, an even greater success than in Denmark.

"A New Caruso" was the headline of Edwin Evans' review the next day: "[Björling] justified all that had been said of him in advance, and confirmed the truth of his gramophone records. He has a glorious voice, and, what is even more important, a perfectly natural unspoiled production." But Evans had some reservations:

> His stocky figure and his businesslike way of advancing to the centre of the stage, more like an athlete than a musician, predisposed the audience in his favour. But it must be confessed that some songs were sung just as one might have expected from that approach—in a competent and businesslike way. Mr. Ivor Newton, at the piano, was hard put to it to make that trout ["Die Forelle"] sufficiently nimble and buoyant. That is Mr. Björling's weakness, as it is of several of his singing compatriots. But of the voice one can say nothing but praise.[4]

This first collaboration with Ivor Newton laid the foundation for a lasting association; he remained Jussi's accompanist for his concerts in the British Isles. Years later, Newton remembered Jussi as

> a man of surprising contradictions: as an artist, he was superb, with a remarkable range and an impeccable style that permitted no musical mistakes and no lapses of memory in its strict fidelity to what the composer had written. As a man, he was obstinate, difficult, taciturn and unusually lazy. He hated to rehearse, and would find endless excuses—his health, the weather, and all varieties of ingenious reasons—to avoid doing so.

Still, he marveled at Jussi's ability to effortlessly navigate the full breadth of musical styles, always hitting the "right vocal tone and color for his wide range of songs," then switching to a "ringing operatic voice for 'Celeste Aida' and 'Nessun Dorma.'" Yes, "Björling, for all his difficulties of his temperament, was . . . a musician to his fingertips; he seemed to do everything right and to do it by instinct."[5]

On 19 November, in the company of the Enwalls, we embarked from Southampton. I greatly looked forward to the trip; Jussi had been to America as a child, but for me it was the first time. Thérèse and I had spent a lot of time preparing our travel wardrobes, and my beautiful bridal gown, dyed and altered, was now sufficiently elegant to be worn with a little jacket for special occasions—until a waiter accidentally spilled tomato sauce down my back. Apart from this, it was a pleasant journey; we passed the gray November days from Southampton to New York playing shuffleboard and table tennis on deck, and we all were elated to see the Statue of Liberty come into view. When I look at the pictures of our arrival in New York, I cannot help but think how touchingly innocent we both look, not quite ready for the thrilling life that awaited us in America.

Jussi's arrival earned him a brief mention in the press. *The New York Times* (26 November 1937), in noting the return, after a seven-month tour, of Lawrence Tibbett, who "said he got his best reception in Sweden," added in the last paragraph: "Opera singers Jussi Bjoerling and Eyvind Laholm arrived on the steamship *Manhattan*." Other articles followed, and Jussi was variously said to be either younger or older than he was. His age was always taken with a grain of salt, and no wonder: notwithstanding the two-decade-long singing career behind him, he was only 26.

We all spoke English, but we were far from fluent. When Louis Biancolli interviewed us at the Hotel Wellington, he was amused that we occasionally had "three-headed huddles in Swedish" before answering some of his questions. He described Jussi as "a short, broad-backed, round-faced, large-headed Swede, with plenty of brawn and a grip of steel."[6] Another reporter, William G. King, wrote that Jussi looked "about 18—a short, heavy-set, moon-faced youth with quiet blue eyes and a slow grin. What seems to be reserve probably is shyness."[7]

Biancolli and others had problems with Jussi's name. After some spelling variations, with and without the diaeresis, most English-language newspapers settled on "Bjoerling," but pronunciation was quite another matter. The ways we heard his name pronounced! Charles Wagner never managed to master the B-j conjunction and always called him "Mr. Jarling." It became a standing joke between him and Alexander Kipnis, who'd ask, "Well, Charles, have you learned to pronounce Jarling's name yet?"[8] The problem diminished in proportion to Jussi's popularity, but only with music lovers. In the late 50s, when Anders tried to reach his father at the Essex House, the operator insisted no such person was registered. We had called Anders earlier, so he *knew* we were at the hotel. "Björling," he kept repeating, "Björling. I'll spell it for you: B-j-o-r-l-i-n-g." "Oh, you mean Ba-Jorling! I'll connect you!"

On 28 November 1937, Jussi sang for the first time as an adult in New York City in the *Sunday Nights at Carnegie Hall* series sponsored by General Motors. I sat in the audience with my fingers crossed so hard they almost broke; as the saying goes, you never get a second chance to make a first impression, and this was the first time tens of thousands of radio listeners were going to hear the voice of Jussi Björling performing live in front of the microphone. Milton Cross, careful not to mispronounce the double consonants of a name entirely new to him, introduced the program.

> The musical public has eagerly awaited the American appearance of the brilliant leading tenor of the Stockholm Opera, Jus-si Björling, whose success in the capitals of Europe has been so sensational. Mr. Björling, only 26 years of age, arrived in New York only last Thursday and makes his first appearance as an exclusive member of the General Motors Concert Company on this program tonight. We are happy indeed to introduce Jussi Björling.

Erno Rapee conducted the General Motors Symphony Orchestra and Chorus, and Jussi sang "Che gelida manina," "La donna è mobile," "Celeste Aida," "Land, du välsignade," and a bilingual duet from *Cavalleria rusticana* with Maria Jeritza, he in Swedish and Jeritza in Italian. The program went exceedingly well, and the *New York Sun* wrote of Jussi's "young, fresh, and powerful voice." He was praised for his great dramatic power and superior musicality shown in the duet with Jeritza. In another review Irving Kolodin made a skeptical reference to Jussi's age. "At present his singing attains an unmistakable effect through the sheer exuberance and vitality of the artist, who is, officially, only in his mid-twenties."[9]

A few weeks and several recitals later, Jussi appeared with the Chicago Civic Opera. He sang the Duke in *Rigoletto* with Lawrence Tibbett and an 18-year-old Chicago schoolgirl, Beverly Lane. It was followed a week later by a performance of *La bohème*. Almost all the reviews were good, some better than others. Music critic Herman Devries wrote, "Jussi Bjoerling can be excused for singing the role of the Duke partly in Italian and then lapsing into his native tongue—Swedish—for here, too, we discovered a tenor such as this city has not heard in many a moon. Adolescent in appearance, the newcomer carries himself with stately demeanor and sings like a demigod."[10] Janet Gunn stated, "Jussi Bjoerling, young Swedish tenor, who is on his way to skyrocket fame, made his Chicago debut, portraying the role of the profligate Duke. He received an ovation for his superb vocal mastery, his truly magnificent range and quality, and for his style and diction, both in Swedish and Italian, inasmuch as he sang his part in the two languages."[11] Robert Pollak observed that Jussi's voice was "poignant, clear and true. The gentleman conducts himself on the stage with appealing simplicity,"[12] while Eugene Stinson proclaimed him "a seasoned and excellent singer, [with] a voice of surpassing pliancy, freshness and brilliance. Indeed, having a voice so brilliant and using it with so much sense of theatrical effect, Mr. Bjoerling himself remains a tenor singularly lacking in elan. Yet his phrasing is a delight, his touch is certain, his manner is modest and his singing is superb."[13]

Jussi followed up his debut with a recital, singing to a nearly all-female audience in the Red Lacquer Room of the Palmer House. It was a morning musicale, scheduled for the ungodly hour of 11 a.m. The footlights beamed straight into his eyes, so Jussi stepped down from the stage and adjusted them himself. "Then he thought his accompanist should have someone to turn the pages so a music teacher from the audience hastily was brought onto the stage," wrote India Moffett, but "any one who sings like Mr. Bjoerling does can afford to be a little temperamental."[14] It made me wonder: if the organizers blind the singer with lights and fail to provide a page turner, why is the singer "temperamental" if he quietly, without making a fuss, does something about it?

Cecil Smith felt similarly about Jussi's singing: "I am certainly not prepared to deny that Mr. Bjoerling is the world's greatest tenor, for I have not heard any living tenor sing better. His voice is fresh, vital, and thrilling in timbre. A vocal method fully adequate to his present needs gives him an unusually even scale, and he has the physical strength (though he is short and roly-poly) to project his splendid top notes with solidity and assurance."[15]

Jussi firmed up the initial impressions a few days later as Rodolfo in *La bohème*, with a sure delivery of its "almost unreasonably lovely music." Edward Barry continued: "Mr. Bjoerling, by the way, has a high C in his bag of tricks. For this reason the aria and the duo were not transposed half a tone downward, as is the custom, but were performed in their original key. Naturally enough, the offstage finish of the duo was genuinely exciting."[16] According to Eugene Stinson, "His was in fundamentals one of the best Rodolfos Chicago has heard, sensitive, poetic and human, though in performance a little indolent in its perfection."[17]

In just three appearances Jussi had conquered the Chicago public, and the city's music lovers received him warmly on all his subsequent returns. Edward Barry summed it up: "The man is only 26. What a career he should have!"[18]

✳

Back in New York, I sent my mother a postcard dated 19 December 1937. "Tonight Jussi is singing at Carnegie Hall and again at 11 a.m. tomorrow. I hope Momo and Anne are as well as we are." (Momo was toddler Anders' attempt at *Mormor*—Swedish for grandmother—and Anne, pronounced An-ne, was his version of his own name. With our family's predilection for nicknames, Anders is still Anne to me.) This morning concert-luncheon was held at the Waldorf-Astoria, the 401st Musical Morning hosted by Albert Morris Bagby, a very short man with a loose front tooth that wiggled the whole time he talked. In the main, these "Bagby concerts" were attended by bevies of wealthy women. Singers are loath to sing that early in the day, but Bagby was a persuasive little man. Besides, so many famous artists had appeared in his series before and since Caruso, including the great man himself, that these concerts attained a special status, and the fee was much higher than singing a whole opera at the Met. But having tried it in Chicago, Jussi didn't have the least desire to sing that early again. Charles Wagner appealed to me to persuade Jussi. "If you want to get along in America, you have to do some of these things," I said. "We need all the engagements we can get, and besides, I think it'd be fun!"

"That's easy for you to say; you don't have to sing!" muttered Jussi. They wanted him to sing the stretta from *Il trovatore* with its high Cs, almost the worst sort of music to attempt so early in the day. Luckily, he didn't have to carry the program alone; the other artist was Lily Pons. They sang a duet from *Rigoletto*. Jussi wore tails; Lily was outfitted in a dress and turban of gold lamé, with a lovely parasol. She was terribly sweet. Her sentiments about singing in the a.m. were the same as Jussi's. "What one won't do for money!" she sighed with an ironic grimace.

But Charles Wagner was happy. Jussi's triumphs validated his own judgment, and it was easy to persuade the Met's general manager, Edward Johnson, to sign Jussi for the following season. "Bjoerling to Sing for Metropolitan" *The New York Times* (22 December 1937) headlined its announcement. With this engagement, Jussi reached the goal he had set for himself long ago; the only thing clouding his joy was that his father hadn't lived to see his predictions fulfilled. Incidentally, the *Times* article, like some others from time to time, made the unequivocal statement that Jussi's father "was also a tenor and sang at the Metropolitan Opera." In later years even Rolf repeated this in a taped interview, but Märta Björling maintains it isn't true. David wasn't at all shy about his accomplishments; had he ever sung on the stage of the Met in a performance he would've told his family—many times.

On 28 December 1937, Jussi gave a recital in St. Paul, Minnesota. What with the recent General Motors broadcast, it was eagerly anticipated, and he received an unusually warm welcome. The year's last concert, in Jamestown, New York, was one of the tour's high points. The reviewer reminded his readers that 19 years earlier the Björling Quartet had to give several unplanned farewell concerts in town to accommodate all who wanted to hear them.

We spent our first New Year's Eve in America at The Stockholm, a restaurant near Rockefeller Center, in the company of Marian Anderson, her Finnish accompanist Kosti Vehanen—described by Marian as "a man of culture and a gentleman"—and the Enwalls. We appreciated Marian's ladylike bearing and quiet charm, but to our surprise, she was totally oblivious where money was concerned. She stuffed her pay into a big purse, which she would leave lying around, though it might contain thousands of dollars. It was probably Vehanen's responsibility to look after it.[19]

The New Year began for us with Jussi's first Town Hall recital, on 4 January 1938. Edward Johnson sat in Charles Wagner's box, and Wagner enjoyed watching his face as he silently sang along with Jussi the *Fanciulla del West* aria. "Three encores were demanded," remembered Wagner. "Bjoerling sang five high Cs that night, and at the conclusion of the recital the audience stood up, cheered, applauded, called him back again and again until finally the curtain had to be rung down and the lights turned out to stop the clamor. Even then the singer was obliged to come before the curtain for more bows."[20] The critics were likewise generous:

> The young singer achieved a success seldom paralleled in our rooms of music, large or small. Mr. Bjoerling's voice not only has substance, sonority and compass to recommend it, but it is the absolutely unspoiled voice of a young man. His breath support is truly magnificent, and he can command a flawless legato of prodigiously long sweep and spin a tone from an imposing *fortissimo* to a vanishing *pianissimo*. He possesses an extraordinarily even scale, his attack is remarkably pure, his *mezza voce* exquisite. And Mr. Bjoerling, unlike most tenors, is unembarrassed in the discreet use of the lower part of his extensive range.[21]

"Mr. Bjoerling's is a lyric tenor that is capable of being projected with amplitude in the grand style," acknowledged *The New York Times* (5 January 1938). "Its range is extensive and it is full throughout the scale with especial brilliance in the top tones. Transpositions downward are not for this young man. He can hit a high C with a cleanness and power and resonance that are stirring."

In the final tally, the tour was extraordinarily successful. Enwall urged us to accept the offers for more performances that were pouring in, but we said no: it was time to go home to Anders. But the tour proved to Jussi his marketability, and he resigned from the Stockholm Opera on 2 February, the day he celebrated his birthday. Beginning with the 1938–39 season, he wanted to be free to accept all guest appearances of his choice. On 4 February, we celebrated Anders' second birthday, then on the 7th, almost like a birthday present, *Fram för framgång* was released. While the film was not a financial success, the domestic reviews were kind.

On 4 April 1938 Jussi introduced his last operetta role, Sándor Barinkay in Johann Strauss' *Der Zigeunerbaron*. It was a pleasant change from standard operatic fare, and he gave the role his special lighthearted touch and quality vocalism. In the last scene his handsome light blue uniform was topped by an enormous fur hat like a Coldstream guard; it gave him height, but he felt ridiculous wearing it. He knew what his features could carry, and his round head wasn't made for stagy headgear. After Barinkay he declared, "I'll never put anything on my head again!"

That included Manrico's helmet, with its visor and enormous plume. Jussi would walk onstage with the helmet under his arm and place it on a stand. There it stayed, even during the stretta. But Svanholm, retrained as a heldentenor and even shorter than Jussi, thought this helmet was really terrific, and to look taller, he always sang "Di quella pira" with it. On one occasion, as he hit the high C, the visor fell down, muffling the sound and destroying his heroic image.

For the remainder of spring and part of the summer of 1938, Jussi was occupied with opera appearances, recital tours, and tours with the Opera; between engagements he had several recording sessions. I didn't accompany Jussi on all his travels around Sweden, as I wanted to stay with Anders as much as possible, but just as we were preparing to return to America together, I discovered I was expecting our second child.

I felt much better physically with this pregnancy, and Jussi took it for granted that I'd come along. The American tour had shown me how tiring travel was and how depressing the long hours could be in a small hotel room in a strange city. If it could be so awful with the two of us, how much more difficult would it be for Jussi to travel alone? With his drinking, it could be disastrous. Jussi had to have me along, emotionally and practically. By his own admission, he depended on having me in the audience to be calm and do his best. But most of all, I wouldn't have missed Jussi's debut at the Metropolitan, even if they had to carry me in on a stretcher!

It would've been heartrending, disastrous, for me to choose between the children's welfare and Jussi's need of me—or for Jussi to choose between his family and his career—but luckily these decisions weren't forced upon us and our marriage survived: my mother gladly stepped in to take care of Anders at our new apartment at Nybrogatan 64, at the corner of Östermalmsgatan. As it turned out, from this time she lavished her love and attention on our children when Jussi and I were absent from Sweden, especially after my father died in 1939. Our tours in the years ahead would sometimes last for six months, and I don't know what we would've done without her.

Jussi's American tour began on 13 November 1938 with a radio concert in Detroit on the *Ford Sunday Evening Hour*, his first appearance on the program sponsored by the Ford Motor Company; José Iturbi conducted. These concerts were held in the enormous Masonic Auditorium, which accommodated nearly 5000 people. Jussi commented, "Ford aimed to invite only the best for these concerts . . . and the soloists were paid fabulous salaries. I received $5000 for 20 minutes—and I was by no means the highest paid."[22]

Soon we returned to New York and the Metropolitan. The year before, we'd visited "every singer's dream," and, to be quite honest, I was very disappointed. The old Met was an ordinary, insignificant, architecturally unimaginative and aesthetically ugly seven-story building of dirty yellow brick, wedged between high-rise office buildings at the intersection of Broadway and 39th Street and utterly lacking any semblance of the dignity and distinction I had expected. The bright lights of the surrounding movie theaters and music halls were much more festive.

Once inside, the impression hardly improved. The backstage was crowded, dirty, and shabby, with narrow, dark hallways; in the tenor's small dressing room, the mirror appeared not to have been cleaned since Caruso's days. But that all the great singers had been here was obvious from the autographs decorating the walls; many had even drawn clever caricatures of themselves, which invaluable mementos, unfortunately, were unceremoniously painted over some years later during the theater's thorough restoration. An indescribable confusion ruled. Stagehands, singers, dressers, dancers ran back and forth, seemingly without purpose, through an all-pervasive odor of dust and greasepaint.

But when one entered the magnificent auditorium, all expectations were fulfilled. The "Diamond Horseshoe," two rows of boxes over the enormous orchestra, glittered with the fantastic gems of New York's millionairesses. In those pre–World War II days the newspapers sent reporters whose sole assignment was to determine the worth of the jewelry on display!

The first opera I saw at the Met was the previous season's *Otello* with Giovanni Martinelli in the title role and Lawrence Tibbett as Iago, both perfection in their roles; my second was *Tristan und Isolde* with the famous Wagnerian pair, Lauritz Melchior and Kirsten Flagstad, a performance that was all legend made it out to be. Trembling, drained, and still somewhat floating in the heaven to which the ethereal music had lifted me, I followed Jussi backstage to meet the two world-famous artists—and was quickly brought back to earth again! Kirsten was in her dressing room, playing solitaire and drinking champagne; Lauritz lay onstage draining a large tankard of beer, now and then clearing his throat and spitting so copiously that I had to watch out not to take a full hit. (Opera singers often spit in the wings if their throats are rough or filled with mucus; from the wings to the stage, cloths were layed out to protect the divas' magnificent trains from being soiled by the large, nauseating spittle.)

The manager of the Metropolitan, Edward Johnson, a Canadian by birth, was an exceptionally engaging and artistically discerning man whom Jussi and I both came to like and admire. Before assuming his administrative duties, he had been a well-known and respected tenor with an international career. Yielding to the prejudices of the times, he Italianized his name and began his singing career in Italy as Edoardo di Giovanni. When he was appointed manager, he wisely left the day-to-day operations of the theater to people with more experience in those areas, Edward Ziegler in particular, reserving for himself the representational and public relations functions outside and within the house. Partly because of his experience as a singer, partly because of his temperament and personality, Johnson understood his artists and spoke their language. The Met under his tenure may have been somewhat disorganized, in some ways even sloppy, but it was home to many fine artists who loved to sing there.

I really appreciated Johnson's kindness in inviting me to be his guest at Jussi's debut. It may have been routine to him, but to me it was a thoughtful gesture. Jussi and I were both overwhelmed by the extraordinary friendliness shown to us; as Jussi put it,

112

All colleagues in America, especially at the Metropolitan, are wonderful. The day before my debut, American tenor Richard Crooks, Italian bass Ezio Pinza, and Australian baritone John Brownlee sent orchids to my wife. There was not a trace of jealousy or rivalry, but only a desire to help. One is met by the same feeling of friendliness whenever one sets foot in America. Sometimes one wishes that a little more of that spirit could also be found at home in Europe.[23]

If we appreciated the spirit among the world-renowned artists, we were unpleasantly surprised by the visit of the chief of the claque. The notion that a singer should ensure his success by hired hands was unthinkable for Jussi, and he dealt with the situation exactly as he always had. He looked the man in the eye and said, "The day I have to pay for applause is the day I quit." The head of the claque nodded. "We'll make an exception for you. You sing so wonderfully well that we'll applaud you as much as if you'd paid us!" Before Jussi and I learned how the claque system worked, we never understood why so many mediocre singers received such applause and shouts of bravo. Once we did, we couldn't fathom how any self-respecting artist took part in such a sham.

The opera chosen for Jussi's debut was *La bohème*; Mafalda Favero, star of Milan's La Scala, was making her North American debut as Mimì, and Marisa Morel hers as Musetta. On that unforgettable evening of Thanksgiving Day, 24 November 1938, New York City was enveloped by the first snowstorm of the season. The wind howled between the skyscrapers, and all traffic was at a standstill. Jussi was obliged to tell the story many times: "It was a blizzard! No taxis around and the subway was blocked, so I had to walk from my hotel at 59th Street and Central Park way down to 39th Street."[24] I trotted alongside my husband in my fanciest evening gown and galoshes. We were both terribly worried, but once we arrived at the theater, everything was fine. Jussi got into costume, and I settled myself in Edward Johnson's box, hardly aware of my surroundings. I didn't hear the hum of the people in the sold-out auditorium or the musicians tuning their instruments. The only thing I felt was the violent beating of my heart.

Finally, the curtain rose and the opera began. The bohemians cursed the cold and burned Rodolfo's manuscript to keep warm; Favero made her entrance; Mimì's candle was blown out by the wind. Then it was Jussi's turn to sing "Che gelida manina," with the high C. His whole future hung in the balance. You make your debut with the Metropolitan Opera only once and carry the judgment of the audience and the verdict of the critics for the rest of your career.

Dreadfully nervous, he began the aria, his left leg shaking violently. I could see that he was trying to calm himself, but the intense trembling continued. Edward Johnson, who had remained backstage for the beginning of the act, had just come into the box. He understood at a glance what was happening, and with a kind and touching gesture, he took my hand. "He's our boy!" he whispered with a nod toward Jussi. Instantly I grew calm, even though Jussi's leg continued to shake even as his high C rang out.

The thunderous applause that followed lasted more than a minute. In an unusual midperformance demonstration, members of the orchestra expressed their approval by rapping their bows against their music stands. With "Che gelida manina" behind him, Jussi's worst trial was over. Mimì's aria followed and was just as enthusiastically received, then the act came to an end with a beautifully phrased duet. When I burst into his dressing room between acts, the first thing Jussi said was "Did it show that my pantleg was fluttering?" Of course it did, but I assured him that the audience couldn't have noticed a thing. The rest of the performance went very well. At the end there were many curtain calls for Jussi, Favero, Morel, and the rest of the cast (John Brownlee, George Cehanovsky, and Norman Cordon), shouts of "Björling! Björling!" and even warm applause from the stagehands for all the debutants.

Jussi did fool the audience after all. "The 26-year-old Swedish tenor lost no time in displaying a voice of exceptional caliber, without any overt hints of debut nervousness," wrote Francis D. Perkins. "The volume is strong and the natural quality pleasing."[25] In the *New York Journal-American*, Grena Bennet spoke of Jussi's "enchanting interpretation." Miles Kastendieck of the *Brooklyn Eagle* thought the opera "marked the debut of the finest tenor to be heard here in many years." But Olin Downes gave Jussi only qualified approval, describing his voice as "both warm and brilliant, and of a sonority which carries best, of course, when he does not tighten and when he has a good reservoir of breath under the tone. The middle part of the voice was uniformly the roundest and warmest last night. There were times when the upper tones became breathy and whitish." He then added, "The sum of it was a tenor of ample tone and quality for the role, with a B-flat which rings and carries, and which has by no means reached the summit of its development."[26]

Mr. Downes and I seemed to have attended different performances, and Jussi and I were baffled by the review. He never sang "white" in his life; if anything, he used too much vibrato. Moreover, he positively never had even a hint of unsupported tones or an insufficient "reservoir of breath." He was a master of breathing technique, and his immense lung capacity was the object of his colleagues' admiration and envy. Finally, he most certainly did not transpose "Che gelida manina" a whole tone down, to B-flat. Not to show off his stupendous high C at his Metropolitan Opera debut would've been artistic suicide. In fact, the C of this aria sat so perfectly in his throat that I believe until his 40s it was easier for him to sing it in the original key. Presumably, other tenors in New York transposed it, so critic Downes, not blessed with perfect pitch, assumed Jussi did likewise. Mr. Downes must've been sitting on his ears, but he was the revered *New York Times* critic and his word was gospel.

Immediately after the Met debut we traveled to Chicago for Jussi's recital at the Opera House. It was our good luck that the day we arrived, we had the opportunity to hear Beniamino Gigli in Verdi's *Aida* with the Chicago Civic Opera. Jussi's voice was often compared to Gigli's, and I preferred that comparison over the one to Caruso.

In this regard Jussi and I had different points of view: for him, there was no greater tenor than Enrico Caruso. When he was interviewed in Budapest, the reporter's first question was "Who is your idol?" Without hesitation Jussi replied, "Caruso."[27] That was the plain truth; he had boundless admiration for the great man. He had many of Caruso's records and would sit and play them over and over again, absorbing everything that could benefit his own singing. He especially admired Caruso's phrasing and legato, and he often tried to emulate the uniquely intense quality of the manly voice, which disturbed me. Caruso had a more powerful and more baritonal tenor voice than Jussi, who, particularly in his youth, was a typical lyric tenor. But now he wanted to sound just as masculine as Caruso, and at times would force his voice too much. Time and again I tried to stop him. If I heard him doing it in an opera or concert, I'd rush to the dressing room during intermission and admonish him: "Too much Caruso. More Gigli, Jussi, more Gigli!"

He knew I was right, but nonetheless he occasionally tried to make his voice sound bigger than it was. Robert Merrill attests he was still at it, years later:

> Jussi sometimes wanted to get dramatic. He'd get excited and would want to sound like Caruso. I'd hear him pushing it—it would change the quality of that beautiful voice. He'd come backstage and say, "Did you hear that Bob? What do you think?" and I'd tell him, "It didn't sound like Jussi Björling! You have a beautiful lyric voice, you should never try to change the quality of your voice!" Then he would say, "I know, I know. I won't do it again."[28]

If he was going to emulate anyone, I would rather it be Gigli, who had always been *my* idol. In my Academy days, I'd shut myself in my room with his records and sing along, so it was with great anticipation that I sat at Jussi's side in Chicago, eager to finally hear Gigli in person. The curtain rose, and a figure in a white toga and golden headdress and arm bands glided onstage. I was puzzled by what I saw. "Who's that? Aida?" I whispered to Jussi.

"You're crazy!" he whispered back. "It's Radamès—it's Gigli!"

"It can't be!" I was shocked. The unfortunate costume made Gigli look exactly like a short fat woman. I was terribly disillusioned, but only briefly. The moment he started to sing it just didn't matter! He had one of the most heavenly voices I'd ever heard, and to this day Gigli remains my favorite singer. Next to Jussi, of course.

Jussi's first meeting with Beniamino Gigli wasn't pleasant. Some time earlier he'd heard Gigli on a radio broadcast from Rome and sent him a telegram of congratulations. Gigli must've heard of Björling too by then because, as Jussi recalled,

> I also received a telegram from him, inviting me to Rome for a singing contest between the two of us. In America our voices were compared as well. [In Chicago] it was my first opportunity to meet him in person, and I looked him up in his dressing room at the Civic Opera, where he was to sing Radamès. I was received by his secretary, who screened his visitors. The secretary knew who I was, and he brought me to Gigli and introduced me with the words: "Here is Jussi Björling." Gigli turned around, looked at me and nodded briefly, saying: "Good luck, *tenore!*"
> That was all, and I wasn't quite sure if I should have felt overwhelmed. Since then, we have met several times, became good friends, and had very good times together.[29]

Jussi held his senior colleague in the highest esteem, unhesitatingly acknowledging the superior place he held among singers. Nobody could deny that Gigli's voice was a God-given instrument with a perfect placement, a technique beyond reproach, and perhaps the most universally appealing timbre of all tenors. Those who objected to his mannerisms, which grew more pronounced in his later years, were arguing only about matters of taste. The admiration and respect Gigli commanded among his colleagues as a singer was complete and well deserved. As an interpreter and technician, both Jussi and I agreed, he was a paragon among tenors.

Jussi's recital on 27 November 1938 went very well. Cecil Smith's review, which singled out Harry Ebert's "unusually musical accompaniments," began with a reference to our visit to the theater the day before.

> At the Saturday afternoon opera matinee of *Aida* a short, rotund young man sat in a box listening with rapt concentration to the singing of Beniamino Gigli. Twenty-four hours later this same young man, whose name is Jussi Bjoerling, sang from the stage of the Civic Opera house in song recital, in a manner scarcely less stirring than that of Mr. Gigli. . . . Still only 27, Mr. Bjoerling is one of the white hopes of tenor singing of the future. His solid, manly voice rounds out into an almost baritone quality in the lower portion and merges smoothly into a dynamic and exciting top register. He sings with ease, with constant tonal beauty, and with a gift for restraint as well as rafter-smashing. On the interpretative side he has not yet come to full maturity, but he is deeply responsive to all the musical meanings he now discovers, and needs only longer experience to become a first-class artist in every regard.[30]

Janet Gunn praised Jussi's "sensitive delivery" and "perfectly molded legato line," but faulted him for forcing his top notes "so that they rang sharp."[31] John Forsell would have seconded her comments! Jussi never sang flat, and only occasionally sharp; as Robert Merrill puts it, "Jussi sang sharp only when he was trying to make his voice bigger, when he tried to sound like somebody else. When he pushed it, yes, it would get a little sharp. But he did that very infrequently; most of the time his musicality was marvelous."[32]

Normally Jussi's intonation was so true to pitch that some conductors in Stockholm remarked that an orchestra could tune by his voice.

Music critic Eugene Stinson was even more generous in his review of the recital. After the inevitable comparison with Gigli, giving both singers their due, he wrote, "Mr. Bjoerling, vibrant and supple as is his magnificent tenor voice, smooth and refreshing as is his use of it, faultless as he is, hasn't possibly yet had enough experience to know how great he is or to make use of that knowledge."[33] Who could ask for more?

Four days after the Metropolitan Opera debut, *The New York Times* (28 November 1938) carried a review of Jussi's film, *Fram för framgång*, which was playing at the Forty-Eighth Street Theatre with English subtitles, describing it as "a pleasant but undistinguished comedy." The reviewer predicted that Jussi's "hearty vocalizing" would prove the most attractive feature of the film.

The next day we had lunch with Helmer Enwall at The Blue Ribbon restaurant. He had come directly from a meeting with Edward Johnson, who was simply bubbling with enthusiasm: "We must strike while the iron is hot. After this enormous success, Jussi must sing not only *Faust* and *La bohème* next season, but also *Rigoletto*!"

"Absolutely not!" Jussi protested when he heard. "It'll be hard enough to learn *Faust* in French, and I know *Rigoletto* only in Swedish. Must I learn that too in Italian? No thank you!"

Helmer and I tried our best to convince him, but Jussi didn't want to listen. We reasoned with him, we argued, but he'd dug in his heels. He wasn't going to do it, and that was that. The food had just been served, but I was so frustrated by his irrational stubbornness that, ignoring my hunger, I left the restaurant in sheer anger and walked the streets for hours. I was too embarrassed to take a cab and admit I was completely lost, and it took me quite some time before I finally found my way back to our hotel. By the time I reached the room, completely exhausted, Jussi was almost overcome with anxiety—to my great satisfaction, I must admit. He had called the hospitals and the police.

"Anna-Lisa, where have you been? I'll sing *Rigoletto*!" he exclaimed, giving me a big hug. Then, innocently, he asked me to bring him the score. It lay on the piano, next to a prettily wrapped little package. "He's not going to get out of it this easy," I thought, and pretended not to notice. Then Jussi took me by the hand and gave me the small box. It contained the most beautiful platinum watch, set with diamonds. I was speechless with joy. Feeling a bit guilty for making him so worried, I rushed all over New York the next day to surprise him with a pocket watch, something he had wanted for a long time. The Met never knew what their new Duke cost us.

Jussi's *Il trovatore* on 2 December was awaited with curiosity. Manrico's music is very different from Rodolfo's, and the Met audience was wondering how "the youthful Swedish tenor" would handle the role of Manrico. Quite well, according to Noel Straus in the next day's *Times*:

117

Mr. Bjoerling's voice is essentially lyric in quality, and not of the dramatic stripe Verdi intended for the protagonist of this opera. Some singers would have resorted to pushing on tones to give them the ample volume required in this work, but Mr. Bjoerling refused to indulge in any such inartistic tactics. And it was far better so. For if Mr. Bjoerling lacked the ringing type of vocalism expected of a Manrico, he found it possible to accomplish much that was highly laudable in those moments of the opera where cantabile work was asked of him.

Soon after the Metropolitan performances, we had our first taste of cross-country travel. Accompanied onstage and off by Harry Ebert, from the first week of January until the 17th we covered the United States from Washington State to New York. At every stop Jussi's success was assured from the first phrase of his opening number, "Adelaide." Even in faroff Tacoma, Washington, his appearance was heralded in a long article, reinforced by a local movie house's showing *Fram för framgång*.

Following a radio appearance in Detroit on the 15th, we returned to New York. Of Jussi's Carnegie Hall performance on 17 January 1939, Pitts Sanborn wrote, "Some of Mr. Bjoerling's singing on this occasion tempts to swollen and empurpled praise. The command of breath and nuance, the jointless legato, the knowledge of style, the masterly phrasing were when combined with freedom and purity of tone irresistible." On the negative side, Sanborn faulted a constricted high C in "Che gelida manina," sung as an encore, and judged that Jussi's singing, particularly in the Flower Song from *Carmen*, was not "deeply charged with feeling." He recognized Harry Ebert as "an excellent accompanist," noting that in a group of solos he played a Ravel piece "with stunning virtuosity."[34]

H. T. of *The New York Times* (18 January 1939) found nothing objectionable in Jussi's singing:

> As at the recital last year, Mr. Bjoerling sang like an artist, with none of the posturing and sobbing that some tenors carry over from the operatic stage into the concert hall. The voice was still fresh and powerful throughout the scale and lustrous in texture. Mr. Bjoerling remembered that his is essentially a lyric tenor, and he did not force and push to achieve dramatic effects. His top tones, nevertheless, in an aria such as "O Paradiso," rang out with all the dramatic impact that the hardiest tenor devotee could desire.

The Carnegie Hall recital was a nice conclusion to Jussi's first extended American tour. The following day, with the satisfaction of a job well done, we sailed home.

# Chapter 8

✳

# COVENT GARDEN

By the time we headed home, I was in my seventh month of pregnancy, and although I'd been determined to complete the tour no matter how I felt, I was extremely relieved that my condition had caused us no complications. I was happy, and Jussi was thoughtfulness personified. He lugged my things around, even those light pieces I'd normally carry myself. On long train trips he saw to it that I was comfortable all the time, and during our stormy transatlantic passage aboard the S.S. *Gripsholm*, when the boat's pitching and rolling were at their worst, he arranged coats and pillows under my bulky stomach as I lay in bed.

It is impossible to describe the happiness I felt when the train rolled into Stockholm's Central Station and I saw my mother holding Anders by the hand. A young child grows and matures with amazing rapidity; the previous October we'd left behind a little toddler and in February 1939 were reunited with a big boy of three.

Now we knew what to expect of childbirth; we weren't as pathetically inexperienced as we'd been the first time around, and at 7:30 p.m. on 16 April 1939, Anders' little brother, Lars-Olof, came into the world. The name Lars came from Jussi's grandfather, Lars Johan Björn, the blacksmith with the large fists and wonderful voice. But we never called our new son Lars, but by his nickname, Lasse. Like Anders before him, he was a beautiful baby and welcomed into the world with love and affection. Julia Svedelius had decorated my room with flowers, and she clucked ecstatically over her latest "grandchild." A real grandmother couldn't have been more proud than Julia was over the little sprout in the crib. Her immense affection for Jussi embraced us all.

⚜

On 8 May 1939, Jussi sang *Faust* on tour to Gothenburg. It was his last performance under contract with the Stockholm Opera, his artistic alma mater, where in nine seasons he learned and sang 52 roles. His farewell wasn't a melancholy affair, for both he and the audience knew that he'd often stand on his old stage again, as a guest artist of new stature: from this moment on Björling was a singing citizen of the music world.

From Gothenburg, Jussi dashed off to London for his first operatic engagement as an independent artist. The musical life of the city at that time was something to be envied. Bracketing Jussi's debut performances at the Royal Opera House, Covent Garden, were *La traviata* and *Aida* with Beniamino Gigli and Maria Caniglia. Concurrently, Arturo Toscanini conducted a series of Beethoven concerts at Queen's Hall. The season's roster also included Lauritz Melchior, Torsten Ralf, and Richard Tauber.

To showcase his debut, *Il trovatore* was brought back to Covent Garden after many years of absence. The lack of preparation showed. When Jussi sang his first Manrico on 12 May 1939, the performance suffered from erratic lighting, makeshift scenery—and Jussi's Lohengrinesque silver tights, brought along from Stockholm, which sorely clashed with the rest of the production. But the performance had a lot to offer. The Leonora, Gina Cigna, had been recommended to David Webster, manager of Covent Garden, by conductor Vittorio Gui himself. In a letter to Webster he wrote, "*Elle n'est plus la Cigna d'il y a 4 années mais encore la meilleure entre les sopranos dramatiques.*"[1] Gui wrote his letters by hand, sometimes in French, sometimes in Italian, with an English translation typed by the Covent Garden staff; in this case it read, "She is no longer the Cigna of four years ago, but yet the best dramatic soprano."

The reviews, all published on 13 May 1939, were mostly in accord. The *Daily Telegraph* noted that "a flowing line, bright clarity of tone, and easy production" were second nature to Björling, and that with Gertrud Pålson-Wettergren's "subtly human" Azucena, the Swedish gypsy had a Swedish son. The *Evening News* complained, "Manrico should be a stalwart soldier-like figure with a voice to match, whereas Björling is of medium height, bears himself modestly and sings like a poet"—an odd criticism given that Manrico is a troubadour. The reviewer then conceded: "His singing appealed irresistibly with its easy flow of beautiful tone, its fine lines and its delicacy. He can sing a melody as few singers do nowadays; and—rarer still—he can send his voice to the middle of every note and keep it there."

The *Times* singled out "Deserto sulla terra" as giving "immediate evidence of a voice of fine and silvery quality and a sense of style in singing. But . . . it was not until [Björling] reached 'Di quella pira' that he showed his true quality and suddenly raised the temperature of the performance with a magnificent piece of singing." The curious compliment that Vittorio Gui "made the orchestra play as if their music really mattered" was in keeping with the lasting British attitude about Verdi. The critic for the *Glasgow Herald* analyzed the many virtues of Jussi's voice, noting that his Manrico was "more troubadour than warrior." The same critic went on: "His artistic home is surely Puccini's Bohemia, and there I hope to meet him some day."

Pålson-Wettergren wrote of Jussi's debut, "Beniamino Gigli, who had just sung a concert in London, sat in the audience, which perhaps contributed to Jussi's nervousness, because he wasn't in his best form."[2] But Gigli must've been impressed because after the performance he went to Jussi's dressing room and embraced him. Gigli appreciated artistic excellence in others, even in rival tenors, and soon after the visit, he sent Jussi a handsome photograph, inscribed *Al tenore Björling—con ammirazione cameradesca* (To the tenor Björling with collegial admiration).

Jussi had to fulfill an engagement in Stockholm before he could return to London in the company of Tullio Voghera for his second Manrico on 23 May. Voghera and Toscanini had been good friends since Metropolitan Opera days, possibly before. On the night of Jussi's Covent Garden debut, Toscanini was conducting a concert, but now, 11 days later, the Maestro was in the audience. Voghera had a happy reunion with his famous countryman and former boss. According to him, Toscanini was enraptured with Jussi's voice, and invited him to sing the Verdi Requiem with him in Lucerne in August, and a month later in London. The Lucerne performance took place; the one in London did not.

※

While the impending outbreak of war filled Europe with grave apprehensions, I lived in my own safe world in neutral Sweden, completely absorbed by my dual role as mother to two small boys and wife to a man—it was quite clear to me by now—who wasn't always so easy to be married to, and who needed my attention as much as the children, if not more. When Jussi and I married, I was hurled into a whirl of constant travel and continual encounters with people of status and achievement, immersed in a world of music created by world-famous musicians, an infinitely rich experience. Jussi's way of living wasn't mine; it turned upside down the simple, predictable, orderly ways I had taken for granted.

After four years of marriage, we were increasingly attuned to one another; we had learned to adapt—at least I had—growing closer, sharing more. Wasn't that what I wanted most in this world? Jussi was in fine form and seemed so happy. Lasse's birth had bound us together even more strongly. This last summer of peace in Europe was our most calm and happy period together, and we looked forward to the wonderful summer that lay before us at Vettershaga, where we had rented a roomy cottage.

In addition to my mother and the nanny, Dolly, our household grew by one: conductor Tullio Voghera—the most important influence in Jussi's evolution from Swedish singer to Italian tenor—joined us for the summer. Jussi owed a great debt to Voghera for imparting his immense knowledge about the musical heritage of his country, a debt he never failed to acknowledge. Tullio supported and encouraged him from the earliest days of their association. "I'll never forget his friendliness toward me during the audition for Forsell, nor the countless words of advice he has given me since," Jussi said.[3]

Tullio was a little gray-haired man with strong features, one of the few coaches whose counsel Jussi accepted completely, without reservations. He depended utterly on the temperamental Italian's knowledge because he knew that Voghera strictly observed the best traditions of Italian opera, which had been handed down by generations of musicians since each work had premiered in the presence of its composer. The Italian operatic idiom practically coursed in Voghera's veins. "A Brazilian couldn't just sing a Swedish folk song," he used to say, "and a Swede cannot just sing Italian opera as it should be sung. One must learn it from someone who knows it from within, one who is Italian."

Tullio Voghera, répétiteur, chorus director, and conductor at the Royal Opera, had a long and distinguished career. He was born in 1879 and completed his musical studies with Enrico Bossi and Giuseppe Martucci at the Conservatory of Bologna. In 1902, at the University of Padua, he earned his Ph.D. with a dissertation on the aesthetics of Richard Wagner. Starting with the 1905–06 season, he served as assistant conductor at the Metropolitan Opera. When Toscanini joined the house in 1908, Tullio became his assistant.

During his years in New York, he also served as accompanist to Bronislaw Huberman and Enrico Caruso. In fact, in 1906 and 1907 he appeared onstage with Caruso in *Fedora* in the mute part of the pianist Boleslav Lazinski, earning $15 for each appearance. Tullio was especially proud of his close association with Caruso; he'd often pull out an expensive gold watch and flash its inscription, *To my dear friend Tullio with thanks, from your affectionate Enrico.* Jussi could never hear enough stories about Caruso, and Tullio had many. Voghera also conducted several performances at the Met, and a *Martha* with Caruso on tour in Cleveland, on 11 April 1910. Only six weeks before, when he conducted *Pagliacci* in the house, the Tonio was his future boss, John Forsell.

Voghera also performed as soloist or accompanist in many Met concerts. He played the piano accompaniment for such notables as Georg Anthes, Alessandro Bonci, Lina Cavalieri, Fedor Chaliapin, Pol Plançon, and Riccardo Stracciari. When a prominent Met boxholder—one of the nails in the Diamond Horseshoe, shall we say—needed a pianist to entertain guests, Tullio Voghera was often the choice, and in this capacity he wound up in the homes of Mrs. Joseph Pulitzer, William Delano, Harry P. Whitney, and Emma H. Gary.

Just how instrumental John Forsell was in Voghera's move to Stockholm in 1910 is a matter of conjecture. Forsell wasn't yet manager of the Opera and was therefore in no position to issue an official invitation, but no doubt he was impressed by the man and influenced his engagement by the Royal Opera. When Voghera married Swedish soprano Iwa Aulin in 1926, Sweden became his permanent home. Except for serving as conductor at the Stora Teatern in Gothenburg from 1924 to 1926, he remained with the Opera till nearly the end of his life in 1943. He also served as conductor at the Royal Opera School, where he was known for his oratorio work. It was here that his collaboration with the teenager Jussi Björling began; Jussi sang *Messiah* with him several times, as well as Beethoven's *Missa Solemnis.*

Jussi worked with Voghera on his Italian and French roles in the original language. After he had learned the phrasing, characterization, and delivery, he might modify some details to fit the spirit of a performance, but he wouldn't deviate from the original concept. His sole objective was to be faithful to the composer's intention as evidenced by the printed score. That was exactly what Voghera imparted to him and the reason Jussi had such a high regard for Tullio. He wanted to present not Jussi Björling's but Puccini's Cavaradossi or Rodolfo, Verdi's Manrico and Duke of Mantua, Gounod's Faust and Roméo. Within the boundaries of an interpreter's prerogatives, Jussi was a faithful servant of the composer in all he did.

Nils Grevillius was another major influence in Jussi's development:

> Conductors in other countries have always expressed their surprise over my ability to know my roles so well and that I always respect the composer and never change anything. Where there is a sixteenth note, I sing a sixteenth note and nothing else. I have Nils Grevillius to thank for that. Never for one moment has he failed to show respect for the composer, and it has been good for me to follow his example.[4]

Jussi's singing and delivery of a role was the fusion of the artistic guidance he received from these two dedicated musicians.

Because I never abandoned hope that I would one day stand onstage with Jussi, I also had lessons with Tullio and so know from firsthand experience what a skillful coach he was. It seemed he knew all the parts of all the world's operas. Like so many conductors, he sang along with his dreadful, hoarse voice, explaining to me precisely how to set the tone; once satisfied I had it, he made me repeat it a hundred times. When I no longer needed to think of language, diction, and technique, the phrase was suddenly filled with feeling.

At Vettershaga that summer of 1939, Tullio had his own room with the famous piano we'd traded for Murre. It could've tried my patience to have an outsider live in our house all summer, but that never happened. We had our great musical interest in common, and Tullio soon melted into our family. We learned to love his cooking, too; he prepared the most delicious pasta, a welcome change from all the pike Jussi caught. Despite his Swedish wife and children and all the years in Sweden, Tullio remained an Italian through and through.

Tullio agreed with me concerning Jussi's attempts to emulate Caruso. He too realized the unique combination of warmth and lightness in Jussi's voice and told him never to jeopardize it by trying to give his voice extra weight. An excellent example of the flexibility of Jussi's voice was the time he managed to sing soprano. During a performance at the Opera in Stockholm, Karin Rydqvist-Alfheim hissed to him in a panic: "I can't sing a note!" She had eaten fish earlier in the day, and evidently a little bone had caught in her throat. When she started to sing, the bone moved forward, and she couldn't continue. "Don't worry," Jussi whispered back. "I'll take over!" He sang the remainder of the soprano's aria and continued to bring it off until intermission.

Jussi was helped by his phenomenal memory—he knew not only his own part but also the part of his supporting actress. When he fully devoted himself to a new assignment, two weeks was the most he needed to commit an ordinary role to memory. He had his own peculiar working method. First he would write the words in the piano score. While his spoken Italian was minimal, he knew what every word in his role meant, and he'd add many of these to his Italian vocabulary. Then he'd rehearse the music with his répétiteur, phrase after phrase. He always learned the words and the music together; he regarded them as inseparable. If he came to a difficult passage, what he called "simple problems," he drew one of his special "heads" with a red or blue pencil. A round blue circle marked where he should enter. A sad face in red, with eyes, nose, and frowning mouth, indicated that just there he should sing with pain and tears in his voice; a smiling face meant he should sound happy. He also marked the length of each phrase, those arching legatos that are the hallmark of every great singer. All these markings were purely mnemonic devices, images he could store in his photographic memory.

When Jussi felt he had the entire role in his mind and his throat, he set aside the score. He then sang through the part several times with Tullio, and by the time rehearsals began, all he needed was the fine-tuning with the conductor. In Stockholm, Jussi learned *all* his roles with months of piano and stage rehearsals, but as time went on, unending general rehearsals were hard on his patience. There were rehearsals for blocking, lighting, costume and makeup, piano and orchestral rehearsals, with and without chorus, with and without the scenery, until everyone, especially Jussi, was bored to death with it all. Jussi had absolutely nothing against learning a role, but the rehearsals! This was particularly true when, in later years, he had already sung a role so many times that he could sing the entire opera, all parts, in his sleep. Jussi then attended rehearsals mainly as a courtesy to his colleagues, to memorize the blocking and to establish a rapport with the conductor and make sure his concept didn't depart from the score. None of the singers interviewed for this book recalled Jussi ever giving less than 100 percent of his attention or cooperation in a rehearsal.

With his part indelibly committed to memory, Jussi might make some slight adjustments of phrasing or gestures during a performance, but these were inspirations of the moment and couldn't be rehearsed. Apart from new productions, the repertory operas were given in a conventional staging everywhere. Many times, at the Metropolitan, La Scala, Covent Garden, or Vienna, a singer was obliged to arrive and step into a performance without a rehearsal. Sixten Ehrling likes to tell about the time a stranger walked up to him at a reception in Hamburg and after a brief introduction explained, "We've already met, Maestro. I was your Iago in *Otello* the other night."

Jussi's ability to imitate helped him. All he needed was the demonstration of an inflection, phrase, or technique, and he could reproduce it with uncanny accuracy. That was how he learned to produce the top notes of his scale from Hislop, whose lessons he never forgot. "To sing a high C," Jussi always said, "is like building a skyscraper. It needs a good foundation to build on!" Gradually, Jussi reached enormous heights; once, I clearly remember, he sang a G above high C. His coloratura technique was fantastic too—every note was well defined and distinct, and he didn't aspirate between the notes. The diabolical thing about it was that he made it all seem so easy!

Jussi had a natural ability to identify with the feelings of the character and express them with his voice and understated acting, without seeming sentimental or affected. By the summer at Vettershaga he was absolute master of his technique, which allowed him to concentrate on the spontaneous expression of emotions with every note and phrase. He created a mood and projected a musical personality with sound alone. It may be this rare gift that makes his recordings so unique. As a large number of live Björling performances emerge, his interpretations are undergoing a critical reassessment, and today's reviewers accord him without reservation some attributes—passion, dramatic involvement, vocal acting—that their counterparts of yore denied.

"It always bothered me when they said Jussi was a cold singer and he had no passion," claims Robert Merrill. "I always said, you listen to the recordings, there is a great deal of passion."[5] Cornell MacNeil agrees. "I think that he was just so technically perfect that he didn't use any of the sobs or swoops to cover up his technical imperfections. Consequently, the singing was so clean that it gave you the impression of something that was perhaps mechanical, as people would say. But cold? I never found that."[6]

At times Jussi may have "walked through" a role, but on many occasions he delivered his role as well as or better than any of his colleagues. His Canio was charged with emotion, and he acted the role from beginning to end with deep involvement. Maestro Kurt Bendix remarked, "People say Jussi couldn't act, but I've conducted him in performances of *Pagliacci* when I thought the walls were going to fall down—what more do people want?"[7] Privately, Jussi never spoke about the longing and despair that now and then came over him, but he could open his heart and express these feelings in song. Perhaps this gave his Canio an extra measure of grandeur: in this part he could release his emotions without restraint, and his Canio was an interpretation that ranked with the best operatic actors of his generation.

By the summer of 1939, it was especially as Roméo, Faust, and Rodolfo that Jussi's ability to live the role came across. In *La bohème* in particular, at the little seamstress' deathbed, he didn't have to feign sorrow. He knew how it felt to watch somebody very dear die. When Jussi's voice broke as he cried "Mimì!" it wasn't a matter of technique but of intuitive identification with another man's despair at the death of his beloved. Helga Görlin used to say there were real tears in his eyes.

Jussi, with his great sensitivity, found it easy to understand the feelings of others, even away from the stage. He was happy for his colleagues when they succeeded, encouraged them when they were gripped by stage fright, calmed and consoled them when they had problems and were unable to concentrate on their roles. Many of them said that when Jussi was in the cast, all other artists were inspired to outdo themselves.[8] I agree; when my own dream to sing with my husband was fulfilled, I felt the same. Jussi's great authority, his self-assurance, and the ring of his wonderful voice seemed to lift and carry me until I could sing as never before. But I had to wait many years for that day.

# Chapter 9

# *Un ballo in maschera*

In August 1939 Jussi appeared at the Opera as a guest artist for the first time, singing Rodolfo, Roméo, Martin Skarp in *Fanal*, and Alfredo in *La traviata*, the latter two roles for the last time in his career. He also sang the Verdi Requiem in Lucerne's Jesuit Church, his first collaboration with Arturo Toscanini, on 16 and 17 August. The other soloists were Zinka Milanov (formerly Kunc), Kerstin Thorborg, and Nicola Moscona. I arrived in time to attend the second performance. It was unforgettable. Jussi knew that Toscanini commanded the highest respect, but even he was impressed by what happened at the performance. "When the Maestro came in, not only did the orchestra rise, but so did the entire audience. There wasn't a sound in the whole auditorium. This was the most impressive tribute an artist ever had."[1]

Jussi told me that once, during a rehearsal, Toscanini abruptly put down his baton. "What's wrong, Maestro?" asked Jussi. He was worried that he'd made a mistake, and he knew how demanding Toscanini was. "Nothing," Toscanini replied. "Sing, Björling, just sing. I'll follow you!"

The mark of a good operatic conductor is that he actually breathes and sings—silently, one hopes—with his singers. Toscanini was one such conductor; Tullio Serafin another. It is a special skill that comes naturally to some musicians, others learn it, some with difficulty and a few not at all. Many years later, Jussi worked with a maestro who lacked this gift. In rehearsal they had no end of trouble staying together in the principal tenor

127

aria. "Look," cried Jussi losing patience, "I have to breathe! I sing this phrase—breathe; next phrase—breathe; next phrase—breathe. Watch!" He took the baton and conducted the orchestra while singing along to demonstrate his point. The conductor, who went on to international acclaim, learned a lot from that lesson.

Toscanini could be a taskmaster. Jussi never had a disagreement with him, but he was often quite harsh or downright rude to those who didn't sing or play according to his high standards. "When were you born?" Toscanini might ask. The unfortunate would name the date. "Is that so? Well, that certainly was a black day in the history of music!" But for Jussi every rehearsal under Toscanini was like a master class:

> Unfortunately, I've never been close friends with Toscanini, but several times I've sat in his room and spoken with him, or more correctly, listened to him speak. His musical instruction was wonderful and when he conducts, he keeps his eyes on the soloist the entire time. I don't understand how he does it, but he is able to hold all the performers in this magic circle—it is like hypnotism. He achieves what he wants like no one else can. ... You have the feeling of being one with him.[2]

In September 1939, the long-dreaded Second World War became a reality, and we didn't know from one day to the next what might happen. I was still nursing Lasse and would've preferred to stay at home with our small boys while Jussi kept his many engagements in the United States and Canada, but he left me no choice: "If you don't come with me, I'm going to cancel the whole trip!" I knew he was prepared to carry out his threat, so once more, my mother moved into our apartment. My children would receive loving and devoted care from her, but even so, it broke my heart when we left them. I knew the many months to come would be filled with constant longing; it was a recurrent sacrifice, and I never learned to overcome the pain.

After a concert at The Hague under the direction of Willem Mengelberg, we traveled on to Bergen; Harry Ebert joined us again. We arrived on a stormy, chilly November evening and hurried into a restaurant to get something to warm us. The place was deserted except for the usual sad trio playing some café music. Rain beat against the windowpanes; a sense of impending doom crept over our party. Just then the musicians began to play "La Paloma."

Jussi hated "La Paloma." He believed that it was a bad omen, and convinced that something terrible would happen if it were played to the end, he jumped up from the table, rushed over to the musicians, and grabbed the bow out of the violinist's hand. He explained that he just couldn't listen to that song, and fortunately, the players were willing to oblige him.

From the time the Spanish composer Sebastián Yradier composed "La Paloma" in 1863, it has been associated with murder, death, and accidents. It's said that the piece was connected somehow with the suicides of Crown Prince Rudolf of Austria and his lover Maria Vetsera at the Mayerling Castle in 1889, and Jussi himself often told about the time the actor Nils Lundell asked the orchestra conductor in a restaurant to play something else. The restaurant owner, his face red with anger, ordered the orchestra to continue. "I'm the owner here, not you!" he yelled at Lundell. The orchestra resumed "La Paloma," and the next moment, the restaurateur was felled by a stroke; he died soon after. Jussi had another story about a good friend of his who died suddenly while listening to the song in the dining room of the Stadshotel in Västerås. His entire life, Jussi was convinced that listening to it spelled disaster.

Like most artists, Jussi attached a great deal of importance to such things. One must never wish an actor "Good luck!" or whistle when he is about to go onstage. This applied to Jussi too, but somewhere he picked up the superstition that before a performance someone had to give him six small kicks on his backside for good luck; he also knocked six times on the nearest piece of wood just before he went on. He always carried a gold-encased rabbit's foot, his personal good-luck charm; his left shoe must go on first; and he could never tolerate two matches laying crossed on top of each other—he would neatly rearrange them side by side. "They call this superstition," he would say, "but it calms my nerves. Superstitions dispel anxiety when one is nervous. We stagechildren have almost convinced ourselves that we can't fail if we carry out these harmless little rituals. It helps us find confidence and strength. If it works as a psychological crutch, why not use it?"

It never occurred to me to try to lessen Jussi's extreme aversion to "La Paloma." The important thing was to make sure that nothing disturbed or upset him. It was entirely possible that if the orchestra had continued to play that night in Bergen, Jussi, impulsive as he was, would've abandoned the entire American tour.

Whether it was the fault of the snippet of "La Paloma" or not, the trip to New York was difficult. Violent weather broke loose sections of the railings on the captain's bridge, and one evening, while we and other passengers struggled to maintain our balance and keep up our spirits dancing to "Boomps-a-Daisy," the latest rage, the boat rolled so much in the wintry waves of the North Atlantic that the heavy piano slid across the floor, and we barely had a moment to jump out of the way before being crushed against the wall. It hadn't helped that before the trip we read in the newspapers about German U-boat attacks against neutral vessels. But now a radio silence was in effect, and we received no information about our country during the entire voyage. Naturally, for 10 trying days, we brooded over whether Sweden would be able to maintain her neutrality. If Sweden were drawn into the hostilities while we were gone, what would happen to our children and my mother?

*The New York Times* noted our arrival on the Holland American liner

129

*Statendam* on 17 November 1939. Upon our arrival, we heard that the Soviets had just bombed Helsinki. Jussi had selected two Sibelius songs for the tour's program, and it may have been this breaking news that caused the public to applaud them so warmly everywhere we went. Jussi also sang Beethoven's "Adelaide" on this tour. The recording he had made of it earlier that summer with Ebert at the piano came to be regarded by many as one of his finest; one critic wrote of it recently, "[Björling varied], with magical skill, the 14 repetitions of that beloved name, . . . providing wondrous changes of tone color at the modulations from B-flat to F, D-flat, and G-flat. Here was a moment of real vocal fulfillment."[3]

On 7 December 1939, Jussi made his Canadian debut in a recital in Winnipeg, and on 28 December he sang his first *Faust* at the Metropolitan with Helen Jepson and Ezio Pinza. Wrote critic R. L.:

> Much of the interest of yesterday's audience was focused on Jussi Bjoerling, who was singing the role for the first time here. . . . [Looking] uncommonly well . . . , he sang ["Salut, demeure"] untransposed, culminating in a high C of ringing beauty. It was regrettable that Mr. Bjoerling shattered the illusion he had created at this point by bowing to the audience, when he could have waited for his richly deserved tribute until the second-act curtain.[4]

Jussi must've momentarily forgotten where he was. According to prevailing stage protocol in Europe, a singer was expected to respond to a demonstrative audience—but not in America: when in New York, *don't* do as the Romans do. Jussi learned his lesson and never again committed the faux pas. In any case, the same critic noted, he delivered his role "with unfailing good taste. As yet, his characterization of Faust is merely a sketch, erring on the side of chivalry and romance. The evil which is inherent in Gounod's version of the character—the lechery of age that sweeps the world in the subtle disguise of youth—was not remotely suggested by Mr. Bjoerling."[5] I couldn't disagree more. I find no trace of lechery in Gounod's sublime music, and the charge that Jussi could convey chivalry and romance but not lechery was high praise indeed!

On New Year's Day 1940, Jussi introduced his Duke of Mantua to Met audiences, a success for which I take a tiny credit: I pushed him to do the role, which fit his voice like a glove, in the first place. The *Rigoletto* was a matinee with Lawrence Tibbett in the title role and Lily Pons as Gilda. Although they had to sing early in the day, without benefit of a full night's sleep and with just a touch of hangover, all three lived up to their reputations. Jussi never forgot the third-act ovations "Parmi veder le lagrime" brought: "I received much praise for both costume and makeup. The only criticism I received was that I wasn't sufficiently cynical."[6] He could live with that shortcoming too!

The next day, on one of the company's Tuesday outings, Jussi appeared in Philadelphia, in *Faust*, once more with Jepson and Pinza. Not for the first time in his life, and certainly not for the last, he sang two demanding roles within 24 hours. Samuel L. Laciar wrote, "Mr. Bjoerling revealed from the opening of the opera that he is a decided acquisition to the Metropolitan forces in that rarest of all voices, tenor. His voice is fresh and youthful, of beautiful quality throughout and possessing great brilliance in the extreme upper register." Laciar made special mention of Jussi's taking "a beautiful high C with the utmost ease" and found his acting "competent but not outstanding."[7] Linton Martin praised Jussi's dazzling top notes, "which have earned him the appellation of 'a second Caruso'" and his "exquisite beauty and purity of tone."[8] But Edwin Schloss found Jussi's "a small voice of good quality used with passionless precision" and his Faust "a lover with two high notes and one gesture."[9]

On 5 January 1940 Jussi was back at the Met, reunited with his Vienna Mimì, Jarmila Novotná, who has vivid memories of the occasion:

> He was a wonderful colleague and I was very happy when *Bohème* was selected for my debut at the Metropolitan Opera and Björling was again Rodolfo. When we saw each other, we had a good laugh as we remembered that in Vienna the custom was to sing all operas in German. But neither of us knew the role in German. So Rodolfo made love to me in Swedish, I sang Italian, and everybody else sang German. Luckily, it was different in New York. We all sang in Italian and the performance was a great success. Björling's aria in the first act was so beautiful that when he finished, the applause stopped the show. The strangest thing happened to him at the end of the first act when he found it necessary to relinquish our unison high C due to a frog in his throat, which normally was a note that many of his colleagues envied him for. He had one of the most beautiful voices and he will never be forgotten.[10]

And Jussi's memory of the evening? "I received, along with praise, the remark that I yielded to the old-fashioned 'tenor habit of hanging onto the high notes as long as my breath and vocal cords would last, whether it was dramatically justified or not.'"[11]

As it turned out, it wasn't merely a frog in the throat but an incipient cold that made Jussi relinquish the duet's high C. His Town Hall concert of 9 January 1940 had to be postponed to February, but by the 15th, he had sufficiently recovered to appear in a second *La bohème*, this time with Bidú Sayão. A charity concert on behalf of Finland followed in Chicago, earning him this compliment: "He owns probably the most beautiful lyric voice in the world. He uses it with limpid clarity and with exquisite taste."[12]

On 30 January Jussi made his first recordings for RCA in the Victor Studio of Manhattan Center. The selections were mostly Schubert songs from his standard concert repertoire, with Harry Ebert at the piano. Harry was a true artist and a real friend. He and Jussi had been working together for many years, and he knew my husband better than most. As Harry described it, even when Jussi was at his lowest, he still had an inner light, something within that was incandescent and indestructible. He used to say that Jussi was "the eternally pure one," simple, naive, untainted and well meaning, like Wagner's Parsifal.

Few people realize how much a skillful and sensitive accompanist contributes to the general success of the recital. Jussi was fortunate to collaborate with the best, and Harry was one of them. He had lived for 20 years in Paris and had studied piano under Maurice Ravel and Sergei Rachmaninoff. He spoke perfect French and English and was competent in Italian and Spanish. He was a prominent soloist, but he enjoyed accompanying, especially someone like Jussi, whom he believed to be a perfect artist and a perfectionist in his work, someone who "didn't know the meaning of carelessness when it came to music." Jussi once told Harry before a number, "I want it transposed." "How low?" Harry inquired. "No, higher. It's the low notes I am worried about."[13]

Harry insisted that Jussi went through his entire role or concert program during the hours before the performance. Before a concert Jussi would sit in his dressing room and concentrate until it was time to go onstage. In those moments he preferred to be alone and didn't want even me to stay with him. Harry didn't want visitors either, but he would be unnerved by the relentless silence; once they were onstage, however, everything fell into place.

Harry believed that Jussi's solo recitals seemed longer than they actually were, that Jussi stretched what was really a small amount of singing over two hours: the recital advertised for 8 p.m. began around 8:10; between numbers Jussi acknowledged the applause and continued to bow until the last handclap died away; he sometimes signaled Harry to take a bow and receive his share of the ovation; between groups of songs he walked offstage at a comfortable, leisurely pace.

While this was indeed his stage routine, Jussi's recitals, with encores, had 18 to 20 numbers—not a short program by any measure. He didn't "stretch" the time; it was unnecessary. When he was in good health, he had 12 to 15 numbers on the printed program. Depending on audience response and how he felt at the moment, he might then sing three to six encores, sometimes more. That was roughly the workout a human throat could comfortably sustain. Listeners always felt they'd received their money's worth.

On 2 February 1940, his 29th "birthday," Jussi delivered the postponed recital at Town Hall. The public was jubilant, but one reviewer noted the lingering effects of the cold. "Mr. Bjoerling's gleaming tenor voice [had] some clouding of texture, mostly noticeable in his lowest register," and in Faust's cavatina "the climactic top tone was rather 'white' in quality."[14] But for others, his "vocal powers [were] in all their undimmed splendor. Top notes rang out like pure gold."[15] "Listeners reveled in the pleasure of hearing an exceptionally fresh, lyric voice used not in the traditional manner of tenors, but in an intelligent and musicianly way."[16]

A week later we were in San Francisco for two concerts on two successive nights conducted by Pierre Monteux. Back in New York, Jussi and Harry Ebert had another recording session on 1 March 1940. It was around this time that we met tenor Jan Peerce. Jussi recognized his qualities as musician and singer and took an instant liking to him, and Jan retained pleasant memories of Jussi:

> The dearest thing that I can remember [is] the first time I met him. There was a supper party being given after one of the spring performances. . . . We went to this party, and Björling came over to me and introduced himself. He was a big star at the time! And the first question he asked was "Why aren't you at the Met?" "Well," I said, "I couldn't tell you." He said, "Wouldn't you like to be at the Met?" I said "Of course I would like to be at the Met!" With that, he took me by the hand and dragged me over to Edward Johnson who was at the party. And he said "Eddie, why isn't he at the Met? He belongs there, he is better than anybody you've got!" Johnson said, "Including you?" He said, "Yes! He is better than I." He was very generous. So Johnson said, "Well, maybe, in the future we'll have him." Jussi said, "Don't wait too long! He belongs there, and you should have him." And we became friends from that moment. He was a human being, a very sweet, wonderful guy.[17]

By mid-March 1940, Jussi and I were back in Stockholm. We could hardly wait to see our Lasse, who was already walking, and we were sorry to have missed Anders' birthday. To make up for our long absence, we decided to give Anders a special treat: he would see his first opera and hear his father sing onstage for the first time. The better to hold a child's attention, we chose the 29 March 1940 performance of the spectacular *Aida*.

My son and I settled into the artists' box over the orchestra pit, where, although the sightlines aren't the best, the stage access allows the singers to come to the box from the wings. For Anders, seeing his papa in an opera meant seeing the man he knew from home. We explained to him the story beforehand, but it was never really clear to him what was going on. As far as he was concerned, all he saw was a crowd of strange figures who ran around singing too much and too loud, trying to be heard over the din of the orchestra right below us. David Björling would surely have disapproved of subjecting the ears of a little child to so much noise.

During the intermission after the triumphal scene, Jussi came to see how his young son was enjoying the performance. He pulled aside the curtain that hung in the doorway of the dimly lit box—and there stood Radamès in his fantastic costume, with a great sword at his side, which strange apparition dreadfully frightened little Anders. He threw himself into my arms, refusing to understand that this ghastly creature was actually his father. Talking gently to his son with his caressing speaking voice, Jussi was able to quiet him down. Anders eventually came to terms with the idea of costume and makeup, and I'm happy to say that this harrowing initiation had no lasting effect. I took him to the opera many times.

✳

The "Winter War" had ended on 12 March with the defeat of the Finns, and many cities and communities lay in ruin. In addition to guest appearances, Jussi sang a charity concert to benefit Finland, a country and a cause that were close to his heart. With his family's ties, he was eager to do what he could to help.

While we were abroad, Konsertbolaget had opened a dialogue with La Scala in Milan. Negotiations for Jussi's debut had progressed so far that his name was printed in the 1939–40 season program booklet, but with the outbreak of war, the engagement was canceled.[18] In 1940 Jussi also went through a period of severe depression and canceled several performances; unfortunately, some of his problems were self-inflicted, due to excessive drinking.

That entire spring and summer, I devoted myself to four-year-old Anders and one-year-old Lasse. Jussi's career was understandably of paramount importance, but we agreed that our young children needed me more just now, and Jussi was willing to compromise. For the first time since 1937, I didn't join him on his American tour. Harry Ebert traveled with him that autumn, and I knew that as a close friend he would take care of Jussi should any difficulties arise.

Jussi was more reluctant to leave home than usual. Seeking to avoid the danger of mines and submarines in the North Atlantic, he and Harry traveled through Germany to Portugal, but that a trip by air wasn't entirely risk-free either became clear when a plane carrying Leslie Howard was shot down by the Germans, who mistook a corpulent passenger on board for Winston Churchill, traveling incognito. By the time they reached Berlin, Jussi wanted to abandon the tour and return home, but Harry and some other friends stopped him. From Berlin they flew to the Azores via Lisbon. On the way to a picturesque mountaintop restaurant, where the airline was treating them to lunch, they shared a taxi with British author Somerset Maugham, who, Harry recalled, "did just two things besides eating. He played bridge with us and another passenger, and he read detective stories."[19] Jussi loved detective stories; he found them relaxing. From then on, if anyone dared to question his literary taste, he replied, "If Maugham can read such trash, so can I."

Several airpockets and 14 more hours of flight later, the weary travelers reached sunny Bermuda, where they took full advantage of the overnight stay, swimming in the Atlantic and sleeping in real beds. From there they flew to New York; *The New York Times* (9 October 1940) reported that Jussi Björling arrived at La Guardia on the Atlantic Clipper and questioned him about his recent stay in Berlin. "He said he saw no air-raid damage there and begged off on questions about butter, eggs, and coffee. 'I must go back by way of Berlin,' he explained."

According to Harry, Jussi was to sing together with basso Alexander Kipnis early the next morning at a Bagby Monday Morning Concert,[20] but this concert cannot be traced in the contemporary press, and Igor Kipnis, the singer's son, has no documentation in his archives.[21] From New York, Jussi and Harry set out on the six-day journey to San Francisco, where the warm autumn days were ideal for a singer's sensitive throat. "In San Francisco you can't help being in top form!" Jussi exclaimed whenever we visited. It was there that my letter of 16 October, written from a ward during my brief hospitalization, reached him.

> My own dear little Jussi! If you could only know how much I've longed for you since you left. It felt so strange that you left without me. But the doctor says that I'll soon be well again. Oh, my own wonderful little Papa, you're my everything, if I had you here now I would give you a big hug. I hope everything is well for you, and that you feel prima. You and Vaje [Harry Ebert] must've had a good time on the trip across, as usual, and it must be going well for you at the concerts and at the Metropolitan. . . . Take good care of yourself. Good night my own wonderful Jussi. A kiss from your own Anna-Lisa.

The letter is signed with lipstick—a kiss on paper.

Jussi debuted with the San Francisco Opera on 18 October 1940 in *La bohème*. His colleagues were Bidú Sayão, John Brownlee (the Marcello of his Metropolitan debut), Margit Bokor (his Nedda from Vienna), and Ezio Pinza. Local audiences had only heard Jussi in concert, and in the words of Alfred Frankenstein, "the promise of sterling operatic achievement suggested by that concert performance was fully born out by Bjoerling's Rodolfo. We have heard plenty of big tenors as the hero of *La bohème*, but rarely tenors whose vocal size is complemented by a freshness and luster, an ease, breadth of range, and youthful robustness equal to Bjoerling's."[22]

A few days later, on 23 October, Jussi sang Riccardo in *Un ballo in maschera*, with hopelessly ill-conceived costumes and outdated scenery. He was made up with a beard, mustache, and wavy hair down to his shoulders and dressed in a quaint musketeer's uniform complete with plumed hat. Half-angry and half-amused by the peculiar costuming, he nonetheless sang well enough to receive glowing reviews. In Frankenstein's judgment, Jussi had made a great debut as Rodolfo but was even better as Riccardo. "His tremendous tenor was youthful and heroic in size, quality and style, and he made one believe that no equal interpreter of Verdi's hero roles has been before the public since the days of Caruso himself."[23] Nice compliment for a role Jussi had performed only twice before in his life, in Stockholm (1934) and in Vienna (1937)!

It was in this *Ballo* performance that Lorenzo Alvary first sang with Jussi. They became friends and spent many a late night playing poker. He was good company and a serious artist, and Jussi appreciated his musicianship. Lorenzo, for his part, seems to have thought the world of Jussi:

> Björling's voice was so absolutely beautiful that it cannot be compared with anyone else's. Nobody, no Italian tenor ever, had that quality before

or after him. He sang effortlessly, and his voice was unique also because it had the same quality from the low octave to the high C. That is very rare, especially among tenors. When Jussi sang, everybody in the audience was absolutely sure that it was going to be the best performance of that particular role. Nobody ever doubted it, and it always was.[24]

Jussi returned to Chicago for a single *Rigoletto* on 16 November 1940, which performance signaled the North American debut of Jussi's colleague from Vienna, Alexander Svéd, as the jester. From Chicago, Jussi proceeded to New York to commence rehearsals for the Met's season opener, a new production of *Un ballo in maschera*.

It was his first opening night at the Met. The international cast consisted of Zinka Milanov as Amelia, Kerstin Thorborg was Ulrica, and Stella Andreva—Jussi's Stockholm Juliette and his very first Oscar in 1934—repeating the Page. Alexander Svéd, who followed Chicago with his Met debut as Renato, was no stranger to opening nights; in 1938 and 1939 he opened La Scala's seasons as Macbeth and William Tell.

*Un ballo in maschera* was last performed at the Met in 1916 with Martinelli. The action for this 1940 production was moved from colonial Boston back to Sweden, as Verdi and his librettist originally intended. Jussi was impressed: "The management wanted to make sure that the sets would be as magnificent and authentic as possible, regardless of the expense. An exact replica of the Hall of State at the Royal Palace in Stockholm had been built and statues of Karl XII and Gustaf II Adolf were brought in, along with real Swedish uniforms and a huge Swedish Coat of Arms center stage."[25] Jussi was costumed in knee-length silk breeches and wore a powdered white wig as had the historic character he was impersonating. The cast was in excellent form, and the public went completely wild.

Jussi sang the role three more times in the house and once in Philadelphia. The second performance on 14 December, a radio broadcast preserved on records, gives an accurate idea of the production, only the sixth time Jussi had sung the role. The esteemed critic Conrad L. Osborne, reviewing a recent CD release, gave high marks to Milanov, but he wrote, "Bjoerling is, if anything, even better. The voice has the same span between a heady fluency for the lyric writing and an almost brawny, ringing core for the dramatic passages that it possessed to the end, but with a slight extra measure of spring and sail." He especially singles out the 90 seconds that conclude the second-act duet. When soprano and tenor "curl your hair with soaring sustained high Cs—we've gone past both the composer and the performers, to the other world inhabited by singing characters."[26]

When the company performed the opera in Philadelphia on 17 December 1940, Jussi's Gustaf struck Linton Martin as "a conventional king, never any too convincing on the dramatic side. But he sang the role with suave, smooth tones, never ruffled or rippled by depth of emotion or feeling. The assassination found him simply a bloodless, papier maché monarch."[27]

Apparently, critic and audience missed the little calamity that nearly ruined the high drama of the final scene. Once, allegedly, a singer had been injured by a gunpowder blast, so Johnson had given orders that in this production the actual shot be fired not onstage but in the wings. When Ankarström drew his pistol and pulled the trigger, everyone, including a nonplussed Svéd and his intended victim waited in vain for his pistol to "fire." The music moved on, and so with remarkable presence of mind Svéd drew his sword—after all, Gustaf had to die! As he plunged the foil into Jussi's breast, a shot went off in the wings.[28] Because the opera was new to audiences, they no doubt believed that the murder weapon was indeed the sword and took the backstage gunshot for some extraneous noise.

*Un ballo in maschera* brought in the highest box office receipts for an opening night in the company's history—$16,943![29] This figure not only prompts one to reflect on the value of the dollar but also the artists' salaries. The breakdown of the *Ballo* soloists' cachets tells it all: Jussi was paid $650, Thorborg $450, Svéd $400, and Andreva $150 for each performance; Bruna Castagna received $350 per week and Milanov $300. For the sake of comparison, it may be instructive to look at what other stars earned in 1940. Top fee went to Licia Albanese at $1200 a performance. The nightly pay of Melchior, Flagstad, Lily Pons, and Tibbett was $1000; Elizabeth Rethberg $900; Martinelli earned $800 in the house and $1000 on tour; Grace Moore and Lotte Lehmann $750; Richard Crooks $700; Pinza $550; Schorr $500; Sayão $400; and Kipnis $300. Composer Italo Montemezzi was paid $250 a performance for conducting his own *L'amore dei tre re*.[30]

On the other hand, a loaf of bread was 8¢ a pound, a quart of milk 13¢, first-class postage 3¢, and an average automobile $700.

※

The most momentous event during this American trip in Jussi's opinion was not his success in *Ballo* but his next collaboration with Toscanini. On 23 November 1940 he sang the Verdi Requiem at Carnegie Hall with Milanov, Castagna, and Moscona, and a month later, on 28 December, Beethoven's *Missa Solemnis* with Milanov, Castagna, and Kipnis; Toscanini conducted the NBC Symphony Orchestra and the Westminster Choir. Both were benefit performances, the Requiem for the Alma Gluck Zimbalist Memorial of the Roosevelt Hospital Development Fund and the *Missa Solemnis* for the National Conference of Christians and Jews.

Toscanini demanded two weeks' rehearsal for each work. It was an inspiring experience for Jussi:

> [We rehearsed the *Missa Solemnis*] for 14 days and we had five orchestra rehearsals. The day before the performance, the general rehearsal was called for 1 o'clock, a dress rehearsal for 6 o'clock, and at 8 o'clock that evening an additional orchestra rehearsal. At noon on the day of the performance, there was one more rehearsal with the orchestra. Everyone participated the entire time with heart and soul. No one stood around, sparing

his energies. As a result, the evening performance was brilliant. I didn't feel the least bit tired until the whole thing was over; then I was quite exhausted.[31]

Jussi said that the devotional atmosphere of the auditorium and the music helped him overcome every trace of nerves. Both performances were broadcast, captured on records, and issued on LP and CD.

Between concerts, Jussi also made a quick trip to Detroit for a *Ford Sunday Evening Hour*, and afterward Jussi and Harry Ebert resumed their recital tour of approximately 30 stops. At one, in Montgomery, Alabama, a 14-year-old girl, Nell, was in the audience. She and her sister had been studying voice with Jeanne Severine-Lorraine, a pupil of Manuel Garcia and an acquaintance of Jean and Édouard de Reszke. Madame Lorraine claimed that she helped the legendary Lilli Lehmann write her book *How to Sing*, mainly by telling her to make it simpler and more accessible. Nell's memories of the night she met Jussi are vivid:

> Madame Lorraine was a great admirer of Jussi Björling—she thought he was the greatest tenor of the day. I began my studies with her at age 13, so when Mr. Björling came to Montgomery, my sister and I went with my mother and father to the concert. After the concert we went backstage, and my sister and I met him and his accompanist.
>
> When we got out of the parking lot, in front of the concert hall, we saw Mr. Björling and his accompanist standing on the street corner waiting for a streetcar, which had stopped running by that time. We were very upset that nobody seemed to think that he needed a ride. We were sure that he was taken for the evening to some big party, but maybe he wanted to get home and had declined the invitation. So we stopped and asked if we could take them somewhere. He seemed delighted, and he said yes.
>
> We took him and his accompanist to the Jefferson Davis Hotel, and he invited us up to his suite. My parents, my sister, and I went up for a while, and we talked about many things, including fishing, that seemed to interest him very much. We asked if he would like to go fishing with us, and he said, "Oh, I would love it!"
>
> We were going to take him up to my uncle's place at Lake Martin, but the next morning it was pouring rain. So my mother called him, and she asked if he and his accompanist would like to come out for lunch. They both came and stayed for five or six hours. He seemed to be enjoying himself, he was very relaxed and quite at home. After lunch I asked if I could sing for him. "Oh, you are an aspiring singer?" "Yes," I said. So he said, "Fine, my accompanist will play for you. What are you going to sing for me?" "O don fatale." "O don fatale!" He was shocked. "Well!"
>
> I told him I was singing it in the lower key—the high note in the original key is a B natural. So I sang "O don fatale" for Mr. Björling, and I tried to do it with as much dramatic flair as I could muster. He complimented me, and he said I must have a very good teacher because I had good high notes, and the line was fine, and I just needed to develop. He then added, "Perhaps one day we'll sing in *Don Carlo* together."
>
> Well, of course that was the most thrilling statement of the day. Then

we played ping-pong, and he told me he loved to play ping-pong with the king, adding "I beat the king of Sweden!" But I was the ping-pong champion of Montgomery, Alabama—which is not saying much—but he was very good and held his own very well. My mother took pictures of us while we were playing ping-pong.[32]

Jussi and Harry stayed over for another day, but the weather didn't improve, so it was more ping-pong and still no fishing. Then they had to move on, and Jussi and Harry said goodbye to Nell and her charming family. Nell remembered Jussi as "a wonderful man, very jovial, very sweet. He did not drink, and he seemed very relaxed in the at-home atmosphere. We were all enchanted with him."[33]

※

Jussi's Town Hall recital on 31 January 1941 drew mixed reviews. Olin Downes acknowledged that his voice was "brilliant without hardness in the upper octave, and warm and beautiful in a lower register," but he found fault with the musical quality of the program's selections.[34] Another critic complained that his renditions of the Brahms, Wolf, and Sibelius selections were "strained and uninteresting" and "had only vocal quality to commend them, and repeatedly not enough of that."[35] At the same time all acknowledged his excellent delivery of the operatic selections.

The radio broadcasts from the Metropolitan, Carnegie Hall, and Detroit gave Jussi unprecedented exposure and prompted more than 300 letters a day—mostly from women. They all wanted his autograph and a photo, so Jussi hired a special secretary to answer these letters and ordered a large supply of postcards with his picture.[36] During his career, Jussi signed several thousand programs, photographs, and record albums—with decreasing enthusiasm as the years wore on. At the end of a strenuous recital or a demanding operatic role he was disinclined to linger for another hour to satisfy the seemingly insatiable expectations of autograph hounds. He could be quite curt with the 50th fan; occasionally, he refused to sign anything. For a while he used a special gimmick to gain a quick getaway: he had his signature printed on calling cards, which he passed out like lollipops. Still, an enormous amount of his signatures are in private hands—and apparently that's where they stay, for in the specialty dealers' catalogs, Björling autographs are the rarest and fetch a staggering price.

During this trip to America Jussi was supposed to sing at the White House for President Roosevelt, but what with the pressures of his office, the deteriorating political situation, and meetings with diplomats and statesmen, the president never had one free evening for such semiformal entertainment. It was also at this time Jussi received an invitation to sing in Rio de Janeiro. The offer was tempting, but he was homesick for his family and eager to return to Sweden the minute the tour was over. When it was, *The New York Times* reported that Björling and Harry Ebert "sailed on the American Export line *Siboney* on March 3 from Jersey City to Lisbon via Bermuda."

"This trip was just as sensational as the clipper trip out, because it went between mines and U-boats," wrote Harry.[37] But the last leg of the journey was uneventful, and after more than five months of separation, the longest since our marriage, I embraced my husband once again.

# Chapter 10

# THE VANISHING TENOR

Jussi spent a large part of the summer of 1941 traveling with the Swedish Army's recreation detail; between military transports, he sang his traditional concerts at Skansen, Gröna Lund, and Copenhagen's Tivoli. But Jussi's beloved Copenhagen was swarming with the German occupation troops, and Jussi soon had enough of the "Heil Hitler" and the outstretched arm. When as he boarded the Oresund's ferry, his German admirers bid him farewell with the usual gesture, Jussi could control himself no longer. He took off his hat, threw it in the air, and shouted: "Long live King Christian!"

It was a melancholy return to Stockholm's Opera. Forsell had retired as manager and was succeeded by Harald André. Jussi found this hard to get used to, and one day, feeling hoarse and completely forgetting about the change in command, he called Forsell to announce he was canceling his performance that evening. "My dear Jussi, I don't give a damn," answered Forsell and hung up.

Forsell died after a short illness on 30 May 1941. Usually Jussi declined to sing at such occasions because he wasn't sure he could control his emotions. But this time he sang. After his father, he owed the most in life to this complex and demanding man. When Forsell died, Jussi lost a father for the second time.

Jussi's 1941–42 Met contract called for 10 performances at a fee of $700 each. A typewritten sheet attached to the contract specifies that his roles were to be Riccardo, Rodolfo, Don Ottavio (crossed out in heavy pencil), Duke of Mantua, Cavaradossi, and Manrico in Italian, and Faust in French.[1] Jussi was scheduled to report for rehearsals on 15 December 1941, and this time I was to come along. Harry Ebert and his French wife, Marguerite, too were looking forward to the trip. At the end of August, as our departure drew near, Jussi felt a growing reluctance about leaving. "Must we go again?" he complained. Although he grumbled about it until the last minute, with a little nudging from me, he agreed to go.

We were to travel by night train to Berlin via Sassnitz, then to Lisbon, and thence on the Clipper to New York. Family and friends came to the Central Station to see us off. When the conductor began to slam the doors shut, the Eberts and I boarded the train. As it started to move, I expected Jussi to push open the door to our compartment any minute—but he never came. The train picked up speed, and still no Jussi. We walked the whole length of the train, searching every compartment. Finally we accepted the incomprehensible: Jussi wasn't on the train. In the last minute he had sabotaged the whole trip.

Our party got off the train in silence at Södertälje, and we took a taxi back to Stockholm. When I opened the door to the apartment on Nybrogatan, my mother met me with the news that Jussi still hadn't shown up. She had been on the train platform, where Enwall and a swarm of journalists, photographers, and others had crowded to say goodbye to us. When the conductor began to walk along the train and shout "Take your places!" Jussi didn't hear him. As one door after another was slammed shut, Jussi stood on the platform, engrossed in conversation. Then the train began to move.

"Hurry up, Jussi, jump!" Enwall shouted. Instead of following his command, Jussi calmly turned around. "No, I won't. You know very well that you're not supposed to jump onto a moving train. You don't want me to break the law, do you?"

In the confusion that followed, as everyone rushed to see what alternative transport could get him to the Trelleborg-Sassnitz Ferry in time, Jussi slipped away. He hopped into a taxi and vanished. "He disappeared from the platform like an arrow," mother explained. "There wasn't a thing we could do to stop him!" Where he went, no one knew. What had really happened? Why had he done this? Where was he now? Although my mother was often highly critical of Jussi's erratic behavior, this time she didn't say a word. She saw how desperate I was, and out of regard for my nerves she kept her thoughts to herself.

It is true that Jussi had protested the trip from the beginning. He may have worried about the unsettled international situation: what if Sweden was drawn into the war by German occupation as Denmark and Norway had been? But how could he do this to us—not the least to his loyal friends

Harry and Marguerite? They had been so happy about the trip! And he must have known that he didn't have any rational reason to cancel the long-planned American tour and Metropolitan season. Usually, I could persuade him to use common sense. This time I didn't have a chance; he had taken us all by surprise.

Eventually, Jussi came home, crestfallen. He told me he had gone directly from the Central Station to the Gyldene Freden restaurant, where he spent the whole evening. But then? What had he done after that? And why had he behaved like this anyway? "Jussi—why? What were you thinking? Please tell me!" He just tightened his lips and refused to respond to my desperate questions. He would not—and probably could not—explain. The far-reaching implications of his action made me insist, until he cut me off. "We're not going to talk about it anymore" was all he said.

I never did receive a real answer. Anger is not a dominant part of my personality, and normally I couldn't be really angry with Jussi, whatever he might do. But this time I took it very hard, and it was a long time before I forgave him. Athough I know it hurt him to hurt me, Jussi's spontaneous nature didn't allow him to foresee the results of his impulsive actions until it was too late.

The incident, predictably and inevitably, exploded in the international press. On 2 September, the American-Swedish News Exchange falsely reported that we were denied transit visas through Germany, and thus a concert tour of 40 American cities and Cuba had to be canceled; this initial version of events may have been based on a release prepared by Konsertbolaget in a simpleminded attempt to salvage the situation and protect Jussi. In any case, on the following day the truth was revealed. "Jussi Bjoerling, Swedish tenor, was said today to have refused to leave for the United States to fill concert engagements," wrote the American press.[2] The Stockholm papers were far less kind. Once details were made public, a terrible uproar ensued, with no end to wisecracks. "Jussi Waited for Peace" read one headline; others were more mocking still, and even the local variety shows ridiculed Jussi's disappearance.

A simple handwritten note was added to Jussi's Met contract for 1941–42: "Artist did not come to U.S."[3] With no acceptable excuse for defaulting on his contracts, we paid a substantial sum in damages. It was a hollow vindication for Jussi that his premonitions were proven right. On 7 December 1941 Japan attacked Pearl Harbor and the United States was forced into the war. Maybe we would have been stranded in the States or perished on our voyage home—who knows?

✳

The canceled trip meant we could spend a wonderful Christmas at home, like a normal family. Jussi was glad that he could be with his boys for a time; he loved them beyond all measure and was indescribably proud of

143

them. Two-and-a-half-year-old Lasse was fair and sunny, quick as a weasel and always into mischief. Anders, nearly six, had grown into a thoughtful little boy, tender and sensitive, with big serious eyes. In the last few years he had spent more time with his grandmother than with us, and naturally he was quite attached to her, which Jussi instinctively resented. "You take the children from me!" I remember him saying to my mother—then he'd add immediately that without her our whole existence would've collapsed, which was perfectly true.

Jussi's first appearance after the Central Station incident was a radio concert, the world premiere of Ture Rangström's Three Ballads. Sixten Ehrling, who took over the orchestra at short notice from an indisposed Grevillius, remembers, "There was no audience; it was a studio concert in the Stockholm Concert Hall. The composer was present, and he gave each of us a big lobster—it was cooked, thank God. Rangström said, 'I think it's stupid to give flowers to a man.' So he gave us these 'flowers.'"[4]

The flak over his aborted tour subsided, the Stockholm public decided they loved having Björling at home during the main season at the Opera. After the *Roméo et Juliette* on 3 February 1942, Jussi tactfully said to a *Dagens Nyheter* reporter: "It is more thrilling to appear here than at any other opera house in the world. No triumphs abroad can take away the respect [I feel] before a performance on the boards where I first learned the difficult art of crossing a stage."[5]

Jussi's last four performances this spring were *Un ballo in maschera* rehearsed and conducted by Vittorio Gui, who led Jussi's London debut. The touch of his experienced hand showed. The audience loved the music, Jussi excelled as Riccardo—not Gustaf—and subsequent press releases exaggerated only mildly by saying a "Björling fever" had swept Stockholm. He was finally a prophet in his own land.

On 9 April 1942 Jussi appeared at the Philharmonie in Berlin, and one might well ask in retrospect why he was willing to sing for the Nazis. The answer lies in Jussi's simple nature. For him, going to Berlin was nothing more than singing to an audience abroad. Sweden remained a neutral country, and we were yet unaware of German atrocities. It wouldn't cross Jussi's mind that his appearance could be construed—or misconstrued—as a political statement. He went to Berlin as a singer, and they applauded him as a singer. "At the end of the recital, listeners rushed the stage in a storm of applause and remained there while Jussi sang five encores."[6]

Jussi had no particular interest in politics. "As a Swede, he didn't have any kind of political convictions," said Lorenzo Alvary. "Outside of singing, nothing was really important to him, all else was only a part of life."[7] This observation oversimplifies the matter. When we boarded the train the day after the Berlin recital, the dignitaries sent us off with a stiff-armed "Heil Hitler!"—which greeting Jussi returned with a casual "Auf wiedersehen." It didn't sit well with our hosts! As we became aware of the cruelty of the Germans beyond the brutality of war, Jussi became outspokenly anti-Nazi.

Newlywed Jussi at his
piano at de Geersgatan 14.

John Forsell, Anna-Lisa, Jussi, and accompanist Harry Ebert after a concert at
Liseberg, Gothenburg.

A young Manrico in
*Il trovatore.*

As Vladimir in two-inch heels, with Chaliapin in
sandals as Khan Konchak and Einar Larson in the
title role, *Prince Igor*, Stockholm, 1935.

*"Bravo pour "Vladimir"* F. Chaliapin,
1935." Photo A. J. Tenhovaara.

An arrogant Turiddu in *Cavalleria
rusticana*. Photo Enar Merkel
Rydberg.

Young Radamès ready to lead his army, Stockholm, 1936. Photo Almberg & Preinitz.

As Canio in a Stockholm *Pagliacci*.

JB as Canio and Alexander Svéd as Tonio, Vienna, 23 February 1937.

Jussi in his dressing room in Stockholm, before a *Trovatore*.

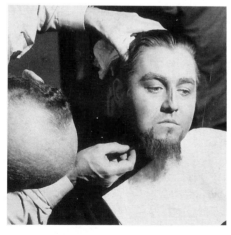

"Young Björling" becoming old Faust.

As old Faust in Boïto's
*Mefistofele*, Stockholm, 1937.

Jussi rehearsing—after all—with Ivor Newton.

Jussi and Anna-Lisa on their way to America for the first time, 1937.

New Year's Eve in Manhattan, 1937. L. to r.: pianist
Kosti Vehanen, Thérèse Enwall, Marian Anderson,
Jussi, Anna-Lisa; Helmer Enwall stands behind Jussi,
next to an unidentified reveler.

Arriving at Idlewild.

As Sándor Barinkay in Johann
Strauss' *Der Zigeunerbaron*,
Stockholm, 1938. Courtesy Jussi
Björling Museum, Borlänge.

A beaming Edward Johnson, pleased as Punch with his new tenor, at Jussi's Met debut, 24 November 1938.

Jussi and the Met's New Year's Day 1940 *Rigoletto* poster.

Lawrence Tibbett inscribed this photo to Jussi "with great admiration and warm friendship." Photo Jane Plotz.

Konsertbolaget director Helmer Enwall, Jussi, and attorney Gösta Hansson, Stockholm, 29 September 1940.

As Gustaf in *Un ballo in maschera*, his first opening night performance at the Met, 2 December 1940.

JB and Elisabeth Rethberg in *Un ballo in maschera*, 23 October 1940. Photo R. Strohmeyer.

The cast of the Met's 1940–41 season opener. L. to r.: Nicola Moscona, Alexander Svéd, Zinka Milanov, Herbert Graf, Edward Johnson, Ettore Panizza, Stella Andreva, JB, Norman Cordon.

Tenor brothers Jussi and Gösta in a *Rigoletto* at the Royal Opera, Stockholm. Photo Pressens Bild.

Jussi and his accompanist Harry Ebert departing for a concert in Copenhagen, April 1941. Photo Aftontidningen.

Jussi in recital at the Redoutensaal, Budapest, 27 November 1942. Photo Inkey Tibor.

Siarö. In 1943 the trees were cleared and the studio was built up the hill from the boathouse, at the same elevation as the house.

Jussi and his boys at the boathouse railing, Siarö.

Young Tullio Voghera sailing in illustrious company aboard the *Kronprinzessin Cecilie*, October 1909. L. to r.: Voghera, Frances Alda, Enrico Caruso, Andrès de Segurola.

A much older Voghera at work with Jussi in the living room at Siarö, at the piano traded for Murre.

King Gustaf and his youngest—*the* youngest—Hovsångaren exchange a conspiratorial smile, 16 June 1944. Courtesy Richard Copeman.

Field artist Jussi Björling,
11 November 1944.
Courtesy Richard Copeman.

During the summer of 1942, Jussi gave benefit concerts for the Red Cross. He spent six months of the year in uniform, doing his military service with the Svea Lifeguard as Field Artist No. 276 in the Army Entertainment Corps headed by Count Folke Bernadotte. He toured the country, gave 20 outdoor concerts in public parks, and he also sang in Denmark and Finland. Partly because of his military service, partly because Harry Ebert wasn't as forgiving of Jussi's recent unaccountable behavior as I, his accompanist on these outings was Sixten Ehrling, a fellow soldier in the Entertainment Corps. Both singer and accompanist traveled and performed in ill-fitting uniforms. Ehrling was a gifted musician, but on one occasion he received an unexpected lesson in voice production.

> One night Jussi wasn't feeling well and he asked me to transpose "Che gelida manina" a semitone down. He hit a gorgeous high B-natural instead of a C, then next came "La donna è mobile," which has a B. So I thought if he could sing a B in *La bohème*, then I don't have to transpose *Rigoletto*, and I didn't. But Jussi didn't have absolute pitch, and as he sang it, he was convinced he was singing it also a half step down, and he cracked on the B-natural at the end.
>
> He was incredibly furious with me, and I deserved it. I said I was sorry and that I thought if he could hit the B in one aria, he can hit it in the next. "Don't you understand, that it's a totally different thing! If I knew I was going to sing a B I would attack it differently. I thought I was going to attack a B-flat!" I didn't know what happens inside a singer's voice and brains, especially not his! Of course I was very apologetic. I think he forgave me eventually. But it was a very strange thing that he could hit the top note in one aria but he couldn't hit the same note in another because he wasn't expecting it to be that note.[8]

On these tours, Jussi's drinking sometimes got out of control, and his behavior became erratic and irrational. Ehrling, a youthful 23, had no experience handling an alcoholic and no intention of serving as a baby sitter to a man eight years his senior. Nevertheless, Jussi met all his obligations—until the end.

> It was late, and he was very tired. We were on our way to Västervik, and all of a sudden he said he didn't want to sing at that city. I sat with the driver and told him to continue, but Jussi said, "No! Turn around! Go back!"
> "Why not? What's wrong?"
> "I can't. I won't."
> "But why, Jussi?"
> "Because my father died there."
> "Your father had died there when you accepted the engagement! Why now?"
> "Because I can't sing there. I am not singing there. Let's turn back."
> We had a terrible argument about it. He had some strange ideas about

> this whole concert, and I remember he said, "How could I possibly sing at that church?" The fact was, he wasn't going to sing at that church at all![9]

Jussi did cancel, and a great deal was written about it. Nobody could understand his sudden change of mind. He knew his itinerary, and he shouldn't have waited until the last minute to cancel. Yet his decision cannot be attributed to a momentary whim—in his adult life Jussi never performed in Västervik.

Jussi stayed with us as much as possible at our new summer place on Siarö, an island north of Ljusterö. Although it had been our first inclination, our lawyer advised us against buying a house on Vettershaga, so we kept our eyes open, and while Jussi was on tour in America in 1940, I spotted an advertisement for a house for rent on Siarö. It seemed to be just what we were looking for.

My mother and I went to view the property, a charming yellow country house with white trim and green shutters, six rooms and a kitchen, situated high on a promontory overlooking easternmost Siarö sound. A big veranda faced the water, and there was a little cabin and bathhouse down by the water's edge. The lot was wide, and the house was surrounded by birches, oaks, and towering evergreens. The view of other tree-lined islands was enchanting, the air salty and clean, and the deep blue waters of the archipelago crystal clear—and full of fish. On the adjacent lot, beyond a fence, cows grazed the meadows.

I rented the place on my own, but Jussi agreed that we couldn't have found anything better. We were completely taken in by the bucolic setting and the decades-old house, which had neither electricity nor indoor bathroom, only a picturesque little outhouse that Jussi immediately christened *Brallemansro* (Bralleman's rest) in fond memory of the little cabin of the same name he shared with Björn Forsell on Stenungsön. Siarö became our summer paradise. There we were a family again, recuperating from the hectic times of the previous season and resting up for the next. It was the one place on earth that Jussi loved above all others, the place where we planned to grow old together.

As soon as the children's vacation began, we moved out to the island. Every evening we fetched fresh milk from farmer David Eriksson, and the boys would climb up on the scrub bench in the kitchen and dunk freshly baked rolls in the still-warm milk. Jussi and the boys would boat or fish in the archipelago, or head for the woodshed where Jussi had his carpenter's bench. There he made birdhouses from old sugar crates; the first was hung up in a big pine tree, which we christened the birdhouse tree, but in the end, innumerable birdhouse trees filled the property. He also carved the most wonderful sailboats for the children. When the weather was nice, we ate on the veranda we called the opera terrace, and afterward we strolled the footpath that wound along the shore, where we often encountered our neighbors, Professor and Mrs. Hult, on their way to the boat landing. They were always most correctly dressed—the professor with spats, cane, and Panama hat, and his wife in muslin with matching umbrella. As in a turn-of-the-century idyll, a cordial exchange of good-evenings followed.

In the autumn of 1941 we bought the house on Siarö, a decision we never regretted. A couple of years later we added a separate music studio, one large room with a 16-foot ceiling, an open fireplace, and a stairway that led to a landing, with a door out to a little round balcony. Jussi didn't exactly know what the stairway and balcony were for, but the house in Karlsarvet had something similar and the setting lent itself to a rehearsal of *Roméo et Juliette*! Here we played the wind-up Victrola, and of course the piano, which had followed us here from Vettershaga.

This music studio became Jussi's workplace and refuge. During summer evenings you could hear his voice through the open windows; my mother and I would sit outside on the kitchen steps, cleaning the carbide lamps and listening to his glorious voice. Quite often passing boaters put down their oars or silenced their motors to hear Jussi practice. As dusk fell and the stars came out, whole flotillas drifted close to shore by our home to listen as his music floated out over the water.

For me, the magical evenings on Siarö epitomize the perfect Swedish summer.

※

In November 1942 we journeyed to Budapest, a fluke engagement. Jussi had been scheduled to return to Vienna's Staatsoper, but in their newfound chauvinism, the Austrians insisted that all operas be sung in German. Apart from our personal hope that a world order where all operas would be sung in German wouldn't prevail, Jussi wouldn't even entertain the notion of relearning any of his roles in translation (other than his native Swedish) on artistic grounds. The Staatsoper administration, unaware of the immovability of a Björling, refused to yield and all negotiations ended. So, as *The New York Times* (20 November 1942) put it, "The tenor has instead gone to Budapest, where there is no objection to the singing of Italian operas in Italian."

Vienna's loss was Budapest's gain, and the Hungarian Royal Opera, eager to welcome Björling back, lined up their very best artists. He was partnered in both *La bohème* and *Faust* by Esther Réthy, back home from Vienna, and György Losonczy, the greatest singing actor of the Hungarian Opera during his 42-year career.[10] The Puccini was conducted by Sergio Failoni, and Gounod's opera by Otto Berg. Both were well received: "One is most impressed by Björling's fantastic professionalism, the smoothness with which he handles his voice, . . . the natural softness of his attack, the perfect breathing; so far, we have not heard anything better from a tenor."[11] Between his own performances, Jussi attended the Opera's production of *Il trovatore*. He liked what he heard, and quite characteristically, he went backstage to congratulate the soloists.[12]

Jussi capped his appearances at the Royal Opera House with a recital on 27 November. It took place in the Redoutensaal, following the recent recitals of Tito Schipa, Set Svanholm, and Helge Roswaenge. One critic found his delivery "cool, [and] elegantly aloof."[13] Another wrote of his "great musicality and a simple delivery void of mannerisms. . . . He is not interested in impressing his listeners with grandiose vocal display. For that reason, he will never be as popular with the less discerning segment of our public as is his countryman, Set Svanholm."[14] We couldn't quite figure out whether this was a dig at Set or Jussi.

Jussi's service to Sweden at home and abroad and the position he occupied in the country's cultural life didn't go unrecognized. On 8 December 1942, he was appointed Knight of the Royal Swedish Order of Vasa. Five days later, he returned to Berns Salong to sing at the Lucia Festival; he had appeared there in 1935, and in 1936 I sung a duet with him on the same occasion. This evening the organizers had seized on Björling's availability as a soloist once again. The guests loved it, and as I listened, I realized how much our lives had been suffused by music. Jussi and I were well matched in most ways, but it was music that had brought us together and kept us going, a constant and inexhaustible source of joy and delight for both of us. Its beauty gave our lives purpose and meaning, content and substance, goal and reward.

*Du holde Kunst, ich danke dir dafür.*

# Chapter 11

# WAR YEARS

The month that began so well ended badly: on Christmas Eve 1942 Jussi came down with pneumonia, and it took him the better part of January to regain his strength.

During the war years, Jussi's activities were mostly confined to Scandinavia, with the exception of Budapest and an invitation from the Maggio Musicale Fiorentino. In late April 1943 Jussi traveled to Florence for four performances of *Il trovatore* at Teatro Comunale. Maria Caniglia, the great Verdian soprano of the interwar years sang Leonora, the role of Azucena was taken by a very young and very gifted Fedora Barbieri, Enzo Mascherini sang Di Luna, and Mario Rossi conducted. At that time I was in the eighth month of pregnancy with our third child and so was unable to accompany Jussi. He assured me he'd take care of himself, and he kept his promise.

The Maggio introduced Jussi to the Italians, and Jussi did his very best to make a good impression. *La Nazione* praised his "extraordinarily modulated voice, so rich in nuances and softness, his great musicality, his convincing insight, and his well-balanced interpretation—all of which place him in the first rank of lyric interpreters."[1]

Many artists converged upon Florence for this festival, a major music event in Italy, and a world-class performer one night was very likely to be sitting in the audience the next. Cellist Gaspar Cassado had seen Jussi in

149

*Trovatore*, and Jussi wanted to catch Cassado's recital but he had to sing that same evening. When Cassado heard about this, he invited Jussi to his apartment and played through his entire program for Jussi alone, saying he wanted to repay Jussi for the pleasure he had given him. The legendary Titta Ruffo also heard Jussi's Manrico, and the grand old man was so impressed that he gave Jussi an autographed photo of himself inscribed *Al giovane celebre tenore Jussi Björling, con ammirazione* (To the celebrated young tenor Jussi Björling, with admiration). Ruffo took Jussi on walking tours of his Florence, where he was living in retirement, and on one of these outings he picked out a silver salt and pepper shaker set in an antique shop. "Take these to your wife—from me," he said. To this day, when I have guests, Titta Ruffo's salt and pepper shakers grace the dinner table.

This engagement was Jussi's last excursion into warring Europe. We followed Jussi's Florentine success in the Swedish press, right up to his safe return from Italy, on 9 May 1943, which was duly noted by *Svenska Dagbladet*. But all his recent artistic laurels were overshadowed by the birth of our daughter on 4 June 1943. "I can't understand why I feel so good," I had exclaimed with wonder to Dr. Claeson, my obstetrician. "Oh yes!" he said with a twinkle in his eye. "Either Mrs. Björling is having an affair, or it's going to be a girl!"

After two boys, a little girl was exactly what we wished for most, and the doctor's jocular prediction was correct. I distinctly heard him announce "It's a girl!" as I came out of the anesthetic, and well mannered as I was, even half knocked out, I politely responded: "Thank you, Doctor!" Dr. Claeson laughed. "Don't thank me!"

Just as we had after Lasse's birth, we went out to the country with the little bundle, whom we called "Lillan" ("Little One"); she was later baptized Ann-Charlotte. This was our third summer on Siarö. In addition to Jussi and me, the children and my mother, we had Tullio Voghera with us again. The whole winter long we had longed for his fabulous spaghetti dishes, and now we could have our fill. In addition to voice lessons, Tullio instructed me in Italian cooking, especially *spaghetti alla matriciana*, but I was only a student—he was the master.

This was the summer we realized that Jussi needed a music studio separate from the main house. He and Tullio had been working in the living room, but it was hard for them to concentrate with the children running around, and Voghera also complained about the room's poor acoustics. So Jussi had his studio built, but poor Tullio never had a chance to enjoy it. This was not only the last summer he spent with us—it was the last year of his life.

⚹

Both Anders and Lasse were musical. Anders, now seven years old, frequently went with his father to the Opera and was completely at home in its labyrinthine backstage. Without any conscious effort on his part, he absorbed most of Jussi's repertoire by hearing him perform onstage there and rehearse at home, and like most artists' children, his proud father showed him off. Anders' showpiece was "La donna è mobile," which he performed standing on a table before a discriminating public consisting of Jussi's admiring colleagues. Once he sang on Sven Jerring's popular radio show *The Children's Mailbox*. When our eldest had finished, quite unexpectedly, Jerring told him, "Now, Anders, you're going to hear some other boys about your age"—and so saying, he played a recording of Jussi and his brothers singing one of David's Psalms. None of us—not even Jussi—recognized the three boy sopranos on the record!

It never occurred to Jussi to train the children's voices. Although his own father began to teach him and his brothers "almost before they'd learned to talk," Jussi was convinced that they were the exception and singing lessons given too early could be injurious to the voice. When the children entered school, Jussi didn't want them to participate in special music programs, only the usual lessons required of every child. Anders was later a member of the Radio Boys Choir, but after his voice changed, he stopped singing and refused to continue his piano lessons. Neither Jussi nor I pressured him to keep at something he so obviously had come to dislike. As it turned out it was Lasse and Ann-Charlotte—tenor and soprano—who continued the family's musical tradition.

Jussi loved our children, but he didn't ignore his obligations to his own first son, Rolf. He tried to look after him, bought him presents, and contributed toward his support. When I first met Rolf, he must have been a boy of six or seven, a flaxen-haired youngster, handsome, and the very image of Jussi. Unfortunately, Rolf resented me from the beginning, which got our relationship off to a bad start. He never accepted me as his father's wife. He was convinced that Jussi's true love was his mother, Linnea, and he went to his grave believing that had I not come between them, Jussi would've married her.

I, in my turn, was protective of my family, and though it would've been better for all concerned if Rolf and I had been closer, naturally my own children came first for me. Nevertheless, Jussi wanted Rolf to know his father and his brothers and sister, and I agreed. As a boy, Rolf came to our apartment regularly to play with his younger siblings. Considerate of his feelings and not wanting to inhibit either him or Jussi on these visits, I usually excused myself to run some errands, giving all the Björlings an unimpeded opportunity to bond. But these efforts failed to awaken in Rolf a sense of belonging. He felt like an outsider—and continued to look upon me as an intruder. It was probably not his fault; I can easily imagine that his mother had few good things to say about Jussi, his young family, and me in particular. But parceling out blame is a pointless exercise, and it is impossible to say which of us was more responsible for the distant and stilted relationship that developed between us.

Jussi's 1943 autumn activities began with concerts in Sweden and Helsinki. On 10 October he gave a very emotional recital at Stora Tuna Church, the site of his parents' and grandparents' graves. Because he sang so often in churches, he put together a special program suitable for the venue, one that usually finished with "Sverige." Without fail, the audience would spontaneously rise as though it were our national anthem. On this occasion, Märta Björling remembers that when he came to the song's closing lines—"*Du land, där våra barn en gång få bo, och våra fäder sova under kyrkohällen*" ("You land, where our children once will live, and our forefathers sleep under the church stones")—tears rolled down his face.[2]

Jussi lent his voice to many charitable causes during these years when the people of Europe were in such appalling need. He initiated performances at the Opera for the children of France, Belgium, and Italy, and he once sang three concerts in two days. Jussi wrote about one particular form of fund-raising, and one especially successful event: "I usually took along 20 or so of my recordings and autographed them, and they would be auctioned off. In the large hall in Helsingfors, one of my concerts brought in 250,000 Finnish Mark for the Finnish invalids."[3] He made a recording exclusively to benefit the Boy Scouts of Sweden; they derived all the income from it. Jussi was moved by the gratitude he received. "It amounts to much more than the relinquished salaries," he used to say.

The war years in Sweden made my husband even better known and more loved there than before. People could hear him now year-round, during the winter months as well. The lines to his performances at the Opera were several blocks long; it was often said that Jussi taught the Swedes to go to the opera. He attracted a new public who without him, perhaps, would never dared to have entered the musical sanctuary of the upper class. Those who went for the first time to a performance of *La bohème* just to hear Björling often returned to see other operas as well.

Jussi's simple, open personality, devoid of posturing or artifice, made him popular far beyond the circle of sophisticated music lovers. Yes, concerning music, he knew—and rightly so—that he was special; false modesty was as alien to him as flaunting the position he had attained among singers. But he was never assertive about it unless challenged, and otherwise no one was more humble than he. Faithful to the timeless traditions of Dalarna, in everyday life he was informal with everyone everywhere, which only added to his popularity. People on the streets recognized him, and sometimes it seemed that he was on a first-name basis with all Stockholm. He drew comments at the Opera by holding doors open for others, cleaning ladies included. Gertrud Pålson-Wettergren remembered him as "always cheerful, uncomplicated, and congenial in the company of good friends. He was no *divo*, he didn't need to be, and, as a matter of fact, didn't know how to be one."[4] Teddy Nyblom's observations ran along the same lines: "The tenor of the world was least of all arrogant; nobility, commoners, peasants, millionaires, cab drivers—they were all [his] buddies on the same level."[5]

In an era when accompanists acknowledged applause two steps behind the singer, Jussi stood side by side with his pianist. He often insisted that his accompanist take a solo bow, sometimes at an awkward point in the recital or even if the accompanist was visibly reluctant to do so. Many singers recall numerous incidents—either as eyewitnesses or as the object of the gesture— when Jussi led a colleague out for a curtain call, then stepped back and disappeared, leaving his fellow soloist to receive the full measure of the ovation.

A large portion of his appeal was his Swedishness. His heart was so obviously in everything he sang in Swedish, and especially when he sang it for Swedes. The constant touring to small communities during the war brought Jussi close to the people and established him as "Sweden's Jussi." Had he continued his American tours every winter, this wouldn't have happened to the same extent or with the same intensity.

⁂

Tragically, Jussi paid a large price for the affection he now received from his countrymen. When he was in Sweden, Jussi turned to alcohol at an alarmingly increased rate. In America he was occupied with musical or travel preparations for the next appearance, but in Stockholm, the singers often gathered after the performance at the bar in the Strand Hotel or at the Opera Bar. One drink led to another as they socialized, and many drinks led to a lot of trouble.

Jussi's drinking made me terribly sad and depressed. I knew he needed to unwind, that he wanted to feel free and unencumbered in his movements, that the expectations of his public were a great pressure. But as the nonalcoholic wife of an alcoholic husband, I didn't understand why he couldn't curb his need for that kind of entertainment. We had a wonderful home life and a happy family. Was that not enough for him?

During this period, I often sat up and sewed almost all night, waiting for Jussi to come home, embroidering pillows and table covers with roses in petit point. It calmed me to think, "One more flower, and he'll be home for sure." Every time I heard a car door slam on Nybrogatan, I jumped. Could it be Jussi? Had he finally come home—and if so, in what shape? In hard moments, it gave me strength to remember my own happy, protected childhood, knowing that I had enjoyed so much of what Jussi had never received.

Sometimes I prayed, and then I felt better. That came from my grandmother and my mother—she too had sat up many a late evening, waiting for my father to come home. But prayer carried me only so far, a temporary and weak remedy in the face of the frequency of the incidents. Many nights I couldn't sleep at all. *I can't cope with this anymore*, I thought. Distressed and distraught, I became completely apathetic and was hospitalized for a deep depression.

153

When things were as bad as they could get, I cried on my mother's shoulder; she'd say, "Go to Madame von Skilondz and try to relax by singing a few hours." Actually, it worked like magic! While singing I almost forgot my unhappiness, and Madame von Skilondz supported and encouraged me: "You should sing! You should be something yourself—stand on your own feet!"

Although she cared for him, many times Mama thought I should leave Jussi. But I couldn't make that decision. In the years Jussi and I had been married, our love had deepened more than I had thought possible. Quite simply, we couldn't exist without each other. And so the troubles continued.

When Jussi finally came home late at night, he was dreadfully tired and, at the same time, abnormally excited and quarrelsome, but I didn't want to argue. "You need to get some sleep," I'd say, and help him to bed. Sometimes he'd brush aside the whole episode and assure me that I shouldn't worry, it wouldn't happen again. Other times he was deeply sorry and would apologize. And yet, between these drinking spells, Jussi was his happy, loving self, the Jussi who'd come home and immediately call out, "Mama, where are you?" then follow me around from room to room while I did housework, then sit and talk with me when I was finished.

Strangely enough, Jussi's physique never seemed to be affected by his destructive drinking habit. He was at the top of his craft, filled with a vitality and lust for life, and onstage it was one success after another. Music critic Teddy Nyblom wrote in *Aftonbladet* that when "timid and innocent" Jussi Björling made his debut 10 years earlier, "certainly no one thought that he would develop so soon into the world-class singer he seems to be in his best moments." He acknowledged that recognition from the Swedish music critics was slow in coming, mainly because of his acting. "Now Jussi has improved even in stagecraft and his Faust and Roméo surprise us with his elegant and spirited interpretations. An air of real theater surrounds everything he does now."[6]

I knew how hard Jussi had worked to improve and how happy this verdict made him. I sent a silent "thank you" to Gösta Ekman.

※

On 2 December 1943 Jussi was struck during a *Faust* rehearsal by stomach pains that turned out to be appendicitis; he was taken to Sophiahemmet to be operated on by Professor Söderlund. Afterward, the nurse told me that as the patient was anesthetized, they heard him murmur in a weak voice, "Greetings, chaste and pure abode!" The nurse was deeply moved by the respectful greeting; she didn't know it was the first line of an aria ("Salut, demeure") from *Faust*. "Mr. Björling is such a fine gentleman," she concluded in awe.

Understandably, Jussi thought a lot about his father's death during all this. He was relieved that his operation went so well, and when he thanked

Professor Söderlund, the doctor took the opportunity to ask Jussi if he'd give a concert for the benefit of Sophiahemmet's nurses' home. "Of course," Jussi replied, without giving it much thought. He kept his promise, but much too soon. He strained so much during the concert that his incision opened and began to bleed. He didn't realize—and the professor should have—that many of the supporting muscles had been cut. After this, he couldn't sing sustained high notes for months, and his programs had to be planned in observance of this problem. But at the Opera's New Year's Eve celebration, the whole company was represented, so Jussi sang too. He couldn't desert his colleagues. Sixten Ehrling conducted a musical farewell to the old year, welcoming the new.

Musically, Jussi filled 1944 with a large number of recitals, some for charity, and 13 performances at the Royal Opera. On 18 and 25 April he sang in the same evening the principal roles of opera's Siamese twins, *Cavalleria rusticana* and *Pagliacci*. Despite their common stylistic roots, Turiddu and Canio are dramatically dissimilar roles, and it requires a lot more than vocal stamina to perform them well: within the span of a 30-minute intermission, one must turn from a two-timing young Sicilian peasant into an aging betrayed husband, driven to murder. On 21 April 1936, the first time Jussi attempted this bravura casting, he was barely 25 years old. He did it well then, and better yet on every subsequent occasion. By his 30s and 40s, Jussi could immerse himself in the roles and give them a dramatic intensity worthy of the music. The 8 December 1954 double bill in Stockholm, which has been preserved, serves as a fair documentary of his interpretation.

Jussi was very patriotic, thus he was especially pleased when he was invited for the first time to sing at the Swedish Flag Day ceremony at the Stadion, on 6 June 1944. Hundreds of Swedish flags fluttered against the blue sky, and Sweden's old King Gustaf V presided in his general's uniform, a symbol of our revered monarchy. Coincidentally, it was D-day, the day the Allies landed at Normandy. After that, the outcome of the war became clearer with each passing day, but the question of how many more lives would be extinguished remained until the inevitable collapse of the Third Reich.

Ten days later, on 16 June 1944, Jussi was appointed *Hovsångare*, at 33, the youngest Royal Court Singer ever; David Björling and *Hovsångaren* John Forsell would've been proud. After the ceremony, King Gustaf and Jussi posed for the cameras. The king liked Jussi as an artist and as a person, and as they shook hands, he advised him, "This is the moment we're supposed to look serious and solemn." They both smirked, the cameras flashed—and the picture with the awkward conspiratorial smiles made all the Stockholm newspapers.

Jussi was often invited to the palace to sing, not only on state occasions but for private dinner parties too.

The first time I couldn't help thinking about the day many years before when three small boys sang in Leksand's Church for the king and queen. Moreover, the first time I sang at the palace—I didn't sing at the palace. It happened as follows: John Forsell was dressed in his beautiful white commissioned officer's uniform with sword and medals, and greeted his protégés. The concert was to take place in the White Room with all the pomp which can still be found at the Stockholm Palace. Forsell had decided that I was indisposed, which to some degree was true but not as much as he would have liked to believe. He came up to me and said thoughtfully: "My dear Björling, if you don't feel well, you shouldn't sing at an occasion like this."

John Forsell himself sang, and he sang exactly what I had planned to sing. This was a bitter experience, but I consoled myself with the thought that life would give me many more opportunities. But Forsell had clearly forgotten that one never applauds at the palace, because when he finished singing and stood waiting for the thunder of applause which never came, he turned to the Royal Court Conductor and said loudly enough for at least the first 10 rows to hear: "By God, I believe they think it's Björling singing!"[7]

Jussi soon received another distinction from the people of Sweden: listeners voted him the most popular radio personality of 1944. In the words of tenor Sture Ingebretzen, Jussi's colleague, "Jussi became popular and all Sweden's idol in the deepest and noblest meaning of the word. Everybody liked him, from prominent musical authorities to ordinary people who instinctively enjoyed his voice. The man in the street, people who had never been to the Opera in their lives, all called Jussi, the world's foremost tenor, by his first name."[8]

Jussi thought that in spite of his unusual childhood and early successes he was too young to write an autobiography, but everyone else felt he had a story to tell and that, with the enormous popular interest in him, he should tell it. With some persuading Jussi gave in, and during the summer of 1944, we had a long-term houseguest at Siarö, Sten Söderberg, who had been hired by the publisher Wahlström and Widstrand to ghostwrite Jussi's autobiography, and whose name, at the publisher's insistence, did not appear in the book.

Day after day the two sat together: Söderberg asked questions and then jotted down Jussi's long answers. He then organized the material, without adding his own or diminishing Jussi's phraseology in the process. Most of the text sounds the way Jussi expressed himself, and in many passages I can hear his voice telling the anecdote, which is why I've incorporated many passages from Jussi's autobiography throughout this narrative: to present Jussi's thoughts and views in his own words.

The collaboration wasn't all work. They took time out for relaxation, including fishing. When Jussi declared that he was the "Pike's Enemy Number One," Söderberg said, "Prove it!" Jussi always rose to a challenge, so they rowed out to the islands around Siarö, cast for the best part of the day, and—nothing. Downcast, they decided to row home. On the way back, reaching the side of the island where he'd never caught a thing before, Jussi said in desperation, "I just have to try once more!"

They stopped for a minute, Jussi took one more cast—and he hooked one of those giant pikes of which fish stories are made, second only to the monster he'd snagged on his very first time out. When he finally managed to lift it with a net into the boat, the fish whipped up its tail. Jussi told Söderberg to put his foot on it, but with one eye on the pike's jaws, the writer refused. In any case, Jussi salvaged his reputation, we had a superb dinner, and the lesser of the two pikes' heads that still "adorn" Jussi's studio proves that the story is true.

Jussi resumed work in August and in September returned to the Opera, appearing in *Ballo in maschera*, *Trovatore*, *Faust*, *Aida*, and *La bohème*. On 20 October 1944, dating it from his 1919 American tour, he celebrated his 25th anniversary as a professional singer at the Stockholm Concert Hall. He shared the stage with his frequent partner, Hjördis Schymberg; Grevillius conducted the Royal Opera Orchestra. It was like an operatic family affair, and everybody toasted Jussi, wishing him another 25 years of singing.

# Chapter 12

# RETURN TO AMERICA

On 27 April 1945 Jussi received the prestigious royal medal *Litteris et Artibus*, and on 6 June he was invited to sing again at the Swedish Flag Day ceremony. World War II had ended, so this year it was a combined celebration of the Allied victory and the guarantee of Sweden's survival as a free and independent nation. A week later Jussi took part in a charity gala for the Danish Resistance movement. Recitals at Skansen and Gröna Lund were followed on 11 August by a charity recital on Ljusterö, the island across the sound from Siarö.

This small-scale affair was his first collaboration with Professor Axel Hugo Teodor Theorell, a Ljusterö summer resident. Hugo, director of a research institute at the Karolinska Institute, was an accomplished violinist and his wife a pianist. Jussi and he spent many musical afternoons together, and a mutual acquaintance suggested they give a joint recital. In Hugo's words,

> Jussi sang as only he could when he felt at his best; my wife and I played in between to give him breathing space. When he was to go on for the second time, he took off his jacket because of the heat. I suggested that perhaps he should take off his suspenders too, and he picked up on the idea immediately. However, Jussi had lost some weight, and his pants had a precarious tendency to slide down. We found some string to tie together the suspender buttons in the back, and the situation was saved. Few seemed to

notice that Jussi went up and down from the podium sideways as well as backing out, persistently turning his back away from the audience.[1]

In September 1945, Jussi's autobiography, *Med bagaget i strupen* (*My Voice Is My Luggage*), was published. Unfortunately, for reasons never made clear, his brother Gösta had decided to write his own book about Jussi with the help of Teddy Nyblom. Jussi was unaware of it, and when *Jussi: boken om storebror* (*Jussi: The Book About Big Brother*) appeared a couple of months before his own effort, Jussi regarded Gösta's literary attempt as a preemptive strike. He was very angry with his younger brother, who knew full well that Jussi was at work on his own book. The unnecessary friction between the two lasted for quite some time, and as his book brought Gösta neither fame nor fortune, I hardly think it was worth the aggravation.

When at war's end America reopened its doors to foreign artists, Jussi, the citizen of a neutral country, was politically the least problematic European import for American impresari. Even before the conclusion of the hostilities, offers began to arrive. Francis C. Coppicus and Frederick C. Schang's Metropolitan Musical Bureau, a division of Columbia Concerts, was eager to secure Björling for its roster. Helmer Enwall and Konsertbolaget worked out the details, and in October 1945, Jussi and I were once more en route to America—this time flying, not sailing, over the North Atlantic. We'd been permitted to join eight other civilian passengers on a big American Skymaster from the Army Air Transport Command, carrying homeward-bound military personnel. Transatlantic civilian air travel from Scandinavia wouldn't begin until Scandinavian Airline System (SAS) started operations in 1946.

The party of civilians included mighty heldentenor Lauritz Melchior and his German-born wife, Maria. The six-foot, four-inch great Dane called his petite companion "Kleinchen" ("Little One"). Wonderful roast beef was served for dinner, the first time in years we had meat without a ration coupon! Late at night, we refueled at the American military base on Iceland; in the early morning we landed at Goose Bay in Labrador to refuel again. Over North America we hit a violent storm with air pockets, and we learned that on the side where Melchior was sitting, a motor had stopped. "It's your fault, Lauritz, you're too heavy!" Jussi teased. "All the weight is on your side!" It was a flight of which nightmares are made.

Luckily, we were near an airport in Maine and were able to make an unscheduled landing to check the motor. By this time, my feet were so swollen from sitting upright in the unpressurized cabin that I couldn't get my shoes on, so my reentry on American soil was made in stockings. Finally, after one and a half days of flight, we landed at La Guardia, where I managed to squeeze my feet into my shoes just as we came face to face with some 25 photojournalists' cameras and bobbing posters that read "Welcome Home!" We were touched. As we were driven off to the Algonquin Hotel, it seemed our return to America was indeed a blessed homecoming.

Of course everybody wanted to know how the war had affected our lives, and Jussi frankly admitted that, in light of what the rest of Europe had suffered, we had weathered the difficult times with a minimum of hardships. The return of the Met's "Swedish tenor" was mentioned in the New York dailies, and *The New York Times* (3 October 1945) announced, "Mr. Bjoerling will go on concert tours taking him through the United States, Canada and Cuba."

Jussi's first postwar appearance, in Detroit on the 7 October *Ford Sunday Evening Hour*, was to be followed by a series of duo recitals with Dorothy Kirsten, the young soprano who had begun to make a name for herself only a few years earlier. Her Met debut was still a couple of months off, and she was completely unknown to us. "Kirsten? Who's that?" Jussi asked our new manager, Frederick C. Schang, suspiciously. "I want to hear her before we perform together!" Schang thought the request reasonable and arranged a luncheon so that the two could get acquainted. It was a most pleasant affair, and afterward Jussi said, "I don't need to hear her sing. As soon as she spoke, I could hear by her voice that she's OK!"

Dorothy and Jussi's first joint recital was in Butte, Montana, on 19 October 1945. (Two earlier bookings in Billings, Montana, on 16 and 17 October, were canceled due to a polio epidemic.) On the evening of the first concert, a telegram from Coppicus and Schang greeted us at Butte's Hotel Finlen: "As you open your American concert season tonight accept greetings from your management and heartfelt wishes that a long and mutually happy and profitable period of collaboration is thus initiated. Kindest regards to you and Mrs. Bjoerling."

The collaboration indeed turned out to be long and happy, and to make sure that it was profitable too, the new management scheduled Jussi for about 70 appearances between October and May, turning him into a cross between a workhorse and a cash cow. But it didn't bother Jussi. He thrived on the exposure, and whereas other artists may have been resentful about singing in so many small towns, Jussi, with his lifelong travels behind him, didn't mind it in the least. San Francisco or Butte, he gave his all every night. Dorothy too retained good memories of their association.

> I was very fortunate early in my career when Columbia Artists arranged a joint concert tour with Jussi. He was already an established artist, and I learned a lot from him. There were rumors at the time of his drinking problems, but I never saw Jussi intoxicated. Anna-Lisa was with us on this tour and perhaps she kept him in tow. Our tour ended in Los Angeles with *La bohème* . . . which was also my debut with the San Francisco Opera. But in all our performances together, Jussi was never less than a gentleman and a fine and warm colleague. I like to think that he had enough respect for me to never let me see him any other way.[2]

While rehearsals for the 9 November *La bohème* were in progress, Dorothy, Jussi, and I were invited to the Melchiors' home, "The Viking," a large house in Beverly Hills overlooking the city. To our dismay, Lauritz welcomed our ravenous threesome in a brocade morning gown with Kleinchen at his side, her face still covered with cold cream. "We'll be with you shortly," Lauritz assured us. "Go out in the garden and eat a little fruit for the time being!"

We ate some green figs in the garden, and a little later we were invited in. After a few cocktails we were treated to greasy lentil soup and other heavy German dishes that Kleinchen's mother prepared for us. We were too hungry to be choosy, so we just gorged ourselves. Just as Lauritz began to play his recordings, the German cuisine began to affect us, and we took turns at the several bathrooms in the house. Even during these sojourns we weren't deprived of Lauritz' voice—he had loudspeakers installed in the bathrooms too. We heard him in songs from his films, "Vesti la giubba" among others. It didn't suit Lauritz' Wagnerian voice at all.

The ordeal—the food, not Lauritz' singing—wore out all three of us. We were so sick we could hardly move. It didn't matter so much to me because I didn't have to sing the next day, but poor Dorothy and Jussi did. In spite of this adverse culinary experience, their *Bohème* at the Shrine Auditorium before 6000 people was an unqualified success. Jussi's "Che gelida manina" stopped the show, and Francesco Valentino, the Marcello of the evening, remembered his high C for decades.[3]

We too thought the performance went exceedingly well—until we read Isabel Morse Jones' review: "Bjorling attained his best moments in the second act. There was too much orchestra for him to dominate in the first and the fact that he has gained weight immoderately has not helped his breathing. The audience was captivated by his arias and he had more applause than the others but Puccini, the composer, was really the man they were applauding."[4] How a slimmed-down Jussi could appear to have gained weight "immoderately" on wartime rationing, and what breathing problems he could possibly have had remained a mystery. We consoled ourselves with the knowledge that Dorothy's "loud voice [was] well managed," as Jones put it. In stark contrast, another review proclaimed that Jussi's return "caused the future to look darker for other tenors."

> With matchless vocal equipment, he is not content to be a mere sound producing mechanism. His Rodolfo was played in his mind as well as in his voice, and there was sensitiveness in his portrayal. . . . True, he occasionally holds up proceedings for the sake of a high note, but why not? It is a quarter of a century since we have heard a tenor's tones swell and pulsate as Bjoerling's do. Any time he wants to linger over a high note, I'll wait for him.[5]

After the performance we were invited to the home of Ingrid Bergman and her husband, Dr. Petter Aron Lindström, in Beverly Hills' Benedict Canyon. It was a typically Swedish place, with an enormous fireplace in the giant living room and the scent of roses wafting in from their beautiful garden. Jussi knew Ingrid through Björn Forsell, and even though this was the first time I met her, it was like greeting an old childhood friend. Our fathers had both sung with The Swedes and had shared an artists' studio; in fact, I had been painted by Ingrid's father, Justus Bergman. When Uncle Justus later switched to photography to earn a better living, he displayed my picture in his showcase on Strandvägen. Justus Bergman too had dreams that his daughter would get into opera, but Ingrid chose dramatic arts and thus we never became classmates. But I had met Petter, a dentist, as his patient. He was a great lover of music.

We left the California sunshine for the cold and windy New York City of late November. For the first time, Jussi was engaged for a radio concert on the *Voice of Firestone*. Richard Crooks had been the star of this program, but he now found it hard to go on with his career because of health problems; with a gallant gesture and a warm recommendation, Richard turned over his place to Jussi, another example of the singular generosity between colleagues that made us feel so at home in America. After a time Richard and his wife, Mildred, became our best friends.

What's more, Richard had brought us together with his gifted accompanist, Frederick Schauwecker. He was the vocal coach of the Chicago Musical College, and during his distinguished career he accompanied many other world-class singers, among them Claire Dux, Ninon Vallin, and Giovanni Martinelli. Freddie had just finished a spring tour with Richard when Coppicus approached him on our behalf. We met for lunch, and the rapport between the two men was instant. Freddie became Jussi's permanent accompanist in America and a friend for life. We asked him to join us for European recitals too, but he preferred to spend summers in the United States with other musical activities.

Years later, when Freddie was asked in an interview how they prepared for recitals, he said that Jussi "loathed rehearsals, but he didn't really need much preparation. Neither did I, for that matter. Outside of having to learn some Scandinavian songs for him, I had no problem."[6] Freddie was a superb musician, with the instincts of a born accompanist who could well support a soloist. As for Jussi, he would vocalize in his hotel or dressing room before a recital, and that was all he needed. "I never knew him to forget a line," remembered Freddie. "In fall of 1945 he sang . . . some joint recitals in Los Angeles with Dorothy Kirsten, plus a performance of *La bohème*. I asked him if he wanted to go over the role, as he'd sung no excerpts from it on the tour, but he said no. He didn't even have the score with him! He just walked into the rehearsal cold."[7] It's true. He sang the role note perfect.

Although Jussi usually sang his repertoire without transposition, a tight schedule and the vagaries of travel made him tired at times. On these occasions he worked out a code with Schauwecker. Borrowing a phrase from Scarpia Jussi would say "da Palmieri," which meant they performed the piece a semitone down; the original key was *simulata*.

❉

The arrangements for Jussi's renewed association with the Metropolitan Opera had been worked out without difficulty; his contract for the 1945–46 season called for seven performances at a fee of $650 each, with the management retaining a five-performance option for the post-season tour at $700 per performance. His roles were to be Riccardo, Rodolfo, Duke of Mantua, Cavaradossi, Faust, and Roméo. Three others—Radamès, Don Alvaro, and Manrico—were also listed but crossed out by mutual agreement. The only restriction imposed by the contract was that it specifically prohibited him from appearing in opera in the designated tour cities.

Jussi returned to the Met in *Rigoletto*, on 29 November 1945. The third performance, one month later to the day, was broadcast on the radio under Texaco's sponsorship. A young Leonard Warren delivered an excellent Rigoletto, and Bidú Sayão was a sweet, girlish Gilda. Around this time Jussi was advised to curl his hair with a curling iron, to make him look more "romantic." His hair was straight, without a ripple, so he did. We all hated it, himself included. Some of his surviving publicity photos as the Duke and Rodolfo sport the unnatural Björling curls.

On 5 December 1945, Jussi sang Mario Cavaradossi in his first Metropolitan *Tosca* with Lawrence Tibbett as Scarpia and Grace Moore in the title role. Grace and Jussi had admired each other ever since they sang together at Carnegie Hall in 1937. Jussi was so young when he became a leading tenor that his partners were often older than he was; the ageless Grace was 12 years his senior, but she was still in top form, both in voice and looks. Moreover, she showed us the same warm-hearted kindness as Richard Crooks. As a welcoming gesture, Grace hung a big Christmas wreath on the door of Jussi's dressing room and placed a bouquet in Swedish colors on his makeup table, complete with little American and Swedish flags.

Gracie was very beautiful, successful as a singer and as a movie actress,[8] and she was known for her steamy love affairs with practically every tenor with whom she sang. She didn't care the least whether they were married, nor did some of the tenors; this appetite for men made her known in music circles as "Crazy Moore." Her attentions made me uneasy in the beginning, but it was soon obvious that this was unnecessary. She wasn't intent on adding Jussi to her tenor conquests, and we became the best of friends. "Your Anna-Lisa is the first tenor-wife I've really liked!" she told Jussi.

Grace Moore's art of seduction wasn't limited to tenors. Once we and some of the other singers were sitting together in the lounge car of the Metropolitan's touring train, and the conversation turned to love affairs. True to the rumors, "Crazy Moore" interrupted, "Oh, Latin lovers really are the best—" At that very moment Ezio Pinza, who was equally renowned for his sexual escapades, stuck his head through the door; devoted to self-promotion, he bragged far and wide about his conquests and his capacity as a lover. Without losing a beat, Grace continued in the same breath, "—except for that one! He just goes zip, zip, zip, and leaves you in the cold!"

I've never seen someone beat a hastier retreat than Pinza. We'd heard that some time before Ezio had moved in with Grace, but after just one week she called off the arrangement and threw him out. Apparently Pinza didn't live up to his reputation or Grace's expectations.

The 5 December 1945 *Tosca* was a big success for the whole cast. The audience responded enthusiastically, throwing heaps of flowers on the stage. It was easy to be a persuasive Cavaradossi to Grace's radiantly beautiful Tosca. Grace had a fantastic glow, her own special aura, and she looked the part, for she always chose costumes that accented her features and complexion. With her excellent sense of timing, the interplay between her and Jussi was natural and compelling. They both had a certain dignity, and they created a harmonious balance between their complementary personalities.

On 15 December we attended Robert Merrill's debut as the elder Germont in *La traviata*. Impressed by his exceptionally beautiful and well-produced voice, we visited him after the performance; he was a nice young man and apparently very pleased that Björling was in the audience. "Anna-Lisa and Jussi came backstage, and they were both very sweet. He said 'Some day I would like to sing with you.'"[9] Merrill later summed up his first impressions of us: Jussi was a "stocky bull of a man with the face of a choirboy; he was buoyant, gracious, and married to one of the most beautiful women in Sweden."[10] The compliment to me may be overly kind, but I take it.

When Christmas Eve rolled around, we celebrated with our operatic fellow Swedes Torsten Ralf and Karin Branzell at her New York home. We were grateful to be able to spend the holiday in Swedish surroundings, but it was small compensation for being away from our own family for the first time in five years. Jussi and I recorded Christmas greetings to be broadcast on the traditional radio program from America to Swedish listeners. He added a few words to the family, and weeks later we received from my mother pathetic photographs of the children's Christmas celebration, which made us feel worse than ever. It nearly broke our hearts to see our brood like a bunch of orphans.

On 8 January 1946, Jussi went with the company to Philadelphia. Stella Roman was to have sung the title role in *Tosca*, but she was indisposed, and a very young Regina Resnik, in her assumption of the role, stepped in to save the performance. On the train ride to Philadelphia she talked to Jussi.

> He was very kind, very sweet. I was quite aware of my good fortune and who my partners were. In one sense I was afraid, in another I was very proud. I always felt the greater the people who sing with you, the greater your performance. I wasn't nervous; I was very well prepared, and I wanted to sing Tosca.
>
> In any case, this *Tosca* was a landmark for me, one of the great experiences of my life. I remember standing onstage in the first-act duet with Björling, and nobody would ever convince me that I wasn't in love with

him and jealous of the portrait he was painting. I was aware that every moment onstage with him was an honor.

Then I remember also Lawrence Tibbett as Scarpia. Although he was on the edge of his decline, his was a presence that gave one the inspiration to act as well. It was a very interesting performance. I realized while it was happening that I had a great actor who was no longer at the top of his career vocally, but who was handing me Act II as an actress on a platter; and I had the greatest living tenor in the world singing Acts I and III with me and giving me all his support vocally. So the inspiration was in a way more than one could bear—overwhelming! I realized then, singing with these artists, that I wasn't even beginning to tap my resources. I was getting the kind of lesson nobody could pay for.[11]

*Tosca* was repeated in the house, and then we set out on a rather long tour, beginning with a return engagement to the *Ford Sunday Evening Hour* in Detroit, conducted by Eugene Ormandy. Next it was Canada, where Jussi appeared on 15 January 1946 at Quebec City's Palais Montcalm, with Schauwecker at the piano. The local newspaper reported, "The Bjoerling voice has a full tenor range, capable of a floating *pianissimo* and a ringing top that spins and shines in brilliance. . . . It is the voice of a musician, used with flawless taste, yet it has the priceless quality of exuberant excitement."[12]

At the next stop, Toronto's Eaton Auditorium, Schauwecker and Jussi shared the platform with the Russian violinist Henri Temianka in two recitals, on 17 and 19 January. Edward W. Wodson's review, "Swedish Tenor Recalls Caruso by Clear Tone," invoked the usual comparison:

He sang as only Caruso used to sing. He is shorter than Caruso, thickset with broad shoulders and deep chest. He stood exactly as Caruso used to stand on the concert platform. As it was with Caruso, so it was with him. He never seemed to breathe. Long, glorious notes—florid passages— wide-ranging intervals—torrents of passionate words—there was no hint [of] faltering tone. He sang through two full octaves—from C to C—and his face as he sang was a living mirror of his song.[13]

We returned to New York for a *Voice of Firestone* radio concert on 21 January, where Jussi shared the microphone with another young soprano, Eleanor Steber. Then, after many stops in the South, Midwest, Canada, and California, we landed in Cuba where Jussi was to give two concerts on 2 and 4 April 1946. I was expecting again, and perhaps exhausted by the strain of travel, I had a miscarriage in Havana.

Everyone in the hospital spoke only Spanish; I couldn't make myself understood and felt very uncomfortable. Jussi was occupied with his obligations, and I had nothing to do but lie in bed. To pass the time, I read over and over again the itinerary for the remainder of the tour and added up the miles we had already traveled by train and plane during our concert tours in the United States and Canada. The total distance would stretch twice around the earth.

It was dreadfully hot in Havana that spring, especially for Swedes. Air conditioning was a thing of the future, and poor Jussi was ready to collapse, singing dressed in tails and starched shirt. As I lay in my hospital bed with the sheets clinging to my body, I listened to him describe how drenched with sweat his tails had been by the end of both concerts. People who read about "triumphant concert tours" picture the artist whisked around in the lap of luxury, protected from heat and cold, rain and sleet. They couldn't possibly imagine what a performer, even a well-paid and well-known artist, had to go through in those days to deliver the goods.

# Chapter 13

# ROMÉO AT THE MET

My hospitalization was relatively brief, and when we flew back to New York I was still so weak that I had to be carried onto the plane. But luckily, Jussi never had to cancel a single appearance for my sake. A short stay in New York was followed by the Met tour, various recitals, and a final Carnegie Hall engagement, a Scandinavian pops concert with other artists.

After Cuba, I began to think things over. Was it absolutely necessary to rove about like this from one end of the United States to the other—and back again? We would board a plane in Miami in summer clothes and sandals and fly directly to a snowstorm in Toronto, then travel south again to the spring slosh of New York. It was an enormous strain for Jussi's sensitive throat. He constantly risked sickness and forced inactivity. In addition, the interclimatic travel was dreadfully cumbersome. It meant having to carry extra luggage, accompanied by eternal unpacking and repacking.

*Oh well*, I thought, *this is how it has to be*. There's no telling how long a human voice will last, and a singer's old age pension comes from his lifetime earnings. Never forgetting the insecurities of his childhood, Jussi wanted to accept as many engagements as he could in order to be able to set aside money for our own and for our children's future. If something were to happen to his voice or to us, he reasoned, with sufficient savings their welfare and education would be secure.

So, we didn't protest. We followed the illogically conceived zig-zag tour itinerary for some time. It was our good friend Lawrence Tibbett who finally set us straight and solved our problem. Larry was an old hand at this game. When we mentioned our exhausting travels, he asked us to bring along our schedule the next time we came to dinner. We did, and when he saw it, his mouth stiffened beneath his elegant little mustache.

"What's this?" he exclaimed. "I thought I knew every little hole in this country, but where is Lake Charles? Where's Edinburg? And here—this is outright swampland! What are you doing there?" He then asked Jussi what fees he received. Larry shook his head when he heard the amount. "Now I understand. They're using you as bait, and they don't even pay you for it!" He explained that Jussi's name was exploited to sell an entire concert package. "If you want Björling, you must take Miss So-and-So!" The gimmick worked, but at Jussi's expense, physically and materially.

"It doesn't have to be like this!" Larry said determinedly. He explained how we should handle matters and even gave us a few pointers on how to negotiate with our manager. Jussi hated to bargain about himself; he had yet to learn to make demands and he didn't like confrontations. It took him some time to understand that he was a highly marketable commodity, that if he didn't assert himself, those who "traded in Björling" were only using him.

So I took it upon myself to go to Columbia Concerts. While we occasionally dealt with Francis C. Coppicus, it was mostly Frederick C. Schang who handled the Björling account. This was our first season with the partners, and we were still at the Mr. Schang–Mr. Björling stage of the relationship. Schang regarded Jussi as just another money machine in the large stable of first-class singers who brought in his profits.

Armed with Larry's thorough instructions, I went up to the Columbia Concerts office and asked to speak with Mr. Schang. When I entered, Schang was sitting with a cigar in his mouth and his feet on his desk—the very image of an American impresario straight out of a B movie. He gave me a brief greeting but didn't budge, as if signaling that I wasn't *the tenor*, only his wife. I was already upset, but at the sight of him I became angry. At the very least he could've taken his feet off the desk!

I then did exactly what Larry said to do. For the first time in my life I used both lies and blackmail. Knowing that it was impossible for him to question the competition to verify my story without jeopardizing his own position, I felt fairly secure with my fib. "Well, Mr. Schang," I began, "We have to talk business. I'm sorry to tell you that Jussi has received an offer from—" and I named a rival agency. "I must also tell you that we've been made aware of how you've been milking us the whole time."

Schang's feet came off the desk in a hurry! We negotiated—or rather renegotiated—fees, schedules, expense allowances. I demanded, Schang squirmed, but I held firm. Jussi and I had been too innocent for too long. Thanks to Larry Tibbett, I understood how American business deals were made. "Give me a moment, let me think," Schang said. He thought it over and then gave in. "OK, you can have the fee you ask." It was simple. Schang couldn't afford to lose Jussi Björling to the competition. It may have been a Hobson's choice, but it was a wise one. The only thing open to him was compromise.

From this time on, we weeded out the remote places on tour and tried to maintain a logical geographical progression, as much as local concert seasons allowed. If it hadn't been for Tibbett, I don't know how much longer we would've roamed back and forth willy-nilly for inadequate fees. Larry only reinforced our image of the typical American—warm, kindhearted, thoughtful, and not the least jealous. As for Schang, it didn't take long for the business relationship to blossom into friendship, and he remained Jussi's American manager for the rest of Jussi's life.

Born in Manhattan in 1893, Schang graduated from Columbia University's Graduate School of Journalism in 1915 and worked as a reporter for the *New York Tribune*. His long experience as impresario of the world's great artists began when he handled some of Enrico Caruso's bookings. He was cofounder and president of Columbia Concerts, Inc., which through his efforts and the hard work of his associates, under the new name of Columbia Artists Management, Inc. (CAMI), eventually became the world's largest concert agency.

Schang was a wonderful person, with a mischievous gleam in his eyes, a hoarse voice, and a tireless gift of gab. Over time, Mr. Schang became Freddie to us and one of our most faithful friends. During the summer of 1987, he came to visit me in Sweden. His mind was still sharp, and he entertained an entire dinner party with his stories. When he left this earth in 1990 at age 96, a significant part of American musical history went with him.

※

During the Met tour in April 1946, Jussi sang for the first time with Licia Albanese, in a *Bohème* in Cleveland. In years to come, Jussi and Licia sang together many times. Their voices and temperament blended well, and because they were the same height, they looked well together onstage.

In Minneapolis, Jussi repeated his Rodolfo with Dorothy Kirsten. He also sang concerts with Eugene Ormandy in Ann Arbor and a *Ford Sunday Evening Hour* in Detroit with Fritz Reiner. But if I had to single out one occasion as particularly memorable, I would choose the 9 May 1946 recital in Montreal. One reviewer pointed out that although this was Jussi's first visit to the city, thanks to his recordings, the house was packed with "young people with strong hands and loud voices . . . and they made ample use of both."[1] In terrific form, Jussi offered a veritable songfest: in addition to pieces by Beethoven, Schubert, Strauss, Tosti, and Leoncavallo, he sang his beloved "Ingemisco," "Addio alla madre" from *Cavalleria rusticana*, "Ch'ella mi creda" from *La fanciulla del West*, the Flower Song from *Carmen*, "La rêve" from *Manon*, "Che gelida manina," "La donna è mobile,"

169

and "Vesti la giubba." The youthful audience nearly lost control, and Jussi enjoyed their response even more than usual.

※

We returned home in late May. Jussi rested for the better part of June and July, then in August he finally made his debut not *at* but *with* La Scala in Milan. The theater itself had suffered damage in a British air raid in August 1943 and was still under reconstruction, so the performances were held at the Palazzo dello Sport.

Although it was a short engagement, I couldn't miss Jussi's Milan debut, so we traveled to Italy together. He sang three performances of *Rigoletto* on 20, 22, and 24 August 1946, with Carlo Tagliabue, Lina Aimaro-Bertasi, and Cesare Siepi making his La Scala debut as Sparafucile. After one of the performances John Gualiani and Leonard Maggett, a South African tenor, went backstage to meet Jussi. "What do the Milanese think of my Duke?" he asked his visitors. "They think you have a lovely voice and you sing well, but your singing is cold." "Well, that is understandable," Jussi replied, "I come from a very cold country!"[2]

While we were still in America, *Svenska Dagbladet* (29 March 1946) had carried the announcement that Jussi was to sing in Australia. Jussi discussed the matter with Enwall and decided he didn't want to travel so far. "Maybe later," he said. Instead, he returned to the Royal Opera in September for three performances, then at the end of the month we sailed again for the United States aboard the Swedish America liner *Gripsholm*.

Four days after our arrival on 1 October, Jussi made his triumphant return to Chicago. In *Rigoletto* "his voice was as fresh and gleaming as if he had done nothing but polish it those six seasons the war forcibly separated him from our opera," wrote one reviewer of his Duke.[3] Dorothy Kirsten, his partner in *La bohème*, departed from tradition and performed the role without a wig, thus turning brunette Mimì into a ravishing blonde. The critical verdict here? "Vocally, of course, the evening was Bjoerling's. . . . His voice isn't the Caruso size that record [of 'Che gelida manina'] led many to believe, but it is pure and shining and it has an exceptionally lovely quality, a Nordic veil of beauty in its own way like the poetic radiance that makes Melchior great and made Flagstad beloved."[4]

After Chicago it was San Francisco Opera, for Rodolfo, Manrico, and Roméo, and a series of recitals. During one of our stops in Los Angeles this autumn we visited Swedish actress Viveca Lindfors on the set of her current Hollywood project, *Night Unto Night*. "Who is your leading man?" we asked. "His name is Ronald Reagan," Viveca answered. "He really isn't very good, and I don't think he enjoys being an actor. But you know how it is; I have to be grateful for the films I can get." Viveca's opinion was later validated by the reviews.[5] I also remember meeting other movie stars, among them Irene Dunne, Van Johnson, Joan Crawford, Tyrone Power, and especially Errol Flynn, as handsome in real life as on the silver screen. I felt sorry for him when Jussi beat him at arm wrestling.

We had been at home with the children only four months this year, and now Christmas 1946 was approaching, the second year in a row we would face it an ocean away from home. Jussi could take it no longer. He called my mother. "Get passports for all of you—please come over with the children!" Mother arranged for the passports, but to get their visas, the children had to go to the United States embassy in Stockholm. There they were led into a big room, where they were made to swear they wouldn't plot to overthrow the United States government or engage in prostitution. Anders, aged ten, Lasse seven, and Ann-Charlotte three, promised under oath to lead a clean and virtuous life while in America.

It was their first trip abroad, and the view of Manhattan from New York harbor was unlike anything they'd ever seen. Electricity in Sweden was still strictly rationed, and quite apart from the immensity of the impressive sky-line, the city, aglow with Christmas lights in the December twilight, seemed a fairyland.

Jussi was even more excited about the usual tourist sights than the children. In his eagerness, he wanted them to see everything of New York, from the Empire State Building and the glittering Radio City Music Hall to his own place of work, the Metropolitan Opera. He and the children spent countless hours roaming the Central Park Zoo and the Bronx Zoo, and we also visited the Statue of Liberty, all the way to the top of the torch in her mighty outstretched arm, even though Jussi was to sing that evening. Most singers would've postponed a trip in the raw sea air to a day when they didn't have a performance, but Jussi wanted to cheer up Anders, who some days earlier had scalded his leg with boiling water while we were making tea in our hotel kitchenette. His leg still hurt and his knee was stiff from the bandages; it was hard for him to go up the steep spiral staircase, and he had even greater difficulty descending. But Jussi was so happy to see our children, he couldn't do enough for them. He backed down the statue's narrow iron staircase, helping his son with every step. A few hours later 3000 people would gather to hear him sing, but he didn't care: his main concern was to please the children and to keep Anders' mind off his burn.

The *Faust* on 23 December was the beginning of a professional collaboration and a lasting friendship with Robert Merrill, who recalled his Swedish colleague fondly:

> [He was] tremendously stimulating and a very musical singer, a joy and an inspiration to work with. Many times I was so bewitched by his golden timbre that I almost lost control. Jussi had the most natural tone formation I'd ever heard. He never forced, or made grimaces when he sang. His mouth was usually held closed, like an O, even on the high notes. Most singers I've known usually open their mouths a trifle for the high notes, but not Jussi; he bent his head back slightly and click! There was a high C without the least effort. I don't think he could ever sing an ugly note.[6]

To celebrate Christmas, we bought a little tree and decorated it and our room at the Hotel Windsor, using the decorations my mother brought from Sweden. For Christmas Eve we were invited to the home of Lennart Nylander, the Swedish consul-general. We adults had a pleasant evening, and the children were loaded down with presents. The boys received cowboy outfits, and poor little Ann-Charlotte was stalked, lassoed, imprisoned, and tied up. Lasse, a rascal of perpetual motion, and Jussi, a willing playmate, initiated many a violent pillow fight, until the feathers flew about the room like snow. A tip to the maid and restitution for the pillows usually restored order.

The children had a wonderful time and overstayed their vacation, giving them a chance to see their father at the Met. They all visited backstage on 19 December 1946 and on 15 January 1947 the boys attended the first of Jussi's two Roméos at the Met. With Bidú Sayão as his adorable Juliette, Gounod himself couldn't have wished for better interpreters. Bidú and Jussi were ideally matched vocally and visually and seemed to possess a special chemistry. Bidú remembers,

> Sometimes they said he wasn't a good actor, but with me he was, because I was really in love with him on the stage. He was such a warm and kind man, and he had this boyish personality—it was so easy to be very amorous with him. It was a great pleasure for me to sing with him. He had the kind of voice that could manage lyric or dramatic roles. My voice was small, a lyric coloratura soprano, but when he sang Roméo or *La bohème* with me, he wouldn't reduce his sound but sing with extreme delicacy never to cover my voice. In the act where Roméo has a very dramatic moment with the high Cs he sounded like a real dramatic tenor, and the voice had unbelievable beauty.[7]

The performance went especially well and the audience was most receptive. But we learned from Noel Straus' review in *The New York Times* (16 January 1947) that Jussi didn't have "Gallic refinement and finesse" in the same measure as Bidú, who "made the deeper impression." That was entirely possible, but Straus went on to complain about Jussi's "tendency to employ power, instead of refining the tones, that kept the tenor's account of the important aria 'Ah, lève-toi, soleil,' from reaching the heights it might otherwise easily have scaled. . . . His voice blended well with that of Miss Sayão, and with greater attention to the sort of vocalism this French opera requires, he would have made a more memorable Roméo than proved the case."

Fortunately, the second performance on 1 February 1947 was broadcast, recorded off-the-air, and released repeatedly on LP and CD. Reviewing one of its vinyl incarnations issued by the Metropolitan Opera Guild, Peter G. Davis wrote, "Bjoerling is in especially magnificent form, positively reveling in a voice that sounded never less than glorious, even on off days."[8] Conrad L. Osborne was even more enthusiastic:

> [A] state-of-grace performance, one of those in which a superb singer is caught at his absolute peak in a role perfect for his voice. . . . [I] regard it

as the finest singing of a complete romantic tenor role, beginning to end, I've ever heard. . . . The voice's perfect registral balance, almost implausibly poised on the fulcrum of the break; the purity of the vowels, even on the most difficult combinations of pitch and dynamic; the free-flowing legato and unvarying vibrato pattern allied to an excellent capacity for floridity—the combination of these factors is found in Bjoerling's singing at (to risk understating the matter) a once-in-a-generation level.[9]

We usually read the reviews—sometimes I even read them aloud to Jussi—knowing that one couldn't just relish praise and ignore censure. He enjoyed the good critiques, and because the unfavorable ones were so few and far between, he paid special heed to valid, well-intentioned criticism. When the adverse comments were on target, he made an effort to correct and eliminate the fault. But at times critics were so wide of the mark, it was useless to be angry or upset, and we could only laugh at their incompetence.

Only a few months before, on 26 October 1946, Jussi deservedly received a lukewarm review after his Manrico at the Shrine Auditorium. He didn't feel well that day, but his reaction was quintessential Jussi: "I'll show them I'm still one hell of a tenor!" Three days later, his Rodolfo was something exceptional, even by his own standards. "This time he sang like a God. This time he was really at his best!" remembered his friend Kjellertz—and so do I.[10]

※

On this New York trip, we would go backstage to meet and greet the artists and, quite frankly, to show off our children. To my surprise, Blanche Thebom, our compatriot by ancestry, still remembers these visits.

> Inasmuch as my parents were Swedish-born and I had been decorated by the queen with the Royal Order of Vasa, [Jussi] was always most cordial and friendly. I found him to be warm, with easy laughter, a man of real presence and style. I remember specifically his bringing his two handsome young sons to be introduced; they were models of correctness in demeanor. They were also beautiful in their black velvet suits—they looked like royalty's children in a painting.[11]

What stands out in the boys' memory, however, is meeting Bidú Sayão. The Brazilian beauty didn't have any children, and with her passionate Latin temperament she went into ecstasies over our sons. The boys still speak of their desperate attempts to dodge her exuberant kisses in the dressing room. They were much too young to appreciate them.

It's noteworthy that Jussi delivered such a fine performance on 1 February because we were still shaken by the previous week's tragedy. On Sunday, 26 January 1947, we were at the Melchiors' apartment for dinner. As theater folks who rise late and stay up late, we talked till way past midnight. When we went home to our hotel in the early morning hours, we heard the paperboys shouting: "Grace Moore is dead!"

A DC-3 had crashed within minutes of takeoff from Copenhagen's Kastrup Airport, and all 22 people aboard perished, among them Prince Gustaf Adolf, heir to the Swedish throne, traveling incognito. The prince had been hunting in the Netherlands at the invitation of Queen Juliana and Prince Bernard, and as a special courtesy, the queen had arranged for a retired KLM chief pilot to fly the party home. Grace no doubt considered it an honor to be allowed to travel with them. It seems that the pilot failed to position the flaps properly on takeoff. Sweden lost a future king, and opera lost a reigning queen.[12]

# Chapter 14

# Mimì Takes a Bow

My mother and the children flew home, and Jussi and I began our spring tour to the West Coast and back. In New York, Jussi was happy to renew his acquaintance with Giuseppe de Luca, who had just returned to America. He and Jussi went to the Mecca Temple to see *Rigoletto* with Giuseppe Valdengo, who wrote,

> According to my diaries, I first met Jussi Björling on 13 April 1947, when he came to see me after the performance in the company of Giuseppe de Luca. The meeting was most cordial, and he was very complimentary about my performance and the color of my voice. Björling was always helpful; he explained to me that one should breathe high in chest and [later] when we sang together, he would sometimes point to his diaphragm to remind me to keep the breath high. He became really angry when he heard once that a singing teacher advised that the sound should sink toward the abdomen. "Jackass!" he exclaimed. "That is the perfect way to ruin the voice!"[1]

Valdengo's recollections confirm Jussi's attitude toward voice teachers. Jussi knew what good teaching was and therefore harbored a deep distrust against voice teachers in general:

> I myself could never be a voice teacher. It demands a special gift. When one teaches the art of singing, there's nothing concrete to hold onto. Something abstract, something unreal, must be transmitted by the teacher to the

175

student. My father had this advice for us: "When a note is perfect, it should lay and vibrate like a metal ball suspended on top of a water fountain." . . . My father also made certain that we never sang anything that didn't suit our voices—that was perhaps his foremost contribution to our future.[2]

✳

I flew home to Sweden, and Jussi sailed on the Cunard liner *Queen Elizabeth* for a series of appearances in England. But they never took place; the mammoth ship ran aground off Southampton and the concerts were rescheduled for September. Meanwhile Jussi had his much needed vacation on Siarö, studying his song and Lieder repertoire with Wilhelm Freund, who was a frequent working guest on the island. Freund was an excellent pianist, a great expert of Lieder, and a permanent coach at the Opera House; in later years he taught Lieder singing at the Music Academy. While he stayed with us, he coached me too.

Freund was a vegetarian and a health food addict. He jogged early every morning, and afterward would lie in the sun on the dock. Once Jussi discovered him lying there naked and got very angry. "How can you do this? Ann-Charlotte could come along!" But Freund, at least, went down to the relative privacy of the water's edge to sunbathe. Our large, stocky Finnish maid, Hille, would strip naked in the morning before we rose and soak up the warm rays only a few feet from the house. One morning Jussi looked out the bedroom window and came face to face—figuratively—with Hille's more than ample charms, spread out on the grass below. He shook me awake, quite alarmed. "Anna-Lisa, come quick! Get Hille away from there before the boys wake up, or they'll never get married!"

In addition to the usual summer engagements, Jussi gave another benefit recital on nearby Ljusterö, joined by Hugo Theorell. It is traditional for every Swedish church to have a crown for brides to wear in wedding services; the quality of workmanship and the cost of the crown reflect upon the congregation. The Ljusterö church didn't yet have one, and Jussi was ready to see that it did. The little hall was too small for their audience, so the doors were thrown wide open to let the music reach everyone standing in the grounds and surrounding meadows. The concert was so successful that from this time on it became an annual event.

Jussi was always available for a good cause. They needed fire protection equipment or a new roof for the community center on Ljusterö? "I'll just yell some more," he'd say and raise the money. At the next recital under the new roof, so many people crowded into the wooden structure that the floor collapsed, so Jussi had to "yell some more" to pay for a new floor. He enjoyed the relaxed atmosphere and the intimate proximity of his audience. When Professor Theorell won the 1955 Nobel Prize in medicine, a famous tenor and a Nobel laureate donating their services made these informal musical events that much more special.

The Duke of Mantua with his wife, 1945.

As the Duke in *Rigoletto* at the Met.

Swedish tenor exports to America: Torsten Ralf and Jussi Björling, with Anna-Lisa, aboard the S.S. *Drottningholm*, May 1946.

Anna-Lisa and Jussi in front of the
*locandina*, La Scala, August 1946.

JB as the Duke of Mantua at his
La Scala debut, 1946.

Anna-Lisa and
mother Emy with
Lasse and Anders
in Edward
Johnson's box,
waiting for the
curtain to rise on
*Roméo et Juliette*,
15 January 1947.

The Björlings and Johnson in Bidú Sayão's dressing room following the performance.

Set Svanholm as Walther von Stolzing, Anna-Lisa, and Jussi on the 25th anniversary of the Opera Soloist Club, November 1947. Photo A. B. Text & Bilder.

Edward Johnson, Amelita Galli-Curci, and JB after the Met's *Trovatore*,
Los Angeles, 16 April 1948. Photo Otto Rothschild.

Jussi and Anna-Lisa saying goodbye to Edward Johnson
at Bromma Airport following his visit to Stockholm and
Siarö, July 1948. Photo Dagens Nyheter.

Anna-Lisa singing with Jussi at Skansen, 4 August 1948.

Anna-Lisa as Mimì at her opera debut, Stockholm, 30 August 1948. Photo Järlås.

Jussi, Anna-Lisa, and Folke Bernadotte following her successful debut in *La bohème*. Photo Stockholms-Tidningen.

Uphill hike in San Francisco, 1948.

Anna-Lisa Björling, publicity still.
Photo Maurice Seymour.

As Faust at the Metropolitan.

A curly-haired Rodolfo at the Met.

Jussi signing autographs in his dressing room at the Met as a wide-eyed Ann-Charlotte looks on, 25 December 1948. Photo Einar Thulin.

Edward Johnson with the Björlings after the Christmas Day 1948 *La bohème*. Photo Einar Thulin.

Pike's Enemy Number One and Ann-Charlotte, just slightly taller than her father's latest catch.

Jussi and Nils Grevillius at the artists' entrance of the Royal Opera, Stockholm.

Posing with leis and ukulele, Hawaii, 1949.

As Des Grieux, 1949. Photo Enar
Merkel Rydberg.

At home at Nybrogatan 64.
Photo Järlås.

Jussi and Anna-Lisa, Houston,
21 February 1949.

No one was more amused by Uno
Stallarholms wickedly funny
caricature than Jussi himself!

Rudolf Bing, of whom Cyril Ritchard cautioned, "Don't be misled—behind that cold, austere, severe exterior there beats a heart of stone." Courtesy Metropolitan Opera Archives.

Robert Merrill as Rodrigo and JB as Carlo in *Don Carlo*, which opened Bing's inaugural season at the Met, November 1950.

JB as Otello and Merrill as Iago in a publicity shot for their *Otello* duet.
Photo Bruno.

Dorothy Caruso inscribes a photograph of her late husband, Enrico, while Jussi, wearing the doublet her husband wore as the Duke in *Rigoletto*, looks on, 1951.

Jussi in front of La Scala, May 1951.

As Riccardo in *Un ballo in maschera*, La Scala, May 1951.

"To the genius, the great singer, Jussi Björling, with gratitude, Jean Sibelius." Photo Fred Runeberg.

Anna-Lisa as Juliette receiving a post-performance kiss from Roméo following her North American opera debut, San Francisco, 27 September 1951. Photo Paul C. Tracy.

Cheerful bohemians George Cehanovsky (Schaunard), JB (Rodolfo), and Giuseppe Valdengo (Marcello), 8 October 1951, San Francisco. Courtesy Giuseppe Valdengo.

Anna-Lisa and Jussi with Gaetano Merola at the Fol de Rol,
San Francisco, 10 October 1951.

Jussi, Olle, and Gösta in 1952.

Jussi and Hjördis Schymberg with a floral tribute from Marguerite and Axel Wenner-Gren after *La bohème*, 28 September 1953. Photo Enar Merkel Rydberg.

Anna-Lisa adjusting Faust's tie before the Met's season opener, 16 November 1953. Photo Einar Thulin.

Faust in tails. Photo Sedge Le Blang.

Basso Nicola Rossi-Lemeni in top hat and tails as Gounod's Devil. Photo Sedge Le Blang.

"To Jussi Björling
with all my best
wishes, Arturo
Toscanini."

Anders with his parents at his graduation from Sigtuna, 1954. Photo Sven Braf.

Apart from his scientific work and violinist's skills, Hugo Theorell was the only man who was Jussi's equal at arm wrestling. When he was three years old, Theorell's legs were paralyzed by polio, but his arms were so strong that he could walk on his hands with ease. When Jussi and Hugo performed together, the evening would end in an arm wrestling match, a war of giants. Jussi won arm wrestling contests even against professional wrestlers. On one unfortunate occasion, locked motionless for a long time with his opponent, Jussi gave a tremendous push, breaking both bones in the man's lower arm.

Jussi's exceptional strength was a constant source of amusement and amazement. The boys remember him opening Coke bottles with his bare hand, or lifting a heavy armchair, loaded down with telephone books, into the air by the tip of its front leg. Nobody could duplicate this feat, although several of our friends tried. Jussi gleefully recalled the time he bested the macho Forsell in *Fanal*.

[I had] an enormous executioner's sword that reached to my chin, and consequently it was very heavy. John Forsell couldn't resist remarking, "Where is that sword taking Mr. Björling?" So I swung it above my head and then handed it to him. With a good deal of effort he managed to lift it. He was also quite amused by my physical strength and my reputation as an arm wrestler. Both on Stenungsön and in Stockholm he challenged people to arm wrestle with me, and if he was successful he would beam with satisfaction, because the outcome was always clear. Am I allowed to brag a little? I'm proud to say that I have never lost in arm wrestling.[3]

Jussi's passion for arm wrestling may have had something to do with the onset of his sciatica. His recurring back pain worsened, and the British tour rescheduled for September 1947 had to be postponed once more. His condition was so bad that he had to cancel his performance at the Opera. That was bad enough, but Jussi considered it an even greater catastrophe that he missed the 50th birthday celebration of his friend and colleague, baritone Einar Larson. On the day of the performance he couldn't even get out of bed.

"You must stand in for me, Anna-Lisa!" he said unexpectedly. I hardly had time to catch my breath before everything was settled. Apart from the token appearances at the Lucia celebrations, Einar Larson's birthday gala was my debut, but not my first offer for an engagement. At a party in New York, I had sung an impromptu duet with tenor Jan Kiepura, who afterward asked me to appear at his theater. Although flattered, I couldn't desert Jussi in the middle of a tour.

Einar Larson's birthday gala was different: I was actually helping Jussi by singing. The gala abounded in real celebrities, and it went very well. I received a hearty welcome from the festive audience. "What a success!" wrote *Svenska Dagbladet*. "What a voice!" It spoke of a musical sensation and of "Einar's and Anna-Lisa's big evening." *Aftontidningen*'s headline read "To Wake Up and Find Oneself Famous!" and other newspapers carried pictures of Einar and me together. Naturally, I was happy about the kind words. Such attention almost embarrassed me, but I was checked by one critic who, referring to the *Bohème* aria, thought I was a little too "suntanned and plump" to be the ideal Mimì.

But poor Jussi wasn't having much fun. On 10 October 1947 he managed to participate in an Opera Gala for the new royal couple, Ingrid and Frederik of Denmark. He sang Radamès in the Nile scene of *Aida*, and, encouraged, he sang a *Faust* on 21 October. That proved to be a mistake. Excruciating back pain forced him to stop all work. During his illness, friends and strangers called regularly to inquire after him and to offer advice. Letters from well-wishers poured in, and the newspapers carried daily bulletins on his condition. It was almost as if Jussi were a member of everybody's family.

Our family doctor, who came to see Jussi daily, was a surgeon and as surgeons are wont to do, he tried to persuade Jussi to undergo an operation, but he refused. His suffering went on for months, and the longer his condition persisted, the more concerned we all became, family, friends, and fans. Then we began to notice that among the many letters of advice we received, a name kept recurring—Tolén. He was a chiropractor on Kungsgatan, and people claimed he could perform miracles. At that time chiropractors didn't enjoy their present status. I almost didn't dare to suggest that we give it a try, but by the time I finally brought it up, Jussi was ready to try anything. With much effort I eased him into a taxi, and off we went.

"Aha!" said Mr. Tolén the minute he opened the door. "I see what the problem is!" Without an examination, Jussi's posture made the whole medical picture clear to him. He asked me to stay in the waiting room, but I couldn't resist sneaking a peek through the keyhole. I couldn't see a thing and began to have second thoughts. What had I made Jussi do? If he became an invalid for the rest of his life, it'd be all my fault! Eventually the door opened and Jussi appeared, jubilant, his whole face beaming. "The pain is gone!" It was unbelievable that only minutes ago he had been hurting so much that he couldn't walk without help. For the first time in months, he was his old self again.

"I've corrected the alignment of the vertebrae that were pinching the sciatic nerve," Mr. Tolén explained. "I'm going to send a bench to Mr. Björling, which you can keep until his spinal column stabilizes itself. I'll come to your home to give him treatments. That way he doesn't have to come here for return visits." Jussi and I were afraid of what our family doctor might say if we told him we'd gone to see a chiropractor; typical Swedes, we didn't want any confrontations, so when he made his calls, we hid the therapeutic bench. But without question, the treatment worked. Jussi was rarely troubled with his back again.

❖

When he felt better, Jussi recorded "O Paradiso" under the baton of Sixten Ehrling for the film *En svensk tiger* (*A Swedish Tiger*). After a Rodolfo and a Cavaradossi at the Opera, we left for America in early December 1947 and *our* "Luciafest" engagement in Minneapolis—my American debut and a foretaste of the many joint ventures Jussi and I would share in years to come.

We flew over from Sweden with Count and Countess Carl Johan Bernadotte. The count was born Prince Carl Johan, Duke of Dalecarlia, and was in line for the Swedish throne, but he relinquished his claim and his title when he married a commoner. That didn't prevent Jussi, an obedient Dalecarlian royalist, to address him whenever they met as "My Duke!"

The count was on friendly terms with the Kriendler brothers—Jack, Max, and Bob—who owned the famous 21 in New York City. Max Kriendler, an opera lover and an amateur singer, asked Count Bernadotte to arrange a meeting with Björling, and so the Bernadottes invited us and Set Svanholm for a late supper at 21. Max Kriendler was so excited that around 10 o'clock he asked the patrons to leave and closed the restaurant. As the evening progressed, the two tenors began to sing. They sang snippets from Swedish folk songs and drinking songs, "singing louder and higher, until the glasses on the table rattled and the chandeliers began to swing! They both wanted to sing better than the other, so you can imagine! It was pretty funny," recalls Count Bernadotte. "By the time we left around three in the morning, Max Kriendler was quite possibly treated to more erratic singing than he could stand."[4]

In the 1947–48 season, Jussi sang a cluster of performances at the Met in late December and early January. His fee rose to $800 per performance. We spent our holiday with a New York audience, in "a Christmas Day *Rigoletto* with Pons, Björling, Warren a sumptuous-sounding Rigoletto, and Székely a virtuoso Sparafucile,"[5] followed by Jussi's first Met Turiddu on New Year's Eve 1947. Although this was the only *Cavalleria rusticana* Regina Resnik ever sang with Jussi, she never forgot the occasion.

> His Turiddu was peerless. It wasn't very Sicilian—he didn't leave his blood on the stage—but the singing was incomparable! The most difficult and most ungrateful piece is the "Siciliana" behind the curtain, and nobody sang it the way he did! The tessitura is high from the start, and it's murderous. Everybody else uses it to warm up, but Jussi just sang as though it were a *romanza*. The ease with which he sang was incredible!
>
> I also remember that before the performance I said to him, "I warn you Jussi: I'm very dramatic and very violent in this part. If you don't give me what I want, I'll drag you all over the stage." So he smiled, wished me luck, and said, "Do whatever you want with me today."
>
> In this performance of *Cavalleria rusticana* I remember a Björling I was seeing onstage for the first time. Because so much was demanded of him, in this *Cavalleria* he was as great a tenor actor as any I ever sang with.[6]

In the first week of 1948 we finalized with the Met Jussi's obligations between March and May. He was to sing eight times at $850 per performance. We then began our exhausting itinerary of some 50 concerts, singing our way to San Francisco and back again to the Met, for a single *Trovatore*. During the entire tour Jussi was in glorious voice, especially so when he sang for his faithful Chicago public on 6 March 1948. Claudia Cassidy's review of this concert was fit for framing:

> It is possible that Jussi Bjoerling does not possess the most beautiful tenor in the world today. But on the basis of Saturday evening's recital in Orchestra Hall I doubt that you could prove it. The Swedish cosmopolite with the gleaming array of decorations almost outsang himself, if that is possible. The timbre of his voice was so burnished, its equilibrium so secure, that whether he cleft the operatic heavens with the sword stroke of arias that disdained transposition, gravely descended a flawless scale, or spun a perfect *pianissimo*, it was singing of a tonal splendor unique in contemporary music.

She further praised the "hint of mischief" in Schubert's "Die Forelle" and the "climactic brilliance" of "Zueignung," adding that Rachmaninoff "would have delighted in the way he sings 'In the Silence of Night.' But the fact remains that Bjoerling comes into his own in the music written in the imperishable tradition of the great operatic tenor."[7]

With our address changing almost daily, the family was unable to write to us during these cross-country tours, and as often happened when we hadn't heard from them for a long time, our longing for the children grew more intense. When we arrived in Chicago and found no letters waiting, Jussi wrote to Lasse from the Bismarck Hotel, 6 March 1948:

> We haven't heard anything from you all for so long, so I thought now I'll write to Lasse, and that will speed up the correspondence. Mama is wondering and asking all the time if we've received any letters from our little darlings. Many other letters come from Sweden, but not the ones we're waiting for. Get going now, Lasse, and be a nice guy. Ask Lillan [Ann-Charlotte] to draw a figure or anything at all, just so she holds the pencil herself. I sing here tonight, so I am alone in the hotel room, resting my throat. Mama is out shopping but will be back soon. Now it won't be long until we're home with you all again, just another three months. Just think how much fun we'll have out in the country—I finish now with the warmest greetings and a big embrace to all of you, from Papa. Lillan gets a kiss as usual. Tell Anne [Anders] that I'm waiting for an answer to my last letter.

Back in New York, on 15 March 1948 Jussi participated for the first time in NBC's *Bell Telephone Hour*, which series of radio concerts always showcased the most prestigious artists. A recital at Carnegie Hall followed, leaving us a few days' rest before we joined the Met's spring tour. Around this time Jussi went to hear Giuseppe di Stefano at the Met. He had a high regard for the young man; he liked his voice and admired his singing. After a particularly successful Des Grieux in Massenet's *Manon*, he invited Di Stefano to the hotel and asked him to repeat the stunning *filatura* from *forte* to *piano* on the A in "Le rêve." Di Stefano was happy to oblige, and as he later reported, Jussi "tried to reproduce it for hours with that voice of his, resplendent like a diamond, without success. He then challenged me with high notes, which were his specialty, and there I was beaten. But that was a private contest between us, a healthy and productive emulation and not seeking any publicity."[8]

The Met tour opened with *La bohème* in Baltimore's Lyric Theater. I was invited to sit in a box with Mr. Carle Jackson, the son of the city's former mayor, and his wife, Mrs. Jackson, the great Rosa Ponselle. During our pleasant conversation, she said that she hadn't heard a tenor voice as distinctive and shimmering as Jussi's since Caruso. But for critic Weldon Wallace, although he allowed that after "Che gelida manina" the audience "set up a demonstration for Mr. Bjoerling," Jussi "sang well within an extremely limited range of color and volume. His voice did not expand freely, and the tones showed strain in the *forte* passages, especially in the upper register." The concluding two-sentence paragraph from Wallace's inspired pen is a classic: "*La bohème* has a simple, unaffected humanity. Therefore, it is merry, and it is sad."[9]

The Met tour took us back to Los Angeles, where Regina Resnik sang her first Leonora opposite Jussi. "My memory of the performance is as clear as though it all happened two minutes ago," declares this remarkable lady:

> They had opened the cut of the little marriage duet. The stage director, Herbert Graf, seated me in my white gown for the bridal scene in front of Björling, so I was watching him very closely. He was not even a foot and a half away. I remember watching him sing the big cavatina ["Ah sì, ben mio"] to me, Leonora, with my back to the audience, looking up at him.
>
> I think that aside from my own studies, it was probably my greatest singing lesson. Suddenly certain words of great teachers and singers came to mind. I used to laugh at that a little bit. Now I tell this story to my students and to professional singers working with me. I remembered clearly reading [Manuel] Garcia, [Mathilde] Marchesi, and all the great singers— the mouth should look like a pear, producing the pear-shaped tone. I looked at Björling, and I never saw the pear disturbed. It either became larger or smaller, but the pear was always there: the rosebud of the upper part of the lip formed the top of the pear; with the upper teeth slightly visible—the mouth and the lower lip, the bottom of the pear.
>
> I say it was my greatest singing lesson: I didn't see him breathe, I didn't see his chest heave, a knee move, a shoulder move—he was so static that he could easily've been taken for being a little removed from the character. He was not intense as an actor—he was a great singer. He sang the text beautifully, his Italian was impeccable. He was an interpreter of the text because his singing and his vocal method made such a beautiful

> statement. Of course, that's completely belied in the live performance of *Manon Lescaut*. If anybody left his heart and his blood on the stage that day, it was Björling as Des Grieux! There is probably nothing as passionate I ever heard from any tenor![10]

Although Jussi was a quick study, sometimes he would flatly refuse to cooperate no matter how easy it would've been for him. One such occasion was this spring of 1948 when he was invited to participate in the May Festival in Cincinnati. The role he was asked to sing was Florestan in *Fidelio*, with Rose Bampton as Leonora and Martial Singher as Rocco. The concert staging was to be conducted by Fritz Busch.

On 20 December 1947 Freddie Schang wrote that he had spoken with the great German maestro, who wanted Jussi to sing the aria, duet, and finale of Beethoven's opera, and two days later a group of songs with orchestra lasting 20 minutes, as part of a matinee performance. Jussi was sent the score to prepare the role, but he refused to learn it.

To tell the truth, he had some justification. The performance came in the middle of the Met tour, on 4 May. Lacking time to leisurely review the role, he had to rely mainly on his memory. This was the lesser problem. The stumbling block was that this *Fidelio* was to be sung in English and Jussi knew it only in Swedish. He had sung the role four times in 1935 and was now asked to relearn it for just one appearance. *Fidelio* was not exactly a repertory piece, and it was unlikely that he'd ever be asked to sing Florestan again in English. Without some special inducement, he was unwilling to devote his time and energies to learning a part he'd have few opportunities to perform again.

Edward Johnson always called on me when he wanted Jussi to do some new assignment, greeting me with "Here comes the most welcome lady at the Met." When everyone else had tried and failed, it fell to me to persuade Jussi to change his mind. This time I too ran into a brick wall of resistance. "But Jussi! Johnson said this engagement was important and you should sing—and it's so easy for you to learn the part!" I couldn't understand how he could turn down such a prestigious invitation just because he had to master a few pages of English text. After all, Florestan's part *is* very short. His irrational stance turned my frustration into anger.

"Oh, I'm so tired of you! I think I'll just go home"—and I walked out, leaving Jussi alone so that my words would sink in. We both remembered the *Rigoletto* incident very well and by the time I returned, he was ready to give in.

"OK Morsan, run down to the drugstore and buy blue and red pencils," he sighed. (When we were alone or among family, Jussi almost always called me *Morsan*—Swedish for Mommy—Mama, or Mamichko.) I never ran so fast; there was always a chance he'd change his mind. But when I returned with pencils in hand and Jussi began to draw his little faces in the piano score, I knew the battle was won.

This was the only time Rose Bampton and Jussi sang together. "I must say I found him most congenial and socially a very nice person to be with," Rose recalls. "He came to dinner at our house one night after a perform-ance that my husband [Wilfrid Pelletier] conducted. He was charming, and he had a great sense of humor, too. He was a very real, wonderful person! People who knew him well loved him. Richard Crooks always spoke so well about him, high praise coming from another tenor!"[11]

During the *Fidelio* rehearsals an amusing incident involving Jussi's English occurred. In the Florestan-Leonora duet, when he was to sing "Day of joy and rapture," he sang "rupture." Rose started to giggle, and Maestro Busch and the musicians burst into laughter. Jussi didn't understand what the matter was, which made everything even more comical. "No, no, Jussi," they explained. "*Rap*ture!"

"Of course," Jussi nodded. When they repeated the passage, he sang of "Day of joy and rape-ture."

"With his perfect diction there was no doubt about *what* he sang," Bampton says. "He was so darling about it, but of course Fritz Busch and I were just in hysterical laughter, it was so funny. Each time it would happen in the rehearsal we'd stop and laugh"—which threw Jussi completely off balance. From that point on he was no longer sure how to pronounce the word correctly. At the end of the last rehearsal, Busch pulled Bampton aside. "Rosie, in the performance he can sing whatever he wants. But don't look at me; regardless of what comes out, you must go on!" Bampton followed the Maestro's instruction and neither of them lost their composure—although Jussi still sang "rupture" in the performance.[12]

The concert was a great success. Rose was in superb voice and sang a stupendous Leonora, and both Edward Johnson and I breathed a sigh of relief. That was Jussi's last Florestan and the only time he sang it in English.

※

In his late 30s, Jussi's capacity for work seemed limitless, but by the end of the Met tour, the punishing schedule and the wear and tear of cross-country travel began to show. We were happy to end the tour on 15 May 1948 with a *Ballo in maschera* in Cleveland and finally head home, sailing aboard the Italian steamer *Conte di Savoia*, in the company of Count Folke Bernadotte.

Count Bernadotte was the son of Prince Oscar, brother of King Gustaf V. A graduate of Sweden's West Point, the officers' school of Karlberg, he served as president of the Swedish-American Society, chief of the Boy Scouts of Sweden, and president of the Swedish Red Cross, exchanging prisoners of war. During the final months of World War II, Count Berna-dotte saved the lives of almost 20,000 inmates of German concentration camps when he obtained Heinrich Himmler's permission to transfer them, first into a single camp under the direction of the Swedish Y.M.C.A. and thence to Sweden. With his reputation for integrity, he became an intermediary, bringing Himmler's offer of surrender from the armies on the western front to the Allies. The Germans wanted to continue fighting on the east but the Allies demanded an unconditional surrender, thus Bernadotte informed Himmler of the rejection the day Admiral Karl Dönitz announced Hitler's death. He must have had his compatriot Raoul Wallenberg in mind when he said, "We Swedes take pride in that in the midst of inhumanity we produced individuals whose humanity transcended the evil around them."[13]

As usual, on this crossing we were special guests at the captain's dinner. We were all relaxed and in high spirits when Jussi turned to me. "We should sing something! Let's do the *La bohème* duet and maybe some others too." We did, and our impromptu concert was the highlight of the evening. "I didn't know Morsan could sing!" Folke exclaimed, picking up Jussi's nickname for me. Our little concert set him thinking, and the next day he reminded Jussi of his promise to sing Rodolfo in a gala performance of *La bohème* in late August, which performance would be attended by international delegates to the Red Cross World Congress. "And now I know who'll sing Mimì," Folke continued. "Anna-Lisa!"

"I couldn't possibly!" I protested. "I've never set foot on an opera stage in my entire life!" Then I glanced over at Jussi. He looked very determined. Jussi was often involved in benefit events organized by Folke and Estelle Bernadotte, and he never declined an invitation from Folke. "If Folke wants it, we'll do it. I'll teach you the role."

As soon as we were settled at home, we headed to the Opera to get the approval of Grevillius, who was to conduct, and Ragnar Hyltén-Cavallius, the director. To my surprise they were both enthusiastic. For the first time I had my own score, my own répétiteur; the music suited my voice, and learning the role was fairly painless. But rehearsals were another story!

During my student years I leaned toward dramatic, even violent stage roles. Murder and mayhem were to my liking—the more emotional outbursts the better! Juliette, with the poison, suicide, and dagger-pierced heart, appealed to me a lot more than Mimì, an ordinary seamstress with a humdrum life. She had to be portrayed naturally, and her actions were simple, too. So simple, in fact, that among other things I had to cross the stage and open a window. If only I could glide—but no, they nagged at me to move naturally. Hyltén-Cavallius maintained that I trudged with bent knees, and the rest of the cast began to mimic me. "This won't work!" I cried.

So poor Jussi worked with me at home. He knew exactly how the role should be played, and he was an excellent teacher of the difficult art of acting with subtlety. He told me not to concentrate so much on technique; I could sing, I had learned that foundation—it should be automatic. "You're no longer a pupil at the Music Academy," he admonished. "Just think of the words and put all your ardent feelings into your singing—then it becomes natural." He made me speak the lines of "Mi chiamano Mimì," then he sang phrases and I imitated him. "Sing the whole phrase as one word," he advised. I tried, and he thought I picked it up very quickly. "You should feel it in your spine, right down to every muscle. Think about the meaning of the words!" he'd urge me over and over.

I was willing to work endlessly to be a worthy partner to Jussi, and he was patiently determined to turn his Anna-Lisa into Rodolfo's Mimì. All day long we rehearsed at the Opera; then half the night, in the living room on Nybrogatan, with my mother serving as a patient, if skeptical, audience, we worked on those passages I found most difficult to act naturally. "It looks completely idiotic," Jussi groaned. "How could I fall in love with you when you move so stupidly?"

"I can't do this!" I cried—but I wanted to do it very much, more than anything in my life. To sing a complete performance with Jussi meant everything to me; I wasn't going to let this opportunity slip by. Finally, he asked my mother to leave the room. "We'll call you when we're ready!"

Unencumbered by an audience, he simply acted out the part erotically, becoming the young poet Rodolfo of a Paris garret trying to sweet-talk Mimì into his arms—and beyond. Succumbing to his great charm, for the first time I understood the words and the music, and I began to live Mimì's awakening love for Rodolfo, to feel it in my own body and in my own heart. We went over the scene a couple of times, then Jussi called for my mother. "Now you may come in!"

We did "O soave fanciulla," the closing duet of Act I, now so intense, so believable that my mother exclaimed, "What have you done with her? It's like another voice, a completely different presentation!" Jussi was triumphant. "Well, this is how it is when she follows my instructions!"

From then on, the daily rehearsals went much better, and 30 August 1948, the day of my debut at the Royal Opera, finally arrived. Red Cross delegates from 48 countries, some of them beautifully dressed in their exotic native costumes, filled the theater. I was less nervous than if it had been the usual critical Stockholm audience sitting in judgment. Our children were with their grandmother in the artists' box. "Just be your natural self and live what you sing" was Jussi's last advice. This time he was nervous for both of us, not only himself.

According to Hyltén-Cavallius, I came up the dimly lit stairs in full view of the audience and knocked on the nearest door. Rodolfo opened it, and there we were, facing each other. "Forgive me, the wind has blown out my candle," I sang. The only problem was that my candle still burned brightly because I had forgotten to blow it out.

I stared at Grevillius, whose arms had frozen in the middle of a beat, waiting for the flame to be extinguished. I didn't know what was the matter. At the last dress rehearsal everything had gone so well. The conductor's white cuffs, hanging in midair, glowed in the dark.

Both Isa Quensel, the Musetta, and I were a little nearsighted, so "Grillet" had rolled up his sleeves so that we could follow the beat by following his cuffs. He was a wonderful man, liked by all, one of those conductors who breathed with singers, became one with them. With him at the podium, we knew we'd get all the support we needed—as long as we saw his hands. But now even he couldn't rescue me.

So Jussi did. "Blow out the candle, for heaven's sake!" I heard him hiss, and I almost lost control, certain that in this moment Jussi regretted a thousand times that he'd ever persuaded me to sing Mimì. I realized what was wrong, blew out the candle, and the action continued. The whole incident lasted only seconds—an eternity for us onstage—but I doubt the audience noticed it.

When the confusion about the candle was over, everything went very well. We sang our respective arias and capped the act with the duet where I was able to convey, effortlessly, that I was falling in love with Rodolfo. But in the second act I couldn't follow Jussi's injunction to "have fun and relax." As I watched Musetta's big scene, the whole time I kept thinking about the third act. I couldn't relax for a second.

I'm sure that Jussi wondered if I would dare to leave the security of the wings, where I waited for my entrance, for I start Act III alone, without another cast member to divert attention from me. Just then, I caught sight of Hjördis Schymberg, our classic Mimì, standing nearby and observing me with a searching look. My legs stopped shaking and before I knew it, I was onstage. Just before I began to sing, I heard Jussi's voice from the wings, full of surprise, "I'll be darned! She's on the stage!"

The rest of the performance went flawlessly, and even Jussi thought I was better than expected. Finally, we reached the sad ending, the little seamstress dying in her lover's arms. By the time I sang my last lines, I was so emotionally drained and physically exhausted that I collapsed very naturally. "Look! I think she really did faint!" the terrified Marcello, Hugo Hasslo, whispered to Schaunard, Arne Wirén, and at the same time, five-year-old Ann-Charlotte screamed from the artists' box: "Mama!" Then I heard my mother calmly reassuring her: "Be quiet, Ann-Charlotte. It's only make-believe!"

At that very moment I felt Jussi taking my hand. He slipped a ring on my finger. Carefully, I peeked from under my half-closed eyelids—it was a ring of diamonds!

"Don't wake up too soon," he whispered.

I didn't want to. My fondest dream had been fulfilled: to stand onstage together with Jussi and to sing at the Royal Opera with him! I pulled myself together and looked just as dead as before, but when I came alive again to accept the applause at Jussi's side, no one could help noticing how giddy I was. This was the second of the two absolutely happiest moments in my life. The first was when I had Anders and knew that I had given birth to a perfect, healthy child.

When we opened the newspapers the next day, my joy was even greater.

"A Remarkable Debut" was the headline from Stockholm's most dreaded critic, *Svenska Dagbladet*'s Kajsa Rootzén.

> Anna-Lisa Björling, though thoroughly trained at the Conservatory, has hidden her light under a bushel, and suddenly she reveals that she too—with the desire and suitable roles—could make a music-dramatic career.
>
> Her voice isn't especially big, but it has much charm and intimacy in its timbre, and her safe conception of Mimì's part was a testimony, pure and simple, of artistic feeling for nuances.
>
> Her singing was beautiful, and as soon as the worst of nervousness had passed, the singing came alive. That this was a debut was obvious in her somewhat strained and impersonal acting, but she could probably overcome such things if she were to perform the role many times—and she should be given the opportunity to do so.

It made me happy to know that my singing pleased the listeners. I had no illusions about being in Jussi's league as a singer, but it gave me great pleasure to sing with him, and I was grateful that I was allowed to have this joy. Neither the public nor the critics ever suggested that Jussi inflicted me upon them. On the contrary, then and after, I was often asked why I didn't sing more often.

But of all the fine reviews and good wishes that streamed in, the one that meant the most to me was a telegram addressed to Opera Singer Anna-Lisa Björling: "We heartily thank you for your pure voice, your cultivated and artistic debut! Greetings to the family! Julia Svedelius." Two days later, Jussi handed me a photograph of himself in a beautiful bronze frame. Across it, like a ribbon, ran a line of music he had cut out of his own score: *Amo Mimì sovra ogni cosa al mondo, io l'amo* (I love Mimì more than anything in the world, I love her).

# Chapter 15

# *Manon Lescaut*

Jussi's pride and relief over my debut knew no bounds: his endeavors as a singing teacher and acting coach hadn't ended badly. Less than a week later, we participated in a charity concert at the Concert Hall. Encouraged by the success of this venture, he suggested we give more recitals together, and Freddie Schang booked us for some more joint concerts in America. It was fun to perform as man and wife—especially when the man was Jussi Björling!

In a way it was as if I had begun a new life, one that Folke Bernadotte had brought about, and my heart was filled with gratitude toward him. Our shock and sorrow were all the greater, then, when 19 days later, on 18 September 1948, the inky block letters of the morning newspapers carried the headline "Folke Bernadotte Murdered During Freedom Mission to Israel."

At the premature end of his long "service to his country and to men everywhere," Folke Bernadotte had entered upon the greatest challenge of his career. Named United Nations Mediator on 21 May 1948, he had the impossible task of bringing about peace between warring Jews and Arabs in Palestine. He was quoted as saying that he knew he had "only a 1 percent chance of success."[1] Ironically, at the time of his death, a second two-month-old truce that he himself had negotiated was in effect.

We learned from the reports that his jeep was ambushed, and he and another United Nations official were killed. Bernadotte's funeral was held in Gustaf Vasa Church on 26 September 1948. Jussi was asked to sing, and it was extremely difficult for him. He struggled with his emotions, his voice about to desert him after every phrase. As he sang the last line of "Sverige," tears streaming down his face, his voice broke into sobs.

※

At the end of the month Jussi flew to San Francisco. He sang Manrico and Rodolfo; in *La bohème* he sang for the first time with Tito Gobbi and Italo Tajo, which famous basso remembered Jussi as a "nice gentleman and a kind colleague with a beautiful tenor voice."[2]

I joined Jussi near the end of the San Francisco season. We then traveled with the company to Los Angeles, where we were happily reunited with our friends Bidú Sayão and her husband, Giuseppe Danise. We all went out to dinner, along with their young protégée, Regina Resnik. Unfortunately, Jussi had had quite a few drinks, and he was getting tense and argumentative, telltale signs of trouble ahead. I hoped in vain that the evening would pass without incident, but the conversation turned to singing and singers. As Regina tells it,

> Danise asked me a question about another singer. I ventured an opinion, and Björling, who had gotten increasingly quiet, suddenly—in a voice and in an attitude I didn't recognize—said, "Who are you to express an opinion? Your nose isn't even dry yet!" And he lit into me. I sat there, and I felt my flesh crawl, getting red to the roots of my hair. I sat very quietly. Anna-Lisa said to him "Oh, you're being very hard, Jussi," or something like that. Danise suddenly became very quiet, and Sayão was very sweet and said, "Oh, don't mind it, Regina, of course you can have an opinion." Then Jussi screamed: "She cannot have an opinion! She is too young to have an opinion!"
>
> Of course the party broke up. Everybody was beginning to realize that probably nothing more could go well. I just waited until Anna-Lisa or Bidú said, "It's getting late."
>
> I didn't sleep that night. I called Sayão the next day and asked if I could come over. She was very reluctant [to discuss it]. I didn't want to speak to Anna-Lisa; I decided to bury it, and it *never* happened again. I never saw this side of Jussi again. When we saw each other, it was as though it never had happened.[3]

Jussi canceled a student matinee of *Il trovatore*, and Kurt Baum took his place. He was also scheduled to sing his first Don Ottavio in 11 years, but although the printed program shows Jussi Björling, Max Lichtegg sang the role. I was sorry that Jussi didn't take part in this *Don Giovanni*; it had a wonderful cast, featuring not one but two Pinzas—Ezio as the Don, and Claudia, his daughter, as Donna Elvira. We didn't have much contact with her, which was probably our fault. "Mr. Björling, I think, kept pretty much to himself" is the way Claudia remembers Jussi. But she added, "The only

189

person with whom my father would talk about singers and singing was the prompter at the Met, Otello Ceroni. And I remember my father and Mr. Ceroni always saying how wonderful Jussi Björling was."[4]

Jussi did take part in the Los Angeles season's closing *La bohème* on 31 October, whereupon critic Albert Goldberg ruefully remarked, "Mr. Bjoerling, after flunking out of two scheduled performances, finally got around to singing for us. . . . He is the most musicianly and vocally refined of all tenors. He never sings a phrase without its appropriate shade of meaning, and his voice is invariably kindness to the ear. And he can act, too, without making too much of a point of it."[5]

On 15 November 1948 Jussi was to open the *Bell Telephone Hour*. When Freddie Schang announced the good news, he added that Jussi should depart from his usual repertoire and sing something new. They tossed around some ideas, trying to find something musically appealing and, quite frankly, showy. Soon after Jussi received a telephone call from Schang. "I've found an old Caruso recording of a number he used to sing as an encore. It could be something for you." Jussi took a taxi to Schang's office, and Freddie placed the 78 rpm record on his phonograph. It was "L'alba separa dalla luce l'ombra," a poem by Gabriele d'Annunzio set to music by Caruso's good friend Paolo Tosti. "Just listen to the way Caruso sings it," Freddie said.

When the record was over, Jussi said, "Play it again!" Freddie did. "Again!" commanded Jussi. This time he took off his tie, unbuttoned his collar, and at the top of his voice sang along with Caruso.

"Anna-Lisa, he sang it with such power that the windows rattled!" Freddie later described it to me. He was reliving the thrill of the moment, and he relived it many more times. This episode became a fixture in Freddie's repertoire of Björling stories.

Jussi took the record from Freddie and listened to it again and again. He frankly modeled his own interpretation on Caruso's, not to imitate him, but as an artistic tribute to the immortal model. His rendition on the *Telephone Hour* created a sensation, and he recorded it the following year. The score, long out of print, was reprinted with the caption "Sung by Jussi Björling."

Jussi listened to the record many times for the pleasure of hearing Caruso's colossal singing. It was always on the Victrola in his studio at Siarö, where it remains to this day.

※

Our engagements kept us in America from October through April. Not to cheat the children out of another family Christmas, we brought my mother and the Björling brood over once more to celebrate the holidays with us in New York. They attended Jussi's performances, including an appropriately scheduled *La bohème* with Sayão on Christmas Day. We went backstage after the performance; the boys had not forgotten to dread Bidú's kisses, but this time they had Ann-Charlotte as a decoy for Bidú to fawn over.

There were no other opera engagements until a *Trovatore* on 3 January 1949, so Jussi spent a lot of time with the children. When they left, on 7 January, we began another strenuous tour of about 40 stops. At his recital in Washington, D.C., on 11 January, Jussi was in excellent form. After the encores, the house lights were turned on, and as French Crawford Smith wrote,

> Pandemonium broke out at Constitution Hall. . . . A few diehards persisted in applauding. Mr. Bjoerling reappeared and obliged with Leoncavallo's showpiece, "Mattinata." Then it happened. The staid old walls reverberated with shouts, applause, whistles and catcalls the likes of which we've never experienced there before. Beaming from ear to ear, the rotund Mr. Bjoerling again obliged—this time with the aria from the last act of *Tosca*. Score: One 13-selection program with 8 encores![6]

Smith also noted Jussi's "pleasing personality . . . his diction is flawless in German, Italian, French and his native Swedish; his English is improving mightily for he fell prey only to the pitfall of most foreigners—the accursed 'v' and 'w.'" On the negative side, "Mr. Bjoerling has not yet overcome his tendency to 'sharp' on high notes," but Smith added it was refreshing to hear a singer sing sharp rather than flat.

Jussi maintained his form for the rest of the tour. Of the 6 February concert in Chicago's Orchestra Hall, Claudia Cassidy wrote, "Perhaps you have sometimes thought of his as a cool voice. I too have heard him sing in magnificent detachment. But here, tho' he retained the serene control of the master singer, that serenity set him free in a warm and glowing world of song. He was, or for the moment seemed to be, all things to all music."[7]

Jussi was reunited with Dorothy Kirsten in San Antonio for a single *La bohème* on 19 February, then two days later we both sang for the Scandinavian Club in Houston. On the following day, the University of Houston appointed Jussi honorary professor. By 2 March we were in Utica, New York, and then flew to San Francisco for a recital at the War Memorial Opera House. I mention all this not so much to track our movements (which this volume's Chronology does so exhaustively) as to convey a sense of the discomforts and fatigue of travel. In those pre-jet days a coast-to-coast flight could take 10 hours. To be buckled into an undersized seat listening to four roaring engines for that long a time was an endurance test in itself, but however grueling the trip, upon arrival the singer is expected to perform with little or no rest.

From San Francisco we visited Los Angeles for a short break, as guests of Dr. Petter Lindström. This time Ingrid wasn't there: a few weeks earlier she had left for Rome to join Roberto Rossellini and begin filming *Stromboli*. Ingrid had become involved with other leading men, but Petter knew that this time his wife had left for good. Alone with his daughter Pia, he was beside himself. He pulled me into Ingrid's dressing room, where everything was just as she had left it in her rush to get away. "Do you think she is sane?" he asked. "She has left everything like this!"

We didn't know what to say. We liked both Ingrid and Petter and didn't want to take sides in their marital conflict. Petter was at ease with us and glad for the opportunity to talk about the greatest disappointment of his life. And it did us a lot of good to be with Petter: for some reason, Jussi was able to talk openly with him about his alcoholism.

For centuries drinking and holding one's liquor was a manly thing, a matter of virtue rather than vice. For my generation, drinking to excess was considered a character flaw at worst, a simple lack of willpower. Only recently has alcoholism been recognized for what it is: a debilitating disease requiring medical attention and treatment. During our long conversations, I finally understood that drinking was a biological imperative for Jussi, that he was unable to control his metabolic needs without expert medical intervention; as Petter explained, it was a compulsion that could be checked only with a great exertion of self-control, which alcoholics, by the very nature of their disease, generally lack. Others have suggested that career pressures drove Jussi to drink. Giorgio Tozzi argues, "When one stops to think of what demands were made upon him because of his immense vocal gift and his art, should it not be at least understood from the sound of humanity in his voice that he was indeed human and subject to some human weakness?"[8]

Yes, always having to excel onstage contributed to his alcohol dependency. But the truth is that Jussi would've drunk had he been a plumber, a bank clerk, or a mailman. He began to drink before he had a career, and he drank more as he scaled the artistic heights. He drank when he had to perform, and he drank when he did not—in fact, especially then! Jussi was a sick man, and his sickness was alcohol. Little by little I recognized that he deserved understanding, not scorn; compassion, not pity; and above all selfless devotion to help him cope, but only now do I understand how desperately he tried to overcome his addiction, how much he suffered because he tried—and repeatedly failed.

It was a relief to be able to speak openly about this problem with a friend. Jussi could briefly lose control, even in America, and when I noticed the danger signs, it was impossible for me to relax. Petter was a kind man, and he understood my situation. "You're so tense all the time," he'd say. "Let your jaw drop, like this—" and he'd illustrate the technique. But the best relaxation therapy was lounging in the sauna of his summer house, or swimming in the pool and lying on the lush lawn, drying off in the California sunshine. One afternoon as I lay by the pool, I heard the most heavenly piano music coming from the open windows of the house next door. "Who's playing so beautifully?" I asked. "Oh, that's Arthur Rubinstein. He's our neighbor," Petter answered.

I clearly remember this moment. As I lay in Ingrid Bergman's garden, listening to Rubinstein's magnificent playing, it hit me, as so many times before, what a fantastic life I had because of Jussi.

⚜

On 29 March, Jussi joined the Met tour for a *Trovatore* in Boston; by 4 April we were back in New York for a *Bell Telephone Hour* concert. It was probably during this time that Jussi passed by Jack Caidin's Record Collector's Shop on 8th Avenue, the gathering place for opera lovers. Caidin played records all day, and the amplified music enticed customers like the sweet smell of a doughnut shop. As the Björling voice filled and overfilled the store, to everybody's surprise Jussi's round face appeared in the doorway. "It's a damn good record," he said, "and the tenor is good too!" By the time the people in the store realized who it was, he was gone.[9]

On 11 April 1949, Jussi participated in a gala charity concert at Carnegie Hall. "Sweden in Music" was conducted by Fritz Busch and Max Rudolf, and the program included our compatriots Joel Berglund and Karin Branzell. Jussi gave a stupendous rendition of "L'alba separa dalla luce l'ombra" at the end; Caruso's encore brought down the house.

Our summer on Siarö that year was interrupted by several recitals in Stockholm and Copenhagen's Tivoli, some by Jussi alone, some by the two of us. Then in mid-August, earlier than usual, we ended our working vacation to return for an all-work-no-play season in the United States. Thanks to Schang's promotion of Mr. and Mrs. Björling's joint performances, on 23 August we sang a "Symphony Under the Stars" concert in the Hollywood Bowl. Although we performed to a capacity audience of 20,000 persons, I wasn't especially nervous. The more the better, I thought. In such a crowd, individuals are lost in a great anonymous mass.

After California, we gave a joint recital in Honolulu, then flew back to San Francisco. Jussi opened the season in *Tosca* with Elisabetta Barbato and Lawrence Tibbett. He also sang Rodolfo and Faust. "Probably there is not another tenor in the world who can sing the difficult 'Salut, demeure' more cleanly and attractively than he did, or with so pure and ringing a high C," wrote Alexander Fried.[10] Alfred Frankenstein credited Jussi for his combination of "the heroic tenor's reserves and the lyric tenor's ease; above everything he has perfect taste in music-making."[11]

In midseason, we gave a joint radio concert on the *Standard Hour* program in the War Memorial Opera House. It was conducted by the manager of the San Francisco Opera, Gaetano Merola. In addition to our solos, we sang the duet from *La bohème* and closed the concert with the bridal chamber duet from *Roméo et Juliette*. Merola was obviously pleased, but we didn't realize then that he had future plans for us.

The highlight of the opera season was Björling's first new part in 11 years, Des Grieux in Puccini's *Manon Lescaut*. (The last role Jussi had added to his repertoire was Vasco da Gama in *L'africaine*, which role he sang six times at the Stockholm Opera in 1938.) His latest creation, the Chevalier Des Grieux, was a remarkable interpretation that never failed to leave a deep impression, then and after.

An incident during *Manon Lescaut* rehearsals revealed another characteristic of Jussi's personality: he wouldn't tolerate abuse of himself, and he wouldn't tolerate injustice toward others either. The comprimario role of Edmondo was taken by Cesare Curzi. For some reason, conductor Fausto Cleva took a dislike to the young man, and he treated Curzi with such angry discourtesy that Jussi went to Merola. "I won't sing the performance unless Cleva apologizes to Curzi in front of the whole company." Merola spoke to Cleva, the apology was delivered, and Jussi was satisfied. Curzi never forgot the gesture.[12]

Puccini's opera hadn't been performed in San Francisco for 22 years, and Alexander Fried felt that some people went to the theater expecting to hear Massenet's *Manon*. Licia Albanese gave a magnificent reading of the title role, "but the opera belongs to the tenor," Fried wrote. "Jussi Bjoerling sang . . . with a thrilling sweep and beauty, and with a romantic passion that was as welcome in him as it was unusual."[13] Frankenstein echoed the sentiment: "Jussi Bjoerling's tremendous vocalism, virility and musicianship have been the subject of verbal rhapsodies in these columns on the occasion of each of his previous appearances. This time, in addition to singing as he always does, he managed to discover some histrionic resources he had never shown before."[14]

Jussi sang the role twice in San Francisco and once in Los Angeles, all three performances with Licia. Then on 23 November he introduced his latest creation at the Metropolitan, this time with Dorothy Kirsten as Manon. The work had been absent from the Met repertoire too, for 19 years, and the revival was "an enormous success." With a stab at humor, Olin Downes described the climax of the Le Havre scene as the moment when "Des Grieux, frantic, casts himself at the captain's feet, in an ear-splitting tenor solo which brings down the house. . . . Mr. Bjoerling was not singing at his best until the latter moment, either, and he certainly is as unromantic a figure as Des Grieux as could readily be imagined. But there was the [gang]-plank and the song. What else mattered?"[15]

H. Wendell Endicott, president of the Boston Opera Association, must have read Downes' review. Failing to see any humor in its gnarled prose and resenting the gratuitous swipe, he was moved to write to Jussi:

> I had the great good fortune to see and listen to two magnificent performances at the Metropolitan last week—*Manon Lescaut* on Wednesday night and *Tosca* on Saturday night. . . . I am a considerably older man of some experience. You are a considerably younger man with a great deal of experience in your art; but when you can bring an audience numbering into the thousands up on to their feet with cheers and bravos, that is a spontaneous acclaim to your performances, and it should bring the deepest gratification as a recognition of your work. Because a few individuals who have access

to the press may think it is smart or funny to make an unworthy remark against any individual, it should be taken by that individual as a matter of no moment whatsoever. Any person in public life (and artists are in public life) is bound to run up against "cheap cracks" or untruths slammed against them. None of us is spared. I get my answer from the knowledge of whether I have done a good job or not. You got your answer both nights from those thousands of people out front, and those are the people that are your critics.[16]

Another letter of interest arrived from Gaetano Merola, who was preparing the 1950 season and was considering including *Turandot*: "The part of Prince Calaf would fit you perfectly, vocally and otherwise; and . . . if we give *Turandot* Mrs. Bjoerling could sing the role of Liù."[17] F. C. Coppicus wrote back to Merola: "This is to confirm the verbal agreement between you and Jussi Bjoerling, according to which the artist places himself at your disposal for the entire 1950 fall season of the San Francisco Opera Association." The letter specified that Jussi would be guaranteed 10 performances in San Francisco and Los Angeles at a fee of $1500 each. If *Turandot* were to be given with Jussi, "his wife, Anna-Lisa, will sing the second soprano role, at a fee of $650.00 per performance and such other roles as may be mutually agreed upon between Mrs. Bjoerling and yourself."[18]

The Texaco broadcast matinee on 10 December 1949 was Jussi's sixth performance as Des Grieux, and the reception on that occasion was overwhelming.[19] But the ultimate approval originated from a most unexpected source. When the performance was over, Jussi was handed a telegram from Rancho Santa Fe, California. It was sent after the Le Havre scene *during* the broadcast: "Am listening in with pleasure. Bravissimo. Galli-Curci."[20]

※

Past experience had taught us that a family Christmas was a precious thing. Rather than yield to the demands of the American agents and public, we insisted that Schang not accept any bookings for the end of December. With transatlantic air travel commonplace, travel time was no longer a factor, and for the first time in years we went home for the holidays.

Besides, Jussi needed a respite from the pressure exerted by impresari worldwide. He had been approached as early as September 1945 to tour Australia and New Zealand.[21] In 1946, there was an exploratory exchange of letters with the Cherniavsky Concert Bureau for a tour of South Africa. Alexander Cherniavsky mentioned that soon direct air service from New York to South Africa would take "only three days," so after brief reflection we abandoned the idea.[22] A similar proposal came from Celebrity Artistes of Johannesburg in 1949, and Opera Nacional of Mexico had made repeated overtures that autumn.[23]

Back home in Stockholm, in the biting, cold weather of the holiday season of 1949, Jussi developed a bad case of laryngitis. A 40-minute radio broadcast on New Year's Day was canceled, and the *Roméo et Juliette* at the Opera postponed from the 2nd to the 8th of January. Afraid to cancel again and provide grist for the rumor mills, Jussi sang, though not very well. Three days later he sang Rodolfo, which didn't go much better.

In those days, the Stockholm Opera started selling tickets on Sundays for the week ahead, including that Sunday night's performance. The box office opened at noon, but for Jussi's performances the queue started forming the night before. Not wanting to disappoint his fans, I called the opera at noon to tell them Jussi was ill and wouldn't be able to sing. As the newspapers meticulously reported, word didn't reach the lady on duty at the box office until 12:29 p.m., and by then she had sold 150 tickets to people who had been in line since 7 o'clock the night before![24]

All hell broke loose. *Aftonbladet* made broad hints about the "nature" of Jussi's illness. In light of the public outcry, Joel Berglund, the manager at that time, had no choice but to demand medical proof. *Svenska Dagbladet* (17 January 1950) reported, "Two doctors have now submitted to the opera manager evidence of Jussi's illness; one is the doctor appointed by the opera, the other Jussi's own throat doctor. Consequently, Björling's illness is considered confirmed, and his failure to appear at Sunday's performance is regarded as lawful."

Berglund told the newspapers, "It is stated in Jussi Björling's contract that he is liable to pay 5000 Kronor if he cancels a performance without lawful excuse. Now, however . . . Mr. Björling has been able to confirm that he was sick." For my part, I was interviewed by phone and in person, it seemed by everybody, giving the same story over and over: I had discouraged him even when he gave his first performance, and he'd felt that he must make every effort not to fail his audience again. As I explained in one interview,

> We sat together at home on Saturday night, and since he felt pretty good then, we both hoped that he'd be able to deliver Sunday's performance. However, by morning it was clear that it would be impossible, and I telephoned the opera manager at noon, when at last we gave up any hope. . . . Today my husband is even worse, he has a fever and such a sore throat he can hardly speak. Because of his illness, our American tour also has to be postponed. It is certain we cannot leave on 22 January as we had planned, and the departure will depend entirely on when he is well.[25]

It didn't help matters that Jussi had been seen about town the night before. But this time it wasn't alcoholic indisposition; he was truly ill and unable to sing. "The Court Singer, who continues to be bedridden with a fever, according to Mrs. Anna-Lisa's bulletin, is very sad about all the disappointment he has caused through his illness," reported the *Stockholms-Tidningen* (18 January 1950). "To make up for the disappointment . . . he is now preparing, together with his wife Anna-Lisa, a farewell concert before they set out on their American tour. It would take place in the Konserthuset

Auditorium and the Master Singer wishes that priority be arranged for all those people who stood in line Saturday night."

But it took weeks for Jussi to recover, and despite our best intentions, the recital didn't take place; in fact, the entire Canadian portion of our tour had to be canceled. By mid-February 1950 we were back in San Francisco, where the milder weather, as always, did Jussi's throat a world of good.

❋

Whenever we had a free moment, I rehearsed with Freddie Schauwecker before my appearances and always benefitted from his valuable advice. I wanted to be especially well prepared for our joint appearance on the *Voice of Firestone* on 6 March 1950, which was to be simulcast on radio and television, a novel experience for audience and artist alike. The medium of live television was a new challenge for performers, who had no idea how to act for the TV camera, nor what they might look like when their whole face filled the screen, giving viewers a ringside view of their teeth, tongue, and larynx.

The *Voice of Firestone* had been a respected NBC radio program since 1928; in 1954 it moved over to the ABC network, where its final 1962–63 season was preceded by a two-year hiatus. On the radio, its main—but by no means only—competitor was the *Bell Telephone Hour*, which aired from 1940 until 1958. The competition was fierce; in 1950 the *Bell Telephone Hour* made a very attractive offer to Jussi for the following season if he'd "agree not to accept Firestone engagements."[26] But Jussi, refusing to be a pawn in industry rivalries, continued to sing on both programs.

The *Voice of Firestone*'s move to television was a minor embarrassment. The sets were minimal, the camera work elementary, and the stage direction inane and often counter to the text or context of the music. The orchestral support under a competent but uninspiring Howard Barlow lent no distinction to the accompaniment; alas, Barlow's striking resemblance to Leopold Stokowski was only physical. Every show opened and closed with signature tunes composed by Idabelle Firestone, "If I Could Tell You" and "In My Garden." Jussi didn't relish singing Idabelle's little gems, but high fees paved the way to many a compromise.

On 11 March, Jussi sang with the Swedish Glee Club in Orchestra Hall in Chicago. In response to Enwall's inquiry from Stockholm, Coppicus wrote him a letter on 16 March 1950, happily quoting Claudia Cassidy's review:

> It is difficult to think of a voice of comparable beauty, so that Bjoerling's rival is Bjoerling at his best. That voice is all a piece and as it mounts a wonderfully flexible scale it opens up with a supercharged brilliance that sets the rafters and the customers ringing. Its quality is extraordinary from the lows to the highest note, so that it encompasses a rare range of song, and has a way of persuading you that whatever Bjoerling is singing is what he sings best.[27]

More recitals followed, then on 30 March Jussi sang Cavaradossi with the Met on tour, partnered for the first time by Ljuba Welitsch. On the following night, 31 March 1950, we joined several of our countrymen at Carnegie Hall in "Night of Swedish Stars," a program that benefitted the Swedish Seamen's Welfare Fund. Jussi sang four Swedish songs, Tosti's "Ideale," and the rediscovered gem "L'alba separa dalla luce l'ombra"; I sang "O mio babbino caro," "Depuis le jour" from *Louise*, and the Waltz Song and bridal chamber duet with Jussi from *Roméo et Juliette*. The two of us closed the concert with an emotional rendition of "Sverige."

This was the first time I sang with Jussi in New York, and I found it impossible to hide the stress of the moment. *Time* magazine (10 April 1950) wrote, "When Anna-Lisa, still slim and pretty at 40, sang her first aria, from Puccini's *Gianni Schicchi*, her bright-colored soprano was tight and quivering with nerves. It loosened up in arias from *Roméo et Juliette* and Charpentier's *Louise*." The article also noted that Jussi "is not his wife's favorite tenor: in her catalogue of greatness, Jussi comes after 60-year-old Beniamino Gigli. Jussi says, 'That's all right, Gigli's my favorite too.'" Well, after Caruso, that is!

Each successive appearance gave me a great satisfaction that I was finally putting my laborious years of vocal training to good use. I was much happier, and Jussi shared my joy. "I used to think that one singer in the family was enough," he once said, "but this joint tour makes me think I was wrong. At our Carnegie Hall debut I was more nervous than my wife was. Maybe it showed too, because they gave her flowers at the end. Me—I got nothing. Seriously, she has such a beautiful voice that it would be a crime not to let her sing."[28]

But during one of our tours, at a concert in Minneapolis, when I came backstage after taking bow after bow to continued applause, Jussi said, "What are you doing? Why do you stand out there carrying on like that?" I didn't know if I should be angry or amused. "But Jussi, I sang well!" Could he really be jealous of the ovation I received? The telegram he sent to Anders after the concert showed that his little outburst was all in good humor: "Mama brilliant success tonight. Papa was there too. Take care. Kisses and hugs. Papa."

I was thrilled to be able to share Jussi's musical life onstage as well as off. Knowing that in our duets he tried to showcase rather than overshadow my singing gave me the inspiration to do my best; I always felt secure singing with him. And I was amply repaid by the generous praise that came my way: no critic ever wrote that I was an unsatisfactory partner to my husband. But I didn't seek artistic glory independently from Jussi; a squeeze of the hand during our curtain calls or a kiss after the concert was worth more than words could ever express. *Prime donne* considered themselves fortunate to sing a few performances with Jussi Björling—I felt privileged to sing so many.

✳

Jussi gave two recitals in Toronto's Eaton Auditorium on 8 and 10 April 1950. Critic Edward Wodson caught the first:

> The first eight notes of his voice—whatever their pitch, high, low, loud or soft—tell the music lover why the whole world today is eager to hear Jussi Bjoerling. There isn't a hurrying, impatient, self-centered, uncertain, unbeautiful tone in it. It is steady as the light of a planet in a sky glittering with starshine. Whatever it sings about—things grave, gay, tragic or reflective and impersonal—it seems the last word to be said on the matter. The listener is at peace with himself and with the singing storyteller. It is music without doubt of any sort—utterly satisfying and beautiful beyond telling.[29]

After Toronto Jussi joined the Met tour in Cleveland, where he partnered Dorothy Kirsten as Des Grieux. A few days later we arrived in New Orleans for two performances of *Ballo in maschera*. Conductor Walter Herbert insisted that Jussi sing Riccardo's third-act aria, "Ma se m'è forza perderti." But Jussi didn't know the aria; it'd been cut from every production he'd ever sung. Coppicus informed Herbert that Jussi had a crowded schedule and didn't have time to learn it, but Herbert refused to accept this. On 31 December 1949 he had written, "We all hope that you will find the time. It should be very easy for you to learn this short aria in a few days. . . . It's not only that we consider the aria an important part of the opera, but our public is eager to hear it from you more than from any other tenor."

Flattery carried no weight with Jussi. He was indeed busy with rehearsals, performances, and travel, thus the upshot of the matter was that he didn't learn Riccardo's aria. But he must have felt guilty about it, so he compensated the New Orleans public with an interpolated high C before the Quintet in the second act and another at the end of the scene where the aria was to have been sung. I don't remember when, if ever, he took such liberties with the music. It was unnecessary and not very artistic, but the audience loved it.

We finished our spring tour with two more performances with the Met in Chicago.[30] In *Rigoletto* Jussi joined Leonard Warren in the title role and Patrice Munsel as Gilda. Ljuba Welitsch repeated her impassioned *Tosca*, but this time the Scarpia was Alexander Svéd, his last performance ever as a Met artist. Upon his return to Hungary the communist government confiscated his passport, thereby ending his international career.

# Chapter 16

# *Don Carlo*

Jussi's voice was widely known over the airwaves by virtue of his radio broadcasts of the late 1940s and the early 1950s. In the United States his popularity was so great that he received the Musical America Award of Achievement for 1950. The text, dated 29 June 1950, read thus: "Musical America has the honor to present this Award of Achievement to Jussi Björling, selected by the music editors and critics of the daily newspapers of the United States and Canada as Radio's Foremost Man Singer in Musical America's Seventh Annual Poll of Music on the Air 1950." When he won the very same award a year later, it was clear that he wasn't just a passing fad. It made him happy to receive this kind of endorsement from such a wide range of listeners.

In the summer of 1950, Jussi and I gave joint recitals in Stockholm at Skansen and Gröna Lund. Jussi also sang in Copenhagen, a charity recital at the Uppsala Cathedral, and a "Stars aus Europa" radio concert in Berlin. A special event was soprano Helga Görlin's 50th birthday celebration. The Opera threw her a party, an affair so lively that when it was over, some of her colleagues weren't yet ready to call it a night. Five tenors, Jussi among them, went over to Hugo Hasslo's apartment to continue the celebration. Mrs. Hasslo, a former ballerina of the Royal Opera, was there.

> It was after 2 o'clock in the morning when they started to sing. All of them! Our neighbor's bedroom was next to the room where the tenors

gave their impromptu recital. He had his windows open all night to hear better, but his wife slept through this wonderful performance. When he told her about it in the morning she became very upset. "The next time anything like this happens, let me know so that I can enjoy it too!"[1]

This wasn't the first time Jussi broke the night with his singing. Our lawyer, Eric Wennerholm, recalls one balmy summer Saturday evening. He and Jussi had just escaped a boring party, and Jussi suggested they go to Eric's place:

> [Jussi] sang and sang in front of the open window. He seemed to enjoy the lack of attention, to escape being the great Jussi Björling. In such moments, among a very few close friends, Jussi was completely free and open, a playful child. . . . [Next day,] my wife began to think that maybe we had disturbed our nice neighbor lady and phoned to offer her apologies. "Disturbed?" she said, "Oh no! I sat for hours at my window and just enjoyed it. It became my Sunday church service."[2]

※

In the 1950–51 season Jussi's fee at the Metropolitan reached $1000 per performance for a minimum of 15 performances. The contract specified Riccardo, Rodolfo, Don Carlo, Don Alvaro, Duke of Mantua, Cavaradossi, Des Grieux, Faust, and Roméo. I no longer recall the significance of only five of the nine roles being underlined, but deducing from the unfolding of the season, Don Alvaro, Des Grieux, and Roméo were only possibilities, included in case the theater decided to stage those operas. I don't remember Jussi's ever studying the role of *La forza del destino*'s Don Alvaro, however.

When we returned to the Metropolitan in October 1950, we found a different environment. Edward Johnson had retired and Austrian-born Rudolf Bing, the former director of the Glyndebourne and Edinburgh festivals, was his successor.

Through Eddie Johnson's last season at the Met, he and Jussi enjoyed an excellent working relationship. They were both singers, both tenors, and they never disagreed. Johnson empathized with all his artists; he spoke their language and promoted harmony within the entire company. During his tenure, discipline may have been lax, chronic financial difficulties meant that rehearsals were few, and scenery was often carelessly erected and in poor repair, but Eddie had taken over the Met in the middle of the Great Depression, brought it back into the "black," and managed it well during the difficult war years. It was unfortunate that now, at the brink of the United States' new prosperity, he no longer felt the requisite stamina to continue. Although we all expected changes with the new management, no one guessed that the unique familial camaraderie among Met artists would be lost forever.

The contract for Bing's first season and his opening night *Don Carlo* had been settled at the turn of the year. Bing wanted Jussi for a longer period than he was willing to give to the Metropolitan; in January 1950 he wrote Jussi "just a personal line to say how glad I am about our agreement. It is not as extensive as I hoped it would be, but at least it is a good beginning." He repeated what he had requested of Helmer Enwall, that Jussi "should please not go away during the rehearsal period for *Carlos*."[3] He stressed the importance of the opening night and that he was counting on Jussi's cooperation. "This must really be superbly rehearsed and it would be disastrous if during this rehearsal period you suddenly wanted to rush off."[4]

Soon after this, negotiations hit a snag. As far as I recall and can reconstruct from correspondence, Rudolf Bing dealt with Helmer Enwall in Stockholm, and Gaetano Merola with Coppicus in New York. No doubt the participants in these negotiations believed that the San Francisco and New York engagements dovetailed when in fact they overlapped. As late as 10 March, clarifying a misunderstanding regarding the timespan he was able to give San Francisco, Jussi wrote, "I also agree to learn the role of [i.e., in] 'Turandot' for the coming season of 1950."[5]

But Jussi was confused with regard to which opera house had prior claim on his services. The conflict came to a head, and the chairmen of the boards in San Francisco and New York, Kenneth Monteagle and George A. Sloan, were involved to resolve it. In a letter to Sloan, Bing explained, "I started my negotiations with Bjoerling direct (not via Coppicus) at exactly the same time—that was in early December [1949], approximately four weeks after my arrival." Unaware of the most recent exchange of letters between Merola and Coppicus, both then and before leaving New York— according to Bing—"[Jussi] asked me to continue negotiations with his Swedish agent in Stockholm, which I did." In the course of a subsequent meeting with Merola, the two managers discovered that they both had a contract with Björling. Bing concluded: "The fact remains that Mr. Bjoerling has inexcusably and irresponsibly entered into two commitments for the same period. This was neither Mr. Merola's fault, nor mine."[6]

I believe a failure of communication between Jussi's transatlantic managers was to blame for the confusion; Jussi knew full well he couldn't sing on both coasts at the same time. In the end, San Francisco gallantly deferred to the new general manager of the Metropolitan, and Jussi learned Don Carlo instead of Calaf. But Bing's assumption that Jussi had dealt with him in bad faith placed their relationship under a permanent cloud.

When Jussi's performance dates were settled, Bing wrote to him again regarding the 1950–51 season: "It would be of the utmost importance to me to have you with us on the tour." Boston would want to hear Jussi again, and "so do other places. Would you very kindly let me know as quickly as you can whether you can be with us so that we can come to a definite agreement. Please make it possible." He then added a postscript asking Jussi not to commit himself in advance for the 1951–52 season "unless we have discussed the matter."[7]

As Bing's next letters to both Jussi and Enwall indicate, he and Jussi had "a long talk . . . about his participation in next year's Metropolitan Opera spring tour." The letters were written the same day, 12 May 1950, thus the conversation must've taken place in Chicago during the Met tour. "As I told you," Bing wrote Jussi, "I am so very anxious that during my first season and tour everything should be successful and happy so please make it possible by accepting what I think is a fair and reasonable suggestion as I have put it to Mr. Enwall."[8] He confirmed to Enwall that the Met wanted Jussi for the whole month of April 1951 with five appearances, "which gives ample time for concerts and I am prepared, if Mr. Bjoerling would finally commit himself now to accept that, to pay his return air transportation from Stockholm to New York."[9]

*Finally*—the word indicates that Bing was running short of patience. He regarded a Met engagement as the axis of every singer's life, around which the rest of his or her activities revolved, and he had little tolerance for a singer who thought otherwise. His attitude, quite correctly, was that a large portion of a singer's remuneration was the honor of appearing at the Met and the enhanced demand such an affiliation produced. But for Jussi, the Met was just another square in a patchwork quilt of engagements; he didn't want to lock himself in until the entire design emerged.

A singer doesn't sing for pleasure alone, he also sings for money. If the pleasure is the same no matter to which audience he sings, it would be foolish not to sing for twice the money. Top salary or not, at the Metropolitan Jussi earned one-third to half of his fees elsewhere, especially in solo recitals. It was a weighty factor, and Jussi didn't take Bing up on his offer.

※

Bing had great plans for the company he took over. Full of energy and enthusiasm, he wanted to inaugurate his tenure with something special. *Don Carlo*, which was last given at the Metropolitan in 1923, seemed to be the perfect vehicle.

By this time Jussi's repertoire was, for the most part, complete. *Un ballo in maschera*, *Rigoletto*, *Trovatore*, *Tosca*, *La bohème*, and *Faust* were among his best classical parts—and the ones for which he was in the greatest demand. Apart from Des Grieux, he hadn't added a new role for years. But Jussi looked upon Don Carlo as a challenge. Moreover, it suited him vocally and histrionically: his voice had gained a dramatic color and weight, and the stage action demanded by playing the heir to the Spanish throne was well within the scope of his restrained acting style. He learned the role specifically for this production.

*Don Carlo* had such a young cast that at the venerable age of 39, Jussi was the senior citizen among the principals. Delia Rigal, the Argentinian soprano who sang Elisabetta, was at age 29 making her Metropolitan Opera debut, as was Fedora Barbieri as Princess Eboli, at barely 30. The baby of the cast was 23-year-old Lucine Amara in her invisible debut singing the

Celestial Voice from the wings. Among the men, Robert Merrill, the Rodrigo of the evening, was 33, and Grand Inquisitor, Jerome Hines, only 29. Youngest among the men was the venerable King Philip, 27-year-old Cesare Siepi, also in his Metropolitan Opera debut. Apart from Amara's, for the other three debutants this was their American debut as well.

Siepi almost missed this historic opportunity. The Met's first choice for the role was Bulgarian Boris Christoff, but under the provisions of the Mac-Carran Act, the U.S. State Department wouldn't issue a visa to the citizen of a communist country. The Met next tried Mihály Székely, who had unwisely returned to his native Hungary at the end of the 1949–50 Met season. With the communist party's recent takeover, Székely too had had his passport permanently revoked. Although he may have been the third choice for the role, Siepi was in his full glory and sang a sensitive, moving King Philip.

Bing had a lot of trouble with his other singers, too. Thanks to the Mac-Carran Act, cast members who were citizens of former fascist countries were subjected to a lot of unpleasantness. Fedora Barbieri and her husband, Luigi Barlozzetti, were first taken to Ellis Island, and baritone Paolo Silveri, Bing's Don Giovanni, and his wife were kept on board ship and questioned late into the night. Upon landing, Silveri found that most of his luggage had been stolen, and what was worse, in the inclement weather he caught a terrible cold. After the first rehearsal he ran a high fever, lost his voice, and had to remain silent for 20 days.[10]

Jussi's collaboration with Bing hit another snag when he arrived late for rehearsals. On 21 October, a very annoyed Bing dispatched a letter—a curious admixture of pleading desperation and implied threats.

> I cannot tell you how upset and discouraged I am. You were one of the first with whom I discussed my hopes for some more teamwork and some more rehearsing, and I was happy and encouraged by your reactions; and now look how the thing starts!
>
> Right from the beginning the artistic discipline is undermined. The Italian artists are here for every rehearsal on the dot and have to rehearse ensembles, duos and everything without a tenor.
>
> I am frightfully sorry to hear that you are not well. If so, why have you not immediately called a doctor? It is not that I mistrust your word, but if I had a doctor's certificate it gives at least some excuse to the others who are already disgruntled and who always have to rehearse without you.
>
> You must know how much I have been looking forward to our collaboration and what enormous value I put on your artistic services to this house, but it simply cannot go on like this. Please let us avoid a major trouble, which will no doubt arise unless you can see your way to attend rehearsals without fail and punctually. It is one of the foremost objectives I have in mind, to establish real rehearsal discipline in this house, and however great my regret may be, I cannot abandon that policy whatever the consequences may be. So please cooperate as you have so kindly promised only the other day again.[11]

Bing, of course, was right, and Jussi joined the cast at the next rehearsal. If Bing allowed anyone to slip from a contractual obligation, he could never consolidate his position of authority. He had just shown his determination to establish control by allowing Lauritz Melchior's contract to lapse on the eve of his 25th Met season, a clear signal that he wouldn't hesitate to act likewise with other artists, regardless of reputation, age, or seniority with the company.

To accommodate the newspapers, a long press conference was held the day before the *Don Carlo* premiere. We had to appear in formal clothes at 11 a.m., and Jussi was furious that anyone could be so inconsiderate as to ask such a thing of him. "I'm not going to do it," he exploded. "I—will—NOT!" Once again it fell to me to coax him. "Freddie Schang says you must be a little more cooperative," I urged. "It goes with the job; the other singers must do it too." I was able to change his mind. But when the reporters wanted to photograph the two of us eating breakfast in bed, Jussi reached his limit. There were no pictures in bed.

The season opened on 6 November 1950. As Jussi was about to leave for the theater, we received a telegram. "Wishing you greatest success [for] your brilliant career. Affectionate regards [to] Anna-Lisa. Edward Johnson." As always, a thoughtful gesture from Eddie, one that Jussi appreciated very much. I arrived to find the auditorium swarming with celebrities dressed to the nines; the installment of the new general manager had sensationalized the premiere, and even I was photographed in my ice-blue strapless evening gown—I tried not to bring shame to my husband.

The performance was televised and carried by nine stations as far away as Chicago.[12] Although the press declared it an improvement over the two previous telecasts, in 1948 and 1949, it still left much to be desired. The underlit scenes were too dark for the cameras, and the large crowd scenes were lost on the small screen; still, "other pictures had a definition and brightness which compared with the finest studio work," wrote Jack Gould in *The New York Times* (7 November 1950). "The best TV came with the close-ups of the principals [who avoided] any excessively broad gestures."

The audience in the theater and the TV viewers at home were witnessing an extraordinary opera production. Vocally and visually the Met delivered its best. Where the performance fell short was "in the pit." Geraldine Farrar, who heard both the opening night telecast and the radio broadcast on 11 November, identified the shortcoming with pinpoint accuracy: "The conductor, Fritz Stiedry had impossible tempi and no clear understanding of Italianate feeling."[13] In light of the excellence of the soloists, it's regrettable that Bing hadn't added the finishing touch of a preeminent Verdi conductor to his first-night cast.

The New York dailies gave extensive coverage to the event, before and after the performance, and the critics couldn't have been kinder in recognizing each cast member's accomplishment in his or her respective role. The performance was so well rehearsed and the ensemble so strong, it was only proper no one was singled out. Yet for Barbieri, Jussi was unique: "The first time I had the pleasure to sing with him in *Don Carlo* I had my mouth open upon hearing that voice pour forth so effortlessly." Remembering their later collaboration, she added,

> It was a pleasure to sing duets with him. . . . He tried not to make mistakes in Italian. If he did, he would apologize, "I am sorry, Fedora," and I would say to him: "Imagine if I would try to sing in your language!" and we would laugh. He was a great friend and a wonderful colleague. I have been singing for 52 years and I have heard, and am hearing, many tenors, [but] I will never forget the performances I sang with him, because there will never be another Jussi.[14]

✳

Jussi really loved operatic work, but at times he doubted whether being an opera singer was worth all the trouble. As a concert artist he was in control of every detail; in opera, on the other hand, he had to contend with theatrical conventions and the rules and restrictions of the house. Still, an operatic performance was such a wonderful combination of music and drama that Jussi would never have been able to give it up.

As Jussi felt more secure with stagecraft, he began to put on his own makeup outside of Sweden. He knew his own features best and how they should be made up for the each role. Here again, less was more. During later years he hardly used a wig, preferring to work with his own hair. According to the stage manager of the Royal Opera, Ryno Wallin:

> Jussi was the most exemplary operatic artist. He was particular about being at the Opera in good time before a performance and making sure that everything was ready. He took care of his own entrances; one could rest assured about him and never needed to call him. He was reliability personified. Before the performance or his entrances he never talked or fooled around but was always completely focused. Thus for his part he always had perfect performances.[15]

The concentration before the evening's performance began in complete silence, in long moments, alone, in front of the dressing table mirror. One could see his lips move as he applied his makeup, as he went over the most important passages of the evening's role. It was then that he mentally became Faust, Rodolfo, Roméo, or Don Carlo.

In the 1950–51 Met season, in addition to eight performances of *Don Carlo*, Jussi sang five *Faust*s and two *Manon Lescaut*s. Jussi's 15th and last performance this season was *Manon Lescaut* on 10 January 1951, with his first Manon, Licia Albanese. Bing attended every performance, Jussi's as well as the others. When he could not, as with the 10 January *Manon Lescaut*, he sent a special note of apology that he was unable to be present because "I was in bed with a frightful cold. However, I hope there will be an opportunity of seeing you before you leave and, of course, I look forward to your return for an equally successful season next year."[16]

But next season was another matter. Bing approached Jussi's agents with details for the 1951–52 season, which Francis Coppicus' letter sent to the Hotel St. Moritz confirms: "As I told you over the telephone, Rudolf Bing just told me that he is very anxious to have you back next season. Since your contract with the San Francisco Opera prevents you from singing in the revival of *Rigoletto*, planned for the first week of the opera season, Mr. Bing offers you the first performance of *Bohème*."[17] But knowing of all the offers his agents received, Jussi asked Coppicus and Schang to let the Met know he wouldn't return the following year. As soon as Bing was informed, he wrote,

> I was very distressed to hear from Mr. Coppicus today that you are contemplating leaving the Metropolitan Opera because apparently you can no longer afford the luxury of singing here. Naturally, I need not tell you, because you must know it, how greatly I would regret your departure and furthermore I am afraid that this is a decision—incidentally, most likely a pretty final decision—which you must make yourself and there is very little I can do about it. You know that you are drawing the highest fee the Metropolitan can pay and I see that in a period of 10 weeks we have guaranteed you 15 performances. It will be a question of repertory and also a question of exactly when you will be at our disposal, and if it would help you greatly I would be willing to say that we would guarantee you 16 or 17 performances during such a period.[18]

Soon after, Alan Kayes, commercial manager of RCA Red Seal Records, was having lunch with Eddie Johnson at the Coffee House, and he mentioned Jussi's intention to leave the Met. Johnson was shocked. "Why don't we go up and see him?" he suggested. "Eddie did this on his own, not to accommodate Bing," asserts Kayes. They went to the Hotel St. Moritz and found Jussi alone. Eddie tried to reason with him, and Kayes explained that if he left the Met it could affect his record sales. Jussi thought it over. After some extensive three-way negotiations between him, Bing, and Coppicus and Schang, Jussi at first agreed to sing only three *Don Carlo*s in the spring of 1952; but no matter how small the initial concession, it was the visit paid by the two men that made a very stubborn Jussi Björling begin to relent. According to Kayes, "He had an enormous respect and affection for Eddie Johnson."[19]

By the end of February 1951 the plans for the 1951–52 Met season were finalized. Jussi was to sing four times in November and December and twice in March, at a fee of $1000 for each performance, with an option for three weeks of spring tour. His roles were to be Rodolfo, Duke of Mantua, Turiddu, and Don Carlo. In the same letter Bing suggested 12 performances for 1952–53, plus the spring tour of 1953. He concluded his letter saying "While I regret that you could only be with us for such a short period next season, I appreciate your difficulty, all the more as you have agreed to compensate us again in the following year by being available for a longer season."[20]

While Bing was negotiating with Coppicus, Jussi was approached directly by a Miss Keller, the representative of Ernesto de Quesada's Sociedad Musica Daniel, concerning extended opera and concert engagements in Rio de Janeiro and Buenos Aires. Jussi told her that he wouldn't be able to make a decision before seeing Helmer Enwall in Stockholm on 15 March.[21] It was the deteriorating South American political situation that, in the end, was responsible for the plan's being abandoned.

Meanwhile, Jussi enjoyed his success at the Met. He was especially pleased when fellow Swedes came to hear him—and positively delighted when Carl Kempe and his wife Marianne, friends of ours from Stockholm, caught the performance one evening. After the opera, they invited us to supper at 21. We had a grand time together. Little did we know that we'd become related years later when our Lasse married their daughter, Veronica.

※

Jussi and Bob Merrill had been good friends, but the *Don Carlo* performances brought them much closer together. As Bill Arneth, Jussi's last publicity agent once observed, "Jussi thought that Merrill was one of the finest baritones in the world—admired him as a person and admired him as a singer."[22] Bob was Jussi's junior by six years, and remembering his own beginnings, Jussi felt a kinship with the young man with the golden throat. I trusted Bob and depended on him in moments of impending crises, as his own recollections prove:

> I'd visit them at the Essex House and when Anna-Lisa had to go out and was a little nervous to leave him alone, she'd call me. "Bob, come and spend some time with Jussi." It was rough. I would try to keep him from drinking, and we'd play poker. When he became involved in the game, he was like a child. Then, I could feel the surge of his sudden desire for a little alcohol. He would order martinis [from room service], not one or two but several. He was able to hold his liquor, but I could see his personality changing. He would become angry and bellicose, though not every time.
>
> I'll never forget the time I took him for a walk. I was concerned that he wanted a drink. It was evening and as we were walking and chatting, we suddenly passed a bar. We could see in the window that a prizefight was on the TV. "Oh," he said, "I want to see the fight." You couldn't hold Jussi back if he wanted to do something, so we went in the bar. We sat, had a beer, *one beer*, watching the fight. I went into the men's room and by the time I came out, there was a martini there and he was arguing with the guy next to him about the fight. Because he never carried money on him, of course I paid.
>
> One night Anna-Lisa called me. She said: "Jussi is drinking, please come over." I tried to change his mind, and for a while I did. Anna-Lisa had a very bad cold, and she suggested I take Jussi out. So we took a cab to 21, and we sat around chatting with the owners. After a while I said

"Come on Jussi, let's go, it's getting late—we have a performance to-morrow night." He just waved me aside and refused to leave. It was very late, and I had a performance to sing! I called Anna-Lisa and I told her I couldn't budge Jussi. So she said, "You go home, I'll come down." This poor woman—she was feverish with the flu or something—had to leave the hotel around 2:30 in the morning to take him home. He was absolutely inebriated.

The next day, the day of the performance, I called Anna-Lisa. "He is sleeping," she said, "he isn't well, he has a hangover." Jussi showed up at 7 o'clock at the opera house, at 8 o'clock he was ready for the perform-ance—I never heard him sing better![23]

※

In the first half of 1950, Freddie Schang tried to negotiate a better recording contract with RCA, at the heart of which was a guarantee of royalties, giv-ing the executives a greater incentive to record Björling. Freddie wrote, "I stuck to my original thesis which is this: as long as they are guaranteeing some of your competitors, you are at a disadvantage because it is human nature to push the recordings of artists guaranteed and let the ones who have no guarantee just take what they can get."[24]

Soon Freddie was able to report that Samuel Chotzinoff of RCA Victor Company wanted Jussi to "rerecord on tape all of the leading tenor repertory so that they can issue it on new speeds. There is no longer a market at the old speed (78 rpm). I stated that I would not discuss repertory with them until they committed themselves on the subject of a guaranteed annual royalty." He continued:

> They flatly refused a guaranteed royalty, but after a negotiation of one hour, came forward with the following proposition, which I consider the opening wedge in a new relationship: they are shortly to record the opera *Carmen* with Risë Stevens and Robert Merrill. They want you to do the tenor role, and they will give you an advance royalty on this one album of $2500. In view of the fact that this sum is more than your U.S. royalties for the last four years, I think it is something. I wish you could cable me on receipt of this letter if you are agreeable to do the *Carmen*, which will be recorded in New York this October as soon as you arrive, and at times you are not rehearsing with the Metropolitan.[25]

Jussi had never sung Don José and at the moment he was working on the title role of *Don Carlo*. It was impossible to switch vocal gears and absorb another role. He agreed to do the recording, but only in 1951.

"I remember that we went together to a luncheon at a restaurant near the old Met," Risë Stevens recalls. "We sat and talked together for a while, about different things. It was such a wonderful meeting, he couldn't have been warmer and sweeter." When the conversation turned to *Carmen*, she told Jussi that she wanted him to sing with her in her recording of the opera.

"'Oh, I don't know that I could do it on the stage, Risë,' he said, 'but I would love to do it in a recording.' Then I had to run to a rehearsal, so our conversation ended there."[26]

During our stay in New York, Jussi made several recordings at the Manhattan Center. Freddie's report notwithstanding, the records were still issued on 78 rpm discs. RCA, seeking to capitalize on the recent success of *Don Carlo*, had Jussi record the first-act duet with Merrill three weeks after the premiere. They recorded four more duets a month later, on 3 January 1951.

Bob vividly remembers the afternoon they spent discussing and rehearsing "Sì, pel ciel," from *Otello*. They listened to the duet as recorded by the finest tenor and baritone voices of the 20th century—Enrico Caruso and Titta Ruffo—which some experts maintain is perhaps the greatest recording of a duet ever made. Jussi certainly thought so, and he appreciated the magnificence of the voices and the interpretations as well. His great fear was that in spite of his best effort he would be unable to do justice to the music. In Merrill's words:

> Before we went to record our famous duet album, we worked at the Essex House. We went over especially the duet from *Otello*. Jussi said, "Bob! Caruso and Titta Ruffo! Let's listen to it." As we kept listening to it and we kept rehearsing, he said, "I want to sound like Caruso. I want it to sound like a Caruso and Titta Ruffo record." I said, "We'll try, but it'll still be Jussi Björling and Robert Merrill."
>
> We went to the studio at the Manhattan Center on 34th Street. We got out of the cab, and he grew quite nervous. He wanted to walk around before we went up because he was quite concerned about it. We did; we walked around and walked around. Then finally he said, "Let's go up and do it!" And he was marvelous! Our voices seemed to blend. He knew it and I knew it, and the public knew it.[27]

Jussi's apprehension served only one purpose: it compelled him to excel, and the end result, no less on Merrill's part than on Jussi's, requires no apology. Jussi was impressed by Merrill's performance. "He said to me, 'Bob, when I do my first Otello, it's going to be with you. I won't sing *Otello* without you.' We shook hands on that."[28] Jussi's admiration for Bob wasn't just a polite remark made in the heady moments of a successfully completed recording. In an interview following our return to Sweden, he described Merrill as "a great star [to emerge] in the last five years."[29]

What mattered most to Jussi was that the duet had shown that the role, in time, wouldn't be beyond his scope. In his autobiography, he wrote, "One more thing tempts me—Otello. But it isn't the right time yet. I want to keep my lyric tone as long as possible, and if I start too soon with the dramatic roles, there is a danger of hurting my voice. I'm very cautious. Many have asked why I don't sing Otello, because they think it was made for me. But I want to wait until my voice changes of its own accord for such a project."[30] Singing the role onstage is quite another matter, but in a recording he could surely sustain it in power and range. As Jürgen Kesting observed, "In the duet Björling's voice rises to a penetrating high A on *per la morte*; it then sinks, effortlessly, to the resonant low C-sharp on *sterminator*."[31] Some reviewers wrote that if the Caruso-Ruffo recording didn't exist, the Björling-Merrill version would be a contender for first choice among recorded versions of this music.

It is interesting to note that the idea of these duets originated with Jussi two years earlier. An interoffice memo to RCA producer Richard Mohr spoke of "a request from Mr. Bjoerling that he very much would like to do the Boïto *Mefistofele* 'Dai campi,' also the *Turandot* 'Non piangere Liù,' and the duets, with Leonard Warren if possible, from *Otello* and the *Pearlfishers*."[32] Jussi never recorded these solos, but with the *Pearlfishers* duet he was on the right track. "Au fond du temple saint" became the most popular recording of this batch, in large part due to Merrill's beautiful singing and the perfect blending of the voices. It has gone through more than 40 reissues on 78 rpm records and LPs, and its amazing popularity now continues on CD.

In January and February 1951, I sang several recitals with Jussi in the United States and Canada. Our joint appearance in Quebec City took place on 31 January 1951 at the Palais Montcalm. The *Quebec Chronicle-Telegraph* accorded Jussi the usual praise, judging that in our duets he was "the guiding star carefully supporting his wife's trained if not powerful soprano."[33] Two days later, on Jussi's 40th "birthday," we sang at the St. Denis Theatre in Montreal. According to critic Eric McLean, who by his own admission left during intermission and reviewed only half of our program, "Mme. Bjoerling has a pleasant but quite limited soprano voice."[34] But Jussi reaped his customary laurels on nearly every occasion, whether it was a joint or solo recital. Claudia Cassidy wrote of his 25 February 1951 appearance at Orchestra Hall in Chicago: "He would have been extraordinary in any age, for topnotch tenors are scarce articles. But in our time he verges on the fabulous."[35]

In addition to Grieg and Schubert songs, Jussi sang arias from both Puccini's and Massenet's *Manon*, "Dalla sua pace" from *Don Giovanni*, "La donna è mobile" from *Rigoletto*, and the Gralserzählung from *Lohengrin*. Singling out the way he captured "the heroic poetry of Lohengrin's narrative," a recent addition to his American concert repertoire, Cassidy summed up Jussi's artistry in a single paragraph better than most:

> It is impossible to be too grateful to Mr. Björling for his tacit acceptance of the fact that the greater the gift, the greater the responsibility. He walks onstage like a man without a care in the world, having done the work offstage. The beautiful voice, as shining in stratospheric brilliance as it is poignantly veiled in shadow, has been polished to technical perfection. His standards of interpretation are the highest, being informed, imaginative, and patrician. In performance he is both generous and eloquent, but

he has an instinctive serenity, a rocklike inner reserve. He is a vastly popular singer who maintains the aristocratic art of song.[36]

On 16 February 1951, Jussi took part in NBC's TV program *We the People*, hosted by Dan Seymour. Dressed as Canio, Jussi sang "Vesti la giubba" from *Pagliacci*. Enrico Caruso's widow, Dorothy, was in the studio. They had a pleasant visit, and Jussi told her about how he and his brothers missed a chance to hear Caruso sing *Pagliacci* because they went to a cowboy movie instead. After the performance, Dorothy gave Jussi the costume her husband had worn as the Duke in *Rigoletto* at the Metropolitan Opera. "You have the old Italian school of singing," she said. "You're the only one worthy to wear his mantle, bear Rico's crown!"[37]

Her statement did not pass unnoticed. As *Time* magazine (5 March 1951) reported, "In Manhattan, Enrico Caruso's widow Dorothy finally came right out and said that the only living tenor who comes close to wearing 'Rico's' crown is the Metropolitan Opera's Swedish-born Jussi Bjoerling. Said Tenor Bjoerling: 'The greatest moment of my life.'"

Mrs. Caruso promised to send a picture of her late husband, but before she had time to go through her collection, she wrote to Jussi: "I shall try to send you the picture of Caruso that he and I liked best, as well as one in costume. . . . It was a pleasure meeting you and your wife even under the amazing circumstances of *We the People*. And it was a joy to me—an extra joy— to have had the opportunity to hear you sing, at that time. . . . I am *so glad* that *Time* quoted exactly what I said about your voice!"[38]

Jussi never wore Caruso's costume in a performance; he thought it would be pretentious to do so.[39] But I know that with the possible exception of Gösta Ekman's silver peacock and its accompanying letter, he had never been so happy about a gift.

From the inception of his international career, Jussi had been hailed as "the Swedish Caruso," but he always felt the comparison, though well intended and highly complimentary, was unfounded and unnecessary. Caruso and Björling were temperamentally different singers, and their highly individualistic timbres little resembled each other. The great Italian's voice was always described as golden; the epithet more often applied to Jussi's voice was silver—two adjectives that suggestively convey the difference between their musical personalities as well: the Neapolitan sunshine of Caruso's golden tones and the Nordic restraint of Jussi's silvery timbre.

In an article devoted to the reissue of Caruso's and Jussi's 78 rpm records, Conrad L. Osborne observed:

> Was Caruso really better than all the other tenors of the century? Was Bjoerling truly superior to his contemporaries? Yes, in both cases. And for all the important differences between them as artists, they shared an elementary vocal virtue which, more than any other, provided a basis for their greatness. This was an unfailing adherence to an unbroken vocal line, a continuity of vibration, which assured them of beautiful, appropriately

colored tone (always postulating an accurate instinct for proper shading, which both possessed to a marked degree) regardless of pitch, dynamic, or vowel.[40]

Jussi was quietly flattered by the parallel drawn between himself and his idol, but he readily acknowledged Caruso's unsurpassable supremacy. No one knew better than he that while Caruso's level of excellence was a model, his vocal attributes were as much inborn as cultivated, and thus remained unattainable. He could only be as good as Jussi Björling could be, and to play on words, he was the best possible Jussi Björling.

❈

On 3 March 1951 Jussi sang a recital at New York City's Hunter College. His Swedish songs were especially praised, and his operatic selections included such a wide range of styles and periods as "Dalla sua pace," "Nessun dorma," "Donna non vidi mai," and the Gralserzählung. He then cut some records in New York and made another appearance on the *Bell Telephone Hour*. Finally, after five months of peregrinations, we returned to Sweden in mid-March.

With an endless string of engagements in the months ahead, Jussi realized that in spite of his fabled memory and his capacity for concentrated work he wouldn't be able to learn Don José in time, to absorb and do justice to a role in French he had never rehearsed or sung onstage. On 25 April Jussi cabled RCA that it was impossible for him to make the *Carmen* recording in June; he proposed that the recording be postponed. Alan Kayes replied by return mail that that too was impossible: the recording was announced as an October release, and "we were so far committed in our arrangements as regards orchestra, chorus, rehearsal and recording studios that we found it necessary to go forward with the project by securing a replacement for you in the role of Don José." Kayes added that Jussi's cable was "a tremendous disappointment," but in view of the expenses incurred in setting up the sessions, RCA "had no choice but to make an arrangement for a replacement in the role and go forward with our plans."[41]

Kayes' letter was followed by another from Edgar Vincent, who was at that time handling Jussi's publicity for the Muriel Francis agency. "We, as everyone else, are really heartbroken at your decision not to come to New York to do the *Carmen* recordings," he wrote. "Somehow I still have hopes that you will change your mind before this letter reaches you. RCA Victor cannot and will not change the date of the *Carmen* recordings."[42]

But Jussi wasn't in a position to reconsider. To make the time to work on Don José and go back to New York he would've had to cancel a whole string of engagements, and he couldn't do that. The *Carmen* recording proceeded on schedule with Jan Peerce, whom Jussi had so enthusiastically recommended to Eddie Johnson. This was the first time Jan replaced Jussi. He sang very well, yet one wonders what that recording would've been like with the voice of Jussi Björling. Risë Stevens, for one, had lasting regrets about the missed opportunity.

> I was getting so excited about it I cannot tell you! I was very disappointed, feeling that he didn't want to do it. Then I found out that wasn't so, but I was never told what had happened. But can you imagine to have him on that record! There was only one Jussi! Anyhow, that was a great disappointment. . . . Our repertoire was so different—I did so many things that call for a dramatic tenor—this would've been the only way we could've sung together. Really, it's such a shame. Years go by very fast, and every time I'd see him, he would say, 'One of these days, Risë!' But it just never happened.[43]

Another engagement that never happened was Jussi's Australian tour. Sometime in 1950, Helmer Enwall notified Jussi that the J. C. Williamson Theatres Ltd. made a firm offer for a tour of Australia from mid-June till late August 1951, with a possible extension to include New Zealand. They were willing to guarantee 12 to 15 concerts at a fee of 50 percent of *gross* receipts with a minimum of 400 Australian pounds per concert. Enwall was certain that the receipts in the Australian concert halls of 1500 to 2500 seats would far exceed the guarantee. The stumbling block was Jussi's serious intention to record *Carmen*—and the seven-day air travel time. He concertized with a lot less strain in America, and if the fees weren't quite as high, it didn't much matter.

✸

On 8 April 1951 Jussi introduced his Des Grieux to Stockholm audiences. In May, he confronted another major challenge, six performances of *Un ballo in maschera* at La Scala. Although he had appeared with the company before, this was the first time he would sing in that historic theater, and he was eagerly looking forward to performing in the world's most revered opera house. This was the one engagement he absolutely refused to break, and the one that forced him to ask for a postponement of the *Carmen* recording.

Jussi traveled to Milan ahead of us for the rehearsals. No sooner had he checked in at his hotel than an earthquake hit. He had never experienced anything like it before, and he was terrified. We had no close friends in Milan; the only person he was able to track down was his Renato-to-be, Paolo Silveri, who was staying elsewhere. Jussi told Silveri he was ready to leave that very minute for Stockholm. "I tried to reassure him, and went to his hotel, bringing with me a bottle of whisky. We spent a couple of hours together, talking about the coming performance and drowning our concerns with a few drinks."[44] Silveri admitted that he needed a few drinks himself to calm his nerves; but he didn't judge that Jussi drank to excess. When Silveri felt that Jussi was sufficiently reassured, he went back to his hotel.

But Jussi was so afraid of aftershocks that he spent the rest of the night in a hired cab. In an interview he gave after he returned home, he said:

> I'm not ashamed to confess that I've never been so frightened in my entire life, and I decided to go home immediately. I got a real shock to my nerves, which I felt for a couple of days, and it didn't make my work any easier. The following day I had a piano rehearsal and then an orchestra rehearsal in the afternoon, and I slept so badly that I couldn't sing at the dress rehearsal but had to limit myself to marking.[45]

In spite of his "earthshaking" arrival in Milan and his frayed nerves, the performances with Silveri, Caniglia, and Cloe Elmo were a success. The audience applauded with the enthusiasm only Italians can show when they are pleased. Toscanini attended the last of the sold-out performances by special arrangement and said that he'd never heard Jussi in better form.[46]

"I have the most beautiful memories of Jussi Björling," Silveri reminisced. "He had a voice of extraordinary quality that I would compare to 'our' Gigli, with whom I sang hundreds of performances. Jussi was a complete artist, he knew how to stand onstage with ease; however, the superb quality of his voice was superior to his interpretative renditions."[47]

On 20 June 1951, Jussi sang at the Sibelius Week in Helsinki. Sibelius often sent telegrams after Jussi's concerts in Finland to thank him for the way he interpreted his music. Something in Jussi's singing, something deep inside him, made one feel that this was the way Sibelius' songs should be performed. Jussi pristinely expressed the light and purity, strength and beauty of Nordic nature, as if Sibelius' music and Jussi's singing sprang from the same source of inspiration. Such attributes can never be learned or acquired—either they are there or they are not. With Jussi, they were there.

The composer was in frail health and unable to attend the concert, but we were honored with an invitation to greet him on his 86th birthday at his home, Ainola. The visit is etched in my mind. I still remember the home's simplicity, the sunshine falling over the broad, freshly scrubbed floor boards, and Sibelius' warmth and cordiality as he received us. His mere presence made a powerful impression. I can still see the old man's hands, violently trembling as he toasted us with champagne; he used a giant glass, so that he wouldn't spill his drink.

When we were ready to leave, Sibelius gave Jussi an inscribed photograph: *To the genius, the great singer, Jussi Björling, with gratitude, Jean Sibelius.* Jussi was deeply moved to receive such a tribute from such a man. He admired Sibelius enormously, and this dedication meant more to him than all the orders and honors he had received. The framed photograph still stands in a permanent place of pride on the piano at our home.

# Chapter 17

# Roméo's Juliette

Jussi kept returning to the notion that we do another complete opera together. On 19 September 1949, Francis Coppicus had written me, "I heard with great pleasure that you are going to sing with Jussi in San Francisco in the *Faust* performance on October 1. Please let me know immediately if this is correct as the Metropolitan Opera is interested." The plan was never realized, but Jussi suggested, "We should sing *Roméo et Juliette* together." Schang approached Gaetano Merola, who liked the idea. Jussi would sing the first Roméo of the 1951 season with Bidú Sayão, and a week later I would take over Juliette from her.

To prepare for my San Francisco Opera debut, I went to Rome alone to study the role with a French coach (whose name I no longer recall). Then in July, when Jussi was to give a concert at the Royal Albert Hall, he sent me to Joseph Hislop's London studio. "Joss is a really excellent teacher! Be sure to sing the Waltz Song for him, and go over the things you are unsure about," Jussi said. Indeed, the one piece that made me nervous was the Waltz Song with its high C—on which I cracked so miserably at the Academy. When I sang it for Joss, he didn't say a word, he just sat quietly and looked at me for a long, long time. We then went over other parts of the role. Joss made many useful suggestions, not merely of the "helpful hints" variety but insightful comments that confirmed Jussi's high regard of his abilities.

"She's much better than you think," Joss said seriously when Jussi came to get me. I would've taken this comment as a polite evasion of saying anything concrete had he not added that I should resume my career in earnest. I had too much to give to the public, it was a waste not to use it, he said. Jussi assured me that Hislop wasn't generous with praise and would never say something he didn't mean. "Then I must still be quite good," I thought, and my self-confidence grew a tiny bit.

Of the first performance of the opera, Howard Fried wrote, "Aside from Bidú Sayão's gentle, affecting Juliet, what stirred the public was the utterly beautiful singing of Jussi Bjoerling in the role of Roméo."[1] According to Alfred Frankenstein, "Jussi Bjoerling's Roméo was remarkable for its stalwart, untiring, invariably just musicianship and its grandly resonant tone."[2] It was a great challenge to sing with Jussi, but to take over a role in which Sayão had excelled bordered on reckless. I was terrified, and I was deeply grateful that Bidú, a sweet and sensitive friend, not wanting to add to my anxiety, did not attend my first performance.[3]

I wasn't worried about the musical aspects of my role. Juliette suited my voice and range very well. Moreover, the dramatic action was much more to my liking than the everyday surroundings of La bohème. The only difficult spot was Juliette's big solo, the role's showpiece, with its coloratura roulades; in this staging I was to dance around and sing at the same time. The other moment I was anxious about was the balcony scene. I was to gracefully toss a rose for Jussi to catch. What if he missed? He calmed my worry: "If I can catch a ball, I can catch a rose!"

The War Memorial Opera House was filled to the last seat on the evening of 27 September, my North American opera debut. The discriminating San Francisco audience was both curious and skeptical. Was this just a publicity stunt? Could Björling's wife really sing a difficult role like Gounod's Juliette? Juliette is one of those parts that requires a lot more than voice— acting, personality, sweetness, charm, and the illusion of innocence and youth. To sing the notes correctly is one thing, to be Juliette is quite another.

As in La bohème, the most important part was the entrance, in which I was led around the stage by my father, Capulet. "See what beauty!" he sang as my smile became stiffer and more artificial with every bow. But as soon as I began to sing, my fears vanished. With every bar of music I felt more secure. The feared high C was in place, and when the first applause broke loose, I knew the audience was pleased. Everything was a breeze after that; I was caught up in the role and I sang better than we two ever could have imagined or the public expected. Their reception of the first act was simply tremendous!

We were both elated, and Jussi, in a rare mood, allowed himself one of his infrequent stage pranks. In the secret marriage ceremony we knelt in front of dear Lorenzo Alvary, the Friar Laurence of the evening, with our backs to the audience. As Lorenzo was about to wed us, with a salacious wink Jussi gave him the easily misinterpretable hand signal of a wedding ring being slipped on a finger. Lorenzo had a hard time preserving his friarly dignity.[4] The dramatic death scene was negotiated without mishaps, although I might have had some trouble from my trick knee. "Welcome, dagger, rest in my breast!" I sang, plunging it into my chest. I fell to the ground and struggled up the 12 steps of a velvet-lined staircase toward the sarcophagus of the dying Roméo. As I was about half way up, I heard my dying French Roméo whisper in Swedish: "Watch out for your knee!"

The evening was a great success. Howard Fried wrote that my voice "has lyrical brightness and appeal. It's a girlish voice . . . fairly in keeping with Juliet's youthful character." He found my acting "extremely naive" with the "saving grace: Mme. Bjoerling is blonde, goodlooking, and sympathetic in appearance."[5]

Even if I turned out to be a singer and not just a curiosity, the star of the evening was Jussi, as was to be expected. "Jussi Bjoerling did the sort of singing that makes opera legends. . . . No opera fan who heard the stocky Swedish tenor will ever forget the perfection of his performance. It was a perfection that combined richness of tone and an absolute, clear mastery in every note he sang. It combined finesse and virility, poetic warmth and high C brilliance."[6]

A gala supper followed at Mama Inga's Little Sweden restaurant. Only five years earlier, Inga Lindholm had been the chef at a summer boardinghouse on Siarö, but with our intervention and material help, she had found her future in San Francisco. Her restaurant was known citywide. Although we'd eaten often at her establishment, this night was special, and our party lasted until early morning, with Jussi standing on a sturdy oak table singing "Sweden's Flag": "Wave proudly against the dusky skies, Sweden's Flag, Sweden's Glory!"

The San Francisco Opera Company's annual fund-raising concert, Fol de Rol, took place soon after in the Civic Auditorium. The 2000 guests around candlelit tables and another 5000 in the galleries enjoyed a concert that could best be described as "crossover," with participating artists venturing as far afield as their talents allowed. Dorothy Kirsten stole the show with "Depuis le jour" from *Louise* and her encore, "The Man I Love"— delivered from her perch atop the grand piano. Jussi and I contributed a selection by Victor Herbert. "Jussi and Anna-Lisa Bjoerling appeared, and people whispered that she has the face of an angel and the voice of a nightingale," wrote Will Stevens. "They sang 'Sweethearts,' and it was a good guess San Francisco would never again hear it sung as the Bjoerlings—a couple of sweethearts themselves—sang it. The crowd cheered a long time."[7] When 7000 music lovers cheer in unison, they make a lot of noise.

Jussi's reviews confirmed that he was in top form during the San Francisco season. He sang Rodolfo, Cavaradossi, and the Duke with lovely Lily Pons, with her "magnetic tone and her high E-flat and E." In such distinguished company Jussi didn't shun a little showmanship of his own.

With the happiest of results, Jussi Bjoerling was in extraordinarily high spirits as the Duke. Frivolity and unscrupulous good humor bubbled out of him. His singing was at all times masterly and thrilling. As a token of his brave mood, he took the liberty (not inscribed by Composer Verdi, but open to all tenors who'll risk it) of soaring with Miss Pons to a lofty D-flat at the end of their Act II "Addio." The note was slightly pinched, by Bjoerling standards, but it was all there.[8]

Jussi had several other engagements to fulfill, among them a Rodolfo, the Duke, and Roméo in Fresno and Los Angeles. We then returned for a joint recital to the San Francisco Opera House on 5 November. Unfortunately, I was indisposed, and Jussi—more than accustomed to handling a whole evening's work by himself!—went on without me. Accompanist Henry Holt and Jussi picked easy substitutions that required no rehearsal, and the audience was well compensated for my absence. After the recital, like a pendulum we swung back to Los Angeles for the *Edgar Bergen Show* on 11 November, where we matched wits with a dummy—Charlie McCarthy. Our performance in San Francisco had generated some unusual invitations along with a lot of publicity!

It was around this time that Jussi had a pleasant visit to Mario Lanza's home. Back in late 1949 or early 1950, Jussi had been asked to audition for the role of Enrico Caruso in a film based on his widow's biography. When Jussi went to Hollywood for the tryout, one studio mogul suggested that he have cosmetic surgery done on his nose to make him look more like Caruso. He refused to even contemplate such a foolish idea; it was as if the movie executives had never heard of nose putty and makeup. They also considered having an actor play the role and dubbing Jussi's voice on the soundtrack. The negotiations never went beyond the discussion stage, but when we returned to Sweden, Jussi told the waiting reporters at Bromma Airport:

> I am in good form, and since the movie people in Hollywood have discovered that I know how to sing, one never knows what surprises may be in store. For now there are only vague plans, and for the present time I have decided to stay in Sweden until October, but you never know. Maybe we will be on our way as soon as August for filming. For now I just want to rest and enjoy myself.[9]

But Jussi wasn't on his way to Hollywood. After auditioning almost every tenor they could think of, MGM settled on Mario Lanza, already under contract with the studio. After two less-ambitious films, he was judged ready to take on the role of Caruso. He made the most of the golden opportunity—the greatest thing about *The Great Caruso* is Lanza's singing. Filming ended in October 1950, and the movie was released in Stockholm in early 1951. Ann-Charlotte asked Jussi to take her to see it. After Mario sang the first few numbers, Jussi leaned over to Ann-Charlotte. "Well, how do you like it?"

"Oh, I love it!" she replied.

219

"You do? How do you like Mario Lanza?"

"Oh, he's so handsome, Daddy!" Ann-Charlotte gushed. "And he sings fantastically!" To this day Ann-Charlotte remembers the expression on her father's face: "Daddy looked like he was going to get up and leave! He was extremely upset with me."

"You really think he is handsome?"

"Oh yes!" Ann-Charlotte insisted.

"And you like his voice?"

"It's beautiful, Daddy!"[10]

"Hmm!" was all Jussi said. But in spite of all the grunting, he recognized Lanza's talent, and I'm told the admiration was mutual. Lanza, for his part, always held Jussi in high regard. Robert Merrill noted that Mario had "very little respect for his own talent or that of other singers. Jussi Bjoerling was the only one he admired."[11] Lanza remarked to another singer in Naples, "That Björling knows how to use his voice."[12]

Jussi's meeting with Mario was arranged through an intermediary. Because Mario's wife, Betty, was unwell, I thought it wiser not to accompany Jussi, but Terry Robinson, Mario's trainer and close friend, was kind enough to supply details of the visit:

George London was visiting us (I lived at Mario's home). George mentioned that Jussi Björling was coming to California to appear in San Francisco, and if he came to Los Angeles, he would love to meet Mario. So Mario gave George his private phone number and said he'd love to meet Mr. Björling. I remember that Mario always felt that Mr. Björling had one of the greatest voices he ever heard. In fact he said, many times, that Mr. Björling should have been an Italian, like Gigli and Di Stefano.

A few months after George left Los Angeles, we got a call from an RCA Victor executive that Mr. Björling was in Los Angeles. Arrangements were made for them to come over to our house in Beverly Hills, a big massive home Mario was renting at this time.

Betty Lanza was pregnant with her third child. She was ill at this time and had a nurse with her, and stayed upstairs in her room. Mario was proud of his big house; he went to the door when Mr. Björling arrived, and the two men embraced. There were good vibrations immediately. (Mr. Björling was accompanied by the RCA Victor executive.) Mario gave them a tour of his home, and then we went into his music room, his private domain where he loved to be. We had the maids set up a huge lunch, and the bar was solid with anything your appetite could desire. After some formalities, food and drink, we started to play records. Gigli, Tucker, Di Stefano—and what surprised me, Tagliavini was not one of their favorites. I am not an opera buff, but I listened in on their conversations, and I was the guy putting on the records.

When half way through the afternoon, drinking now more than eating, we played *Tosca* arias by Lanza ["Recondita armonia"] it brought tears to their eyes. It was an emotional time.

I looked at both men, and they had a great resemblance in their attitudes, not in looks but in feelings, sort of cut from the same cloth. At this time they were both pretty deep into alcohol and both sleepy. The RCA Victor man said, "I better get Mr. Björling back to his hotel, he has an affair to attend tonight." So, within 20 minutes, they left. Mr. Björling was all smiles and half asleep. Mario said goodbye from his chair. I walked them to the front door, and when I came back to the music room, Mario was asleep in his chair. Mr. Björling probably slept in the car, going back to his hotel. This was the only time they met.[13]

※

Our California stay was followed by another spell of cross-country travel. On 19 November 1951 Jussi appeared on another of the simulcast *Voice of Firestone* programs in New York. The shows were underrehearsed, and when the moment of the live broadcast arrived, all Jussi could do was follow the elementary blocking. Most of the time he just stood there and sang, as surviving videotapes document. The sleeve notes of the videotapes state: "In an age when first-class tenors were in abundance, Jussi Bjoerling was in a class by himself." The *Voice of Firestone* excerpt proves that in spite of the shortcomings of television, given the semblance of a stage set and left alone without the support of oh-so-cute extras, Jussi could deliver a creditable "Vesti la giubba." His acting in this scene, although a shadow of the tremendous impact of his Canio in the theater, begs no indulgence. Viewers who never heard him in the flesh can still marvel, as all his contemporaries did, at the natural and effortless way he produced those wonderful sounds.

On 2 December we were back in Los Angeles for a second *Edgar Bergen Show*. Unfortunately, with all the travel, climate changes, and crowds, Jussi picked up some "bug" and the first week of December 1951 found him indisposed. Bing, who'd fought so hard to settle the 1951–52 Met season with Jussi back in February, insisted on a doctor's certificate, which Dr. Bruno Griesman duly supplied.[14] The indisposition cost him *Cavalleria rusticana*. Bing wrote,

> It seems impossible to me that you should appear in a part which you have not done here for a long time and never in the current production without adequate rehearsals. These rehearsals have been scheduled for you but, unfortunately, you could not be available, nor have you been in the audience to watch either the rehearsals or the performance. . . . I am afraid, therefore, that we cannot cast you as Turiddu. I very much regret that, because I feel sure that this would be another excellent and successful part for you.[15]

The 9 December concert Jussi sang in Orchestra Hall in Chicago was completely sold out. Seats had even been placed on the stage, and he didn't want to cancel, so he walked onstage with a temperature of 102. Claudia Cassidy found out about it and felt compelled to mention it in her review, calling his performance one deserving a decoration for "gallantry in action above and beyond the call of duty." She also noted that being a superlative singer with a superlative voice, Jussi was able to deliver his entire printed program. "He made no explanations, offered no alibis, and I know the circumstances only because I was worried about him and inquired." She warned the listeners who heard him for the first time that they were hearing him at half mast, adding "To be sure, Bjoerling at half mast, under fur-lined wraps can sing circles around most of the competition. In quality, timbre, range, brilliance and style he is unique in a world where singing is less and less likely to be a great art."[16]

# Chapter 18

✠

# Jussi Björling, Alcoholic

When people talk about Björling, once past remarks about his voice and singing, they often add "but he had a drinking problem." Others may say with less tact and more directness, "He was an alcoholic," and those with more malice than tolerance will say, "He was a drunkard."

Though the labels may vary, Jussi's affliction was acute alcoholism in the most precise clinical sense. But even those who understand the term can hardly have a full appreciation of the nature of the disease, the power of its grip, and the extent to which it destroys the health, happiness, and human environment of its victim. Even at this distance it's too painful for me to speak of it. Yet I must, for I don't want to reinforce distorted hearsay or exaggerated anecdotes by my silence. The truth is gruesome enough.

After we married, it didn't take me long to discover the pattern to Jussi's drinking. When he excused himself from the table at a restaurant, the bar and the men's room were equally likely destinations. A trip to the hotel lobby provided either the daily newspaper or the daily martini. When he left, I never knew for sure where and how he'd end up, for one drink could lead to another—and nothing more—as easily as it could to another six. In time, I learned to read the danger signals; I knew when it was time to worry, and it's sad satisfaction that my anxiety was usually justified.

When sober, Jussi was the most pleasant, kind, jovial, easygoing, sensitive, lovable, and loving person imaginable for weeks or months on end.[1]

Then suddenly, as if someone had flicked a switch, his mood would shift, a change I've described, for want of a better word, as restlessness. His features tightened, he seemed preoccupied and became irrationally quarrelsome. Anders thinks it was perhaps the projection of his inner struggle against the irrepressible craving for alcohol; whatever it was, Ann-Charlotte believes her father suffered, knowing what he was putting us through. When his frustration peaked and he could take it no longer, he had to drink, and Jussi knew, Lasse maintains, that no matter how hard he tried, he'd never completely give it up.

As much as I could, I stalled the onset of major incidents. We played games: Jussi smuggled liquor into the house and hid it; I found it and hid it from him, then he searched it out and hid it again, and so on. Or I'd dilute the hard liquor with water, but of course he wasn't fooled and would only drink more. Eventually he looked for a fight, an excuse to storm out of the house in an artificial fury. This phase could go on for hours or days, until the tension nearly drove us out of our minds. We knew exactly what was about to happen, but we all felt as if we were submerged in a diver's bell, gasping for air. We couldn't breathe until he was gone.

Invariably our momentary sense of relief turned into anxious concern. We hoped his disappearance would last only the day, and sometimes it did. But many times he didn't come home for two or three days, often longer. Then we knew it was time to look for him, for by then he'd be so hopelessly drunk, he was too ashamed to come home and face his family.

His habitual watering holes were relatively few; they included a handful of public places and the homes of a score of "friends," the majority of whom were of a low social strata, dating back to Jussi's impecunious student days. Jussi was good company to his sauce-brethren: a visit from the famous and affluent Björling guaranteed a spell of free-flowing booze.

I finally resorted to an arrangement we both found distasteful but necessary. I handled our finances; his pay from the Opera was sent directly to the bank. Jussi carried only enough pocket money to pay for cab fare and a lunch or dinner with beer perhaps, but not enough for daily and daylong casual drinking. No matter, he managed to find money, and he usually greeted his cronies with some cash, ready to get rip-roaring drunk. After that money was gone, they financed the next stage of the drinking spree by pawning his gold watch, ring, cufflinks, tie clasp. Some well-meaning buddy would stick the receipts in his pocket so Jussi could redeem them later. As the days wore on, Jussi signed I.O.U.s, and with his mind increasingly clouded, the amounts grew larger. Afterward, when the party was over, these people brought the I.O.U.s to me. Out of sheer embarrassment, I paid.

Of course, this defeated the whole purpose of our domestic "no cash" policy. On one occasion, when somebody brought me an I.O.U. large enough to pay for several rounds of akvavit for the entire Swedish merchant marine, I refused to pay—and made it clear I wouldn't pay in the future either. I had no choice; I had to play the "heavy" in our private drama. The people involved, perfectly willing to speed the self-destruction of Sweden's foremost lyric talent, now began to spread stories about me in the city. The unadorned facts were true—I did refuse to pay; the malicious embellishments were not.

When Jussi hadn't shown up for a number of days, our search began with a round of phone calls to the three or four places where he might be. Sometimes this produced results. The answering party admitted Jussi was there—and they were ready to see him leave. After a few days of nonstop drinking Jussi Björling was unfit company for man or beast. If the calls turned up nothing, I'd ask a close family friend—often Sven Salén, a great music lover whose songs Jussi had recorded, or Pastor Tore Norrby—to accompany me to the predictable spots. Even as a young boy, Anders came with me on these sad missions. Later Lasse and eventually Ann-Charlotte were my support.

If we had to go to a private home, we first listened through the door for the telltale sounds of a drinking party. Often we heard Jussi's voice, talking or singing in a nearly unrecognizable baritone. The scene was usually depressing beyond description, with a small group of heavily intoxicated people. We'd go up to Jussi, embrace and comfort him. Ann-Charlotte would gently say, "Daddy, it's time to go home." The sight of Jussi's condition could inspire no other emotion but pity. Once Sven Salén, who loved Jussi like a brother, started to cry: "I cannot see him in this state! I cannot!"

Most of the time Jussi didn't protest but came along without objection. He had been ready to come home perhaps for days, he just didn't dare. He knew that he may have been a celebrated tenor for the world, but to the children he was just Daddy. He had to earn their respect at home, away from the stage. The helpless drunk we furtively packed into a cab wasn't the father he wanted his children to remember. It filled him with shame and self-loathing to be seen by his family in that condition.

When we finally brought him home, he was always dreadfully sick, his body ravaged by the massive alcohol intake. He slept in the darkened bedroom for a day, sometimes two, depending on his condition. Anders remembers one occasion when he came home and just passed out, and the only thing we could do was haul him to bed. When Jussi was in this condition, I felt I was more than granted my early wish to become a nurse, to help the sick. He didn't want any of us to see him in that state; I was the only one allowed into the darkened bedroom. Ann-Charlotte, like the rest of us, has indelible memories of these depressing times.

> The first day I'd only be allowed to knock on the door and say, "How are you, Daddy?" He'd answer something, and I'd leave. Then the next day I'd come home from school, and he'd be in bed, the blinds closed. I'd be allowed to stand on the threshold of his dark room and talk to him. "Hello, Daddy, how are you?" And he would say "I'm all right, but stay where you are, don't come in."
>
> So I'd come back the next day, and maybe the third day he'd say

"Come in, sit and talk to me," but still in the dark. He didn't want me to see what he looked like. Finally, in another day, the blinds were pulled up and I would think, "How nice! He must be better. Thank you, dear God." But when I sat with him he would turn away so I wouldn't see the shame and humiliation in his face. Then slowly he'd turn and look at you, and I felt his sad, sad eyes wanted to say "Please love me anyway!"

It was more than a human being could endure. No matter how much you put your arm around him and reassured him that it wasn't his fault, it didn't help. A person so sweet, kind, and so loving to have this plague! It was so unfair to him and to those he loved![2]

I cannot possibly enumerate the number of times this happened. Nor could I place these incidents with any degree of accuracy into this account of our life together. It could happen monthly, two to three times a summer, or not at all for half a year or more. The frequency, if not the regularity, of recurrence makes it impossible and unnecessary for me to interrupt the flow of this narrative with time out for another incident, and yet another. Even a cursory overview of the Chronology of Jussi's performances shows many gaps when he didn't perform at all. Suffice it to say that a fair number, specifically in Sweden, could carry an entry for drinking.

In the United States and on tour elsewhere, it was a different story. Contrary to the rumors, I don't think he had more than a couple of incidents of really bad drinking in America. Yes, he might drink excessively at a dinner party, and yes, he went off to bars. He could have a few drinks in him, or more than a few, without ever showing any signs of intoxication or suffering more than a bad hangover. But he didn't have a circle of sycophants and fellow alcoholics in America, to encourage him by their own participation.

The full effect of Jussi's alcoholism can be rendered palpable only by a negative statement: had he never touched alcohol, we would have had the most balanced, most harmonious, most happy home life imaginable. The proof of this lies in the long spells when we were exactly like that. When the storm passed and Jussi fully recovered from the latest episode, when he tried so hard to be for us and for himself the husband and father he always wanted to be, our little family experienced a rare bliss. Each time, we prayed that it would remain so, that it would last, but we knew all along that it wouldn't —and it never did. All we could hope for was longer and longer stretches between incidents.

Especially in the summers on Siarö, our life was simply idyllic—after the storms. Sobered up once more, Jussi was so remorseful that he just couldn't do enough to atone for the upheaval he had caused. In the evenings, when the children went to bed, he sat and talked to them about his life, his childhood, his travels with their grandfather. Other times he just sat quietly on their beds, then they would say their evening prayers together. They had their own prayer, but something was always added for the moment. Anders' eyes still fill with tears when he talks about such times. Sometimes the calm and peace lasted, many times it did not.

In the hardest times, in Jussi's most tormented moments, Pastor Norrby came to us like a guardian angel. It was so infinitely reassuring when Tore sat on the edge of Jussi's bed, held his hands, and spoke with him for a long while. It calmed his spirit, and then they read together "God, to whom all children are dear, look after me who is so small." Because he never received his first communion, Jussi felt like an outsider to religion, but I believe he may have been unaware of the depth of his faith. He had a deep-rooted unspoken belief in God and a great inner spirituality. It didn't make him a churchgoer, but rather a man who believed, a man who could distinguish between good and evil, a man who possibly in his entire life didn't consciously commit a mean act. It was manifested in his uncompromising quest for truth and sincerity. He shared his father's values: love for his country, strong feelings for nature, and the innate goodness of a warm heart.

But Jussi's sickness was a heartrending tragedy. To stop himself from drinking, he subjected himself to a special treatment. He took Antabuse tablets daily, a drug that would make him violently ill if he drank any alcohol. The treatment worked; the only way he could drink was by *not taking* the pill. After a while, that was exactly what happened.

Both Anders and Lasse were very protective of me; they knew how Jussi's drinking made me suffer. When Jussi's darker side came to the fore, Anders especially took it very hard; as the eldest, he was too early thrown into situations a boy of his age shouldn't have had to confront, and I often sought his advice when making important decisions. With all the stress at home, his school performance suffered, and when he saw his report cards from the 1951–52 academic year, he knew he had to do something. He had only two years left until graduation, and his grades had to improve if he was to be admitted to a university. He asked us to let him go to Sigtuna, a boarding school. We agreed, and his grades shot up.

As he matured, Anders stood up to his father about his drinking, which only infuriated Jussi. It wasn't a matter of exercising his parental authority; it was his frustration over knowing that Anders was right and he, Jussi, was wrong. Once, after a particularly bad incident, Anders completely lost control.

> I saw what Dad's drinking did to Mother and how desperate and helpless she was. We had a terrible scene. I yelled at Dad, called him names, and I said why doesn't he just pack up and go away, get out of our lives and leave us alone. It was awful, and I wish I had never said all those horrible things. I would do anything if I could take them back, if I could undo what happened. It hurts me even now the way I hurt Dad.[3]

Yes, Jussi was deeply hurt, but it was true. For years I intuitively handled our many crises correctly, as Lasse attests: "When he came home, Mother was happy to see him safely back. She wouldn't start screaming, she never scolded him afterward, she would just try to put him to bed. Mother was not a nag, she was very wise in that respect. Of course she was hurt, but her first concern was to take care of Dad."[4]

Nevertheless by late 1951, after years of the dreadful problems his drinking had caused us, I reached the breaking point. I realized that the vicious circle of sobriety, drinking, remorse, recovery, and fresh promises of restraint—only to be broken—would never change. It was like sitting on a powder keg, never knowing when its dangling fuse might be ignited. My nerves were frayed and my endurance depleted. I had been hospitalized with nervous exhaustion on two separate occasions, and although I'd considered it before, in a state of total desperation, I decided to file for divorce.

It was an agonizing decision, but the only solution, I felt. I had to do it, if not for myself then for the children. The atmosphere Jussi created tore the family apart. It was destructive to us all, and it had to stop somehow. My mother hadn't encouraged me to take this step, but she agreed with my decision. Lasse and Anders too were solidly on my side, which hurt Jussi. Only Ann-Charlotte was opposed. At the young age of eight, it was for her unthinkable not to have her Daddy in the home.

Jussi realized I was serious when I asked our family lawyer to draw up the divorce papers. He was deeply shaken, and frankly, so was I. I was about to take a momentous step, perhaps even more significant than when I married him. I was dressed to leave the house to keep my appointment with the lawyer. But I didn't go. I can put it in no other way: I just couldn't go through with it. I could not imagine life without Jussi. We loved each other, and we had been through too much together. We were bonded for life, for better or worse, in sickness and health. Without him I would have had tranquility and serenity—but without him I would have had no life at all.

# Chapter 19

# *Il trovatore*

Trying to keep Jussi in line in America, collecting him in Stockholm after his binges, preparing for and then canceling a divorce—all these things took their toll. In mid-December 1951, I was again hospitalized with a nervous collapse, a horrifying experience I'd never want to repeat. Word about my condition reached our closest friends, and on 2 January 1952 Freddie Schang sent us a telegram to inquire about my health. A week later Freddie acknowledged Jussi's return telegram. "We were all very much relieved to know that Anna-Lisa was better, and we heard from other sources that she had been able to go home Christmas Eve for a couple of hours." In the same letter, Schang listed Jussi's forthcoming engagements from 2 February through 10 March. The stops were Topeka, San Antonio, Houston, Palm Beach, St. Petersburg, Havana (two recitals), Tampa, Sarasota, and Kingston, Jamaica.

In late January 1952, Jussi (who hadn't sung with Olle and Gösta since the Björling Male Quartet disbanded) and his two brothers made a 78 rpm recording of "Sommarglädje." One side was the dubbing of their acoustic recording, and on the reverse the same voices sang the same song 30 years later. One copy of this unique recording was given away as a prize in a radio contest for listeners. Except for that, my own copy, and a few more in the Swedish Radio Archives, I believe less than half a dozen are in private hands.

Then Jussi returned to New York alone; in my condition, it was unthinkable I'd accompany him. Freddie Schauwecker was to meet him in Topeka, but when he arrived there, he was informed that Jussi hadn't shown, the recital had been canceled, and that he should proceed to San Antonio. He found the opera manager in Texas likewise frantic. "Jussi hadn't shown up there either! Jussi had never left his New York hotel room. He was ill, some sort of nervous ailment affecting his memory if I remember correctly. He returned to Sweden without doing that Southern tour at all. But this had nothing to do with his drinking."[1]

Schauwecker probably didn't want to disclose the real reason for the cancellations. Jussi was worried about me, and he felt that even if he kept his concert dates and sang, it would be a disaster. Schang understood; he let him cancel, concocted some medical excuse, and on 7 February Jussi came home. But my condition improved daily and, reassured, he returned to New York in time for the recording sessions of his first complete opera, *Il trovatore*. After *Rigoletto* and *Carmen*, this was to be the third opera RCA would bring out on the new long playing medium. Recording began on 22 February and ended on 30 March. The cast—Zinka Milanov, Fedora Barbieri, Leonard Warren—was the best that could be assembled.

During this time, Jussi's regular, affectionate correspondence enabled me to follow his travels at a distance—and showed him to be on his best behavior. Once more, he was trying very hard to curb his drinking. To ease my mind, I'd packed for him a supply of Antabuse, hoping that he would take it daily. I believe he did. The earliest note I was able to locate from this period was written in the last week of February, soon after he had settled in New York.

> My dearest little Mama! Now I'm finally on the move again, that is, I'm installed in my hotel room, which by the way is much nicer and less expensive than the one I had last time. I have already rehearsed *Il trovatore* with Cellini, that was yesterday; today at 2:30 p.m. I rehearsed with *Firestone* and tonight at 7:30 recording session with RCA. . . . It was really sweet of you, dearest little Mama, to write those words in my red book. I don't think that I needed the pills, but you were so thoughtful and sweet about it, so I took one immediately and am going to continue doing so. God bless you, my darling.
>
> I'm writing to you in pencil, because I don't have a fountain pen handy, but only you will read my chicken scratches, including spelling errors, so it probably doesn't matter.
>
> I don't have more time to write now. Say hello to our little darlings and kiss them for me. Take really good care of yourself, dear little Mama. Bye for now, and please write soon. Kisses and hugs, Papa

For the first time in his experience, he wrote me soon after, he seemed to enjoy the recording process because the music wasn't chopped up into segments of three or four minutes' duration. "I've had two recording sessions of *Il trovatore*. 'Di quella pira,' in the correct key of course, I've never sung it this well. That was fun, you can imagine. Hope that it continues as well." Jussi also kept a diary on this trip. His brief entry for 7 March reads: "Recording *Trovatore*, 11 a.m. I have sung 'Ah sì, ben mio' and stretta. It was a real hit. Have never been in better form."

It's amazing that Jussi sang the recording as well as he did while sustaining a nonstop schedule in New York. As his diary entries show, between recording sessions, he rehearsed for the 10 March *Voice of Firestone* engagement, and rehearsals for *Don Carlo*, some of them all-day affairs, took place on 8, 11, 12, 15, 17, 18, 19 (orchestral rehearsals), and 20 (dress rehearsal) March. He was even able to squeeze in a social engagement, lunch with Dorothy Caruso, on 14 March.

On 21 and 24 March Jussi sang the first two of his three scheduled performances of *Don Carlo*, the sum total of his appearances with the Met that season. His diary entry for the 21 March performance reads, "Miracle! Bing overjoyed. Wished me 'welcome home' before the performance and expressed his great enthusiasm after each act. He, the Boss, cannot possibly imagine a season without Björling." But Jussi's very next mention of Bing offers a clue of his distrust and dislike of the man. Satisfied that Björling had attended the rehearsals and sang as scheduled, Bing showed no further interest in him, whereupon Jussi noted, "Have met and seen Bing several times. He, on the other hand, doesn't seem to have a notion of my existence. One cannot figure that man out." Edward Johnson must've felt the same; he once confided to us, "There's nothing in the world I have regretted so much as recommending this man as manager for the Metropolitan."

Jussi's continued unwillingness to make himself unconditionally available to Bing permanently soured the relationship between him and the general manager. It was incomprehensible to Bing that Jussi took a pragmatic attitude toward the Met—the pinnacle of achievement for most singers—weighing it as mere income: could he afford to sing there? Also, when Jussi learned of special deals being secretly made with some artists, he felt offended that his services were implicitly devalued vis-à-vis his colleagues.

Jussi sensed right away that Bing's measured courtesy and calculating formality were self-serving, the means to make his singers agree to his terms. Beyond that, he had no interest in him or anyone, as an artist or a person, and this behavior alienated Jussi. What's more, his Swedish, British, and American agents already turned down more offers than they accepted, which didn't exactly predispose Jussi to make concessions for the "Boss."

After the second *Don Carlo*, Jussi began his East Coast tour with Freddie Schauwecker. On 26 March he traveled to Canada and was driven on to Trois-Rivières for a recital on 27 March. He wrote me that day, reminding me of our last Canadian visit and our walk from the railway depot to the hotel in a snowstorm and subzero temperatures. Before he went to bed that night, Jussi noted in his diary: "Returned to Montreal by car after the concert, almost three hours. How hellish." Hellish or not, the next day he had to return to New York.

I wrote to Jussi fairly regularly, keeping him informed about my health and asking him to continue with his pills. No doubt when he felt like having a drink he had one, but I believe that Freddie's presence checked his drinking. Freddie was a friend, and he took care of Jussi beyond an accompanist's call of duty. To reassure me, he wrote, "Dearest Anna-Lisa, you do not know how happy I am to hear from Jussi himself that you are feeling fine again! That is the best news of the month!! Jussi is also in top form, looking healthy and happy. We expect to have some very fine concerts. My love to you and your dear mother and the children."

Jussi's entry for 30 March notes "Bob Merrill's wedding" along with "RCA FINAL Recording 5:30." It must've been a happy day, for on 31 March 1952 he wrote me, on his own very impressive, personalized Metropolitan Opera stationery, and proudly reported,

> Last night we completed the recording of *Trovatore*. We worked for four hours from 5 to 9, but now it's ready and it has gone surprisingly well. You can hear it yourself when I come home, I think that you'll like it.
>
> Tomorrow I sing in Washington, April 1, April 4 in Chattanooga, 7th in Lexington, the 8th I return to N.Y. to complete my guest appearance at the Met on the 9th, Carlos. Something new has been added since I wrote you last. RCA wants me to record a "Björling Concert." There will be 10 to 12 songs, depending on their length. Naturally I shall choose the ones both you and I like best. Isn't that fun? The recording will take place on the 11th from 2 to 5 and 8 to 10, so I certainly have more than enough to do....
>
> I look for letters from you every day. Write one more little letter, please, just a few lines. Hope you are all fine and that you take care of yourselves. I feel, knock on wood, excellent, but oh, oh, oh, how I long to come home to you my darlings.

The *Trovatore* recording was indeed impressive, and it stood the test of time. Philip Hope-Wallace thought that Björling "though not mysterious and seldom quite romantic enough, is so much the best Manrico available that one makes no objections at all; 'Di quella pira' is the genuine article, the romantic passages have a strong individual timbre, and always he is in there singing with a genuine large Verdian style and a fine line."[2] More than three decades later, Jürgen Kesting wrote, "His Manrico projected not only grace in 'Deserto sulla terra,' and elegance in 'Ah sì, ben mio,' a natural cantabile in 'Mal reggendo' and 'Ai nostri monti,' but also provided energetic attacks at the dramatic high points.... He sings the stretta with explosive élan, precise *gruppetti*, great resonance and tonal intensity."[3]

❊

By this time Jussi had turned into a model correspondent, and I was reassured by the consistently upbeat mood of his letters. His private letters were written in a simple but personal style, naturally and with spontaneity. He had a wonderful way of expressing himself in Swedish. His letters to the children were warm and affectionate, and those he wrote to me often contained so much feeling and self-revelation that they made me cry. In business matters, too, Jussi attended to his own correspondence, although he did not enjoy it. I never ghostwrote any of his letters; when I handled business correspondence with Schang, I wrote in the first person over my signature, even if I was speaking for Jussi.

Preparing for his evening recital, Jussi closed his first letter from Washington with "Now I will rest a little before the crowing." This "crowing" took place in Constitution Hall, and in his own words, he received "a thunderous ovation. I sang 10 encores, the audience roared and shouted like in the noisiest football stadium. It was fun, you can imagine. Tonight I will sing for the wounded from Korea, a very worthwhile cause as you know."

Jussi's next letter is dated 4 April 1952, The Read House, Chattanooga, Tennessee: "The hotel is very fine, nice rooms, we, you and I, supposedly have been here twice before." I was amused by this comment. Obviously, he didn't have the slightest recollection, and I could very well identify with his lapse of memory. In our gypsy lives we had been to so many places, large and small, that between the two of us we couldn't have remembered half of them.

In his next long letter, after reporting that the concert "went great," my lonely husband complained, "I haven't heard anything from you for so long, there are probably letters waiting in New York. I hope and believe that you are all in good health and are doing well. Oh how I miss you!!! A thousand kisses and hugs along with the warmest greetings from your Jussi." The next day, 6 April, he wrote from Lexington, Kentucky with this tongue-in-cheek comment: "Today at 4:30 there is a big tea party, hordes of ladies who want to catch a glimpse of the miracle—you know, one of those receptions I'm so particularly enchanted by. Last time, two years ago, the concert took place in a hall that seated 1500 people. Now there's a new arena seating 15,000—how about that!"

In his diary entry for 8 April Jussi noted, "Return flight to New York 10 a.m. Not enough time to make it back in time for rehearsal of Carlos. All principal parts have been reassigned except mine. It will work nevertheless. Typical of Met!" He closed with personal remarks: "No letter from Anna-Lisa. Worried. Anders' letter made me very happy." Apparently, my telegram wishing him well for the upcoming performance arrived late in the day. When he received it, he replied by telegram on 9 April 1952. "Thank you darling for the telegram. Stay calm now. Singing tonight Carlos. Feeling fine, warmest greetings, Papa." When he finally received my letter on the 10th, he replied immediately by return mail.

> Thanks little sweet one for the letter, which I've just read. You can't imagine how happy I am. Now there are just six days left until I come home. Oh how wonderful it will be to relax from singing and music for a while. I really need it. It sounds as if I should be completely worn out, but not at all. I feel first rate. I sang for the last time yesterday at the Met, Carlos, and it wasn't catshit either, you can be sure of that. I don't think I have ever

sounded better, that was everyone's opinion. . . . Cuba and Jamaica aren't going to happen this time, possibly in a year or so. Everything is set for my return home on the 17th, Thursday.

Today, I had a long talk with Bing, which you will hear about when I come home. I was out and strolled on Madison. When I noticed the time was short, I tried to get a taxi, and one came quickly enough and stopped in front of me. It was occupied by an older lady, but she was paying the fare so I assumed that it was going to be available. The lady stared at me the whole time, and I thought that perhaps she thought that I was impolite for not opening the car door. I did so and to my surprise she addressed me by my name and said that she had seen and heard me both on the radio and at the Met, and that she was a great admirer of mine. Then she said, you perhaps will recognize me when I say who I am, my name is Frida [sic] Hempel. Mrs. Hempel asked me to telephone her so that we could agree on a meeting. Can you believe it, the great Frida Hempel, one of the greatest singers there has ever been. I had no idea that she was still alive. I shall tell you more about her when I come home.

I learned upon his return that he did indeed visit Frieda Hempel; they had a pleasant discussion about singing and singers, Caruso in particular.

Jussi wound up his New York stay with a marathon recording session on 11 April. "Recording RCA Björling Concert. 2:00–5:00 and 7:00–10:00 p.m. The recordings went brilliantly well. I sang 16 selections between 2:00–6:00. That has never been done before. I'm very satisfied." He then flew to Houston on the 13th, sang a concert on the 14th, and flew back to New York on the 15th. Even an ocean away, he jotted in his diary, "Lasse's birthday" on the 16th, and on the next day he made the triumphant entry: "Return home. FINALLY!!!!!"

⚒

Back in Stockholm, Jussi kept his drinking under control. He didn't abstain —that was beyond him—but he did stay sober. In May, June, and July of 1952, he gave recitals in England, Denmark, Finland, and Sweden. He was active, but his schedule was not especially strenuous. Then on Siarö, in the last days of August, he developed a pain in his stomach. We didn't think it was dangerous, and he endured it for some days. We suspected that a combination of stress and alcohol may have aggravated his ulcer, but he was booked for a concert in Norrköping on the following Sunday evening, and so he tried to treat the ulcer himself with diet, bed rest, and relaxation.

Then on 31 August he suddenly took ill. We were all alone; my mother had gone back to Stockholm with the children for the school year. I called for an ambulance, and with the help of neighbors we transported Jussi to the Östanå dock. The ambulance took him to the Red Cross Hospital, where he was diagnosed with a bleeding ulcer. After we had checked him in, I called to cancel the concert in Norrköping. The organizers wondered if I could sing in his place, and Jussi urged me to accept the invitation, so I jumped in a taxi to Norrköping to be his stand-in. The concert, conducted by Bertil Bokstedt, was a success.

Jussi was hospitalized for two weeks. His condition improved, and he sang four recitals in Sweden in October and two in Iceland in November. Royal Festival Hall and Albert Hall engagements followed, and it was possibly the latter that Regina Resnik attended. She used to come to Jussi's performances in New York, but this was the first time she heard him abroad.

> I remember vividly going to the Albert Hall to hear a concert by Björling. I also remember that he stood onstage in his particular pose, very round-chested, and holding his lapels with both hands. It seemed to support him at the beginning of the concert. I looked at the program and I didn't believe that he was starting with "Ingemisco." It took my breath away.
>
> I watched the process of getting his voice and body ready to sing. It took 10 seconds before he sang "Ingemisco." I watched him breathe, open his mouth, and sing. There was always thought behind his singing, which was totally natural, thought out, and technically beautifully mastered, but never obvious. He never gave me the sensation that he was thinking *how* he was singing. What could be more beautiful than watching this singer? This "Ingemisco" was probably one of the most beautifully sung five minutes that I have ever, ever heard in my life. So much so that I sat there crying like a child.
>
> I went backstage to see him, and he said, "If I have encores, what do you want?" I said, the Flower Song. And he said, "You shall have it." I remember that with great tenderness. At the end of the concert he said in English, "I dedicate this Flower Song to a very special young singer." And he looked at me, I was there in the third row. It was one of those many nice gestures to me from Björling that I remember that remain unforgettable.[4]

Between and after the London engagements, Jussi performed in Manchester, Glasgow, and Dublin to excellent reviews. He had no health problems and performed extremely well during this British tour. Everywhere his recitals sold out, and he enjoyed the warmest reception an artist could imagine. At the end of each program the people went crazy, screaming, ecstatic—perfect illustrations of how "fanatics" had come to be known as "fans."

Jussi's success was even greater in London. I believe this was the recital Teddy Nyblom was referring to when he wrote,

> I was in his audience in the Albert Hall in London, packed with people even on the stage. I whispered to Anna-Lisa that Jussi ought to sing something in English. Up to then he kept to German, French, Italian and Swedish. Anna-Lisa agreed with me and rushed behind the stage. . . . [Jussi] asked for silence, and said: "Because you have been so nice to me this evening, I will now sing for you—'Because'!" Tremendous applause broke out.[5]

After the recital, as I made my way to the car that was to take us to the Savoy, I got lost in the crush of people. Normally, when we became separated from one another in public, we members of the Björling family whistled our special signal: Siegfried's Leitmotif from Wagner's *Ring*. It never failed to rally the clan, but now it was impossible to be heard over the jubilant cries of the people who had gathered on the street. "Calm down!" Jussi screamed at the crowd. "I have to find my wife!" Eventually, I received some assistance from British bobbies, who escorted me back to him. Some people jumped up on the hood of the car, and the rest followed us all the way back to the Savoy.

Charlie Chaplin was also staying at the Savoy, a favorite spot for artists, and he asked if we could find a way for him to attend the second sold-out London recital. Naturally, we arranged for him to be our guest, and afterward, he invited us to supper at the Coq d'Or. When we all arrived back at the hotel, he asked us up to his suite.

We found out that he had come to London with his wife Oona and their children to attend the premiere of his film *Limelight*. On the passage over, Chaplin was tremendously upset to receive a telegram informing him that he was suspected of being a communist sympathizer and would have to appear before the House Un-American Activities Committee. He'd decided not to return to a country that treated him so. They would settle in Switzerland, and Oona had just flown back to California to retrieve their valuables from their safe deposit box. Chaplin was worried that Oona might be interrogated when she reached the United States and wouldn't be able to bring back what they needed to begin a new life in Switzerland. He was nervous and didn't want to be alone, so he asked us to keep him company.

It was an unforgettable night. Chaplin told us about his life, the hardships of his youth, his career difficulties, his happiness with Oona and his family, his love of music. That he was very musical was evident from the music he composed for *Limelight* as well as some of his earlier films. He kept us entertained until early morning with his stories. The entire time he talked about himself and, if possible, he was even funnier, more entertaining in private than in his films. His all-night monologue was animated to the point of being acted out. When he finally let us go to our room, we'd had nearly 12 hours of Chaplin—and collapsed into bed.

Soon after, Oona came back to London, her delicate mission complete. The family continued their trip to Paris and thence to Switzerland, where they settled in Vevey. Charlie lived out his days there in peace and tranquility. A charming bronze statue of the little tramp near the shores of Lake Geneva commemorates the illustrious English-American expatriate.

※

Jussi never took the approval of his audiences for granted. He knew he had to earn his laurels every night, that he was only as good as his last review and tonight's performance. Contrast this attitude with that of Mario del Monaco: once, when a reporter in Berlin asked him for his opinion about his tenor colleagues, Mario replied, "Colleagues? What colleagues? I only had two, Caruso and Gigli, and they are both dead."[6] The unintentional humor of this towering conceit is best enjoyed if one imagines Gigli returning the compliment: "I had only two colleagues, Caruso and Mario del Monaco."

Jussi was incapable of making such a statement, even in jest. Ivor Newton described him as "genuinely modest." On one occasion, as they drove home after an Albert Hall recital, Newton asked him why he had been so nervous before the concert; after all, he was in splendid form. Jussi pointed at the giant letters on the posters over his name: *The World's Greatest Tenor.*

> "That's what frightens me," he said. "Can you imagine what it's like to sing to a vast crowd of people who have come to hear the 'world's greatest tenor'?"
>
> "You know," I replied, "you *are* the world's greatest tenor."
>
> "Nonsense," he said almost embarrassed by my words.
>
> "Well then," his manager, Victor Hochhauser asked, "tell me who is."
>
> He thought deeply for a moment. "Gigli," he said. "No, he is too old. Schipa? No, he can't sing Lieder."
>
> And he went on through the list, deciding that there was something wrong with all his rivals. "Perhaps you are right," he said at length, with a little gratified smile. "Perhaps I *am* the world's greatest tenor."[7]

# Chapter 20

# Faust in Tails

In December 1952, Jussi and I sang *La bohème* in Helsinki, and on 2 January 1953 Jussi sang *Rigoletto* in Stockholm. We then had to rush to New York, where we barely had time to settle at the Hotel St. Moritz before the three-week-long recording sessions of *Cavalleria rusticana* and *Pagliacci* began on 9 January. On the same day, Jussi signed his contract for the 1952–53 Met season for only two performances, a Turiddu and a Duke in February 1953. The contract didn't carry the Met's option for the tour.

The day the contract was signed, Rudolf Bing sent a cordial letter "as an 'aide memoire' before we will make out the actual contract form" confirming the verbal agreement for the 1953–54 season. According to the letter, Jussi would appear in *Faust*, *Bohème*, *Trovatore*, "and if at all possible as Ottavio in *Don Giovanni* in Italian." Bing stressed that the 18 guaranteed performances hinged on the assumption that he would sing a few performances of the Mozart opera. He closed the letter in an especially friendly tone. "I assure you that I am very happy indeed that we will have you with us again on such an extensive basis and that you will return to your rightful place at the Metropolitan. It is with great pleasure that I look forward to the renewal of our collaboration and I appreciate your making yourself available for such an extended period."[1] But Jussi declined, once more, to sing Don Ottavio, and the guarantee in the contract, dated 5 February 1953, was reduced to a minimum of 16 performances.

RCA had mustered the best cast possible for the January 1953 recording sessions: *Cavalleria rusticana* had Zinka Milanov and Robert Merrill, and in *Pagliacci* Jussi's partners were Victoria de los Angeles, Leonard Warren as Tonio, and Robert Merrill as Silvio. The *Pagliacci* in particular was an artistic success. In an article comparing 20 complete recordings of this opera made between 1907 and 1988 David McKee wrote, "Canio here rejoices in a voice of incomparable beauty: Jussi Björling at the top of his game. . . . His 'Un tal gioco' should be a model for all aspiring Canios, and the Swedish tenor offers the noblest 'Vesti la giubba' with but a hint of a sob."[2]

Canio was, as I said before, the role I most loved to hear Jussi sing. As the desperate clown he gave everything he had: the great loneliness he carried deep inside and the suffering and tragedy that became more and more a part of his last years. All these emotions were in his voice, and his dramatic sense peaked in this role. Every time I heard him as Canio, his rendition was so gripping that I could barely hold back my tears. In the Stockholm staging, after a profoundly emotional delivery of "Vesti la giubba," he staggered up the steps of the traditional commedia dell'arte stage and pulled the curtain aside. He paused for a second, stepped through the opening, then with a violent gesture pulled the curtain closed behind himself. As he disappeared from the audience, the proscenium curtain fell. The scene made such a strong impact on the audience that in some performances it took a few moments before the violent applause broke loose. Not only the spectator was left shaken by the performance; Jussi too was completely exhausted every time he sang Canio.

The boys couldn't miss school, but nine-year-old Ann-Charlotte was with us in New York for a post-Christmas vacation while the 1953 recording of *Cavalleria rusticana* was being made. Jussi let her come along to the recording studio, and with her captivating ways, it didn't take long before she made friends with the distaff choral contingent.

> At first I just stood there, but I was uninhibited, so I walked up to the ladies in the chorus. They let me stand with them, and when the music reached *A casa, a casa amici!* I couldn't restrain myself and began to sing along. I didn't know the words of course, but I picked up the melody from the rehearsals and made up sounds resembling Italian. Dad was about to launch into the Brindisi when he noticed me standing there, singing along to my heart's content. He knew that I had never heard *Cavalleria* before— he was so surprised that instead of starting to sing, he said, "What are you doing there, Lillan?"

There was a long silence. In lieu of an explanation Ann-Charlotte gave him her innocent blue-eyed gaze. "OK. You may stay as long as nothing strange will be heard on the record."[3]

It wasn't easy to stifle our daughter's tenacious desire to sing, but I don't hear anything unusual on this famous recording. Not even our family can tell that Ann-Charlotte is singing with the chorus.

Soon after our return to Stockholm, we both participated in a benefit concert for Dutch flood victims on 22 February 1953. In Paris, Jussi sang a gala recital for the Parisian press on 12 March, but he developed bronchitis and his long-awaited debut as Roméo at the Paris Opéra had to be canceled.

Fortunately, he was well enough the following week to honor his commitments in Glasgow and London, which city was preparing for the coronation of Queen Elizabeth II. London's theaters and concert halls were vying with each other to turn the coronation season into something memorable, and in the lobby of the Savoy we bumped into Beniamino Gigli, Maurice Chevalier, and Charlie Chaplin—we were all registered guests! In the course of pleasant conversation with Gigli (how I was struck by the extraordinary beauty and sweetness of my idol's speaking voice—to listen to my two favorite tenors conversing was a musical experience!), we discovered that on 22 March, Gigli was to sing a matinee in the Royal Festival Hall, while Jussi was to give a concert that evening in the Albert Hall. "Not a bad combination," Gigli exclaimed, "a Björling and a Gigli concert the same day!" But it was a poor combination as far as we were concerned. We would've loved to attend Gigli's recital, but Jussi needed his rest and my loyalty made me stay with him. Talk about mixed emotions!

Set Svanholm accompanied me on this occasion. Albert Hall is round, and Jussi turned to sing some encores to the audience who had been at his back all evening. When the program reached that point, Svanholm said: "Let's go up to the highest spot and listen to how he sounds!" We were both interested in acoustics, and so we went up together and heard his voice, unaltered in clarity and undiminished in power. Jussi firmly believed that every competent singer knew how to project his voice. "There is no such thing as bad acoustics, only bad singers," he maintained.[4] Robert Merrill confirmed this. "I sat in the audience sometimes, in dress rehearsals, and you could hear Jussi's voice in the back row! The voice wasn't small. It wasn't Del Monaco's, a dramatic tenor, he was a spinto. Sometime these big dramatic voices don't project, but you could hear Jussi all over the house."[5]

The Albert Hall recital went well, but the infection returned and Jussi's throat problems persisted well into April, when he resumed his concert schedule with a recital in Gothenburg on the 29th. Finally in July and August we could vacation at Siarö. The autumn season began in September with a series of recitals, followed by only two performances at the Stockholm Opera before our trip to America. In *Tosca*, on 25 September 1953, the title role was taken by a very young Birgit Nilsson.

> He was the most considerate and unpretentious colleague I could imagine. Then when he opened his mouth, pouting his lips in that Björlingesque way and began to sing, I almost completely lost it. It was a flow of tones of indescribable beauty, and it all seemed so easy! I dare say that I've sung with the foremost tenors of our time. Perhaps I've sung with some who

were more impassioned onstage, but I've never been so overwhelmed by a sweet sound coming from a human throat before or since.[6]

Although Jussi immediately recognized Birgit's extraordinary talent, neither of us foresaw the position she would occupy in the world of opera for the next quarter century. Jussi was always interested in up-and-coming singers, and he often attended the Opera School recitals. On one such occasion he heard the young Nicolai Gedda. When some less discerning members of the audience dismissed the tall man with the tiny voice, Jussi was upset. It was a magnificent instrument, he declared, and as for power and volume, that would come later.[7] Jussi, of course, was right. Nicolai acquired a flawless technique, and with his musicianship, linguistic skills, and innate intelligence he built a spectacular career, one that continues into a fifth decade.

※

Before returning to the Met, Jussi gave concerts in Detroit, Hartford, and New York. For some reason Freddie Schauwecker wasn't available, and it was George Trovillo who accompanied him at the Hunter College recital. The critic for *The New York Times* (2 November 1953) summed up the recital in one word: magnificent. He commended Jussi's phenomenal breath control, ease of singing, *messa di voce*, and enunciation, especially his skill with the "impure vowels" of the English language that "put most English-speaking singers to shame. . . . A modest and (as tenors go) self-effacing performer, Mr. Bjoerling lets the music speak for itself."

The *Faust* that opened the Metropolitan's 1953–54 season was the creation of 29-year-old Peter Brook in his directorial debut with the Met. He placed the action in the early 19th century, and in this new staging, instead of the traditional tights and velvet, both Mephisto and Faust wore tails. Jussi stuck to his no-hats policy, but the poor Devil had to wear a shiny black top hat. Nicola Rossi-Lemeni, a bass with a remarkable voice and even more impressive acting skills, didn't seem to mind—he had a ball with the role! It was his Met debut and he made the most of it. Victoria de los Angeles sang Marguerite and Robert Merrill Valentin. Pierre Monteux, at age 78, conducted, and Rolf Gérard designed the sets and costumes.

This *Faust* was to have been Boris Christoff's Met debut as well. After missing the 1950 *Don Carlo*, he was offered Don Basilio in *Il barbiere di Siviglia* but declined, feeling that he should debut in a bigger role. Bing agreed, and he invited the basso to sing Mephisto in Peter Brook's *Faust*. New production or not, when Christoff learned the details of Brook's conception, down to the top hat and tails, he declined to have any part of it. Bing then decided that Christoff was "a difficult artist" (his standard term for a singer who disagreed with him) and declared that he didn't think another invitation would be forthcoming. He kept his word; Christoff never sang at the Metropolitan.[8]

When exactly the tyranny of directors began is difficult to pinpoint. It has recently become customary—and routinely tolerated—for a person of modest gifts to superimpose his ideas on the work of a recognized genius in order to capture a few rays of reflected glory. To reinterpret a universal theme—as René Clair did with Faust in his *Le beauté du diable*—is one thing; to move a period-specific medieval tale a few centuries forward doesn't add one iota to the audience's enjoyment, understanding, or appreciation of the text or the music. With the composer's and librettist's intentions distorted, first-time audiences are deprived of seeing the work as it was conceived by its creators.

The Met's old production designed by Joseph Urban had been in service since 17 November 1917. The new *Faust*, with a total production cost of $85,000, was described as unconventional, daring, and many other adjectives. Olin Downes called the entire production a "desperate resolve" on Brook's part to do "something different," no matter the cost to dramatic possibilities.

As befits a professional, Jussi didn't speak against the production during its run at the Met. On the contrary: knowing what was expected of him, in an interview conducted by Ruby Mercer in November 1953, he actually mouthed a few stock phrases of praise; but years later he allowed himself a candid remark about it in faraway San Francisco, and his comment found its way into print. "There are so many fine operatic masterpieces that will always stay popular," Jussi said, "if they will not try to make them modern. The Metropolitan's new *Faust* by Gounod, putting it in the same era as Hoffmann's *Tales*, is ridiculous. . . . These anachronistic flights of fancy are aberrations, and disturbing; they are out of character with the opera and help to defeat opera's purpose."[9]

But in 1953 Jussi kept his thoughts to himself and cooperated fully during the long rehearsals—up to a point. Brook had engaged a fencing master to teach those clumsy opera singers how to deliver a realistic third-act duel. After a couple of hours of lessons in intricate choreographed moves, Jussi had had enough. He told Bing he came to sing, not to fence like Errol Flynn. He'd never had a bad notice because of his fencing, and whatever he'd done in the duel scene all his life would have to do. Bing agreed.

Jussi wasn't alone in his low regard for the production; De los Angeles too found working with Peter Brook a "very strange experience." The cast members went to talk to Bing about it, but he said that Brook was hired to direct the production and thus had the last word about the details. Brook should've at least made a token effort to explore what it takes to sing and act at the same time. De los Angeles remembers imploring him, "'Please, Mr. Brook, don't make us sit down now. It really is going to be rather difficult to get up *and* maintain a note just at this moment.' . . . Björling and I lost many a battle that way."[10]

Jussi had worked with Victoria in the recording studio earlier in the year, but this was their first onstage collaboration. He appreciated her exquisite singing, and this Marguerite was no less impressed by her Faust.

I don't think he ever knew (at the time I was an extremely shy person) but in our performances together the greater joy for me was to hear his sound around me. Whereas I always felt reluctant to listen to other singers, in his case I would stay around, behind the wings, when in most cases I should have been back in my dressing room getting ready for the next scene. His singing remains unequalled to me and in his particular case no recording will ever convey the unforgettable experience it was to hear him on the stage.[11]

On the day of the premiere, 16 November 1953, the line of standees began to form so early in the day that Bing ordered coffee for them at 11 a.m. instead of the usual midafternoon. Publicity manager Valentino anticipated that I too would be in the spotlight and that to make the most of it, I should wear real jewels for the photographers. He casually announced, "They'll bring some jewelry from Tiffany's for first night and to take pictures." I was deathly afraid that something might happen to the borrowed riches, but Valentino reassured me. "Don't worry. Everything's insured to the limit."

When I'd seen other singers' wives adorned with dazzling gems, I innocently thought they were their own. I didn't know one could actually rent jewelry! I liked to dress up in beautiful gowns, as much for myself as for my husband, but I thought this was a bit much. Now I was able to see the effect, and I had to admit that it was probably the smart thing to do. The photographers crowded around me and the diamond necklace from Tiffany's was kept ablaze by the flash of their cameras.

I was terribly nervous before this premiere. In the past, when I settled in Edward Johnson's box, his wonderful personality and elegant presence calmed me, but now I sat in the orchestra, unescorted, without support. After the intermission I didn't go back to my place but stood outside in the foyer and listened with the door ajar to the auditorium. As the violins softly introduced "Salut, demeure," I could hear my own heartbeat. Aware of the high expectations, I hardly breathed while Jussi sang. Not until he sang the high C in the cavatina—and I heard the tumultuous shouts of bravo at the aria's conclusion—did I dare to go back to my place.

All participants reaped their share of laurels for the evening's success. Olin Downes wrote in *The New York Times* (17 November 1953), "Mr. Björling headed the list of five voices with his wonted mastery of the vocal art. One could not claim for this gifted exponent of song a romantic appearance or histrionic power. But when he communicates the amorous sentiment and soaring line of Gounod's music, or looses the high C that most other tenors may vainly envy him, . . . the singer will cast his spell."

Jussi was in excellent voice when the opera was repeated twice more in November. On one of these occasions he almost forgot to enter on cue. In Brook's staging, Marguerite appears to Faust in the Walpurgis Night. Originally, a red ribbon symbolizing blood was tied around Marguerite's neck, but when dancer Sallie Wilson took over the part, she strove for more realism. "The highlight of my time at the Met was in the Walpurgis Night scene in *Faust*," she recalls. "I was the vision of Marguerite and, after a mad scene you wouldn't believe, I threw myself at Jussi Bjoerling's feet, frothing at the mouth and with blood painted all over my neck. Bjoerling was so nonplussed the first time that he almost couldn't sing."[12]

This wasn't the only time Jussi found Miss Wilson at his feet. When he sang *Cavalleria rusticana* on tour, she swelled the ranks of choristers as one of the villagers. Turiddu sings the "Siciliana" with the curtain still lowered, so she could sit on the floor next to the harp and listen to the serenade. "His singing was so heavenly, I just wanted to hear it up close."[13]

# Chapter 21

# Vocal Problems

It was a great relief to have the first *Faust* behind us; the attendant tension had been immense. As I wrote to Lasse on 18 November 1953, "You cannot imagine how good it feels that the opening night is now over, especially as it was such a big success. It's such a strain each time, because if the reviews, in *The New York Times* say, aren't so good, the whole world will know about it. But this time Dad got the best reviews of all the ones who performed, with a fine headline, 'Bjoerling scores in role of Faust.'"

The family had our itinerary, and when we were scheduled to stay in any one place long enough, they would write to us. The special joy to receive letters from the children is clearly reflected in Jussi's reply to "Lassegubben" (another of Lars' nicknames, impossible to render in English) on 23 November 1953.

Thank you for the letter. It was mighty fun to get a letter from you. I hope you'll write again soon. You mustn't think badly of my writing in pencil, but mother is out and she took along both fountain pens. It's nice to hear you say that school goes so well, and what you say about getting honors is magnificent no end. Yes, we'll soon be home with you all again. Just think how much fun we'll have. Tomorrow I am singing Faust again. The weather is dreadful here, fog and rain, warm and suffocating, it's almost impossible to keep the throat well, but one must manage, just barely.

Say hello to everybody. Mama just came home. She wants you to know that in spite of the lousy weather we are in fine shape.

245

Lousy weather and overheated interiors caught up with Jussi. When he sang at a United Nations soiree on 2 December, he was struggling with the onset of laryngitis. What he did sing was fine, but he had to cut his program short. The next day, he received a letter from Vijaya Lakshmi Pandit, president of the General Assembly:

> It was a great pleasure indeed to listen to your beautiful singing last night. You contributed greatly to the success of the evening. I would like you to know that we understood perfectly well that you felt compelled to cancel part of your programme. I wish again to express my appreciation for your kindness in being with us despite your indisposition and my warm thanks for your memorable performance.

Jussi's condition didn't improve. He was to sing the first two radio broadcasts of the season, but on 5 December Eugene Conley had to replace him as Faust, and a week later Jan Peerce flew down from Toronto to take over the Duke. Jussi canceled his *Faust* in Philadelphia on 15 December specifically to give himself a chance to get better for his next scheduled performance. When that day came, both Jussi and his throat specialist, Dr. Bruno Griesman, thought that he had sufficiently recovered to sing. In fact, assistant general manager Max Rudolf called the doctor, who confirmed that Jussi would be able to go on. Still, as a precaution, Rudolf sent Dr. Griesman a pair of seats for that evening, 17 December, and invited him backstage for a last-minute checkup.

All concerned hoped that everything would go well, but as the act progressed, I could tell that Jussi was in trouble. Near the end of the Kermesse scene, on the phrase "Je t'aime!" he took the exposed high B-flat an octave low. Author Bert Wechsler, an extra at the Metropolitan in the 1950s, stood only a dozen feet from Jussi. "There were palpable shock waves from the audience," he remembers.[1]

When the curtain fell, Dr. Griesman examined Jussi and declared him unfit to continue. The reversed medical opinion was a mere formality; everybody present knew that he couldn't finish the performance. Luckily, soon after the opera began, Rudolf had sent word to Thomas Hayward, Jussi's understudy, to come immediately to the opera house, and executive production manager David Pardoll announced that Hayward, winner of the 1945 Opera Auditions of the Air, would substitute. Hayward had never sung the role at the Metropolitan but had attended the rehearsals and had worked with stage director Peter Brook; according to reviews, he sang the role with confident ease, and his high C in the cavatina was enthusiastically applauded.

Having to withdraw mid-performance was terribly depressing for Jussi. To his distress, the problem persisted, and more engagements had to be canceled, most painfully for him the concert performance of *Un ballo in maschera* with 87-year-old Arturo Toscanini. This wasn't the first time Jussi missed a chance to sing an opera under Toscanini. On 28 December 1949 Schang cabled us: "Toscanini broadcasts April Two Nine, Verdis Falstaff.

Does Jussi know tenor role." Jussi did not, but in this case he would've learned the part to please the Maestro and for the pleasure of working with him. He was forced to decline only because he couldn't reconcile his bookings with the long weeks of rehearsals Toscanini demanded.

Toscanini always had a high regard for Jussi. Giuseppe Valdengo hasn't forgotten what Toscanini said to him in 1948:

> "You know, Valdengo, yesterday I listened to Björling on the radio from the Metropolitan Opera. What a beautiful voice and what fine singing, all on the breath, a perfect technique. It is all tied together and his diction is very good too. Bravo!" . . . He was right. Björling's voice had an Italian color and the high notes shone like the purest sapphires. I went to hear him at the Met whenever I could, because hearing him was like a singing lesson. . . . Toscanini would have liked to conduct an opera with Björling, and he confided to me that he had thought about *Aida*. It is a pity that the Maestro's dream could not be realized because Björling was unavailable, and he had to be satisfied with Tucker. "You see, Valdengo," the Maestro said to me, "Tucker has a fine voice and secure high notes, and perhaps he will be a little more dramatic. Yes, but Björling's voice has a more Latin color!"[2]

Now it had seemed Toscanini would finally have Björling in one of his recordings. According to plans, Jussi was to sing Riccardo in a two-part broadcast of *Un ballo in maschera* to be recorded by RCA. The concerts were scheduled for 17 and 24 January 1954.

Before laryngitis struck, we were invited for coaching sessions to Toscanini's home in Riverdale. Every day Jussi was hoping to be closer to a recovery, but each new day brought fresh disappointment. The condition persisted; his voice was coarse, and straining it could cause lasting damage. But Jussi tried. One newspaper reported that two days after the unfinished *Faust*, "Mr. Bjoerling, still wishing to sing the *Ballo in maschera* broadcast, rehearsed with Mr. Toscanini and the NBC Symphony, singing half-voice."[3]

In this terrible predicament we agreed there was nothing to do but go back to Sweden so that Jussi could rest quietly at home in his own bed until he was well again. In an interview with Ruby Mercer, he said that we were scheduled to fly home on 18 December: "I'm coming back earlier than I expected, because I'm doing a broadcast and recording with Maestro Toscanini. We went through the *Masked Ball*, the whole business."[4]

Christmas and New Year's came and went, the date of the performance drew nearer, and Jussi's voice did not improve. It was obvious that he'd be unable to sing the role, either to the Maestro's or his own satisfaction. To his immense regret, with the performance a little over a week away, he withdrew from the project.

Jussi's cancellation put Toscanini in a most awkward position. The only tenor who could step in as a last-minute replacement was Jan Peerce. It appears Toscanini himself had asked for Björling to sing Riccardo, but Jan believed that he "had been promised the role . . . when Toscanini did it on NBC radio."[5] Jussi was unaware of this, or he never would've accepted the assignment. Adding insult to injury, Jan had to find this out in the newspapers; "For its own contractual, political, and recording reasons, however, RCA wanted my friend Jussi Bjoerling to sing the part."[6]

Jan had been so hurt that he now refused to cooperate. According to his own account, the crisis reduced Toscanini to begging on the telephone. To save face, he claimed that the cast change was RCA management's idea, not his. Jan felt so sorry for his old mentor that he acted as if he believed him; he finally gave in and sang. Jussi would've been mortified had he known the extreme embarrassment he had inadvertently caused the Maestro he so revered.

We came back to New York at the end of the month. *The New York Times* (27 January 1954) reported that Björling had arrived at Idlewild the day before to resume his interrupted concert tour: "Mr. Bjoerling said his doctors pronounced him fit to sing after his four-week rest in Sweden." The notice mentioned that the tenor would sing in Monday evening's performance of *La bohème* at the Metropolitan—but first Jussi had to switch planes and fly on to Milwaukee to deliver a recital on 27 January.

I stayed behind in New York to set up our mini-household, thereby avoiding a tiresome complication. A snowstorm diverted Jussi's plane to Chicago, and he and Freddie had to take the train to Milwaukee the next afternoon and give a performance the same evening. Jussi sang his printed numbers and many encores. "Mr. Bjoerling, despite reports of recent bouts with laryngitis, was in magnificent voice," wrote Richard S. Davis.[7]

The review and his own assessment reassured him that he was back on track, and he returned to New York with renewed confidence. In the *Bohème* of 1 February 1954 Jussi was surrounded by friends: Licia Albanese, Robert Merrill, Cesare Siepi, and George Cehanovsky. The tiny role of Parpignol was sung by the outstanding Otello of the coming decade, James McCracken. Alfred Hubay, an usher that night, maintains, "There wasn't a singer or a singing teacher in New York with his or her aspiring young pupils who wasn't in the theater that night. I couldn't believe my eyes. The combination of Björling and Albanese must have excited every voice buff."[8]

"I never heard him sing better!" Bob Merrill recalls. "He wanted to show that his voice was still intact, that all the rumors he was finished were groundless. He was just fantastic! It was one of the most exciting, most memorable performances. The audience would not leave the theater that night! The curtains parted a dozen times, the lights were turned out in the theater, and people wouldn't leave. I'd say it was a good half hour, maybe 45 minutes that we were in that house and the people would not leave."[9]

The next day we read that his solidly attacked and sustained high B of Rodolfo's aria had "set at rest any doubt" about his voice.[10] But the reviewer's satisfaction over the recovery was premature. Jussi suffered a relapse; perhaps he caught it from Licia, who was recovering from a cold herself. Jan Peerce stepped in again to sing the Duke, and in light of his recent illness and his withdrawal from the Toscanini broadcasts, Jussi's cancellation was a news item once more. "Bjoerling Ill Again" read *The New York Times'* headline.

I was desperate over my husband's inability to shake his affliction—and convinced that his throat would get better if he could just escape the New York winter and travel to some place where it was warm. Our close friends Marguerite and Axel Wenner-Gren owned a wonderful home on Paradise Island in the Bahamas; it occurred to me that a sunny island stay would be the perfect cure for Jussi. I telephoned Marguerite, telling her that Jussi was to sing *Il trovatore* in Miami in a few weeks, and that it was essential he should be well in time for the performance. "Could we come tomorrow?" I pleaded. Axel and Marguerite received us with open arms and spoiled us utterly during our week in Nassau. It was wonderful to be able to relax so completely.

"Jussi," Axel mused one day, "have you ever thought of leaving Sweden and emigrating to the Bahamas? You could save a fortune in taxes!" Axel was involved in land development on Andros Island, and if we followed his advice, he said, we could pick our own lot and build a house. "Get your emigration papers in order as soon as you go home!"

We were tempted. We bought some property, and I even went to the parish registrar's office to get the necessary forms. But when it was time for Jussi to sign, he backed out. "I can't do it," he said. "If I move out of the country, I cannot stand at Skansen and sing 'Land du välsignade' ('You Blessed Land'). How could I sing 'Be it remembered that I was a Swede'? No! It just won't work!"

In outlook, thinking, temperament, and tastes Jussi was Swedish to the core, and he could never permanently transplant himself into the soil of another land. The Swedish landscape has its own special flavor; its unspoiled natural beauty, the clean lines of the white-trimmed wooden houses, the majestic lakes, crisp air, and rich forests of Dalecarlia were in his blood. The countryside, the land, the people meant home. If we had moved to the Bahamas, we would've saved a great deal of money, but Jussi couldn't sell himself. He loved America and his profession made him a cosmopolite, but Sweden was his country, and his Swedishness was not for sale.

We thanked Marguerite and Axel for their hearty hospitality and returned to Florida, where on 27 February Jussi sang *Il trovatore* with the Miami Opera Company. It was the only time he was paired with Astrid Varnay. As she remembers, "Word was out about Mr. Björling's fragile health, and I just hoped he would make it through the performance. Much to my surprise, his Manrico was yet another major achievement of that stalwart Swede."[11] It was obvious to Jussi, however, if not the audience, that despite the brief period of recuperation on Paradise Island, he still had a problem. Jussi decided to cancel the two remaining performances in Miami.

Jussi's cancellations were the subject of much gossip. Perhaps he canceled more often than the average singer, certainly more often than singers who stay and perform within a narrow geographical area. But he had a sensitive throat, he was susceptible to colds and laryngitis, and interclimatic travel placed his voice in constant jeopardy. When he knew he couldn't satisfy the public's immense expectations, he refused to sing; he would rather not disappoint them and humiliate himself. But the moment he canceled the talk began, and too many times it was attributed to his drinking. While this undeniably happened, the fact is that during his career the majority of his cancellations were *not* alcohol related.

Jussi knew the rumors and resented it. With shame and regret he would own up to an alcohol-related cancellation. But to have every laryngitis, flu, appendicitis, ulcer, and sciatica equated in the public mind with drinking was painful and depressing. The accusations were patently unfair. As the chronology of his performances shows, Jussi was immensely productive. Yes, he had many cancellations, but drinking was involved no more than roughly 10 percent of those times. Bert Wechsler was closer to the truth when he said, "For heaven's sake, the man was a singing machine!"[12]

Jussi felt pretty miserable as he sat in Miami Beach's Sea Isle Hotel, waiting for the time to pass and his condition to improve. But he tried to sound upbeat in his letter to the children, on 1 March 1954.

> You cannot imagine how slow it is and how much we long for you. Papa had a rather large misfortune after the *Bohème* performance at the Met, but we can talk about that when we return home. Mother is very tanned. She feels and looks radiant. Papa is just tanned.
>
> Just imagine, little girl, you have sung on the radio and had a real success, and on Papa's birthday no less. [A reporter had coaxed Ann-Charlotte into singing during a taped interview.] Well, not everybody gets such a birthday present. Uncle Axel showed me a newspaper, *Sweden News*, which is published once a week. There was a long rigmarole first about my *Bohème* and then about Lillan, with a photo and very lavish praise. Daddy is probably somewhat inflated ordinarily, but the question is if, when he read about Lillan, there wasn't a danger that he might burst with pride. Congratulations, Lillbullan ["Little Bun"]. We'll talk about recordings when we return home. I'll probably want to be along in a corner to make sure that everything turns out the way it ought. You should make a few bucks too. Maybe they're trying to take advantage of my not being at home, but they are very mistaken. When you come of age you ought to be able to have a nice little bank account, which you have earned all by yourself. I'll see to that.
>
> I hope you're all being really good and sweet and obey Mormor [grandmother] in every way and make it as easy as possible for her. She is not 50 years old anymore, you have to remember that.
>
> Just think, Anders will soon start the baccalaureate exams, and Lasse

is heading for high school, no doubt feeling a little proud to be such fine fellows.

Mama is out shopping, and I'm in bed with a head cold and cough, that is why I'm writing with a pencil, but I'll soon be well again, so that I can sing together a few bucks for you, my little darlings.

I have so much to tell about when we come home. We have bought a place in the Bahamas. What fishing! I have been out three times. Among other fish I caught a 30-pound barracuda, a relative of the northern pike with much bigger teeth, dangerous, which is killed with a club in the water and provides good food for the locals. My second-largest catch was a grouper, shaped like a perch, 25 pounds, somewhat on the heavy side, you can imagine. The really big ones I was able to bring in only to 25–30 meters [26–31 yards]. They just took the bait, a 6-foot steel leader and the whole works. I just wasn't able to handle those boys, but I'll learn, you can be sure, and then those 200- to 600-pound guys will come. You can imagine how frustrating but thrilling it was.

Write us soon, just a few lines about how you feel and how school is. Be careful when you are out. Mama and Papa always pray an evening prayer for their little darlings far away on the other side of the ocean, but for prayers and thoughts there are no distances, we are always with you wherever we are.

In spite of our hopes, Jussi did not improve sufficiently to sing. He had no choice but to disappoint his public and incur the wrath of Rudolf Bing. On 10 March 1954 Jussi informed the Met that on account of his physical condition he was unable to finish the season and participate in the spring tour.[13] We packed our luggage and booked a flight home, grateful for the accuracy and fairness of *The New York Times* (13 March 1954) in stating that after many cancellations "due to bronchitis, Björling, accompanied by his wife, left for Stockholm from Idlewild on 12 March 1954 to recuperate."

The forced idleness in March and April wasn't good for Jussi. The dreaded restlessness took over in full force, and I became sick with worry for him. I lay awake at night; at times I could hardly get a bite of food down. Gradually the worst seemed to be over. The laryngitis had lost its grip, and Jussi was again in prime form. In late April he gave some trial recitals, in May he sang once at the Stockholm Opera and at a concert in the Royal Albert Hall in London, and in June and July, for thousands of listeners, Jussi's voice rang out with undiminished beauty under the starlit skies at Skansen and Gröna Lund.

In another arena, our sensitive, contemplative Anders had come through his difficult teenage years and was graduating from Sigtuna School that spring with excellent marks. Lasse vividly recalls his older brother's commencement exercises. In Sweden a high school graduate receives a white school cap. He wears it all his life at every ceremonial occasion, no matter how old and yellowed the cap may become.

When Anders took his baccalaureate and earned his cap, we all attended the graduation ceremonies. The school made Dad an honorary alumnus and gave him a school pin. One of Anders' classmates took notice of it and tactlessly remarked, "Then it is just the white cap that is missing!" The sting of it spoiled all the fun for Dad, who always regretted that he didn't have any formal education.[14]

⬧

By 1954, the LP was a well-established medium, making the recording of entire operas possible and profitable. Every record company was intent on building a comprehensive catalog of the standard operas, and competition was fierce as the labels vied with each other to obtain the best casts, orchestras, and conductors for each project. Angel had the magnificent partnership of Maria Callas and Giuseppe di Stefano, London/Decca boasted a formidable duo in Renata Tebaldi and Mario del Monaco, and RCA had Milanov and Björling under contract. Encouraged by initial successes, RCA began an ambitious program of recording complete operas, but cost considerations led the company to transplant their major recording projects to Rome's Opera House. London/Decca followed suit, taking advantage of the acoustics of the Accademia di Santa Cecilia.

With the traditional winter season of opera houses, such large-scale recording endeavors were possible only in the summer months. Even then it required organizational skills bordering on wizardry to have soloists, conductor, orchestra, and chorus assemble on schedule and give an outstanding performance with a minimum of rehearsals within the shortest time possible. Singers in demand could work year-round, and those who wanted to capitalize on their vocal assets in the most productive years of their career had to give up their leisure time.

According to producer Richard Mohr, in those days singers wanted to record all their major roles, and record them immediately. But not Jussi. He was interested in preserving his voice for future generations, but he wasn't hounding the powers-that-be for new projects and often had to be persuaded to record. Even when a recording date was firmly set, Siarö and fishing continued to hold a much greater attraction for him then yet another three weeks' work. But by the mid 1950s, Jussi too had to make a choice: rest or record. It seems that our relaxing stays at Siarö—our refuge from agents, impresari, celebrity hounds, and even well-meaning friends—ended with the summer of 1954; from then on, a greater part of Jussi's summers went into recording.

Knowing Jussi's alcohol problem was exacerbated by too much free time, I didn't discourage him. Weighing the moderate stress of recording against extended outings with his drinking buddies and the horrendous toll each such incident took on his system, I felt it was better to have him focused on his work. It was a hard choice, but the merits of the one option clearly outweighed the other. Surrounded by colleagues and stimulated by the task at hand, he was less likely to lose control. Paradoxically, it seemed that work was better for his health than relaxation.

So as not to deprive ourselves of being with the children during these new versions of summer, we let them accompany us whenever they wished. But our perennial travel companion was Ann-Charlotte, who took a keen interest in the recording process. She was always around during Jussi's recordings.

Jussi's first complete opera recorded in Rome was *Manon Lescaut*, the first of three recordings with Romanian maestro Jonel Perlea. Jussi had looked forward to recording with Merrill and Albanese, but with the health crises just behind him and a tour of South Africa ahead, he was loath to break up his July and go to Rome. I think it was nothing more than sheer bullheadedness that prompted him to attempt to withdraw from the recording. "We were all in Rome waiting to begin, and he sent us a cable saying he wasn't coming," remembers Dick Mohr.[15]

Licia Albanese and her husband, Joe Gimma, were among our closest friends. Joe was a successful businessman with a lot of "street smarts." He knew that if the recording was to go forward with Jussi Björling, swift and drastic action was necessary. According to Licia, "My husband sent him a telegram [in the name of RCA] telling him that if he didn't complete the recording, he would have to pay all the expenses of the artists—soloists, chorus and orchestra."[16] Dick confirms:

> The story of the telegram is quite true, and Jussi was there the next day. I had no idea whatsoever why he wasn't willing to come. There was never any explanation. He just came in as if he had never sent the cable and he had never received Joe's; he was just a day late. Once I saw him there, I was diplomatic. I never said, "What was wrong with you?" There was no indication of drinking; he showed up cold sober and stayed cold sober throughout the whole recording. No problems with drinking—not at that time.[17]

I was grateful to Joe for his ruse, and as Licia testifies, Jussi held no grudges: "When he found out that Joe had sent him the telegram—he was a good sport and told that incident to everyone with great laughs. He would say 'You know, that Joe Gimma is a clever one.'"[18]

It would've been a great loss if the *Manon Lescaut* recording had not been made; the cast sang admirably, and the ensemble really jelled under Perlea. According to Dick Mohr, "[Jussi's] best acting, vocally, is in the *Manon Lescaut* recording, in that duet with Albanese when they finally get into 'Dolcissimo soffrir.' I mean, it's practically indecent!"[19] Jussi, too, liked this recording very much, and although unfortunately he and Licia didn't make more records together in the years ahead, their singing on *Manon Lescaut* counts as one of my favorite pairings. Licia wrote,

> To have shared the operatic stage with Jussi Björling will ever remain among the most precious and memorable of my musical experience. The

smooth flow of his velvety voice, applied to a complete command of his roles, was so captivating that even while onstage with him I found myself listening intently to his glorious tones, adding myself to his enraptured audience. Indeed, it was with effort that I had to suppress my urge to join in the applause. However, in our recording sessions of Puccini's *Manon Lescaut* there was no stage discipline to interfere with my giving expression of his exquisite artistry, and I did so, gratefully and enthusiastically.[20]

Rome in July is hot as an oven. I remember how wonderful it was to come in from the heat and pedestrian crush of the street to the relatively cool spaciousness of the opera house, with its faint smell of mothballs. Jussi, worried about alternating the heat of the Roman summer with the cold air of the Grand Hotel, had the air conditioning turned off in our room, but we kept the windows open, and in the evening we listened to the impromptu concerts of the patrons at the trattoria across the street. "How about those tenors?" remarked Ann-Charlotte, to which Jussi replied, "Oh my God! If we had so many good tenors in Sweden, I'd be out of a job!"

Jussi took good care of himself in Rome, with one near exception, as Robert Merrill tells it:

> We had one more session to do, and when we went into the lobby of the Grand Hotel, he said, "Bob, let's have a drink!" I said, "No, Jussi, you know we have to record." I tried to change his mind. He then suddenly disappeared into the men's room, and from there he went to the bar and started to drink. I said, Lord, if he couldn't finish the last session, it's over! The orchestra is gone, the singers have commitments—so I called Joe Gimma, and Joe and I dissuaded him from drinking. But it was a very close call.[21]

One unforgettable Roman afternoon, Licia and Joe, Bob and his wife Marion, Dick Mohr, and we gathered for a little party on the terrace of the Grand Hotel. We were in a happy mood. It so happened that some street musicians came in to entertain the guests, and soon Licia, Bob, and Jussi joined in. Licia sang "Core'ngrato," Bob contributed "Torna a Surriento," and Jussi burst in with "O sole mio." Jussi was in fantastic voice. The terrace wasn't crowded, but one by one the windows opened and guests leaned out to enjoy the concert.

Dick remembers the moment. "The waiters just stopped what they were doing and slowly started to come out on the terrace. They stayed at a respectable distance and listened, but they were leading all the applause."[22] "He wasn't drinking that evening," notes Bob, adding that Jussi's singing gave him "goosebumps. I mean the sound! It was the most glorious sound you ever heard! It sounded like Caruso singing the song."[23] Bob later wrote, "It was more than *bel canto*. That magic day in Rome—Marion and I recall it often—Jussi Bjoerling sang as I have heard no other mortal sing."[24]

# Chapter 22

# SOUTH AFRICA

Jussi was booked for 12 concerts in South Africa in August 1954. He had been invited to sing in the Soviet Union, but Columbia Artists Management advised us not to go. If we did, they thought, we might later be denied an entry visa to the United States. Their precaution was a reflection of the times; it was the height of the McCarthy era, so with regrets, we had declined the invitation.

Jussi had protested violently when the tour was first proposed. He never had global ambitions; in fact I was more eager to spread his fame than he was. This time I enticed him to overlook the wearying distance we must travel by saying that Ivor Newton would make arrangements for a safari. Jussi loved animals and never missed visiting a zoo when his time allowed. In the end, though somewhat reluctantly, he succumbed to the temptation of seeing lions and other wild animals roaming free in their natural habitat—but he told Enwall that the main reason he was giving in was because he wanted to buy me a large diamond. What wife wouldn't be thrilled at such a prospect?

The trip to the cape was tediously long and very uncomfortable. We flew from Sweden to Rome, where we stayed overnight; the next day the plane stopped in Crete and Khartoum, where even in the middle of the night the air was boiling hot. After Khartoum it was a nonstop flight to Johannesburg. To ensure a measure of comfort, Jussi had insisted on a sleeper; it helped, but sleeper or not, he was tired and not in the best of moods upon arrival. Being attacked by waiting journalists did little to improve his disposition, and as often happened, I had to step in to meet the press.

In his memoirs, Ivor Newton recorded that unlike other singers, Jussi wouldn't vocalize before a concert. When asked why not, Jussi gave a simple explanation: "When I'm well, it's not necessary. If I'm not well, what good does it do?"[1] But in South Africa a rehearsal was out of the question. Instead of arriving four days before the first concert to accustom himself to the 6000-foot altitude of Johannesburg, as contracted, Jussi had chosen to arrive only one day before the first recital. It didn't take him long to realize what the elevation did to his breathing, and I asked Ivor to not even suggest a rehearsal. Before they went onstage, Jussi told him: "Don't expect me to breathe after every word; I'll be breathing after every syllable."

We both liked Newton. He had many friends in London's high society, and his lofty connections seemed to extend even to South Africa. He had arranged a special pass for us to tour Zululand in a chauffeur-driven Daimler, but Ivor and I went alone because Jussi had to rest for the concert. He would've loved it: the local people and the flora and fauna were all simply fascinating.

The first concert in South Africa took place in Johannesburg's Plaza Theatre. One reviewer, after noting the Johannesburg music lovers' "enthusiastic, almost hysterical applause," explained that Jussi's singing was in a class by itself,

> not only because the singer has one of those god-gifted instruments which come all too rarely in the human race, but because he uses it with very special art. . . . Unlike other famous singers, particularly of the Latin schools, he did not display the mechanics of his craft. He showed only the finished article. There were no slides toward the upper reaches, no exhaustion in the sustained top note, no breathless breaks, no wild gesticulation. . . . And what partnership from Ivor Newton! One hardly missed the orchestra, the piano was so eloquent.[2]

The *Natal Daily News* lamented that Jussi's "ringing, wonderfully beautiful tones" were repeatedly drowned by the listeners' "rousing applause, bravos and foot stomping." Everywhere, Jussi's audiences displayed such a fever pitch of excitement that even he was astonished. Enwall attributed the violent ovations to the South African public's being unaccustomed to hearing singers in their prime. Singers usually put South Africa, so far off the beaten track, on their itinerary in their declining years.

Jussi sang two more recitals and a radio concert in Johannesburg. Because the programs varied so from recital to recital, many return customers filled the sold-out houses. In addition to opera arias by Handel, Mozart, Donizetti, Verdi, Gounod, Bizet, Mascagni, Puccini, and Giordano, Jussi performed songs by Beethoven, Schubert, Brahms, Liszt, Grieg, Sibelius, Rachmaninoff, Foster, Morgan, and Spross. He gave his listeners a generous sampling of his art.

The concert held at the Durban City Hall on 24 August included such gems as "Celeste Aida," "Nessun dorma," and "Dies Bildnis ist bezaubernd schön." When it was over, the audience refused to leave, and Jussi was obliged to sing three encores. "Beauty of tone, the clearest articulation in the most strenuous of passages, and unfailing flexibility of phrasing were the outstanding characteristics of all that he did."[3]

Jussi appeared twice in Cape Town. At the second recital he sang "Ombra mai fu" and three Grieg songs with Newton at the piano. The orchestra then accompanied him in "Ingemisco," "Una furtiva lagrima," "Come un bel dì di maggio," and "Addio alla madre." "Singing of sheer delight and perfection was heard last night," began the review the following day. "Mr. Bjorling possesses a voice of rare beauty, with qualities rich and golden, sweet and silver. These were coupled with perfect musicianship and taste, amazing and superb breath-control, and excellent diction."[4]

The last concert took place in Pretoria on 3 September, and the cries of "Bravo!" and "Encore!" seemed to go on forever. It was a remarkably successful concert tour, one of his most jubilant ever, and Jussi was especially happy when at the end he received his reward: a safari in Kruger National Park.

And I received mine. One evening in Johannesburg, while we were dining as the guests of Ernest Oppenheimer, the man who controlled the global diamond trade, Ivor cleverly steered the conversation a certain way. "You know, Mr. Oppenheimer, Mr. Björling told me that he wants to buy a diamond for Anna-Lisa."

"Well, he has come to the right place. Come to my office tomorrow, and my assistant will help you."

We went, and we were shown the most fabulous stones outside of crown jewels, museums, and Tiffany rentals. The assistant must have had special instructions from Mr. Oppenheimer, because the prices were lower than we'd expected. Jussi had been thinking of buying me a six-carat diamond, but in his extravagance, he decided on a beautiful seven-carat stone. How could I ever say no to my husband?

�֎

While we were waiting for our plane home, a little girl from the Swedish colony walked up to Jussi. She curtsied prettily and presented him with a basket containing her gift: a little black poodle pup. Ever since we had given up Murre we'd wanted another pet, but because we traveled so much, we never got one. Now, faced with a faît accompli, we were overjoyed. There was only one problem—the tiny, wriggling bundle was supposed to be quarantined. I went to the airport manager and asked him to help us. "Take him with you on the plane," he said. "But don't tell anyone that I gave you permission."

The puppy became the darling of the whole plane. Just before landing in

Copenhagen, we gave him a sleeping pill, and then I handed him to Jussi. "I took care of him the whole way; now it's your turn!" Jussi took the basket and draped his camel's hair coat over it. The puppy slept all the way to Stockholm. At Bromma Airport a swarm of journalists met us, one of whom asked in the midst of the huge commotion, "May I help you?"

"Yes," Jussi replied casually, "take this!" and he handed over the basket and the coat. The reporter felt something stir under the coat, but he didn't say a word, and that is how our contraband poodle made his grand entrance into Sweden. Our faithful friend Bongo, as we called him, had a long and happy life, and he learned enough Swedish to obey—or ignore—some commands. He was a wonderful comfort to me in the dreadful emptiness that followed Jussi's death.

※

During the winter of 1954–55, the first since the war that we didn't travel to America, Jussi sang in Germany, Yugoslavia, Finland, Denmark, and England. On 27 January 1955 Jussi sang his first Radamès in eight years and his only one opposite Birgit Nilsson in the title role, with Sixten Ehrling on the podium. Jussi's decision to sing Radamès in Stockholm was a wise one. He was scheduled to record the role that summer, and the intensive rehearsals with Maestro Ehrling refreshed the role for him. While Ehrling found Jussi's offstage persona hard to take at times, he had nothing but admiration for the singer.

> The man had an incredible musical intuition. He was also very cooperative with the conductor. Occasionally he would say that he heard Caruso do it this way, would it be OK [if he tried it]? He was willing to listen to advice regarding interpretations, [but] he might not be quite as willing to follow the dynamic instructions. Singers like to make sure we hear them. Dynamically they always tend to be louder than the composer intended. For instance, how many times do you hear the *pianissimo* at the end of "Celeste Aida?" Never! The audiences expect [a *forte*], they're used to it. Actually, if he had sung it the way it was written they would've booed him!
>
> But when he opened his big mouth, you just fell into a trance. More than anything else, I remember one rehearsal of *Manon Lescaut*. Grevillius was conducting, and I sat in the auditorium. He just stood there and sang "Donna non vidi mai" marking, in other words he didn't give full voice. When he sang that aria, whispering, oh my God! It was fabulous! It was even more beautiful then when he gave full voice, I thought. To me it was the absolute epitome of beauty. His voice would go across the orchestra like an arch, even in *pianissimo*. The way he sang that rehearsal, that was my most unforgettable moment.[5]

Birgit Nilsson recalls that Jussi "sang a great Radamès with me in Stockholm. The opera house, which holds 1180 people, was just right for his voice. I heard his Radamès once in Chicago but found his voice a bit small for that role in the big auditorium."[6] Of course, next to Birgit's, every voice seemed small. Ehrling remembers her Aida:

> At that time her voice was so enormous that a most distinguished colleague of hers used to call it *eine Naturkatastrophe*, a natural disaster. Jussi was a fantastic singer and had a beautiful voice, but at the end of the second act, when they sing in unison, her top notes were so enormous that actually she was covering Jussi too much, I thought. So I said, "Birgit, I love the sound you make and I love Jussi's sound, but could you—?"[7]

Moses Pergament, who had followed Jussi's career from its inception, found a lot to praise in his presentation.

> I'm convinced that Jussi, with a little goodwill, would have been able to take the last high note in Radamès' first aria exactly the way Verdi prescribed: in a dying-away *pianissimo* [*morendo*]. He preferred the easier and surefire audience-grabber—an intensive, brilliant *fortissimo*. But if one puts the many merits on the other side of the balance, the feverish personal engagement in the Nile scene, the scales tip. So much is welcome and positive that, in spite of artistic overscrupulousness, one gives oneself over body and soul—greedily partaking of the nectar it has pleased our Lord to let flow from this substantial vessel.[8]

Another reviewer noted Jussi's gesture as he was about to take a curtain call with Birgit: "Jussi, in the last moment, sneaks back and leaves Birgit by herself with the ovations. And Birgit Nilsson certainly deserves such attention. . . . Jussi's vocal health is evidently on a respectable and reliably high level, and even if Radamès presently—or shall we say for the time being—is somewhat too much of a heldentenor role for Jussi, his performance deserves our admiration."[9]

During the spring Jussi sang his only joint recital with Elisabeth Schwarzkopf in Oslo, on 2 June 1955. It was such a great triumph for both that Schwarzkopf's husband, Walter Legge, suggested Elisabeth and Jussi record duets together. For the time being it remained just a thought.

July arrived and we were to travel to Rome, but for reasons known only to him, Jussi was in no mood to record. He had simply taken off with the boat and disappeared, and now he was somewhere out in the archipelago, carousing with his buddies. Days passed; I grew more anxious as our time of departure drew near. Finally, some friends and I rounded him up and got him into shape to travel. It wasn't easy.

Meanwhile, the Rome crew's apprehensions paralleled mine. Zinka Milanov liked to sing with Jussi, but she had a very low tolerance for his drinking habits. So did her brother and travel companion, Božidar Kunc, who wrote from Rome to Eleanor Morgan, Milanov's secretary in New York, saying that the whole cast of *Aida* had arrived—except Björling. RCA had just completed sessions of *Madama Butterfly* excerpts with Albanese and Jan Peerce, and as concern mounted, Zinka asked Jan whether he knew the role of Radamès. Peerce said yes.[10] Remembering his *Carmen* with Risë Stevens and the Toscanini *Un ballo in maschera* mess the year before, Jan must have wondered whether he'd be called upon to deputize for his friend once more.

But it wasn't necessary. We arrived a little late, and the sessions proceeded as scheduled. This was the first time the Milanov-Warren-Björling-Barbieri team was reunited since their pioneering *Trovatore*. All were in top form, and while Jussi's Radamès may not be a milestone recording, it is a fine interpretation. He only regretted, as he later told Arthur Jacobs, that he hadn't sung the closing B of "Celeste Aida" *piano*.[11] Jussi felt he couldn't go against popular taste in the theater, but he should have risked it in a recording.

Although Warren had one of the largest voices in the business, his wife, Agatha, worried that his voice would get lost in the ensembles. More than once she complained to Dick Mohr during playback, "I can't hear Leonard!" But Leonard himself was like a big lovable child: simple, gentle, and kind. The Warrens had no children, which may be why Leonard took such an interest in ours. This time Anders and Ann-Charlotte accompanied us to Italy, and Ann-Charlotte especially has fond memories of him. "When I developed a rash and had to stay in bed, Leonard sat by my bedside for hours while I was sick. When I mentioned that the strap on my new sandals had broken, he called down to housekeeping and ordered them up with needle and thread. He sat at my bed, and with his big clumsy hands sewed my sandal strap together. It was so sweet of him!"[12]

Boris Christoff, the Ramfis of the recording, too was quite taken with our very pretty 12-year-old daughter. Finding her name too long and insufficiently descriptive for an angel, he immediately rechristened her Angela and asked Jussi if he could take her around at night to show her Rome. It was no doubt an innocent suggestion, but Jussi didn't think it was a good idea. "Angela" and Boris didn't experience Rome together.

Our stay in Rome had amusing sidelights too, many of them thanks to Milanov. A dear person and a fine colleague, Zinka's eccentricities were more entertaining than annoying. When we dined out, she would collect the leftover squares of butter, wrap them in a paper napkin, and oblivious to the heat, slip the bundle into her purse. "Why do you do that, Zinka?" Ann-Charlotte asked. "It's for my complexion," Zinka explained. "Botter is better than any cold cream!" She must have been right. I have been told that when she passed away at age 83, her face was smooth, wrinkle-free, and without blemish.[13]

One day we decided to ride home from the session in a *carrozza*. Zinka and Božidar faced us in the open horse-drawn carriage, and Dick Mohr and Ann-Charlotte sat up on the bench next to the coachman. As we drove by the Colosseum, Ann-Charlotte felt Zinka tugging at her skirt from behind. "Now ven you go back to Stockholm, you can tell all your classmates that you rode through history in a *carrozza* vith the great Zinka Milanov."

Ann-Charlotte covered her mouth to stifle a guffaw. "Don't fall off," Dick advised her, and Jussi and I struggled to remain straightfaced. Zinka, of course, meant every word. It never occurred to her that the young girl wasn't that easy to impress—she'd been riding all her life with her father, the great Jussi Björling. Dick Mohr observed, "That was Zinka. She wasn't really boasting or bragging, she was just naive enough to say that. She used to stand in front of a mirror at the Grand Hotel, look at herself full length, pat her stomach and pat her behind, then say, 'Not so bad!'"[14]

That was indeed Zinka. Dr. Hugh Davidson, her family doctor, likes to tell of the time he met her on Central Park South. Two starstruck girls interrupted their conversation with, "Oh, Madame Milanov, excuse us, but could we have your autograph?" She obliged and the girls ran off. She then turned back to Dr. Davidson and sighed, "Excuse me, doctor, but vat can you do ven you are a Gott?"[15] Zinka never paused to consider the effect her "Milanovisms" might have on others. She once saw very religious Kurt Baum crossing himself before the third act of *Trovatore*. Zinka just looked at him and said, "If you don't know it Baum, Gott ain't gonna help you."[16]

While we were in Rome, the Gobbis often had us over for lunch or dinner. Tito was an excellent conversationalist, Tilde a charming hostess, and their daughter, Cecilia, a lovely young girl just Ann-Charlotte's age; they had a lot of fun together. One day we accepted their kind invitation to spend the day at their beach house at Santa Severa. Ann-Charlotte and I usually went to the sessions, so I asked Dick to look after Jussi this time. As he tells the story, when the afternoon session was over, Jussi said,

"Now you come back to the hotel Richard, and we'll have a drink." I said, "Oh, Jussi, you don't want to have a drink." But he insisted, "Yes, yes! We must celebrate, it was a good session." So I went back with him, I thought maybe I can curb this if he gets going. Jussi was in the habit of ordering double martinis with beer chasers. He would drink a double martini practically in one gulp, and it would take two or three before you could see any discernible effect.

I forget how many he had, and I kept saying, "No, Jussi, that's enough. You have to record tomorrow." "Oh, I'll be fine," he assured me. Then he got very jolly, and he said "Let's go down the hall and call on Zinka!" I said, "*That* is not a good idea," because Zinka was always as nervous as a cat when she was recording. If you even looked at her crooked, she had an explosion. Once, when she was complaining how hard it was to record all these sessions, George Marek said to her, "You know, London/Decca has Tebaldi recording at morning, noon, and night of the same day!" And she blew up and said, "Go get Tebaldi then, damn it!"

But Jussi insisted on calling on Zinka. He got up, and I tried to keep him back. I was wearing rubber-soled shoes, and on the marble floors of the Grand Hotel, I could get no traction. Even if I could have, I would've been no match for him. He was strong as an ox, and he started pushing me along the corridor toward the suite. He continued pushing me backward right to Zinka's door.

> We stopped there and I said, "Jussi, I beg you by all that is sacred, do not knock on that door!" And he looked at me, and he said, "All right, Richard!" and like a child, like a good little boy, went back to his room. I stayed another 15 minutes, and fortunately Anna-Lisa and Ann-Charlotte arrived. He was such a sweet man; it was such a shame that he had that problem.[17]

Although Jussi wasn't big on pranks, sometimes he would see the potential humor of a situation and indulge himself. One night we came home late, and he noticed the shoes neatly lined up in the hallway outside of each door, waiting to be polished. "Daddy was in a high old mood, and a wicked idea flashed through his mind," remembers Ann-Charlotte. "He gave me a mischievous wink, then quickly moving from door to door, he reshuffled several pairs. He chuckled over the thought of each husband's reaction when he was to find his wife's shoes next to a strange man's pair in front of another room."[18]

We also visited Ingrid Bergman in Santa Marinella, an idyllic fishing village north of Rome, where she lived with Roberto Rossellini and their children. Ingrid served a wonderful Italian meal, and Jussi got his fill of homemade spaghetti. Anders, who spent the afternoon snorkeling, had the misfortune of stepping on a sea urchin. Later, he could tell his school friends about his adventure—and that Ingrid Bergman had pulled the thorns out of his foot!

Ingrid's private life was her own affair, and it had no bearing on our friendship. We were impressed by her courage to begin a new life in a new land. She appeared to be thriving and was very happy. We saw her often during the following summers too, and she remained my friend through the years. The last time we met was in London, six months before she died.

※

Following our return from Rome, Jussi gave two recitals in Furuvik on Dalarna Day. One of Jussi's monumental binges followed, putting him out of commission for the rest of the summer of 1955. "At Gröna Lund, a long-standing tradition has been broken," complained one newspaper. "He had sung faithfully there for many years. This is the first time a Gröna Lund concert has been canceled."[19]

It was detrimental for Jussi to be forced into inactivity without any obligations ahead—and thus began another of those stressful periods. As always, his state of mind affected the whole family, and the children were concerned that I didn't feel so well either. Anders had just been drafted into the army at LV 3 in Norrtälje, and after he moved out, it was Lasse and later Ann-Charlotte's turn to help me cope. I know how much was expected of them, how valiantly they stood by me in every crisis, and I am grateful for all they did.

Sven Salén too continued to be a support. I well remember an ill-fated dinner party at his and his wife Dulli's summer home. Sven, trying to be thoughtful, didn't serve Jussi even a glass of wine, which made Jussi very angry. He got up and left the table. I thought that he would come back after he calmed down, but he did not. Several days later, Jussi showed up at Siarö with a newly acquired luxury yacht, complete with captain and crew. He explained that he had gone down to the dock, caught sight of the yacht, and took off sailing in the archipelago. He liked the boat so much that he'd purchased it. I made an agitated phone call to Sven and explained the situation; he was able to make the necessary arrangements with the former owner to cancel the transaction.

�֎

Jussi's alcoholism was the persistent misfortune of our lives, turning our harmonious existence into long spells of crises. But most of the time we were really happy people, Jussi, our children, and I. Jussi was a wonderful father. He was close to the children and intensely interested in their development. Eventually they came to realize that a person who had as much to give as their father often had weaknesses, but the trips, the visits to the opera, the many interesting people they met, and all the fun we experienced together compensated a great deal for the troubled times.

Jussi believed that the children and I should have the best of everything, and I often had to rein in his well-intentioned but impulsive spending. One day, in the store where he purchased his fishing supplies, Jussi bought the finest, most expensive bicycle he could find for Anders. It had a coaster brake, two hand brakes, and a gear shift—an unheard of novelty at that time. Anders, just 10 years old, was completely dumbfounded. He hadn't yet learned to ride, and the bike was too large—he couldn't even reach the pedals. I'll never forget the sight of my son pedaling back and forth on Östermalmsgatan, while my short, stocky husband ran alongside, with one hand on the carrier to keep him balanced. They were blissfully happy, like children at play.

When Anders turned 14, Jussi bought him a very expensive silk robe. Another time, Jussi bought a rifle with real cartridges for Lasse, who was much too young for such a gift; we exchanged the rifle for an air gun. Jussi was generous with friends too. One day's mail brought a large bill for a camel's hair overcoat, shawl, hat, and gloves. When I asked Jussi about it, he confessed that Grevillius, who had admired his coat so much, was not in a position to buy one, so—

On Siarö, Jussi and the boys often fished together. Whether at an inlet a half hour distant or just the nearby weed bed, the two marveled at how their father could pinpoint with uncanny accuracy where the pike were, depending on the time of day, the angle of the sun, or the temperature of the water. He cast so skillfully that the lure wound up exactly where he wanted it—behind a rock or next to a blade of seaweed, and he almost always got a nibble. Ann-Charlotte claims he could lure the fish just by whistling to them.

"Please, Papa, play the perch tune," she'd begged. Then Jussi whistled a special melody and to Ann-Charlotte's delight, "the fish came like arrows from all directions straight to the dock!"[20]

Jussi kept a large wooden fish chest underneath the dock for the fish they caught. He was careful not to let the fish suffer too long; if they brought home more than we could eat in a day or too, he'd turn them loose. As dinner time approached he'd ask me, "What size do you want?" I would then "order" a six-pounder. Over the years, I served our family many a pike fillet: poached or boiled, served with horseradish or chopped hardboiled eggs in melted butter; baked in the oven with mushrooms; even pike soufflé. No matter the variations, Ann-Charlotte had her fill of pike. Now she won't touch it.

On one occasion, Jussi didn't return a contract for a concert in spite of repeated follow-ups from Konsertbolaget. Erik Järnklev lost patience and called us at Siarö. Holding the receiver I told Jussi what the call was about, and he said, "Tell Järnklev there are so many nibbles that I cannot let go of my fishing pole just now." As Järnklev later observed, "It was hard to take him away from his family and Siarö. . . . That those nibbles cost him many a thousand-Kronor banknote obviously didn't bother him."[21]

In the city, ignoring his father's admonishments, he took the children to the movies, usually to the "shoot'em ups" he loved. When they grew older, it was a lot of thrilling Hitchcock films and detective stories. Some films in Sweden had an age restriction for children, but Jussi ignored it. He sailed through, holding his little charge by the hand. Lasse admits he was so nervous at such times that he walked on tiptoes to appear a little taller, but they were never turned away or asked to leave, and it gave them a delicious sense of triumph. When they came home, I always heard a jubilant "We did it!" After they settled into the plush seats of the cinema and the newsreel began, Jussi put the ticket stubs in the hand of whichever child was with him. This little ritual was repeated, without fail, every time, beginning with Anders and continuing with Lasse and Ann-Charlotte.

When Jussi had to perform in the evening, he napped in the afternoon; the house had to be completely quiet from about 2 to 4 p.m. Sometimes, before he lay down to rest, Anders or I read aloud to him. I'd try to pick something low key and soothing, but Anders always chose the wildest adventure stories.

It wasn't easy to be the child of a well-known radio personality. I know that at his first school, the Broms-Ullmans School on Sturegatan, Anders was often bullied during recesses. The boys would surround him, not letting him pass. "Sing something Anders!" they taunted. "Sing like your father!" His famous father and uncommon experiences, including foreign travel, made Anders different—and the boys resented that. We were aware of this but decided not to interfere; applying pressure through the school authorities would only have made things worse. Anders learned to fend for himself, and as he grew older and stronger, the harassment stopped.

The children didn't appreciate the frequent photo-interviews either. Having to dress up and look well-behaved in the most artificial settings was the silliest thing they could imagine. These small inconveniences were topped by being recognized from the newspapers. As they grew older, the boys complained that whenever they got into any mischief, they were always found out because people recognized "Jussi's boys."

When Anders became interested in girls, like all parents, we became a little apprehensive. Jussi, no doubt recalling his own youth said, "Anders, remember: don't make me a grandfather while I'm still singing Roméo!"[22] Once, during their teenage years, the boys went out on a double date in the big mahogany boat we anchored at Djurgården. Anders and Lasse wanted to impress the girls, so they went full speed ahead through the Djurgårdsbrunn channel despite its five-knot speed limit. Jussi found out in short order because both his boat and his boys were recognized. For once, he became terribly angry. He never spanked the children, but this time the boys got a royal scolding—and Jussi knew how to do it!

Something else Jussi never tolerated was when Anders and Lasse teased Ann-Charlotte. The boys once suggested that the three of them play hide-and-seek in the meadow on Siarö. They stood Ann-Charlotte behind a tree and told her to count to 500 before coming to look for them. Little Ann-Charlotte did as she was told, but her brothers had disappeared. They were gone for the entire day. When that happened, Jussi was unmerciful. If he had a weakness for anyone, it was for his little girl Lillan.

Jussi's relationship with each child was different. Anders was the gentlest by nature. He inherited my trick knee and Jussi's physique; he was more quiet and studious and participated less in sports. Lasse on the other hand, the daredevil of the family, thrived on physical activity. Jussi admired athletic prowess, which only egged Lasse on. Ann-Charlotte was the baby and the only girl, and Jussi always had a soft spot for her. In his autobiography he wrote, "One isn't supposed to have a favorite among one's children, but I wonder if my heart beats warmest for my little two-year-old daughter, Ann-Charlotte, when with her dark blue eyes and blond curls and her sweet smile she comes toddling and calls out, 'Hi, Papa!'"[23]

As she was growing up and the boys were preoccupied with teenage matters, it was Ann-Charlotte who followed Jussi backstage at the Opera, just as Anders and Lasse had done before her. She loved to watch her Dad made up by Atos Berg, the only stipulation being that she sit on a little stool in the corner and not ask any questions.

Berg worked with Jussi practically from his first years until his own retirement in the late 50s. "[Jussi] was always very kind and friendly and never interfered with his makeup," Berg said. "[He] wasn't difficult to make up, except that it involved trying to minimize his round face, getting it to seem more slender. He always wanted a little extra nose."[24] Jussi, who had a typically Swedish low ridge, wanted a more noble profile. Once, when the makeup was finished for some romantic role, Ann-Charlotte spontaneously exclaimed: "How beautiful Papa looks!"[25] A big thrill awaited her after the performance: she was allowed to take a thread and slice off the nose.

When Berg finished, Erik Sundin would take over. Sundin, Jussi's dresser from 1945 onward, recalled,

> As a rule, he was a man of few words and detested visits to his dressing room before the performance or between acts. Plainly, he wanted to concentrate in peace and quiet. . . . Like many artists, he was quite superstitious. For example, it would never do to come with the right shoe or stocking first. . . . Whistling in the hallway was a mortal sin, or to be in the stage area with a hat on. . . . He knocked on wood before he went onstage. Before he entered the stage, even if he had been off only for a moment, he wanted to have one or two glasses of Pommac [a soft drink] at room temperature.[26]

Before the performance began, Uncle Sundin escorted Ann-Charlotte to the spot backstage where she could see and hear her Daddy best. She especially liked the second act of *Tosca*, when the executioner led Jussi as Cavaradossi into the offstage torture chamber. Atos Berg was waiting in the wings, and while Jussi screamed on cue, Berg painted blood and bruises on his face. Sometimes Ann-Charlotte helped out, and Jussi never looked so dreadfully mauled as when his little girl had a hand in the makeup. She always wanted "more blood, more bruises!" The torture ended with Jussi emitting a hellish howl, which fascinated Ann-Charlotte no end. "He made it so funny!" she told me. "When he roared out his last scream, he took a stranglehold on his own throat and pulled it back and forth to make it rattle."

Anders Näslund, the executioner who was to carry the "fainted" Jussi back onstage, took a look at him one particular night and calmly announced, "Jussi, you look too damned awful. It's all Ann-Charlotte's fault. I think we should take her instead!" He then took hold of her and began to drag her toward the stage, while Jussi grabbed her feet and pulled in the opposite direction. Ann-Charlotte, who wasn't quite sure if this was a joke or not, was less generous with the blood thereafter.

As she grew older, Jussi enjoyed her interest and was happy to have her around. "Daddy, what's a phrase?" Ann-Charlotte might ask, and Jussi would patiently sit down to the piano to explain. I later discovered that Ann-Charlotte and Jussi were also partners in less edifying activities:

> Daddy was almost always on a diet, and mother very loyally prepared his dietetic meals. One day we were expecting a journalist at Siarö, so Dad and I took the motorboat across the bay to pick him up at the bus. While we sat there waiting, Dad asked: "Do you think the store's open?" "Yes, I think so," I said. "Why don't you go and buy some of the chocolate *you* like. Buy a whole bunch."
>
> So I bought a big bag of chocolate pralines. Our guest must've missed the bus because he never showed, and while we sat there waiting, we ate it all. On our way back Daddy said: "Don't tell Mommy." Of course I didn't, and Dad dutifully ate his carefully prepared dietetic lunch.[27]

Of necessity, only a limited number of Jussi's suits accompanied us on our travels, but in Stockholm, where he had access to his entire wardrobe, he always dressed impeccably—particularly when he went out with Ann-Charlotte. He looked especially dashing one day when he picked her up at the French School. "It was very unusual because he was usually away during the school year," remembers Ann-Charlotte.

> I was about 12, and I was very happy when he told me he would come and fetch me. It was early spring, and he had a light coat on with a beautiful silk scarf around his neck. He looked very elegant; he must've worked on it a long time. I don't know how long he must have been waiting. He greeted me with an eager "Here you are! How lovely you look!" My classmates were very curious to meet my famous father, but he grabbed hold of me and rushed me around the corner. "For heaven's sake, get a taxi, quick!" "Why, what's the matter?" "I'm freezing! I put on no sweater and the thinnest coat to look as slim as possible! I'm scared I'll catch a cold!"[28]

When the weather was pleasant, Jussi and Ann-Charlotte went on walks. "People often laughed at us, two pals, when we were out for a stroll," she says. "No doubt we looked funny together, walking the same way with our feet pointing out, our tummies a little forward, and both of us round-faced, short, and chubby." To stay in lockstep, they whistled while they walked, or one would sing "tiri-diri-dee," while the other chimed in with "Oom-pah-pah, oom-pah-pah." It didn't help the image that just for fun, for long stretches, they walked with one foot on the sidewalk and the other in the gutter. Sometimes I came along on these crazy walks and joined in the folly. The Royal Court Singer and his family must've been quite a sight!

We also had a family vocabulary, our own special words and funny expressions, some of them in the Dalarna dialect. It originated with Jussi and me, but the children picked it up as soon as they could talk. We had terrific fun, carrying on a whole conversation among ourselves—the uninitiated Swede wouldn't have the slightest idea what we were saying. It's a pity that it's untranslatable.

Ann-Charlotte says that with the passage of years, the mischievousness that so often surfaced in her father earlier was lost. She was right, of course. The growing demands imposed upon Jussi made him more serious and less able to set aside all care. When life's pressures weighed him down, it hurt me to see him carry the burden.

"My memories of my father are like a strand of pearls," Ann-Charlotte says, "some are lighter, some darker, like so many pearls. But light or dark, sad or gay, it makes no difference—the inside of every pearl is the same, a deep feeling of love."[29]

# Chapter 23

# CALLAS

By September 1955 Jussi was well enough to travel; he marked his return to the United States with a sold-out Carnegie Hall recital on 24 September. He hadn't performed on the North American continent for 18 months, and speculation about the condition of his voice was rampant. But his fans worried needlessly; it appeared that Jussi's voice was indestructible. "Björling Is Back" rejoiced the headline of *The New York Times* (26 September 1955) and "the cheers reached almost football stadium proportions." His voice "had lost none of its usual splendor" and "[his] control of his vocal resources was, if anything, rather more precise than before." Miles Kastendieck wrote: "By intermission the audience's cheers equalled its applause."[1] The concert, with Freddie Schauwecker at the piano, was recorded and (most of it) released by RCA Victor.

At the same time it was evident that with a noticeable decline in its lyricism, Jussi's voice had grown more solid and more powerful. Contemplating some new and heavier roles was now a logical progression of his art. Around this time Irving Kolodin wrote, "There is, perhaps, no real reason why a singer who can make a handsome living as Manrico and Faust, Rodolfo and Don Carlo should burden himself with Lohengrin or Walther von Stolzing. But is it too much to hope that before he ends his still flourishing career Bjoerling may oblige us by showing how a real lyric Wagner tenor might sound?"[2]

In November 1955, in the first and only pairing of their careers, Jussi sang with Maria Callas in two successive performances of *Il trovatore* at the Chicago Lyric Theater. Caruso allegedly said that all you needed for *Trovatore* was the four greatest voices in the world. With Björling, Callas, Ebe Stignani, and Ettore Bastianini, the Lyric Opera of Chicago came very close to proving that maxim right.

Years before their paths had almost crossed when Giovanni Zenatello offered Jussi Enzo Grimaldo in *La Gioconda* for the Arena di Verona's first postwar season, in 1947. Jussi didn't know the role and had too many commitments to learn it on short notice, so he turned the offer down, thus missing the opportunity to share the stage with a young unknown in her Italian debut.[3] The honor fell to Richard Tucker to partner Callas on this historic occasion, making his own Italian debut.

Callas may not have had the most beautiful voice, but it had an indescribable quality that cast a spell over the listener. Her voice was not as large in the theater as it was on closely miked records, yet it was clear and well projected. While Jussi commanded attention, almost royally, by vocal means, Callas had to be seen as well as heard—a great part of her magic lay in her appearance and acting. She had a charged radiance, a magnetic stage presence that mesmerized the audience so that they hardly noticed anyone else.

What Jussi appreciated most in Callas was that she tried to be faithful to the composer's intentions. She observed all the markings, never deviated from the score, never held a note longer than she should. It was clear from the outset that both Maria and Jussi were driven—not by the vanity of seeking not to be outshone by a partner of equal artistic stature but rather by their high expectations of themselves and each other.

The performance of 5 November 1955 attained a legendary status in opera lore, and it's a great loss that this singular constellation of stars was not immortalized on tape. Rumor has it that one of the two performances— supposedly—was secretly taped; if so, the recording has yet to surface. A highly placed member of the company, who prefers to remain anonymous, recently admitted,

> Unfortunately, I'm the man who unplugged the machine by mistake. Nobody knew it was being taped, even I didn't know it until [co-manager] Larry Kelly told everybody years later. He came to me and said "Where is the cord?" I said "What cord? There was something people were tripping on, so I took the thing out of the socket." He said, "That was our recording!" I said, "I had no idea." If they had only told me what they were doing! I don't really know when this was, whether it was the first or second performance. They were very strict in those days—it was long before record piracy began to flourish. The Lyric was not being broadcast, and it wasn't possible to record in the house as easily as it is now. There were only bulky reel-to-reel machines, the audio cassette had not yet been invented.[4]

It is possible that Kelly discovered the blunder when he went to change reels and plugged in the machine for the last act. This may explain rumors that a tape of the Miserere does exist.[5]

Claudia Cassidy was ecstatic about *Trovatore*. "I'm not quite sure I ever heard such applause as this Lyric audience lavished on our new opera in the big style," she wrote. Callas didn't tell anyone that in the first act she was still trying to cope with the aftereffects of an injection a dentist gave her while working on a broken front tooth. No matter:

> [She sang "Tacea la notte"] superbly in line and style, and her fourth act was a wonder of the western world. Her aria was so breathtakingly beautiful it stopped the show. . . . [Ebe Stignani's] Azucena did its share to bring the house down [and] Bastianini's baritone and good looks are perfect for Luna. . . . No one will claim that [Björling's] is the robust tenor to pierce the operatic din. It just plain gets lost. But his love song in gentle mood is matchless in sheer beauty, and his "Di quella pira" glitters like his flashing sword.[6]

Cassidy also quoted Jussi as saying, "[Callas'] Leonora was perfection. I have heard the role sung often, but never was there a better one than hers."[7] That remark got him in a lot of hot water. Every Leonora gave him hell for putting Callas *hors concours*.

The second performance three days later went even better. Claramae Turner and Robert Weede replaced Stignani and Bastianini. According to Cassidy, both Callas and Jussi "outsang their first *Trovatore* [with] more freshness and more of that ring that makes Verdi triumphant." And Jussi in particular? He "sang like Bjoerling, which is like a Nordic archangel equipped with a celestial high C."[8]

The presence of Rudolf Bing and his assistant manager, Francis Robinson, gave special glitter to this performance. They were like a pair of hands, the iron fist and the kid glove—Bing aloof, precise, formal, and stiletto-sharp, Robinson relaxed, smooth, and reassuring, with the soothing tones of a southern preacher. Bing was in Chicago on a mission: after some tough negotiations with Meneghini, he had finally signed Callas to open the Met's 1956–57 season.

In addition to Manrico, Jussi sang several performances of *Rigoletto*, *Faust*, and *Un ballo in maschera*. His Marguerite was a very young Rosanna Carteri, in excellent form; Nicola Rossi-Lemeni was Méphistophélès; Amelia was taken by Anita Cerquetti in her American debut; and in both *Ballo* and *Rigoletto* Jussi was partnered by Tito Gobbi. Audiences had a lot to cheer about. The other singers received their share of excellent notices, but reviewers vied with each other to describe Jussi's singing. His "Salut, demeure" in *Faust* "was the most exquisite art song within opera that the stage can know. The resonance—not only of tone but of feeling—that Bjoerling bestows upon the French language is a wonder of the lyric theater," wrote Seymour Raven.[9] Irving Sablosky ranked him "probably the finest Faust of our day."[10]

By this time the pattern for my relationship with Rolf, Jussi's first son, had been set, and neither of us made an effort to reestablish it on an adult footing. It was no secret within our circle of friends that I found parts of his character less than admirable, and he wasn't about to change at age 26. For those who knew Rolf and only his perception of the situation, I was a most unlikable person, exclusively responsible for our poor relationship. The problem was this: he talked about me, but I didn't talk about him, so my side was never known. I simply accepted the consequences.

Jussi knew how Rolf and I felt about each other. Although it mattered to him, he never pressured either of us into a familial relationship. He always treated Rolf affectionately and continued to help him financially. When the boy was old enough to work, he found him a good position in Stockholm.

In his early 20s, Rolf immigrated to the United States. In 1955 he was living in Chicago with his wife and child, studying voice with well-known Romanian tenor Dimitri Onofrei. While we were there and during subsequent visits, Jussi saw his son from time to time, sometimes with my knowledge, sometimes without. Although Rolf's feelings about me never changed, he unconditionally loved Jussi: "I had the most fantastic, wonderful father anyone can have."[11]

Chicago was a regular stop on Jussi's tours, and we grew to like the city, the audiences, and our professional associates, particularly Danny Newman, the publicity director for the Lyric Opera, Allied Arts Corporation, and the Metropolitan's visits to Chicago. "He made his successes overwhelmingly through his voice and by innate musicianship," Danny wrote of Jussi. "Within what was the usual level of theatrical competence as exhibited by opera singers in that era, he was above average. However, the sheer beauty of his voice and his astonishing vocal prowess set him apart." Once, when Jussi was passing through Chicago, he unthinkingly wired ahead to Danny, asking him to meet his plane. It was pre-dawn, but Danny was there. "When he got off the plane and saw me waiting, he began to cry. I asked, 'Jussi, why are you crying?' He replied, 'You came to meet me so early in the morning?' I protested, 'Jussi, you sent me a telegram!' Perhaps he did not realize that a cable from him meant a command performance from me."[12]

We developed an even closer relationship with Sarah and Harry Zelzer, who managed Jussi's Chicago concerts after 1950 through their Allied Arts Corporation (formerly Harry Zelzer Concerts). We often dined with them at restaurants or at their home, and they became dear friends over the years. I could always count on Sarah and Harry; if Jussi disappeared for a suspicious length of time, the Zelzers helped me find him before a "situation" developed. Sarah, who attended nearly all Jussi's Chicago recitals, recalls the times:

> We were friends, and we were quite close to them. Jussi was a very pleasant, very stubborn man, with a peculiar sense of humor. He was a great artist, and he got along well with his colleagues. He never knocked them; he was always very willing to help other people. Until his recital was on,

we would have to watch him, and we got used to it. Sometimes when we were having dinner at one of the restaurants, all of a sudden Jussi would disappear, and we would discover he was catching up on drinks. But it never interfered with his concerts. He was one of my favorite singers. As he stood there, perfectly still, and that glorious voice would come out of this not too tall, slightly overweight man, you sometimes even wondered where it all came from.[13]

※

The Chicago season was followed by recitals in Atlanta, Houston, and New Orleans, culminating with a joint appearance on 20 December 1955 with Renata Tebaldi at Carnegie Hall, Leonard Bernstein conducting. Jussi admired Renata greatly, and he always welcomed the opportunity to sing with her. They performed the love duet from *Tosca* and the closing duets from *Aida* and *Manon Lescaut*. Tebaldi vividly recollects: "People went on applauding for at least 20 minutes and refused to leave the hall! And both of us were in excellent vocal form. If we only had a tape of that concert!"[14]

Even before the Chicago and New York performances affirmed that Jussi Björling was still among the world's best tenors, singing with undiminished resources, Freddie Schang, with our tacit approval, had initiated negotiations with the Met and obtained a partial concession regarding the tour. He felt that Jussi was inadequately compensated at the Met: with his preeminence and his drawing power, reasoned Freddie, Jussi should be paid more. Bing wrote to Freddie "to confirm our understanding" that the Met will "exercise our option on Mr. Bjoerling's services for the 1957 Spring Tour, we will then pay Mr. Bjoerling an additional Five Hundred ($500) Dollars over and above the fee stipulated for every performance sung on tour. It was agreed that this arrangement would be kept confidential."[15] The additional $500 fee was a significant jump from the $50 daily allowance we had previously received on tour.

The Met contract Freddie negotiated for 1956–57 specified a minimum of five performances, and two weeks' participation in the spring tour. Jussi wanted to leave the first half of the season open for concertizing, and Max Rudolf, on behalf of Bing, conditionally accepted this: "Subject your giving us 10 weeks between January 28 April 21 1957, agree release you early part season."[16] A letter from Bing to Freddie Schang, dated 31 December 1955, specified *Un ballo in maschera* in Boston and two unspecified performances in Cleveland. The Met's notice of exercising their option for 1956–57 was dated 30 January 1956.

※

Jussi and I had long considered moving to more spacious quarters in Stockholm; we wanted something more practical than our uncomfortably crowded albeit cozy old apartment, but it never came about because we were away from home so much. In addition to living room, sitting room, and den, we had three bedrooms, one for us and two for the children, and only two narrow closets, which didn't allow enough room for broad-shouldered Jussi's suits to hang straight. Before he could put one of his suits on, I'd have to iron it, and on one occasion I must've complained about him wrinkling it afterward, for I left this apologetic note for him: "Sweetheart of mine, you can wrinkle your best suit as much as you want. I will never again scold the most wonderful Papa in the whole world." In any case, one day early in 1956, in a fit of frustration, Jussi posed the rhetorical question: "Is this the way a world tenor should live?"

The obvious answer was no, and the search was on. I went to a housing agency and mentioned some addresses, among them Karlavägen 11, where one of our friends lived. Our time in Stockholm was short; at the end of January, we were due back in New York for a televised concert. But one morning before 9 o'clock, the rental agency called. "You're in luck, Mrs. Björling! There's an apartment available at Karlavägen 11!"

It belonged to an elderly widow, a Mrs. Nauckhoff. Her husband, a general, had died a year earlier in an automobile accident; she wanted to move to a smaller place and might be interested in swapping with us. Could she come right over? Of course I said yes, and although Jussi was to sing that evening, for once, without mercy, I forced him out of bed. "Hurry up—someone is coming to look at the apartment!"

Our home had aged over the years, and a lot of quick cosmetic improvements were required to make a good first impression. We polished the brass doorhandles, and since the general's wife had asked if we had a balcony, we scrubbed away the calling cards the pigeons had left behind. I even rushed out to buy bunches of flowers. When everything was in order and every vase was filled, the whole apartment looked like a respectable florist's establishment.

Jussi took it upon himself to charm the lady—he was a master at that when he wanted to be. But he took success for granted, believing we were destined to get our dream apartment at Karlavägen 11 because the number 11 was the year of his birth. His superstitious expectation was met. Mrs. Nauckhoff was very happy with our apartment, and we with hers. The place had good feelings about it. Before we left for America, we moved into Karlavägen where I still live, four floors up, close by Engelbrekt's Church.

We were absolutely certain we'd made the right move. It was wonderful to have seven spacious, sunny rooms, and for the first time in their lives, all three children had a bedroom. As the movers unloaded our furniture, they placed a big flower vase on our little secretaire. It was from Mrs. Nauckhoff. Her handwritten note said, "I wish you and Jussi to be as happy as I was with my husband here."

We were overjoyed and began furnishing our new home straightaway. One day I came home and told Jussi that I'd seen two exquisite antique armchairs at Bukowski's Auction House. "But they're too expensive," I added. "I really don't think we should spend that much for two chairs, no matter how beautiful they are."

"What do they look like?" Jussi asked. Though he never really cared for material objects, he liked to be surrounded by lovely things.

"Rococo, with oyster-colored silk," I answered a little vaguely. "They're really very nice."

That same evening the doorbell rang, and I opened the door to find a delivery man from Bukowski's with the two chairs. I called for Jussi, but he was nowhere to be found. Just as I was about to say that there must have been some mistake, he jumped out from his hiding place behind the door: "Are these the chairs?"

He was thrilled like a child when he could surprise someone with a present. Every time it happened, I believe that my boundless gratitude made him truly happy.

※

On 30 January 1956, Jussi took part in the *Festival of Music* program on American television, hosted by Charles Laughton.[17] The roster of singers included Marian Anderson, Zinka Milanov, Mildred Miller, Jan Peerce, Roberta Peters, Risë Stevens, Renata Tebaldi, Blanche Thebom, and Leonard Warren, and violinist Isaac Stern, cellist Gregor Piatigorsky, and pianist Arthur Rubinstein all performed.

My memory of Rubinstein's heavenly playing, heard poolside in Ingrid Bergman's garden, still lingered. When I met him, unfortunately, the good impression evaporated. That Renata and Jussi sang their respective arias from the first act of *La bohème* as well as the closing duet was too much for Rubinstein, who played only one Chopin polonaise. He apparently felt that he deserved more air time, and he turned red in the face. The terrible noise I heard coming from his dressing room sounded like furniture being thrown around or smashed. This was the only time we experienced this kind of jealousy from a great artist.

Jussi signed a new contract with RCA Victor on 9 February 1956. The terms were standard and not especially favorable: the contract was to run for three years, with "two (2) successive options to renew for periods of one (1) year." It specified five complete operas: in addition to the imminent *La bohème*, Jussi was to record *Tosca, Rigoletto, Roméo et Juliette*, and *Turandot*.

An especially significant provision of the contract spelled out RCA's option to permit Jussi to record complete operas "for another company." The contract further specified, "We [RCA Victor] previously agreed to your recording *Otello* for the Angel Label." RCA already had the Arturo Toscanini–Ramon Vinay *Otello* in their catalog, and they didn't want to compete with themselves. A vast repertoire of operas had yet to be recorded, and the time of multiple recordings of the same work by the same company was yet to come. Jussi still hoped to sing *Otello* one day, at least on records, so he wanted to leave this option open.

The "monarchy went back on the gold standard when Björling resumed one of his best parts on February 17,"[18] Kolodin wrote of the last *Un ballo in maschera* of the 1955–56 season. Apart from Jussi's return, it was a special event. When conductor Dimitri Mitropoulos walked out to the orchestra pit, he found Rudolf Bing in his place on the podium. Bing asked the audience to join him as he "led the orchestra in a performance of 'Happy Birthday' in honor of the maestro's 60th birthday."[19] It was a rare, endearing gesture, the sort of thing Bing ought to have indulged in more often, if not for his own satisfaction then as a boost for company morale. It put everybody in a good humor, and when Jussi appeared onstage, someone in the audience shouted "Welcome back!"

# Chapter 24

# CRISSCROSSING AMERICA

From mid-February to April 1956, Jussi sang eight performances with the Metropolitan in the house and on tour. In between his Met commitments, his bookings took us all the way to Pasadena, with several stops on the way. As usual, his accompanist and our travel companion was Freddie Schauwecker.

How well I remember these endless tours! Most people imagine the life of a great artist is filled with ovations, glittering parties, and endless tributes. Certainly these are part of an operatic celebrity's experience, but the everyday reality is completely different. The touring artist's is a strenuous and abnormal life.

A singer must protect his voice; both the singer and those around him become slaves to this sensitive instrument, constantly fearing drafts or catching colds. One didn't have to travel far to undergo a dangerously sudden switch in temperature: in New York, for example, we left a wind-whipped 28-degree sidewalk for a 78-degree hotel; in Miami, we left air-conditioned lobbies for steaming-hot 90-degree streets. Something as simple as dining out could be a risk; I always carried a sweater or jacket for Jussi to put on in a chilly restaurant, and we'd try to find a table as far from the air-conditioner registers as possible. If someone nearby smoked, we changed tables again. Sometimes we moved around a dining room three or four times, and the whole time we felt the guests' eyes on us for the wrong reason—if people had no idea who Jussi was, he had to be crazy; if they did, he was being temperamental. In New York the little German restaurant Blue Ribbon on 44th

Street was our particular hangout, where we went for *Eisbein mit Sauer-kraut* and good German beer. The staff did all they could to make it pleasant for us; before they served the beer, they checked it with a thermometer to make certain it was the right temperature for Mr. Björling's throat.

When Jussi and I first came to America, we lived simply and inexpensively, staying at the Hotel Alden on Central Park West or the Windsor on 58th Street. When the weather was too rough to go out, I ran down to the nearest delicatessen to buy coldcuts for our supper, and we'd order something warm to drink from room service. The accommodations could be quite primitive. I remember one stay in a little suite of two rooms in the old part of the Hotel Wellington. We'd just come home from a trip; it was late, and we dined in our room on ham and jelly rolls. We went to bed, and in the middle of the night I heard Jussi call out, "What are you doing, Mamichko? Are you eating?" When he flicked on the light, two mice ran down the lamp cord. No, there was no luxury to speak of in the beginning. Later, when we had accumulated the safety net of a bank account, we were able to afford better hotels with more amenities and no mice.

Whenever possible, I arranged for monthly rates. When we came back to New York after the war, we rented an efficiency apartment at the charming old Algonquin. I bought pots and pans and table settings and hung up my apron and colorful potholders to make everything look as homey as possible. Then we lined up the photographs we had brought with us—the one of the children was always placed on Jussi's nighttable.

The children never realized how painful it was for us to be separated from them, how we waited for their letters. Reports from home were red-letter days for us. It wasn't easy for my mother either. She maintained her own apartment and stayed at our home when we were gone. Although she did it gladly, looking after three youngsters, no matter how well behaved, disrupted her own quiet existence. And we two were so close that she too counted the days until our return. "My life has been one long yearning," she'd say.

An upright piano the Metropolitan lent to their soloists made things even more homelike. On the days he performed, Jussi rested his voice, and one could hardly say a word to him requiring a response, but on his days off, he spent several hours practicing and perhaps took in a Western or an Abbott and Costello farce. These last entertainments weren't to my taste, and I often felt restless, locked up in the little apartment high in a New York skyscraper, especially if I too was to sing that evening. Then I would pass the time washing clothes. Jussi's shirts went to the cleaners for overnight service, but on wash day our whole bathroom was filled with stockings, handkerchiefs, and underwear, hung to dry. It relaxed me to spend time with such simple chores in the middle of a roaring metropolis.

Other singers were surrounded by a swarm of servants and admirers; Caruso had an entire staff with him, and Gigli even brought his own cook. But Jussi and I had only each other. Sometimes we played gin rummy, or he entertained me with card tricks. When a TV set became standard in hotels, we watched television or otherwise spent a quiet evening together, enjoying each other's company. We could have a nice time in absolute silence, so long as we were together.

As Jussi's celebrity grew, he found it uncomfortable to go to the opera and be recognized in the audience, but we'd occasionally go to the theater or the movies, relatively certain of our anonymity. Sometimes we dined with or at the homes of Jussi's colleagues. We spent a lot of time with Alexander Kipnis and his lovely wife, dining out in restaurants. Licia and Joe Gimma too had us over many times. I especially remember Licia's lasagna, the best I ever had, and Joe's advice on stock investments. After Bob Merrill got married, we were invited to his and Marion's home in New Rochelle. I asked Bob not to serve any liquor, which put him in an awkward position, as he later recalled:

> We were sitting around, and Jussi began "Bob! Let's have a beer. Let's have a drink, c'mon Bob!" I said, "Jussi, you know we don't drink!" We kept stalling him, talking, telling stories, hoping that he'd change his mind. But after dinner he says again, "Bob! C'mon! Let's have a drink!" I asked Anna-Lisa if I could give him a beer. So he had a beer before they left, and that was it. It was a strain for both Marion and me, but I liked him very much as a person and as an artist. There was so much good in him, and really, I felt worried that this great talent, this great voice should not go astray.[1]

I remember our very first dining experience in an Italian restaurant in New York; it was the Caruso restaurant, and we were Ezio Pinza's guests. I'd never had *spaghetti verdi* before—I didn't know it came green too! But Jussi didn't care for Pinza because he was very flirty. Once he came to the Hotel Wellington when Jussi was singing *Faust*. I was on my way down and who should I see pacing around in the lobby—Pinza! He knew that Jussi was at the theater and I was alone. I hurried back to the room and when the front desk clerk called up to announce Mr. Pinza's arrival, I said, "Say I'm not here. Tell him I've gone out." When I ran into him later, he said, "Why weren't you there? We could've had a grand time." Jussi didn't appreciate that Pinza, 19 years his senior, was trying to make a pass at his wife, but the basso's efforts were just too pathetic and funny to make an issue of them.

On another occasion, Pinza sent us tickets to *South Pacific*. Jussi had sung the night before and preferred to rest, but he insisted I go. Pinza knew where our seats were, and he easily picked out my blonde head in the audience. When he saw that I was by myself, he sang "Some Enchanted Evening" *right to me*! It was a strange feeling, and frankly, it upset me. Another time, he had us over for dinner. In the middle of the meal the doorbell rang. Crowded at the door were some female admirers who had come to ask the sexiest opera star for his autograph, face to face. Lasse remembers his father being very impressed that girls actually came knocking at Pinza's door: "And he's not even a tenor!"[2]

We could've been at parties every night if we were so inclined, but we turned down many more invitations than we accepted. Jussi never sought the company of the rich and famous nor to mix in high society. He wasn't loquacious by nature or particularly adept at meaningless small talk, and to engage in nonstop chatter with dozens of strangers about nothing was not his idea of fun. Too, attending parties, especially in New York winters, meant more exposure to the triple threats of chills, illness, and smoke. No matter where one went, people smoked without the slightest regard to a singer's presence, and many prominent artists refused to stay at a public gathering if there was smoking. Jussi often asked me to go to these affairs without him, mainly for my sake, so that I'd have some diversion. Almost always I declined—willingly.

Jussi especially hated obligatory social engagements. Although he graciously managed to hide his true feelings most of the time, he loathed having to be pleasant to a multitude of people at post-performance receptions. He wasn't antisocial; he simply preferred to unwind alone and undisturbed. Some singers develop a high tolerance for these obligations, some even crave the affection of fans. For Jussi it wasn't a necessity. He wrote, "I know of nothing that irritates me more than lively conversation after a performance."[3]

But it was often unavoidable that we meet patrons and benefactors at a reception or gala supper after a performance. When Jussi could take it no longer, he had a signal that never failed to make me break off a conversation and determinedly explain that, unfortunately, we must be getting home so my husband could get some rest.

Jussi had a vast supply of riddles and jokes, most of them far from clean. On these occasions he always used the same one: it began with a question posed to the jewel-bedecked society ladies who'd gathered round to catch every golden word that escaped their hero's lips. "Do you know how to kiss a hen's ass without touching the feathers?"

When the answer came back no, he continued. "You take her like this"—and when I saw this gesture from the other side of the room, I knew the clock had struck—"take a deep breath and blow," and here followed the unmistakable sound of a rush of air and a smack. "But you must be quick, you know!" Then, if not before, it was time to go home!

※

I remember our first trips to America with two closet-size wardrobe trunks with "Jussi Björling, Metropolitan" painted across them. Drawers for shoes and wigs were on one side, and the costumes hung on the other. Those colossal trunks went everywhere with us, not to mention the music briefcase, stuffed full of scores and heavy as lead. It held all the music in Jussi's active repertoire; we didn't dare leave it for a porter to carry and always struggled with it ourselves.

Looking after the costumes was my responsibility, and when new costumes were made, it was I who consulted with the tailor and costumer about the pattern and material. We established an excellent rapport over time; they and Jussi's dresser became my best friends backstage. It was also my duty to plan and pack our luggage for the tours. We were prepared for any eventuality: long underwear, wool pants, and galoshes for Milwaukee and Saskatoon, and shorts, bathing suits, and sandals for Miami and the Bahamas.

Shortly after our first arrival in America, we were told that Jussi should have a so-called publicity manager. It wasn't enough to sing well—it was also important to have advertising and publicity in the newspapers. Jussi being who he was, he usually received sufficient publicity from the organizations that employed him. In Chicago it was Danny Newman; in New York CAMI arranged for the services of William V. Arneth. In a letter dated 21 February 1955, Arneth advised Bing, "I now arrange [Björling's] publicity here in America. His management remains, of course, Frederick C. Schang." But we had no desire to spend more money, so on tour I assumed the role of Jussi's publicity agent.

As soon as we arrived in a new city, we were met by the local manager, who should have arranged everything, but the well-meaning and inexperienced soul often fell disappointingly short of the task. Much too often I had to make sure everything was in order. I went around to the department and music stores to make sure that Jussi's posters were plastered everywhere and that his records were displayed along with his picture. It was tiring but essential. During the afternoon, while Jussi rested or took a long walk, the accompanist and I visited the performance site to try out the piano and see that it was properly tuned. Then I'd check the dressing room to see if the heat was adjustable. Too cool, and he risked catching a cold; too warm, and his throat would be dry. I also saw that hot tea or water would be available. I went through the same routine even when I was to sing with him in the evening's recital.

Jussi went to the concert hall a couple of hours ahead of time, usually alone, unless I was needed to keep the photographers or autograph seekers at bay and explain that they could come back after the performance. The hours before the concert were very important for him. Everything had to go according to a predetermined ritual, which included all the superstitions I've already mentioned. He always carried a spray apparatus filled with Cloriton inhalant, and before singing—to the children's everlasting horror—he'd take a needle, poke a hole in the end of three or four raw eggs, and suck out the contents. I know from experience: raw egg is both nutritious and soothing for the throat.

He was always perfectly prepared, yet before he went onstage, Jussi's hands were ice cold from nerves. He once told Anders about a recurring nightmare he had. He is standing in his dressing room at the Opera, putting on his makeup and changing his clothes. But when he tries to take off his pants, he can't get the suspenders off his shoulders no matter how he tugs and pulls at them. Curtain time is drawing near, and he isn't ready. Panic washes over him, he breaks out in cold sweat—and he wakes up.

A few minutes before his entrance, I'd stop by to see that everything was in order—and to give him the six good-luck kicks in the seat of his pants. Then I'd take my place in the audience. During the first songs I was always so nervous that my heart raced and I had a hard time breathing. High expectations increased in proportion to Jussi's success, and his concern to constantly improve and surpass himself became greater with each passing year. As the recital continued, the audience's warm enthusiasm growing with each successive number, our worry subsided—his onstage and mine in the house. Immense tension was replaced by a sublime feeling of contentment and happiness. "Jussi Björling sang like a god" once more.

※

We didn't exactly enjoy those neverending train rides crisscrossing America, but we made the most of them. On the Met spring tours we traveled on the company's special train, which had pullman cars for singers and staff and special freight cars for the scenery. When the train left Grand Central Station, everyone from the orchestra members to the big stars suddenly became a close-knit family. Everyone was kind, cordial, generous, and completely relaxed. We had great fun, sitting all together in large open cars with tables and comfortable chairs, talking, playing cards, and telling stories for hours on end. I was particularly at ease, because now I didn't have to worry about Jussi: his time was filled with work.

During the Met tours we stayed each night in a first-class hotel, courtesy of the Metropolitan. Everywhere the red carpet was rolled out; we were met by the local organizers, and the soloists especially were treated like royalty. After the performance the entire company would be invited to a wonderful supper or a big party at the home of a wealthy opera sponsor.

During Jussi's concert tours everything was on a much simpler scale. Our traveling party consisted of just we two and Freddie Schauwecker. Our home was the train compartment, where we spent the entire day and where we slept every night. In the American pullman wagons of that period one could reserve "drawing rooms," big compartments that were furnished with a table and sofas. It was pleasant to lounge in that living room on wheels and watch the changing landscape as the high-speed train swallowed the miles. During the night two bunk beds could be lowered together to form a wide double bed in the other part of the compartment. By tour's end Jussi and I were so attuned to the train's light, rhythmic movements that when we came back to our hotel in New York, we had difficulty sleeping in a bed that didn't rock.

On the day of a recital none of us would eat anything after four o'clock. By the time the performance was over, we were starved! The organizers would usually arrange for a little coffee and cookies to be served at a post-concert reception, but we needed a full meal, a real supper. I remember one occasion when the other guests were served the usual light fare after the concert, while we were seated at a table in a corner, enjoying a big juicy steak. Everyone stared at us; we felt like animals in a zoo at feeding time, but it couldn't be helped. Jussi lost three or four pounds during a performance, and he needed something substantial to restore his energy.

The best time of the day was when we finally reboarded the train, settled in our compartment, and closed the door behind us. Now we could relax! We'd continue to snack, play cards, discuss the concert, and talk about the people we'd met at the reception. We were fortunate that Freddie was such a pleasant travel companion, a colleague and a friend. There was never any friction between us.

I often consider the thin line that divides art and hype, comparing our little threesome traveling from town to town with the gigantic well-oiled promotional machinery upon which today's superstellar careers rest. Over breakfast at Villa Pace, Licia Albanese remarked to Stella Roman and Bidú Sayão, who had likewise gathered to celebrate Rosa Ponselle's 80th birthday, "In our day, singers had to make their careers on the stage, and not with big-time managers doing everything for you."[4]

Jussi too made his career on the stage and created his own publicity by his singing. He felt it ought to be enough to be able to sing well and had a hard time getting used to the public relations aspect of an artist's life. As early as August 1941, he remarked to a Danish newspaper reporter, "The U.S. is not so easy. The publicity can kill a tenor, or at least his voice." By his own choice, the promotional work done on his behalf was notably less than what was done for many of his colleagues. Onstage he was Björling, famous Swedish tenor. But when the applause died away and he signed the last autograph, he was—and only wanted to be—Jussi, the boy from Dalarna. I cannot help thinking how today's music world would react if they had Jussi Björling in their midst. The overpromotion of megaconcerts, the full commercial exploitation would enable him to reach a wider audience in a single television appearance than he had reached in a decade or more. But my contemplation isn't prompted by sour grapes. Jussi deserved and enjoyed a full measure of success—without seeking publicity and, in fact, in spite of shunning it.

The spring of 1956 brought one of those happy coincidences when every detail falls into place. It was suggested to Sir Thomas Beecham that he record *La bohème* with Victoria de los Angeles as Mimì. He agreed, provided a first-class cast could be assembled. For once, the powers-that-be moved with unprecedented alacrity, and cast, chorus, and orchestra were brought together in record time. The recording sessions at the Manhattan Center began on 16 March and were finished on 6 April 1956.

In the middle of the recording sessions, Jussi's back pain returned. Sir Thomas Beecham remarked that to the best of his knowledge the spine wasn't the organ a tenor used for singing, but his calculated sarcasm notwithstanding, the session had to be interrupted. Bob Merrill sent us off in a taxi to his own chiropractor. After the treatment, similar to the one Jussi had received in Sweden nine years earlier, we rode back to the studio, and Jussi continued the recording.

Dick Mohr recalls the haste with which the recording was set up, to exploit the New York presence of a choice cast *and* Sir Thomas:

> There was not a prior performance onstage. Sir Thomas was at his crotchety best. In the third act, de los Angeles didn't want to cough. It would ruin her vocal line, she claimed. After the first take, when she had not coughed, Sir Thomas said, "Young lady, now we're going to do that again, and if you don't cough, we will later, after the tape is put together, hire a professional cougher, and you may not be able to hear a note you sing!" We did another take—and she coughed.[5]

She delivered a beautiful, touching Mimì, and as Rodolfo, in my opinion, Jussi was a poet's poet, conveying a sufficient mix of dramatic involvement, unaffected charm, and ardent lyricism. The recording has won favor with the critics, and this version of *Bohème* has been held up as a paragon against which all others are measured. In Jürgen Kesting's opinion, "No one has sung the first act more luminously, more tenderly, and the fourth act with more restrained sentiment, than the Swede."[6]

※

Jussi worked nonstop during this period. On the days he wasn't on call at the recording studio, he was rehearsing or performing at the Metropolitan. He continued to sing so well that at the close of the season Irving Kolodin wrote: "With all respect for those who have done the lion's share of roaring at the Metropolitan this season, Bjoerling brings something individual, refined, and cherishable into the operatic jungle."[7]

This critique was in stark contrast to the one Jussi received on the first stop of the 1956 spring tour. Weldon Wallace, Baltimore's best, was disappointed by Jussi's Cavaradossi. "His singing has neither the variety of color nor the brilliance of former years. His phrases were well put together but hardly rich in shape."[8] Poor Jussi. Eight years earlier he'd had an "extremely limited range of color" in Wallace's esteemed opinion, and now he had lost even that! Happily, Wallace found some compensation in the chorus' singing "rousingly."

A highlight of the tour was a wonderful performance of *Un ballo in maschera*, on 17 April in Boston. This was the only time Jussi sang with Marian Anderson, an artist he had long admired. Jussi always regretted that they'd never sung together at the Metropolitan, and he was happy to have the memory of at least this single occasion.

# Chapter 25

✳

# GENTLEMEN'S AGREEMENT

On 19 April 1956, *Hovsångaren* Jussi Björling was elected a member of the Royal Swedish Music Academy in the category of vocal arts. Another distinction followed when on 6 June he was made Commander of the Swedish Order of Vasa. Within an hour of the ceremony's conclusion, he met Irving Kolodin for an interview over lunch. He proudly told Kolodin that this latest honor was "something I never expected before I was 50" and talked with admiration of Mario del Monaco, Jan Peerce, and Richard Tucker. His highest praise, however, was reserved for Giuseppe di Stefano. "If that boy put his mind to it, he could be No. 1 in the world." Kolodin asked why he didn't sing at the Met more often. "I have at most five good years left," Jussi replied, "and that is why I sing more concerts than opera these days. It pays better, and I have to think of my family."[1]

Three days later, on 9 June, he was invited to sing at a luncheon in the City Hall for Queen Elizabeth during her state visit. It was an occasion and honor he especially treasured.

✳

In late June, accompanied by Lasse and Ann-Charlotte, we were in Rome to record *Rigoletto* with Roberta Peters, Robert Merrill, and Giorgio Tozzi. Jussi was at ease with Giorgio and at times would ask him about Italian pronunciation. "He liked me as a person," Tozzi recalled, "and I am very happy to say the greatest accolade I could receive was to know that he also respected my talent."[2] That was certainly true, as Bill Arneth could attest: "Tozzi was a great favorite of Jussi's. He believed that Tozzi would become one of the great singers of the future."[3] And the admiration was mutual: according to Giorgio, "Whenever [Jussi] sang, one had the feeling that this man was born to sing, that he knew how to sing, and that his greatest joy in life was singing."[4]

The *Rigoletto* recording progressed smoothly until the Quartet in the fourth act, when Jussi upset the balance by covering the other singers. They all objected, and poor Dick Mohr was caught in the middle.

> It was a monaural recording, and those were the days when everybody was crowded around one microphone. After the first take of the Quartet he was very pleased with himself, but it wasn't very good, because it was all Jussi.
>
> I took him to one side and said, "Jussi, this isn't your solo, it's a quartet. It's your solo at the beginning of each verse. Then the other three come in, and you have to be balanced. You must let the others have their share of the microphone." So he said, "Well, let's hear it." We all went into the control room, and after he heard it, he took me aside and said, "You're right, Richard, I'll do it right now." So we recorded it again and used the second take.[5]

"Richard Mohr was a very bright man," says Lasse, "the only one who could make Dad change his mind."[6]

Of the final product, one reviewer found Jussi occasionally sharp of pitch but concluded nonetheless: "In spite of its flaws, Bjoerling's performance is one to treasure. The nobility of style and the grace of the phrasing are in a class by themselves."[7]

❋

On 13 September Jussi opened the 1956 San Francisco season in *Manon Lescaut* with Dorothy Kirsten in the title role, under the baton of Oliviero de Fabritiis; he also sang *Tosca* with Tebaldi and *Il trovatore* with Eileen Farrell. Devoted San Franciscans, who hadn't seen him since 1951, were happy to have him back. It was noted that he returned "30 pounds thinner, looking svelte and singing as well as any tenor within memory, Enrico Caruso excepted. In addition to all this, Mr. Bjoerling brings a personal trait to his art that is, once again, almost unique, and that is humility. With this combination of talents and character, Mr. Bjoerling couldn't very well occupy any position but the one at the top."[8]

On 3 October 1956 Jussi took part once again in Fol de Rol, the annual fund-raiser. As Kurt Binar personally ushered one elegant, late-arriving couple to their table, he advised them that Warren had just sung the Prologue, and Licia Albanese and Giuseppe Campora the Cherry Duet from

*L'Amico Fritz.* "Did Björling sing yet?" When Binar replied no, the man turned to his wife with a smile and said, "That's all right, dear. We haven't missed anything."[9] While this incident is complimentary to Jussi, the guest was unkind to the other artists. The lineup that night—which also included Boris Christoff, Leyla Gencer, Dorothy Kirsten, Leonie Rysanek, Elisabeth Schwarzkopf, and Renata Tebaldi—was designed to satisfy the most discriminating taste. Jussi and Dorothy were the only singers to perform two numbers: he sang "L'alba separa dalla luce l'ombra" and "Mattinata," and she Magda's aria from Puccini's *La rondine* and Gershwin's "The Man I Love."

After the artists sang, they returned to their table. Jussi had settled beside me to enjoy the rest of the program when someone accidentally tipped over a candle, catching our centerpiece on fire. In an instant, Jussi doused the flames with a couple of glasses of water, and the guests greeted his fireman's performance with applause, which Jussi acknowledged with a gracious little bow.[10] But Jussi always had great presence of mind and could react with amazing speed. Once he was traveling by train to a recital in Furuvik. As his stop approached, Jussi heard the conductor announce that the train wouldn't be stopping in Furuvik. Jussi leapt from his seat and pulled the emergency brake. "Then the train stopped very quickly," he told Teddy Nyblom. "There was a 50 Kronor fine, but it would've cost some money to take a taxi to Furuvik, plus the wasted time. And time is money."[11]

On 19 October Jussi and Dorothy repeated *Manon Lescaut*, the last time they had the pleasure of singing together. Dorothy paid wonderful tribute to Jussi in her autobiography:

> The gentleman from Sweden, Jussi Björling, was, in my opinion, the greatest tenor of my generation. His voice was the most perfect technique and the most glorious sound I have ever known. Never did I hear him sing a note that was not absolutely on pitch and well produced. . . . Jussi's voice was truly a magnificent one, but this was not his only gift. He gave the feeling that every phrase was expressed with his heart. . . . Björling's vocal magic in opera was such that, although his acting ability was limited, and his figure too full at times, it did not matter. I remember so well the last performance of *Manon Lescaut* we ever sang together at the Metropolitan [6 January 1951]. After our meeting in the first act when he sang "Donna non vidi mai," I could not hold back my tears. Seldom has the house "come down" like it did after this aria by Jussi Björling.[12]

Chicago followed Los Angeles once again that year. At the Lyric Jussi's Tosca was again Renata Tebaldi, radiantly beautiful and in glorious voice, and Scarpia the superb Tito Gobbi. It was a thrill to watch these great artists create magic onstage. Jussi also sang Rodolfo and a couple of Manricos.

The New York City Opera was also on tour, and Jussi accepted their invitation to sing the Duke in *Rigoletto* in Detroit on 7 November 1956. The title role was taken by baritone Cornell MacNeil, whom Jussi had held in high regard since he heard him on Broadway as John Sorel in Menotti's *The Consul*, a role MacNeil created on 1 March 1950, in Philadelphia.

This *Rigoletto* was not a happy experience for the participants, mainly because of Maestro Erich Leinsdorf. While in Detroit, Jussi stayed with the family who owned Detroit's Stockholm restaurant, and conductor and soloists rehearsed in the large living room there. "It became clear early on that Leinsdorf didn't know *Rigoletto*," remembers MacNeil.

> He would do a few pages, then get into a musical philosophy sort of dis-cussion about *Rigoletto*. I realized after the third or fourth time that while he was carrying on this conversation, he was thumbing through the score for about 10 to 12 pages and memorizing them. He would say "OK, let's go ahead," and then we would have another philosophical discussion. It was a remarkable example of what a fine musician's mind like Erich's could do. But he should have done it before he got there.
>
> Jussi had sung the night before in Chicago, and as I remember, he said, "Singing *Tosca* last night with Tebaldi was like singing it with two sopranos." So in the rehearsal, because he was tired, Jussi did what we call marking. Except—I stood there in amazement—he did not concede a breath, he never opted, he never sang it down an octave. He took a full breath, he took the full attack, the whole physical-mechanical process of taking the breath and delivering the sound was intact, as if he were singing a performance. It was an example of what good vocal technique was and is to this day. I will never forget that. It was one of the most impressive things I have ever seen. I stood there and watched him; I had trouble watching Leinsdorf, because it was much more sensible to watch Jussi![13]

It was a poor performance, and Jussi, who felt a cold coming on, cut his second-act aria. But at evening's end Leinsdorf, quite pleased with himself, put down his baton and said to the orchestra, "This is the way *Rigoletto* should be conducted." It was the last performance of his one-year tenure with the company.

Back in Chicago, Jussi was scheduled to appear in a gala concert with Tebaldi, Simionato, and Bastianini on 10 November. Unfortunately, Jussi "had to withdraw on doctor's orders," and Bastianini, who was also under the weather, could only appear in "the second half of the concert." Jussi was replaced by "no less a tenor than Richard Tucker."[14] The concert, conducted by Georg Solti, was a smashing success; it was recorded and released on London records. Unfortunately, Tucker was a Columbia artist and could not be represented in the recording.

His throat condition persisted, and Jussi had to cancel the first *La bohème* with Tebaldi and Bastianini on 14 November 1956. "They'll say I am drunk," he moaned to Byron Belt, assistant manager of the Chicago Lyric Opera. "Not if I make the announcement, they won't!" Byron said. He remembers it clearly: "Björling was ill! He had laryngitis, plain old laryngitis. He never missed a performance with us because of drinking; as a matter of fact I never saw him inebriated."[15] Cornell MacNeil confirmed this. "I knew all of these stories, but I *never* saw him drunk, and I never saw him like he had a hangover."[16]

The Lyric Opera called in up-and-coming tenor Barry Morell to sing Rodolfo. We were all staying at the Bismarck Hotel, as Jussi's young replacement recalls: "As I was going down into the lobby, Mr. Björling came over to me and said, 'Oh, you are Barry Morell! I wish you well tonight; I'm sorry I can't sing—do well, and good luck!' He was sick! He was certainly not drunk."[17] Morell took Jussi's advice; without benefit of rehearsal and with only the briefest conference with conductor Bruno Bartoletti, he sang very well that evening. Jussi recovered sufficiently to reclaim the spot opposite La Tebaldi for the closing *La bohème* of the season.

*The New York Times* (26 November 1956) found Jussi "in uncommonly fine voice" on the occasion of his 24 November 1956 concert at Hunter College: "Occasionally a tone emerged that appeared to surprise and delight even Mr. Bjoerling himself. One such was at the repetition of 'jedes weiche Herz' in Schubert's 'Ständchen.' The tone was exactly right, focused to pinpoint accuracy, and on Mr. Bjoerling's face appeared the cherubic smile of the singer who knows his stuff is working. Such are the innocent joys of vocalism."

The last American concert of the year was on 11 December at the Brooklyn Academy of Music, and on the 12th we flew home. Just before we left, I spoke briefly to Bing. In a letter of the same day, which reached us at home, he said he was reassured of Jussi's intention to return in the spring. Bing also enclosed a signed TV contract for Jussi's 17 February 1957 appearance on the *Ed Sullivan Show* and mentioned his hope that in the 1957–58 season Jussi would sing Radamès and Cavaradossi, offering a fee of $1500 per performance plus an extra $250 for each *Aida*.

※

As soon as we arrived in Stockholm, Set Svanholm, the director of the Opera, reminded Jussi that he had agreed to sing command performances at the Stockholm Festival on 2 and 4 June. On 4 June Jussi was scheduled to sing Manrico in Montreal for the Met.

Svanholm sent a telegram to Bing describing a "gentlemen's agreement" he had with Jussi and asking for Bing's cooperation. Bing cabled his reply to Svanholm, saying that although Jussi signed his contract in May 1955, no doubt preceding this gentlemen's agreement, he would release him from the Montreal date but would absolutely insist on him singing in Toronto on 29 May 1957.[18] The telegram was followed by an exceedingly polite letter addressed to Jussi, repeating in more complete sentences the contents of the telegram. He begged Jussi not to disappoint both the Met and the Toronto audiences.

On Christmas Eve, Jussi sent a telegram to Bing: "Thanks for your cooperation Stockholm Festival. Letter follows soon as possible regarding your proposition. Happy holidays."[19]

Bing's letter of 31 December 1956 confirmed the dates of the 1957 Met tour at the original $1000 fee. It was obviously written for the open-access file, because attached to Bing's letter was a separate note of the same date from Max Rudolf, reaffirming the confidential agreement regarding an extra payment of $500 for each performance. Such special deals with major singers, presumably, were not uncommon at the Metropolitan Opera—nor were they anything new. One outstanding early example is Gatti-Casazza's *sub rosa* arrangement with Enrico Caruso to defray the tenor's substantial income tax obligations, which in 1920 alone amounted to $37,350.[20]

During the festive Christmas season Jussi had a lot of time to reflect about giving the Met eight weeks as Bing had insisted, but whatever his reason, no letter followed. Bing waited as long as he could, then on 17 January 1957 he sent off an angry telegram, stating how upset he was that Jussi's promised reply had failed to arrive and asking for an immediate confirmation of the terms contained in his letter of 12 December. Typically, he had the telegram sent with a prepaid reply.

But unbeknownst to him, we left Stockholm for Zurich the day before his telegram arrived. As part of the Swedish Week celebrations, on 19 January, Jussi sang *Tosca* with Birgit Nilsson and Sigurd Björling; a very young Montserrat Caballé was in the audience that night. Upon our return, Jussi had two days of recording sessions back to back, on the 22nd and 23rd. I'm not sure he had time to read the accumulated mail.

On 22 January a second, shorter telegram from Bing arrived, his fury unconcealed: "Incomprehensible discourtesy, no acknowledgement letter or reply. Paid cable. Please advise immediately. Rudolf Bing." Jussi replied the next day: "Very sorry cannot accept your proposition for next season. Most interested discuss the matter further on my arrival February. Regards. Jussi Bjoerling."[21]

Poor Bing hit the ceiling! He answered by return telegram within hours: "Deeply shocked your going back on what I understood was gentlemens agreement outlined in my letter December twelfth." He stated he couldn't wait to discuss matters until February and wanted a telegram reply *now*! Jussi thought he'd made himself clear, that it was pointless to exchange telegrams if he'd be in New York in three weeks. But Bing thought otherwise: "Grateful if you would consider answering cable January twentythird," he cabled on 1 February 1957.[22] Very well, thought Jussi, and stubbornly sticking to the timetable he had set for himself, he repeated his stand on the matter: "Sorry could not answer your telegram before. Just returned from Switzerland. The first part next season seems impossible. About second part of season, I want to discuss on my arrival in New York. Best regards. Jussi Bjoerling."[23]

Bing was so nonplussed by this affront that he wrote *Schweinerei!*—a

289

mild expletive in German—across the telegram. He wrote another letter to Jussi, and left with no alternative, he waited impatiently for our return. Meanwhile Jussi sang Radamès to Aase Nordmo-Løvberg's Aida in Stockholm. We arrived in New York in time for Jussi's appearance on the *Ed Sullivan Show* on 17 February.

He then faced Rudolf Bing. At the urging of Freddie Schang, Jussi asked for more money, which I believe in retrospect was the main reason Jussi delayed finalizing his commitments. Unfortunately, they couldn't come to terms. By this time it was demonstrably a financial sacrifice for Jussi to sing at the Met. His fees in solo recitals ranged from $3000 to $5000, and the time he was obliged to spend in New York prevented him from pursuing lucrative bookings elsewhere. In an eight-week period he could easily sing 20 or more recitals, while in the same timespan he might deliver 8 to 12 performances at the Met for half the nightly fee. It was simple arithmetic.

Jussi had a sense of his own worth, but he wasn't greedy. After all, he sang concert after concert in small Swedish towns for fees that can only be described as symbolic. He regularly lent his voice for a good cause and happily gave charity concerts throughout his career. No, what irked Jussi was the knowledge that many top singers were given large sums of money under the table. Jussi was a simple man but nobody's fool. His own open, honest personality allowed him to see through people and their motives, and he deeply resented anyone's taking advantage of him. He had learned long ago to look out for himself.

Alan Kayes says that Jussi's idea of negotiating was stating his demands, staring at you in silence, and refusing to yield until he received what he wanted, which obstinacy must have driven Bing up the wall.[24] One such negotiation evidently took place in early March 1957, for in his letter of 4 March Bing expressed his pleasure that Jussi was willing to give the Met "approximately seven weeks next season." He confirmed that if any of those appearances should be Radamès, Jussi would be paid an extra $500.

Jussi must have declined the offer, because on 12 March Bing wrote him a mournful letter, regretting that Jussi wouldn't be returning to the Met the following season. But Bing didn't give up easily, and he had Jussi as a captive audience on the train when the company rode to Philadelphia for a *Trovatore* on 19 March. Three days later Bing summarized in a letter their latest understanding. Jussi agreed to give five weeks to the Met split between November-December and February, and he was guaranteed seven performances, two of which would be *Aida*. His cachet was set at $1500 per performance, with an extra $500 for each *Aida*; his travel allowance would be a total of $3500, up from the $2500 he had been offered on 4 March 1957. The 1957–58 season seemed to be settled, but negotiations were eventually broken off. In the end, Jussi did not sign a contract with the Met for the coming season.

Officially Jussi and the Met split over the question of money, but it was more a break between Björling and Bing, two incompatible personalities. In the final tally, it was everybody's loss.

✳

Meanwhile, Jussi sang a few recitals and on 27 February 1957 a stupendous *Tosca* with Renata Tebaldi and Leonard Warren. The audience was ecstatic. Although Bill Arneth noted that previously "Mme Milanov and Jussi set the house record for curtain calls at 25 at the Metropolitan," in this performance, "Björling and Tebaldi had 28 curtain calls that set a modern record for the Metropolitan which has not been surpassed to this day. The previous record was in the 1930s with Flagstad and Melchior."[25] When asked about this, Tebaldi responded, "I do not remember if Jussi established a curtain call record at the Met *Tosca*, but I would not be surprised if he did."[26] Actually, the record was set by *both soloists* together.

By her own admission, Renata regrets that she and Jussi sang so few performances together. "Our voices blended so well harmonically that in duets our voices seemed like one." She found Jussi a "very introverted, solitary person, difficult to engage in conversation, yet he was very kind, very courteous, and a good colleague."[27]

Jussi's next operatic performance, a *Don Carlo* on 16 March 1957, was no doubt routine for him, but the Eboli, Irene Dalis, was making her Metropolitan Opera debut. For her, the night and everything leading up to it was unforgettable:

It is hard to describe my feeling the day I was escorted to the roof stage of the old Metropolitan for the first rehearsal of *Don Carlo* and saw Jussi Björling standing before me. My only contact with him was as a standee when I was working on my master's degree at Columbia University. For me, he was *the premier tenor* in the world. Even yet, there has never been another voice to equal his. He was a singer's singer. . . . Max Rudolf, the artistic administrator, had escorted me up to the roof stage to introduce me to the cast, and I stood in the doorway, absolutely immobile. I, literally, could not move. I could not believe that I was actually going to be part of this cast. When I finally recovered my senses, I remember my first words were to Jussi. "It is a great honor to meet you and a greater honor to be onstage with you!"

From that moment on, he was my strongest supporter. He was a sensitive man and understood my apprehension and fear. Even though I was the leading mezzo-soprano at the Berlin Opera at the time, this was going to be my debut in the revered temple of opera at that time, the Metropolitan Opera. The closer we came to the first night, 16 March 1957, the more nervous I became . . . and finally I arrived at a rehearsal partially hoarse.

This is when Jussi took me aside, told me about his own personal throat doctor, took me to a pay phone, called Dr. Bruno Griesman, and made me talk to him. Even the moment brings a smile to my face, for Dr. Griesman's first words on the telephone were, "Open your mouth!" I was ever so grateful to Jussi for guiding me to that excellent doctor and remained his patient for most of my career.

The big night came. At the old Met the male singers' dressing rooms were at stage right, and the ladies' dressing rooms on stage left; so it was a long walk and quite a chore to greet a colleague. But before the performance there was a knock at my door, and it was Jussi Björling himself. It is a moment I will never forget, for this great man, this legend among performing artists said, "I want you to know that it will be an honor for *me* to be onstage with *you* tonight."

He taught me that night just how genuinely humble a great artist is. His concern for a young singer set an example for me, and I remember thinking that it would be wonderful if I could, one day, encourage and help a young singer the way he did that night. That may very well have been the beginning of Opera San José [California], the company I founded upon my retirement from the stage.[28]

---

I cannot say exactly when Jussi's heart trouble began for, not wanting to cause me anxiety, he'd kept his true condition from me. But I believe it was around this time in 1957 that I became aware of how severe Jussi's arrhythmia was. Spells grew more frequent, and each lasted longer.

Arrhythmia is an alarming sensation, especially before one knows what is happening. First, the heart seems to hesitate, skipping a beat; the terrified patient wonders whether the heart has stopped altogether—and in severe, advanced cases it has. When the heart resumes pumping, the next beat comes as a violent jolt, causing an abnormal pressure in the chest. Depending on the frequency of skipped beats and the duration of the attack, the victim can experience weakness, lightheadedness, and an overall sense of malaise.

"It's so wonderful when my heart returns to normal that it's almost worth the suffering," poor Jussi would say. "It's nothing to worry about," his doctor reassured him. "Many people have it. It'll pass. I'll give you some pills that will suppress the symptoms. Just take them when it flares up and try to take it easy for a while." For Jussi this meant no engagements, no work. It'd mean that while he relaxed, the old restlessness would steal over him. And when that happened—he was caught in a trap. For the time being we didn't have a choice; he was booked for years ahead.

When the attacks of arrhythmia and shortness of breath occurred—and they could happen at any time—I tried to get him to bed. He'd sit up with pillows piled behind his back, and I'd stayed with him until the trouble passed. If we were in Stockholm, I sent for a doctor to care for him. Between attacks he felt well and looked completely, deceptively healthy.

Another thing that strained his heart was his weight. At five feet, seven inches tall, even his usual weight of 200 pounds was too much, and with his love of home cooking, he could reach 220 pounds. I too needed to lose weight, and over the years we'd sometimes dieted together. But now he announced, "I'm tired of always hearing that I'm too fat." Determined to reach the weight the doctor had set for him, he went on a rigorous diet. It was frightening to see how the pounds fell away—he lost 35 pounds in less than five months—but I kept telling myself that weight loss under a doctor's supervision couldn't be dangerous, it was good for his heart that he weigh less. Nevertheless, I was shaken by the results. His round, happy face became drawn and serious, its lines more defined. His age was showing.

Jussi sang two more performances of *Don Carlo*, on 29 March and 4 April 1957. Meanwhile, his arrhythmia persisted. When it occurred offstage he could cope with it, but during a performance it made him dreadfully uncomfortable. After the second *Don Carlo*, he began to feel worse; he visited Dr. Griesman, who, alarmed by his blood pressure, forbade him to go on tour. Knowing Bing, Jussi insisted on having something in writing, so Dr. Griesman duly wrote Bing on 8 April 1957: "Mr. Jussi Bjoerling is suffering from an attack of raised blood pressure. He needs a rest of about three weeks."

If he was to do nothing for three weeks, Jussi preferred to be under the care of his own physician in Stockholm. We flew to Sweden, and indeed the medical attention and the home environment seemed to help. Within days, Freddie Schang forwarded the Metropolitan's inquiries about his return. Jussi was uncertain about facing the strain and discomfort of the Met tour. Although he knew quite well that it would incur Bing's wrath, he first contacted assistant manager Max Rudolf in Cleveland to tell him about his condition and then confirmed it in a telegram to Schang on 24 April 1957: "Thanks telegram letter. Understand perfectly Mr. Bing anxious know whether I am coming or not. Sorry cannot tell you 100% surely about possibilities. Therefore if more preferable to Mr. Bing my canceling immediately I will do so. Please inform him about this sad matter telling him how sorry I am about situation. Sending him letter. Regards. Bjoerling."[29]

Schang kept a copy and had the original telegram delivered to Bing, who had foreseen this outcome. A day earlier, he had cabled Earle R. Lewis in Atlanta to have Kurt Baum ready to take over some of Jussi's roles.

In response to the telegram, on 25 April 1957, Bing wrote Jussi a simple, straightforward letter. He stated that under the circumstances it was best if the Met accepted his suggestion and canceled his participation immediately rather than at the last minute. He closed his letter with a polite wish for a full recovery.

Both gentlemen were convinced that Jussi Björling would never again stand on the stage of the Metropolitan Opera.

# Chapter 26

# CHICAGO AGAIN

Jussi had no engagements from April until early June 1957. He then sang Radamès, Manrico, and Rodolfo at the Royal Opera, his rested voice in fantastic condition.

King Gustaf V was very musical, and during his reign young singers from the Opera House were often invited to evening soirees at the palace to entertain the other guests; the Court Singers especially were expected to sing, and the king always asked Jussi to attend. When Gustaf VI Adolf ascended the throne, he continued the tradition. Marit Gruson remembers that around this time, after a small dinner party at the palace, "Bertil Bokstedt sat down to the piano, and Jussi sang as only Jussi could. Then he said to Bokstedt, 'Now we'll make their ears ring' and delivered the Gralserzählung from *Lohengrin* with such power, beauty, phrasing, eloquence that one could almost envision him standing there in silver armor instead of a tuxedo."[1]

In July it was Rome once more, this time to record *Tosca* with Zinka Milanov and Leonard Warren. To capitalize on the availability of the Rome Opera orchestra and chorus and the house itself, where the recording took place, RCA decided to record two Puccini operas concurrently (the other was *Madama Butterfly* with Anna Moffo and Cesare Valletti), with sessions scheduled for 2 p.m. on alternate days—which left Jussi idle every other day. Unfortunately and almost inevitably, he wandered down to the hotel bar on his days off. This led to some trouble, but luckily he didn't go over the edge in Rome; none of the sessions were canceled on his account.

The taxing task of simultaneously recording two complete operas was assigned to Erich Leinsdorf. According to his autobiography, Leinsdorf thought that Cesare Valletti's voice, for all its outstanding qualities, was "too light" for the role of Pinkerton, and one day, as he and the cast were listening to a take of the love duet, "a very drunk Jussi" showed up in the playback room and began to sing into his ear "how the tenor part *should* be sung."[2] The more the embarrassed conductor tried to silence him, the angrier Jussi became. Božidar and I were called to collect him. Regrettably, this was typical behavior for Jussi at a certain stage of his inebriation, but I have difficulty accepting Leinsdorf's view of his motives. Drunk or sober, Jussi wouldn't be abusive toward a colleague—it wasn't in his makeup.

Another minor conflict was caused by Leonard Warren, who could be unpleasantly overbearing at times. He kept interrupting and giving instructions, and when he did it once too often, forcing Zinka to repeat some passages, she exploded. "Leonard! That's enough! I am not a young woman anymore, and these high Cs don't grow on trees, you know!"[3] But in Leinsdorf's words, "Whatever frictions and fights were part and parcel of these recording days, all was washed down at a dinner, given for the casts of both operas by George Marek on the final night."[4]

In a taped interview, Zinka told her longtime friend and accompanist Bruce Burroughs that Jussi was "behaving strangely" in Rome "and he was drinking all night, you know, that's why he didn't sing as well as he could."[5] Yet when the recording was reviewed, Jussi garnered more praise than criticism. Conrad L. Osborne had some reservations, but he found the last act "ravishing from beginning to end, and of course Björling at his worst brings a loveliness of quality and smoothness of line which most tenors at their best would envy."[6]

Of Milanov, theater and music critic Roger Dettmer declared she delivered "her party-record share of hooting, whooping and screaming [along with] some secure, tonally rich singing," especially in the first act, that as Scarpia Warren was "puffing-up vowels and chewing off consonants," and that Erich Leinsdorf was, in brief, "miscast." As for my husband, Dettmer quipped that although Puccini had called it *Tosca*, thanks to Jussi's "impassioned participation," record buyers might just be asking for the opera *Cavaradossi*: "Bjoerling's Cavaradossi is his best recording since the duet disk with Robert Merrill."[7]

⚜

Our stay in Rome was touched with sadness, for Beniamino Gigli was very ill. He too suffered from a weak heart, and as a diabetic, his kidneys had deteriorated. He now required two insulin shots daily. As his close friend Metropolitan tenor Gabor Carelli wrote in his memoirs, Gigli's doctor described his condition as a *collasso completo* (complete collapse) of the body. Medication that helped one organ harmed the other. When Carelli last saw Gigli, he overheard the sick man hum the *Pearlfishers* romance. *"Vedi, la voce c'è, è il cuore che non va"* ("See, the voice is there, it's the heart that doesn't work").[8]

Jussi, Ann-Charlotte, and I called upon the enfeebled, visibly ill Gigli at his home. Soprano Rina Gigli, who often sang with her father, well remembers our visit.

> The great Swedish tenor, Jussi Björling, had the courtesy to visit and pay his respects to my beloved papà at our villa on Via Serchio in Rome. It was a particularly sad period for us. My father was already very ill, not only physically but emotionally as well. Only very few of his friends, admirers, and colleagues from happier days came to visit and keep him company. Among those who did not forget him in those sad moments I remember Gino Bechi, Maria Caniglia, Tito Gobbi, Maria Huder, Aldo Ferracuti, and Maestro Luigi Ricci.
>
> My father had very few artistic contacts with Jussi Björling, therefore he was very touched and moved by his noble gesture. Björling was in Rome to record *Tosca*, and he came with the express intention to pay homage to an artist "whom everybody still considered the true grand master of bel canto," as Björling referred to him in the course of their meeting.
>
> I was able to participate only briefly in their conversation. They spoke about singing, interpretations, opera houses. I remember that my father mentioned that in 1924 Puccini cabled him in San Francisco asking him to create Calaf in *Turandot* at La Scala. My father said that he was proud to be asked, but nothing came of it after Puccini's death.[9] My father recalled his first two concerts in Stockholm in May 1925, and his return there and to Gothenburg in 1949. Finally, he mentioned his *Tosca* at the Royal Opera opposite Birgit Nilsson, in 1952.
>
> My father [seldom] had a chance to hear Björling in the theater, but I remember that he held him in high esteem and had a most favorable opinion of his records. I must say my father was always very careful and precise in his judgment of other artists; he never used disparaging terms and [only] few praises. By nature he was more inclined to give good advice, suggest ways to support the voice or how to interpret this or that romance. He was a great artist, but certainly a great man, respecting qualities in others, never in competition with other singers.
>
> I think I agree with my father's judgement that Jussi Björling was a great lyric tenor who left wonderful memories in the world of opera. I have always maintained that his *Turandot* with Nilsson was, without a doubt, one of the greatest interpretations of Puccini's opera.[10]

Ann-Charlotte remembers that when we said our goodbyes, Jussi hugged Gigli warmly but ever so tenderly, as if he were afraid of hurting the sick man's fragile frame. We were glad to have paid this visit to Jussi's illustrious colleague, but we came away with heavy hearts, knowing we wouldn't see him again. One by one, the living legends were leaving us to become dead immortals. Arturo Toscanini died on 6 January and Ezio Pinza on 9 May 1957. We didn't dare say it, but we all knew that Beniamino Gigli, the tenor with the angelic voice, would join the heavenly chorus before long.

✖

We spent August on Siarö, then in September returned to Florence to record *Cavalleria rusticana* with Renata Tebaldi and Ettore Bastianini. This was the first time Jussi was released by RCA to record for London/Decca, and he was pleased to finally be making a recording with Renata.

We flew to America on 9 October 1957 for a tour that was to begin with a series of performances in Chicago. Upon our arrival in New York, an attendant gave me a telegram from Stockholm addressed to Jussi, who was momentarily not at my side. I knew instinctively that it contained bad news, and if that were true, it would be better if Jussi heard it from me. My fears were confirmed when I opened the telegram: Jussi's younger brother Gösta had died of a stroke at Bromma Airport, on 9 October. Faced with a most difficult decision, one I didn't want to make alone, I called our friend at the Lyric Opera, publicity director Danny Newman, for advice. According to his recollection,

> Anna-Lisa phoned me from the New York airport in the late evening. They had just landed and upon descending from the plane, Anna-Lisa was handed a cable, informing her that Jussi's brother, Gösta, had just died. She said nothing to him, but went to a phone booth immediately and called me saying the following: "What should I do? If I tell him, he will turn around, go back to Sweden right away and will not come back for the Chicago season." While from the Lyric Opera standpoint, I would like to have asked her not to tell him, but to do so after they arrived in Chicago the next day, I felt this was too self-serving, and I told her that she must make up her own mind as to how to handle it. There was a pause and she then said, "I will not tell him now. Meet us at the plane tomorrow morning in Chicago." He came, did his grieving here along with rehearsals, and fulfilled his contract.[11]

We had begun to lose our closest friends, and now Gösta, Jussi's dearest brother, was gone too. He had become one of the most important artists at the Opera in his repertoire and in fact was about to fly to Helsinki to sing Rodolfo when he was stricken. Elisabeth Söderström, who sang with Gösta many times in both opera and operetta, knew his voice well:

> The timbre was very much like Jussi's, but Gösta had a shorter pillar of sound inside him and his voice didn't have the same power. He was a very secure artist musically, with great art of characterization. I think he was a fantastic actor, and he did cameo roles to perfection. I remember singing many times either Frasquita or Mercedes to his Remendado. Especially with Sixten Ehrling, we rehearsed the smugglers quintet until we were ready to die. He would rehearse the ensemble even during intermission,

297

and if you sang one eighth note wrong the whole evening was spoiled for him![12]

I told Jussi about his brother's death in Chicago, preparing him for it as gently as I knew how, but such a blow cannot be softened. He took it hard—but agreed it was pointless to return to Sweden. Rather, he channeled his fresh emotions over the death of a loved one into singing. His first performance was *La bohème* with Pennsylvania-born Anna Moffo, who had launched her career in Europe and was returning to her homeland armed with voice, acting, intelligence, personality, and beauty. She had been scheduled to make her American debut as Lucia di Lammermoor, but because Giuseppe di Stefano canceled, her debut role was Mimì:

> Björling was very dear to me. He was special to a lot of people, but to me as a very young debutante, [he] was very important. I had of course heard Björling for many years, before I even thought of being a singer. When I was finally sitting at the table as he was singing his aria, I thought I won't be able to utter a sound when he is finished! Because his "Che gelida manina" was—I mean the house came down! It seemed like 20 minutes of applause, and to follow him as a debutante and sing "Sì, mi chiamano Mimì" when my whole mindset was for Lucia!
>
> Anyway, it worked out very well. He was so kind and so dear; without his support I wouldn't have been able to get through my debut, certainly not! No one ever was so supportive.[13]

Anna weathered the stress of her debut quite nicely, and she had a well-deserved success. No matter how helpful Jussi may have been, it was her singing and charm that conquered the audience.

The 1957 season at the Lyric Opera had a glittering roster. Another of his leading ladies, Renata Tebaldi, inspired Jussi in all three performances of *Manon Lescaut*. In his review Seymour Raven wrote,

> Renata Tebaldi brought to Manon that rare combination of abundant beauty and warm musicality. In Jussi Bjoerling, Miss Tebaldi had a lover who reached heights not easily attainable in this opera. . . . That Mr. Bjoerling's voice was ablaze with passionate music is hardly the surprise, tho even for him it must have been a night to remember. What he brought to bear on the role of Des Grieux was that most elusive skill of opera singing, . . . acting with the voice, achieving that synthesis of song and sound which is at the heart of opera and from all else flows. That a slim and youthful looking Bjoerling also tore loose with the most emancipated physical performance I have ever seen him give is the more evidence of his profound artistic motivation as initiated in song.[14]

Jussi's Des Grieux impressed not only the audience, but his colleagues too. Cornell MacNeil never forgot the first time he sang Lescaut with Jussi this season. "Before I knew Jussi and worked with him, a lot of people, particularly the Italians, would say he was cold, which is a lot of nonsense! I remember a performance of *Manon Lescaut* in Chicago, when in the scene where he sings 'No! Pazzo son!' I forgot to sing my responses. I was just astounded watching him, both as an actor and a singer."[15] Andrew Foldi, the Naval Captain, agrees. Jussi's delivery of the scene was "indeed heartrending to the point of having to fight back tears onstage."[16] Foldi also has a personal memory about the first *Manon Lescaut*:

> I was warming up at home, extremely nervous. I was in very poor voice and decided to go to the kitchen to get a glass of water. As I passed the closed room where my children, aged four and six, were playing, I overheard my four-year-old daughter say to her brother, "Boy, am I glad I don't have to pay to hear Daddy sing tonight!" With that ringing in my ear, I had to go onstage with Björling and Tebaldi. I honestly do not believe that my legs shook like that before or since.[17]

Foldi was a young basso then excelling in comprimario roles with the Lyric Opera. Once Jussi asked Foldi if he could go with him and his wife to hear a new young German singer, Dietrich Fischer-Dieskau. "He further asked that, if possible, he would like to stay very inconspicuous," Foldi tells the story. "So we got three box seats, and he sat behind us in the second row of the box. After Fischer-Dieskau finished his second song (if memory is right, it was 'Adelaide') Björling leaned forward and whispered to me, 'A very talented tenor!'"[18]

Jussi's two performances of *Un ballo in maschera* were conducted by Georg Solti. "This was the first time I met Björling," Solti recalls, "and I thought he was absolutely splendid. There were no problems at all."[19] Foldi sang Tommaso both evenings, and he confirmed that the *Ballo* rehearsals "went very well with Solti. I honestly do not remember anything specific about them and surely no disagreements of any sort."[20] But Claudia Cassidy had many reservations: "Except for Mr. Bjoerling, who was in magnificent voice to toss off a spectacular 'Barcarolle,' and who stood alone in the ease and elegance of the grand style, this was not a distinguished performance."[21]

*Tosca* came next on 29 November with Eleanor Steber and Tito Gobbi. "The star was not so brightly shining," wrote Dettmer of Jussi. "Probably because Bruno Bartoletti seldom synchronized the stage and pit, he sang with some restraint, with a measure of untypical caution." However, Gobbi's Scarpia "again was the oleaginous butcher, the elegant satyr, of former seasons—at its best, one of contemporary opera's great impersonations."[22]

Jussi's last Chicago performance was *Don Carlo* on 30 November. I don't recall what brought about Jussi's performing Cavaradossi and Carlo on two subsequent evenings, perhaps the unavailability of Di Stefano for the former or Brian Sullivan for the latter role. In any case, Jussi joined a most spectacular cast headed by brothers-in-law Boris Christoff and Tito Gobbi, the latter also singing two nights in a row. Anita Cerquetti was Elisabetta, and Claramae Turner, the mezzo-soprano scheduled to sing Eboli, had to withdraw for health reasons and was replaced by Nell Rankin. Georg Solti remembers this performance too as trouble-free; he may have been unaware that the singers grumbled about his heavy-handed, Germanic approach to Verdi's score. Curiously, Claudia Cassidy placed the blame for the mediocre performance on the singers, who, in her view, "botched the Verdi ensembles beyond recognition."[23]

This was the first and last time Jussi sang onstage with the great Boris Christoff. The two enjoyed an excellent rapport and held each other in the highest esteem, according to Christoff's wife, Franca. "Jussi was always most kind to Boris, who considered Björling's voice and singing perfect, the most beautiful voice among living tenors. Björling was not a great actor, but his singing would most movingly express the spirit of the character."[24]

As the artists relaxed in their respective dressing rooms after the performance, Nell Rankin came tapping on Jussi's door:

> He told me that he'd like me to come to Sweden and sing *Don Carlo* with him. When he said he liked my performance—because I wasn't going to tell him if he didn't like it!—I said that when I was young, I had met him. I knew that he wouldn't remember it, but some pictures would bring it to mind. I got out my little portfolio and showed him the pictures my mother took of the two of us playing ping-pong. He didn't remember the exact place, but he did remember the incident. "Oh yes! You were that child who played ping-pong with me in the South!" I said, "Do you remember the kid that tried to sing 'O don fatale' for you and you said perhaps we would sing this together?" And he laughed and said "Well, I do remember you singing for me."[25]

Jussi must be forgiven for not remembering the exact details. In the nearly 17 years that had passed since their first meeting, little Nell had grown into a beautiful woman with huge charcoal eyes, a lovely figure, and a powerful, rich, well-schooled voice. Jussi was genuinely happy to see her, and he was touched when she urged him to keep one of the old photographs.

※

An especially bright spot of this stay in Chicago was a visit from Anders and his fiancée. After completing his military service, Anders had traveled to the United States on an American-Scandinavian Foundation scholarship and enrolled at Gustavus Adolphus College in St. Peter, Minnesota, where he spotted a lovely girl working part time in the college bookstore. His English literature course required 14 paperbacks, and it occurred to him that if he bought one book at a time, he'd have at least 14 opportunities to chat with Miss Janet Neidt of Waterloo, Iowa. A few purchases later, he summoned the courage to ask her out on a date. The attraction was mutual, and Janet happily confided to her roommate that a Swedish boy named Anders had asked her out. "He says his father is some kind of a singer," she added.

"What does he sing?" her roommate asked.

"Opera. He says he's quite well known."

"What's his name?"

"Björling." The roommate, a music major, fell back on the bed in mock faint.

"You were asked out on a date by the son of Jussi Björling?!"

"Oh, you've heard of him?"

Janet recounted the incident to Anders, who was happy to learn his appeal had nothing to do with his famous father. The relationship blossomed, and they decided to marry. We'd first met Janet in New York in the spring of 1957, and now again in Chicago, where we celebrated their intention with a quasi-engagement party at the Ambassador East Hotel, a happy occasion for all.

We thought we'd leave Chicago in an upbeat mood, but as we looked for the review of *Don Carlo* in the morning, we confronted the front page's headline: "Gigli, Famous Italian Tenor, Dies in Rome."[26] Even if we'd met only seldom, Gigli, the artist, was a real presence in our lives. He was a singer we both admired, and we mourned the passing of a uniquely gifted colleague.

Jean Sibelius, another great musician, had died at age 92 on 20 September 1957, and Jussi was invited to participate in a concert dedicated to his memory at Carnegie Hall, on 8 December 1957. Jussi considered it a privilege to be able to pay his musical respects to the august composer's memory. Sibelius' songs accompanied him throughout his career.

# Chapter 27

# BING VS. BJÖRLING

After the Sibelius concert we sailed home on the S.S. *Stockholm*, arriving in Gothenburg on 19 December 1957. In early February 1958 Jussi participated on a television program in Stockholm, and on 17 February sang *Il trovatore*. His Azucena was young Swedish mezzo-soprano Kerstin Meyer, whose career was beginning to take flight around this time:

> I started to travel in 1958. When [Jussi and I] sang *Trovatore* together I had a long journey behind me, and I was tired. Right before the performance when he greeted me and asked "How are you?" I said, "I don't know, Jussi, my voice isn't good tonight. I wonder if I'm going to make those top notes." He said, "Relax, you'll be all right."
>
> Azucena's big scene in Act II was rather difficult. There *are* quite a few top notes and they have to be there, and they came. The role ends in the prison, when Manrico gently lays Azucena down on the cot and she falls asleep. During the applause after "Ai nostri monti," Jussi bent over me and whispered, "So what was wrong with those top notes?" I thought that was rather sweet.
>
> For my generation, Jussi Björling was *the* singer. I had his records, I played them as a child, I grew up with that sound. He belonged to all Sweden, everybody loved him. The sound of his voice and his personality went through the whole society, all classes in Sweden. People living Godknows-where, as soon as they had a radio, they'd listen to him and knew his voice. They loved his personality, the way he sang, his repertory,

everything. Of course, for anybody who was interested in music, his singing was an example because he was so absolutely perfect.

He was a very good colleague, and he could see when you needed
support. He was always helpful, really, and it was a joy to sing with him.
He had enormous generosity onstage, and in a way, you really had a feeling you never sang better than when Jussi was there because the sound he
created and the open flow of his voice made everybody relax. You never
sang as well as when you had Jussi onstage. He was a legend and rightly
so.[1]

※

On 2 March 1958, Jussi gave a recital at Carnegie Hall. "Jussi Bjoerling Is
at Top of His Form in Carnegie Hall Song and Aria Recital," *The New York
Times* headlined its review. The recital was recorded, but it remained mis-
placed in the RCA vaults for 34 years. At the insistence of Cantor Don Goldberg, executives located the tape in 1991. Released on compact disc in 1992,
it shows Jussi in splendid form. "The Swedish tenor opened his program
with a stupendous performance of the 'Ingemisco' from the Verdi Requiem
that left hearers in the hollow of his hand for the remainder of the program."
The reviewer noted a "new solidity of the lower register," adding that the
voice "seemed to have gained in power and intensity since last heard. The
adjective 'magnificent' should be used sparingly, but in this case it seemed
justified."[2] He concluded that one couldn't help thinking that listeners would
be able to tell their grandchildren that they heard Björling at the height of his
powers. Louis Biancolli observed, "It was refreshing to hear a tenor in Carnegie Hall who not only produced round, golden tone at will, but produced
it with such obvious enjoyment of the very act of singing."[3]

Close on the heels of the Carnegie Hall recital, Jay S. Harrison conducted a lengthy interview with us. Jussi was in an expansive mood, and
they touched on a wide range of subjects. What did Jussi think of Tebaldi?
"She is fantastic, supreme. Since Maria Caniglia there has never been such
a person." Did he like the Met audiences? "My greatest response from the
public has always been at the Metropolitan. When I make my entrance
onstage, there is always such a demonstration that I almost choke up with
tears." Any new roles? "Now I am studying Don José; next year it will be
something else. But I will tell you this: I have one favorite role. It is Otello.
What a part for a tenor! What an opera! What music! But you know something? I will never sing it.[4] It would damage my voice. I would not like that
to happen." Which was easier, opera or solo recitals?

Opera really is easier than recital work. In . . . opera you deal with only one
composer at a time, so you can have the same style of singing all night. In
recital, each number is by someone else, and you must approach it with a
different musical style. Then, too, in opera you deal with other people, so
there are moments when they are singing and you can rest. Not in recital—

there you are alone and must work constantly. Also, if you don't feel well while working in opera, someone is always around to replace you. But if you get sick before a concert there is no understudy and you can't send out your pianist to play solos.[5]

This balanced, well-organized interview wouldn't have attracted special attention had Harrison not ventured to say that if Björling's name didn't appear on the Met roster next year, "it will amount to another one of those scandals that the Metropolitan has never been able to explain to anyone's satisfaction."

This gratuitous swipe at the Met was like throwing tacks in the lion's cage and then waiting for the roar. Harrison didn't have to wait long. Rudolf Bing's vitriolic rebuttal appeared exactly a week later. Calling Harrison's statement "an impertinence," Bing went on:

The "Bjoerling scandal" is, if perhaps not satisfactorily, easily explained. The Metropolitan Opera a year or so ago increased its top performance fee for principal artists by 50 percent. I am aware that certain other American opera companies are paying higher fees; but they have neither the prestige nor the publicity value nor the artistic standard to offer that makes an engagement by the Metropolitan Opera still one of the most highly prized attainments for any singer. There are a few singers who in my view are entitled to our top fee and they are also entitled to feel that nobody else gets more. It is on that basis of mutual trust and understanding that artists like Mmes. Milanov, Tebaldi, Callas, Messrs. Tucker and Del Monaco, to mention only a few, have signed with the Metropolitan. Mr. Bjoerling demanded for this season a very substantial increase over and above what the here-named and a few other leading artists have accepted.

When weeks of discussions brought no result, I wrote to Mr. Bjoerling on March 12, 1957, a letter from which I quote: "It is a matter of great disappointment to us that you have not seen fit to accept our offer for next season. All of us—the management, your colleagues, the public—have looked forward to celebrating in 1958 the 20th anniversary of your debut here and perhaps to years ahead in the new house.

"I don't have to tell you what you have meant and continue to mean to the Metropolitan. We have given you no more than you have given us so I am implying no debt of gratitude when I point out that the Metropolitan has contributed in large measure to your success, particularly in America. Our only obstacle is that you simply have demanded more money than we can pay. . . .

"Time is almost on us when we shall have to make some announcement of our plans. One of the first questions will be why are you not returning and we will have to give the reason. For both our sakes I hope no such necessity will arise, that before then you will have accepted our terms, offered, believe me, in the highest esteem."

The reply was the same: Mr. Bjoerling insisted on his increase. Since I am unable to increase so drastically all our top artists' fees and unwilling to betray them by singling out Mr. Bjoerling, his name does not appear on this season's roster nor will it be there next season. The departure of any distinguished singer is regrettable but the Metropolitan Opera is bigger than its parts: it has survived Caruso's and Flagstad's departures.[6]

Appended to Bing's response was Harrison's apology for referring to the situation as a scandal; he excused the tone of his article on the grounds that he was apparently misinformed about the matter.

Bing noted in his autobiography that Jussi always talked about being "unable to afford" to sing at the Met.[7] From a certain perspective, that was true. Jussi wanted to maximize his earnings before his vocal decline set in. He felt he couldn't give more time to the Metropolitan than he did. It wasn't for publicity's sake that he said he loved his Met audiences; they'd been truly wonderful to him. But he could serve them just as well elsewhere—at two or three times his Met fees and even greater multiples in solo recitals.

Even so, I'm certain that Jussi would gladly have made even financial sacrifices for a friend like Edward Johnson. The heart of the matter was that he simply didn't like Rudolf Bing. A perfect gentleman in manner and bearing, Bing wore an impenetrable social armor that kept even his close associates at arm's length. His aura, a calculated projection of aloof unapproachability and cold condescension, made it impossible to warm up to him. Bing prided himself on this point: "I hardly knew any of my artists. It was very deliberate; I never set foot in any artist's apartment, they never set foot in mine, we were friendly but totally professional."[8] He didn't want to be loved—he wanted to be obeyed, and inevitably, he paid the price for it. Such an aspiration can be achieved only in the military, or in a relationship of total economic dependency. Jussi was a civilian—and didn't depend on Rudolf Bing's Metropolitan Opera for his income.

My independent-minded husband, the most unpretentious and least self-important artist Bing could engage, would've responded well to some truly human caring instead of socially correct words devoid of warmth and feeling. Bing, for his part, would've preferred a star tenor who could be told when to report, what to sing, and how long to stay in town.

In his memoirs Bing unintentionally captures his own persona—and his attitude toward Jussi—in the recounting of an incident from 1949, while he worked with Edward Johnson. Jussi, as Des Grieux, was "troubled with a backache and didn't feel like getting up to fetch some water for the dying Manon." Instead, the "ever obliging Licia Albanese" got up and fetched water for him.[9] If Bing had bothered to find out about the back pain Jussi had endured during the performance and the supreme effort he made to avoid a cancellation and sing, he would've been less judgmental. Licia only tried to help him get through the performance. Loyalty and friendship is a two-way street. For Eddie Johnson Jussi suffered but sang. Under his successor he would've canceled and let Bing do the suffering.

More understanding and compassion could have saved Bing a lot of aggravation in his dealings with his other artists too. Unable to accept that a singer wasn't just another musical instrument to be taken out nightly from a carrying case to perform, he took every deviation from his edicts as an act of disobedience and every cancellation as a personal affront. Jussi's alcoholism always placed his indispositions under a cloud of suspicion, so Bing was even less predisposed to be accommodating. He never accepted that Jussi could be really and truly ill. Yet I unequivocally insist that all Jussi's Met cancellations were for medical reasons.

For better or worse, Bing did not manage so much as rule his company. The late Francis Robinson, Bing's assistant manager for public relations, was often encouraged to write his memoirs. He always refused, and on at least one occasion, he gave a simple explanation: "If I wrote an autobiography, I'd have to call it *My Life in the Fourth Reich*."[10] Robinson liked his boss and admired his many unique qualities, but he had no illusions about his administrative style.

***

In early March 1958, we flew to Toronto for another recital. As we checked in at the Canadian airport for the flight to our next stop, Cleveland, the clerk at the control desk took one look at Jussi's passport and said, "This has expired. You cannot enter the United States with an expired passport." Some frantic phone calls resolved the matter, and we reached Cleveland in time. Our zigzag tour took us back to Ottawa, followed by Chicago, and then we left the frozen north for Miami. Jussi sang a recital in Fort Lauderdale on 21 March, and the next day, Saturday, he rewarded himself with a deep sea fishing jaunt. On Sunday, he had another attack of stomach bleeding, worse than before. He was driven unconscious to the emergency room in Fort Lauderdale.

On the 27th, the day he was released from the hospital, he was to have sung a recital in Gainesville, Florida, but that same evening he was rushed back to the hospital, this time for a stay of more than a week. Only when the crisis passed was I informed that for a time his condition had been critical.

Jussi came home to our hotel on 5 April with express orders for a strict diet and bed rest for at least three weeks, which convalescence forced the cancellation of the remainder of the tour: New Orleans, Greenville (Texas), Houston, Whittier (California), two recitals in Berkeley, San Francisco, Portland, Seattle, Vancouver, Pasadena, and China Lake (California). Our loyal friend Freddie Schauwecker took care of everything and sat with me every evening, his gently reassuring presence calming my tattered nerves.

While recuperating, Jussi had a lot of time to think; it disturbed him that his acrimonious relationship with Bing had become public. Schang felt it was time to declare a truce, and after some persuasion, Jussi agreed to extend the olive branch. After discussing the matter over the phone, Jussi authorized Freddie to compose a conciliatory letter on 19 April 1958. It is worth quoting in full, as indeed it led to an eventual reconciliation and Jussi's return to the Metropolitan in the 1959–60 season.

During my recent illness in Florida I had a chance to give considerable thought to the situation at the Metropolitan with respect to myself. The more I thought about it the more clearly I understood your problem with respect to fees and the factors preventing you from offering me the same fees that I have accepted or received for performances in Chicago and San Francisco.

Nevertheless I feel, on the eve of my departure for Sweden, that it would be unfortunate indeed if this were to be the sole obstacle standing in the way of a renewal of a cherished association with the Metropolitan.

I realize you had to plan your season on the assumption that I would be available for performances and I, of course, have made commitments for guest performances, concerts, recitals, etc. But there are still some open periods in my own schedule, specifically, the week December 7th of this year, and several weeks in February, 1959, and I would be available for a few performances at least on the terms originally offered me, namely, round-trip passage for two, a fee of $1750 per performance, and $2000 for an Aida performance.

Then, of course, I would also grant an option for the 1959–60 season, for a longer period of time to be agreed upon, on the same terms as above.

The recent publicity only seems to have contributed to a misunderstanding which I hope this letter will rectify. I am sure we both agree that any further publicity or public statements would serve no purpose whatsoever.

I shall go directly to Stockholm from here but my attorney, Mr. Gustave Kwaldin, will receive a copy of this letter and will know how to proceed with an acknowledgement in my absence.[11]

※

As we had anticipated, news of Jussi's illness was carried in the press and spread through the music world. We could do nothing but wait and so flew home on 20 April; Freddie Schang, who had been deeply concerned about Jussi's condition, notified us of the effect of the cancellations on 21 April 1958:

I trust you have returned safely and that your own doctors will find your situation improved. Of course you realize that the wide reports of your serious illness, your detention in the hospital, and the cancellation of 14 dates, has affected the outcome of our bookings for the spring of 1959.

Whereas last year we had at this time all of our bookings in hand for your present tour just canceled, we now have for 1959 13 contracts according to the list attached hereto. It seems likely that we will get several more, particularly if you are able to come to the San Francisco and Chicago Opera seasons next fall.

More than anything, Jussi had returned to Sweden so that he could attend Lasse's graduation. Although he had learned a great deal over the years, Jussi regarded the knowledge that had come to him through his travels, his musicianship, his gift for languages, and his associations with people from all walks of life as nothing out of the ordinary. In his mind only the learning acquired in school had real value, and he was extremely proud that his boys, unlike himself, had received a formal education.

This deep-seated inferiority complex manifested itself in strange ways. For instance, Anders recalls that they could be discussing something; Anders would know he was right, but even if Jussi knew his son was right, he wouldn't give in. They were both stubborn, and the whole day would be ruined with their falling out. Once Jussi and Lasse argued over some trifle at lunch, and it made Jussi upset. "Don't disagree with Papa," I begged Lasse. "Remember his blood pressure—you know he has a performance tonight!" Lasse backed down, and Jussi soon left for the Opera. Just before we were to leave, Jussi called. "Hi, Lasse, it's Papa. We're still friends, aren't we?" Such a simple, considerate gesture—typical of Jussi. He could flare up, but afterward he was always filled with regret.

Lasse's outdoor graduation ceremony took place in mid-May. It was a happy day, and we stood in the schoolyard and waited under unfriendly gray skies. I was so proud of Jussi—he had lost weight and looked well, but his resistance was low and his constitution weakened by the ulcer and the strict diet. The chilling wind that blew that afternoon was bad for him, and by the time he was to sing *Tosca* with Birgit Nilsson on 20 May, he had a sore throat. He should've canceled, but it was a special performance in honor of the Princesses Sibylla and Margaretha, who were to occupy the royal box.

Birgit remembers that at the rehearsal the day before, "Jussi said his throat didn't feel right, but he trusted his doctor, and if he said he could sing, he would go on."[12] On the day of the performance his throat specialist reassured him that he was fit to perform: "Your throat is just a little red. Don't worry, it'll be fine."

It was not. More nervous than usual, Jussi told Grevillius that something in his chest didn't feel right. The opera began, and he got through "Recondita armonia" with great difficulty. At that point he changed the blocking to be able to say to Bengt Peterson, the stage director standing in the wings, "I can't continue." He knew no understudy stood by and they'd need some time to make arrangements. The management rushed Einar Andersson, who was fortunately at home, to the Opera.

Within minutes of the aria, Jussi's voice grew worse. He could barely manage the brief exchange with Angelotti, and by the time Tosca entered, it was all over for him. In Birgit's words, "After a few bars it was quite obvious that Jussi was indisposed. He had a cold coming on, and after 15 minutes he had no voice left. With great effort, he spoke his lines through the first act. I suffered very much with him, because I knew how anxious he was to sing and sing well."[13]

He struggled, voiceless, vainly trying to talk his way through the long love duet, until the curtain mercifully fell. The lights came on, and we rushed backstage. Jussi sat in his chair, deathly silent, crushed and desperate. Without saying a word, without a whisper, he got dressed and we went home. After a long intermission the performance continued with Einar Andersson.

Late that night, Jussi called Grevillius, crying like a child. "Such things should never happen," Jussi said to him between sobs.[14] There was nothing to do except get him to bed, give him lemon and honey water, and let his voice rest. Full-blown bronchitis forced him to cancel a host of concerts at home and abroad.

On 7 June, almost as a test, Jussi gave his annual summer recital at Skansen. With that, both he and his voice needed another couple of weeks' rest. We didn't want to jeopardize Jussi's recovery, and Lasse was satisfying his military service, so Ann-Charlotte and I traveled alone to Anders' wedding in Waterloo, Iowa, the only mother-daughter overseas trip we took together. In New York we had a grand time shopping and visiting friends, and in the evenings we had cozy chats together. Jussi's consolation prize, as it were, was the notification that on 1 June 1958, "the Board of Directors of Gustavus Adolphus College conferred the Doctor of Music degree upon Jussi J. Björling." He was to collect the citation at a later date.

The wedding of Anders and Janet on 14 June 1958 was a major social item in the local papers. Some of the confused reporting was unintentionally funny—one of them announced that Janet had married the great opera star, Jussi Björling!

Jussi resumed his activities in the last days of June, giving recitals at Gothenburg, Stockholm, London's Royal Albert Hall, and Copenhagen's Tivoli. On 11 August 1958 he participated in another charity collaboration on Ljusterö with his violinist friend Hugo Theorell, now a Nobel laureate in medicine; and on 19 August he sang at the opening ceremony of the European Athletics Championship.

Then, in the autumn of 1958, Jussi had his first heart failure. According to Dr. Per Holmström's health certificate, 15 September 1958: "This is to certify, that Mr. Jussi Björling has been in absolute need of hospital care during the time 6/9–12/9 1958 [6–12 September] because of heart failure (Tachycardia paroxysmalia + Hypertonia) and is strongly recommended to avoid hard physical exercise." Because this was written in English, I assume the canceled concerts—or perhaps a recording session—were in London or the United States, or involved RCA.

The doctor called it a mild incident. If Jussi took it easy as much as his lifestyle and profession allowed, and especially if he stopped drinking, he could lead a normal life. The experience, so soon after Gösta's death, frightened Jussi terribly. With remarkable self-control, he quit drinking cold turkey, for a time. I didn't dare believe that he had completely overcome his illness, but for nearly a year Jussi drank only occasionally, without incident.

"That was a very long period," remembers Lasse, "and I thought it was the end of the whole problem. It wasn't, it came back later, but this was perhaps the longest since his teens. He looked happy, relaxed, and he felt good about himself."[15]

When the doctor declared him fit to travel, we flew to San Francisco. His first performance, *Il trovatore* on 26 September 1958, had the special significance of being his first collaboration with Leontyne Price.

Incomprehensible as it has always been to us Swedes, the racial barriers in the United States extended to the arts too. Rudolf Bing had taken a firm stand on the race issue in courageously bringing Marian Anderson to the Metropolitan in 1955, and Kurt Herbert Adler closed ranks with Bing when he engaged Price in 1957 for the title role in *Aida*. When we asked why this was regarded as another civil rights milestone, we were told that to bring the divine Marian Anderson to the Met in the role of the black fortuneteller Ulrica was one thing; to make an African-American Aida or Leonora the love interest of a white Radamès or Manrico was quite another. Also, while Anderson was a recognized star of the concert stage with a long international career, Leontyne was at the dawn of hers.

Whatever the breakdown of these invisible barriers signified, Jussi, who didn't know the meaning of prejudice or discrimination, was pleased to partner such an immensely gifted singer. Price's Leonora, a role she was to perfect in years ahead, was already sensational. As the reviews confirmed, "She sang with utmost purity, musical grace and profound feeling. She was beautiful to see, and beautifully costumed. She acted her role with a finesse and eloquence equal to that of her singing."[16] When she finished "D'amor sull'ali rosee" in the fourth act, "conductor Georges Sebastian threw down his baton and led the stunned audience in the applause."[17]

✳

After San Francisco, Jussi sang three *Trovatore*s in Chicago with marvelous Italian mezzo Giulietta Simionato. "He was more a singer than an actor," was her impression. "He more internalized rather than externalized his character according to his own sensibility. His voice had the purity of the finest crystal and the sweetness of honey. It was moving."[18] Jussi, for his part, liked Giulietta's easygoing cheerfulness, her beautiful voice, and dramatic intensity. Communication between them was difficult because she had a limited command of English, and Jussi spoke only in snippets from opera librettos, the Italian of Piave, Cammarano, and Illica:

> His admiration for me was almost embarrassing. . . . I remember he spoke to me in halting Italian or in English, or paraphrasing some phrases from opera, like *"Vicino a te s'acqueta l'irrequieta anima mia"* ("Near you my restless soul grows calm") [from *Andrea Chénier*], indicating that with me near onstage he could give his best. He was a kind colleague, friendly, cordial—a gentleman! It was not easy [to be one] in a theatrical environment![19]

310

Cornell MacNeil recalls Jussi's Manrico on these occasions:

> Ettore Bastianini was singing Di Luna, but I didn't come in to hear that, although I might well have. I really came in every night and stood in the wings to hear Jussi sing "Ah sì, ben mio" and then do "Di quella pira," two almost completely opposed—in terms of what most tenors do with it technically—styles of singing. Jussi sang a stylistically beautiful "Ah sì, ben mio," and then went on without destroying his vocalism, without pushing, without screaming, and sang "Di quella pira" just exactly as his voice should've produced it. It was spectacular as a lesson in technique and style, and moving from lyrical to dramatic singing. When I heard the dress rehearsal sitting out in the house, I knew I wanted to be closer, so that's why I went to the wings to watch him do it.[20]

In the middle of the Chicago season Jussi sang Manrico, Don Carlo, and the Duke in Los Angeles. We then flew back to Chicago to complete the engagement with two performances of *Rigoletto*, one with Tito Gobbi and the other with Cornell MacNeil. Anna Moffo was a lovely Gilda both times.

This was a tranquil period for us. I could happily report to my mother on 19 November 1958, "Jussi is in top form and he has never been in better humor. If he could always be so kind and in control, one could never complain. I actually believe that the heart palpitations finally scared him. . . . He hasn't touched a drop since we left home, and I don't believe he's going to either."

Jussi concluded his Chicago season with three performances of *Aida*, the only time North American audiences heard his Radamès. The magnificent cast included Leonie Rysanek, Giulietta Simionato, and Tito Gobbi. Although the audiences roared, the critics had reservations. René Devries wrote, "Björling, who made his début here 21 years ago as a light tenor and has now become a *tenor robusto*, sang with a great deal of tonal beauty, but did not find Radamès . . . one of his most fortunate roles vocally, nor one that moved him to act other than perfunctorily for the most part."[21] In a sense, these Chicago performances were experimental. Both Rudolf Bing and Kurt Herbert Adler wanted to present Björling as Radamès, but Jussi continued to resist, and this remained the last time he undertook the role anywhere.

Jussi believed that most of Radamès' music was more lyrical than dramatic, thus calling for a Manrico voice rather than an Otello voice: "Radamès is not a dramatic part, it's a spinto part, and it has lyric passages that for a dramatic tenor, I tell you, would be very difficult to sing."[22] But Jussi was an objective critic of his own singing and never nurtured false illusions about his voice's properties. He knew he couldn't produce the robust sound the public had come to associate with Radamès. For that kind of delivery he always considered the weight, power, and brilliance of Mario del Monaco's voice ideal, and he didn't want his more lyric interpretation to suffer in comparison with the stentorian rendition of his Italian colleague.

The year 1959 would be another active one for Jussi, and he was obliged to turn down many offers, including a concert performance of *Il pirata* with the American Opera Society at Carnegie Hall on 27 January—an especially exciting occasion, as it signaled Callas' first appearance in New York after Bing had fired her. Although Jussi was offered the part of Gualtiero opposite Callas, he confessed in an interview, "Unfortunately, I cannot do it. I don't have the time." When pressed about other roles, Jussi said, with a noticeable edge to his voice, that if he did everything he wanted to do and the public wanted him to do, he'd have to study and rehearse "till I am finished!"[23]

During our few days' stay in New York, Jussi met with John Gutman, one of Bing's assistant managers, and they came to terms regarding the 1959–60 season. Gutman carried the details of the discussion back to Bing and sent us a letter by messenger to the Essex House.

> I had occasion to discuss the details of our talk yesterday with Mr. Bing and I am pleased to say that I do not foresee any further difficulty in our signing a contract with you for next season. I know that you had occasion to talk with George Marek last night and . . . as soon as they have made a definite decision on a possible recording of *Faust*, I shall of course discuss details with you.[24]

The recording Gutman referred to was the planned stereo remake of the 1954 recording with Boris Christoff, Victoria de los Angeles, and the young Nicolai Gedda. Because Jussi wasn't available for the remake, the same trio recorded *Faust* in stereo in 1959.

Gutman also sent a revised contract for eight performances. The amusing conclusion of his letter reveals the administration's eagerness not to give Björling a chance to change his mind and get away: "I feel that the attached contract represents in every way what you had requested and I wonder whether we could not expedite matters by your signing the three copies of the contract (and the three repertory sheets, please) right away and give it back to our messenger. That would be wonderful and it would save us further correspondence and other delay."

Jussi smiled at the request, signed the contract, and handed it to the messenger. His promise to return to the Metropolitan after two seasons' absence was signed, sealed, and hand delivered.

# Chapter 28

✻

# RETURN TO THE MET

In the first week of December 1958 we were back in Sweden. The Christmas holiday separated two *Manon Lescaut*s at the Opera, with Elisabeth Söderström in the title role. On the threshold of a remarkable international career, she considered it a special occasion to be cast opposite Björling.

> I grew up with the sound of Jussi Björling, because my father was an amateur tenor and he loved the sound of Jussi. I didn't see him in the auditorium very often because that was too expensive, but I heard him in his outdoor concerts or, as a student at the Opera School, from the wings. Then I was given the part of Manon Lescaut, and when Jussi came for guest appearances, to my shock and delight I was going to sing with him.
>
> What I remember of the *Manon Lescaut* is that he was never out of character onstage. He lived the part without too many gestures, without trying to look different than he was. But in his eyes and the concentration *he was* the person. He was Des Grieux, not Jussi Björling. So it was very easy to work with him as an actress in spite of the fact that he didn't perhaps look like the slim young man that Des Grieux should be.[1]

We made a brief excursion to London on 4 January 1959; Jussi sang two arias on the television program *Sunday Night at the Palladium*. Back in Stockholm, another *Manon Lescaut* followed, but two days later his heart felt so bad that he had to be hospitalized for eight days. This forced him to cancel a *Tosca* and a *La bohème*, accompanied by the usual rumors regarding the cause. Jussi returned to the stage in mid-February with a Cavara-dossi and one more Des Grieux. Recalls Söderström,

> Of course, I would never say "Jussi" to him, I called him *Hovsångaren*. After the last performance, during the curtain calls we had been kissing and embracing and the people were shouting, and Jussi brought me out with him. I said, "It's your applause, I shouldn't really enjoy it," but he said "Come along here." And then I said, "May I call you Jussi?" and he said, "I've been waiting for that for a really long time!"[2]

On 21 February we flew to New York. In the absence of a Metropolitan engagement, Jussi was free to concertize the whole spring. He was in espe-cially good form at Hunter College on 7 March, singing encores after each group throughout the concert, as he often did when he felt well. Reviewing the recital, Eric Salzman wrote, "Control and precision were always at the service of the music and even the operatic arias were a long way from the shouting bravura style some opera stars think necessary to bring down the house. Mr. Bjoerling brought it down just the same."[3]

I was also glad that Jussi remained in control. As I reported to my mother on 8 March 1959, "After the concert in New York he drank a couple of cocktails—probably to relax from the stress which always comes with a concert in New York. But the next day it was orange juice again. And that's the way it'll be the rest of the tour, so you can remain calm."

Since Anders' college years and marriage, Lasse and Jussi had grown much closer. They'd take in a movie and afterward would sit at the kitchen table and talk, exactly as Jussi and I did in our quiet, reflective moments. Lasse recalls their exchanges fondly: "These kitchen sessions [were] long father-son conversations. We took advantage of the time we could have together, both of us knowing that we'd lost so much time over the years. He loved the movies, he loved the simple little things. He never played the great tenor at all; I wish he would have."[4]

Jussi, who often found it difficult to put his feelings into words, talked to his boys easily, not lecturing them but rather trying to give them ideals and values to live by, in particular his deep-seated passion for truth. Many times I heard him say: "Remember: truth, truth, truth!" I sometimes resorted to little fibs and white lies in difficult situations, but Jussi—never! He'd rather say nothing than tell a lie—which is why his broken promise to his father haunted him so all his life. "Look how I kept my solemn oath, sworn to him on his deathbed!" he'd say to the boys, shaking his head. "I don't want to extract a promise from you like my father did from me and my brothers. Just remember: you must be careful with alcohol!" Sometimes, lately more often than before, he hinted at his own condition. "Well, Lasse," he'd say, "I won't live to an old age. I have burned the candle at both ends."

At this time, in the spring of 1959, Lasse was wrapping up his military service. He wrote to Jussi, assuring him he'd know how to conduct himself when the farewell party came around. Still, Jussi thought some fatherly advice was in order. So while I wrote to my mother, he wrote to his son, admonishing him in an old-fashioned, formal style, just as his father or John Forsell would've written to him many years ago.

My dear son,
You wonder, of course, why your father has taken up the pen, as they used to say in the olden days, and writes to his son. It's quite simple. I constantly long for you and Ann-Charlotte. These are the moments before your so-called farewell-to-the-military party. I am no saint, as you know. I don't need to explain—But promise me, Lasse. Don't forget what you said to me the last time we sat at the table: "There are going to be those who will get drunk, but I have two friends who think the same as I do—so there!"
   That's enough about that. I hope you are all fine, and now that spring is approaching, may you keep your good health. Keep well and take care of yourself.

Your father

Lasse explains: "As we grew older, Dad became increasingly embarrassed by his inability to write stylishly, by his spelling errors, that he didn't have the same schooling as we were getting. Even so, when he did write, he wrote very well. Only his lifelong inferiority complex about his lack of education made him feel that he was not a good writer. It is possible that he didn't write as many letters as he would have for this very reason." Anders agrees.[5]

In March and April we again toured America. On 19 and 21 March Jussi sang Manrico twice for the Tulsa Opera Company. After that, he concertized in Charlotte, Corpus Christi, Beaumont, Baton Rouge, Kansas City, Atlanta, and San Francisco. Gustavus Adolphus College, Anders' alma mater, planned a special convocation to confer upon him the honorary doctorate of music, but we couldn't fit this new stop into our itinerary. The recitals were scheduled too closely, every three days, and Jussi was either singing, traveling, or resting. Instead, he proposed to postpone the ceremony till March 1961, when he was scheduled to sing in Minnesota.

On our way to the West Coast, Jussi met Janet's parents for the first time in Sioux City, Iowa. It was a most pleasant visit, allowing us to celebrate together the birth of our first grandchild, Peter Anders. Anders and Janet had moved to Sweden after their graduation, and Janet delivered the baby in Stockholm only the day before, on 6 April.

One evening a few days later, a bellboy handed Jussi a special delivery letter from Anders. Somehow he knew he should be alone when he opened it, so he went into the walk-in closet, turned on the light, and read. The telegram brought tragic news: Anders and Janet's firstborn had died. "Jussi, where are you?" I called. He came back into the room. "Let's go and sit down. You must try to be strong now," he said. "Why? What happened?"

With great gentleness, he read me the letter. We were devastated. We were so happy about our first grandson—it was a terrible shock. We both cried, then I called my mother for details. Our first reaction was to go home, but we realized it would serve no purpose; cancellations would only make a lot of people unhappy. I don't know how Jussi could sing his recital the following day, but he did. When the show goes on, as it must, the public never knows what happened in a singer's life that day. His job is to walk out on the platform regardless of how he feels and enchant an audience of 3000.

※

Following Jussi's recital in San Francisco on 20 April 1959, Alexander Fried wrote,

> [Björling's] great voice reached its old peak over and over again. Only at times was it apparent that time has worn a bit of gloss off his tones here and there. His singing was masterfully sure and flexible. His taste in interpretation . . . was fine. His vocal mood was, if anything, warmer than it used to be. His top tones—in Don José's Flower Song from *Carmen*, for instance—pealed out with exciting clarity and power.[6]

Jussi sang two recitals in Berkeley, on 23 and 24 April, to make up for his cancellation the year before. We had a pleasant business lunch with Kurt Herbert Adler, then on 26 April we flew to New York—our first transcontinental flight by jet. It took four hours and 40 minutes, cutting the travel time in half.

The spring tour culminated with a Gala Benefit Concert for the Swedish Seamen's Welfare Fund at Carnegie Hall on 29 April. In May he sang in Sweden, Norway, and England, and we spent June on Siarö, interrupted only by the usual summer appearances, including—yes, again—Skansen and Gröna Lund. Jussi stayed up until 3 a.m. on 27 June to hear the broadcast of the Ingemar Johansson–Floyd Patterson fight. He had met "Ingo" and was in his corner on this occasion. The show of Swedish muscle greatly appealed to him, and Jussi was proud and happy when Johansson won.

Apart from a little fishing, this summer Jussi had little time for relaxation. Maestro Bertil Bokstedt moved out to the island with us to work with Jussi on Calaf in *Turandot*. Jussi was preparing the part for a recording in July with two great sopranos, Birgit Nilsson and Renata Tebaldi, both London/Decca artists. A complex arrangement had been made to have the three of them participate in the same recording: RCA borrowed Nilsson and Tebaldi for this recording, and in return, Jussi had already recorded *Cavalleria rusticana* with Tebaldi two years earlier and would eventually sing *Un ballo in maschera*, both for London/Decca.

Bertil remembers this summer fondly: "It was one long intense musical party. . . . Actually one should have paid to be able to play for him."[7] "We worked every day for over two weeks. Anna-Lisa prepared wonderful meals, and Jussi was in good humor. He always sang in full voice; after he had the music committed to memory he wanted to feel the full sound as we rehearsed. We had the door of the studio open, and people would stop with the boats. I'm not surprised; I don't think anybody can sing 'Nessun dorma' like Jussi."[8]

We flew to Rome on 30 June. *Turandot* was Jussi's first complete opera to be recorded in stereo, but the engineers couldn't yet manipulate the channels at a control panel to create the full stereo effect for the characters' movement; rather, the singers had to walk among three microphones positioned at the apron of the stage. Ann-Charlotte thought the singers looked very funny as they tiptoed around the stage, careful not to make the boards creak.

We followed the rehearsals from the control room, but when it was time for "*In questa reggia,*" Jussi asked Ann-Charlotte to sit in a box farthest back in the auditorium. "Listen. Now you're going to hear something!" he said. Birgit Nilsson's mighty sound came over the system so loudly that it almost frightened her—she had never heard anything like it! Jussi joined her in the line "*Gli enigmi sono tre*" with the high C in unison. It was something to behold, Ann-Charlotte remembers: "Papa took a stance that went down to the tips of his shoes. His face turned completely red, but singing in the same microphone, he matched Birgit's volume note for note."[9]

Birgit wrote, "Jussi sang a marvelous Calaf. It is a pity that the engineer manipulated the controls to enlarge his voice. It is quite obvious, and it was really not needed."[10] I don't think the engineers had artificially enlarged Jussi's voice, but I know he had to give full throttle to hold his own against the ladies. Dick Mohr offers his recollections of these sessions:

> On playback we played the takes at a high level because the singers all felt they could better detect a mistake or a flaw in their performances. Actually, Jussi's was not really a large voice. If you heard him at the old Met after hearing it on some of the records, you'd always be slightly disappointed. You'd think "Where is this huge voice?" It was really a lirico-spinto tenor, but it carried, and he had a marvelous projection.
>
> In that *Turandot*, when he did "Non piangere, Liù," that was a one-take aria. When he listened to it, he was almost crying, because it's so sad. Leinsdorf wanted to repeat it; he said "It's too slow." And Jussi said, "That's the way I feel it," and that was the end of it. I always feel that regardless of the music, an opera aria or anything else Jussi ever sang, underneath it all there was always this tone of sadness. He could sing "Funiculì, funiculà," and I could hear sadness in it. I don't know why, I just think it was a basic quality of the voice. I don't think it was a matter of interpretation so much as some inherent quality in the vocal equipment. But that is almost the favorite aria I ever recorded, "Non piangere, Liù" in that complete *Turandot*.[11]

Many people who worked or sang with Jussi, and many of his listeners commented on the sadness, the hidden tear, that gave his singing a special quality.[12] Reminiscing about him, Blanche Thebom said,

> As to his singing—there has absolutely never been such a unique quality. No one ever sounded like Jussi and he never sounded less than magnifi-

cent. His high C retained the same beauty as the rest of his voice, and his vocal technique and sophisticated musicianship was a marvel. Additionally, there was a heartrending pathos in that sound—you find it in Sibelius too. I have never been able to play his recordings without breaking into tears. There is always the depth of impending melancholy in that glorious golden tone. What an inspired and inspiring singer he was![13]

This was Jussi's last recording produced by Dick. During a full decade of collaboration, we enjoyed his friendship, benefitted from his competence, and appreciated his gentlemanly ways, his patience, his tact and diplomacy. He guided Jussi's recording projects with expert hands, and all the artists knew they could trust and depend on him.

> In my experience, Jussi was always a complete gentleman. I would say he was gentle—he was like an overgrown boy, very stolid. I remember when he'd stand and talk to you with his hands at his side, [they were] doubled up in little fists, like a child's. He wasn't a voluble talker, but he laughed a great deal. He had an easy sense of humor, he appreciated having fun, and he liked good food, as you can see by some of those pictures.
> At those sessions none of us ever felt much like joking. He was totally cooperative, he'd come to rehearsals on time, or would call in advance and say "I'll be a little late." We *never* began a rehearsal wondering, "Where is he?" When he'd come to the sessions he would be fine; I don't recall Jussi ever blowing up or having temper tantrums. Musically he was always exactly what you would expect: A-plus. I never heard a bad performance from Jussi onstage at the old Met.[14]

There was not a weak element in the *Turandot* recording; Leinsdorf brought out the best in the cast and the Rome Opera House forces. According to Conrad L. Osborne, the recording had the best cast that could be found for the respective roles. Nilsson, he wrote, "sails through the altitudinous title role with even, powerful tone." He admired Tebaldi's "sumptuous Liù" and Giorgio Tozzi's "rolling, round bass . . . just right for Timur." Of Jussi, he wrote, "The astounding Bjoerling gives us another object lesson in pure singing, combining his ringing, gradually deepening tone with an incomparably lyrical treatment of the line. His Calaf would not, I suspect, hold its own in the opera house opposite voices of the Nilsson/Tebaldi caliber, but we've got it on records, and it's brilliant."[15]

Osborne wasn't alone in his opinion. The recording won the very first Grammy for best classical performance, operatic or choral, in 1960. It has stood the test of time, too; when it was rereleased on compact disc in 1987, the announcement called it *The Turandot*.

※

I have no recollection of what may have brought it about, but after the *Turandot* recording, Jussi's period of relative sobriety came to an end. In Ann-Charlotte's words,

An alcoholic just flips. The person you know and love when he is sober becomes someone else—he changes in front of your eyes when he becomes possessed of a need for alcohol.

Dad would pick a fight to have a reason to go away from home. We'd turn ourselves inside out to agree with him to avoid a fight. If he said day was night, black was white—we'd agree. "Yes, Daddy, whatever you say." This game went on until he found an excuse to leave, and usually by then we were so worn out we were glad that he was gone.

Nobody could predict when the next episode would occur. Neither could he, for that matter. And when it happened, nothing could stop him. On one such occasion I just went crazy. It happened at Karlavägen. In a last desperate effort to stop him, I yelled at him. Hoping that it would hold him back, I said something like "Well, go away then, you—drunk."

He froze and just stared at me. The great sadness, the sorrow and disappointment in his blue eyes were so profound, so desperate, so pitiful, that I can see it as clearly as if it had happened today. His gaze, that look will follow me to the grave. If there is one thing in my life I could change or undo, it would be this.[16]

Jussi stayed away his usual week or so, Lasse remembers. "He came home after several days of drinking—he looked horrible! After he sobered up in three or four days, he came to me to apologize. I remember he went down on his knees, took my hand, and said 'Lasse, I will try to stop! I promise!' Can you imagine? A father in front of his son goes down on his knees! He looked me in the eyes—you couldn't help loving him!"[17]

During the summer of 1959, Jussi's heart condition worsened. By a strange coincidence, on 11 August, as he was about to fly to Gothenburg to sing a concert at Liseberg, he had another episode of heart fibrillations at Bromma Airport, where Gösta was stricken two years before. I was able to care for him at home, and by the 20th he was well enough to keep his Gröna Lund engagement, singing without effort. We were relieved that the concert went so well, but four days later, he suffered another, more serious episode and was rushed to the Red Cross Hospital by ambulance. After a week's stay there, he continued to convalesce at home, with me serving as his round-the-clock nurse, as I had so many times before.

His strong constitution prevailed once more. Jussi seemed sufficiently recovered, the doctor saw no reason why he should not travel, and so in the third week of September Jussi left for Rome to record *Madama Butterfly*, his second recording project of the summer. The role of Pinkerton is neither long nor strenuous; the duets with Sharpless are short and light, only the love duet and "O fiorito asil" require any effort. As I recall, *Butterfly* was the reason Jussi withdrew at the last minute from joining the Royal Opera Company of Stockholm on their guest appearance in Edinburgh.[18] The preliminary program of the summer festival, printed and disseminated months in advance, shows Björling as one of the participants. As much as he regretted being unable to support his "home team," it was impossible to turn down the opportunity to record both Puccini operas.

319

After Cavaradossi, Des Grieux, Rodolfo, and Calaf, Lt. F. B. Pinkerton was Jussi's last Puccini role on records. Conrad L. Osborne observed that because *Madama Butterfly* is an opera that can be carried by one star, an opera company will seldom lavish three stars on it.[19] Recording is a different matter, however, and this ensemble had a star casting with Victoria de los Angeles in the title role and Mario Sereni as Sharpless.

As always, Jussi was well prepared for the recording. He had sung the role a dozen times between 1936 and 1939, and with his amazing memory he needed only to refresh a score he once knew intimately. To help the process, he had EMI send him a pair of custom pressed 78 rpm records of the love duet with Beniamino Gigli and Toti dal Monte. Always willing to learn from a superior model, he listened to that classic recording over and over until our family knew the love duet as well as he did. But he always found his own interpretive solutions; Jussi was never accused of copying anyone, the only exception being his deliberate tribute to Caruso, the recording of "L'alba separa dalla luce l'ombra."

The heat in Rome not only aggravated Jussi's precarious state of health, it may well have contributed to more heart problems. Jussi collapsed while recording the love duet, and the sessions were rearranged to allow him to recover. In a few days he was well enough to resume, and the pattern of his life continued: his health problems had no effect whatsoever on his voice. He sang amazingly well, and the recording was finished with minimal delay.

In a recent interview, de los Angeles said that onstage it was very clear how involved Jussi was in the emotion of the performance: she saw his hand tremble with the intensity of it. Even in the studio, in *Pagliacci*, she found it moving simply to watch him record his "Vesti la giubba." Remembering his Pinkerton, she said, "When people say to me 'Oh, he's so cold—he was a *cold* singer,' I say 'Then you should have *seen* him sing.' And if you listen to him you will hear a *passionate* person inside him."[20]

When the set was released, Conrad L. Osborne called Victoria's singing "most beautiful . . . consistently pure and lovely." He added,

> Lovers of fine singing will find little to complain of in de los Angeles' work; and unless their standards are superhuman, they will find nothing whatever to complain of in the work of Bjoerling. . . . What a difference it makes to have Pinkerton's role sung this way! . . . He gives us a liquid outpouring of ringing, bronzed tone, phrased and shaped with consummate taste and musicianship. This is genuinely great singing, and constitutes, I think, an even better Pinkerton than Gigli's.[21]

Once again, Osborne picked well. *Butterfly* earned the 1961 Grammy for best classical performance, operatic or choral. This was Jussi's third—and posthumous—Grammy. The first Grammy ever given for best classical performance, vocal soloist, went to Renata Tebaldi in 1958 for her *Operatic Recital*; Jussi won the prize in the following year for his *Björling in Opera* (RCA), between the *Turandot* and *Butterfly*.

✳

Back in Stockholm, his heart stabilized once more, Jussi refused to contemplate an extended rest and resumed his fall schedule as routinely as if he had been in good health. But he was not, and when he sang *Manon Lescaut* on 1 November, his last, his colleagues onstage were quite alarmed by his physical condition. His old friend tenor Sture Ingebretzen distinctly recalls that in Act I, the chorus watched him with so much concern that they could barely go through the motions of merrymaking.[22] Hjördis Schymberg, his Manon, recalled, "Jussi didn't kneel down as he used to do. Rather, he sat partially on a rock, and I remember that when I was lying there, against his chest, I could feel his heart beating incredibly underneath the heavy costume. He must have felt very uncomfortable, but he still sang a brilliant performance."[23]

As usual, the voice was fine. Gertrud Pålson-Wettergren listened to the radio broadcast: "I was so overwhelmed by the brilliance and freedom of his singing that I rushed to the telephone and called the opera stage manager." Jussi returned the call. "When I told him how much I'd enjoyed his singing, he became so happy, and told me again that same evening how happy my telephone call had made him."[24]

But when Gertrud met Jussi at the NK department store, she too noticed how wan he looked. He'd been dieting, and the weight loss showed in his face. She warned him: "Jussi, it isn't good to diet so much." He smiled pensively and replied, "I'm not going to grow old either—like Gösta."[25]

✳

In November 1959, Jussi made his triumphant return to the Metropolitan, singing eight performances—Turiddu and Cavaradossi three times, and Faust twice—in five weeks. Thanks to some enthusiastic fan, his reentry performance, the *Cavalleria rusticana* on 16 November 1959, has been recorded. Turiddu sings the "Siciliana" before the curtain is raised and so it passed without an audience reaction, but when the agitated introduction to the Santuzza-Turiddu duet began—and Jussi appeared onstage for the first time since 1957—the auditorium exploded in applause that stopped the show.

Jussi never had a memory lapse, but on this particular occasion the prompter confused him. Responding to Santuzza asking where he was the night before, he sang, correctly, *before* prompting, "A Francofonte." The prompter ignored it, gave him the cue, and Jussi, so prompted, unnecessarily repeated the phrase. In the in-house recording, his own surprise at what he had done is clearly audible in his voice.[26]

The performance went gloriously well. The ovation that followed was more than one could ask. Partnered with such an electrifying artist as Giulietta Simionato, Jussi acted up a storm, once again artistically thumbing his nose at critics who condemned his stagecraft. The two of them made the confrontation between Santuzza and Turiddu throb with vibrant passion.

This was one of Giulietta's great roles vocally and histrionically, and she brought the flesh-and-blood verismo character fully to life. When Turiddu made his exit on Santuzza's curse, conductor Verchi tried to proceed but the audience lost control. Their shouting, howling, clapping, and stomping drowned out the music, and the performance stopped in its tracks.

Jussi, by then totally immersed in the drama, sang a fiery Brindisi and closed with perhaps the most Italianate "Addio alla madre" I ever heard him deliver. For once it was complete with sobs that seemed to flow naturally from the music. It was a remarkable performance, but the hot-blooded Sicilian Turiddu was always a showpiece for "cold, Nordic-type" Jussi Björling. As for Giulietta's recollection of their collaboration, she recently wrote, "I can assure you that Jussi Björling is among the most beautiful memories of my life as a singer."[27]

Cornell MacNeil, the Scarpia that afternoon, recalled Jussi's Cavaradossi of 21 November:

> *Tosca* was so underrehearsed that in the second act, in his fight with the henchmen, as he was screaming '*Carnefice! Carnefice!*' Jussi broke loose. He acted too violently and fell to the ground with a big thump. I stood there and I wanted to help him, but I knew I couldn't! You are Scarpia, for God's sake, you can't go lift the prisoner! I remember the anxiety I had for the rest of that scene wondering if he had hurt himself. In his later years he was considered a better actor than as a young singer, and I could see at close range why.[28]

The stage business seemed to go much better in the next performance, this time with Leonard Warren as the police chief. Cantor Don Goldberg was in the audience that night, savoring every detail.

> In the second act after Cavaradossi sings "*Vittoria!*" Jussi picked up a chair to throw at Scarpia. Warren, standing behind the desk, literally seemed to turn white! He immediately motioned Sciarrone and Spoletta to go after him, and they grabbed Jussi, with the chair raised high in his hand. He was still fighting as they dragged him out. Then just before reaching the exit, his body slumped as if he were dead. He wasn't taken out, he was *dragged out*! When I saw that, knowing of his health problems, I said "Oh my God! He's had another heart attack!" What made it even more dramatic was that Jussi didn't come out for a curtain call.
>
> But Act III began on time, and after his scene with the Jailer, Jussi sang an unforgettable "E lucevan le stelle." When he took the first A-natural and did a diminuendo down to nothing, there wasn't a sound in the house. People were holding their breaths. And when he finished the aria with such bravura, the applause was almost like a standing ovation—so many in that audience rose to their feet. Jussi was in magnificent voice, and it was simply perfect.[29]

Jussi honored every commitment regarding the Met performances, but not without effort. He felt ill at ease a lot more than he let on; he didn't want to worry me. In order to conserve his energy for the performances, he canceled several rehearsals. Bing, unaware of his state of health, wrongly regarded each incident as the ongoing antics of a recalcitrant Björling. It happened once too often, and Bing dashed off an angry letter on 26 November 1959.

> Dear Jussi,
> Needless to say, we are all very much disturbed not only at the fact that you have canceled practically every rehearsal so far, but, if you forgive my saying so, also at the way you have handled these cancellations. There are some other singers involved in your performances and you can imagine the sort of friendly feeling it engenders when you cancel five minutes or 10 minutes before the start of a rehearsal when none of the other artists, today including Zinka Milanov, can be notified. May I add that *Faust* must have you at the scheduled stage and orchestra rehearsals. If you feel too tired, and I certainly hope you won't, I would be grateful if you would let me know in good time, so that we can begin to make other plans for the performance. The work has not been onstage now for more than two years and needs careful rehearsing. I am sure you yourself, who have been out of this performance for so long, would not wish to go on without appropriate rehearsals.
>
> Yours sincerely,
> Rudolf Bing

Jussi had every intention of attending his scheduled rehearsals. Contrary to Bing's interpretation, his last-minute cancellations were an expression of goodwill; he was hoping to the very last moment to be able to participate, and he did take part in the single rehearsal the Met accorded to *Faust*.

Bing's attitude may be partially excused: Jussi wasn't prone to complaining, and he kept the details and magnitude of his health problems to himself. Unfortunately, he still fortified himself with the occasional drink in the hotel bar, which didn't help matters. During the first intermission of the 19 December *Faust*, Robert Merrill was walking downstairs to the stage when he heard someone yell "The pills! The pills!" He went into Jussi's dressing room and fetched the little box of tablets. "I ran down and put one in his mouth. I swear to God, I could see his heart beating through his costume! It was a most frightening moment. He took the pill, and after his heart calmed down and the act began, he sang 'Salut, demeure' with the high C like you never heard before! Nothing could effect that voice! He always sang well."[30]

In *Faust* Jussi was reunited with Elisabeth Söderström. "Between her first role in Italian and her third in German," Irving Kolodin wrote, "Söderström showed her typical Scandinavian adaptability by singing another in French on December 8."[31] Her Italian turn had been Susanna in *Le nozze di Figaro*, a role she'd been singing since her debut in it a decade ago, but because it was a new staging by Cyril Ritchard, it was rehearsed for four solid weeks. *Faust*, on the other hand, was a traumatic experience for Elisabeth; as an old production, it didn't receive the same treatment.

I'd never sung the part in my life. I got one rehearsal before the perform-ance [on 8 December]. Then came a live broadcast [on 19 December] with Jussi, Cesare Siepi, and Robert Merrill, a wonderful star-studded cast, and *I was scared to death*! I remember being so nervous that I didn't know what my name was! Then Jussi said, "You have nothing to be nervous about—nobody expects anything from you! For me it's much worse. Because I've been away for a long time, people want to see if I am finished or not."

But even if he was nervous, he had enough time and care to watch over me. And then to sing next to Jussi sort of released forces within you that you didn't know you owned. I think it comes from the way of breath-ing. If you stand next to a person who has this wonderful, deep breathing then you yourself start to breathe the same way, and it helps you relax.[32]

When asked about her career goals on a radio interview soon after, Elis-abeth's response was totally spontaneous: "The day before yesterday I sang Marguerite in *Faust* at the Metropolitan with Jussi Björling in the title role, and that was something that I would never have dared to hope for in my wildest dreams."[33] Elisabeth didn't say that to ingratiate herself with the public or Jussi. As an internationally acclaimed prima donna on the brink of retirement, 33 years later, she repeated the sentiments: "Listening to Björ-ling has always been my ultimate pleasure. He never made an ugly sound, and yet his voice was the most human, emotional instrument. . . . Although he didn't move much onstage, his mime and his eyes told you he was always in character."[34]

✳

There was always an affinity between Jussi and the Metropolitan public. In this 1959–60 season, the audience seemed to express its special apprecia-tion, as if thanking him for his return; the reception at every one of his per-formances was as vociferous as at the first. Their enthusiasm pleased Jussi, and he was glad that he had come back.

When in the midst of the fanfare *Opera News* interviewed him, Jussi made predictions about our children, allowing with an honest shrug of his shoulders that Anders "has a voice, but—" Quite true! Anders is the con-troller at Gustavus Adolphus College. "Lasse will be a diplomat. He is so intelligent. His Latin! Ann-Charlotte, our youngest, she is 16, she will be the singer of the family."[35] Lasse didn't become a diplomat. After a stint in the banking business, he followed in his father's footsteps and over the years has accumulated recital and operetta performance credits; Ann-Charlotte too became a successful operetta and concert singer in Sweden.

In the same article, Jussi mentioned how much he enjoyed singing *Roméo et Juliette* and announced, "Next year I plan to record it." That was true, although when it was suggested that he record *Roméo et Juliette*, Jussi had the same apprehensions about the language as he'd had when in 1955 he declined to be Victoria de los Angeles' Des Grieux in her recording of Massenet's *Manon*. This role would've been new to Jussi, and he was worried about his ability to sing in correct French. This may also have been why he didn't record *Faust*. In the decades ahead, critics lamented that Jussi's artistic conscience about authentic pronunciation wasn't shared by the generation of tenors who came after him.

Jussi signed his last contract with the Metropolitan Opera Association on 21 November 1959 for a minimum of 12 performances between 24 October and 21 December 1960. He was scheduled to sing in *Manon Lescaut* on 25 October 1960, in opening week. In addition to $1500 a performance, he was to receive a single payment of $1000 rehearsal expenses. The compact time block appealed to Jussi. Having established a truce with Bing, he said he was glad to return to the Met in the following year. None of us realized at the time that when the curtain fell and the tumultuous applause died away after the last *Cavalleria rusticana* on 22 December 1959, the period some fans fondly call the Björling era at the Met had come to an end.

# Chapter 29

# SINGING IS MY LIFE

Ann-Charlotte and Lasse joined us for the 1959 holiday season in New York, and we all had a very special dinner at Giorgio Tozzi's home. As Giorgio tells the story,

> I remember at one Christmas having invited Jussi and his wife Anna-Lisa and their two children over to our home. We had an apartment at the time on 71st Street in New York. I didn't think that Jussi would accept the invitation, feeling that perhaps being such a famous person he already had been invited many times over. I was delighted when he accepted.
>
> He came to our home, and we asked him to say grace, and he made a little toast. He said, "You know, of all the years that I have been coming to the United States, this is the first time that anyone ever invited us into their home for one of the holidays." I was quite surprised. But then thinking it over, I remember that I myself was very hesitant to invite him, because I felt that such a famous man certainly would have been invited by so many people that it would have been rather futile for me even to ask him. I imagine that is the reason why he never was invited. Probably others thought the same way I did. I thank God now that I had the courage to override my own false consideration of the situation and invite him. It was a beautiful day and a very happy day, I must say.[1]

Giorgio was not the only one who thought that we were inundated with invitations. "I was somewhat in awe of Jussi," Cornell MacNeil admits. "He never treated me in a manner that would lead me to be in awe other than my admiration for his voice and his vocalism, [but] the thought of having social contact with him just never occurred to me."[2]

Jussi closed the autumn tour with a recital at Hunter College on 27 December 1959. His popularity and drawing power were such that he and Schauwecker had been invited back for this "concert extraordinary" only nine months after their previous appearance. It was a capacity house; many people had to be seated on the stage behind him, but as always, Jussi sang at least one number or a couple of encores facing them. Cornell MacNeil recalls the night, the last time he heard Jussi sing.

> He sang this glorious concert with encores, all the things that everybody wanted him to sing. Jussi felt about himself that he was pretty damned good, and he gave you the impression as a concert singer that he could do everything that he wanted to do. He varied his approach to fit the piece of music. Jussi was a stylist. He was relaxed, he would talk to the pianist, turn around, smile, announce his encores, and the audience would break into applause. [After the recital] there was this adulation and incredible applause. When I went backstage, I was just in tears. He staggered me with his vocalism; I found it an extremely emotional experience.[3]

John Briggs' review in *The New York Times* (28 December 1959) made special mention of his diction, now holding up his English as a model even to native singers: "Certainly nothing that he does seems studied or labored; it appears as effortless as breathing." David Björling would've relished reading this line about his son; it's fitting that Jussi's very last recital in New York received such high praise.

Following a few weeks' vacation in Puerto Rico, our family returned to Stockholm. Jussi had been feeling quite ill; his heart was acting up again, and the attacks of arrhythmia and palpitations were more frequent. Nonetheless, on 6 March 1960, only four months short of his debut on the same stage 30 years before, he sang the strenuous *Il trovatore*, his 133rd guest appearance at the Royal Opera House since 1939. Hjördis Schymberg was Leonora, Hugo Hasslo Di Luna, and Kerstin Meyer Azucena. Since Jussi's first Rodolfo at the side of Hjördis' Mimì on 13 October 1934, the two of them had enthralled Stockholm audiences, singing together so wonderfully and so often that they'd come to be regarded as a team. Although he didn't know it, singing this engagement with her, in a performance conducted by Herbert Sandberg—the maestro who had accompanied him at his audition in front of the Board of the Music Academy in 1928—completed the circle. This was his final appearance at the Royal Opera.

The performance, broadcast and captured on tape, has recently been released on CD.[4] Jussi's voice is veiled and below its customary brilliance, with a pronounced baritonal hue, an impression reinforced by the transposition of "Di quella pira" by a full tone. But his musically and interpretively correct and ardently heroic Manrico suggests his ripe readiness to record Otello.

327

Publicity director Bertil Hagman always treated Jussi with the utmost respect. Normally he didn't disturb Jussi in his dressing room, but this time he was expected: Jussi had agreed to sit for a series of photos in the pose of the stretta, sword in hand, for a future portrait to be executed by the photographer's brother, the painter Sven "X:et" Erixson. But the performance had left Jussi so exhausted that he refused. Reminded of his promise, he turned angry. "No! I don't want to do it! I'm tired, don't you understand that? I am ill."

Ann-Charlotte stepped in. "Daddy wouldn't you like to?" she began. "No!" said Jussi. "Please try to do it, the man has brought his equipment." "I said no," Jussi retorted. "It won't take long." Jussi shook his head. "Daddy, please?"

Jussi gave in and posed for the pictures on the set, but in a very bad humor. The next day, sorry for putting Hagman in an awkward position, he sent him an inscribed photo. As always, he regretted his bad temper; he just couldn't let anyone be angry with him.

Ill or not, the day after *Trovatore* Jussi flew to London for rehearsals at Covent Garden commencing 8 March, negotiations for which return had begun as early as 10 November 1950, when Harold Holt, Jussi's British representative at the time, advised Sir David Webster, manager of Covent Garden, to contact Konsertbolaget in Stockholm. Webster and Helmer Enwall began an exchange of letters on 30 December 1950; the exploratory correspondence continued, and on 10 August 1951, Holt wrote to Webster:

> I spent much time with [Björling] and his prima donna wife during their few days in London and I learned with interest that during the coming season they will appear together at the Royal Opera House, Stockholm singing the principal roles in *Romeo and Juliet*. This seems to me a grand idea to have the actual husband and wife singing these roles and I am sure it would create tremendous interest in London.[5]

Nothing came of Holt's suggestion of our joint appearance (I'm not even sure we were aware of his efforts in this direction), but then and later, Jussi's return engagement to Covent Garden was repeatedly discussed and postponed. On 5 August 1958, Webster's assistant wrote to Set Svanholm: "Mr. Webster asked me to write a line to know if there is anything that you can do to persuade Jussi Björling to come to us for *Tosca* in January. We have been trying for some long time to make such a visit possible."[6]

On 1 October 1958, Jussi's current British agent, Victor Hochhauser, transmitted to Webster the contents of a letter he received from Stockholm. "Before Jussi's departure for USA he quite agreed to give some performances at the Covent Garden, but he absolutely insisted upon a fee of at least £600 [$1680]."[7]

In his letter of 12 December 1958 to Hochhauser, Webster accepted the terms adding, "We are very glad that Mr. Jussi Bjorling can appear here at Covent Garden next summer." Although an agreement in principle had been reached, the problem of fitting the performances into Jussi's bookings remained. The contract that was signed with Covent Garden on 14 August 1959 specified four performances of *La bohème* between 8 and 22 March 1960, at the stipulated £600 per performance. According to *The Scotsman* (18 March 1960) Jussi's fee was "higher than any other artist—even Callas."

✼

After a 21-year absence, Jussi would sing at Covent Garden, and I planned to be there for his long-awaited return on 10 March 1960, but a few days before our scheduled departure, my mother became ill. On 7 March, as we were about to bid her goodbye, I discovered she had a temperature of 104 and had her admitted to Roslagstull's Hospital, where she was diagnosed with pneumonia. Of course, I wanted to stay with her until she was out of danger, so that day Jussi flew to London without me.

Jussi's Mimì was the delightful Rosanna Carteri. Although communication between the two of them was limited ("My English wasn't so good, nor was his Italian," Carteri recalled), she retained pleasant memories of their collaboration. "I still remember his kindness to me," she recently wrote.

> Although many years have passed by, those evenings in Covent Garden are still fairly clear in my memory. To sing with Jussi Björling has been a very important experience for me because he was an artist of a very high level and a singer with a magnificent voice. Even though at the time he wasn't young anymore, his voice was pure and sweet, in line with the Italian school. I also remember his perfect technique, his excellent Italian diction, and his style that only a few singers managed to have. His voice and his acting were measured, and the performance he gave was always in good taste.[8]

In spite of the timely arrival of the principals, the *Evening Standard* (11 March 1960) complained about the first night's poor ensemble work under Edward Downes: "The show had been thrown together with the minimum of rehearsal." *The Stage and Television Today* (17 March 1960) acknowledged that Jussi, as a singer, was magnificent but called him "about as Bohemian as an elderly family solicitor, in dress, makeup and deportment, and as romantically passionate as a benevolent uncle."

Philip Hope-Wallace gave a balanced review of the performance. He wrote that Jussi's "acting was correct deportment rather than anything naturalistically convincing. But what an artist he is vocally. His phrasing was most unusually sensitive." Adding that the voice was less powerful than he had remembered, he remarked on the "beautiful riding strength" of the climax of "Che gelida manina" as Jussi was "turning his head and as it were spinning the note right out round the house. He was at his best in the third act, especially in the quartet."[9]

In an article entitled "The Return of Jussi Björling," Desmond Shaw-Taylor was no less objective: "The voice is remarkably well preserved: equable, steady, produced without violence or strain." He noted that Jussi "wisely" transposed "Che gelida manina" a semitone down. "His singing of the aria, as of the entire role, was thoroughly accomplished, and delightfully free of the routine Italian vices: no sudden yells, no gulps or sobs or wobbles, no interminable top notes. Such a feeling for style is too rare and valuable to be dismissed as a merely negative virtue." In his opinion too, where Jussi failed to hit the mark was the physical aspects of the role. "Mr. Björling's stage deportment—it would be absurd to call it acting—resembled that of a frock-coated Victorian solicitor interviewing a young lady in distress. . . . I have never seen a Rodolfo take less trouble to find Mimì's key—or pounce on it more obviously when found."[10]

"Rosanna Carteri, a newcomer from Italy was an accomplished and satisfying Mimì," wrote critic Leslie Ayre; in Anthony Gerrard's opinion, her "rich and resonant soprano voice thrilled the house."[11] The other bohemians, John Shaw's Marcello and Geraint Evans' Schaunard, were also warmly praised, but judging from the enthusiasm and the unwavering unanimity of every critique, it was Marie Collier as Musetta who stole the show. Desmond Shaw-Taylor wrote, "Marie Collier, who seems to gain in verve and assurance with each role she now takes up, gave us a Musetta of such tearing high spirits as to stop the show in the Café Momus scene. It may be regrettable, but an audience will always rise to a performance so warm and richly histrionic as this; even Mr. Björling looked astounded."[12]

※

The second presentation was a routine performance, but the third *La bohème*, on 15 March 1960, my birthday, almost made tragic history. Jussi arrived at the theater at 6 p.m. He got into his costume and makeup, then sat motionless for a long time in his dressing room. At 7:30 stage manager William Bundy rang his bell: "On stage, Mr. Björling." Jussi tried, but he had to come back to his dressing room. He had had an acute attack of heart fibrillations, he felt terrible, and he said he could not go on. Webster and his associates rushed to him; the physician that was summoned gave Jussi a stimulant and following a brief examination declared his patient was "suffering from acute heart strain. He needs a long rest." Geraint Evans saw an ashen-faced Jussi lying in the dressing room. "I thought he was dead," he later confessed.[13]

The few minutes that passed would have been insignificant under normal circumstances, but they were not when an audience of several thousand filled an auditorium, waiting for the curtain to rise. What made the situation even more tense was that Her Majesty Queen Elizabeth, the Queen Mother, was in attendance. A messenger was sent to the royal box to explain the cause of the delay. At first, Jussi planned to follow the doctor's advice and cancel the performance, but he felt obliged to rise to the occasion. He got up from his couch and insisted, "For the Queen Mother I will continue."[14]

The audience grew impatient, and around 7:40 some slow handclapping was heard in the auditorium. Jussi went onstage again but returned to the dressing room, asking the anxious staff to give him a few more minutes' rest. If he felt just a little better, he'd sing. At 7:50, the circle of a spotlight flashed across center stage, and house manager John Collins stepped in front of the curtain. "I have to tell you that Jussi Björling has been unwell all day. Five minutes ago there was some doubt if he would be able to go on. There was some doubt whether he would be able ever to sing again. But if you will be patient, he says he will try. Once more, our apologies."

As the minutes ticked on, the chest pains began to subside. Finally, Jussi felt reassured enough to say that he'd be able to sing. At 8:03, Sir David Webster addressed the audience. "I have to report that Mr. Björling has had a heart attack. But so that you will not be disappointed, he says that he will sing." A prolonged applause greeted this announcement. The Queen Mother joined in from the royal box. Webster then added, "He has been sitting and resting, trying to get ready for the performance. I am sure with your warmth and sympathy Mr. Björling will see it through. A substitute tenor is standing by and will take over if required. Mr. Björling believes this may not be necessary."

It was not. The curtain rose 36 minutes late, and then, according to James Horrocks, "As Björling sang I recalled the golden days of Caruso." This well-intentioned exaggeration notwithstanding, Jussi sang well, at full power, but very carefully. The medicine had some side effects, and he felt almost numb during the first act. He took "Che gelida manina" slower than usual and broke up some of his phrases. At times he sacrificed his legato to add an extra breath in mid-phrase, but the audience was supportive and he received a "tremendous ovation." As the evening wore on, he felt increasingly better. Reassured that he'd make it through, he improved from act to act.

"Once the performance began," writes Rosanna Carteri, "his voice didn't seem to have suffered, only his acting was slowed, almost as if he was afraid of getting physically tired. Naturally everybody onstage was trying to help him but, if I remember correctly, he didn't get too tired. In the end, the public rewarded him with a long and loud applause,"[15] including the royal guest.

After the performance the Queen Mother wished to come and thank Jussi personally in his dressing room, but he thought that was out of the question—he should be the one to go and greet her. She then invited him to go to her box, if he felt well enough. Carteri recalls, "The two of us, still dressed in our costumes, went to meet the Queen Mother, who kindly received us with a big smile and words of compliment and admiration."[16] Because this wasn't a gala performance, the singers were received in the antechamber of the box,[17] where they had a pleasant 10-minute conversation. Wishing Jussi a speedy recovery, Her Majesty said, "That was without parallel. . . . I appreciate the fact that you could perform at all. I thought you were very good."[18]

Jussi's fear that his every indisposition would be ascribed to alcoholism followed him beyond the grave. As late as 1993, author Charles Osborne retold this incident, speaking as a personal witness and making the uninformed statement that Björling was "absolutely drunk out of his mind and they were busily pouring black coffee into him."[19] By contrast, in addition to the many newspaper accounts that give the precise sequence of events, Rosanna Carteri unequivocally states, "I sincerely believe that on those occasions, he *did not drink*," adding her unconditional assurance "that he was very calm and in control even during the performance of his illness."[20]

Only 11 days earlier, on 4 March, Leonard Warren sang his last performance at the Metropolitan. The opera was *La forza del destino* (*The Force of Destiny*). Leonard was in fine form and had just acknowledged the applause after his big aria, "Urna fatale del mio destino" ("Fatal urn of my destiny"). As he was to begin the cabaletta, he turned to Roald Reitan, the Chirurgo (Surgeon) in the opera, and said "Help me!" In the next moment he lost his balance and toppled over like a giant log, falling headlong and hitting the ground with such force that he broke his nose. Within moments, Dr. Adrian Zorgniotti, the physician on duty, had rushed onto the stage. The curtain was lowered, and minutes later Dr. Zorgniotti pronounced Warren dead. He first suspected a cerebral hemorrhage but concluded that Warren suffered a myocardial infarct.[21] Warren was 48 years old, only two months younger than Jussi.

We all liked Leonard, and when the news reached us in Stockholm, just before Jussi left for England, he'd taken it very hard. Surely the parallel between their conditions had occurred to him; Jussi must have realized that he was gambling with his life that night in London. No matter: he was a trouper to the core and would meet his commitments. Yet he too could have died of a heart attack in the middle of the performance.

Jussi felt much better the next day, resting in his suite at the Savoy. Calls poured in from every possible source, even "officials from Clarence House inquired about his health on behalf of the Queen Mother."[22] It was a kind gesture on the part of the beloved "Queen Mum."

Everybody was concerned about Jussi's condition, and a succession of reporters requested interviews. The reporter with the *Star* (16 March 1960) was relieved to find him "gay and confident" about his final appearance and awaiting the arrival of his wife the following day. "I am quite recovered, I feel fine," he was quoted in the *Evening News* (16 March 1960). Looking forward to singing to another sold-out house, he added, "I shall be all right; there is no question of my not being able to sing on Friday."

Jussi didn't hesitate to admit to the *New Chronicle* (17 March 1960):

"Of course I was worried, but only because I might have to let down a fully sold-out house. But this has happened before, and I always have my pills with me." When the reporter asked him about possible retirement, he laughed. "Of course I do not plan to stop singing. You cannot let these things worry you. Singing is my life. I have no intention of giving it up."

By this time my mother was out of danger. I had been so preoccupied with her, staying by her and making sure she received the best possible care, that I had no idea what was going on beyond the hospital—and the family was thoughtful enough to keep the news from me. I brought Mother home from the hospital on 16 March, and when I flew to London to join Jussi the next day, I was blissfully unaware of what had transpired at Covent Garden.

Jussi met me at the airport with a giant bouquet of lilies-of-the-valley. He seemed his usual self, and fortunately for me, I heard for the first time the details of his ordeal directly from him. I was terribly concerned and kept asking how he felt, but he just waved my anxious questions aside: "For heaven's sake, I'm fine now!"

He didn't want to worry me, especially now that the worst was over. But a few months later, when Gertrud Pålson-Wettergren asked him about that near-fatal evening in London, he confessed, "Nothing more horrible has ever happened to me. It's a riddle to me how I ever got through that evening."[23]

Because of Jussi's heart problems in August and September of 1959, we'd asked Freddie Schang not to book a concert tour for him in the coming season. He had only five engagements to honor, three in San Francisco and two in southern California.

Our trip from London to New York was our first transatlantic flight by jet, trimming the overnight journey to a mere eight hours. We stayed at the Essex House and spent the next couple of days in business meetings. When we dined with our old friend Harald Thelander, he observed that Jussi seemed quite subdued.[24] It was true; now that we were only a mile from the Met, Leonard Warren's death loomed large in Jussi's mind. It brought his London ordeal into full focus. "Next time it's my turn," he said. I was horrified and scolded him for saying such a thing. As it turned out, Jussi was right—his time was running out.

We arrived in San Francisco on 24 March. Jussi was to appear with the Cosmopolitan Opera, a company in implicit competition with the San Francisco Opera. The Cosmopolitan had an ambitious repertoire and a roster of internationally acclaimed singers. As a matter of policy, the company focused its investment on soloists rather than productions. Jussi was their highest paid tenor at $4000 for each performance.[25]

In *Il trovatore* on 29 March 1960, Jussi's partners were Cornell MacNeil, Margherita Roberti, and a wonderful young mezzo, Irene Kramarich. "Periodic reports about Jussi Bjoerling's ill health must be greatly exaggerated," Howard Fried began his review, paraphrasing Mark Twain. Calling him "the veteran Swedish tenor"—a sobering epithet—Fried praised his "vocal mastery, quality and fire." He found the lower range of his voice "a shade short of its best luster," but he still marveled at the feeling and graceful phrasing of "Ah sì, ben mio." In the stretta, Fried added, Jussi's "top C brought down the house."[26]

Three days later, Jussi sang the title role in *Faust*. Pavel Lisitsian, the magnificent Russian baritone in stupendous form as Valentin, sang his second of only two opera performances in America, the other being a single Amonasro at the Met on 3 March 1960—the night before Leonard Warren died. A very young Norman Treigle sang Méphistophélès; years later Treigle reportedly remarked that while he acted his heart out—and he did indeed—Jussi just stood there, and with his incredible singing had the greatest possible success.

We were glad that this engagement went so well. Mercifully, neither of us knew that this *Faust* was to be his last operatic performance.

After a recital at the War Memorial Opera with Freddie Schauwecker, we traveled to Pasadena. The recital on 5 April at the Civic Auditorium was the next to last stop on our American itinerary. To our alarm, Jussi's heart problem flared up before curtain time. His heart racing, all he could do was take his pills and wait. He soon felt better, and despite my protestations, he insisted on singing. The concert started half an hour late, but Jussi sang very well.

"Bjoerling Tired But Masterful" was the headline of Roy Copperud's review. Jussi, he wrote, looked "tired and drawn. When he began to sing, however, a light came into his eyes and an expression of pleasure played over his features."[27] But after the first three numbers he had to leave the stage, and impresario Elmer Wilson was obliged to announce, "Mr. Bjoerling has asked to rest for five minutes." Freddie played two solos, and although the breaks between the subsequent groups of songs were longer than usual, Jussi finished the program and even capped it with two encores. No wonder Copperud observed, "The circumstances made all the more remarkable a performance that was impressive for its serene fullness; nothing was skimped." Albert Goldberg confirmed in the *Los Angeles Times* (7 April 1960), "Mr. Bjoerling was in his finest form. . . . At no time was there any evidence of physical distress either in Mr. Bjoerling's appearance or in his singing. The voice sounded uncommonly fresh and pure, and his artistry was as distinguished as ever." The recital in Santa Monica, on 7 April, went without complications, and with that last obligation fulfilled, we said goodbye to Freddie and flew home, so Jussi could rest before his next engagements.

Lasse volunteered to accompany Jussi to Amsterdam while I stayed home with my mother, who was still weak. They had a grand time together in the mild spring weather, taking long walks through the tulip fields and along the canals, and visiting Haarlem and the Rijksmuseum. Lasse recalls, "It was fun to be traveling with Dad and to have him all to myself. When we went to the Concertgebouw for the first rehearsal, we were greeted like royalty." Jussi had an interminable wait before it was his turn to rehearse, however, and then the plan was to have him go down the steep staircase that leads to the stage and climb back up between his two numbers. In his condition, mixing stairs and singing had to be avoided at all cost, but Jussi knew that if he complained it'd be taken for arrogance. Lasse quickly sized up the situation.

> Father did it, but he really felt the strain. So I immediately said, "This must be changed. You must realize that Mr. Björling is not in the best of health and he cannot take this." Father just looked at me; but he looked so happy, so relieved. So I took charge, and I had them reschedule the program. Dad came downstairs, sang his two arias, acknowledged his applause, and *then* went up the steps—once.[28]

⚜

By now, Jussi had learned to live with daily spells of arrhythmia. Although he was quite dependent on his pills, he felt better after his Dutch outing with Lasse, which was like a vacation for both of them. Frankly, he needed a long rest, but among other commitments, more recording sessions awaited him; in 1960, Jussi's vacation had to wait until September. Then we'd be off to the Met and thence to Japan and Australia.

It was the first time Jussi had three recording projects scheduled for one summer. He was to sing the tenor part in the Verdi Requiem in Vienna, and after that he was expected in Rome for two recordings in succession. One, an unusual choice in respect to Jussi's active repertoire, was Luigi in Puccini's *Il tabarro*. Jussi at least had sung Luigi early in his career, but his colleagues, Leontyne Price and George London, would be new to their roles of Giorgetta and Michele.

During our most recent stopover in New York, at the Essex House, we had received Dick Mohr's 23 March letter specifying that Jussi had to be in Rome no later than 25 June and confirming the casting. A second letter, dated 13 April, reached us in Stockholm with the complete recording schedule. It would have been an interesting recording, but it was never made. Neither Dick Mohr nor Alan Kayes of RCA, nor Nora London (George's widow), nor I can remember when Jussi canceled the recording.[29] The only documentation I have is the undated handwritten text of a telegram from Jussi to Dick: "Regret very much to inform you that I cannot record *Il tabarro*. Have to rest between other recordings, doctors orders. Sorry to disappoint you. Bjoerling."

Canceling the recording so late, most likely in May, I can only conclude that Jussi had a doctor's certificate confirming his poor health and recommending the rest. If he were to exert himself with a recording project, it made more sense to save his energy for the major undertaking of *Un ballo in maschera*.

✳

In June, on the occasion of our silver wedding anniversary, Jussi presented me with a large arrangement of lilies-of-the-valley, the same flowers I'd carried in my bridal bouquet. We'd had 25 fantastic years together, in spite of all the difficulties, and it was a fitting time to take stock of our future.

Every music lover who bought a ticket to hear Björling expected him to deliver what Cornell MacNeil called "that glorious consistency . . . I don't know a singer who so universally and continuously, and without exception maintained his vocalism regardless of the situation in which he was singing."[30] Kurt Bendix, who conducted many of Jussi's performances at the Royal Opera, believed Jussi was apparently incapable of making a musical mistake.[31]

Aware of what he owed his public, Jussi wouldn't go onstage unless he was able to give a performance worthy of Jussi Björling. Having to live up to that expectation at all times over a long career, in spite of abusing himself with alcohol, was an awesome responsibility, an artistic achievement, and a physiological miracle—each and every night of a 20-, 30-, or 40-recital tour. Traveling by boat, train, and plane; changing time zones and climates sometimes within hours; performing—it required the stamina of an athlete. It had been easy to sustain such a demanding lifestyle in the prime of our lives, while we were both healthy and had the requisite physical endurance, but since his brother's death, Jussi had grown increasingly aware of his own mortality and the limits of a singing career. He derived much pleasure from performing, but no matter how much he enjoyed singing, with his 50th birthday approaching, it was time to slow down. It was unnecessary to wear himself out earning more money. With his hard work and my careful handling of our finances, we had enough savings to assure us a pleasant life and a secure future for the children.

Of course, he didn't plan to stop entirely. Singing indeed *was* his life, and his voice was still in excellent shape. If he paced himself right, he could keep going for another decade. Most of all, if he accepted fewer engagements, only those with particular musical, artistic, or financial appeal—and preferably all three—he could finally devote the necessary time to the roles he had always longed to sing: Lohengrin and Otello. His voice had attained the proper weight, and at last he had the requisite artistic maturity to do these demanding parts justice.

He felt ready. He *was* ready.

✳

Jussi and Lasse fishing off Siarö.

Anna-Lisa and Jussi making an excursion in style in South Africa.

Birgit Nilsson and JB in *Tosca*, 14 January 1955.

"Your tiny hand is frozen," sings an ardent Rodolfo to Tebaldi's Mimì, televised 30 January 1956. Courtesy Renata Tebaldi.

JB, Richard Mohr, and Robert Merrill confer during the *Rigoletto* recording, Rome, June 1956. Courtesy Richard Mohr.

Dinner party at Alfredo's, Rome, June 1956. L. to r.: Jussi, Ann-Charlotte, Marion Merrill, Anna-Lisa, Richard Mohr, Lasse, unidentified guest, Robert Merrill. Courtesy Richard Mohr.

Anna-Lisa, Jussi, Robert Merrill, and Ann-Charlotte, sunning on a balcony at the Grand Hotel, Rome, 1956.

Leonard Warren as Scarpia in a photo inscribed to Jussi, wishing "sincere best wishes to my good friend and colleague." Photo Paul A. Hesse.

Beniamino Gigli echoes Warren's sentiments, 1953. Photo Lo Bianco.

Gigli and JB at the HMV Salon in Gothenburg, 25 April 1951. Photo H. T. Bild.

Gigli in the garden of his Roman villa, September 1957.

Anna Moffo in her American debut as Mimì with JB as Rodolfo in *La bohème*, Chicago, 16 October 1957. Courtesy Danny Newman.

Renata Tebaldi and JB in *Manon Lescaut*, Chicago, 21 October 1957. Photo Lannes.

At Chicago's Como Inn, 1957. L. to r.: Tito Gobbi, Tullio Serafin, Renata Tebaldi, JB. Courtesy Danny Newman.

Anna-Lisa, Jussi, Anders, and Janet, in the dressing room before *Manon Lescaut*, Chicago, 9 November 1957. Photo Lannes.

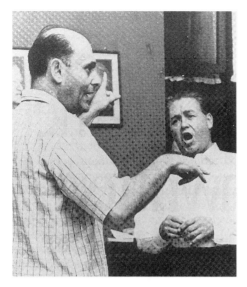

Rehearsing with Georg Solti, Chicago, November 1957.

Boris Christoff as King Philip and JB as Don Carlo in *Don Carlo*, 30 November 1957. Courtesy Danny Newman.

Nell Rankin as Eboli in *Don Carlo*. Courtesy Nell Rankin.

Anna-Lisa backstage with Manrico—sporting a noble profile thanks to nose putty.

Ann-Charlotte with Jussi, Swedish Flag Day, 1957.

On 27 December 1959, shortly after what would be their last project together, Dimitri Mitropoulos inscribed this photo to Jussi "in remembrance of our collaboration. From a very grateful and appreciative partner."

Cornell MacNeil, a vicious Scarpia. Courtesy Cornell MacNeil.

Ingrid Bergman visiting Jussi in his dressing room at the Royal Opera, Stockholm, 1959. Photo Enar Merkel Rydberg.

Jussi with Bongo
in front of the
studio at Siarö,
1959. Photo Bertil
S-son Åberg.

Jussi and Victoria
de los Angeles
take a break from
recording at the
Trevi Fountain,
Rome, September
1959. Photo
Parioli.

Hjördis Schymberg (Leonora) and JB (Manrico) at his last performance at the Royal Opera, Stockholm, 6 March 1960.

Rosanna Carteri and JB in *La bohème*, Covent Garden, 10 March 1960. Courtesy Richard Copeman.

Marie Collier as Musetta in Act II of *La bohème*, Covent Garden, 10 March 1960. Photo Houston Rogers.

Lasse left his seat to snap this photo of his parents' silver wedding anniversary dinner at Karlavägen 11. L. to r.: Anders, maid, Emy Berg, Anna-Lisa, Jussi, Janet; front center: Ann-Charlotte.

Jussi enjoying his favorite pastime, in a quiet moment at Siarö. Photo Erik Collin.

Jussi with arm raised at the *Un ballo in maschera* session, Rome: "Maestro! I would like to rerecord that last phrase!" Photo Hans Wild.

A very distressed Jussi, moments later. The dime-store Chinese fan, momentarily at rest, leans against the music stand. Photo Hans Wild.

Poster announcing Jussi's death.

The Jussi Björling Museum in Borlänge.

One of numerous costume exhibits at the museum.

"This is where we will grow old together." Photo Erik Collin.

On 6 June 1960, Flag Day, Jussi gave a recital at Skansen before a record-breaking crowd; on the 9th he joined several colleagues from the Opera at Gröna Lund. With these obligations out of the way, we traveled to Vienna for the Verdi Requiem. He regretted not having had more opportunities to sing it in his career, but he'd had little choice in the matter; when people engaged Jussi Björling, they'd rather have him in a solo recital or in opera.

The sessions were set for 12 to 19 June. Fritz Reiner conducted the Vienna Philharmonic, and the other soloists were Leontyne Price, Rosalind Elias, and Giorgio Tozzi—a well-chosen quartet of premier voices. This was the only recording Jussi made with Leontyne Price, and the last with Giorgio Tozzi. Rosalind had a high regard for Jussi; when asked about him, she replied, "Hey! If you mention Jussi Björling, you cannot speak about anybody else! He was incomparable. He was unique!"[32] The day Jussi was to record "Ingemisco" he seemed very nervous, Tozzi remembers:

> I tried to allay his anxiety by saying that after all, this was a recording session, and that if he was not satisfied with any part of his work, he could rerecord. He said to me that it was not that simple, because the orchestra was the Vienna Philharmonic, and if he did not sing well that day, by tomorrow all of Vienna would know about it, and soon the rest of the world would know! I could certainly understand what he meant. After all, people had come to expect only the greatest performances of him. However, he did record "Ingemisco" magnificently, as the recording attests.[33]

Indeed, the Requiem recording shows Jussi's voice in optimal condition. Ann-Charlotte watched him record each day, sitting in front of the loudspeakers in the control room, listening to every detail of the playback. Her memories of this session are more personal: "The 'Ingemisco' was so incredibly good, I just sat there and thought, who is this? And then the realization came: this is my father! I always regarded Daddy's singing with certainty—it was a given that he sang well. But then, suddenly, it was so much more than what I had expected. It was a strange feeling."[34] The experience left a deep impression on Ann-Charlotte; she says that this was probably the only time she separated her Daddy from the singer in her mind. When the sessions were over, she asked Jussi for the Requiem score. It is now in her collection, bearing the inscription *Till Lillan från Pappa. Wien 15.6.1960* (To Little One from Papa. Vienna 15 June 1960).

While in Vienna, Erik Smith, a member of the recording team, took it upon himself to entertain our high-spirited daughter, not exactly an unpleasant task. It was all quite innocent—after all, Ann-Charlotte was a 17-year-old schoolgirl—but one night they were out much later than expected. Jussi got anxious and resorted to the only solution open to him at the moment: he began to drink. He went to the Decca engineers' suite to look for Ann-Charlotte. Producer John Culshaw mentions in his memoirs the absurd experience of waking to find a heavily intoxicated Jussi Björling standing at the foot of his bed, "uncontrollably drunk."[35] Apart from it being untrue, he obviously hadn't the slightest idea what an uncontrollably drunk Jussi Björling looked like.

This incident excepted, Jussi's drinking in Vienna was fully under control. Erik remembers that when he picked Jussi up before the "Ingemisco" recording, he was very nervous. On their way to the Sofiensaal he suggested that they stop somewhere for a beer, but Erik managed to talk him out of it.[36]

In the middle of our stay, Set Svanholm arrived in Vienna to sing the title role of Wagner's rarely performed *Rienzi* in a concert production. Then director of the Royal Opera, Svanholm brought with him the royal medal *Litteris et Artibus*, which the king of Sweden had bestowed upon Birgit Nilsson, who was in town for a series of Brünnhildes in a new production of *Götterdämmerung* at the Staatsoper. Birgit invited us and some other of her friends to the Die drei Hussaren restaurant in Grinzing, the famous *Heuriger* district outside Vienna, for Svanholm's "official" presentation of the medal.

Erik Smith and Ann-Charlotte met us there. According to Erik, as they approached the restaurant, "We heard Jussi's voice even at a distance, singing 'Dein ist mein ganzes Herz' with the little *Schramml* band."[37] Other members of the recording team were present, and one of them came up with the idea of creating a gala concert for Prince Orlofsky's ball in the London/Decca *Fledermaus* then being recorded with Herbert von Karajan. The executives were intrigued, and recording sessions were quickly set up for soloists then in Vienna. Before we left town, Jussi contributed a bilingual "Dein ist mein ganzes Herz" in Swedish and German from Lehár's *The Land of Smiles*. The "Gala *Fledermaus*" was a hit with record buyers, and Prince Orlofsky's ball was later released on a separate LP.

# Chapter 30

# SOLTI

Jussi rested at home following the Requiem recording, just as the doctor ordered. He participated only in a special program in Rättvik, honoring the United States on the 4th of July, American Independence Day. After the celebrations, Jussi gave his last recorded interview to Anthony Baird. On the surviving tape he sounds tired; his speech has a measured cadence. But when asked about the training of the younger generation, Jussi was roused.

> I would say this: it seems to me that nowadays if you have a voice and you have a top C or things like that, then nothing else matters. They put you onstage whenever you're ready for a top C; nothing else means anything. And that's *absolutely wrong*. And I can assure you of one thing—that is never going to last, absolutely not. For two, three, four, five, seven years, but you can be sure, that's all.[1]

When Baird asked him about operas written by modern composers, Jussi replied, "Some of them are very good and interesting, but I really don't understand that kind of work." A frank admission, but Jussi could never pretend. Modern music—or rather new compositions that passed for music—held no interest for him.

On 8 July we flew to Rome for the recording of *Un ballo in maschera*, giving Jussi a full day's rest before the first rehearsal, set for the 10th. Erik Smith was there to greet us, we were happy to see; he and Jussi had enjoyed such an excellent rapport while working on the Requiem that Culshaw, the producer of *Ballo*, suggested to Erik that he "come along and look after the [Björlings] as a family friend." According to Erik, "I didn't really have a role, I wasn't doing the recording. Being with Decca and not having a particular recording at that time, John thought it would be nice if I sort of looked after them a bit."[2]

In Rome, Erik had some pleasant conversations with Jussi, who naturally recounted his work on *Ballo* with Toscanini. "The Maestro asked him to put in a rhythmic laughter in the quintet 'È scherzo od è follia,' actually beating his baton in the rehearsal to try and get a completely musical, rhythmic version of a laugh."[3] Jussi told Erik that Toscanini had given him an old 78 rpm record, so he could hear how Alessandro Bonci sang the laughing *staccati* of the piece.

In spite of the stifling summer heat, we were all in excellent spirits, Jussi in particular. Riccardo was one in his handful of favorite roles, and he was unbelievably happy finally to be recording *Ballo*. His unavoidable withdrawal from the Toscanini performances had loomed large in his mind ever since, and he regarded this opportunity as a second chance. Moreover, Verdi's opera on a Swedish theme had two Swedish singers: Birgit Nilsson as Amelia, and Jussi Björling as Gustaf III/Riccardo.

Originally London/Decca wanted Renata Tebaldi for Amelia,[4] and Jussi had looked forward to working again with the great diva. At this late date Tebaldi no longer recalls why she didn't, in the event, participate in the recording, offering only that she had "studied Amelia's two arias in the early 60s and recorded them for London records in 1965."[5] According to Birgit, it was Jussi who recommended her for this recording,[6] but I don't think she required anybody's good word. She was an exclusive London/Decca artist and had had a great success as Amelia in Chicago in 1959—from the company's standpoint, an excellent choice.

But it was never a question who was to be the star of this recording; the opera was cast from strength. In addition to Birgit and Jussi, Cornell MacNeil was to sing Renato, Giulietta Simionato was Ulrica, and Sylvia Stahlman Oscar. An assembly of this much talent under Georg Solti's leadership promised to produce a milestone recording, and London/Decca had assigned the project to their most capable producer, John Culshaw.

Solti began his career as a concert pianist and conducted his first opera in 1938. He conducted only three more performances before he obtained his first full-time engagement as a conductor in 1946. The turning point of his career came in 1958, with the release of London/Decca's pioneering stereophonic recording of Wagner's *Das Rheingold*. It was produced by John Culshaw, the man who believed that stereo recordings would eventually replace live opera. *Das Rheingold* was designed to prove his point. Its sonic attributes and special effects did nearly as much for stereophonic recording as Enrico Caruso did for the gramophone half a century earlier.

Stereo, first regarded a costly gimmick, now revealed its potential. Anyone who heard the Vienna Philharmonic play Wagner under Solti—and Donner's thunderclap as produced by John Culshaw—was converted for life. Solti's masterly way with the score catapulted him into a position of preeminence, a position he was determined to hold and consolidate with every new assignment. The company relished his sudden celebrity and was eager to capitalize on his talents. While preparing for *Siegfried*, the next installment of Wagner's mighty *Der Ring des Niebelungen* to be recorded, Solti was given a Verdi assignment.

There is no point in comparing the relative standing of Jussi Björling and Georg Solti in the music world. As accomplished musicians in their respective fields, they could both rightly anticipate they'd be treated with professional and social courtesy by the other. With no problems between them in Chicago in 1957, it was reasonable to expect another harmonious, respectful collaboration.

Jussi was not a newcomer to the role of Riccardo. His acclaimed interpretation had been learned under the expert tutelage of Tullio Voghera and refined with Vittorio Gui and Gennaro Papi. By 1960, he had performed it 38 times with such eminent conductors as Fritz Busch, Josef Krips, Dimitri Mitropoulos, Ettore Panizza, Nicola Rescigno, Egisto Tango, and Bruno Walter. He had benefitted by Toscanini's coaching of him in the part. Audiences and critics loved Jussi's Riccardo, but for some reason, as he soon was to find out, it didn't correspond to Solti's conception. He wanted to produce a different *Ballo*, and he made it clear from the very beginning that this was to be *his* recording.

On 10 July orchestra and chorus assembled at the Accademia di Santa Cecilia for the first rehearsal. According to Culshaw, "An hour or so before the first piano rehearsal Mrs. Björling rang to say that her husband was suffering from 'palpitations' doubtless brought on by the heat and would not be able to attend."[7] Mr. Culshaw's ironic quotation marks notwithstanding, Jussi did have palpitations and was suffering more than usual from his arrhythmia. He was cold sober and his voice was fine, but that morning he simply couldn't face the strain of a rehearsal in the non-air-conditioned confines of Santa Cecilia. Remembering his heart problems before and during the *Madama Butterfly* sessions 10 months earlier, we agreed that he shouldn't push himself. They could easily dispense with his services on the very first day.

Solti took Jussi's absence as a bad omen, and he told Culshaw, "John, we must work, this cannot go on."[8] Culshaw came to our hotel. It was beastly hot. Jussi's condition hadn't improved, and he suggested to Culshaw that instead of going to Santa Cecilia twice a day, there should be only one rehearsal, immediately preceding the recording session. To be in the best physical shape for the actual recording, he didn't want to tire himself with extra rehearsals. He politely explained that he knew his role well and didn't think he'd need much rehearsal beyond the ensembles.

Culshaw had his own interpretation of what he heard, and it lost something in the translation to Solti. As Solti tells it, the message from Jussi that reached him and remained with him all these years was this:

> "No, I don't want to rehearse, I don't need a rehearsal! I cannot work as much, I just want to come [to the recording]. During the orchestra rehearsal playback we will see what we are getting, and talk about it during that time,"—or words to that effect. This is not a way to make a recording. This is not the way, until today, that I ever recorded an opera, and I am approaching [my] 50th [recording]. Never![9]

It also appears that Culshaw led Solti to believe that Jussi was drunk. When reminded this wasn't true, Solti said "I know now it was a heart condition, but I didn't know it at that point! I asked him to have a piano rehearsal, I always do that with everybody. Before I record a bit, I sit at the piano and rehearse, and then we go to the orchestra. But he refused to do that, and I thought this is very impolite! I didn't realize what it was."[10]

Although he didn't feel much better, Jussi attended rehearsal on 11 July. Of the principal soloists only Cornell MacNeil and Sylvia Stahlman were present. It was a piano rehearsal; Solti conducted and a most capable man by the name of Pedrazzoli played the accompaniment. Pedrazzoli was completely bilingual, and an excellent musician. It was his assignment to serve as assistant maestro and prepare the cast.

The piano rehearsal took place in the hall, among the musical instruments. On such occasions the maestro conducts the vocalists and the pianist. At one point, Pedrazzoli felt the beat wasn't right, and he didn't quite follow. When he tried to explain, Solti exploded and yelled at him in his limited Italian, "*Mio* maestro, *mio* maestro!" Pedrazzoli, in his quiet little way, said nothing. He just got up and walked out. He went outside for a while, then came back, sat down at the piano, and without a word went ahead with the rehearsal.

The orchestra didn't fare much better. After the previous day's rehearsal, conductor and instrumentalists should've been attuned to each other, but they weren't. Part of the problem was that the players' innate understanding of the Italian operatic idiom and Solti's were in conflict. For a time it appeared doubtful Solti would get what he wanted from the orchestra, but he wasn't one to compromise. With some struggle, he got the musicians to play together; after some further battling, they were finally ready to record. Cornell MacNeil picks up the story:

> Jussi sang "La rivedrò nell'estasi," I think beautifully—absolutely—the whole thing.[11] At the end, when the red light went off, Jussi said: "Maestro, I would like to sing that last phrase again!" I don't know what he thought was wrong with the final phrase; as always, I was astounded with it. At that point, over the loudspeaker from the control room came Cul-

shaw's voice: "Oh Jussi, we'll record this many, many more times. Don't worry about it."

As Solti went back to fighting with the orchestra, Jussi turned to me and said, very humbly: "Don't they think I know what I am doing?" I said: "Jussi, he's having a battle with the orchestra, you can see that. Come on, let's go out in the garden, we'll sit down and talk."

We were called back in, and Jussi recorded the same piece again, with the same result. I don't know how often these little breaks went on, but we went into the garden many times, because it was cooler out there. As we discussed what was going on inside, I began to worry when Jussi changed from "Don't they think I know what I am doing?" to "Do you think they know what they are doing?"[12]

That ended the first day's recording session. It was very late, and everybody was tired. The performers dispersed and were expected to return for the next day's rehearsal. Cornell MacNeil, an astute and analytical observer of human nature, went home very disturbed that night.

I don't write letters very often. But I was so upset, that I had to get it out of me somewhere. So I wrote a letter to my good friend Otto Guth, an assistant to Kurt Herbert Adler in San Francisco. He was a Viennese gentleman and a fine coach whom I loved dearly. "Otto, I am desperate!" I wrote, "I don't know what to do. Between Solti and Culshaw, they are going to drive Jussi out of this recording, and there is absolutely nobody in the world with whom I would rather make a recording." I am a lousy correspondent, but I was upset enough to write that letter. Here was a man who recorded pretty much for one recording company his entire life, where they treated him incredibly well, and these people were simply ignoring him completely, tromping all over what I thought was a remarkable talent and singer, paying no attention to him and dismissing him over the loudspeaker.[13]

Solti remembers listening to the tapes with Culshaw the next morning: "When we listened to the playback of the first session, I thought that this is not what I want! It was very good singing, but of course it was totally different from what I wanted. In a way it was another conception. So I said to Culshaw: 'This is really not what I would like, let's ask him to come to rehearse. You go and speak to him.' I didn't talk to him, John Culshaw did."[14]

When exactly Culshaw was to have spoken to Jussi isn't clear. But in Culshaw's judgment and long after the fact, "It was evident immediately that [Björling] was not going to get on with Solti because he was beyond the stage where he was prepared to reconsider any aspect of his performance."[15] Indeed, Jussi had not the slightest doubt that his interpretation was correct, entirely in line with the Italian style and the opera's tradition. He felt Solti's suggested departures from it would've been wrong. "Why should I change?" he said to me. "And why does Solti treat me like a schoolboy?" he added, no less upset with the Maestro than Solti was with him.

Unknown to us, by the third day, 12 July, they had already made inquiries to find another tenor. According to John Culshaw, neither Carlo Bergonzi nor Giuseppe di Stefano was available.[16] MacNeil tells what happened when he arrived at the recording session that morning:

> Terry McEwen, who had recently been appointed the American representative for London records, came to me (I was out in the garden again because I was upset) and said: "Don't you think it would be great if we could get Mario del Monaco?" I just couldn't answer. [Riccardo] wasn't a thing for Mario to sing. . . . [McEwen also said,] "Isn't it too bad that Jussi is drinking again?" Well, that is absolutely untrue. All the time that he was in Rome he was completely sober.[17]

Jussi was a few minutes late for the morning rehearsal. It may well have been a Roman traffic jam that delayed our cab, but it didn't matter. Being late cast a shadow over the proceedings. The final unpleasantness began to build when Solti, cold and aloof, waved Jussi to the rehearsal area. "Björling! Come here! We rehearse the barcarola."

Both Ann-Charlotte and I witnessed the scene, and Solti's voice still rings clearly in our ears. It was the tone of a schoolmaster addressing one of his pupils. In 1960, Solti had yet to make his permanent move from the German- to the English-language territory, to change his domicile from Frankfurt to London. Limited though his command of English was, however, it wasn't the words but the tone that made his command offensive. Had he spoken German and used the polite form: "*Herr* Björling! *Kommen Sie hier, bitte!*" his intonation would still have made it sound like a curt command.

Solti, for his part, probably didn't mean his manners to offend, and his singers and musicians in Frankfurt must have been used to them. But Jussi, who was treated by everyone with deferential courtesy, was not. Ann-Charlotte and I held our breaths, waiting for his reaction. Unaccustomed though he was to being ordered around in that tone of voice, he said nothing. He did as he was told.

They began to rehearse "Di tu se fedele." Jussi was astounded to find that Solti wanted to change everything—tempo, phrasing, dynamics, nuances. He tried to object and explain, even reason and argue. He had very few artistic disagreements in his long career. If a difference of opinion came up, he was open to persuasion, and usually so was the other party. This time it was different.

Solti failed to convince Jussi to depart from singing the piece the way he believed was right. The exchange made it clear to Jussi that his opinion didn't matter in the least. Having come to that realization, his frustration reached the limit. Suddenly he was walking toward and past us. "Let's go! We're going back to the hotel." Ann-Charlotte and I followed him out of the hall. Jussi hailed a cab, and we drove off.

Allegedly, Jussi's parting words to Solti were these: "You go home and study your part—I know mine!" We didn't hear him say this, and 33 years later, Maestro Solti himself had no recollection that this statement was ever made.[18] Nevertheless Jussi must've said something like it, because Birgit Nilsson distinctly remembers that it was repeated to her within hours over the telephone. It was also cited in print as recently as 1993, but the source of the citation has never been identified.[19]

⋇

No one questions that the conductor must be the unifying force of a musical undertaking. Within the overall framework of the production, however, the way a role is interpreted—phrasing, dynamics, coloring, inflection—ought to be the singer's prerogative. His reputation is made, maintained, or destroyed by his performance. If the interpretation is a failure, he cannot issue a public statement: "The conductor made me do it."

It was Jussi's suitability and reputation as Riccardo that had prompted London/Decca to negotiate with RCA for his release. He had always sung the role as written, or his conductors would've objected. None ever did. It is highly improbable, if not downright impossible, that on this occasion he would've deviated so much from Verdi's markings that Solti had to bring him back in line. As long as he faithfully followed the printed score, there oughtn't have been any question of whose concept of Riccardo should be preserved on records: Jussi Björling's or Georg Solti's. When it comes to the interpretation of a role, on recorded collaborations we admire Chaliapin's Boris Godunov, not Eugene Goossens'; Riccardo Stracciari's Figaro, not Lorenzo Molajoli's; and for that matter, Beniamino Gigli's Riccardo, not Tullio Serafin's.

Solti was best recognized in the German repertoire; Jussi, for his part, always excelled in Italian opera. Just as Jussi was prepared to bow to the conductor's intentions regarding the performance as a whole, he expected the Maestro to reciprocate the artistic courtesy and listen with an open mind to his ideas about the role. After all, Jussi had sung Riccardo more often in his career than Solti had conducted *Un ballo in maschera* in his.

⋇

Jussi was angry and upset. He had never had an experience like this. Not one to easily take offense, he felt insulted and humiliated by the offhanded treatment. Riccardo was one of his best roles, and after all, he wasn't just any singer, but an opera singer of the first rank. It was not he who said so but the critics, in unanimity, on three continents. While it was of no particular importance to him to sing under Solti, his presence in the cast was of major musical value.

But the record company obviously thought otherwise. As MacNeil observed,

Commercially, Solti was more important to London/Decca than any of the rest of us were. They would cater to him well beyond anything they would do for anybody else, particularly a tenor they had borrowed! I did not expect people to kiss [Jussi's] hand and bow in obeisance to him, but certainly at that point of his career he deserved some consideration and I never saw any evidence of it. Whatever he asked in my presence, they trampled all over [him].[20]

MacNeil's assessment of Jussi's relative importance was correct. Independently, we had reached the same conclusion. It was clear to us that Solti wouldn't change his position and that he enjoyed John Culshaw's unconditional support. If the recording was to take place, it was Jussi who must compromise and that is exactly what he did. "I'll do anything he wants, just so this recording gets done," Jussi said to me. Quite simply, he didn't want anything to go wrong again with *Un ballo in maschera*.

But going along with Solti's interpretation was no longer enough—we were told that he also wanted an apology. Both Ann-Charlotte and I clearly remember that this demand was made, yet Maestro Solti firmly maintains that he never asked for one.[21] Perhaps the apology was Culshaw's idea; he may have wanted to force Jussi to bow to Solti to ensure his cooperation. In any case, Jussi wanted this recording so much, he swallowed his pride: he would agree to the changes Solti wanted *and* would give him an apology.

Our contact person had been John Culshaw, but this time we thought we should try to reach Solti more directly. I wanted to stay with Jussi to help him maintain his equilibrium and control, so Ann-Charlotte was given the delicate assignment of communicating Jussi's concession to the Maestro. "Solti was very unpleasant to me, too," she says. "I think for that reason I was not a very good go-between because I got mad at him also."[22] When Ann-Charlotte delivered Jussi's message, Solti's response was curt and final.

"It's too late." The sessions had been canceled, there would be no recording. In the Maestro's words, "Culshaw and I decided that's enough. We [would] finish, and we [would] get another tenor."[23]

As neither Giulietta Simionato nor Birgit Nilsson had arrived in Rome yet, they had to be notified immediately. Birgit remembers the circumstances quite clearly:

During that time I was rehearsing the *Ring* performances in Bayreuth. The "London team" were very cooperative, and they arranged the recording to fit my Bayreuth rehearsals. They were going to start with those scenes where I had nothing to sing, and they would concentrate on my scenes when I was there so that I could go back to Bayreuth in time for further rehearsals.

I remember so well the last day in Bayreuth before going to Rome. We worked very hard the whole day, and I came home late at night and started to pack for Rome. At 1 o'clock in the morning London Records called and said that the recording was canceled. The man said that Jussi had a fight with the conductor, Georg Solti.

Jussi was tired, and he did not want to rehearse. He felt that he knew the part since he had studied it with Toscanini. After a few rehearsals in that terrible heat, when Solti was constantly interrupting, Jussi finally shouted: "You go home and study your part, I know mine!" Whereupon Solti said "Thank you very much." That was the end. I am sorry I was not in Rome, maybe I could have done something to save the recording. Nevertheless, in producer John Culshaw's book one can read [that after the cancellation] "Nilsson was quick off the mark in wanting money for what had been recorded so far."[24] He also says in the book how drunk Jussi was, which also was not true.[25]

In addition to the artistic and personality conflicts between conductor and tenor, Solti knew that within the allotted schedule he couldn't extract from the orchestra a performance that would meet his high standards. Secretly, he must have longed for the disciplined virtuosi of the Vienna Philharmonic. Still, to be unwilling to compromise in musical matters is one thing; to refuse to consider another person's interpretive views and sacrifice an entire musical endeavor is quite another. One of his singers wrote, "There was about Solti a streak of magnificent selfishness. Nothing else mattered to him except his performances and everything else took second place to them."[26] Nilsson said the same thing in different words: "Sir Georg is a very demanding conductor. I like him very much, but he *must* have it his way. If you are not willing to work under his conditions, you just forget it."[27]

Looking back at this demoralizing experience, I'm sorry that Jussi offered to compromise. His remark to Solti, if indeed it was made, was out of line, but Jussi didn't flare up easily, and if he lost control it was prompted by Solti's rigid refusal to amicably resolve a *bona fide* difference of artistic opinion. Had Solti not turned it into a contest of wills, the situation would never have reached the point it did.

Maestro Solti, in his turn, maintains that when Jussi said to Culshaw, "No, I can't. I'm too tired, I can't work," he never gave the reason he felt unwell. Had he known Jussi was ill, the Maestro added,

At that point I would accept that, and somehow we would make a record. Somehow—whatever! But I thought he is out drinking too much, or he is [being] stubborn, doesn't want to work. That's why I was so very upset. If I had known the truth I would have finished it! I don't know how good or how bad it would have been, but I would have finished it, under any condition. I am not a monster, not a cruel person. I would have said "All right, just do what you can." Björling was a good singer, absolutely, and I liked his singing. When I heard him in Chicago I thought [he was] wonderful. That's the reason why we chose him. I knew he had an alcohol problem, but I didn't know he had a heart condition. Two months later he died, and of course, I was very sorry. Then I realized what had happened; it wasn't that he didn't want to rehearse, *he could not!*[28]

John Culshaw didn't serve his Maestro well. He filtered the facts through his own prejudices, and to placate Solti and reassure him that *he* was in charge, he created the impression that they had on their hands an intoxicated, uncooperative tenor who had to be replaced. After all, Solti was the up-and-coming conductor of the company, and they had nothing to gain by trying to accommodate a tenor on loan. He was dispensable. In the tense atmosphere—and admittedly not helped by Jussi's heart problems—advancing any consideration to the most senior, most experienced, and I dare say most famous and respected artist of the entire team did not occur to any of the participants.

Looking at the photographs taken during these sessions, I have to admit that nobody would've guessed how ill Jussi was. Slimmed down and healthfully tan, he still had his boyish countenance. He didn't complain about the oppressive heat of the hall, just kept his checkered shirt open at the neck and his dime-store Chinese fan going most of the time. He behaved as a real professional, the good trouper that he was.

※

With the sessions halted and the project in pieces, Culshaw laid all the blame on an unbending Björling, at first to his superiors and then in his public writings. He first discussed the incident in a magazine article[29] and later in his posthumously published memoirs, *Putting the Record Straight*. The two narratives partially contradict each other, and they significantly deviate from the truth on crucial points, far too numerous to refute here. The one detail that deserves to be most emphatically discredited relates to Jussi's heavy drinking. Culshaw claimed that when he came to our hotel, Jussi was "sprawled on the bed, along with an empty bottle of whisky and one that was half finished."[30] The fact is that until the recording was canceled, Jussi didn't touch alcohol in Rome. If Ann-Charlotte's and my assertions are insufficient, eyewitnesses Cornell MacNeil, Erik Smith, and even Sir Georg Solti agree that Jussi's comportment showed no signs of intoxication. The surviving photographs of the sessions show him energetic, alert, focused, and openly unhappy. By inventing such a colorful lie, Culshaw only reinforces his culpability.[31]

The whole affair was as terribly sad for every participant as it was for music lovers, for this *Ballo* promised to be a superb recording. Aborting it proved to be a lost opportunity not only for Jussi but for Solti, who would have presided over a potentially historic recording with a brilliant cast and the most suitable interpreter of the role of Riccardo. I cannot help but think that with another team in charge, what happened would never have occurred. Although the drama that unfolded lasted only two days, it left such bitter memories that Ann-Charlotte and I can hardly speak of it even today.

# Chapter 31

# Jussi Död

As we flew home on 15 July 1960, I was hoping against hope that once on Siarö Jussi would calm down and put the Rome episode into perspective. But that didn't happen. More than ever before, he retreated into a world where no one could reach him.

Jussi never got over what happened to him in Rome. It remained with him like a festering sore, darkening his last days. He didn't rage, he didn't condemn Solti, but he found no outlet for his feelings, not even in his beloved fishing, and his drinking took on monumental proportions. We were in despair, totally powerless; it was simply awful. Nothing we could do or say consoled him. "His spirit was broken somehow," says Ann-Charlotte. "Mommy would hide the bottle, and when he'd start demanding it, something would materialize to make him stay. But it wouldn't be enough."[1]

The next time he was about to walk out, Ann-Charlotte begged him not to leave, desperately trying to reason with him, but he was adamant. He stayed away for several days at one of his haunts; as always, none of his "friends" called to let us know that Mr. Björling was with them. The drinking bout ended in the usual round of sickness, hangover, malaise, recovery, and profound remorse.

In spite of all this and his persistent heart trouble, Jussi sang at Gröna Lund on 28 July, and on 5 August he participated, in stupendous voice, in a radio concert, his last, at the Concert Hall in Gothenburg. The concert was taped and later released by RCA Victor. "The *Lohengrin* excerpt is incredible," wrote Alan Rich. "One thinks immediately of a young Melchior, in the ring and purity of Bjoerling's tones. Here is a genuine lyric Wagnerian tenor, not a reconverted baritone. Björling planned to add Lohengrin to his repertory, but did not live to achieve his goal; on this record we have the one foretaste of unrealized glory."[2]

Nils Grevillius conducted the Gothenburg Symphony Orchestra, our dear "Grillet," who had followed Jussi since he first auditioned for Nathanael Broman on the radio. He was like an anchor in Jussi's career, the one fixed point in his musical universe. He was at the helm of the Royal Opera Orchestra at Jussi's very first appearance onstage, he led the orchestra on many of Jussi's 78 rpm and LP recordings, and now, he was the conductor at Jussi's last orchestral concert.

Incidents of arrhythmia—lengthier and more frequent and discomforting—didn't let up during this concert. Grevillius recalled that backstage Jussi suddenly pointed at his chest: "It feels so strange here sometimes—it feels as if my heart were standing still."[3] Björn Forsell, who was in the audience, said, "Jussi, old friend, great to see you! You sounded so good, and how healthy and tan you look!" "Yes," answered Jussi, "that part is fine, but this old pump [pointing to his heart] is a little bad."[4] According to Björn: "We had decided to make a joint appearance in *Otello* on the radio in the fall. It would've been the first step toward Jussi's last coveted role."[5] Gösta Kjellertz, another friend from student days, was also there. To his inevitable "How are you?" Jussi complained once again about his heart, but tentatively agreed to sing some charity concerts with him in September.

After the Gothenburg concert Jussi was hospitalized so that his heart could be regulated under a physician's supervision, and a scheduled charity recital with Hugo Theorell on Ljusterö, this time to raise money to refurbish the kitchen of the community hall, was postponed six days. When it finally took place, on 17 August, the hall couldn't accommodate the crowd, and all the windows and doors were thrown open so the large audience gathered outside could hear him. It was a sunny summer afternoon, and with a "Well, it's a warm day," Jussi took off his jacket, opened his shirt, and sang. Relaxed and happy, he sang a long concert effortlessly. They just wouldn't let him go.[6]

On 20 August Jussi sang on Solliden's stage at Skansen, his 53rd performance there, including three recitals we sang together. It was doubtful to the last minute whether he'd be able to go on, as he'd had a few drinks beforehand and his heart was bothering him, but he did. While he wasn't at his best, more so from chest pains than anything else, I don't think the audience sensed that anything was amiss. As Gösta Berg, the manager of Solliden, proudly stated, "He never deserted us. All contracted concerts were performed as scheduled."[7] This was Jussi's last public appearance. His next concert at Gröna Lund was rained out.

Meanwhile, we received artistic director Robert Herman's confidential list of Jussi's Met performances for the coming season. In addition to six

Des Grieux and four Roldolfos, the schedule included two *Madama Butterfly*s. Jussi didn't care for the role of Pinkerton onstage, and he sent a cable to the Met: "Regret but don't sing *Butterfly*. Regards."[8]

Herman's woeful letter—"I am terribly distressed to have received a cable from you this morning"—followed by return mail. Herman, who couldn't have known anything about Jussi's state of health, much less his state of mind, reminded Jussi of the agreement he'd made at the 20 November 1959 meeting, when the Met consented to an "enormous increase in fee," and Jussi "agreed to include *Butterfly* and *Aida*." The bottom of the letter carried Bing's handwritten message: "Dear Jussi, *please* do these 2 more Butterflies! Kindest regards, Rudolf Bing." The letter, dated 24 August 1960, was sent to Karlavägen 11. Jussi never read it.

When Gösta Kjellertz called on Monday, 5 September, to remind Jussi of the charity concerts, he said, "No Gösta, I can't risk it, I'm not feeling well. My heart is irregular, it's not too good, Gösta. I will be happy to do it some other time."[9]

※

Siarö meant so much to us all. When we were together as a family, in good times and in bad, it was usually there, and to this day "home" for Ann-Charlotte means Siarö, not Stockholm. But it was high time we modernized our summer place and added some comforts that we took for granted in the city; we expected the repairs to keep us busy through mid-September.

I watched as Jussi worked alongside the carpenters. It seemed he had momentarily regained his inner harmony, and after a full day of hammering and sawing, he felt contented. My mind returns often to what he told me that last evening, 8 September 1960, as twilight fell: "This is where we will grow old together."

Just a few hours later, word of Jussi's death came over the radio's morning news. Although I wasn't there to see it, as the sun rose over the deep blue water, Ljusterö's flags were already flying at half-mast.

※

When my initial paralysis passed, I called our neighbor Otto Sjöberg. He didn't answer; I found out later he thought somebody had dialed the wrong number in the middle of the night. I then called Mr. Sundman, another resident on the island who lived a little farther away. "Jussi's very ill. Could you please come over?"

As soon as he saw Jussi, he understood. "It's too late, Mrs. Björling." I could see he was right, but I refused to believe it. At first, I didn't want to call home and say what had happened—if I did, I would've had to admit the truth. But I had to do something. I finally pulled myself together enough to call Ann-Charlotte.

I already started school, so Mother called me at Karlavägen. Her voice was panicked. She said "You have to come and fetch us, because Daddy is very ill." She didn't say that Daddy was dead, she couldn't accept it, but I knew something was terribly wrong.

It would've been difficult to find a physician at that hour, so I called Dr. Sander Itzikowitz, the psychiatrist who lived on the floor below us. He arranged for a car and a helicopter, and I called mother to tell her we were on our way. We arrived in about two hours.

We ran into the house. Daddy seemed asleep, and I couldn't tell just by looking at him that he wasn't alive. I ran up to him and took his hand—it was quite cold. But Mommy refused to understand what had happened. She just blocked it out. Somehow she felt that if she didn't admit it, then it wasn't true.

They removed Daddy with great difficulty on the narrow staircase and lifted him into the helicopter. It had a large bay; Mother, the doctor, and I were on one side, and the body with the medics on the other. Bongo sat by the head of his master. Mommy, still clinging to a miracle, asked the medics to put the oxygen mask on Daddy; I think it was nice of them that they did.

Both Mother and I were totally numb. We didn't cry; it took a long time before the tears came. I remember gazing at father's body. The windows were just above him, and I could see the whole archipelago. As we flew toward Stockholm, the air was clear and the sun was rising higher and higher—this sad day had dawned on the most beautiful September morning![10]

We flew to Bromma Airport, and Jussi's body was taken to the Karolinska Hospital; only there did I finally accept that Jussi was dead. Even if I had wanted to deny it, I could not—it was staring at me from everywhere. Somebody had notified the newspapers, and by the time we left the hospital, kiosks throughout the city were covered with giant posters: "Extra! Jussi Dead This Morning."

Not Royal Court Singer, not Jussi Björling, just Jussi. Everybody's Jussi. Our Jussi. My Jussi.

I hardly recall the hours and days that followed. Not wanting them to learn of the tragedy from the news media, Ann-Charlotte called Anders and Janet, who were vacationing in Dalarna. Now the head of the family, Anders took charge, and helped by his wife, who was expecting again, and Ann-Charlotte, he tried to spare me all burdens. They handled the complex arrangements for the funeral and made provisions for an autopsy, which revealed that it was a miracle Jussi had survived as long as he did: his enlarged heart had been ravaged by the heart attacks. The official cause of death was *functio laesa cordis. Morbus arterioscleroticus cordis.*[11] The one consoling thought in this great sorrow was that Jussi had died peacefully, in his sleep. God granted him the greatest mercy.

Lasse was working in a bank in Paris, and Ann-Charlotte notified him by phone. "My father was sad that I was leaving that summer; he must've had some premonition. I will never forget the day when I was sitting in the office working, and the call came from Stockholm. My sister was on the phone, and she said, 'Father is dead.' It was as if someone had turned off the lights. I didn't expect it; none of us did, it was a complete shock."[12] Anders contacted Rolf in Chicago; he arrived in time for the funeral.

Flags at the Royal Opera House flew at half mast. From the summer palace near Hälsingborg, King Gustaf VI Adolf expressed his deep sorrow. Every Stockholm newspaper—and every major publication around the world, I've been told—carried a notice of Jussi's death. His obituary in *The New York Times* (10 September 1960) was the first of several articles about him; it quoted Rudolf Bing, who'd heard the news in Paris, as graciously saying of Jussi, "He was one of the great tenors of our time. We were proud that he sang for some 25 years at the Metropolitan, and that is where he really built his career."

Newspapers worldwide carried the Associated Press' report of Jussi's funeral, which was broadcast by radio and television.[13] Services were held on 19 September 1960, in Engelbrekt's Church, a block away from our home on Karlavägen; Pastor Norrby, our close friend, officiated. "The Opera was making a guest appearance in London when the sad news came," wrote Sture Ingebretzen. "Thus we from the Opera Chorus weren't given the chance to sing at the funeral. Otherwise, it would've been our right, our way to say 'thank you' for all the times we were able to accompany him in so many operas."[14]

I have no clear recollection how I got through it, but photographs show me at the head of the funeral procession on the arm of Pastor Norrby. Lasse and Ann-Charlotte followed, then came Anders and Janet, and my mother with Rolf. Jussi's old friends Sigurd Björling, Conny Söderström, Einar Larson, and Erik Sundquist served as honor guard at the coffin. More than 1200 people filled the church, and a throng gathered outside. Pastor Norrby's moving eulogy to "a divinely gifted singer" was punctuated by stifled sobs from the congregation.

The following day, Jussi's remains were interred in the Stora Tuna churchyard, his headstone, a plain granite slab with his name and dates, just a few paces away from his brother Gösta's. Jussi was a great artist but a simple man, and as he avoided all ostentation in life, we felt that he would have wished for dignified simplicity in death.

In the summer of 1989, Anders and his family drove to the cemetery in a driving rainstorm. They almost turned back, but it was the last day of their stay in Sweden and they wanted to pay their respects at the family graves. The familiar steeple came into sight, they pulled up in front of the gate—and the rain stopped. In a grey mist, they visited the gravesites of the grandparents, great-grandparents, Kalle and Gösta, but as they approached Jussi's grave, the clouds parted and through a widening swath of blue sky, the brilliant arch of a rainbow appeared on the horizon. At the focal point of the radiant illumination stood the simple granite headstone with angular Dalecarlian red letters in the style of Nordic runes—*Jussi Björling*. "Dad rests in peace," said Anders.

A week after Jussi's death, Harold C. Schonberg described his voice as "the greatest lyric instrument since Gigli's."[15] Dorothy Kirsten wrote, "I felt a great loss when I received the shocking news of his death. He was much too young and still had so much to give. In my career, I have sung with most of the great tenors, but Jussi will always be very special."[16] A couple of weeks after the funeral, a personal note from our dear friend Licia Albanese appeared in *The New York Times* (2 October 1960).

> With Jussi Bjoerling's death, the world of music has lost a great voice, and I a great friend. We sang together for 19 years, beginning with a *La bohème* at the Met in 1941. A more considerate colleague would be impossible to find. He was always charming and helpful and never lost his sense of humor. I don't know of anyone who brought more sunshine into a room than he did, and every time he came into my home with his wife for luncheon or dinner, he told his wonderful stories and always ended by singing to us Swedish and Neapolitan songs that he sang from the heart. He knew the styles of Gounod, Verdi and Puccini inside out, and the tenderness with which he imbued his roles will haunt me always.

The memory of Jussi Björling, tenor and colleague, remains incandescent for many. Birgit Nilsson said, "I feel that he very much continues to live among us. No other singer who has been gone so long is heard so often on the radio. He was really a national saint and a national hero, the like of which we shall not experience again."[17] Johannes Norrby, director of the Stockholm Concert Hall, summed up the sentiments of many when he said, "I willingly admit that when I heard Jussi and when I hear him now on record, I am so affected, touched, and moved that I get tears in my eyes. This is because he lives not only in our mind's ear but in our hearts. That is where he will live, now and for all time—the Swedish Jussi."[18]

# *Postlude*

The whole family was in a state of shock, unable and unwilling to believe that this sudden tragedy had actually occurred. Our lives revolved around Jussi, and my life was his. Without him I didn't know what to do. It was like walking on ice—one tries to keep one's balance and remain upright. Family and friends called and visited often, but one person deserves special mention for her determination to help me through the darkest days of my bereavement: Marguerite Wenner-Gren, one of the few close friends who knew all about Jussi's alcoholic excesses and my efforts to hold the man, the family, the career, and our marriage together. I'll never forget her compassionate understanding, her many private, thoughtful gestures, and especially the public tribute she paid me when she wrote, "Jussi's death has brought Anna-Lisa and us even closer together. If all Jussi's admirers in the world knew what she meant to him, his name would never be mentioned without hers."[1]

Time passed, and in 1961, just as I was beginning to regain my equilibrium, I faced the death of my mother, my friend and my inexhaustible source of strength in moments of crisis. Losing her was almost too much to bear; I was inconsolable and could only reason that she had had a long life and did not die in her prime like Jussi. But curiously, this double loss strengthened me. Losing the love, companionship, and protection of Jussi and the gentle, caring, affectionate support of my mother forced me to realize that I was on my own. I couldn't spend the rest of my days pitying myself.

Soon after I received unexpected help from Pastor Norrby, who called on me from time to time. His visits were always a comfort, but on one particular occasion he made an unusual proposition: "You should start singing again, Anna-Lisa, it'd be good for you." I was only 51, and my voice was still intact, so when he pointedly invited me to sing the soprano role in Handel's *Messiah* at his church, I considered and agreed. It was hard work at first, but Tore was right: singing again was like stepping over a threshold. I began to sing regularly in the choir at Gustaf Vasa Church, which forced me to keep a schedule. No longer could I lie in bed all day, feeling sorry for myself. What solace music can bring; with it, one forgets for the moment all that weighs one down. Music, which had brought Jussi and me together, continued to exercise its healing power when he was no longer with me. I never recovered from my loss, but music helped me to carry on without him.

Jussi was featured so much on the radio, it was inevitable I'd hear him that way, but it took some time before I could actually play his records again. It was our sons who urged me to listen to their father's voice—"You mustn't hide from it!"—and I'm glad they did. I had to go far away in the apartment, where I'd hear the voice very softly, at a distance. At first I was unable to control my tears. Hearing his silvery voice, the one I had listened to and sung with so often, I expected him to be there, to be able to touch him. I closed my eyes—and felt that if I opened them, I would see his smiling face again. It was agony.

Soon I listened to the records on my own, appreciating the soothing warmth of that singular voice and its ability to bring closure to an emotional wound. These sessions became a very private ritual, a musical communion. It was like spending a little time with Jussi, as if he could still speak to me through his records. His voice was no longer disturbing; rather, it brought me comfort and peace.

Throughout these reminiscences, I felt it wasn't my place to praise Jussi or draw comparisons between him and other tenors. These things were better left to the critics and his colleagues; through their words, favorable or not, I hoped to show how he was regarded from his debut to his death. However, I think I can make some objective observations about the physical attributes of the voice without the cloud of personal bias.

The purity of his voice was as remarkable as its range; even more impressive, it was perfectly equalized. While the entire range and timbre of Jussi's voice was that of a tenor, his lower notes were strong and secure, an unbroken extension of his upper octave. A single note, regardless of pitch or volume, could be identified as a note *from the same scale*, whereas the top or low notes of some singers sound as if they've been grafted onto the midrange and are often of a different texture. Jussi was fortunate in this regard: nature gave him and his technique made him, physically, a one-of-a-kind musical instrument, like a violin. He could do with his voice as he pleased, following the composer's demands or his own conception of how the music should be sung. He could execute Almaviva's coloratura and Radamès' outbursts, deliver Manrico's stretta and Riccardo's barcarola, and sing Rodolfo's or Faust's cavatina or Rossini's "Cujus animam" as written. He was equal to all the dynamic and technical demands of the music in his repertoire.

※

Jussi's recording career spanned 40 years. He grew up with the medium as possibly the only artist who made both acoustic and electric 78 rpm records, *and* monophonic and stereophonic LPs. In this respect too he was fortunate; his voice and his artistic development are well preserved. His recorded legacy is the monument of a life spent in the service of music, and the public's appreciation of Jussi's art remains undiminished. His recordings never left the catalogs; the 78 rpm records have been repeatedly reissued and his LPs have migrated to CDs. And thanks to the widespread use of off-the-air recording devices, a truly amazing number of his live performances, both concerts and opera broadcasts, were captured and continue to surface. A large number of these have been released, many of them on the Bluebell label.[2]

And so Jussi is being rediscovered by successive generations of opera lovers, and the life's work of the "cold" tenor who couldn't act is undergoing a reassessment. The prevailing view is best summed up by critic Alan Blyth, who in his review of a recent CD release of half a dozen of Jussi's performances wrote, "It would be hard to deny, that this set [*Roméo et Juliette*] enshrines some of the most glorious tenor singing ever heard. Indeed, after listening to six sets devoted to the great Swede you might have difficulty denying that he is, taking everything into account, the greatest tenor of the century."[3]

One hopes that eventually all Björling recordings in the vaults of record companies and in private hands will be shared with those who heard him in person and those who wish they did. As for myself, I am delighted to experience anew Jussi's peculiar talent for creating an aural landscape for the mind in long-forgotten recitals and opera performances. In them, Jussi's voice rings forth with unequalled brilliance, reinforcing his reputation and attesting once again that he never gave a substandard performance.

"Stylistically Björling was in a class of his own among the tenors of three decades," wrote John Steane.[4] As Regina Resnik put it,

> The purity of the tone, the clarity was always there. I heard differences in performances in quantity of sound, but never in quality! Never! He had something extremely personal in the *passaggio* that no other tenor had. There came a change in the sound of his voice when it switched from the *passaggio*. When he put on volume, there was a throb in his voice. It changed into a quality where I thought that he seemed to manufacture

more space in his head. I never heard that from anybody, except Caruso. This, of course, is "the mystery." It is more than a gift. It is undefinable![5]

Jussi died before his time by any standard, popular or actuarial, but because of the peculiarities of his life one cannot speak of a short career. He began performing before he was five years old, and even if we date his career from the beginning of the American tour in 1919, he sang through 41 of his 49 years. A 30-year operatic career without a discernible diminution of powers is by no means the rule in any epoch; regrettably, it is becoming the exception in ours.

※

Jussi had 55 roles in his repertoire in addition to oratorio parts. A handful of these were small roles, the rest he gradually winnowed down to about a dozen. He was so successful in those parts that audiences—and in response to their demand, impresari—wanted him to sing only those. At times people would remark it was a pity that Jussi stopped singing Roméo. He did not; he was no longer asked to do it because *Roméo et Juliette* dropped out of the repertoire. When Sayão, the last great Juliette of Jussi's generation, stopped singing the role, there was no one to take her place.

When he was young, Jussi sang anything and everything he was assigned; experience later showed him which roles suited him best, and he stuck with those. He was especially successful with two French roles, Gounod's Faust and Roméo, and excelled in Verdi and Puccini. In later years he may have grown somewhat indifferent to learning new parts, but it didn't stem from laziness. To learn major roles required more time and uninterrupted concentration than he was able—and willing—to devote to it, and he was disinclined to just step into a routine performance and perform an important new role "cold." Although Andrea Chénier and Don José are both meaty enough roles to require long study, Jussi wouldn't be given the necessary rehearsal time to get inside them unless they were to be a part of a new production.

Some roles he was offered were not alluring enough to be worth the effort in terms of artistic satisfaction or frequency of performances. Fenton in *Falstaff* and the single performance of *Il pirata* fell in this category, even if the former was to be with Toscanini and the latter opposite Maria Callas. But when he felt challenged, he rose to the occasion, as when in 1949 he added Puccini's Des Grieux and in 1950 the title role for the Met's new *Don Carlo*. Nine years later he enthusiastically learned Calaf for the pleasure of recording it with Nilsson and Tebaldi, and without any concrete plans to perform it onstage.

Jussi's death put an end to a number of projects that were planned for the year ahead. He signed a contract on 26 October 1959 for a stereo remake of *La bohème* with Victoria de los Angeles and Sir Thomas Beecham. The contract specified that it would be recorded between 1 April and 31 October

1960, but scheduling problems forced the sessions to be postponed until 1961. As David Bicknell wrote to Jussi on 18 July 1960, "It is regrettable that so much time was wasted this year in wrangling with RCA Victor as to whether you were or were not free to do this work. As your contract with them runs out early next year, I hope we can now definitely fix the dates for 1961."

What would've been Jussi's first complete opera in French, a *Roméo et Juliette*, also with de los Angeles and Beecham, was discussed repeatedly. Alan Kayes wrote to me on 16 April 1959: "Beecham is making some difficulties about the recording of *Romeo and Juliet*." He added that in case the recording didn't go forward, Jussi had suggested doing a highlights record with me in Sweden.

Another project that fell victim to scheduling was a duet record with Elisabeth Schwarzkopf. If I'm not mistaken, it was as much a matter of finding a mutually convenient time as working out the contractual arrangements between RCA and EMI/Angel Records. The times that were tentatively set for the recording couldn't be met, and the opportunity to record with Elisabeth Schwarzkopf passed, never to be recaptured. It is most unfortunate, because most of the chosen selections would have presented both artists outside their standard repertoire, such as the first- and fourth-act duets from *La bohème*, "Lontano, lontano" from *Mefistofele*, "Parle-moi de ma mère" from *Carmen*, "Già nella notte densa" from *Otello*, "Der Lenz ist gekommen" from *Marta*, the Cherry Duet from *L'amico Fritz*, and last but by no means least, the love duet from *Madama Butterfly*. In addition, in 1959 and 1960, Jussi began to be interested in Walther von Stolzing, too. It is a great loss that he didn't record or sing in concert some of Walther's music, at least the Prize Song.

Most of all, time did not allow Jussi to fulfill his twin dreams of recording *Otello* and *Lohengrin*. Whether or not Jussi's vocal stamina could have sustained these roles in a performance, we are the poorer for him not having recorded them. What held him back with the first was his artistic judgment: he wanted to let the natural aging process ripen his voice to the proper weight, to let his timbre darken and the silver sheen take on a layer of burnished gold. Once, questioned on the subject of future recordings, Jussi singled out *Otello*, stressing: "Recording, I say, recording. I am not that spinto, you know!"[6] His 1951 recording of "Sì, pel ciel," the role's most dramatic part, left no doubt about his ability to do justice to Otello's music, at least on record.

Regarding Lohengrin, time and again he mentioned that he expected to sing the role. The last such statement he made to Arthur Jacobs in May 1960.[7] His concert recordings of the Gralserzählung show his suitability for the role—the color, the Nordic purity of his voice would have given the silver knight an aural dimension few other impersonators possessed. Of the 5 August 1960 Gothenburg concert under Nils Grevillius, Howard Klein wrote, "The *Lohengrin* excerpt nevertheless teases the imagination, for his

Lohengrin probably would have been one of unparalleled sensitivity and nuance."[8]

Taking on these roles was never a question of endurance. Jussi sang Turiddu and Canio in the same evening on several occasions; while neither role is excessively taxing by itself, the two added together in one evening separates the merely competent vocalist from the accomplished professional. The sum total of seven verismo arias and an extended duet are demanding and comparable to Otello's three arias and three duets. The formidable "Esultate" would have shown the brilliance of Jussi's voice, and for once, I would have cheered him on to give "more Caruso." *Lohengrin* was a different matter. The title role encompasses long stretches of singing, and poor Lohengrin has nearly as much music to sing in the third act alone as the entire tenor role of some Italian operas.

With the cancellation of *Un ballo in maschera*, Jussi's last complete recording became, quite fittingly, Verdi's Requiem. The set was released posthumously, within a month after he died. It was as if he had sung at his own funeral.

※

No matter how long Jussi has been dead, it seems that he never really left us. We are surrounded by his portraits, the piano he used, the objects he touched, and the photographs inscribed to him by composers, artists, and public personages. Friends and relatives talk about him, professional people call, fans write. After Jussi's death, we received mail from all over the world. Although the pieces diminished in number and frequency as the years passed, even now, more than three decades later, my children and I continue to receive letters, inquiries, even mementos. They show what Jussi meant to so many, as a singer and as a person. In 1971, Gustavus Adolphus College named its new concert hall after Jussi; Robert Merrill sang the dedication recital. The Jussi Björling Museum in Borlänge (established in 1994) and the publications of the Swedish Jussi Björling Society and the Society in London keep his memory alive.

I feel privileged and grateful to have been able to stand beside Jussi and share the whole of his life, not just the happy and successful times, but those moments too when he so desperately needed my love and support. During the years since Jussi died I've often asked myself: Did I do enough? Did I really understand him? Was I overprotective in my zeal to bring about a secure environment for him? I will never know the answers. I'm certain of only one thing: I devoted my life to him—as a wife, a helpmate, the other half of a team—and the love between Jussi and me was so strong that it overcame all our difficulties.

After Jussi died, I was stunned to find in his wallet several of the little notes I tucked in his luggage when he traveled without me. I never realized they meant so much to him. As I reread them, I was moved not so much by the profound love I had tried to express in my simple words, but by the discovery that he had kept my words with him. "I cannot live without you, my sweetheart. Kiss, Mama," reads one note, and another: "Sleep well my dear one, and welcome home again. Hug and—" the lipstick mark of a kiss. Jussi carried with him for 16 years even the brief message that accompanied a photo I'd sent him of him and Ann-Charlotte when our daughter was still a baby. "Hi Little Darling! Isn't our little angel pretty, but then you do look proud. I think of you all the time. Kiss and hug, your Anna-Lisa." The note was dated 20 November 1944.

I am comforted by the thought that Jussi saw his children grow up. What is most painful for me is that he didn't live to see our delightful grandchildren and they never knew their grandfather. Their loss is immense, greater than they could ever comprehend. But Jussi is with me today and every day, in my heart. He has always been there and will always be there.

# NOTES

*Da Fine al Capo*

1. In Swedish the suffix *ö* or *ön* denotes an island. Thus "Siarö" means "Siar Island."
2. Telephone conversation between Ann-Charlotte Björling and Andrew Farkas, 21 July 1995.

CHAPTER 1

1. Letter from Adelina Patti to her brother-in-law Gustaf Cederström, 16 September 1910. Italics hers. Courtesy John F. Cone.

CHAPTER 2

1. J. Björling 1945, 5.
2. Conversation between Märta Björling-Kärn, Don Goldberg, Harald Henrysson, and Bertil Bengtsson, 17 June 1992, Mora, Sweden.
3. The most common transliteration of the great Russian basso's name. *Andrew Farkas*
4. Märta Björling-Kärn heard an elderly lady speak on a radio program about David, who had worked in her home in New York as a male orderly.
5. According to family lore, Enrico Caruso was present when David auditioned for the Opera School. Impressed by what he heard, he offered to give David lessons

362

and correct the defects of his unschooled voice. After some time, the lessons, for unspecified reasons, abruptly ended. While a personal encounter with Caruso was chronologically possible and the tenor making some helpful hints on a visit to the Opera School probable, Caruso taking on a student is neither. He'd just made his Metropolitan Opera debut and teaching was the last thing on his mind. This must be regarded for what it is: Björling family legend.

6. J. Björling 1945, 7.
7. Conversation between Märta Björling-Kärn and Andrew Farkas, 19 August 1993, Mora, Sweden.
8. Photocopies of the midwife's engagement book and birth register are in the Jussi Björling Museum in Borlänge.
9. Unidentified clipping, courtesy Harald Henrysson.
10. Unidentified clipping.
11. Conversation between Märta Björling-Kärn and Andrew Farkas, 19 August 1993, Mora, Sweden.
12. J. Björling 1945, 5. A marble plaque affixed to the wall commemorates the architect of the church, and concludes with the statement that the brothers Jussi, Gösta, and Olle Björling appeared there in public for the first time. Information courtesy Enrique Gilardoni.
13. This report was copied by Gunnar Boman, head physician at the Lung Clinic, University Hospital, Uppsala, at the request of Lennart Ekman. The authors thank them for making this document available.
14. Conversation between Märta Björling-Kärn and Andrew Farkas, 19 August 1993, Mora, Sweden.
15. Conversation between Ann-Charlotte Björling and Andrew Farkas, August 1993, Stockholm.
16. In 1957, Märta was awakened by a vivid dream: Gösta was embracing her with his arms around her neck, just as he used to do when he was a little boy. It was as if Gösta were taking a last farewell; a few hours later he died of a stroke.
17. Conversation between Märta Björling-Kärn, Don Goldberg, Harald Henrysson, and Bertil Bengtsson, 17 June 1992, Mora, Sweden.
18. Unidentified clipping.
19. According to Märta Björling-Kärn, Jussi combined two incidents from his childhood. David and Olle did go to the Metropolitan to hear Caruso, and the two smaller boys stayed at the hotel. The two tickets cost $11, a small fortune in those days. A few years later, when they were on a tour in Copenhagen, they passed a cinema on their way to the hotel. A Western was playing, and the boys begged their father to let them see it. David asked a hotel porter to take them to the movies.
20. Hagman, 49–50.
21. Henrysson 1993, 159–160.
22. J. Björling 1945, 8.
23. *Willmar Tribune*, 4 August 1920.
24. David Björling's booklet was reprinted and published by Eriks Förlaget in 1978 from a surviving copy in the collection of the late Rolf Björling.
25. J. Björling 1945, 9.
26. Ibid., 30.
27. Ibid., 8.
28. A.-L. Björling, 81–82.

29. J. Björling 1945, 9.
30. Ibid.
31. Ibid., 13–14.
32. Ibid., 16.
33. Ibid., 17.

CHAPTER 3

1. J. Björling 1945, 18–19.
2. Ibid., 20.
3. Hagman, 117.
4. J. Björling 1945, 21.
5. Ibid.
6. Hagman, 52.
7. Ibid.
8. Ibid., 53.
9. J. Björling 1945, 22.
10. Henrysson 1993, 16.
11. Hagman, 79.
12. Quoting this passage in his autobiography, Jussi couldn't help remarking parenthetically, "I think Aunt Julia remembers incorrectly: I was really always very particular about my appearance, because Papa often called me 'Beautiful Jonathan.'" J. Björling 1945, 28.
13. Svedelius, 245–246.
14. Courtesy Royal Theater Archives, Stockholm.
15. Svedelius, 248–251.
16. Courtesy Royal Theater Archives, Stockholm.
17. J. Björling 1945, 42.
18. Ibid., 37.
19. Ibid., 38.
20. Ibid., 41.
21. *The Björling Saga*, televised documentary.
22. Hagman, 61.
23. J. Björling 1945, 45.
24. Hagman, 98–99.
25. *The Björling Saga*, televised documentary.
26. J. Björling 1945, 45
27. Ibid., 47.
28. Ibid., 131.
29. Ibid., 25–27.
30. Ibid., 52.
31. Ibid., 55.
32. Ibid., 52.
33. *Svenska Dagbladet*, 21 August 1930.
34. J. Björling 1945, 83.
35. According to reports, Adolphe Nourrit, like all his contemporaries, sang the high notes as head tones. It was his younger colleague, Gilbert Duprez, who introduced the *ut de poitrine*, the high C from the chest.

CHAPTER 4

1. Svedelius, 252.
2. J. Björling 1945, 111.
3. Quoted in the sleeve notes of *The Art of Jussi Björling* (EMI, RLS 715).
4. J. Björling 1945, 49.
5. *Aftonbladet*, 30 September 1931.
6. Hagman, 84.
7. *The Björling Saga*, televised documentary.
8. *Svenska Dagbladet*, 9 November 1931.
9. *Dagens Nyheter*, 26 February 1932.
10. *Aftonbladet*, 26 February 1932.
11. *Svenska Dagbladet*, 26 February 1932.
12. Set Svanholm quotes the same punchline in Hagman, 77.
13. *The Björling Saga*, televised documentary.
14. J. Björling 1945, 48.
15. *The Björling Saga*, televised documentary.
16. *Stockholms-Tidningen*, 23 August 1933.
17. *Svenska Dagbladet*, 23 August 1933.
18. Hagman, 66.
19. J. Björling 1945, 48.
20. *Svenska Dagbladet*, 20 October 1933.
21. Hagman, 175–176.
22. Ibid., 111–112.
23. *The Björling Saga*, televised documentary.
24. J. Björling 1945, 127.
25. Conversation between Marit Gruson and Andrew Farkas, 8 December 1992, New York City.
26. *Svenska Dagbladet*, 27 August 1934.
27. *Arbetaren*, 26 August 1934.
28. *Dagens Nyheter*, 14 October 1934.
29. *Svenska Dagbladet*, 14 October 1934.

CHAPTER 5

1. Cook, 7; also J. Björling 1945, 48.
2. J. Björling 1945, 93.
3. *Stockholms-Tidningen*, 18 August 1935.
4. *Nya Dagligt Allehanda*, 18 August 1935.
5. Hagman, 31.
6. *Stockholms-Tidningen*, 18 September 1935.
7. *Aftonbladet*, 18 September 1935.
8. *Dagens Nyheter*, 13 October 1935.
9. *Svenska Dagbladet*, 13 October 1935.
10. In the vast storehouse of Chaliapin anecdotes concerning his eccentricities and demands regarding costuming and staging, not one indicates that his seemingly capricious demands were self-serving. He insisted on changes, rearranged sets and props, conducted conductors, cursed and sulked, but with only one artistic end in mind: to improve the quality of the performance. *Andrew Farkas*

11. Lauri-Volpi, 205. In the 1920s at the Metropolitan, in addition to Lauri-Volpi himself, Chaliapin's Fausts were Giovanni Martinelli, Mario Chamlee, and Armand Tokatyan. The reader is invited to choose which of the three was the "blooming idiot." *Andrew Farkas*
12. Conversation between Märta Björling-Kärn and Andrew Farkas, 19 August 1993, Mora, Sweden.

CHAPTER 6

1. Unidentified clipping, 15 March 1936.
2. J. Björling 1945, 77.
3. Ibid.
4. *Szinházi Élet*, no. 11 (1937): 32.
5. *Stockholms-Tidningen*, 27 September 1936. Actually, the aria has nine Cs.
6. Hagman, 31.
7. Ibid., 97.
8. Wagner, 365.
9. Ibid.
10. Hagman, 123.
11. *Dresdner Anzeiger*, 10 February 1937.
12. *Dresdner Neueste Nachrichten*, 10 February 1937.
13. Clipping from an unidentified Dresden newspaper, 12 February 1937.
14. *Neues Wiener Journal*, 15 February 1937.
15. *Neues Wiener Journal*, 18 February 1937.
16. Ibid.
17. *Neues Wiener Journal*, 26 February 1937.
18. Incident related by Otniel Sobek to Enrique Gilardoni, 30 September 1970, Buenos Aires; information courtesy Enrique Gilardoni. Verdi composed the stretta without *any* high Cs; it was allegedly Enrico Tamberlick who introduced it in the mid-19th century with Verdi's tacit approval.
19. *Neues Wiener Journal*, 6 March 1937.
20. Unidentified clipping.
21. *Neues Wiener Journal*, 18 March 1937.
22. Incident related by Otniel Sobek to Enrique Gilardoni, 30 September 1970, Buenos Aires. Information courtesy Enrique Gilardoni.
23. *Pesti Hirlap*, 28 February 1937.
24. *Pester Lloyd*, 28 February 1937.
25. *Ujság*, 10 March 1937.
26. Having listened to nearly all Björling's commercial and private recordings, I found only two mispronunciations in his postwar output. In the stretta from *Il trovatore* he would sometimes sing "corro a salvar*mi*" instead of "salvar*ti*," and in "Parmi veder" in *Rigoletto* he would sing "a*g*neli" for "a*n*geli." Others may turn up a couple more instances, but on the whole, as many critics observed, Björling's diction and pronunciation in seven languages were correct. *Andrew Farkas*
27. Hagman, 78.
28. Bertil Bokstedt, program notes to "Jussi Björling Memorial Concert," 9 September 1985. After Jussi's death, Maestro Bokstedt became manager of the Royal Opera.

29. Letter from Hugo Alfvén to Jussi Björling, 11 June 1957.
30. For a detailed narrative of the plot, see Henrysson 1993, 178–179.
31. Jussi's version of the aria with the middle B can be heard in the live recording of the performance in New Orleans on 22 April 1950, and in the film *Fram för framgång*. Nearly all other tenors take a higher option. *Andrew Farkas*
32. Hagman, 34–35.
33. Ibid., 67.
34. Hugo Hasslo, program notes to "Jussi Björling Memorial Concert," 9 September 1985.
35. Douglas, 11.
36. Letter from Birgit Nilsson to Andrew Farkas, 2 February 1993.
37. Metropolitan Opera, 31 March 1956.
38. Telephone conversation between William Seward and Andrew Farkas, 3 February 1992.
39. Hagman, 65.

CHAPTER 7

1. Hagman, 35.
2. Britons had first heard him over the airwaves in a live broadcast of Act II of Kurt Atterberg's opera *Fanal* on 2 April 1937. It was a concert performance broadcast by the BBC from the Royal Opera in Stockholm in the presence of the composer.
3. *Daily Mail*, 16 November 1937.
4. *Daily Mail*, 17 November 1937.
5. Newton 1966, 199–201.
6. *New York World Telegram and Sun*, undated clipping.
7. Unidentified clipping, 1 December 1937.
8. Information courtesy James A. Drake.
9. Unidentified clipping, 29 November 1937.
10. Unidentified clipping.
11. *Chicago Herald and Examiner*, 9 December 1937.
12. *Chicago Times*, 9 December 1937.
13. *Chicago Daily News*, 9 December 1937.
14. *Chicago Tribune*, 14 December 1937.
15. Ibid.
16. *Chicago Tribune*, 16 December 1937.
17. *Chicago Daily News*, 16 December 1937.
18. *Chicago Tribune*, 16 December 1937.
19. J. Björling 1945, 153.
20. Wagner, 366.
21. *New York World Telegram*, 5 January 1938.
22. J. Björling 1945, 78.
23. Ibid., 152.
24. Interview of Jussi Björling by Alan Wagner for WNYC, 2 December 1958 (first broadcast 14 December), Essex House, New York City.
25. *New York Herald Tribune*, 25 November 1938.
26. *The New York Times*, 25 November 1938.
27. *Szinházi Élet*, no. 11 (1937): 32.

28. Conversation between Robert Merrill and Andrew Farkas, 16 March 1992, New Rochelle, N.Y.
29. J. Björling 1945, 149.
30. *Chicago Tribune*, 28 November 1938.
31. *Chicago Herald and Examiner*, 29 November 1938.
32. Conversation between Robert Merrill and Andrew Farkas, 16 March 1992, New Rochelle, N.Y.
33. *Chicago Daily News*, 28 November 1938.
34. *New York World Telegram*, 18 January 1939.

CHAPTER 8

1. Letter from Vittorio Gui to Sir David Webster, 27 February 1939, from Budapest. Courtesy Royal Opera House, Covent Garden Archives.
2. Hagman, 85.
3. J. Björling 1945, 79.
4. Ibid., 80.
5. Conversation between Robert Merrill and Andrew Farkas, 16 March 1992, New Rochelle, N.Y.
6. Taped reminiscences prepared by Cornell MacNeil for Andrew Farkas, 18 October 1992, Denver.
7. Douglas, 11.
8. Several artists interviewed for this book confirmed this, among them Hugo Hasslo, Sture Ingebretzen, Cornell MacNeil, Robert Merrill, Kerstin Meyer, Regina Resnik, Elisabeth Söderström, and Giuseppe Valdengo. *Andrew Farkas*

CHAPTER 9

1. J. Björling 1945, 73.
2. Ibid., 75.
3. Kesting 1986, 1606.
4. *New York Herald Tribune*, 29 December 1939.
5. Ibid.
6. J. Björling 1945, 162.
7. *Evening Public Ledger*, 3 January 1940.
8. Unidentified clipping, 3 January 1940.
9. *Philadelphia Record*, 3 January 1940.
10. Letter from Jarmila Novotná to Andrew Farkas, 26 February 1993.
11. J. Björling 1945, 162.
12. *Chicago Times*, 22 January 1940.
13. *The Björling Saga*, televised documentary.
14. *New York Herald Tribune*, 3 February 1940.
15. *New York World Telegram*, 3 February 1940.
16. *New York Sun*, 3 February 1940.
17. Interview of Jan Peerce by James A. Drake, 1974. Courtesy James A. Drake.
18. Information courtesy John Gualiani, who saw a copy of the program listing Björling among the visiting guest artists.
19. Hagman, 140.
20. Ibid., 141.

21. Telephone conversation between Igor Kipnis and Andrew Farkas, 9 October 1994.
22. *San Francisco Chronicle*, 19 October 1940.
23. *San Francisco Chronicle*, 24 October 1940.
24. Conversation between Lorenzo Alvary and Andrew Farkas, 6 December 1992, New York City.
25. J. Björling 1945, 165.
26. *Keynote* (January 1982): 38.
27. *Philadelphia Inquirer*, 18 December 1940.
28. Jussi told this story many times, including in an interview given to Bo Teddy Ladberg in Stockholm, 30 October 1959.
29. Courtesy Metropolitan Opera Archives.
30. Ibid.
31. J. Björling 1945, 74–75.
32. Conversation between Nell Rankin and Andrew Farkas, 29 April 1993, New York City.
33. Ibid.
34. *The New York Times*, 1 February 1941.
35. Unidentified clipping, 1 February 1941.
36. J. Björling 1945, 166–167.
37. Hagman, 139–140.

CHAPTER 10

1. Courtesy Metropolitan Opera Archives.
2. *The New York Times*, 3 September 1941.
3. Courtesy Metropolitan Opera Archives.
4. Conversation between Sixten Ehrling and Andrew Farkas, 28 April 1993, New York City.
5. From an undated publicity sheet.
6. G. Björling, 121.
7. Conversation between Lorenzo Alvary and Andrew Farkas, 6 December 1992, New York City.
8. Conversation between Sixten Ehrling and Andrew Farkas, 28 April 1993, New York City.
9. Telephone conversation between Sixten Ehrling and Andrew Farkas, 29 November 1992, confirmed in a conversation on 28 April 1993, New York City.
10. Losonczy was Jussi's partner in all his operatic appearances in Budapest, in 1937 and 1942.
11. *Pester Lloyd*, 24 November 1942.
12. *Szinházi Magazin*, no. 49 (1942): 8.
13. *Pesti Hirlap*, 29 November 1942.
14. *Pester Lloyd*, 28 November 1942.

CHAPTER 11

1. Hagman, 129.
2. Conversation between Märta Björling-Kärn and Andrew Farkas, 21 August 1993, Mora, Sweden. Harry Ebert tells the same story in Hagman, 142.

3. J. Björling 1945, 96.
4. Hagman, 86.
5. Ibid., 163.
6. A.-L. Björling, 176.
7. J. Björling 1945, 91–92.
8. Hagman, 102.

CHAPTER 12

1. Hagman, 170.
2. Statement dictated by Dorothy Kirsten to her secretary, Vicki Hillebrand, in 1991, and transmitted to Andrew Farkas.
3. Letter from John Gualiani to Andrew Farkas, 9 March 1992.
4. *Los Angeles Times*, 10 November 1945.
5. *Los Angeles Examiner*, 10 November 1945.
6. *Opera News* (26 February 1972): 30.
7. Ibid.
8. Grace Moore made four films: *New Moon*, 1931, with Lawrence Tibbett, *Love Me Forever*, *One Night of Love*, and an abridged version of Charpentier's *Louise* with Georges Thill under the composer's supervision.
9. Conversation between Robert Merrill and Andrew Farkas, 16 March 1992, New Rochelle, N.Y.
10. Merrill, 169.
11. Conversation between Regina Resnik and Andrew Farkas, 8 December 1992, New York City.
12. *Quebec Chronicle-Telegraph*, 16 January 1946.
13. *The Evening-Telegram*, 18 January 1946.

CHAPTER 13

1. *Montreal Daily Star*, 10 May 1946.
2. Letter from John Gualiani to Andrew Farkas, 9 March 1992.
3. *Chicago Tribune*, 6 October 1946.
4. *Chicago Tribune*, 8 October 1946.
5. *The New York Times*, 11 June 1949.
6. Conversation between Robert Merrill and Andrew Farkas, 16 March 1992, New Rochelle, N.Y.
7. Telephone conversation between Bidú Sayão and Andrew Farkas, 1 November 1992.
8. Davis 1984, 54.
9. *Opus* (December 1984): 32.
10. *The Björling Saga*, televised documentary. Kjellertz and his wife were living in Los Angeles at the time.
11. Letter from Blanche Thebom to Andrew Farkas, 23 August 1992.
12. Details obtained in a conversation between Count Carl Johan Bernadotte, brother of the late Prince Gustaf Adolf, and Andrew Farkas, 12 April 1994, Ponte Vedra Beach, Fla.

## CHAPTER 14

1. Letter from Giuseppe Valdengo to Andrew Farkas, 5 April 1994.
2. J. Björling 1945, 87–89.
3. Ibid., 50.
4. Conversation between Count Carl Johan Bernadotte and Andrew Farkas, 12 April 1994, Ponte Vedra Beach, Fla.
5. Kolodin 1968, 475.
6. Conversation between Regina Resnik and Andrew Farkas, 8 December 1992, New York City.
7. *Chicago Tribune*, 8 March 1948.
8. Di Stefano, 10.
9. *Baltimore Sun*, 31 March 1948.
10. Conversation between Regina Resnik and Andrew Farkas, 8 December 1992, New York City.
11. Telephone conversation between Rose Bampton and Andrew Farkas, 12 August 1992.
12. Ibid.
13. *The New York Times*, 18 September 1948.

## CHAPTER 15

1. *The New York Times*, 18 September 1948.
2. Letter from Italo Tajo to Andrew Farkas, 12 October 1992.
3. Conversation between Regina Resnik and Andrew Farkas, 8 December 1992, New York City.
4. Telephone conversation between Claudia Pinza and Andrew Farkas, 21 October 1992.
5. *Los Angeles Times*, 1 November 1948.
6. Unidentified clipping, probably *The Evening Star*, 12 or 13 January 1949. Courtesy Robert Morrison.
7. *Chicago Tribune*, 7 February 1949.
8. Letter from Giorgio Tozzi to Andrew Farkas, 24 August 1992.
9. Conversation between tenor Salvatore Randazzo and Andrew Farkas, 14 March 1992, New York City.
10. *San Francisco Examiner*, 3 October 1949.
11. *San Francisco Chronicle*, 3 October 1949.
12. Information obtained from Cesare Curzi by John Gualiani and transmitted to Andrew Farkas, 9 March 1992. Confirmed by Kurt Binar, 10 December 1994.
13. *San Francisco Examiner*, 9 October 1949.
14. *San Francisco Chronicle*, 9 October 1949.
15. *The New York Times*, 24 November 1949.
16. Letter from H. Wendell Endicott to Jussi Björling, 28 November 1949.
17. Letter from Gaetano Merola to Jussi Björling, 3 December 1949.
18. Letter from F. C. Coppicus to Gaetano Merola, 5 December 1949.
19. Authors Thomas G. Kaufman and John F. Cone were eyewitnesses and happily recalled the occasion for Andrew Farkas.
20. Telegram from Amelita Galli-Curci to Jussi Björling, stamped 10 December 1949, 3:40 p.m. EST.

21. Letter from P. L. Brady, an impresario in Wellington, New Zealand, to Jussi Björling, 15 September 1945.
22. Letter from Alexander Cherniavsky to Jussi Björling, 25 March 1946.
23. Letters from Antonio Caraza Campos, director general of the Opera Nacional, to Jussi Björling, 10 August and 3 November 1949.
24. *Dagens Nyheter*, 16 January 1950.
25. *Svenska Dagbladet*, 17 January 1950.
26. Telegram from F. C. Coppicus to Jussi Björling, delivered 1 March 1950.
27. *Chicago Tribune*, 12 March 1950.
28. Kupferberg, 43.
29. *The Telegram*, 10 April 1950.
30. Björling's fees for the two performances were $900 each.

CHAPTER 16

1. Conversation between Mrs. Hugo Hasslo and Andrew Farkas, 1 September 1991, Stockholm.
2. Hagman, 157.
3. The original French libretto of Verdi's opera used the Spanish spelling, *Don Carlos*, for the title. Although in the Italian translation the title character became Carlo, because he was a historical personage, he is usually referred to by the Spanish form of his name.
4. Letter from Rudolf Bing to Jussi Björling, 26 January 1950.
5. Letter from Jussi Björling to Paul Posz, San Francisco Opera Association, 10 March 1950.
6. Letter from Rudolf Bing to George A. Sloan, 10 April 1950. Courtesy Metropolitan Opera Archives.
7. Letter from Rudolf Bing to Jussi Björling, 27 April 1950.
8. Letter from Rudolf Bing to Jussi Björling, 12 May 1950.
9. Letter from Rudolf Bing to Helmer Enwall, 12 May 1950.
10. Silveri 1983, 116; Silveri 1993, 125.
11. Letter from Rudolf Bing to Jussi Björling, 21 October 1950; Bing, 167–168.
12. Unfortunately, no copy of the television broadcast has been located.
13. Farrar, 141.
14. Letter from Fedora Barbieri to Andrew Farkas, 8 August 1992.
15. Hagman, 177.
16. Letter from Rudolf Bing to Jussi Björling, 11 January 1951.
17. Letter from F. C. Coppicus to Jussi Björling, 25 January 1951.
18. Letter from Rudolf Bing to Jussi Björling, 29 January 1951.
19. Telephone conversation between Alan Kayes and Andrew Farkas, 14 April 1994.
20. Letter from Rudolf Bing to Jussi Björling, 27 February 1951.
21. Letter from Ernesto de Quesada to Helmer Enwall, 3 February 1951.
22. Radio interview, William Arneth and Walter Stegman, WNYC, 2 February 1962, New York City.
23. Conversation between Robert Merrill and Andrew Farkas, 16 March 1992, New Rochelle, N.Y.
24. Letter from F. C. Schang to Jussi Björling, 14 July 1950.
25. Letter from F. C. Schang to Jussi Björling, 12 September 1950.

26. Telephone conversation between Risë Stevens and Andrew Farkas, 6 November 1992.
27. Conversation between Robert Merrill and Andrew Farkas, 16 March 1992, New Rochelle, N.Y.
28. Ibid.
29. Interview of Jussi Björling by Per Lindfors, broadcast 1 April 1951, Stockholm.
30. J. Björling 1945, 85.
31. Kesting 1986, 1604.
32. Company correspondence from Constance Hope to Richard Mohr, 24 November 1948.
33. *Quebec Chronicle-Telegraph*, 1 February 1951.
34. *Montreal Daily Star*, 5 February 1951.
35. *Chicago Tribune*, 26 February 1951.
36. Ibid.
37. Note that Dorothy Caruso made this statement in 1951, before the ascendancy of Richard Tucker. It has been reported that shortly before her final illness, upon presenting Tucker with one of Caruso's Canio costumes, she said that among the tenors she had heard, Tucker's timbre came the closest to her husband's. *Andrew Farkas*
38. Letter from Dorothy Caruso to Jussi Björling, 9 March 1951. Italics hers.
39. The costume is now on display at the Jussi Björling Museum in Borlänge.
40. *High Fidelity* (August 1961): 64–65.
41. Letter from Alan Kayes to Jussi Björling, 26 April 1951.
42. Letter from Edgar Vincent to Jussi Björling, 30 April 1951.
43. Telephone conversation between Risë Stevens and Andrew Farkas, 6 November 1992.
44. Letter from Paolo Silveri to Andrew Farkas, 28 October 1992.
45. *Aftonbladet*, 27 June 1951.
46. Hagman, 45.
47. Letter from Paolo Silveri to Andrew Farkas, 28 October 1992.

CHAPTER 17

1. *San Francisco Examiner*, 23 September 1951.
2. *San Francisco Chronicle*, 23 September 1951.
3. Confirmed in a telephone conversation between Bidú Sayão and Andrew Farkas, 1 November 1992.
4. Conversation between Lorenzo Alvary and Andrew Farkas, 6 December 1992, New York City.
5. *San Francisco Examiner*, 29 September 1951.
6. Ibid.
7. *San Francisco Examiner*, 11 October 1951.
8. *San Francisco Examiner*, 22 October 1951.
9. *Svenska Dagbladet*, 19 May 1950.
10. Conversation between Ann-Charlotte Björling and Andrew Farkas, 31 August 1991, Siarö.
11. Merrill, 166.
12. Letter from John Gualiani to Andrew Farkas, 20 August 1992.
13. Letter from Terry Robinson to Andrew Farkas, [4 May 1992].

14. Letter from Rudolf Bing to Fred Schang, 5 December 1951; medical certificate addressed to Max Rudolf by Bruno L. Griesman, 6 December 1951.
15. Letter from Rudolf Bing to Jussi Björling, 5 December 1951.
16. *Chicago Tribune*, 10 December 1951.

## CHAPTER 18

1. Everyone interviewed unequivocally confirmed that Jussi Björling was "the nicest man," "the sweetest guy," the most congenial and helpful colleague one could ever meet. Most of these direct quotes have been omitted intentionally; they would have been repetitive, monotonous, and, perhaps in some readers' opinions, self-serving. *Andrew Farkas*
2. Conversations between Ann-Charlotte Björling and Andrew Farkas, 31 August 1991, Siarö, and August 1993, Stockholm.
3. Conversations between Anders Björling and Andrew Farkas, August and September 1991, Siarö and Stockholm.
4. Conversation between Lars Björling and Andrew Farkas, 2 September 1991, Ekolsund.

## CHAPTER 19

1. *Opera News* (26 February 1972): 31.
2. *The Gramophone* (March 1954): 400.
3. Kesting 1986, 1602.
4. Conversation between Regina Resnik and Andrew Farkas, 8 December 1992, New York City.
5. Hagman, 168–169.
6. Alemanno, 32.
7. Newton 1966, 201.

## CHAPTER 20

1. Letter from Rudolf Bing to Jussi Björling, 9 January 1953.
2. David McKee, "Pagliacci on Disc," *The Opera Quarterly* 9, no. 3 (spring 1993): 38.
3. Conversation between Ann-Charlotte Björling and Andrew Farkas, August 1993, Stockholm.
4. J. Björling 1945, 92.
5. Conversation between Robert Merrill and Andrew Farkas, 16 March 1992, New Rochelle, N.Y.
6. Hagman, 87.
7. Information shared in a conversation between Marit Gruson and Andrew Farkas, 8 December 1992, New York City.
8. After the fact, this sequence of events was verified by George Jellinek in two separate interviews with Boris Christoff and Rudolf Bing. Information courtesy George Jellinek.
9. Cook, 7. Quotation marks notwithstanding, the phrasing sounds more Cook than Björling. *Andrew Farkas*

10. Roberts, 107.
11. Sleeve notes, *The Art of Jussi Björling* (EMI, RLS 715).
12. Wechsler, 22.
13. Telephone conversation between Sallie Wilson and Andrew Farkas, 26 May 1993.

CHAPTER 21

1. Letter from Bert Wechsler to Andrew Farkas, 16 April 1993.
2. Letter from Giuseppe Valdengo to Andrew Farkas, 5 April 1994.
3. Unidentified clipping, 13 January 1954.
4. Interview of Jussi Björling by Ruby Mercer for WNYC, on 11 December 1953, at the Essex House, New York City.
5. Levy, 128.
6. Ibid., 129.
7. *Milwaukee Journal*, 28 January 1954.
8. Conversation between Alfred Hubay and Andrew Farkas, 7 December 1992, New York City.
9. Conversation between Robert Merrill and Andrew Farkas, 16 March 1992, New Rochelle, N.Y.
10. *The New York Times*, 2 February 1954.
11. Information dictated by Astrid Varnay and transmitted to Andrew Farkas by Donald Arthur, 17 August 1995.
12. Conversation between Bert Wechsler and Andrew Farkas, 26 April 1993, New York City.
13. Letter from Max Rudolf to Hyman R. Faine, 24 March 1954.
14. Conversation between Lars Björling and Andrew Farkas, 2 September 1991, Borlänge.
15. Conversation between Richard Mohr and Andrew Farkas, 7 December 1992, New York City.
16. Letter from Licia Albanese to Andrew Farkas, 15 January 1993.
17. Conversation between Richard Mohr and Andrew Farkas, 7 December 1992, New York City.
18. Letter from Licia Albanese to Andrew Farkas, 15 January 1993.
19. Conversation between Richard Mohr and Andrew Farkas, 7 December 1992, New York City.
20. Sleeve notes, *The Art of Jussi Björling* (EMI, RLS 715).
21. Conversation between Robert Merrill and Andrew Farkas, 16 March 1992, New Rochelle, N.Y.
22. Conversation between Richard Mohr and Andrew Farkas, 7 December 1992, New York City.
23. Conversation between Robert Merrill and Andrew Farkas, 16 March 1992, New Rochelle, N.Y.
24. Merrill and Dody, 258–259; Merrill, 171.

CHAPTER 22

1. Newton 1966, 199.
2. *Rand Daily Mail* (Johannesburg), 16 August 1954.

3. *National Mercury* (Durban), 25 August 1954.
4. *Cape Times*, 2 September 1954.
5. Conversation between Sixten Ehrling and Andrew Farkas, 28 April 1993, New York City.
6. Letter from Birgit Nilsson to Andrew Farkas, 2 February 1993.
7. Conversation between Sixten Ehrling and Andrew Farkas, 28 April 1993, New York City.
8. *Aftontidningen*, 29 January 1955.
9. *Dagens Nyheter*, 28 January 1955.
10. Information supplied in a letter from Bruce Burroughs to Andrew Farkas, 19 February 1993.
11. Jacobs, 597.
12. Conversation between Ann-Charlotte Björling and Andrew Farkas, 31 August 1991, Siarö.
13. Information courtesy Bruce Burroughs.
14. Conversation between Richard Mohr and Andrew Farkas, 7 December 1992, New York City.
15. Conversation between Hugh Davidson and Andrew Farkas, 29 April 1993, New York City.
16. Conversation between Richard Mohr and Andrew Farkas, 7 December 1992, New York City.
17. Ibid.
18. Conversation between Ann-Charlotte Björling and Andrew Farkas, August 1993, Stockholm.
19. A.-L. Björling, 249–250.
20. Conversation between Ann-Charlotte Björling and Andrew Farkas, August 1993, Stockholm.
21. Hagman, 116.
22. Conversation between Anders Björling and Andrew Farkas, 31 August 1991, Siarö.
23. J. Björling 1945, 109.
24. Hagman, 178–179.
25. Ibid., 179.
26. Ibid., 180.
27. Conversation between Ann-Charlotte Björling and Andrew Farkas, 31 August 1991, Siarö.
28. Ibid.
29. Conversation between Ann-Charlotte Björling and Andrew Farkas, August 1993, Stockholm.

CHAPTER 23

1. *New York Journal-American*, 26 September 1955.
2. Kolodin 1955, 28.
3. Confirmed in a letter from John Gualiani to Andrew Farkas, 9 March 1992.
4. Telephone conversation with Andrew Farkas, 28 April 1992.
5. Henrysson 1993, 235.
6. *Chicago Tribune*, 7 November 1955.
7. Davis 1966, 238–239.

8. *Chicago Tribune*, 9 November 1955.
9. *Chicago Daily News*, 16 November 1955.
10. Ibid.
11. Conversation between Rolf Björling and Ronald L. Davis, 21 February 1981, Dallas. Courtesy Ronald L. Davis.
12. Letter from Danny Newman to Andrew Farkas, 4 March 1992.
13. Telephone conversation between Sarah Zelzer and Andrew Farkas, 20 April 1992.
14. Letter from Renata Tebaldi to Andrew Farkas, 20 May 1994.
15. Letter from Rudolf Bing to F. C. Schang, 6 October 1955.
16. Cablegram from "Max Rudolf Bing" [i.e., Max Rudolf and Rudolf Bing] to Jussi Björling, 30 December 1955. Courtesy Metropolitan Opera Archives.
17. This television program, broadcast 30 January 1956 on New York City's Channel 4, was a part of the *Producer's Showcase* series. *The New York Times* (31 January 1956) referred to it as *Festival of Music*.
18. Kolodin 1968, 567.
19. Jay S. Harrison, unidentified clipping, probably *New York Herald Tribune*.

CHAPTER 24

1. Conversation between Robert Merrill and Andrew Farkas, 16 March 1992, New Rochelle, N.Y.
2. Conversation between Lars Björling and Andrew Farkas, 2 September 1991, Borlänge.
3. J. Björling 1945, 169.
4. This remark was made on 23 January 1977, in the presence of James A. Drake, Ponselle's biographer. Courtesy James A. Drake.
5. Conversation between Richard Mohr and Andrew Farkas, 7 December 1992, New York City.
6. Kesting 1986, 1605.
7. Kolodin 1956, 37.
8. *Baltimore Sun*, 11 April 1956.

CHAPTER 25

1. Kolodin 1960, 45.
2. Giorgio Tozzi on Provo, Utah's KBYU, broadcast 15 November 1978.
3. Radio interview, William Arneth and Walter Stegman, WNYC, 2 February 1962, New York City.
4. Giorgio Tozzi on Provo, Utah's KBYU, broadcast 15 November 1978.
5. Conversation between Richard Mohr and Andrew Farkas, 7 December 1992, New York City.
6. Conversation between Lars Björling and Andrew Farkas, 2 September 1991, Borlänge.
7. *High Fidelity Annual: Records in Review 1958* (Great Barrington: The Wyeth Press, 1959), 191.
8. Cook, 7.
9. Conversation between Kurt Binar and Andrew Farkas, 6 November 1995, San Francisco.

Notes

10. Details confirmed by eyewitness Kurt Binar.
11. Hagman, 166.
12. Kirsten, 83–84.
13. Conversation between Cornell MacNeil and Andrew Farkas, 20 October 1992, Charlottesville, Va.
14. *Chicago Daily News*, 12 November 1956.
15. Telephone conversation between Byron Belt and Andrew Farkas, 12 October 1991.
16. Conversation between Cornell MacNeil and Andrew Farkas, 20 October 1992, Charlottesville, Va.
17. Telephone conversation between Barry Morell and Andrew Farkas, 2 November 1992.
18. Cablegram from Rudolf Bing to Set Svanholm, 17 December 1956. Courtesy Metropolitan Opera Archives. Bing refers to the contract signed in 1955, which contained the options regarding the tours.
19. Courtesy Metropolitan Opera Archives.
20. Letter from treasurer Frank Garlichs to Giulio Gatti-Casazza, 12 February 1921. Information courtesy Metropolitan Opera Archives and Dr. Adrian Zorgniotti.
21. Courtesy Metropolitan Opera Archives.
22. Ibid.
23. Ibid.
24. Telephone conversation between Alan Kayes and Andrew Farkas, 14 April 1994.
25. Radio interview, William Arneth and Walter Stegman, WNYC, 2 February 1962, New York City. Alan Wagner cited the same occasion in his interview with Björling, 2 December 1958, New York City.
26. Letter from Renata Tebaldi to Andrew Farkas, 20 May 1994.
27. Conversation between Renata Tebaldi and Connie DeCaro, 22 October 1994, San Marino. Courtesy Connie DeCaro.
28. Letter from Irene Dalis to Andrew Farkas, 23 August 1992.
29. Courtesy Metropolitan Opera Archives.

CHAPTER 26

1. Conversation between Marit Gruson and Andrew Farkas, 8 December 1992, New York City.
2. Leinsdorf, 167.
3. Telephone conversation between eyewitness Roger Gross and Andrew Farkas, 5 January 1995.
4. Leinsdorf, 170.
5. Taped conversation between Zinka Milanov and Bruce Burroughs, 12 May 1989, New York City. Courtesy Bruce Burroughs.
6. *High Fidelity* (September 1964).
7. Undated clipping, *Chicago American*, presumably November 1957.
8. Carelli, 176–177.
9. The role of Calaf was sung by Miguel Fleta at the world premiere at La Scala, 25 April 1926. Gigli never sang the role.
10. Letter from Rina Gigli to Andrew Farkas, 15 November 1992.
11. Letter from Danny Newman to Andrew Farkas, 4 March 1992.

378

12. Conversation between Elisabeth Söderström and Andrew Farkas, 29 August 1991, Stockholm.
13. Telephone conversation between Anna Moffo and Andrew Farkas, 10 December 1992.
14. *Chicago Tribune*, 22 October 1957.
15. Conversation between Cornell MacNeil and Andrew Farkas, 20 October 1992, Charlottesville, Va.
16. Letter from Andrew Foldi to Andrew Farkas, 27 October 1992.
17. Ibid.
18. Ibid.
19. Conversation between Sir Georg Solti and Andrew Farkas, 3 December 1993, Washington, D.C.
20. Letter from Andrew Foldi to Andrew Farkas, 27 October 1992.
21. *Chicago Tribune*, 16 November 1957.
22. *Chicago American*, 30 November 1957.
23. *Chicago Tribune*, 1 December 1957.
24. Letter from Franca Christoff to Andrew Farkas, 21 September 1992.
25. Conversation between Nell Rankin and Andrew Farkas, 29 April 1993, New York City.
26. *Chicago Tribune*, 1 December 1957.

CHAPTER 27

1. Conversation between Kerstin Meyer and Andrew Farkas, 3 September 1991, Stockholm.
2. *The New York Times*, 3 March 1958.
3. *New York World Telegram and Sun*, 3 March 1958.
4. Jussi meant "I'll never sing it *onstage*."
5. *New York Herald Tribune*, 9 March 1958.
6. *New York Herald Tribune*, 16 March 1958.
7. Bing, 168.
8. Interview of Rudolf Bing by James A. Drake, 5 October 1982, New York City. Courtesy James A. Drake.
9. Bing, 168.
10. Conversation between Dr. Adrian Zorgniotti and Andrew Farkas, 16 March 1992, New York City.
11. An indication that Jussi didn't type this letter himself is that his lawyer's name was Kvalde, not Kwaldin. Jussi wouldn't have let such a crude error pass.
12. Letter from Birgit Nilsson to Andrew Farkas, 2 February 1993.
13. Ibid.
14. Hagman, 74.
15. Conversation between Lars Björling and Andrew Farkas, 2 September 1991, Borlänge.
16. *San Francisco Examiner*, 28 September 1958.
17. Lyon, 80.
18. Letter from Giulietta Simionato to Andrew Farkas, July 1992.
19. Ibid.
20. Conversation between Cornell MacNeil and Andrew Farkas, 20 October 1992, Charlottesville, Va.

21. *Opera* (February 1959): 100–101.
22. Interview of Jussi Björling by Alan Wagner, for WNYC, 2 December 1958 (first broadcast 14 December), Essex House, New York City.
23. Ibid.
24. Letter from John Gutman to Jussi Björling, 2 December 1958.

CHAPTER 28

1. Conversation between Elisabeth Söderström and Andrew Farkas, 29 August 1991, Stockholm.
2. Ibid.
3. *The New York Times*, 9 March 1959.
4. Conversation between Lars Björling and Andrew Farkas, 2 September 1991, Borlänge.
5. Conversations between Anders and Lars Björling, and Andrew Farkas, 1991 and 1993, Stockholm.
6. *San Francisco Examiner*, 22 April 1959.
7. Bertil Bokstedt, program notes to "Jussi Björling Memorial Concert," 9 September 1985.
8. Conversation between Bertil Bokstedt and Andrew Farkas, 3 September 1991, Stockholm.
9. Conversation between Ann-Charlotte Björling and Andrew Farkas, August 1993, Stockholm.
10. Letter from Birgit Nilsson to Andrew Farkas, 2 February 1993.
11. Conversation between Richard Mohr and Andrew Farkas, 7 December 1992, New York City.
12. Nigel Douglas mentions that after his BBC program *Singer's Choice*, a woman wrote to him about Björling: "To me it is a voice heavy with unshed tears." Douglas, 3.
13. Letter from Blanche Thebom to Andrew Farkas, 23 August 1992.
14. Conversation between Richard Mohr and Andrew Farkas, 7 December 1992, New York City.
15. *The Sixth High Fidelity Annual: Records in Review 1960* (Great Barrington: The Wyeth Press, 1961), 233.
16. Conversation between Ann-Charlotte Björling and Andrew Farkas, August 1993, Stockholm. In her everlasting regret over what she said to her father, Ann-Charlotte comes very close to echoing the words of her brother Anders before her.
17. Conversation between Lars Björling and Andrew Farkas, 2 September 1991, Borlänge.
18. *Opera* (August 1959): 495.
19. *High Fidelity* (January 1961): 62.
20. *The Gramophone* (July 1992): 27.
21. *High Fidelity* (January 1961): 62.
22. Conversation between Sture Ingebretzen and Andrew Farkas, 28 August 1991, Stockholm.
23. *The Björling Saga*, televised documentary.
24. Hagman, 84.
25. Ibid., 86.

26. The performance has been issued on a two-record CD set (Myto, 2 MCD 931.73) as a companion to *Manon Lescaut*.
27. Letter from Giulietta Simionato to Andrew Farkas, July 1992.
28. Conversation between Cornell MacNeil and Andrew Farkas, 20 October 1992, Charlottesville, Va.
29. Conversation between Don Goldberg and Andrew Farkas, 19 March 1992, New York City.
30. Conversation between Robert Merrill and Andrew Farkas, 16 March 1992, New Rochelle, N.Y. The high C was actually a B-natural, however, as can be heard on the CD release of the performance.
31. Kolodin 1968, 631.
32. Conversation between Elisabeth Söderström and Andrew Farkas, 29 August 1991, Stockholm.
33. Hagman, 91.
34. *Sunday Telegraph*, 19 July 1992.
35. *Opera News* (19 December 1959): 32.

CHAPTER 29

1. Giorgio Tozzi on Provo, Utah's KBYU, broadcast 15 November 1978.
2. Conversation between Cornell MacNeil and Andrew Farkas, 20 October 1992, Charlottesville, Va.
3. Ibid.
4. Bluebell, ABCD 045.
5. Correspondence in Royal Opera House, Covent Garden Archives.
6. Ibid.
7. Ibid.
8. Letter from Rosanna Grosoli Carteri to Andrew Farkas, 20 November 1993.
9. *Opera* (May 1960): 363.
10. *The Sunday Times*, 13 March 1960.
11. *West London Press*, 18 March 1960.
12. *The Sunday Times*, 13 March 1960.
13. Conversation between Geraint Evans and Enrique Gilardoni, 4 September 1962, Buenos Aires. Courtesy Enrique Gilardoni.
14. This detail and the account of events that follow were reconstructed from Jussi's narrative of what had transpired and from James Horrocks' report in the *Daily Express*, 16 March 1960.
15. Letter from Rosanna Grosoli Carteri to Andrew Farkas, 20 November 1993.
16. Ibid.
17. Confirmed in a letter from the comptroller to the Queen Mother, Queen Elizabeth, written at Her Majesty's bidding, to Andrew Farkas, 2 June 1993.
18. *Daily Mail*, 16 March 1960.
19. Texaco Opera Quiz, Metropolitan Opera broadcast, 13 April 1993. Unfortunately, Charles Osborne (not to be confused with Conrad L. Osborne) is not the only one to have fanned the flames of this fabrication. Nigel Douglas wrote that during these performances "rumours were rife that the drink problem was getting out of hand" and when Jussi started the third performance half an hour late, "not everybody was convinced by the official announcement that Björling was suffering from a strained heart." Douglas, 17.

20. Letter from Rosanna Grosoli Carteri to Andrew Farkas, 28 January 1994. Italics hers.
21. Conversations between Dr. Adrian Zorgniotti and Andrew Farkas, 1992 and 1993, New York City.
22. *Evening News*, 16 March 1960.
23. Hagman, 86.
24. Thelander, 30.
25. The contract was signed 11 January 1960.
26. *San Francisco Examiner*, 31 March 1960.
27. *Star-News*, 6 April 1960.
28. Conversation between Lars Björling and Andrew Farkas, 2 September 1991, Borlänge.
29. Leontyne Price was not available for comment.
30. Conversation between Cornell MacNeil and Andrew Farkas, 20 October 1992, Charlottesville, Va.
31. Douglas, 7.
32. Conversation between Rosalind Elias and Enrique Gilardoni, 24 June 1966, Buenos Aires. Courtesy Enrique Gilardoni.
33. Letter from Giorgio Tozzi to Andrew Farkas, 24 August 1992.
34. Conversation between Ann-Charlotte Björling and Andrew Farkas, 31 August 1991, Siarö.
35. Culshaw 1982, 239.
36. Telephone converation between Erik Smith and Andrew Farkas, 24 August 1993.
37. Ibid.

CHAPTER 30

1. Interview of Jussi Björling by Anthony Baird, broadcast 5 July 1960, Rättvik, Sweden.
2. Telephone conversation between Erik Smith and Andrew Farkas, 24 August 1993.
3. Ibid.
4. On 17 December 1959, Alan Kayes, manager of Red Seal Artists and Repertoire, wrote to Jussi at the Essex House, New York City: "Dear Jussi: I am confirming your acceptance of the recording of Masked Ball for Decca during the first half of July 1960 with the cast that I gave to you by telephone yesterday—yourself, Tebaldi, MacNeil, Simionato, Ratti, with Solti conducting—and am advising Mr. Rosengarten accordingly."
5. Letter from Renata Tebaldi to Andrew Farkas, 20 May 1994.
6. Letter from Birgit Nilsson to Andrew Farkas, 2 February 1992.
7. Culshaw 1982, 240.
8. Conversation between Sir Georg Solti and Andrew Farkas, 3 December 1993, Washington, D.C.
9. Ibid.
10. Ibid.
11. An inquiry to Sir Georg Solti first resulted in a telefacsimile reply from his secretary, Charles Kaye, to Andrew Farkas, 26 February 1992. Kaye indicated that the Maestro "does remember that Björling recorded some parts of the music, but

he does not remember exactly which." In the subsequent conversation between Maestro Solti and Andrew Farkas, the Maestro firmly stated that two takes of the "first entrance of Riccardo" were recorded.

12. Conversation between Cornell MacNeil and Andrew Farkas, 20 October 1992, Charlottesville, Va.
13. Ibid.
14. Conversation between Sir Georg Solti and Andrew Farkas, 3 December 1993, Washington, D.C.
15. Culshaw 1973, 57.
16. Culshaw 1982, 242.
17. Telephone conversation between Cornell MacNeil and Andrew Farkas, 28 September 1992.
18. Conversation between Sir Georg Solti and Andrew Farkas, 3 December 1993, Washington, D.C.
19. Letter from Birgit Nilsson to Andrew Farkas, 10 October 1992; also Lebrecht, 170–171.
20. Conversation between Cornell MacNeil and Andrew Farkas, 20 October 1992, Charlottesville, Va.
21. Conversation between Sir Georg Solti and Andrew Farkas, 3 December 1993, Washington, D.C.
22. Conversation between Ann-Charlotte Björling and Andrew Farkas, 31 August 1991, Siarö.
23. Conversation between Sir Georg Solti and Andrew Farkas, 3 December 1993, Washington, D.C.
24. Culshaw 1982, 241. The ledger sheets for the Rome sessions show that Birgit Nilsson was paid a total of 6000 Italian lira, then the equivalent of $10. The expense is identified as a hotel bill, thus this minuscule sum might have been a token deposit on her room. Information courtesy Michael Gray.
25. Letter from Birgit Nilsson to Andrew Farkas, 2 February 1993.
26. Lebrecht, 170–171.
27. Letter from Birgit Nilsson to Andrew Farkas, 2 February 1993.
28. Conversation between Sir Georg Solti and Andrew Farkas, 3 December 1993, Washington, D.C.
29. Culshaw 1973, 55–58.
30. Culshaw 1982, 241.
31. Culshaw was no more honest with his superiors at London/Decca. According to his memoirs, when he reached his boss, Maurice Rosengarten, by phone in Switzerland, Culshaw told him that they had recorded the entire opera "apart from the scenes involving the tenor." Just how that was accomplished in a single completed session without the soprano and the mezzo-soprano, Culshaw does not explain.

CHAPTER 31

1. Conversation between Ann-Charlotte Björling and Andrew Farkas, August 1993, Stockholm.
2. *High Fidelity* (May 1965): 81.
3. Hagman, 74.
4. Ibid., 62–63.

5. Ibid., 64.
6. Ibid., 171.
7. Ibid., 114.
8. Cablegram from Jussi Björling to Robert Herman, 24 August 1960. Courtesy Metropolitan Opera Archives.
9. *The Björling Saga*, televised documentary.
10. Conversation between Ann-Charlotte Björling and Andrew Farkas, 31 August 1991, Siarö.
11. Information taken from the death certificate, issued by the Engelbrekt församling in Stockholm, signed by Alvar Cedermark, *Komminister*.
12. Conversation between Lars Björling and Andrew Farkas, 2 September 1991, Borlänge.
13. *The New York Times*, 20 September 1960.
14. Hagman, 103.
15. *The New York Times*, 18 September 1960. Reprinted in the liner notes to *Jussi Bjoerling: Volume I—Great Recordings of the Century* (COLH 148), 1964.
16. Statement dictated by Dorothy Kirsten to her secretary, Vicki Hillebrand, in 1991, and transmitted to Andrew Farkas.
17. Birgit Nilsson, program notes to "Jussi Björling Memorial Concert," 9 September 1985.
18. *The Björling Saga*, televised documentary.

## *Postlude*

1. Hagman, 152. Freddie Schang was no less generous when he closed his tribute to Jussi with these words: "In all of his worldwide travels Bjoerling was accompanied by his lovely wife Anna-Lisa, stalwart companion of trials and triumphs, mother of three surviving children. No record of Bjoerling's career can be complete without a tribute to his dedicated spouse, whose Viking courage was an ever-present reservoir of strength for which the tenor had periods of need." Schang, 22.
2. This statement is made for informational, not promotional purposes. Lest the Björling family be accused of commercialism, it should be noted that royalty payments accrue only from the manufacture and sale of records issued by RCA/BMG. *Andrew Farkas*
3. *Opera* (January 1994): 30.
4. Steane, 371.
5. Conversation between Regina Resnik and Andrew Farkas, 8 December 1992, New York City.
6. Interview of Jussi Björling by Alan Wagner, for WNYC, 2 December 1958 (first broadcast 14 December), Essex House, New York City.
7. Jacobs, 597.
8. *The New York Times*, 16 May 1965.

# BIBLIOGRAPHY

Albert, Jürgen. 1971. "Erinnerungen an Jussi Björling." *Collegium Musicum* (March): 19–22.

Alemanno, Osvaldo. 1988. *Mario del Monaco.* N.p.: Matteo Editore.

Bergquist, C. Hilding. 1974. "Jussi Björling." *Record Research* 129–130 (October/November): 5.

Bing, Rudolf. 1972. *5000 Nights at the Opera.* New York: Doubleday & Company.

Björling, Anna-Lisa. 1987. *Mitt liv med Jussi.* Stockholm: Bonnier.

Björling, David. 1978. *Hur man skall sjunga.* Reprint, Stockholm: Eriks Förlaget.

Björling, Gösta. 1945. *Jussi: boken om storebror.* Stockholm: Steinsvik.

Björling, Jussi. 1945. *Med bagaget i strupen.* Stockholm: Wahlström and Widstrand.

———. 1950. "Singers, Too, Are Human." *Music News* (September): 15.

"Björling Returns." 1945. *Opera News* 10, no. 2 (5 November): 12–13.

Blyth, Alan. 1985. "Jussi Björling, 1911–1960." *Opera* 36 (September): 994–997.

———. 1994. "Polishing the Past." *Opera* 45 (January): 30–31.

Boas, Robert. 1958. "The Great Interpreters No. 15: Jussi Björling. Appreciation." *Gramophone Record Review* 55 (May): 571–572.

Brahms, Caryl. 1960. "Björling in *Bohème.*" *John O' London's* (24 March): 350.

Bruun, Carl L. 1960. Discography to *Jussi Björling, en minnesbok* by Bertil Hagman, 187–208. Stockholm: Albert Bonniers förlag.

Carelli, Gábor. 1979. *Utam a Metropolitanbe.* Budapest: Zeneműkiadó.

"Career No. 2." 1950. *Time* 55 (10 April): 77–78.

Cassidy, Claudia. 1979. *Lyric Opera of Chicago.* Chicago: Lyric Opera of Chicago.

Clough, F. F., and G. J. Cuming. 1945. "Jussi Bjoerling: Discography." *American Record Guide* 12, no. 4 (December): 87–90, 95.

———. 1958. "The Great Interpreters No. 15: Jussi Björling, Discography." *Gramophone Record Review* 55 (May): 572, 633–635; 56 (June): 706.

Cook, J. Douglas. 1956. "Jussi Bjoerling: The Supreme Operatic Tenor." *The Argonaut* (21 September): 7.

Culshaw, John. 1973. "Fragments from an Unwritten Autobiography." *High Fidelity* (June): 55–58.

———. 1982. *Putting the Record Straight.* New York: Viking Press.

Davidson, Gladys. 1955. *A Treasury of Opera Biography.* New York: Citadel Press.

Davis, Peter G. 1984. "If You Knew Jussi." *New York* 17 (6 August): 54–55.

Davis, Ronald L. 1966. *Opera in Chicago.* New York: Appleton-Century.

Di Stefano, Giuseppe. 1989. *L'arte del canto.* Milan: Rusconi.

Douglas, Nigel. 1992. *Legendary Voices.* London: André Deutsch.

Dzazópulos, Juan, and Enrique Gilardoni. 1995. "Inolvidable Jussi." Parts 1–3. *Correo Musical Argentino* 164:8; 165:8; 166:8.

E. B. 1948. "Jussi Bjoerling, Tenor, Carnegie Hall, March 21" *Musical America* 68, no. 5 (April): 34–35.

Eaton, Quaintance. 1937. "More Singers from the Royal Opera." *The American-Swedish Monthly* (October): 8–9.

Elfström, Mats. 1974. "Swedish National Discography: Jussi Björling and Related Research." *Record Research* 125–126 (February): 11.

———. 1975. "Erik Odde." *Skivsamlaren* 1 (November): 4.

———. 1976. "Jussi Björling: First Records and Research on the Comedian Harmonists and von Eichwald Labels." *Record Research* 137–138 (February/March 1976): 13.

Emmons, Shirlee. 1983. "Voices from the Past." *NATS* [*National Association of Teachers of Singing*] *Bulletin* (January/February): 23–27.

Ewen, David. 1940. *Living Musicians.* New York: H. W. Wilson Company.

———. 1978. *Musicians Since 1900: Performers in Concert and Opera.* New York: H. W. Wilson Company.

F. S. 1959. "Swedish Match." *Opera News* 24, no. 7 (19 December): 14, 32.

Farrar, Geraldine. 1991. *All Good Greetings, gf.* Ed. Aida Craig Truxall. Pittsburgh: University of Pittsburgh Press.

Favia-Artsay, Aida. 1961. "Tributes to Bjoerling and Bori." *Hobbies* 66 (October): 30.

———. 1967. "Historical Records." *Hobbies* 67 (February): 30.

Fellowes, Myles, ed. 1940. "Good Singing is Natural." *Etude* 58 (October): 655–656, 698.

Flaster, Don. 1949. "Opera Star Interviewed." *The Chat* (18 March): 2.

G. J. 1961. "Memories of the Young Bjoerling." *Hi Fi Stereo* (April): 57–58.

Gelatt, Roland. 1960. "Music Makers." *High Fidelity* (November): 71.

Goldberg, Don. 1988. "50 Years Ago—The Met Debut of Jussi Bjoerling." *Opera News* 53, no. 10 (10 December): 44.

———. 1991. "The Masked Ball Mystery." *Opera News* 55, no. 9 (19 January): 34–35.

Hagman, Bertil. 1960. *Jussi Björling, en minnesbok.* Stockholm: Albert Bonniers förlag.

Hamilton, David. 1983. "A New Jussi Bjoerling Discography." *ARSC* [*Association for Recorded Sound Collections*] *Journal* 14, no. 4:98–99.

Henrysson, Harald. 1975. *Förteckning (till sin huvuddel engelskspråkig) över lju-*

*dupptagningar med Jussi Björling och utgåvor av dessa.* Borås, Sweden: Bibliotekshögskolan.

———. 1993. *A Jussi Björling Phonography.* 2nd ed. Stockholm: Svenskt Musikhistoriskt Arkiv.

Henrysson, Harald, and Jack W. Porter. 1984. *A Jussi Björling Phonography.* Stockholm: Svenskt Musikhistoriskt Arkiv.

Himmelein, Fred T. 1967. "The Bjoerling Recordings: A Selective Discography." *Le Grand Baton* 4, no. 1 (February): 13–18.

Jacobs, Arthur. 1960. "Passing Notes." *The Gramophone* (May): 597.

"Jussi Björling." 1947. In *Current Biography.* New York: H. W. Wilson Company.

Jussi Björling Appreciation Society. 1958– . *Newsletter.* London: Jussi Björling Appreciation Society. (Irregular.)

Kesting, Jürgen. 1973. "Konkretisierte Erinnerungen an bessere Tage des Gesangs: Jussi Björling und seine Schallplatten." *Opernwelt* 1973, no. 4 (April): 43–47.

———. 1986. *Die grossen Sänger.* 3 vols. Düsseldorf: claassen Verlag.

Kirsten, Dorothy. 1982. *A Time to Sing.* Garden City, N.Y.: Doubleday & Company.

Kolodin, Irving. 1955. "A Doll, a Bird, and a Tenor." *Saturday Review* 38, no. 41 (8 October): 27–28.

———. 1956. "Bjoerling in Opera, City Center, Lipton." *Saturday Review* 39, no. 15 (14 April): 37.

———. 1960. "Jussi Bjoerling." *Saturday Review* 43, no. 39 (24 September): 45.

———. 1968. *The Metropolitan Opera 1883–1966: A Candid History.* New York: Knopf.

Kupferberg, H. 1951. "Mama, Sing With Papa." *Colliers* 127 (17 February): 42–43.

Lauri-Volpi, Giacomo. 1960. *Voci parallele.* N.p.: Garzanti.

Lebrecht, Norman. 1991. *The Maestro Myth.* [New York]: Birch Lane Press.

Leinsdorf, Erich. 1976. *Cadenza: A Musical Career.* Boston: Houghton Mifflin Company.

Levy, Alan. 1975. *The Bluebird of Happiness: The Memoirs of Jan Peerce.* New York: Harper & Row.

Lyon, Hugh Lee. 1973. *Leontyne Price: Highlights of a Prima Donna.* New York: Vantage Press.

Merrill, Robert. 1976. *Between Acts: An Irreverent Look at Opera and Other Madness.* New York: McGraw-Hill.

Merrill, Robert, and Sandford Dody. 1965. *Once More from the Beginning.* New York: Macmillan.

Miller, Richard. 1993. *Training Tenor Voices.* New York: Schirmer Books.

Natan, Alex. 1963. *Primo Uomo: Grosse Sänger der Oper.* Basel: Basilius Presse.

Newton, Ivor. 1960. "Stubborn—But a Musician." *Music and Musicians* (10 November): 9, 14.

———. 1966. *At the Piano—Ivor Newton: The World of an Accompanist.* London: Hamilton.

Osborne, Conrad L. 1961. "Instruction in Almost Every Phrase." *High Fidelity* 11 (August): 64–65.

Pease, Edward. 1972. "A Jussi Björling Discography, Part I: Low-priced Recordings Currently Available from Normal Retail Sources in the United States." *NATS [National Association of Teachers of Singing] Bulletin* 29, no. 2 (December): 12–15.

———. 1975. "A Jussi Björling Discography, Part II: Full-priced Recordings Currently Available from Normal Retail Sources in the United States." *NATS* [*National Association of Teachers of Singing*] *Bulletin* 32, no. 2 (December): 6–11.

Roberts, Peter. 1982. *Victoria de los Angeles*. London: Weidenfeld & Nicolson.

"Rolf." 1964. *Newsweek* 63 (30 March), 51.

Schang, F. C. 1960. "Jussi Bjoerling." *Opera News* 25, no. 3 (19 November): 22.

Seemungal, Rupert P. 1959–64. *A Complete Discography of Jussi Björling*. 1–3rd ed. Trinidad.

Silveri, Paolo. 1983. *Paolo Silveri nella vita e nell'arte*. Rome: Bardi Editore.

———. 1993. *The Fantastic Life of Paolo Silveri*. Rome: Romagrafik.

Skandrup Lund, Eyvind, and Herbert Rosenberg. 1969. *Jussi Björling: A Record List*. Copenhagen: Nationaldiskoteket.

Smith, Cecil. 1949. "Manon Lescaut Revived at the Metropolitan." *Musical America* 69, no. 15 (1 December): 5.

Springer, Morris. 1972. "On the Road with Jussi." *Opera News* 36, no. 14 (26 February): 30–31.

Steane, J. B. 1974. *The Grand Tradition*. New York: Charles Scribner's Sons.

Stroff, Stephen M. N.d. *Guldstrupen: Jussi Björling—en biografi*. Stockholm: Bokád Bokförlag.

———. 1988. "Young Jussi Björling." *Antiques & Collecting Hobbies* 93 (October): 60–64.

Stubington, Ken. 1959–1960. "Discography." *Record News* 4, no. 4 (December): 120–128; 4, no. 5 (January): 176–187.

Svedelius, Julia. 1934. *År och människor*. Stockholm: Bokförlaget Natur och Kultur.

Svengalis, Kendall F. 1986. "Jussi Björling Remembered." *Nordstjernan Svea* (20 March).

Thelander, Harald. 1961. "His Voice Shall Live Forever." *The American-Swedish Monthly* (April): 29–31.

Thielen, Hugo. 1975. "Jussi Björling: Schallplattenverzeichnis." *Fono Forum*, no. 4 (April): 338–343.

Trimble, L. 1960. "Farväl Guldstrupan!" *Musical America* 80 (October): 34–35.

Vegeto, Raffaele. 1964. Discography to *Le grandi voci: dizionario critico-biografico dei cantanti con discografia operistica*, Rodolfo Celletti, ed. Rome: Istituto per la collaborazione culturale.

Vernier, David. 1992. "Mirror, Mirror on the Wall." *CD Review* (November): 26–28.

Wagner, Charles L. 1940. *Seeing Stars*. New York: G. P. Putnam's Sons.

Wechsler, Bert. 1982. "Survivor: Sallie Wilson." *Ballet News* 3, no. 10 (April): 20–23.

Win, Godfrey. 1960. "People." *Women's Illustrated* (18 June): 28.

"Your Vocal Problem." 1950. *Etude* 68 (June): 21.

Zelzer, Sarah Schectman, with Phyllis Dreazen. 1990. *Impresario: The Zelzer Era 1930 to 1990*. Chicago: Academy Chicago Publishers.

# A Jussi Björling Chronology

by
Harald Henrysson
CURATOR, JUSSI BJÖRLING MUSEUM

## Jussi Björling's Opera, Operetta, and Oratorio Repertoire

The information below identifies the number of times JB performed the works listed, and the date of his first and last appearance in each role. Unless otherwise indicated, the first performance took place in Stockholm. The abbreviations given for the roles are used in the chronology of performances.

*L'africaine* (G. Meyerbeer): JB as Vasco da Gama. 6 performances Oct. 4, 1938–Oct. 17, 1938 (Stockholm).
Sélika (S), Inès (I), Nélusko (N)

*Aida* (G. Verdi): JB as Radamès. 31 performances Oct. 12, 1935–Nov. 29, 1958 (Chicago); only act 3 sung two times, in Stockholm.
Aida (Ai), Amneris (Amn), Amonasro (Amo), Ramfis (R), King (K)

*Arabella* (R. Strauss): JB as Count Elemer. 6 performances Dec. 30, 1933–Feb. 14, 1934 (Stockholm; it is doubtful JB sang the role at the last performance.).
Arabella (A), Zdenka (Z), Matteo (Mt), Mandryka (Mn)

389

*Un ballo in maschera* (G. Verdi): JB as Riccardo/Gustavus. 38 performances Apr. 18, 1934–Nov. 18, 1957 (Chicago).
Amelia (A), Oscar (O), Ulrica (U), Renato (R), Samuel (S), Tom (T)

*Il barbiere di Siviglia* (G. Rossini): JB as Count Almaviva. 26 performances Nov. 7, 1931–Jan. 20, 1937 (Stockholm).
Rosina (R), Berta (Be), Figaro (F), Bartolo (Br), Basilio (Bs)

*Bellman* (E. Ziedner): JB as Näktergal. 1 performance July 25, 1930.
Ulla (U), Bellman (B), King Gustaf (G), Mowitz (Mw), Mollberg (Ml)

*La bohème* (G. Puccini): JB as Rodolfo. 114 performances Oct. 13, 1934–Mar. 18, 1960 (London).
Mimì (Mi), Musetta (Mu), Marcello (Ma), Schaunard (S), Colline (C)

*I cavalieri di Ekebù* (R. Zandonai): JB as Ruster (a minor role, not in the original Italian version). 11 performances Apr. 19, 1931–Mar. 2, 1936 (Stockholm).
Anna (A), Major's Widow (W), Giosta Berling (B)

*Cavalleria rusticana* (P. Mascagni): JB as Turiddu. 31 performances Feb. 14, 1935–Dec. 22, 1959 (New York).
Santuzza (S), Lola (Lo), Lucia (Lu), Alfio (A)

*La damnation de Faust* (H. Berlioz): JB as Faust. 10 performances Feb. 1, 1936–Apr. 23, 1936 (Stockholm).
Marguerite (Ma), Méphistophélès (Mé), Brander (B)

*Djamileh* (G. Bizet): JB as Haroun. 6 performances Sep. 6, 1933–Nov. 26, 1933 (Stockholm).
Djamileh (D), Splendiano (S)

*Don Carlo* (G. Verdi): JB as Don Carlo. 16 performances Nov. 6, 1950 (New York)–Nov. 4, 1958 (Los Angeles, S. F. Opera).
Elisabetta (El), Celestial Voice (V), Eboli (Eb), Rodrigo (R), Filippo (F), Grand Inquisitor (I)

*Don Giovanni* (W. A. Mozart): JB as Don Ottavio. 10 performances Aug. 20, 1930–Sep. 14, 1937 (Stockholm).
Donna Anna (A), Donna Elvira (E), Zerlina (Z), Don Giovanni (G), Leporello (L), Masetto (M), Commendatore (C)

*L'elisir d'amore* (G. Donizetti): JB as Nemorino. 6 performances Nov. 9, 1932–Feb. 19, 1933 (Stockholm).
Adina (A), Belcore (B), Dulcamara (D)

*Engelbrekt* (N. Berg): JB as Bishop Sigge. 3 performances Mar. 21, 1931–May 7, 1931 (Helsinki, Stockholm Opera).
Ingrid (I), Karin (K), Cecilia (C), King Erik (KE), Engelbrekt (E), Puke (P)

*Die Entführung aus dem Serail* (W. A. Mozart): JB as Belmonte. 4 performances Jan. 26, 1935–Mar. 17, 1935 (Stockholm).
Constanze (C), Blonde (B), Osmin (O), Pedrillo (P)

*Evgeny Onegin* (P. Tchaikovsky): JB as Lensky. 8 performances Jan. 14, 1933–Dec. 10, 1935 (Stockholm).
Tatyana (T), Olga (Ol), Filipyevna (F), Onegin (On), Gremin (G)

*Fanal* (K. Atterberg): JB as Martin Skarp. 23 performances Jan. 27, 1934–Aug. 26, 1939 (Stockholm).
Rosamund (R), Jost (J), Duke (D)

*La fanciulla del West* (G. Puccini): JB as Dick Johnson. 9 performances Dec. 29, 1934–Feb. 25, 1937 (Vienna).
Minnie (M), Jack Rance (R), Jake Wallace (W)

*Faust* (C. Gounod): JB as Faust. 70 performances Aug. 25, 1934–Apr. 1, 1960 (San Francisco, Cosmopolitan Opera).
Marguerite (M), Siebel (S), Valentin (V), Méphistophélès (Mé)

*Fidelio* (L. v. Beethoven): JB as Florestan. 4 performances Mar. 26, 1935–Apr. 10, 1935 (Stockholm); one abridged concert performance May 4, 1948 in Cincinnati.
Leonore (L), Marzelline (M), Jacquino (J), Fernando (F), Pizarro (P), Rocco (R)

*La fille du régiment* (G. Donizetti): JB as Tonio. 9 performances Sep. 26, 1936–May 17, 1937 (Stockholm).
Marie (M), Duchess (D), Marchioness (Mc), Sulpice (S)

*Die Fledermaus* (J. Strauss): JB as Alfred. 10 performances Sep. 17, 1935–Sep. 2, 1936 (Stockholm).
Rosalinde (R), Adele (A), Orlofsky (O), Eisenstein (E), Falke (Fa), Frank (Fr)

*Der fliegende Holländer* (R. Wagner): JB as Erik. 4 performances Sep. 29, 1931–Apr. 24, 1933 (Stockholm).
Senta (S), Mary (M), Steersman (St), Dutchman (Du), Daland (Da)

*Guillaume Tell* (G. Rossini): JB as Arnold. 11 performances Dec. 27, 1930–Jan. 3, 1932 (Stockholm).
Mathilde (M), Jemmy (J), Hedwige (H), Tell (T), Walter (W), Gesler (G)

*Das Herz* (H. Pfitzner): JB as A Young Cavalier. 3 performances Apr. 14, 1932–Apr. 25, 1932 (Stockholm).
Helge (H), Modiger (M), Athanasius (A), Wendelin (W)

*L'illustre Fregona* (R. Laparra): JB as Tomas. 22 performances (+ one containing only acts 1 and 3) Jan. 16, 1932–Jan. 2, 1937 (Stockholm).
Fregona (F), Carmencita (C), Lope (L)

*Knyaz Igor* (A. Borodin): JB as Vladimir Igorevich. 36 performances Mar. 11, 1933–Aug. 30, 1937 (Stockholm).
Yaroslavna (Ya), Konchakovna (Ka), Igor (I), Galitsky (G), Konchak (Kk)

*Kronbruden* (T. Rangström): JB as Mats. 3 performances Apr. 6, 1933–Nov. 30, 1934 (Stockholm).
Kersti (K), Brita (B), Midwife (M), Constable (C), Neck (N)

*Louise* (G. Charpentier): JB as The Song-writer. 8 performances Nov. 29, 1930–Sep. 11, 1931 (Stockholm).
Louise (L), Mother (M), Julien (J), Father (F)

*Madama Butterfly* (G. Puccini): JB as B. F. Pinkerton. 12 performances Sep. 5, 1936–Apr. 21, 1939 (Stockholm). Only act 1 sung Feb. 6, 1945 in Stockholm.
Butterfly (B), Suzuki (Su), Goro (G), Sharpless (Sh)

*Manon Lescaut* (G. Puccini): JB as A Lamplighter and Chevalier Renato Des Grieux. 6 performances as Lamplighter July 21, 1930–Mar. 15, 1932 (Stockholm). 25 performances as Des Grieux Oct. 7, 1949 (San Francisco)–Nov. 1, 1959 (Stockholm).
Manon (M), Des Grieux (DG), Lescaut (L), Geronte (G)

*Martha* (F. v. Flotow): JB as Lyonel. 3 performances Sep. 30, 1933–Oct. 11, 1933 (Stockholm).
Harriet (H), Nancy (N), Plumkett (P)

*Mefistofele* (A. Boito): JB as Faust. 2 performances Sep. 30 and Oct. 3, 1937 (Stockholm).
Margherita (M), Elena (E), Marta (Mt), Mefistofele (Me)

*Messa da Requiem* (G. Verdi). 4 performances Apr. 28, 1937–Nov. 23, 1940 (New York).

*Messiah* (G. F. Handel). 7 performances Dec. 6, 1930–Dec. 5, 1936 (Stockholm).

*Mignon* (A. Thomas): JB as Wilhelm Meister. 10 performances Oct. 8, 1932–Jan. 31, 1937.
Mignon (M), Philine (P), Frédéric (F), Lothario (L)

*Missa Solemnis* (L. v. Beethoven). 8 performances Apr. 5, 1931–Dec. 28, 1940 (New York).

*La notte di Zoraima* (I. Montemezzi): JB as A Voice in the Night. 5 performances Oct. 16, 1931–Jan. 13, 1932 (Stockholm).
Zoraima (Z), Muscar (M), Pedrito (P)

*Pagliacci* (R. Leoncavallo): JB as Canio. 20 performances Jan. 11, 1936–May 9, 1955 (Stockholm).
Nedda (N), Beppe (B), Tonio (T), Silvio (S)

*Resa till Amerika* (H. Rosenberg): JB as The Bargeman. 5 performances Nov. 24, 1932–Feb. 1, 1933 (Stockholm).
She (S), He (H)

*Das Rheingold* (R. Wagner): JB as Froh. 1 performance Jan. 17, 1933.
Fricka (F), Erda (E), Loge (L), Mime (M), Wotan (W), Alberich (A), Fasolt (Fs), Fafner (Ff)

*Rigoletto* (G. Verdi): JB as the Duke of Mantua. 56 performances Feb. 25, 1932–Nov. 19, 1958 (Chicago).
Gilda (G), Giovanna (Gv), Maddalena (M), Rigoletto (R), Sparafucile (S)

*Roméo et Juliette* (C. Gounod): JB as Tybalt and Roméo. 3 performances as Tybalt Aug. 30, 1931–Feb. 1, 1932 (Stockholm). 44 performances as Roméo Aug. 22, 1933–Oct. 29, 1951 (Los Angeles, S. F. Opera); only act 4 sung 4 times in Stockholm.
Juliette (J), Stéphano (S), Roméo (R), Tybalt (T), Mercutio (M), Friar Laurent (L)

*Rossini in Neapel* (B. Paumgartner): JB as Gioacchino Rossini. 6 performances Nov. 26, 1936–Dec. 26, 1936 (Stockholm).
Colbran (C), Barbaja (B)

*Sadko* (N. Rimsky-Korsakov): JB as A Hindu Guest. 11 performances Nov. 17, 1934–Apr. 13, 1936 (Stockholm).
Volkhova (V), Sadko (S), Tsar of the Ocean (O), Venetian Guest (Ve), Viking Guest (Vi)

*Salome* (R. Strauss): JB as Narraboth. 5 performances Dec. 29, 1931–Oct. 3, 1932 (Stockholm).
Salome (S), Herodias (Hi), Herodes (He), Jochanaan (J)

*Saul og David* (C. Nielsen): JB as Jonathan. 14 performances Jan. 13, 1931–Mar. 23, 1932 (Stockholm).
Mikal (M), David (D), Saul (S), Samuel (Sm)

*Il tabarro* (G. Puccini): JB as Luigi. 4 performances Oct. 20, 1934–Dec. 13, 1934 (Stockholm).
Giorgetta (G), Michele (M)

*Tannhäuser* (R. Wagner): JB as Walther von der Vogelweide. 12 performances Aug. 8, 1931–Sep. 30, 1932 (Stockholm).
Elisabeth (E), Venus (V), Tannhäuser (T), Wolfram (W), Hermann (H)

*Te Deum* (A. Bruckner). 1 performance Apr. 29, 1930.

*Tosca* (G. Puccini): JB as Mario Cavaradossi. 51 performances Oct. 19, 1933–Dec. 16, 1959 (New York).
Tosca (T), Scarpia (S), Sacristan (Sa)

*La traviata* (G. Verdi): JB as Alfredo. 14 performances Jan. 5, 1933–Aug. 29, 1939 (Stockholm).
Violetta (V), Flora (F), Germont (G)

*Tristan und Isolde* (R. Wagner): JB as A Young Sailor. 4 performances Feb. 15, 1932–Apr. 6, 1935 (Stockholm).
Isolde (I), Brangäne (B), Tristan (T), Steersman (S), Kurwenal (K), Marke (M)

*Il trovatore* (G. Verdi): JB as Manrico. 67 performances Aug. 17, 1935–Mar. 29, 1960 (San Francisco, Cosmopolitan Opera).
Leonora (L), Azucena (A), Di Luna (DL), Ferrando (F)  ,

*Die Zauberflöte* (W. A. Mozart): JB as Tamino. 5 performances Dec. 15, 1933–Dec. 8, 1936 (Malmö, Stockholm Opera).
Pamina (Pm), Queen of the Night (Q), Papagena (Pa), Papageno (Po), Sarastro (S)

*Der Zigeunerbaron* (J. Strauss): JB as Sándor Barinkay. 7 performances Apr. 4, 1938–Aug. 26, 1938 (Stockholm).
Saffi (S), Arsena (A), Czipra (C), Zsupán (Z)

## Jussi Björling's Public Performances

This chronological table comprises JB's known public performances. As a rule, "concert" stands for orchestral accompaniment (with the conductor's name indicated, if known) and "recital" for piano accompaniment. The list excludes JB's performances as a boy together with his brothers—a great number of performances in Sweden between 1915 (December 12) and 1927 and in the US between 1919 (November 20) and 1921—and his performances as a conservatory student at the

Royal Academy of Music in Stockholm (17 student concerts between October 5, 1929 and April 25, 1931). Radio concerts sung without an audience, excluded here, can be found in *A Jussi Björling Phonography*.

The country is indicated after a city name only in a few cases, mainly for European non-capital cities. The country is never given for Swedish, British, US, or Canadian cities. State names are added for only those US and Canadian cities which may not be known to international readers. Names of opera houses are given only when it is necessary in order to avoid confusion (e.g., in Prague, where JB sang both at the National Theater and at the New German Theater). Where no locality is indicated, Stockholm performances were given at the Royal Opera House, New York performances at the Metropolitan Opera House. The locality for a recital or concert, if known, is as a rule indicated only for cities which played an important role in JB's career and where he sang frequently (e.g., some of the largest Swedish cities: Stockholm, Gothenburg [Göteborg], Malmö, Helsingborg, Uppsala, and Lund; the other Scandinavian capitals (Copenhagen, Oslo, and Helsinki); London; and some US cities: New York, Chicago, San Francisco, Detroit, etc.). Unless otherwise noted ("w. other soloists," "joint w."), a concert or recital was a solo performance. At a "festival," "soiree," "cabaret program," or "radio program," JB was, as a rule, joined by other artists.

The list of opera performances is assumed to be complete. I was able to verify 931 complete opera and operetta performances between 1930 and 1960 (including two where JB was replaced after the first act). The information about some American recital tours is far from complete, due to a lack of sources. Documentation for a great number of recitals and concerts has been found in the Björling family archive and other sources after the corresponding list in *A Jussi Björling Phonography* was compiled. Several Swedish recitals are no doubt still missing, especially those outside the largest cities. Researching JB's career has been rendered difficult by the fact that several times he cancelled performances after a program had been printed. Programs exist for some performances which did not take place; one such example is a *Don Giovanni* in Los Angeles in 1948. Whenever possible, my ambition has been to verify that scheduled performances actually took place. Performances followed by (?) are regarded as uncertain (e.g., there may be no other evidence for them than the itinerary of a planned tour).

I am grateful to many persons who have been helpful with information for this list. I owe special thanks for assistance with opera performances to Dr. Bergljot Krohn Bucht, Royal Opera Archives, Stockholm, and to Mr. Tommy Eriksson, Karlstad. Mr. Bertil Bengtsson, Gothenburg, has checked the manuscript. Any additions or corrections from readers will be much appreciated. They can be sent to The Jussi Björling Museum, Borganäsvägen 25, S-784 33 Borlänge, Sweden.

Harald Henrysson
Borlänge, Sweden

## 1930

| | |
|---|---|
| Apr. 29 | Stockholm, Concert Hall. *Te Deum*. E. Lundin, E. Widmark-Lundblad, J. Kyhle; V. Talich, cond. |
| May 11 | Stockholm, Hasselbacken Restaurant. Recital (Konstnärsringen spring banquet). |
| July 21 | Stockholm. *Manon Lescaut* (Lamplighter). G. Söderman (M), E. Beyron (DG), C. Richter (L), Å. Wallgren (G); N. Grevillius, cond. |
| July 25 | Stockholm. *Bellman*. G. Pålson-Wettergren (U), D. Stockman (B), O. Strandberg (G), B. Biguet (Mw), C. Molin (Ml); N. Grevillius, cond. |
| Aug. 11 | Stockholm. *Manon Lescaut* (Lamplighter). As July 21 except H. Görlin (M). |
| Aug. 20 | Stockholm. *Don Giovanni* (gala for 2nd International Congress of Pediatricians). K. Sundström-Bernstein (A), I. Wassner (E), H. Görlin (Z), J. Forsell (G), J. Berglund (L), E. Benktander (M), Å. Wallgren (C); A. Järnefelt, cond. |
| Sep. 25 | Stockholm. *Don Giovanni*. As Aug. 20 except C. Richter (G). |
| Nov. 29 | Stockholm. *Louise*. H. Görlin (L), G. Pålson-Wettergren (M), E. Beyron (J), L. Björker (F); N. Grevillius, cond. |
| Dec. 1 | Stockholm. *Louise*. As Nov. 29. |
| Dec. 4 | Stockholm. *Louise*. As Nov. 29. |
| Dec. 6 | Stockholm, Storkyrkan. *Messiah*. H. Görlin, E. Larcén, J. Berglund; T. Voghera, cond. |
| Dec. 10 | Stockholm. *Louise*. As Nov. 29. |
| Dec. 13 | Stockholm. *Louise*. As Nov. 29. |
| Dec. 26 | Stockholm. *Louise*. As Nov. 29. |
| Dec. 27 | Stockholm. *Guillaume Tell*. A. Ohlson (M), E. Ekendahl (J), B. Ewert (H), J. Berglund (T), L. Björker (W), E. Stiebel (G); H. Sandberg, cond. |
| Dec. 30 | Stockholm. *Guillaume Tell*. As Dec. 27. |

## 1931

| | |
|---|---|
| Jan. 4 | Stockholm. *Louise*. As Nov. 29, 1930. |
| Jan. 13 | Stockholm. *Saul og David*. B. Hertzberg (M), C. Arnesen (D), E. Larson (S), Å. Wallgren (Sm); A. Järnefelt, cond. |
| Jan. 15 | Stockholm. *Saul og David*. As Jan. 13. |
| Jan. 17 | Stockholm. *Guillaume Tell*. A. Ohlson (M), E. Ekendahl (J), B. Ewert (H), J. Berglund (T), L. Björker (W), J. Herou (G); H. Sandberg, cond. |
| Jan. 18 | Stockholm. *Saul og David*. As Jan. 13. |
| Jan. 25 | Stockholm. *Guillaume Tell*. As Jan. 17. |
| Jan. 27 | Stockholm. *Don Giovanni* (gala on Mozart's 175th birthday). R. Althén (A), I. Wassner (E), H. Görlin (Z), J. Forsell (G), J. Berglund (L), E. Benktander (M), Å. Wallgren (C); A. Järnefelt, cond. |
| Feb. 8 | Stora Tuna. Recital (JB sang w. piano in concert by local orchestra). |
| Feb. 8 | Domnarvet. Recital (as above). |
| Feb. 20 | Stockholm. *Guillaume Tell*. As Dec. 27, 1930. |
| Feb. 21 | Stockholm. *Saul og David*. As Jan. 13 except K. Bernstein-Sundström (M), D. Stockman (D). |

| | |
|---|---|
| Feb. 23 | Stockholm. *Saul og David*. As Feb. 21. |
| Feb. 24 | Stockholm. *Guillaume Tell*. As Dec. 27, 1930. |
| Feb. 25 | Stockholm. *Saul og David*. As Feb. 21. |
| Feb. 27 | Stockholm. *Guillaume Tell*. As Dec. 27, 1930. |
| Mar. 2 | Stockholm. *Guillaume Tell*. As Dec. 27, 1930. |
| Mar. 8 | Stockholm. *Saul og David*. As Feb. 21. |
| Mar. 20 | Stockholm. *Saul og David*. As Jan. 13 except D. Stockman (D). |
| Mar. 21 | Stockholm. *Engelbrekt*. E. Larcén (I), H. Görlin (K), E. Ekendahl (C), S. Edwardsen (KE), E. Larson (E), S. Herdenberg (P); A. Järnefelt, cond. |
| Mar. 25 | Stockholm. *Engelbrekt*. As Mar. 21. |
| Apr. 5 | Stockholm. *Missa Solemnis*. R. Althén, E. Larcén, J. Berglund; T. Voghera, cond. |
| Apr. 19 | Stockholm. *Cavalieri di Ekebù*. B. Hertzberg (A), K. Thorborg (W), E. Beyron (B); N. Grevillius, cond. |
| Apr. 24 | Stockholm. *Cavalieri di Ekebù*. As Apr. 19. |
| Apr. 29 | Stockholm. *Guillaume Tell*. As Dec. 27, 1930. |
| May 6 | Helsinki (Stockholm Opera). *Don Giovanni*. As Jan. 27 except K. Bernstein-Sundström (A), S. d'Ailly (M); H. Sandberg, cond. |
| May 7 | Helsinki (Stockholm Opera). *Engelbrekt*. As Mar. 21 except R. Nordström (C); H. Sandberg, cond. |
| May 8 | Helsinki (Stockholm Opera). *Cavalieri di Ekebù*. As Apr. 19 except G. Pålson-Wettergren (W). |
| May 9 | Helsinki (Stockholm Opera). *Don Giovanni*. As May 6. |
| July 22 | Gothenburg, Liseberg. Recital. |
| July 29 | Copenhagen, Tivoli. Concert; F. Schnedler-Petersen, cond. (partly recital w. piano). |
| July 31 | Porla. Recital. |
| Aug. 8 | Stockholm. *Tannhäuser*. B. Hertzberg (E), I. Wassner (V), E. Beyron (T), E. Larson (W), Å. Wallgren (H); A. Järnefelt, cond. |
| Aug. 14 | Stockholm. *Cavalieri di Ekebù*. As May 8. |
| Aug. 17 | Stockholm. *Tannhäuser*. As Aug. 8. |
| Aug. 30 | Stockholm. *Roméo et Juliette* (Tybalt). H. Görlin (J), K. Rydqvist (S), D. Stockman (R), S. Herdenberg (M), L. Björker (L); N. Grevillius, cond. |
| Sep. 1 | Stockholm. *Tannhäuser*. As Aug. 8 except C. Molin (W), L. Björker (H). |
| Sep. 5 | Stockholm. *Manon Lescaut* (Lamplighter). H. Görlin (M), E. Beyron (DG), C. Richter (L), Å. Wallgren (G); N. Grevillius, cond. |
| Sep. 11 | Stockholm. *Louise*. As Nov. 29, 1930. |
| Sep. 13 | Stockholm. *Tannhäuser*. As Aug. 8 except L. Björker (H). |
| Sep. 15 | Stockholm. *Manon Lescaut* (Lamplighter). As Sep. 5. |
| Sep. 16 | Stockholm. *Saul og David*. As Feb. 21. |
| Sep. 22 | Stockholm. *Saul og David*. As Feb. 21. |
| Sep. 29 | Stockholm. *Der fliegende Holländer*. I. Wassner (S), E. Larcén (M), S. Edwardsen (St), J. Berglund (Du), L. Björker (Da); H. Sandberg, cond. |
| Oct. 3 | Stockholm. *Tannhäuser*. As Aug. 8 except G. Ljungberg (E), O. Ralf (T), C. Molin (W). |

Oct. 7     Stockholm. *Roméo et Juliette* (Tybalt). As Aug. 30 except M. Mandahl (S), E. Beyron (R).
Oct. 16    Stockholm. *Notte di Zoraima*. K. Rydqvist (Z), E. Beyron (M), E. Larson (P); N. Grevillius, cond.
Oct. 18    Stockholm. *Notte di Zoraima*. As Oct. 16.
Oct. 22    Stockholm. *Tannhäuser*. As Aug. 8 except N. Larsén-Todsen (E), L. Björker (H).
Oct. 24    Stockholm. *Notte di Zoraima*. As Oct. 16.
Oct. 28    Stockholm. *Manon Lescaut* (Lamplighter). As Sep. 15.
Nov. 2     Stockholm. *Notte di Zoraima*. As Oct. 16.
Nov. 7     Stockholm. *Barbiere di Siviglia*. A. Ohlson (R), E. Larcén (Be), S. Svanholm (F), E. Stiebel (Br), Å. Wallgren (Bs); H. Sandberg, cond.
Nov. 10    Stockholm. *Barbiere di Siviglia*. As Nov. 7.
Nov. 11    Stockholm. *Saul og David*. As Feb. 21.
Nov. 15    Stockholm. *Barbiere di Siviglia*. As Nov. 7.
Nov. 16    Stockholm. *Der fliegende Holländer*. As Sep. 29 except N. Larsén-Todsen (S).
Nov. 20    Stockholm. *Barbiere di Siviglia*. As Nov. 7.
Nov. 22    Stockholm. *Guillaume Tell*. As Dec. 27, 1930.
Nov. 27    Stockholm. *Barbiere di Siviglia*. As Nov. 7.
Dec. 2     Stockholm. *Barbiere di Siviglia*. As Nov. 7.
Dec. 5     Stockholm, Storkyrkan. *Messiah*. As Dec. 6, 1930.
Dec. 29    Stockholm. *Salome*. K. Rydqvist (S), G. Pålson-Wettergren (Hi), O. Ralf (He), C. Richter (J); A. Järnefelt, cond.

**1932**

Jan. 3     Stockholm. *Guillaume Tell*. As Dec. 27, 1930.
Jan. 6     Stockholm. *Salome*. As Dec. 29, 1931, except B. Ewert (Hi).
Jan. 9     Stockholm. *Tannhäuser*. B. Hertzberg (E), I. Wassner (V), M. Öhman (T), E. Larson (W), Å. Wallgren (H); A. Järnefelt, cond.
Jan. 13    Stockholm. *Notte di Zoraima*. As Oct. 16, 1931.
Jan. 16    Stockholm. *Illustre Fregona*. R. Nordström (F), C. Olsson Åhrberg (C), F. Cembraeus (L); N. Grevillius, cond.
Jan. 18    Stockholm. *Illustre Fregona*. As Jan. 16.
Jan. 23    Stockholm. *Illustre Fregona*. As Jan. 16.
Jan. 24    Stockholm. *Tannhäuser*. As Jan. 9 except K. Bernstein-Sundström (E), C. Molin (W), L. Björker (H).
Jan. 25    Stockholm. *Salome*. As Dec. 29, 1931.
Jan. 30    Stockholm. *Illustre Fregona*. As Jan. 16.
Feb. 1     Stockholm. *Roméo et Juliette* (Tybalt). R. Nordström (J), M. Mandahl (S), D. Stockman (R), S. Herdenberg (M), L. Björker (L); N. Grevillius, cond.
Feb. 6     Stockholm. *Barbiere di Siviglia*. A. Ohlson (R), E. Larcén (Be), S. Svanholm (F), E. Stiebel (Br), Å. Wallgren (Bs); L. Blech, cond.
Feb. 10    Stockholm. *Illustre Fregona*. As Jan. 16.
Feb. 15    Stockholm. *Tristan und Isolde*. H. Trundt (I), G. Pålson-Wettergren (B), E. Beyron (T), S. Herdenberg (S), C. Molin (K), Å. Wallgren (M); L. Blech, cond.

397

| | |
|---|---|
| Feb. 17 | Stockholm. *Tristan und Isolde*. As Feb. 15. |
| Feb. 22 | Stockholm. *Barbiere di Siviglia*. As Feb. 6. |
| Feb. 25 | Stockholm. *Rigoletto*. A. Ohlson (G), E. Larcén (Gv), I. Björck (M), E. Larson (R), L. Björker (S); L. Blech, cond. |
| Feb. 26 | Stockholm. *Barbiere di Siviglia*. As Feb. 6. |
| Feb. 28 | Stockholm. *Illustre Fregona*. As Jan. 16. |
| Feb. 29 | Stockholm. *Rigoletto*. As Feb. 25. |
| Mar. 2 | Stockholm. *Illustre Fregona*. As Jan. 16. |
| Mar. 11 | Stockholm. *Saul og David*. As Mar. 20, 1931. |
| Mar. 13 | Stockholm. *Barbiere di Siviglia*. As Feb. 6 except H. Sandberg, cond. |
| Mar. 15 | Stockholm. *Manon Lescaut* (Lamplighter). M. Flor (M), E. Beyron (DG), C. Richter (L), Å. Wallgren (G); N. Grevillius, cond. |
| Mar. 16 | Stockholm. *Saul og David*. As Mar. 20, 1931. |
| Mar. 18 | Stockholm. *Rigoletto*. As Feb. 25 except K. Bendix, cond. |
| Mar. 23 | Stockholm. *Saul og David*. As Mar. 20, 1931. |
| Mar. 25 | Stockholm. *Missa Solemnis*. As Apr. 5, 1931. |
| Mar. 30 | Stockholm. *Rigoletto*. As Mar. 18. |
| Apr. 3 | Stockholm. *Tannhäuser*. As Jan. 9 except O. Ralf (T), L. Björker (H). |
| Apr. 9 | Stockholm. *Tannhäuser*. As Apr. 3 except C. Richter (W). |
| Apr. 14 | Stockholm. *Herz*. B. Hertzberg (H), S. Edwardsen (M), J. Berglund (A), I. Björck (W); A. Järnefelt, cond. |
| Apr. 16 | Stockholm. *Illustre Fregona*. As Jan. 16. |
| Apr. 21 | Stockholm. *Herz*. As Apr. 14. |
| Apr. 25 | Stockholm. *Herz*. As Apr. 14. |
| May 6 | Stockholm. *Illustre Fregona*. As Jan. 16. |
| June 8 | Copenhagen, Tivoli. Concert; F. Schnedler-Petersen, cond. (partly recital w. piano). |
| June 10 | Copenhagen, Tivoli. Concert. As June 8. |
| June 14 | Copenhagen, Tivoli. Concert. As June 8. |
| June 15 | Malmö, Folkets Park. Recital. |
| June 16 | Copenhagen, Tivoli. Concert. As June 8. |
| July 6 | Gothenburg, Liseberg. Recital. |
| Aug. 9 | Stockholm. *Tannhäuser*. As Apr. 3 except C. Molin (W); H. Sandberg, cond. |
| Aug. 12 | Stockholm. *Barbiere di Siviglia*. As Feb. 6 except H. Sandberg, cond. |
| Sep. 3 | Stockholm. *Barbiere di Siviglia*. As Aug. 12. |
| Sep. 6 | Copenhagen, Tivoli. Joint concert w. V. Schiøler, piano; F. Schnedler-Petersen, cond. |
| Sep. 10 | Copenhagen, Tivoli. Concert; F. Schnedler-Petersen, cond. (partly recital w. piano). |
| Sep. 24 | Stockholm. *Salome*. As Jan. 6 except G. Ljungberg (S); K. Bendix, cond. |
| Sep. 28 | Stockholm. *Barbiere di Siviglia*. As Aug. 12. |
| Sep. 30 | Stockholm. *Tannhäuser*. As Aug. 9 except G. Ljungberg (E), C. Richter (W), Å. Wallgren (H). |
| Oct. 2 | Stockholm. *Illustre Fregona*, acts 1 and 3 (part of gala for the Prince of Wales). As Jan. 16. |
| Oct. 3 | Stockholm. *Salome*. As Sep. 24. |
| Oct. 5 | Stockholm. *Illustre Fregona*. As Jan. 16. |

| | |
|---|---|
| Oct. 8 | Stockholm. *Mignon*. H. Görlin (M), A. Ohlson (P), O. Strandberg (F), J. Berglund (L); H. Sandberg, cond. |
| Oct. 16 | Stockholm. *Mignon*. As Oct. 8 except K. Rydqvist (M). |
| Nov. 2 | Stockholm. *Mignon*. As Oct. 8 except J. Forsell (L). |
| Nov. 9 | Stockholm. *Elisir d'amore*. H. Görlin (A), S. Herdenberg (B), E. Stiebel (D); H. Sandberg, cond. |
| Nov. 16 | Stockholm. *Elisir d'amore*. As Nov. 9. |
| Nov. 20 | Stockholm. *Mignon*. As Oct. 8. |
| Nov. 24 | Stockholm. *Resa till Amerika*. H. Görlin (S), J. Berglund (H); H. Rosenberg, cond. |
| Nov. 27 | Stockholm. *Illustre Fregona*. As Jan. 16. |
| Nov. 28 | Stockholm. *Resa till Amerika*. As Nov. 24. |
| Dec. 1 | Stockholm. *Resa till Amerika*. As Nov. 24. |
| Dec. 3 | Stockholm, Storkyrkan. *Messiah*. As Dec. 6, 1930. |
| Dec. 7 | Stockholm. *Resa till Amerika*. As Nov. 24. |
| Dec. 12 | Stockholm. *Rigoletto*. As Mar. 18 except S. Andreva (G). |
| Dec. 27 | Stockholm. *Rigoletto*. As Dec. 12. |

**1933**

| | |
|---|---|
| Jan. 5 | Stockholm. *Traviata*. H. Görlin (V), A. Ohlson (F), E. Larson (G); L. Blech, cond. |
| Jan. 11 | Stockholm. *Traviata*. As Jan. 5. |
| Jan. 14 | Stockholm. *Evgeny Onegin*. K. Rydqvist (T), B. Ewert (Ol), E. Larcén (F), E. Larson (On), L. Björker (G); H. Sandberg, cond. |
| Jan. 17 | Stockholm. *Rheingold*. G. Pålson-Wettergren (F), E. Larcén (E), F. Cembraeus (L), S. Edwardsen (M), J. Berglund (W), E. Stiebel (A), C. Molin (Fs), L. Björker (Ff); L. Blech, cond. |
| Jan. 21 | Stockholm. *Evgeny Onegin*. As Jan. 14. |
| Jan. 30 | Stockholm. *Traviata*. As Jan. 5. |
| Feb. 1 | Stockholm. *Resa till Amerika*. As Nov. 24, 1932. |
| Feb. 3 | Stockholm. *Elisir d'amore*. As Nov. 9, 1932. |
| Feb. 5 | Stockholm. *Traviata*. As Jan. 5. |
| Feb. 6 | Stockholm. *Evgeny Onegin*. As Jan. 14. |
| Feb. 8 | Stockholm. *Elisir d'amore*. As Nov. 9, 1932. |
| Feb. 9 | Stockholm. *Tristan und Isolde*. B. Hertzberg (I), G. Pålson-Wettergren (B), E. Beyron (T), S. Herdenberg (S), C. Molin (K), Å. Wallgren (M); L. Blech, cond. |
| Feb. 12 | Stockholm. *Evgeny Onegin*. As Jan. 14. |
| Feb. 14 | Stockholm. *Elisir d'amore*. As Nov. 9, 1932. |
| Feb. 19 | Stockholm. *Elisir d'amore*. As Nov. 9, 1932. |
| Mar. 11 | Stockholm. *Knyaz Igor*. H. Görlin (Ya), G. Pålson-Wettergren (Ka), E. Larson (I), Å. Wallgren (G), J. Berglund (Kk); N. Grevillius, cond. |
| Mar. 12 | Stockholm. *Barbiere di Siviglia*. As Aug. 12, 1932. |
| Mar. 13 | Stockholm. *Knyaz Igor*. As Mar. 11. |
| Mar. 16 | Stockholm. *Knyaz Igor*. As Mar. 11. |
| Mar. 18 | Stockholm. *Knyaz Igor*. As Mar. 11. |
| Mar. 19 | Stockholm. *Knyaz Igor*. As Mar. 11. |
| Mar. 23 | Stockholm. *Knyaz Igor*. As Mar. 11. |

| | |
|---|---|
| Mar. 25 | Stockholm. *Knyaz Igor*. As Mar. 11. |
| Mar. 26 | Stockholm. *Missa Solemnis*. As Apr. 5, 1931. |
| Mar. 30 | Stockholm. *Knyaz Igor*. As Mar. 11. |
| Apr. 5 | Stockholm. *Knyaz Igor*. As Mar. 11. |
| Apr. 6 | Stockholm. *Kronbruden*. B. Hertzberg (K), E. Larcén (B), R. Nordström (M), J. Berglund (C), E. Larson (N); A. Järnefelt, cond. |
| Apr. 9 | Malmö, Palladium. Recital w. Sångarcirkeln choir. |
| Apr. 12 | Stockholm. *Knyaz Igor*. As Mar. 11. |
| Apr. 15 | Stockholm. *Knyaz Igor*. As Mar. 11. |
| Apr. 19 | Stockholm. *Barbiere di Siviglia*. S. Andreva (R), G. Allard (Be), S. Svanholm (F), E. Stiebel (Br), Å. Wallgren (Bs); H. Sandberg, cond. |
| Apr. 20 | Stockholm. *Der fliegende Holländer*. K. Bernstein-Sundström (S), E. Larcén (M), S. Edwardsen (St), J. Berglund (Du), L. Björker (Da); H. Sandberg, cond. |
| Apr. 24 | Stockholm. *Der fliegende Holländer*. As Apr. 20. |
| Apr. 26 | Stockholm. *Traviata*. As Jan. 5 except H. Sandberg, cond. |
| Apr. 27 | Stockholm. *Knyaz Igor*. As Mar. 11 except S. Herdenberg (G). |
| May 5 | Copenhagen (Stockholm Opera). *Knyaz Igor*. As Mar. 11. |
| May 6 | Copenhagen (Stockholm Opera). *Don Giovanni*. K. Bernstein-Sundström (A), I. Wassner (E), H. Görlin (Z), J. Forsell (G), E. Stiebel (L), F. Cembraeus (M), L. Björker (C); H. Sandberg, cond. |
| May 8 | Kristianstad (Stockholm Opera). *Barbiere di Siviglia*. As Apr. 19 except A. Ohlson (R). |
| May 10 | Copenhagen, Tivoli. Concert by Stockholm Opera; (JB's part: H. Sandberg, cond. ?). |
| May 16 | Stockholm. *Knyaz Igor*. As Mar. 11. |
| May 26 | Stockholm. *Knyaz Igor*. As Apr. 27. |
| July 12 | Copenhagen, Tivoli. Concert; F. Schnedler-Petersen, cond. (partly recital w. piano). |
| July 14 | Copenhagen, Tivoli. Concert. As July 12. |
| July 17 | Malmö, Folkets Park. Concert; G. Schnéevoigt, cond. |
| July 19 | Copenhagen, Tivoli. Concert. As July 12. |
| July 21 | Copenhagen, Tivoli. Concert. As July 12. |
| Aug. 3 | Stockholm. *Knyaz Igor*. As Mar. 11 except R. Althén (Ya), S. Herdenberg (I). |
| Aug. 15 | Stockholm. *Cavalieri di Ekebù*. B. Hertzberg (A), G. Pålson-Wettergren (W), E. Beyron (B); N. Grevillius, cond. |
| Aug. 16 | Stockholm. *Knyaz Igor*. As Aug. 3. |
| Aug. 22 | Stockholm. *Roméo et Juliette*. S. Andreva (J), E. Ekendahl (S), S. Edwardsen (T), S. Herdenberg (M), L. Björker (L); H. Rosenberg, cond. |
| Aug. 23 | Stockholm. *Cavalieri di Ekebù*. As Aug. 15. |
| Aug. 25 | Stockholm. *Knyaz Igor*. As Aug. 3. |
| Aug. 27 | Stockholm. *Roméo et Juliette*. As Aug. 22. |
| Aug. 30 | Stockholm. *Barbiere di Siviglia*. As Apr. 19 except E. Larcén (Be). |
| Sep. 6 | Stockholm. *Djamileh*. B. Ewert (D), F. Cembraeus (S); K. Bendix, cond. |
| Sep. 7 | Stockholm. *Knyaz Igor*. As Aug. 3. |
| Sep. 9 | Stockholm. *Djamileh*. As Sep. 6. |

Sep. 10     Stockholm, Skansen. Recital (benefit for Barnens Dag).

Sep. 14     Stockholm. *Djamileh*. As Sep. 6.

Sep. 20     Stockholm. *Roméo et Juliette*. As Aug. 22.

Sep. 27     Stockholm. *Cavalieri di Ekebù*. As Aug. 15.

Sep. 30     Stockholm. *Martha*. A. Ohlson (H), B. Ewert (N), J. Berglund (P); H. Rosenberg, cond.

Oct. 1     Stockholm. *Djamileh*. As Sep. 6.

Oct. 4     Stockholm. *Martha*. As Sep. 30.

Oct. 5     Stockholm. *Knyaz Igor*. As Aug. 3 except E. Larson (I).

Oct. 11     Stockholm. *Martha*. As Sep. 30.

Oct. 16     Helsingborg, Concert Hall. Recital w. Kvartettsångsällskapet (Quartet Song Society); O. Lidner, cond. (partly recital w. piano).

Oct. 19     Stockholm. *Tosca*. K. Rydqvist (T), C. Richter (S), E. Stiebel (Sa); N. Grevillius, cond.

Oct. 22     Stockholm. *Barbiere di Siviglia*. As Aug. 30.

Oct. 27     Stockholm. *Tosca*. As Oct. 19.

Oct. 29     Stockholm. *Djamileh*. As Sep. 6.

Oct. 29     Stockholm. *Illustre Fregona*. As Jan. 16, 1932.

Oct. 30     Stockholm. *Roméo et Juliette*. As Aug. 22.

Nov. 6     Stockholm. *Don Giovanni* (gala on J. Forsell's 65th birthday). As May 6 except R. Althén (A).

Nov. 8     Stockholm. *Roméo et Juliette*. As Aug. 22.

Nov. 12     Stockholm. *Mignon*. H. Görlin (M), S. Andreva (P), O. Strandberg (F), Å. Wallgren (L); H. Sandberg, cond.

Nov. 26     Stockholm. *Djamileh*. As Sep. 6.

Nov. 29     Stockholm. *Knyaz Igor*. As Oct. 5.

Dec. 1     Stockholm. *Knyaz Igor*. As Oct. 5.

Dec. 2     Stockholm, Storkyrkan. *Messiah*. H. Görlin, G. Pålson-Wettergren, J. Berglund; T. Voghera, cond.

Dec. 4     Stockholm. *Knyaz Igor*. As Oct. 5 except S. Herdenberg (G).

Dec. 11     Stockholm. *Cavalieri di Ekebù*. As Aug. 15.

Dec. 15     Stockholm. *Zauberflöte*. K. Rydqvist (Pm), A. Ohlson (Q), E. Ekendahl (Pa), F. Cembraeus (Po), L. Björker (S); H. Rosenberg, cond.

Dec. 29     Stockholm. *Knyaz Igor*. As Aug. 3.

Dec. 30     Stockholm. *Arabella*. H. Görlin (A), S. Andreva (Z), E. Beyron (Mt), E. Larson (Mn); H. Sandberg, cond.

## 1934

Jan. 2     Stockholm. *Arabella*. As Dec. 30, 1933.

Jan. 5     Stockholm. *Arabella*. As Dec. 30, 1933.

Jan. 8     Stockholm. *Zauberflöte*. As Dec. 15, 1933.

Jan. 9     Stockholm. *Arabella*. As Dec. 30, 1933, except D. Stockman (Mt).

Jan. 15     Stockholm. *Arabella*. As Dec. 30, 1933.

Jan. 18     Stockholm. *Knyaz Igor*. R. Althén (Ya), B. Ewert (Ka), E. Larson (I), S. Herdenberg (G), J. Berglund (Kk); N. Grevillius, cond.

Jan. 27     Stockholm. *Fanal*. H. Görlin (R), J. Berglund (J), L. Björker (D); N. Grevillius, cond.

Jan. 29     Stockholm. *Fanal*. As Jan. 27.

[1934]
| | |
|---|---|
| Feb. 1 | Stockholm. *Fanal*. As Jan. 27. |
| Feb. 3 | Stockholm. *Fanal*. As Jan. 27. |
| Feb. 13 | Stockholm. *Fanal*. As Jan. 27. |
| Feb. 14 | Stockholm. *Arabella*? (JB's participation uncertain). As Jan. 9. |
| Feb. 26 | Stockholm. *Fanal*. As Jan. 27. |
| Mar. 2 | Stockholm. *Fanal*. As Jan. 27. |
| Mar. 11 | Stockholm. *Fanal*. As Jan. 27. |
| Mar. 13 | Gävle (Stockholm Opera). *Barbiere di Siviglia*. As May 8, 1933 except J. Forsell (Bs). |
| Mar. 20 | Stockholm. *Fanal*. As Jan. 27. |
| Mar. 24 | Stockholm. *Knyaz Igor*. As Jan. 18 except H. Görlin (Ya). |
| Mar. 28 | Stockholm. *Fanal*. As Jan. 27. |
| Apr. 3 | Stockholm. *Fanal*. As Jan. 27. |
| Apr. 6 | Stockholm. *Kronbruden*. B. Hertzberg (K), E. Larcén (B), R. Nordström (M), J. Berglund (C), E. Larson (N); H. Sandberg, cond. |
| Apr. 7 | Stockholm, Opera House. Concert by Royal Opera soloists; N. Grevillius, cond. |
| Apr. 8 | Stockholm. *Tosca*. K. Rydqvist (T), C. Richter (S), E. Stiebel (Sa); N. Grevillius, cond. |
| Apr. 11 | Gävle. Concert; H. Sandberg, cond. |
| Apr. 12 | Gävle. Concert; H. Sandberg, cond. |
| Apr. 18 | Stockholm. *Ballo in maschera*. I. Köhler (A), S. Andreva (O), G. Pålson-Wettergren (U), E. Larson (R), C. Molin (S), L. Björker (T); H. Sandberg, cond. |
| May 7 | Västerås. Joint recital w. S. Svanholm. |
| May 26 | Oslo (Stockholm Opera). *Don Giovanni*. B. Hertzberg (A), I. Wassner (E), H. Görlin (Z), J. Forsell (G), J. Berglund (L), C. Molin (M), L. Björker (C); H. Sandberg, cond. |
| May 27 | Oslo (Stockholm Opera). *Fanal*. As Jan. 27. |
| May 31 | Stockholm. *Fanal*. As Jan. 27. |
| June 29 | Copenhagen, Tivoli. Concert by Stockholm Opera soloists (*Fanal* excerpts); N. Grevillius, cond. |
| July 6 | Malmö, Folkets Park. Gala concert; O. Morales, cond. |
| July 11 | Copenhagen, Tivoli. Concert; F. Schnedler-Petersen, cond. (partly recital w. piano). |
| July 13 | Copenhagen, Tivoli. Concert. As July 11. |
| July 18 | Copenhagen, Tivoli. Concert. As July 11. |
| July 20 | Copenhagen, Tivoli. Concert. As July 11. |
| July 21 | Copenhagen, Tivoli. Operetta concert; S. C. Felumb, cond. |
| Aug. 10 | Stockholm. *Fanal*. As Jan. 27. |
| Aug. 14 | Stockholm. *Knyaz Igor*. As Mar. 24 except G. Pålson-Wettergren (Ka). |
| Aug. 19 | Gothenburg, Slottsskogsvallen. Concert w. Västergötland Singers' Union. |
| Aug. 25 | Stockholm. *Faust*. H. Görlin (M), E. Ekendahl (S), E. Larson (V), J. Berglund (Mé); N. Grevillius, cond. |
| Aug. 28 | Stockholm. *Faust*. As Aug. 25. |
| Aug. 29 | Stockholm, Gröna Lund. Recital. |
| Aug. 30 | Stockholm, Gröna Lund. Recital. |

| | |
|---|---|
| Sep. 3 | Stockholm. *Faust*. As Aug. 25. |
| Sep. 5 | Stockholm. *Faust*. As Aug. 25 except C. Richter (V). |
| Sep. 7 | Stockholm, Drottningholm Palace Theater. Soiree. |
| Sep. 8 | Copenhagen, Tivoli. Concert; N. Grevillius, cond. |
| Sep. 9 | Helsingborg, Folkets Park. Recital. |
| Sep. 9 | Malmö, Realskolan. Recital. |
| Sep. 11 | Stockholm. *Faust*. As Aug. 25. |
| Sep. 16 | Stockholm. *Faust*. As Sep. 5. |
| Sep. 20 | Stockholm. *Fanal*. As Jan. 27. |
| Sep. 22 | Stockholm. *Faust*. As Aug. 25. |
| Sep. 25 | Stockholm. *Faust*. As Sep. 5 except K. Bendix, cond. |
| Sep. 26 | Stockholm. *Tosca*. As Apr. 8 except I. Köhler (T); K. Bendix, cond. |
| Sep. 28 | Stockholm. *Barbiere di Siviglia*. As Apr. 19, 1933. |
| Oct. 1 | Fagersta (Stockholm Opera). *Barbiere di Siviglia*. As May 8, 1933. |
| Oct. 5 | Stockholm. *Faust*. As Aug. 25. |
| Oct. 7 | Stockholm. *Tosca*. As Apr. 8 except D. Giannini (T), E. Larson (S). |
| Oct. 13 | Stockholm. *Bohème*. H. Schymberg (Mi), S. Andreva (Mu), E. Larson (Ma), C. Richter (S), L. Björker (C); N. Grevillius, cond. |
| Oct. 16 | Stockholm. *Bohème*. As Oct. 13. |
| Oct. 20 | Stockholm. *Tabarro*. G. Pålson-Wettergren (G), C. Molin (M); N. Grevillius, cond. |
| Oct. 22 | Stockholm. *Faust*. As Aug. 25. |
| Oct. 23 | Stockholm. *Tabarro*. As Oct. 20. |
| Oct. 25 | Stockholm. *Knyaz Igor*. As Aug. 14. |
| Oct. 27 | Stockholm. *Bohème*. As Oct. 13 except S. Herdenberg (Ma). |
| Oct. 29 | Stockholm. *Bohème*. As Oct. 13 except H. Görlin (Mi). |
| Nov. 2 | Stockholm. *Barbiere di Siviglia*. I. Quensel (R), G. Allard (Be), S. Svanholm (F), E. Stiebel (Br), L. Björker (Bs); H. Sandberg, cond. |
| Nov. 3 | Stockholm. *Faust*. As Aug. 25 except K. Bendix, cond. |
| Nov. 6 | Stockholm. *Faust*. As Sep. 25. |
| Nov. 10 | Stockholm. *Faust*. As Sep. 25. |
| Nov. 17 | Stockholm. *Sadko*. S. Andreva (V), E. Beyron (S), J. Berglund (O), E. Larson (Ve), L. Björker (Vi); N. Grevillius, cond. |
| Nov. 18 | Stockholm. *Fanal*. As Jan. 27. |
| Nov. 20 | Stockholm. *Sadko*. As Nov. 17. |
| Nov. 23 | Stockholm. *Faust*. As Nov. 3. |
| Nov. 30 | Stockholm. *Kronbruden* (gala on T. Rangström's 50th birthday). As Apr. 6 except B. Ewert (B), M. Mandahl (M). |
| Dec. 1 | Stockholm, Storkyrkan. *Messiah*. As Dec. 2, 1933. |
| Dec. 2 | Stockholm. *Sadko*. As Nov. 17 except L. Björker (O), S. Herdenberg (Ve); H. Sandberg, cond. |
| Dec. 5 | Malmö (Stockholm Opera). *Tosca*. As Apr. 8 except O. Ralf (Sa). |
| Dec. 7 | Ystad (Stockholm Opera). *Tosca*. As Dec. 5. |
| Dec. 8 | Kristianstad (Stockholm Opera). *Tosca*. As Dec. 5. |
| Dec. 10 | Stockholm. *Tabarro*. As Oct. 20. |
| Dec. 13 | Stockholm. *Tabarro*. As Oct. 20 except K. Bendix, cond. |
| Dec. 15 | Örebro. Recital (benefit for "Uncomplaining Poverty"). |
| Dec. 16 | Stockholm, Sports Palace. "Aquacade" (charity gala), joint w. A.-L. Berg (later Björling). |

| | |
|---|---|
| Dec. 26 | Stockholm. *Sadko*. As Dec. 2. |
| Dec. 29 | Stockholm. *Fanciulla del West*. H. Görlin (M), J. Berglund (R), F. Jonsson (W); N. Grevillius, cond. |

**1935**

| | |
|---|---|
| Jan. 1 | Stockholm. *Fanciulla del West*. As Dec. 29, 1934. |
| Jan. 3 | Stockholm. *Fanciulla del West*. As Dec. 29, 1934. |
| Jan. 5 | Stockholm. *Fanciulla del West*. As Dec. 29, 1934. |
| Jan. 8 | Stockholm. *Fanciulla del West*. As Dec. 29, 1934. |
| Jan. 11 | Stockholm. *Bohème*. As Oct. 29, 1934. |
| Jan. 16 | Gothenburg, Lorensberg's Cirkus. Recital. |
| Jan. 19 | Stockholm. *Bohème*. H. Schymberg (Mi), R. Nordström (Mu), E. Larson (Ma), C. Richter (S), L. Björker (C); N. Grevillius, cond. |
| Jan. 20 | Stockholm. *Fanciulla del West*. As Dec. 29, 1934. |
| Jan. 26 | Stockholm. *Entführung aus dem Serail*. S. Andreva (C), H. Schymberg (B), L. Björker (O), S. Edwardsen (P); H. Sandberg, cond. |
| Jan. 28 | Stockholm. *Fanciulla del West*. As Dec. 29, 1934. |
| Feb. 1 | Stockholm. *Traviata*. S. Andreva (V), G. Allard (F), E. Larson (G); H. Sandberg, cond. |
| Feb. 3 | Stockholm. *Faust*. H. Görlin (M), E. Ekendahl (S), C. Richter (V), J. Berglund (Mé); N. Grevillius, cond. |
| Feb. 6 | Stockholm. *Traviata*. As Feb. 1. |
| Feb. 8 | Stockholm. *Faust*. As Feb. 3 except K. Bendix, cond. |
| Feb. 9 | Stockholm. *Sadko*. S. Andreva (V), E. Beyron (S), L. Björker (O, Vi), S. Herdenberg (Ve); N. Grevillius, cond. |
| Feb. 11 | Stockholm. *Entführung aus dem Serail*. As Jan. 26. |
| Feb. 14 | Stockholm. *Cavalleria rusticana*. K. Rydqvist (S), B. Ewert (Lo), G. Allard (Lu), C. Molin (A); S.-Å. Axelson, cond. |
| Feb. 16 | Stockholm. *Cavalleria rusticana*. As Feb. 14. |
| Feb. 18 | Östersund (Stockholm Opera). *Tosca*. I. Köhler (T), C. Richter (S), O. Ralf (Sa); N. Grevillius, cond. |
| Feb. 22 | Stockholm. *Cavalleria rusticana*. As Feb. 14. |
| Feb. 24 | Stockholm. *Entführung aus dem Serail*. As Jan. 26. |
| Feb. 26 | Stockholm. *Knyaz Igor*. As Mar. 24, 1934. |
| Mar. 1 | Stockholm. *Cavalleria rusticana*. As Feb. 14. |
| Mar. 3 | Stockholm. *Barbiere di Siviglia*. As Nov. 2, 1934. |
| Mar. 5 | Uppsala, University. Concert; N. Grevillius, cond. |
| Mar. 6 | Stockholm. *Fanciulla del West*. As Dec. 29, 1934. |
| Mar. 9 | Stockholm. *Evgeny Onegin*. B. Hertzberg (T), B. Ewert (Ol), G. Pålson-Wettergren (F), E. Larson (On), L. Björker (G); H. Sandberg, cond. |
| Mar. 11 | Stockholm. *Evgeny Onegin*. As Mar. 9. |
| Mar. 14 | Stockholm. *Evgeny Onegin*. As Mar. 9 except K. Rydqvist (T). |
| Mar. 16 | Stockholm. *Fanal*. As Jan. 27, 1934. |
| Mar. 17 | Stockholm. *Entführung aus dem Serail*. As Jan. 26. |
| Mar. 19 | Stockholm. *Fanal*. As Jan. 27, 1934. |
| Mar. 25 | Stockholm. *Missa Solemnis*. R. Althén, B. Ewert, J. Berglund; T. Voghera, cond. |

| | |
|---|---|
| Mar. 26 | Stockholm. *Fidelio*. I. Köhler (L), H. Schymberg (M), S. Edwardsen (J), S. Herdenberg (F), J. Berglund (P), L. Björker (R); L. Blech, cond. |
| Mar. 29 | Stockholm. *Fidelio*. As Mar. 26. |
| Apr. 1 | Stockholm. *Fidelio*. As Mar. 26. |
| Apr. 3 | Stockholm. *Cavalleria rusticana*. As Feb. 14. |
| Apr. 5 | Stockholm. *Cavalleria rusticana*. As Feb. 14. |
| Apr. 6 | Stockholm. *Tristan und Isolde*. B. Hertzberg (I), G. Pålson-Wettergren (B), E. Beyron (T), S. Herdenberg (S), C. Molin (K), L. Björker (M); L. Blech, cond. |
| Apr. 8 | Falun. Joint recital w. E. Larson. |
| Apr. 10 | Stockholm. *Fidelio*. As Mar. 26. |
| Apr. 11 | Västerås. Joint recital w. E. Larson. |
| Apr. 14 | Eskilstuna. Joint recital w. E. Larson. |
| Apr. 15 | Karlstad. Joint recital w. E. Larson. |
| Apr. 16 | Jönköping. Joint recital w. E. Larson. |
| Apr. 19 | Gothenburg, Lorensberg's Cirkus. Joint recital w. E. Larson. |
| Apr. 20 | Helsingborg, Concert Hall. Joint recital w. E. Larson. |
| Apr. 21 | Malmö, Realskolan. Joint recital w. E. Larson. |
| May 16 | Riga (Stockholm Opera). *Don Giovanni*. As May 26, 1934. |
| May 18 | Riga (Stockholm Opera). *Cavalieri di Ekebù*. B. Hertzberg (A), G. Pålson-Wettergren (W), E. Beyron (B); N. Grevillius, cond. |
| May 19 | Riga (Stockholm Opera). *Fanal*. As Jan. 27, 1934. |
| May 23 | Stockholm. *Roméo et Juliette*, act 2 (part of Royal Wedding gala). H. Görlin (J); N. Grevillius, cond. |
| June 19 | Copenhagen, Tivoli. Concert; S. C. Felumb, cond. (partly recital w. piano). |
| June 21 | Copenhagen, Tivoli. Concert. As June 19. |
| June 24 | Copenhagen, Tivoli. Concert. As June 19. |
| June 26 | Copenhagen, Tivoli. Concert; S. C. Felumb, cond. |
| June 28 | Malmö, Folkets Park. Recital. |
| June 28 | Falsterbo. Recital (?). |
| July 2 | Brussels. Joint concert w. other Swedish artists (at World Exhibition). |
| July 10 | Stockholm, Gröna Lund. Recital. |
| July 31 | Stockholm, Gröna Lund. Recital. |
| Aug. 6 | Stockholm. *Faust*. As Feb. 3 except E. Larson (V). |
| Aug. 8 | Stockholm. *Sadko*. As Feb. 9 except H. Schymberg (V). |
| Aug. 9 | Stockholm. *Bohème*. As Jan. 19 except H. Görlin (Mi), I. Quensel (Mu). |
| Aug. 16 | Stockholm. *Sadko*. As Aug. 8 except H. Sandberg, cond. |
| Aug. 17 | Stockholm. *Trovatore*. I. Köhler (L), G. Pålson-Wettergren (A), E. Larson (DL), L. Björker (F); H. Sandberg, cond. |
| Aug. 20 | Stockholm. *Trovatore*. As Aug. 17. |
| Aug. 21 | Stockholm. *Bohème*. As Aug. 9 except S. Herdenberg (Ma). |
| Aug. 25 | Stockholm. *Faust*. As Feb. 8. |
| Aug. 27 | Stockholm. *Bohème*. As Aug. 21. |
| Aug. 29 | Stockholm. *Cavalleria rusticana*. As Feb. 14. |
| Aug. 30 | Stockholm. *Knyaz Igor* (gala for Nordic Administrative Council). As Mar. 24, 1934. |
| Sep. 4 | Stockholm. *Bohème*. As Aug. 21. |

405

| | |
|---|---|
| Sep. 5 | Stockholm. *Fanal*. As Jan. 27, 1934. |
| Sep. 9 | Stockholm, Gröna Lund. Recital. |
| Sep. 14 | Stockholm. *Cavalleria rusticana*. As Feb. 14. |
| Sep. 15 | Stockholm, Skansen. Joint concert w. H. Görlin, J. Berglund; N. Grevillius, cond. |
| Sep. 17 | Stockholm. *Fledermaus*. B. Hertzberg (R), I. Quensel (A), G. Pålson-Wettergren (O), E. Beyron (E), F. Cembraeus (Fa), E. Stiebel (Fr); N. Grevillius, cond. |
| Sep. 18 | Stockholm. *Fledermaus*. As Sep. 17. |
| Sep. 23 | Stockholm. *Rigoletto*. H. Schymberg (G), G. Allard (Gv), I. Björck (M), E. Larson (R), L. Björker (S); K. Bendix, cond. |
| Oct. 2 | Stockholm. *Fanal*. As Jan. 27, 1934. |
| Oct. 12 | Stockholm. *Aida*. H. Görlin (Ai), G. Svedman (Amn), E. Larson (Amo), F. Jonsson (R), L. Björker (K); K. Bendix, cond. |
| Oct. 16 | Stockholm. *Aida*. As Oct. 12. |
| Oct. 21 | Stockholm. *Aida*. As Oct. 12 except I. Björck (Amn). |
| Oct. 23 | Växjö (Stockholm Opera). *Tosca*. As Feb. 18 except S. Björling (Sa). |
| Oct. 27 | Stockholm. *Aida*. As Oct. 12 except B. Ewert (Amn). |
| Oct. 30 | Stockholm. *Illustre Fregona*. A. Ohlson (F), C. Olsson-Åhrberg (C), F. Cembraeus (L); N. Grevillius, cond. |
| Oct. 31 | Stockholm. *Barbiere di Siviglia*. I. Quensel (R), G. Allard (Be), G. De Luca (F), E. Stiebel (Br), L. Björker (Bs); H. Sandberg, cond. |
| Nov. 1 | Stockholm. *Illustre Fregona*. As Oct. 30. |
| Nov. 4 | Stockholm. *Illustre Fregona*. As Oct. 30. |
| Nov. 10 | Stockholm. *Illustre Fregona*. As Oct. 30 except S.-Å. Axelson, cond. |
| Nov. 11 | Stockholm. *Fledermaus*. As Sep. 17. |
| Nov. 13 | Stockholm. *Faust*. As Aug. 6. |
| Nov. 15 | Stockholm. *Fledermaus*. As Sep. 17 except I. Köhler (R), E. Ekendahl (O), D. Stockman (E). |
| Nov. 17 | Stockholm. *Bohème*. As Aug. 21. |
| Nov. 20 | Stockholm. *Illustre Fregona*. As Nov. 10. |
| Nov. 22 | Stockholm. *Illustre Fregona*. As Nov. 10. |
| Nov. 24 | Stockholm. *Mignon*. H. Görlin (M), A. Ohlson (P), O. Strandberg (F), C. Molin (L); S.-Å. Axelson, cond. |
| Nov. 26 | Stockholm. *Knyaz Igor*. H. Görlin (Ya), B. Ewert (Ka), E. Larson (I), F. Chaliapin (G, Kk); K. Bendix, cond. |
| Nov. 27 | Stockholm. *Illustre Fregona*. As Nov. 10. |
| Nov. 29 | Stockholm. *Knyaz Igor*. As Nov. 26. |
| Nov. 30 | Stockholm, Storkyrkan. *Messiah*. H. Görlin, B. Ewert, J. Berglund; T. Voghera, cond. |
| Dec. 1 | Stockholm. *Bohème*. As Jan. 19 except I. Quensel (Mu). |
| Dec. 3 | Stockholm. *Faust*. B. Hertzberg (M), E. Ekendahl (S), E. Larson (V), F. Chaliapin (Mé); K. Bendix, cond. |
| Dec. 10 | Stockholm. *Evgeny Onegin*. As Mar. 9 except G. Allard (F); A. Coates, cond. |
| Dec. 13 | Stockholm, Berns Salong. Lucia festival. |
| Dec. 15 | Malmö (Stockholm Opera). *Mignon*. As Nov. 24 except J. Berglund (L). |
| Dec. 16 | Malmö (Stockholm Opera). *Mignon*. As Dec. 15. |

Dec. 17　Malmö (Stockholm Opera). *Mignon.* As Dec. 15.

Dec. 26　Stockholm. *Fledermaus.* As Sep. 17 except E. Ekendahl (O).

**1936**

Jan. 2　Stockholm. *Cavalleria rusticana.* K. Rydqvist (S), B. Ewert (Lo), G. Allard (Lu), S. Björling (A); S.-Å. Axelson, cond.

Jan. 4　Stockholm. *Faust.* B. Hertzberg (M), E. Ekendahl (S), C. Richter (V), J. Berglund (Mé); N. Grevillius, cond.

Jan. 5　Stockholm, Concert Hall. Pops concert; A. Wiklund, cond.

Jan. 6　Stockholm. *Fledermaus.* B. Hertzberg (R), I. Quensel (A), E. Ekendahl (O), E. Beyron (E), F. Cembraeus (Fa), E. Stiebel (Fr); S.-Å. Axelson, cond.

Jan. 11　Stockholm. *Pagliacci.* K. Rydqvist (N), O. Strandberg (B), E. Larson (T), C. Richter (S); H. Sandberg, cond.

Jan. 11　Stockholm, Fenix-Kronprinsen. "TSO:s plundringsnatt," cabaret program.

Jan. 19　Stockholm. *Pagliacci.* As Jan. 11 except S. Svanholm (S).

Feb. 1　Stockholm. *Damnation de Faust.* H. Görlin (Ma), J. Berglund (Mé), E. Stiebel (B); N. Grevillius, cond.

Feb. 3　Stockholm. *Damnation de Faust.* As Feb. 1.

Feb. 6　Stockholm. *Damnation de Faust.* As Feb. 1.

Feb. 8　Stockholm. *Damnation de Faust.* As Feb. 1.

Feb. 9　Stockholm. *Illustre Fregona.* As Nov. 10, 1935.

Feb. 11　Stockholm. *Damnation de Faust.* As Feb. 1.

Feb. 12　Stockholm. *Sadko.* H. Schymberg (V), E. Beyron (S), L. Björker (O, Vi), S. Herdenberg (Ve); H. Sandberg, cond.

Feb. 14　Stockholm. *Sadko.* As Feb. 12.

Feb. 15　Stockholm. *Damnation de Faust.* As Feb. 1.

Feb. 15　Stockholm, Felix-Kronprinsen. "Soaré dansant," cabaret program.

Feb. 17　Stockholm. *Sadko.* As Feb. 12.

Feb. 18　Stockholm. *Damnation de Faust.* As Feb. 1.

Feb. 25　Stockholm. *Damnation de Faust.* (gala for International Music Week). As Feb. 1.

Feb. 27　Stockholm. *Cavalieri di Ekebù* (gala for International Music Week). B. Hertzberg (A), G. Pålson-Wettergren (W), E. Beyron (B); N. Grevillius, cond.

Mar. 2　Stockholm. *Cavalieri di Ekebù.* As Feb. 27.

Mar. 4　Stockholm. *Damnation de Faust.* As Feb. 1.

Mar. 9　Stockholm. *Trovatore.* I. Köhler (L), G. Pålson-Wettergren (A), E. Larson (DL), C. Richter (F); L. Blech, cond.

Mar. 13　Vienna, Concert Hall. Recital.

Mar. 17　Prague, National Theater. *Faust.* A. Staškievicuté (M), Ž. Napravilová (S), J. Konstantin (V), V. Zítek (Mé); M. Zuna, cond.

Mar. 19　Prague, National Theater. *Traviata.* M. Kočová (V), B. Kozlíková (F), J. Křikava (G); F. Škvor, cond.

Mar. 23　Copenhagen, Odd Fellow Palace. Recital.

Mar. 25?　Århus (Denmark). Recital.

Mar. 27　Stockholm. *Faust.* As Jan. 4 except H. Görlin (M).

[1936]

| | |
|---|---|
| Mar. 29 | Stockholm. *Fledermaus*. As Jan. 6 except D. Stockman (E). |
| Apr. 9 | Stockholm. *Bohème*. As Aug. 21, 1935. |
| Apr. 10 | Stockholm. *Missa Solemnis* (benefit for Royal Opera pension fund). As Mar. 25, 1935. |
| Apr. 13 | Stockholm. *Sadko*. As Feb. 12. |
| Apr. 13 | Stockholm. *Fledermaus*. As Mar. 29 except K. Rydqvist (A). |
| Apr. 21 | Stockholm. *Cavalleria rusticana*. As Jan. 2 except C. Molin (A). |
| Apr. 21 | Stockholm. *Pagliacci*. H. Schymberg (N), O. Strandberg (B), S. Björling (T), G. Kjellertz (S); S.-Å. Axelson, cond. |
| Apr. 23 | Stockholm. *Damnation de Faust*. As Feb. 1. |
| Apr. 28 | Stockholm. *Zauberflöte*. H. Görlin (Pm), A. Ohlson (Q), E. Ekendahl (Pa), F. Cembraeus (Po), L. Björker (S); F. Weingartner, cond. |
| May 8 | Stockholm. *Pagliacci*. As Apr. 21 except S. Svanholm (S). |
| May 12 | Stockholm. *Roméo et Juliette*. H. Schymberg (J), E. Ekendahl (S), S. Edwardsen (T), S. Herdenberg (M), L. Björker; N. Grevillius, cond. |
| May 16 | Stockholm. *Roméo et Juliette*. As May 12. |
| May 20 | Prague, National Theater. *Aida*. M. Žaludová (Ai), M. Krásová (Amn), M. Linka (Amo), J. Huml (R), J. Munclingr (K); M. Zuna, cond. |
| May 23 | Brno (Czechoslovakia). *Bohème*. A. Cvanová (Mi), V. Strelcová (Mu), N. Cvejič (Ma), V. Síma (S), V. Jedenáctic (C); M. Sachs, cond. |
| May 28 | Vienna. *Trovatore*. M. Németh (L), K. Thorborg (A), F. Ginrod (DL), C. Bissuti (F); C. Alwin, cond. |
| June 1 | Vienna. *Bohème*. M. Perras (Mi), A. Kern (Mu), H. Duhan (Ma), V. Madin (S), N. Zec (C); C. Alwin, cond. |
| June 3 | Vienna. *Trovatore*. As May 28 except V. Schwarz (L), A. Svéd (DL). |
| June 7 | Vienna. *Aida*. M. Németh (Ai), K. Thorborg (Amn), A. Svéd (Amo), L. Hofmann (R), N. Zec (K); V. de Sabata, cond. |
| June 12 | Prague, National Theater. *Trovatore*. M. Kočová (L), M. Krásová (A), J. Křikava (DL), H. Thein (F); J. Charvát, cond. |
| July 23 | Stockholm, Gröna Lund. Recital. |
| July 25 | Smedjebacken. Recital. |
| July 29 | Copenhagen, Tivoli. Concert; T. Jensen, cond. (partly recital w. piano). |
| July 31 | Copenhagen, Tivoli. Concert. As July 29. |
| Aug. 7 | Stockholm. *Bohème*. As Aug. 21, 1935. |
| Aug. 14 | Stockholm. *Faust*. As Mar. 27 except E. Larson (V). |
| Aug. 16 | Stockholm. *Fledermaus*. As Mar. 29 except I. Köhler (R). |
| Aug. 18 | Stockholm. *Roméo et Juliette*. As May 12. |
| Aug. 20 | Stockholm. *Bohème*. As Aug. 21, 1935. |
| Aug. 23 | Stockholm. *Pagliacci*. As Apr. 21. |
| Aug. 27 | Stockholm. *Fanal*. As Jan. 27, 1934. |
| Aug. 29 | Stockholm. *Faust*. As Aug. 14. |
| Sep. 1 | Stockholm. *Aida*. I. Köhler (Ai), G. Pålson-Wettergren (Amn), E. Larson (Amo), F. Jonsson (R), L. Björker (K); K. Bendix, cond. |
| Sep. 2 | Stockholm. *Fledermaus*. As Aug. 16. |
| Sep. 5 | Stockholm. *Madama Butterfly*. H. Görlin (B), B. Ewert (Su), S. Edwardsen (G), S. Herdenberg (Sh); N. Grevillius, cond. |

| | |
|---|---|
| Sep. 6 | Stockholm. *Cavalleria rusticana*. As Apr. 21 except I. Wassner (S). |
| Sep. 11 | Stockholm. *Madama Butterfly*. As Sep. 5 except H. Sandberg, cond. |
| Sep. 13 | Stockholm. *Aida*. As Sep. 1 except B. Ewert (Amn). |
| Sep. 15 | Stockholm. *Bohème*. H. Schymberg (Mi), I. Quensel (Mu), E. Larson (Ma), E. Stiebel (S), L. Björker (C); N. Grevillius, cond. |
| Sep. 20 | Stockholm. *Trovatore*. As Mar. 9 except L. Björker (F); H. Sandberg, cond. |
| Sep. 26 | Stockholm. *Fille du régiment*. E. Ekendahl (M), R. Ostenfeldt (D), G. Allard (Mc), E. Stiebel (S); K. Bendix, cond. |
| Sep. 28 | Stockholm. *Traviata*. E. v. Bandrowska-Turska (V), G. Allard (F), E. Larson (G); H. Sandberg, cond. |
| Sep. 30 | Stockholm. *Fille du régiment*. As Sep. 26. |
| Oct. 2 | Stockholm. *Traviata*. As Sep. 28. |
| Oct. 11 | Stockholm. *Fille du régiment*. As Sep. 26. |
| Oct. 13 | Stockholm. *Aida*. I. Wassner (Ai), B. Ewert (Amn), E. Larson (Amo), C. Molin (R), J. Berglund (K); B. Walter, cond. |
| Oct. 16 | Stockholm. *Fille du régiment*. As Sep. 26. |
| Oct. 20 | Stockholm. *Fille du régiment*. As Sep. 26. |
| Oct. 22 | Norrköping (Stockholm Opera). *Roméo et Juliette*. As May 12. |
| Oct. 23 | Norrköping (Stockholm Opera). *Roméo et Juliette*. As May 12. |
| Oct. 26 | Stockholm. *Fille du régiment*. As Sep. 26. |
| Oct. 28 | Uppsala, University. Recital. |
| Oct. 31 | Stockholm. *Madama Butterfly*. As Sep. 11. |
| Nov. 1 | Stockholm. *Trovatore*. As Mar. 9 except B. Ewert (A); K. Bendix, cond. |
| Nov. 3 | Stockholm. *Cavalleria rusticana*. As Sep. 6. |
| Nov. 3 | Stockholm. *Pagliacci*. As Apr. 21. |
| Nov. 8 | Stockholm. *Madama Butterfly*. As Sep. 11. |
| Nov. 12 | Stockholm. *Fille du régiment*. As Sep. 26. |
| Nov. 15 | Stockholm. *Madama Butterfly*. As Sep. 11. |
| Nov. 26 | Stockholm. *Rossini in Neapel*. H. Görlin (C), E. Stiebel (B); H. Sandberg, cond. |
| Nov. 29 | Stockholm. *Fille du régiment*. As Sep. 26. |
| Nov. 30 | Stockholm. *Rossini in Neapel*. As Nov. 26. |
| Dec. 2 | Stockholm. *Rossini in Neapel*. As Nov. 26. |
| Dec. 5 | Stockholm, Storkyrkan. *Messiah*. H. Görlin, I. Aulin-Voghera, J. Berglund; T. Voghera, cond. |
| Dec. 7 | Malmö (Stockholm Opera). *Zauberflöte*. As Apr. 28 except H. Sandberg, cond. |
| Dec. 8 | Malmö (Stockholm Opera). *Zauberflöte*. As Dec. 7. |
| Dec. 10 | Stockholm. *Rossini in Neapel*. As Nov. 26. |
| Dec. 13 | Stockholm, Berns Salong. Lucia festival (w. A.-L. Björling). |
| Dec. 15 | Paris, Cité Universitaire. *Bohème*, act 1 (part of theater inauguration gala). H. Dosia (Mi), A. Gaudin (Ma), L. Musy (S), C. Got (C); G. Szyfer, cond. |
| Dec. 17 | Stockholm. *Rossini in Neapel*. As Nov. 26. |
| Dec. 26 | Stockholm. *Rossini in Neapel*. As Nov. 26. |
| Dec. 30 | Stockholm. *Illustre Fregona*. As Nov. 10, 1935. |

**1937**

| | |
|---|---|
| Jan. 2 | Stockholm. *Illustre Fregona*. As Nov. 10, 1935. |
| Jan. 7 | Stockholm. *Faust*. B. Hertzberg (M), E. Ekendahl (S), C. Richter (V), J. Berglund (Mé); K. Bendix, cond. |
| Jan. 11 | Stockholm. *Roméo et Juliette*. As May 12, 1936. |
| Jan. 19 | Sundsvall (Stockholm Opera). *Barbiere di Siviglia*. H. Schymberg (R), G. Allard (Be), G. Kjellertz (F), E. Stiebel (Br), L. Björker (Bs); H. Sandberg, cond. |
| Jan. 20 | Östersund (Stockholm Opera). *Barbiere di Siviglia*. As Jan. 19. |
| Jan. 24 | Stockholm. *Madama Butterfly*. H. Görlin (B), B. Ewert (Su), S. Edwardsen (G), S. Herdenberg (Sh); H. Sandberg, cond. |
| Jan. 29 | Stockholm. *Faust*. As Jan. 7 except H. Görlin (M). |
| Jan. 31 | Stockholm. *Mignon*. H. Görlin (M), A. Ohlson (P), O. Strandberg (F), C. Molin (L); H. Sandberg, cond. |
| Feb. 4 | Nuremberg. *Pagliacci*. T. Eipperle (N), E. Kurz (B), W. Schmid-Scherf (T), J. Herrmann (S); M. Pitterroff, cond. |
| Feb. 6 | Berlin, German Opera House. *Bohème*. K. Nettesheim (Mi), A. Frind (Mu), K. Schmitt-Walter (Ma), E. Heyer (S), L. Windisch (C); W. Lutze, cond. |
| Feb. 8 | Dresden. *Bohème*. M. Cebotari (Mi), E. Wieber (Mu), P. Schöffler (Ma), L. Ermold (S), W. Bader (C); K. Striegler, cond. |
| Feb. 10 | Dresden. *Rigoletto*. M. Cebotari (G), W. Vogel (Gv), I. Karen (M), M. Ahlersmeyer (R), K. Böhme (S); W. Czernik, cond. |
| Feb. 14 | Vienna. *Bohème*. J. Novotná (Mi), M. Bokor (Mu), H. Wiedemann (Ma), V. Madin (S), N. Zec (C); J. Krips, cond. |
| Feb. 16 | Vienna. *Trovatore*. M. Németh (L), R. Anday (A), A. Svéd (DL), C. Bissuti (F); F. Weingartner, cond. |
| Feb. 17 | Vienna. *Madama Butterfly*. J. Novotná (B), D. With (Su), H. Gallos (G), H. Wiedemann (Sh); J. Krips, cond. |
| Feb. 23 | Vienna. *Pagliacci*. M. Bokor (N), A. Dermota (B), A. Svéd (T), G. Monthy (S); C. Alwin, cond. |
| Feb. 25 | Vienna. *Fanciulla del West*. E. Flesch (M), A. Jerger (R), G. Monthy (W); H. Duhan, cond. |
| Feb. 27 | Budapest. *Aida*. M. Németh (Ai), E. Némethy (Amn), G. Losonczy (Amo), M. Székely (R), T. Vitéz (K); A. Fleischer, cond. |
| Mar. 2 | Vienna, Concert Hall. Recital. |
| Mar. 5 | Vienna. *Trovatore*. E. Flesch (L), K. Thorborg (A), F. Ginrod (DL), C. Bissuti (F); J. Krips, cond. |
| Mar. 7 | Vienna. *Faust*. E. Réthy (M), D. Komarek (S), A. Svéd (V), A. Kipnis (Mé); J. Krips, cond. |
| Mar. 9 | Budapest. Recital. |
| Mar. 12 | Vienna. *Pagliacci*. As Feb. 23 except R. Sallaba (B), F. Ginrod (S). |
| Mar. 14 | Prague, New German Theater. *Aida*. Z. Kunc (later Milanov) (Ai), L. Kindermann (Amn), J. Schwarz (Amo), M. Andersen (R), J. Hagen (K); F. Zweig, cond. |
| Mar. 17 | Vienna. *Ballo in maschera*. E. Flesch (A), M. Perras (O), K. Thorborg (U), A. Svéd (R), N. Zec (S), C. Bissuti (T); J. Krips, cond. |
| Mar. 20 | Vienna. *Rigoletto*. M. Perras (G), P. Paalen (Gv), D. With (M), F. |

410

|  |  |
|---|---|
| | Ginrod (R), H. Alsen (S); H. Duhan, cond. |
| Mar. 22 | Vienna. *Trovatore*. As Mar. 5 except A. Svéd (DL). |
| Apr. 1 | Stockholm. *Faust*. As Jan. 29 except N. Grevillius, cond. |
| Apr. 7 | Stockholm. *Roméo et Juliette*. As May 12, 1936. |
| Apr. 12 | Stockholm. *Madama Butterfly*. As Jan. 24 except N. Grevillius, cond. |
| Apr. 17 | Stockholm. *Aida*. I. Köhler (Ai), G. Pålson-Wettergren (Amn), E. Larson (Amo), C. Molin (R), J. Berglund (K); K. Bendix, cond. |
| Apr. 28 | Stockholm, Concert Hall. *Messa da Requiem*. I. Souez, F. Elsta, L. Björker; F. Busch, cond. |
| May 8 | Gothenburg (Stockholm Opera). *Bohème*. H. Schymberg (Mi), E. Ekendahl (Mu), S. Herdenberg (Ma), C. Richter (S), L. Björker (C); N. Grevillius, cond. |
| May 14 | Gothenburg (Stockholm Opera). *Knyaz Igor*. H. Görlin (Ya), G. Pålson-Wettergren (Ka), E. Larson (I), S. Herdenberg (G), J. Berglund (Kk); K. Bendix, cond. |
| May 17 | Stockholm. *Fille du régiment*. As Sep. 26, 1936. |
| May 21 | Stockholm. *Faust*. As Jan. 7 except M. Delin (M), E. Larson (V). |
| May 26 | Stockholm. *Aida*. As Apr. 17 except H. Nyblom (Ai), F. Jonsson (R). |
| May 29 | Stockholm. *Knyaz Igor*. As May 14 except B. Ewert (Ka). |
| June 6 | Stockholm, Skansen. Recital (on Swedish Flag Day). |
| June 12 | Paris, Champs-Élysées Theater. Swedish concert (w. other soloists); N. Grevillius, cond. |
| June 13 | Paris, Champs-Élysées Theater. Swedish concert (w. other soloists); N. Grevillius, cond. |
| July 29 | Stockholm, Gröna Lund. Recital. |
| Aug. 5 | Stockholm. *Bohème*. As May 8 except E. Larson (Ma). |
| Aug. 8 | Stockholm. *Bohème*. As Aug. 5. |
| Aug. 10 | Stockholm. *Madama Butterfly*. As Apr. 12. |
| Aug. 15 | Stockholm. *Pagliacci*. H. Schymberg (N), D. Stockman (B), S. Björling (T), G. Svensson (S); S.-Å. Axelson, cond. |
| Aug. 18 | Stockholm. *Roméo et Juliette*. As May 12, 1936. |
| Aug. 21 | Stockholm. *Faust*. As Apr. 1 except E. Larson (V), S. Björling (Mé). |
| Aug. 24 | Stockholm. *Roméo et Juliette*. As May 12, 1936. |
| Aug. 25 | Stockholm. *Knyaz Igor*. As May 14 except C. Molin (Kk). |
| Aug. 30 | Stockholm. *Knyaz Igor*. As Aug. 25 except R. Althén (Ya). |
| Aug. 31 | Stockholm. *Cavalleria rusticana*. As Sep. 6, 1936. |
| Sep. 4 | Stockholm, Skanstull's Amusement Park. Recital. |
| Sep. 5 | Stockholm, Gröna Lund. Concert (in connection w. production of the film *Fram för framgång*); N. Grevillius, cond. |
| Sep. 14 | Stockholm. *Don Giovanni*. I. Köhler (A), I. Wassner (E), K. Rydqvist (Z), E. Pinza (G), E. Stiebel (L), C. Molin (M), L. Björker (C); H. Sandberg, cond. |
| Sep. 16 | Stockholm. *Bohème*. As May 8. |
| Sep. 24 | Stockholm. *Rigoletto*. H. Schymberg (G), G. Allard (Gv), M. Sehlmark (M), L. Tibbett (R), L. Björker (S); K. Bendix, cond. |
| Sep. 30 | Stockholm. *Mefistofele*. H. Görlin (M), I. Wassner (E), M. Sehlmark (Mt), L. Björker (Me); H. Sandberg, cond. |
| Oct. 3 | Stockholm. *Mefistofele*. As Sep. 30. |
| Oct. 27 | Uppsala, University. Recital. |

| | |
|---|---|
| Nov. 12 | Copenhagen, Odd Fellow Palace. Recital. |
| Nov. 16 | London, Queen's Hall. Recital. |
| Nov. 28 | New York, Carnegie Hall. General Motors radio concert (joint w. M. Jeritza); E. Rapee, cond. |
| Dec. 1 | Springfield, MA. Joint recital w. A. de Saint-Malo, violin. (First performance on this US tour, which included about 12 recitals.) |
| Dec. 5 | New York, Carnegie Hall. General Motors radio concert (joint w. D. Dickson, G. Moore); E. Rapee, cond. |
| Dec. 8 | Chicago. *Rigoletto*. B. Lane (G), M. Barron (Gv), A. Paggi (M), L. Tibbett (R), N. Ruisi (S); R. Moranzoni, cond. |
| Dec. 13 | Chicago, Palmer House. Recital. |
| Dec. 15 | Chicago. *Bohème*. M. Claire (Mi), J. Paull (Mu), G. Czaplicki (Ma), S. Giglio (S), N. Ruisi (C); R. Moranzoni, cond. |
| Dec. 19 | New York, Carnegie Hall. General Motors radio concert (joint w. H. Jepson); E. Rapee, cond. |
| Dec. 20 | New York, Waldorf-Astoria. Bagby Musical Morning (joint recital w. L. Pons). |
| Dec. 28 | St. Paul, MN. Recital. |
| Dec. 30 | Jamestown, NY. Recital. |

**1938**

| | |
|---|---|
| Jan. 4 | New York, Town Hall. Recital. |
| Feb. 4 | Stockholm. *Bohème*. H. Görlin (Mi), E. Ekendahl (Mu), E. Larson (Ma), C. Richter (S), L. Björker (C); N. Grevillius, cond. |
| Feb. 6 | Stockholm. *Faust*. H. Görlin (M), E. Ekendahl (S), E. Larson (V), J. Berglund (Mé); K. Bendix, cond. |
| Feb. 14 | Uppsala, University. Recital. |
| Feb. 16 | Malmö, Hippodrome. Recital (benefit for SDS Fund). |
| Feb. 17 | Copenhagen. Radio concert; N. Malko, cond. |
| Feb. 19 | Stockholm. *Pagliacci*. K. Rydqvist (N), D. Stockman (B), E. Larson (T), G. Svensson (S); S.-Å. Axelson, cond. |
| Feb. 19 | Stockholm. *Cavalleria rusticana*. I. Wassner (S), B. Ewert (Lo), G. Allard (Lu), S. Björling (A); S.-Å. Axelson, cond. |
| Feb. 22 | Stockholm. *Rigoletto*. H. Schymberg (G), G. Allard (Gv), M. Sehlmark (M), E. Larson (R), L. Björker (S); K. Bendix, cond. |
| Feb. 25 | Gävle (Stockholm Opera). *Faust*. As Feb. 6 except S. Björling (Mé). |
| Feb. 26 | Gävle (Stockholm Opera). *Faust*. As Feb. 25. |
| Feb. 28 | Stockholm. *Rigoletto*. As Feb. 22. |
| Mar. 2 | Stockholm. *Aida*. I. Köhler (Ai), J. Claussen (Amn), E. Larson (Amo), F. Jonsson (R), L. Björker (K); K. Bendix, cond. |
| Mar. 4 | Stockholm. *Roméo et Juliette*. H. Schymberg (J), K. Rydqvist (S), S. Edwardsen (T), S. Herdenberg (M), L. Björker (L); S.-Å. Axelson, cond. |
| Mar. 6 | Stockholm. *Tosca*. I. Köhler (T), C. Richter (S), E. Stiebel (Sa); S.-Å. Axelson, cond. |
| Mar. 8 | Stockholm. *Roméo et Juliette*. As Mar. 4. |
| Mar. 9 | Gothenburg, Concert Hall. Recital. |
| Mar. 11 | Stockholm. *Roméo et Juliette*. As Mar. 4. |

| | |
|---|---|
| Mar. 16 | Norrköping (Stockholm Opera). *Faust*. As Feb. 25 except C. Richter (V). |
| Mar. 20 | Stockholm, Concert Hall. Pops radio concert; L.-E. Larsson, cond. |
| Mar. 23 | Stockholm. *Pagliacci*. As Feb. 19 except S. Björling (T), G. Kjellertz (S). |
| Mar. 23 | Stockholm. *Cavalleria rusticana*. As Feb. 19 except C. Molin (A). |
| Mar. 25 | Stockholm. *Roméo et Juliette*. As Mar. 4. |
| Mar. 28 | Stockholm. *Aida*. As Mar. 2 except B. Ewert (Amn). |
| Apr. 4 | Stockholm. *Zigeunerbaron*. I. Köhler (S), I. Quensel (A), M. Sehlmark (C), E. Stiebel (Z); K. Bendix, cond. |
| Apr. 5 | Stockholm. *Zigeunerbaron*. As Apr. 4. |
| Apr. 9 | Stockholm. *Zigeunerbaron*. As Apr. 4 except B. Hertzberg (S). |
| Apr. 12 | Copenhagen, Odd Fellow Palace. Recital. |
| Apr. 15 | Stockholm. *Missa Solemnis*. R. Althén, B. Ewert, J. Berglund; T. Voghera, cond. |
| Apr. 16 | Stockholm. *Zigeunerbaron*. As Apr. 4 except G. Pålson-Wettergren (C). |
| Apr. 18 | Stockholm. *Cavalleria rusticana*. As Feb. 19. |
| Apr. 20 | Stockholm. *Bohème*. As Feb. 4 except H. Schymberg (Mi), E. Stiebel (S). |
| Apr. 27 | Stockholm. *Zigeunerbaron*. As Apr. 4 except O. Ralf (Z). |
| Apr. 30 | Stockholm. *Zigeunerbaron*. As Apr. 4. |
| May 10 | Malmö (Stockholm Opera). *Roméo et Juliette*. As Mar. 4 except E. Ekendahl (S); N. Grevillius, cond. |
| May 11 | Malmö (Stockholm Opera). *Faust*. As Mar. 16 except N. Grevillius, cond. |
| May 13 | Stockholm, Concert Hall. Opera Evening w. Royal Opera soloists (JB opposite H. Schymberg; N. Grevillius, cond.). |
| May 15 | Stockholm, Concert Hall. Opera Evening w. Royal Opera soloists (JB opposite H. Görlin, J. Berglund; N. Grevillius, cond.). |
| May 27 | Stockholm, Concert Hall. Opera Evening w. Royal Opera soloists (JB opposite I. Björck, H. Schymberg; N. Grevillius, cond.). |
| July 14 | Stockholm, Gröna Lund. Recital. |
| Aug. 11 | Stockholm. *Aida*. As Mar. 28 except C. Molin (K). |
| Aug. 15 | Stockholm. *Bohème*. As Feb. 4 except H. Schymberg (Mi), I. Quensel (Mu), S. Herdenberg (Ma). |
| Aug. 17 | Stockholm. *Aida* (gala for Nordic Parliamentary Meeting). As Mar. 28. |
| Aug. 24 | Stockholm. *Madama Butterfly*. H. Görlin (B), B. Ewert (Su), S. Edwardsen (G), S. Herdenberg (Sh); N. Grevillius, cond. |
| Aug. 26 | Stockholm. *Zigeunerbaron*. As Apr. 4. |
| Aug. 31 | Malmö, Hippodrome. Recital (benefit for SDS Fund). |
| Sep. 2 | Stockholm. *Bohème*. As Feb. 4 except E. Norena (Mi), I. Quensel (Mu). |
| Sep. 4 | Stockholm, Skansen. Concert (benefit for Barnens Dag); N. Grevillius, cond. |
| Sep. 6 | Stockholm. *Traviata*. E. Norena (V), G. Allard (F), C. Molin (G); H. Sandberg, cond. |
| Sep. 9 | Stockholm. *Faust*. E. Norena (M), G. Lemon-Bernhard (S), C. Rich- |

413

|  | ter (V), J. Berglund (Mé); N. Grevillius, cond. |
|---|---|
| Sep. 11 | Stockholm. *Traviata*. As Sep. 6 except E. Larson (G). |
| Sep. 25 | Örebro. Festival soiree. |
| Oct. 4 | Stockholm. *Africaine*. I. Köhler (S), H. Schymberg (I), S. Björling (N); K. Bendix, cond. |
| Oct. 6 | Stockholm. *Africaine*. As Oct. 4. |
| Oct. 8 | Stockholm. *Africaine*. As Oct. 4. |
| Oct. 11 | Stockholm. *Africaine*. As Oct. 4 except G. Lemon-Bernhard (I). |
| Oct. 14 | Stockholm. *Africaine*. As Oct. 11. |
| Oct. 17 | Stockholm. *Africaine*. As Oct. 4. |
| Oct. 20 | Västerås (Stockholm Opera). *Faust*. As Sep. 9 except B. Hertzberg (M), S. Björling (Mé). |
| Nov. 13 | Detroit, Masonic Auditorium. "Ford Sunday Evening Hour," radio concert; J. Iturbi, cond. (First performance on this US tour.) |
| Nov. 24 | New York. *Bohème*. M. Favero (Mi), M. Morel (Mu), J. Brownlee (Ma), G. Cehanovsky (S), N. Cordon (C); cond. G. Papi. |
| Nov. 27 | Chicago, Opera House. Recital (benefit for The American Daughters of Sweden). |
| Nov. 30 | New York. *Bohème*. As Nov. 24. |
| Dec. 2 | New York. *Trovatore*. Z. Milanov (L), B. Castagna (A), C. Tagliabue (DL), J. Gurney (F); G. Papi, cond. |
| Dec. 7 | Bridgeport, CT. Recital. |
| Dec. 9 | Philadelphia, Academy of Music. Recital. |
| Dec. 10 | New York. *Trovatore*. As Dec. 2. |
| Dec. 13 | Pittsburgh. Recital. |
| Dec. 15 | New York, Waldorf-Astoria. Joint recital w. E. Morini, violin. |
| Dec. 19 | New York, Waldorf-Astoria. Bagby Musical Morning, joint recital w. Z. Milanov and E. Zimbalist, violin. |
| Dec. 19 | New York, Brooklyn Academy of Music. Recital. |

## 1939

| Jan. 5 | Tacoma, WA. Recital. |
|---|---|
| Jan. 6 | Seattle, Music Hall. Recital. |
| Jan. 11 | Maryville, TN. Recital. |
| Jan. 13 | Princeton, NJ. Recital (?). |
| Jan. 15 | Detroit, Masonic Auditorium. "Ford Sunday Evening Hour," radio concert; F. Reiner, cond. |
| Jan. 17 | New York, Carnegie Hall. Recital. (Last performance on this US tour.) |
| Feb. 4 | Stockholm. *Bohème*. As Aug. 15, 1938. |
| Feb. 6 | Stockholm. *Bohème*. As Aug. 15, 1938. |
| Feb. 8 | Stockholm. *Aida*. I. Köhler (Ai), G. Pålson-Wettergren (Amn), S. Björling (Amo), F. Jonsson (R), C. Molin (K); L. Blech, cond. |
| Feb. 11 | Stockholm. *Faust*. H. Görlin (M), G. Lemon-Bernhard (S), C. Richter (V), J. Berglund (Mé); N. Grevillius, cond. |
| Feb. 13 | Gothenburg, Concert Hall. Concert; T. Mann, cond. |
| Feb. 15 | Stockholm. *Pagliacci*. I. Quensel (N), O. Strandberg (B), S. Björling (T), G. Kjellertz (S); S.-Å. Axelson, cond. |

| | |
|---|---|
| Feb. 19 | Stockholm. *Faust*. As Feb. 11 except B. Hertzberg (M), E. Larson (V). |
| Feb. 22 | Stockholm. *Roméo et Juliette*. H. Schymberg (J), G. Lemon-Bernhard (S), S. Edwardsen (T), S. Herdenberg (M), L. Björker (L); N. Grevillius, cond. |
| Feb. 25 | Stockholm. *Bohème*. As Aug. 15, 1938. |
| Mar. 7 | Stockholm. *Traviata*. As Sep. 11, 1938. |
| Mar. 9 | Stockholm. *Bohème*. H. Schymberg (Mi), I. Quensel (Mu), S. Herdenberg (Ma), C. Richter (S), F. Jonsson (C); N. Grevillius, cond. |
| Mar. 12 | Stockholm. *Bohème*. As Mar. 9 except E. Larson (Ma), E. Stiebel (S). |
| Mar. 18 | Stockholm. *Roméo et Juliette*. As Feb. 22. |
| Mar. 25 | Stockholm. *Faust*. As Feb. 11 except B. Hertzberg (M), S. Björling (Mé); K. Bendix, cond. |
| Apr. 1 | Stockholm. *Cavalleria rusticana*. H. L. Göransson (S), B. Ewert (Lo), G. Allard (Lu), C. Molin (A); S.-Å. Axelson, cond. |
| Apr. 4 | Örebro. Recital. |
| Apr. 7 | Stockholm. *Missa Solemnis*. H. Schymberg, B. Ewert, J. Berglund; T. Voghera, cond. |
| Apr. 8 | Stockholm. *Bohème*. As Mar. 9 except H. Nyblom (Mi). |
| Apr. 12 | Stockholm. *Cavalleria rusticana*. As Apr. 1 except M. Sehlmark (Lu). |
| Apr. 18 | Stockholm. *Madama Butterfly*. T. Kiwa (B), B. Ewert (Su), S. Edwardsen (G), S. Herdenberg (Sh); H. Sandberg, cond. |
| Apr. 20 | Stockholm. *Faust*. As Feb. 11 except E. Larson (V). |
| Apr. 21 | Stockholm. *Madama Butterfly*. As Apr. 18. |
| Apr. 23 | Stockholm. *Cavalleria rusticana*. As Apr. 12 except G. Svensson (A); H. Sandberg, cond. |
| May 3 | Gothenburg (Stockholm Opera). *Roméo et Juliette*. As Feb. 22. |
| May 5 | Gothenburg (Stockholm Opera). *Bohème*. As Mar. 9 except B. Hertzberg (Mi), L. Björker (C). |
| May 8 | Gothenburg (Stockholm Opera). *Faust*. As Feb. 11 except E. Ekendahl (S). |
| May 12 | London. *Trovatore*. G. Cigna (L), G. Pålson-Wettergren (A), M. Basiola (DL), C. Zambelli (F); V. Gui, cond. |
| May 17 | Stockholm, Concert Hall. Opera Evening w. Royal Opera soloists (JB opposite H. Schymberg; N. Grevillius, cond.). |
| May 23 | London. *Trovatore*. As May 12 except E. Stignani (A), A. Borgioli (DL). |
| June 8 | Hilversum (Netherlands). Radio concert; F. Weissmann, cond. |
| June 11 | The Hague. Concert; E. Ansermet, cond. |
| July 31 | Stockholm, Gröna Lund. Recital. |
| Aug. 2 | Gothenburg, Liseberg. Recital. |
| Aug. 6 | Furuvik. Recital. |
| Aug. 10 | Stockholm. *Bohème*. As Mar. 9 except I. Köhler (Mu). |
| Aug. 16 | Lucerne (Switzerland), Jesuit Church. *Messa da Requiem*. Z. Milanov, K. Thorborg, N. Moscona; A. Toscanini, cond. |
| Aug. 17 | Lucerne, Jesuit Church. *Messa da Requiem*. As Aug. 16. |
| Aug. 23 | Stockholm. *Roméo et Juliette*. As May 3 except B. Lemon-Brundin (S). |

Aug. 26    Stockholm. *Fanal*. As Jan. 27, 1934.

Aug. 29    Stockholm. *Traviata*. H. Schymberg (V), G. Allard (F), C. Molin (G); H. Sandberg, cond.

Oct. 19    Stockholm, Concert Hall. Recital.

Oct. 22    Stockholm, Concert Hall. Recital (benefit for Save the Children and air-raid precautions).

Oct. 25    Helsingborg. Recital.

Oct. 27    Copenhagen, KB Hall. Recital.

Nov. 4    The Hague. Concert; W. Mengelberg, cond.

Nov. 20    Provo, UT. Recital.

Nov. 27    Seattle, Music Hall. Concert; N. Sokoloff, cond.

Nov. 30    Lindsborg, KS. Recital.

Dec. 4    Ann Arbor, MI. Recital.

Dec. 7    Winnipeg. Recital.

Dec. 13    Pittsburgh. Recital.

Dec. 28    New York. *Faust* (benefit for Near East College Association). H. Jepson (M), L. Browning (S), J. Brownlee (V), E. Pinza (Mé); W. Pelletier, cond.

## 1940

Jan. 1    New York. *Rigoletto*. L. Pons (G), T. Votipka (Gv), I. Petina (M), L. Tibbett (R), N. Moscona (S); G. Papi, cond.

Jan. 2    Philadelphia (Met). *Faust*. As Dec. 28, 1939.

Jan. 5    New York. *Bohème*. J. Novotná (Mi), M. Dickson (Mu), J. Brownlee (Ma), G. Cehanovsky (S), N. Cordon (C); G. Papi, cond.

Jan. 15    New York. *Bohème*. As Jan. 5 except B. Sayão (Mi), E. Pinza (C).

Jan. 21    Chicago, Opera House. Recital (benefit for Finland).

Jan. 22    Grand Rapids, MI. Recital.

Jan. 24    Newark, NJ. Recital.

Jan. 26    Dayton, OH. Recital.

Feb. 2    New York, Town Hall. Recital.

Feb. 9    San Francisco, Opera House. Concert; P. Monteux, cond.

Feb. 10    San Francisco, Opera House. Concert; P. Monteux, cond.

Feb. 16    Chicago. Recital (?).

Feb. 23    Enid, OK. Recital (?).

Feb. 26    Troy, NY. Recital.

Feb. 28    Springfield, MA. Recital.

Mar. 21    Stockholm. *Bohème*. H. Schymberg (Mi), I. Köhler (Mu), S. Herdenberg (Ma), C. Richter (S), L. Björker (C); N. Grevillius, cond.

Mar. 25    Stockholm, Concert Hall. Recital (benefit for Finland).

Mar. 27    Stockholm. *Roméo et Juliette*. H. Schymberg (J), B. Lemon-Brundin (S), S. Edwardsen (T), S. Herdenberg (M), L. Björker (L); N. Grevillius, cond.

Mar. 29    Stockholm. *Aida*. I. Köhler (Ai), G. Pålson-Wettergren (Amn), E. Larson (Amo), F. Jonsson (R), L. Björker (K); K. Bendix, cond.

May 7    Stockholm, Concert Hall. Recital.

May 13    Stockholm. *Bohème*. As Mar. 21 except B. Hertzberg (Mi), F. Jonsson (C); K. Bendix, cond.

| | |
|---|---|
| May 21 | Stockholm. *Roméo et Juliette*. As Mar. 27. |
| May 25 | Stockholm, Skansen. "Försvarslånets medborgarfest" (War Bonds Festival). |
| June 16 | Stockholm, Skansen. Recital. |
| July 18 | Stockholm, Gröna Lund. Recital. |
| Aug. 4 | Eskilstuna. Recitals (2). |
| Aug. 22 | Gothenburg, Liseberg. Recital. |
| Sep. 5 | Stockholm, Gröna Lund. Recital w. other soloists (benefit for Barnens Dag). |
| Sep. 16 | Malmö, Realskolan. Recital. |
| Sep. 18 | Helsingborg, Concert Hall. Recital. |
| Sep. 27 | Uppsala, University. Recital. |
| Sep. 30 | Lund, University. Recital. |
| Oct. 18 | San Francisco. *Bohème*. B. Sayão (Mi), M. Bokor (Mu), J. Brownlee (Ma), G. Cehanovsky (S), E. Pinza (C); G. Papi, cond. |
| Oct. 23 | San Francisco. *Ballo in maschera*. E. Rethberg (A), M. Bokor (O), S. Sten (U), R. Bonelli (R), L. Alvary (S), R. Sellon (T); G. Papi, cond. |
| Oct. 26 | Seattle, Civic Auditorium. Recital. (One of the first of about 30 recitals on this US tour.) |
| Oct. 29 | San Francisco. *Bohème*. As Oct. 18. |
| Nov. 4 | Los Angeles (S. F. Opera). *Ballo in maschera*. As Oct. 23. |
| Nov. 12 | Pasadena, CA. Recital (?). |
| Nov. 16 | Chicago. *Rigoletto*. J. Tuminia (G), H. Fix (Gv), L. Summers (M), A. Svéd (R), D. Beattie (S); L. Kopp, cond. |
| Nov. 23 | New York, Carnegie Hall. *Messa da Requiem* (benefit for Roosevelt Hospital). Z. Milanov, B. Castagna, N. Moscona; A. Toscanini, cond. |
| Dec. 2 | New York. *Ballo in maschera* (Met season opening). Z. Milanov (A), S. Andreva (O), K. Thorborg (U), A. Svéd (R), N. Cordon (S), N. Moscona (T); E. Panizza, cond. |
| Dec. 8 | Detroit, Masonic Auditorium. "Ford Sunday Evening Hour," radio concert; E. Ormandy, cond. |
| Dec. 12 | New York. *Trovatore*. N. Greco (L), B. Castagna (A), F. Valentino (DL), N. Moscona (F); F. Calusio, cond. |
| Dec. 14 | New York. *Ballo in maschera*. As Dec. 2 except B. Castagna (U). |
| Dec. 17 | Philadelphia (Met). *Ballo in maschera*. As Dec. 2 except G. Papi, cond. |
| Dec. 21 | New York. *Ballo in maschera*. As Dec. 17. |
| Dec. 25 | New York. *Faust*. H. Jepson (M), H. Olheim (S), L. Warren (V), N. Moscona (Mé); W. Pelletier, cond. |
| Dec. 28 | New York, Carnegie Hall. *Missa Solemnis* (benefit for National Conference of Christians and Jews). Z. Milanov, B. Castagna, A. Kipnis; A. Toscanini, cond. |
| Dec. 30 | New York. *Trovatore*. As Dec. 12 except A. Kaskas (A), A. Svéd (DL). |

## 1941

| | |
|---|---|
| Jan. 8 | New York. *Ballo in maschera*. As Dec. 2, 1940, except F. Valentino (R). |

| | |
|---|---|
| Jan. 11 | New York. *Trovatore*. As Dec. 12, 1940. |
| Jan. 31 | New York, Town Hall. Recital. |
| Feb. 8 | New York. *Rigoletto*. J. Tuminia (G), T. Votipka (Gv), B. Castagna (M), L. Tibbett (R), N. Moscona (S); G. Papi, cond. |
| Feb. 16 | Chicago, Opera House. Recital. |
| Feb. 22 | Stillwater, OK. Recital. |
| Feb. 27 | New York. *Rigoletto*. As Feb. 8 except H. Reggiani (G), R. Weede (R). |
| Mar. 27 | Stockholm, Auditorium. Recital. |
| Apr. 3 | Stockholm, Opera House. Soiree (benefit for Salvation Army). |
| Apr. 5 | Stockholm. *Roméo et Juliette*. H. Schymberg (J), G. Lemon-Bernhard (S), S. Edwardsen (T), S. Herdenberg (M), L. Björker (L); N. Grevillius, cond. |
| Apr. 10 | Stockholm. *Bohème*. H. Schymberg (Mi), I. Köhler (Mu), S. Herdenberg (Ma), A. Wirén (S), L. Björker (C); N. Grevillius, cond. |
| Apr. 12 | Stockholm. *Roméo et Juliette*. As Apr. 5 except B. Lemon-Brundin (S). |
| Apr. 17 | Uppsala, University. Recital. |
| Apr. 23 | Copenhagen, KB Hall. Recital. |
| Apr. 30 | Stockholm. *Pagliacci*. I. Köhler (N), D. Stockman (B), E. Larson (T), G. Svensson (S); S.-Å. Axelson, cond. |
| May 3 | Stockholm. *Bohème*. As Apr. 10 except F. Jonsson (C). |
| May 5 | Stockholm. *Roméo et Juliette*. As Apr. 12. |
| May 16 | Örebro. Recital. |
| July 1 | Boden. Recital. |
| July 2 | Övertorneå. Recital. |
| July 17 | Stockholm, Gröna Lund. Recital. |
| Aug. 1 | Solna, Haga. Stockholm Garrison Festival. |
| Aug. 3 | Furuvik. Recital. |
| Aug. 17 | Borås. Opening concert for Ryavallen sports ground. |
| Aug. 22 | Copenhagen, Tivoli. Recital. |
| Sep. 21 | Stockholm. *Bohème*. As May 3 except B. Hertzberg (Mi). |
| Sep. 24 | Stockholm. *Aida*. H. Guermant-de la Berg (Ai), B. Ewert (Amn), S. Björling (Amo), R. Persidsky (R), L. Björker (K); H. Sandberg, cond. |
| Sep. 26 | Stockholm. *Tosca*. B. Hertzberg (T), S. Björling (S), E. Stiebel (Sa); N. Grevillius, cond. |
| Sep. 28 | Stockholm. *Bohème*. As Sep. 21 except I. Quensel (Mu), S.-O. Sandberg (Ma). |
| Sep. 30 | Gothenburg, Concert Hall. Recital. |
| Oct. 3 | Halmstad. Recital. |
| Oct. 4 | Stockholm, Opera House. Recital w. other soloists (benefit for victims of naval catastrophe). |
| Oct. 7 | Gothenburg (Stockholm Opera). *Bohème*. As Sep. 28 except H. Schymberg (Mi). |
| Oct. 10 | Karlstad. Recital. |
| Oct. 12 | Östersund. Recital. |
| Oct. 14 | Sundsvall. Recital. |
| Oct. 21 | Helsingborg, Concert Hall. Recital. |
| Oct. 24 | Malmö, Amiralen. Recital. |

## 1942

| | |
|---|---|
| Feb. 3 | Stockholm. *Roméo et Juliette*. H. Schymberg (J), B. Lemon-Brundin (S), S. Edwardsen (T), S. Herdenberg (M), L. Björker (L); S.-Å. Axelson, cond. |
| Feb. 8 | Stockholm. *Rigoletto*. H. Schymberg (G), G. Allard (Gv), B. Ewert (M), A. Wirén (R), S.-E. Jacobsson (S); K. Bendix, cond. |
| Feb. 15 | Stockholm. *Bohème*. H. Schymberg (Mi), I. Köhler (Mu), S. Herdenberg (Ma), A. Wirén (S), F. Jonsson (C); K. Bendix, cond. |
| Feb. 18 | Stockholm. *Rigoletto*. As Feb. 8 except M. Sehlmark (M). |
| Feb. 21 | Stockholm, Concert Hall. Concert w. other soloists (benefit for children of Finland). |
| Feb. 23 | Stockholm. *Roméo et Juliette*. As Feb. 3 except G. Lemon-Bernhard (S); N. Grevillius, cond. |
| Mar. 5 | Stockholm. *Ballo in maschera*. H. Guermant-de la Berg (A), H. Schymberg (O), M. Sehlmark (U), S. Björling (R), A. Wirén (S), S.-E. Jacobsson (T); V. Gui, cond. |
| Mar. 8 | Stockholm. *Ballo in maschera*. As Mar. 5. |
| Mar. 11 | Stockholm. *Ballo in maschera*. As Mar. 5. |
| Mar. 15 | Stockholm. *Ballo in maschera*. As Mar. 5. |
| Mar. 17 | Gothenburg, Concert Hall. Recital. |
| Mar. 19 | Uppsala, University. Recital. |
| Mar. 22 | Copenhagen, Odd Fellow Palace. Recital. |
| Mar. 24 | Malmö, Realskolan. Recital. |
| Mar. 26 | Helsingborg, Concert Hall. Recital. |
| Mar. 28 | Gothenburg, Concert Hall. Recital. |
| Mar. 31 | Örebro. Recital. |
| Apr. 9 | Berlin, Philharmonie. Recital. |
| Apr. 17 | Gothenburg, Concert Hall. Recital. |
| May 5 | Stockholm, Concert Hall. Concert; N. Grevillius, cond. |
| May 9 | Stockholm. *Aida*. I. Wassner (Ai), G. Pålson-Wettergren (Amn), E. Larson (Amo), F. Jonsson (R), L. Björker (K); H. Sandberg, cond. |
| May 13 | Stockholm. *Roméo et Juliette*. As Feb. 3 except N. Grevillius, cond. |
| May 16 | Stockholm. *Rigoletto*. As Feb. 18. |
| May 18 | Helsinki, National Theater. Recital (benefit for war invalids). |
| May 19 | Helsinki, Invalid Hospital. Recital before patients. |
| May 24 | Furuvik. Recital. |
| May 31 | Täby, Hägernäs. Recital (benefit on Air Force Day). |
| June 14 | Stockholm, Skansen. Recital. |
| June 28 | Örnsköldsvik. Recital. |
| July 16 | Malmö, Folkets Park. Recital. |
| July 21 | Båstad. Recital (?). |
| July 24 | Copenhagen, Dyrehaven. Recital. |
| July 26 | Karlskrona. Recital. |
| July 30 | Stockholm, Gröna Lund. Recital. |
| Aug. 5 | Solna, Haga. Stockholm Garrison Festival. |
| Aug. 8 | Stockholm, Skansen. Recital. |
| Aug. 12 | Ystad. Recital. |
| Aug. 26 | Gothenburg, Liseberg. Recital. |

| | |
|---|---|
| Aug. 27 | Stockholm, Gröna Lund. Recital. |
| Aug. 28 | Södertälje. Recitals (2). |
| Sep. 17 | Copenhagen. *Rigoletto*. E. Wilton (G), E. Nielsen (Gv), E. Brems (M), H. Skjær (R), E. Nørby (S); E. Tango, cond. |
| Sep. 19 | Copenhagen. *Bohème*. E. Oldrup (Mi), K. Rendsberg (Mu), H. Skjær (Ma), P. Wiedemann (S), E. Nørby (C); J. Hye-Knudsen, cond. |
| Sep. 20 | Copenhagen. *Rigoletto*. As Sep. 17. |
| Sep. 27 | Stockholm. *Roméo et Juliette*. As May 13. |
| Sep. 29 | Stockholm. *Bohème*. As Feb. 15 except N. Grevillius, cond. |
| Oct. 2 | Stockholm. *Rigoletto*. As Feb. 8. |
| Oct. 8 | Stockholm, Concert Hall. Joint recital w. H. Schymberg, E. Larson. |
| Oct. 12 | Gothenburg, Concert Hall. Recital. |
| Oct. 25 | Malmö, Palladium. Recital. |
| Oct. 26 | Gothenburg, Concert Hall. Recital. |
| Nov. 22 | Budapest. *Bohème*. E. Réthy (Mi), J. Osváth (Mu), G. Losonczy (Ma), O. Maleczki (S), E. Koréh (C); S. Failoni, cond. |
| Nov. 25 | Budapest. *Faust*. E. Réthy (M), K. Horányi (S), I. Palló (V), G. Losonczy (Mé); O. Berg, cond. |
| Nov. 27 | Budapest. Recital. |
| Dec. 8 | Stockholm, Concert Hall. Concert (benefit for Red Cross); N. Grevillius, cond. |
| Dec. 13 | Stockholm, Town Hall. Lucia festival. |

**1943**

| | |
|---|---|
| Jan. 31 | Kalmar. Recital. |
| Feb. 2 | Gothenburg, Concert Hall. Recital. |
| Feb. 4 | Lund, University. Recital. |
| Feb. 7 | Kristianstad. Recital. |
| Feb. 9 | Malmö, Realskolan. Recital. |
| Feb. 11 | Karlshamn. Recital. |
| Feb. 12 | Karlskrona. Recital. |
| Feb. 17 | Stockholm. *Aida*. H. Guermant-de la Berg (Ai), G. Pålson-Wettergren (Amn), E. Larson (Amo), F. Jonsson (R), L. Björker (K); H. Sandberg, cond. |
| Feb. 21 | Helsinki. *Bohème* (benefit for opera pension fund). A. Mutanen (Mi), A.-C. Winter (Mu), E. Eirto (Ma), K. Ruusunen (S), L. Wager (C); L. Funtek, cond. |
| Feb. 24 | Stockholm. *Rigoletto*. As Oct. 2, 1942. |
| Feb. 26 | Stockholm. *Faust*. H. Görlin (M), B. Lemon-Brundin (S), G. Svedenbrant (V), J. Berglund (Mé); K. Bendix, cond. |
| Feb. 28 | Stockholm. *Bohème*. H. Schymberg (Mi), I. Köhler (Mu), S. Herdenberg (Ma), A. Wirén (S), F. Jonsson (C); H. Sandberg, cond. |
| Mar. 2 | Västerås. Recital. |
| Mar. 7 | Stockholm. *Roméo et Juliette* (benefit for N. Grevillius on his 50th birthday). As May 13, 1942. |
| Mar. 10 | Uppsala, University. Recital. |
| Mar. 21 | Mora. Recital. |
| Mar. 23 | Älvdalen. Recital. |

| | |
|---|---|
| Mar. 25 | Orsa. Recital. |
| Mar. 27 | Rättvik. Recital. |
| Mar. 28 | Leksand. Recital. |
| Apr. 1 | Stockholm. *Faust*. As Feb. 26 except H. Schymberg (M); N. Grevillius, cond. |
| Apr. 4 | Stockholm. *Bohème*. As Feb. 28 except I. Quensel (Mu); N. Grevillius, cond. |
| Apr. 8 | Stockholm. *Trovatore*. S. Amundsen (L), G. Pålson-Wettergren (A), S. Björling (DL), S.-E. Jacobsson (F); L. Blech, cond. |
| Apr. 11 | Stockholm. *Trovatore*. As Apr. 8 except H. Guermant (L), B. Ewert (A), E. Larson (DL). |
| Apr. 24 | Florence. *Trovatore*. M. Caniglia (L), F. Barbieri (A), E. Mascherini (DL), D. Baronti (F); M. Rossi, cond. |
| Apr. 28 | Florence. *Trovatore*. As Apr. 24. |
| May 2 | Florence. *Trovatore*. As Apr. 24. |
| May 6 | Florence. *Trovatore*. As Apr. 24 except C. Sassoli (L). |
| May 10 | Stockholm, Concert Hall. Joint recital w. H. Schymberg (for Swedish Association of Staff Managers). |
| May 13 | Stockholm. *Roméo et Juliette*, act 2 (part of "För Europas barn," Swedish Radio gala soiree, benefit for children of Europe). H. Schymberg (J); N. Grevillius, cond. |
| May 23 | Stockholm, Stadion. Recitals (2, at sports event). |
| June 30 | Stockholm, Gröna Lund. Recital. |
| July 15 | Stockholm, Gröna Lund. Recital. |
| Aug. 10 | Solna, Haga. Stockholm Garrison Festival. |
| Aug. 12 | Malmö, Folkets Park. Recital. |
| Aug. 18 | Copenhagen, Tivoli. Concert; T. Jensen, cond. |
| Aug. 20 | Copenhagen, Tivoli. Concert; T. Jensen, cond. |
| Aug. 28 | Stockholm, Skansen. Recital. |
| Sep. 3 | Stockholm, Gröna Lund. Recital (benefit for Barnens Dag). |
| Sep. 14 | Umeå. Recital (benefit for new concert hall). |
| Sep. 17 | Stockholm. *Rigoletto*. H. Schymberg (G), G. Allard (Gv), M. Sehlmark (M), A. Wirén (R), S.-E. Jacobsson (S); K. Bendix, cond. |
| Sep. 20 | Stockholm. *Rigoletto*. As Sep. 17 except B. Ewert (M). |
| Sep. 23 | Stockholm. *Trovatore*. As Apr. 8 except H. Guermant (L). |
| Sep. 27 | Stockholm. *Aida*. As Feb. 17. |
| Sep. 30 | Stockholm. *Trovatore*. As Sep. 23. |
| Oct. 7 | Helsinki, Messuhalli (Mässhallen). Recital (benefit for Red Cross). |
| Oct. 10 | Stora Tuna. Recital. |
| Oct. 10 | Falun. Recital. |
| Oct. 12 | Gothenburg, Concert Hall. Recital. |
| Oct. 14 | Stockholm, Concert Hall. Recital. |
| Oct. 22 | Stockholm, Royal Tennis Hall. Inaugural ceremony; A. Wiklund, cond. |
| Oct. 26 | Malmö, Realskolan. Recital. |
| Oct. 29 | Lund, University. Recital. |
| Oct. 31 | Helsingborg, Concert Hall. Concert; S. Frykberg, cond. |
| Nov. 7 | Luleå. Recital. |
| Nov. 9 | Boden. Recital. |

| | |
|---|---|
| Nov. 11 | Piteå. Recital. |
| Nov. 15 | Härnösand. Recital. |
| Nov. 19 | Östersund. Recital. |
| Nov. 27 | Stockholm, Town Hall. Recital (contribution to choral concert, benefit for children of Scandinavia). |
| Dec. 1 | Stockholm. *Roméo et Juliette*. H. Schymberg (J), B. Lemon-Brundin (S), S. Edwardsen (T), S. Herdenberg (M), L. Björker (L); N. Grevillius, cond. |
| Dec. 31 | Stockholm, Opera House. New Year's Vigil; S. Ehrling, cond. |

**1944**

| | |
|---|---|
| Jan. 17 | Stockholm, Engelbrekt Church. Sophiahemmet 60th anniversary celebration. |
| Jan. 25 | Stockholm, Concert Hall. Concert (benefit for Swedish Red Cross in Denmark and Norway); N. Grevillius, cond. |
| Feb. 2 | Kristinehamn. Recital. |
| Feb. 12 | Gothenburg, Concert Hall. Concert (benefit for Swedish Red Cross in Denmark and Norway); N. Grevillius, cond. |
| Feb. 13 | Borås. Recital. |
| Feb. 17 | Växjö. Recital. |
| Mar. 2 | Stockholm, Concert Hall. Norden Association 25th anniversary. |
| Apr. 14 | Stockholm. *Faust*. H. Schymberg (M), B. Lemon-Brundin (S), G. Svedenbrant (V), J. Berglund (Mé); N. Grevillius, cond. |
| Apr. 18 | Stockholm. *Pagliacci*. G. Lemon-Bernhard (N), A. Ohlson (B), S. Björling (T), G. Svedenbrant (S); S. Ehrling, cond. |
| Apr. 18 | Stockholm. *Cavalleria rusticana*. R. Moberg (S), I.-G. Norlin (Lo), M. Sehlmark (Lu), E. Sundquist (A); S.-Å. Axelson, cond. |
| Apr. 21 | Stockholm. *Trovatore*. H. Guermant (L), G. Pålson-Wettergren (A), S. Björling (DL), S.-E. Jacobsson (F); L. Blech, cond. |
| Apr. 23 | Karlsborg. Recital. |
| Apr. 25 | Stockholm. *Pagliacci*. As Apr. 18 except S. Edwardsen (B). |
| Apr. 25 | Stockholm. *Cavalleria rusticana*. As Apr. 18. |
| Apr. 29 | Stockholm, Concert Hall. Recital w. B. Hertzberg, S. Björling, and other soloists (benefit for Blå Stjärnan). |
| May 4 | Linköping. Recital. |
| May 6 | Åtvidaberg. Recital. |
| May 14 | Stockholm. *Aida*, act 3 (part of gala, benefit for Red Cross). H. Guermant (Ai), S. Björling (Amo), F. Jonsson (R); H. Sandberg, cond. |
| May 21 | Stockholm, Skansen. Recital (at Djurgårdsmässan). |
| June 6 | Stockholm, Stadion. Swedish Flag Day ceremony. |
| June 29 | Stockholm, Gröna Lund. Recital. |
| July 27 | Stockholm, Gröna Lund. Recital. |
| Aug. 6 | Stockholm, Enskede Sports Field. Recital. |
| Aug. 10 | Ljusterö. Recital (benefit for bridal crown fund). |
| Aug. 13 | Varberg. Recital. |
| Aug. 15 | Falkenberg. Recital. |
| Aug. 16 | Gothenburg, Liseberg. Recital. |
| Aug. 27 | Södertälje. Recitals (2). |
| Sep. 3 | Borås. Recital (Elfsborg Sports Club 40th anniversary). |

| | |
|---|---|
| Sep. 9 | Stockholm, Eriksdal Hall. Recital at election meeting. |
| Sep. 19 | Stockholm. *Ballo in maschera*. H. Guermant (A), H. Schymberg (O), G. Pålson-Wettergren (U), S. Björling (R), E. Sundquist (S), S.-E. Jacobsson (T); H. Sandberg, cond. |
| Sep. 22 | Stockholm. *Trovatore*. As Apr. 21. |
| Sep. 25 | Stockholm. *Faust* (benefit for children of France). As Apr. 14 except H. Görlin (M). |
| Sep. 28 | Stockholm. *Aida*. H. Guermant (Ai), G. Pålson-Wettergren (Amn), E. Larson (Amo), F. Jonsson (R), L. Björker (K); H. Sandberg, cond. |
| Oct. 3 | Stockholm. *Bohème*. H. Görlin (Mi), I. Köhler (Mu), S. Herdenberg (Ma), A. Wirén (S), F. Jonsson (C); N. Grevillius, cond. |
| Oct. 20 | Stockholm, Concert Hall. Joint concert w. H. Schymberg; N. Grevillius, cond. |
| Oct. 26 | Stockholm, Concert Hall. Gala evening w. other soloists (benefit for Finland); A. Järnefelt, cond. |
| Oct. 29 | Helsingborg, Concert Hall. Concert; S. Frykberg, cond. |
| Nov. 4 | Stockholm. *Roméo et Juliette*, act 2 (part of gala for Swedish Theater Union). H. Schymberg (J); N. Grevillius, cond. |
| Nov. 10 | Stockholm, Concert Hall. Radio concert; T. Mann, cond. |
| Nov. 19 | Växjö. Recital. |
| Nov. 21 | Malmö, Realskolan. Recital. |
| Nov. 22 | Lund, University. Recital. |
| Nov. 24 | Jönköping. Recital. |
| Nov. 28 | Gothenburg, Concert Hall. Recital. |
| Dec. 5 | Uppsala, Cathedral. Joint recital w. actor A. De Wahl (benefit for student scholarship fund). |
| Dec. 13 | Stockholm, Svea Artillery Regiment. Lucia festival. |
| Dec. 13 | Stockholm, Town Hall. Lucia festival. |
| Dec. 31 | Stockholm, Opera House and Concert Hall. New Year's soirees. |

**1945**

| | |
|---|---|
| Jan. 16 | Stockholm. *Aida* (gala, benefit for children of Belgium). As Sep. 28, 1944. |
| Jan. 28 | Stockholm, Concert Hall. Barnavännerna 75th anniversary. Recital w. other soloists (benefit for children of Europe). |
| Feb. 6 | Stockholm. *Madama Butterfly*, act 1, and *Trovatore*, act 3, scene 2 (part of gala, benefit for children of Italy). *Butterfly*: H. Görlin (B), B. Ewert (Su), S. Edwardsen (G), G. Svedenbrant (Sh); N. Grevillius, cond. *Trovatore*: H. Guermant (L); N. Grevillius, cond. |
| Feb. 11 | Linköping. Recital. |
| Feb. 13 | Gothenburg, Concert Hall. Joint concert w. H. Schymberg; S. Westerberg, cond. |
| Feb. 17 | Helsinki, Conservatory. Recital w. other soloists (benefit for Porkkala refugees). |
| Feb. 17 | Helsinki, Messuhalli (Mässhallen). Opera artists' carnival (benefit for opera pension fund). |
| Feb. 18 | Helsinki, Swedish Theater. Recital w. other soloists (benefit for war invalids). |
| Feb. 22 | Stockholm, Bromma läroverk. Recital. |

| | |
|---|---|
| Mar. 9 | Falun. Recital w. A.-L. Björling and other soloists (benefit for Blå Stjärnan). |
| Mar. 11 | Mora. Recital (in connection w. skiing competition Vasaloppet. Partly concert; G. Leijd, cond.). |
| Mar. 13 | Östersund. Recital. |
| Mar. 15 | Sundsvall. Recital. |
| Mar. 17 | Härnösand. Recital. |
| Mar. 20 | Umeå. Recital. |
| Mar. 25 | Luleå. Recital. |
| Apr. 6 | Stockholm. *Faust*. H. Görlin (M), B. Lemon-Brundin (S), G. Svedenbrant (V), S. Björling (Mé); N. Grevillius, cond. |
| Apr. 10 | Stockholm. *Roméo et Juliette*. H. Schymberg (J), B. Lemon-Brundin (S), S. Edwardsen (T), S. Herdenberg (M), L. Björker (L); N. Grevillius, cond. |
| Apr. 13 | Stockholm. *Bohème*. H. Schymberg (Mi), I. Köhler (Mu), C.-A. Hallgren (Ma), A. Wirén (S), F. Jonsson (C); N. Grevillius, cond. |
| Apr. 15 | Stockholm. *Bohème*. As Apr. 13 except R. Moberg (Mi). |
| Apr. 18 | Stockholm. *Ballo in maschera*. H. Guermant (A), H. Schymberg (O), G. Pålson-Wettergren (U), S. Björling (R), E. Sundquist (S), A. Wirén (T); H. Sandberg, cond. |
| Apr. 21 | Stockholm, Concert Hall. Concert w. other soloists (benefit for Blå Stjärnan); S. Waldimir, cond. |
| Apr. 24 | Stockholm. *Rigoletto*. H. Schymberg (G), G. Allard (Gv), M. Sehlmark (M), A. Wirén (R), S.-E. Jacobsson (S); K. Bendix, cond. |
| Apr. 27 | Stockholm, Concert Hall. Simfrämjandet 10th anniversary. |
| June 6 | Stockholm, Stadion. Swedish Flag Day ceremony. |
| June 15 | Stockholm, Opera House. Gala evening (benefit for Danish Resistance Movement); N. Grevillius, cond. |
| June 19 | Solna, Råsunda Stadium. Recital (benefit for Barnens Dag). |
| June 27 | Stockholm, Skansen. Recital. |
| July 19 | Stockholm, Gröna Lund. Recital. |
| Aug. 2 | Stockholm, Gröna Lund. Recital. |
| Aug. 5 | Furuvik. Recitals (2). |
| Aug. 11 | Ljusterö. Recital (benefit for Ljusterö Community Center). |
| Aug. 29 | Stockholm, Skansen. Recital. |
| Sep. 10 | Stockholm. *Roméo et Juliette*. As Apr. 10 except C.-A. Hallgren (M). |
| Sep. 12 | Stockholm. *Rigoletto*. As Apr. 24. |
| Sep. 14 | Stockholm. *Trovatore*. H. Guermant (L), G. Pålson-Wettergren (A), S. Björling (DL), S.-E. Jacobsson (F); L. Blech, cond. |
| Sep. 16 | Stockholm. *Bohème*. As Apr. 13 except G. Lemon-Bernhard (Mu). |
| Sep. 20 | Stockholm, Concert Hall. Concert; N. Grevillius, cond. |
| Sep. 23 | Copenhagen. *Ballo in maschera*. E. Schøtt (A), E. Oldrup (O), I. Steffensen (U), H. Skjær (R), E. Nørby (S), A. Føns (T); E. Tango, cond. |
| Oct. 7 | Detroit, Masonic Auditorium. "Ford Sunday Evening Hour," radio concert; D. Mitropoulos, cond. (First performance on this American tour, which lasted until May and included more than 70 concerts and recitals.) |
| Oct. 19 | Butte, MT. Joint recital w. D. Kirsten. |
| Oct. 22 | Great Falls, MT. Joint recital w. D. Kirsten. |

424

| | |
|---|---|
| Oct. 25 | Spokane, WA. Joint recital w. D. Kirsten. |
| Oct. 27 | Walla Walla, WA. Recital. |
| Oct. 30 | Portland, OR. Recital. |
| Nov. 1 | Salem, OR. Joint recital w. D. Kirsten. |
| Nov. 3 | Seattle, Moore Theater. Recital. |
| Nov. 5 | Eugene, OR. Recital. |
| Nov. 9 | Los Angeles (S. F. Opera). *Bohème*. D. Kirsten (Mi), N. Connor (Mu), F. Valentino (Ma), G. Cehanovsky (S), L. Alvary (C); G. Merola, cond. |
| Nov. 13 | Ogden, UT. Recital w. Ogden Tabernacle Choir. |
| Nov. 19 | New York, Rockefeller Center. "Voice of Firestone," radio concert; H. Barlow, cond. |
| Nov. 29 | New York. *Rigoletto*. B. Sayão (G), T. Altman (Gv), M. Lipton (M), L. Warren (R), N. Moscona (S); C. Sodero, cond. |
| Dec. 5 | New York. *Tosca*. G. Moore (T), L. Tibbett (S), S. Baccaloni (Sa); C. Sodero, cond. |
| Dec. 10 | New York. *Rigoletto*. As Nov. 29. |
| Dec. 20 | New York. *Tosca*. As Dec. 5. |
| Dec. 29 | New York. *Rigoletto*. As Nov. 29 except N. Cordon (S). |

## 1946

| | |
|---|---|
| Jan. 1 | New York. *Bohème*. B. Sayão (Mi), F. Greer (Mu), J. Brownlee (Ma), A. Kent (S), N. Cordon (C); C. Sodero, cond. |
| Jan. 6 | New York, Met. Concert w. other soloists (benefit for Mizrachi); P. Breisach, cond. |
| Jan. 8 | Philadelphia (Met). *Tosca*. R. Resnik (T), L. Tibbett (S), S. Baccaloni (Sa); C. Sodero, cond. |
| Jan. 11 | New York. *Tosca*. As Jan. 8 except G. Pechner (Sa); P. Cimara, cond. |
| Jan. 13 | Detroit, Masonic Auditorium. "Ford Sunday Evening Hour," radio concert; E. Ormandy, cond. |
| Jan. 15 | Quebec. Recital. |
| Jan. 17 | Toronto. Joint recital w. H. Temianka, violin. |
| Jan. 19 | Toronto. Joint recital w. H. Temianka, violin. |
| Jan. 21 | New York, Rockefeller Center. "Voice of Firestone," joint radio concert w. E. Steber; H. Barlow, cond. |
| Jan. 25 | Atlanta. Joint recital w. D. Kirsten. |
| Jan. 26 | Birmingham, AL. Joint recital w. D. Kirsten (?). |
| Jan. 28 | New Orleans. Recital. |
| Jan. 30 | Lake Charles, LA. Recital (?). |
| Feb. 2 | El Paso, TX. Recital (?). |
| Feb. 7 | Eureka, CA. Recital. |
| Feb. 11 | San Francisco, Opera House. Recital. |
| Feb. 13 | Fresno, CA. Recital. |
| Feb. 15 | Los Angeles, Occidental College. Recital. |
| Feb. 17 | San Diego, CA. Recital. |
| Feb. 20 | Pasadena, CA. Recital. |
| Feb. 22 | Claremont, CA. Recital. |
| Feb. 26 | Los Angeles, Philharmonic Auditorium. Recital. |

| | |
|---|---|
| Mar. 3 | Chicago, Orchestra Hall. Recital. |
| Mar. 6 | Ottawa. Recital. |
| Mar. 8 | Kitchener, Ontario. Recital (?). |
| Mar. 11 | London, Ontario. Recital. |
| Mar. 13 | Hamilton, Ontario. Recital (?). |
| Mar. 18 | Rockford, IL. Recital. |
| Mar. 20 | Decatur, IL. Recital (?). |
| Mar. 25 | New York, Rockefeller Center. "Voice of Firestone," radio concert; H. Barlow, cond. |
| Mar. 27 | Baltimore. Recital (?). |
| Mar. 29 | Richmond, VA. Recital. |
| Apr. 2 | Havana. Recital. |
| Apr. 4 | Havana. Recital. |
| Apr. 15 | New York, Rockefeller Center. "Voice of Firestone," radio concert; H. Barlow, cond. |
| Apr. 17 | New York. *Ballo in maschera*. Z. Milanov (A), P. Alarie (O), M. Harshaw (U), L. Warren (R), N. Cordon (S), L. Alvary (T); B. Walter, cond. |
| Apr. 20 | New York. *Rigoletto*. J. Antoine (G), G. Zeiher (Gv), M. Lipton (M), L. Warren (R), N. Cordon (S); C. Sodero, cond. |
| Apr. 23 | Clemson, SC. Recital (?). |
| Apr. 25 | Knoxville, TN. Recital (?). |
| Apr. 28 | Cleveland (Met). *Bohème*. L. Albanese (Mi), F. Greer (Mu), F. Valentino (Ma), G. Cehanovsky (S), N. Cordon (C); C. Sodero, cond. |
| May 2 | Ann Arbor, MI. Concert; E. Ormandy, cond. |
| May 4 | Minneapolis (Met). *Bohème*. As Apr. 28 except D. Kirsten (Mi), J. Brownlee (Ma). |
| May 9 | Montreal. Recital. |
| May 12 | Detroit, Masonic Auditorium. "Ford Sunday Evening Hour," radio concert; F. Reiner, cond. |
| May 15 | New York, Carnegie Hall. Scandinavian "Pop" Concert w. other soloists; S. Parmet, cond. |
| May 29 | Gothenburg, Liseberg. Recital. |
| July 27 | Stockholm, Skansen. Recital. |
| July 31 | Stockholm, Gröna Lund. Recital. |
| Aug. 12 | Stockholm, Skansen. Concert; A. Järnefelt, cond. |
| Aug. 20 | Milan. *Rigoletto*. L. Aimaro-Bertasi (G), L. Lauri (Gv), W. Madonna (M), C. Tagliabue (R), C. Siepi (S); F. Molinari Pradelli, cond. |
| Aug. 22 | Milan. *Rigoletto*. As Aug. 20 except L. Gennai, cond. |
| Aug. 24 | Milan. *Rigoletto*. As Aug. 22. |
| Aug. 28 | Copenhagen, KB Hall. Recital. |
| Sep. 11 | Stockholm. *Tosca*. R. Moberg (T), E. Larson (S), S.-E. Jacobsson (Sa); N. Grevillius, cond. |
| Sep. 13 | Stockholm, Stadion. Olympic Festival (benefit for Greece). |
| Sep. 15 | Stockholm. *Trovatore*. H. Guermant (L), G. Pålson-Wettergren (A), C.-A. Hallgren (DL), S.-E. Jacobsson (F); L. Blech, cond. |
| Sep. 18 | Stockholm. *Bohème*. H. Schymberg (Mi), I. Köhler (Mu), C.-A. Hallgren (Ma), A. Wirén (S), F. Jonsson (C); N. Grevillius, cond. |
| Oct. 5 | Chicago. *Rigoletto*. J. Antoine (G), J. Pabst (Gv), W. Heckman (M), |

426

|          | L. Warren (R), V. Lazzari (S); N. Rescigno, cond. |
|----------|----------|
| Oct. 7   | Chicago. *Bohème*. D. Kirsten (Mi), F. Greer (Mu), E. Mascherini (Ma), W. Engelman (S), V. Lazzari (C); N. Rescigno, cond. |
| Oct. 14  | San Francisco. *Bohème*. S. Roman (Mi), M. Sa Earp (Mu), M. Harrell (Ma), G. Cehanovsky (S), N. Moscona (C); P. Cimara, cond. |
| Oct. 16  | San Francisco. *Trovatore*. S. Roman (L), M. Harshaw (A), F. Valentino (DL), N. Moscona (F); K. H. Adler, cond. |
| Oct. 18  | Carmel, CA. Recital. |
| Oct. 21  | Ventura, CA. Recital. |
| Oct. 25  | Spokane, WA. Joint recital w. D. Kirsten (?). |
| Oct. 26  | Los Angeles (S. F. Opera). *Trovatore*. As Oct. 16. |
| Oct. 29  | Los Angeles (S. F. Opera). *Bohème*. As Oct. 14 except B. Sayão (Mi); G. Merola, cond. |
| Oct. 30  | Portland, OR. Recital (?). |
| Nov. 3   | Los Angeles (S. F. Opera). *Roméo et Juliette*. B. Sayão (J), E. Knapp (S), A. De Paolis (T), J. Brownlee (M), L. Alvary (L); P. Breisach, cond. |
| Nov. 6   | Omaha, NE. Recital. |
| Nov. 11  | Minneapolis. Recital. |
| Nov. 17  | Washington, Constitution Hall. Recital. |
| Nov. 19  | Troy, NY. Recital. |
| Nov. 20  | Los Angeles. Concert (?). |
| Nov. 23  | New York, Columbia University. Recital. |
| Nov. 26  | Buffalo, NY. Recital. |
| Nov. 28  | Detroit, Music Hall. Concert; K. Krueger, cond. |
| Nov. 29  | Detroit, Music Hall. Concert; K. Krueger, cond. |
| Dec. 2   | Montreal. Recital. |
| Dec. 5   | Toronto. Recital. |
| Dec. 7   | Toronto. Recital. |
| Dec. 19  | New York. *Bohème*. As Jan. 1 except G. Cehanovsky (S), G. Vaghi (C). |
| Dec. 23  | New York. *Faust*. R. Mazella (M), M. Stellman (S), R. Merrill (V), E. Pinza (Mé); L. Fourestier, cond. |

**1947**

| Jan. 15  | New York. *Roméo et Juliette*. B. Sayão (J), M. Benzell (S), T. Hayward (T), J. Brownlee (M), N. Moscona (L); E. Cooper, cond. |
|----------|----------|
| Jan. 17  | Montclair, NJ. Joint recital w. D. Kirsten. |
| Jan. 25  | New York. *Bohème*. L. Albanese (Mi), F. Greer (Mu), F. Valentino (Ma), G. Cehanovsky (S), G. Vaghi (C); C. Sodero, cond. |
| Jan. 27  | New York. *Trovatore*. S. Roman (L), M. Harshaw (A), F. Valentino (DL), G. Vaghi (F); C. Sodero, cond. |
| Feb. 1   | New York. *Roméo et Juliette*. As Jan. 15. |
| Feb. 6   | Fort Wayne, IN. Recital (?). |
| Feb. 8   | Chattanooga, TN. Recital (?). |
| Feb. 10  | Louisville, KY. Recital. |
| Feb. 14  | Springfield, IL. Recital (?). |
| Feb. 17  | Denver. Recital (?). |

427

| | |
|---|---|
| Feb. 23 | San Francisco, Opera House. Recital. |
| Feb. 28 | Santa Barbara, CA. Recital (?). |
| Mar. 3 | Los Angeles, Philharmonic Auditorium. Recital (?). |
| Mar. 5 | Bakersfield, CA. Recital (?). |
| Mar. 10 | Albuquerque, NM. Recital. |
| Mar. 12 | Lubbock, TX. Recital. |
| Mar. 15 | Austin, TX. Recital. |
| Mar. 17 | Dallas. Recital. |
| Mar. 21 | Akron, OH. Recital. |
| Mar. 24 | Kalamazoo, MI. Recital (?). |
| Mar. 26 | Saginaw, MI. Recital (?). |
| Mar. 29 | Chicago, Orchestra Hall. Recital. |
| Mar. 31 | Mason City, IA. Recital (?). |
| Apr. 5 | New York. *Trovatore*. D. Ilitsch (L), M. Harshaw (A), L. Warren (DL), N. Moscona (F); C. Sodero, cond. (One of the last performances on this American tour.) |
| June 17 | Solna, Råsunda Stadium. Charity gala (benefit for Barnens Dag); I. Gustafsson, cond. |
| July 17 | Stockholm, Gröna Lund. Recital. |
| July 26 | Ljusterö. Joint recital w. H. Theorell, violin (benefit for Ljusterö Community Center). |
| July 30 | Stockholm, Skansen. Recital. |
| Aug. 14 | Stockholm, Gröna Lund. Recital. |
| Aug. 18 | Oslo, Calmeyergatens Misjonshus. Joint recital w. J. Berglund (benefit for prisoners of war). |
| Aug. 23 | Stockholm, Skansen. Recital. |
| Aug. 29 | Gothenburg, Liseberg. Recital. |
| Aug. 30 | Stockholm, Skansen. Recital (benefit for Barnens Dag). |
| Oct. 10 | Stockholm. *Aida*, act 3 (part of gala for king and queen of Denmark). H. Guermant (Ai), M. Bergström (Amn), S. Björling (Amo), F. Jonsson (R); N. Grevillius, cond. (Program shows act 4, but advertisement act 3; Amonasro's presence confirms the latter.) |
| Oct. 21 | Stockholm. *Faust*. H. Görlin (M), B. Lemon-Brundin (S), E. Larson (V), J. Berglund (Mé); N. Grevillius, cond. |
| Nov. 29 | Stockholm. *Bohème*. H. Görlin (Mi), H. Guermant (Mu), H. Hasslo (Ma), A. Wirén (S), F. Jonsson (C); N. Grevillius, cond. |
| Dec. 1 | Stockholm. *Tosca*. As Sep. 11, 1946. |
| Dec. 7 | Cincinnati. Recital. |
| Dec. 9 | St. Louis, MO. Recital. |
| Dec. 11 | Manhattan, KS. Recital. |
| Dec. 13 | Minneapolis. "Luciafest" recital. |
| Dec. 25 | New York. *Rigoletto*. L. Pons (G), E. Sachs (Gv), I. Petina (M), L. Warren (R), M. Székely (S); P. Cimara, cond. |
| Dec. 27 | New York. *Trovatore*. As Jan. 27 except L. Warren (DL); E. Cooper, cond. |
| Dec. 31 | New York. *Cavalleria rusticana*. R. Resnik (S), I. Jordan (Lo), C. Turner (Lu), F. Valentino (A); G. Antonicelli, cond. |

**1948**

| | |
|---|---|
| Jan. 3 | New York. *Bohème*. B. Sayão (Mi), M. Benzell (Mu), J. Brownlee (Ma), H. Thompson (S), N. Moscona (C); G. Antonicelli, cond. |
| Jan. 8 | New York. *Ballo in maschera*. S. Roman (A), P. Alarie (O), M. Harshaw (U), L. Warren (R), N. Moscona (S), L. Alvary (T); F. Busch, cond. |
| Jan. 10 | New York. *Rigoletto*. M. Benzell (G), E. Sachs (Gv), L. Browning (M), L. Warren (R), G. Vaghi (S); P. Cimara, cond. |
| Jan. 13 | Hickory, NC. Recital (?). |
| Jan. 15 | Spartanburg, SC. Recital (?). |
| Jan. 19 | Havana. Recital. |
| Jan. 21 | Havana. Recital. |
| Jan. 24 | Shreveport, LA. Recital (?). |
| Jan. 26 | Fayetteville, AR. Recital (?). |
| Jan. 30 | Edinburg, TX. Recital. |
| Feb. 3 | San Francisco, Opera House. Recital. |
| Feb. 7 | Seattle, Moore Theater. Recital. |
| Feb. 9 | Vancouver. Recital. |
| Feb. 11 | Portland, OR. Recital. |
| Feb. 13 | Moscow, ID. Recital (?). |
| Feb. 16 | Missoula, MT. Recital (?). |
| Feb. 20 | Helena, MT. Recital (?). |
| Feb. 23 | Fargo, ND. Recital. |
| Feb. 26 | Ottumwa, IA. Recital (?). |
| Mar. 1 | New York. *Trovatore*. D. Ilitsch (L), C. Elmo (A), R. Merrill (DL), G. Vaghi (F); E. Cooper, cond. |
| Mar. 6 | Chicago, Orchestra Hall. Recital. |
| Mar. 8 | Indianapolis. Recital. |
| Mar. 11 | Bloomington, IN. Recital. |
| Mar. 15 | New York, Rockefeller Center. "Telephone Hour," radio concert; D. Voorhees, cond. |
| Mar. 21 | New York, Carnegie Hall. Recital. |
| Mar. 23 | Bethlehem, PA. Recital (?). |
| Mar. 30 | Baltimore (Met). *Bohème*. As Jan. 3 except L. Albanese (Mi), F. Greer (Mu), G. Cehanovsky (S). |
| Apr. 3 | Atlanta (Met). *Bohème*. As Mar. 30 except G. Vaghi (C). |
| Apr. 8 | Dallas (Met). *Ballo in maschera*. D. Ilitsch (A), I. Manski (O), C. Elmo (U), L. Warren (R), G. Vaghi (S), L. Alvary (T); F. Busch, cond. |
| Apr. 16 | Los Angeles (Met). *Trovatore*. R. Resnik (L), C. Elmo (A), L. Warren (DL), J. Hines (F); E. Cooper, cond. |
| Apr. 21 | Los Angeles (Met). *Ballo in maschera*. As Apr. 8 except S. Roman (A). |
| Apr. 28 | Lincoln (Met). *Tosca*. R. Resnik (T), J. Brownlee (S), S. Baccaloni (Sa); G. Antonicelli, cond. |
| Apr. 30 | St. Louis (Met). *Cavalleria rusticana*. S. Roman (S), M. Lipton (Lo), C. Turner (Lu), J. Brownlee (A); G. Antonicelli, cond. |
| May 4 | Cincinnati, Music Hall. *Fidelio* (abridged concert performance). R. |

|        | Bampton (L), S. Russell (M), F. Bens (J), M. Harrell (F), J. Macdonald (P), M. Singher (R); F. Busch, cond. |
|--------|----|
| May 6  | Cincinnati, Music Hall. Concert w. other soloists; F. Busch, cond. |
| May 8  | Minneapolis (Met). *Trovatore*. As Apr. 16 except N. Moscona (F). |
| May 11 | Battle Creek, MI. Recital (?). |
| May 13 | Cleveland (Met). *Trovatore*. As Apr. 16 except S. Roman (L), R. Merrill (DL). |
| May 15 | Cleveland (Met). *Ballo in maschera*. As Apr. 8 except F. Greer (O), F. Valentino (R), N. Moscona (S). |
| June 16 | Stockholm, Skansen. Gala concert (on King Gustaf V's birthday); N. Grevillius, cond. |
| July 4 | Stockholm, Skansen. Recital (on US Independence Day). |
| July 7 | Stockholm, Skansen. Recital. |
| July 22 | Stockholm, Gröna Lund. Recital. |
| Aug. 4 | Stockholm, Skansen. Joint recital w. A.-L. Björling. |
| Aug. 15 | Gothenburg, Liseberg. Recital. |
| Aug. 24 | Stockholm, Gröna Lund. Recital. |
| Aug. 30 | Stockholm. *Bohème* (Red Cross Conference gala). A.-L. Björling (Mi), I. Quensel (Mu), H. Hasslo (Ma), A. Wirén (S), F. Jonsson (C); N. Grevillius, cond. |
| Sep. 5 | Stockholm, Concert Hall. Gala soiree, joint w. A.-L. Björling (benefit for women's organizations). |
| Sep. 16 | Stockholm. *Tosca*. As Sep. 11, 1946. |
| Sep. 24 | Stockholm. *Cavalleria rusticana*. A.-G. Söderholm (S), I.-G. Norlin (Lo), M. Sehlmark (Lu), G. Svedenbrant (A); H. Sandberg, cond. |
| Sep. 24 | Stockholm. *Pagliacci*. I. Quensel (N), A. Ohlson (B), S. Björling (T), C.-A. Hallgren (S); H. Sandberg, cond. |
| Sep. 26 | Stockholm, Gustaf Vasa Church. Funeral service for Count Folke Bernadotte. |
| Sep. 26 | Stockholm. *Roméo et Juliette*. H. Schymberg (J), K. Löfgren (S), S. Edwardsen (T), C.-A. Hallgren (M), L. Björker (L); N. Grevillius, cond. |
| Sep. 29 | Copenhagen, KB Hall. Joint recital w. A.-L. Björling. |
| Oct. 9 | Sacramento (S. F. Opera). *Trovatore*. S. Menkes (L), C. Elmo (A), L. Warren (DL), N. Moscona (F); D. Marzollo, cond. |
| Oct. 12 | San Francisco. *Bohème*. L. Albanese (Mi), L. Hartzell (Mu), T. Gobbi (Ma), G. Cehanovsky (S), I. Tajo (C); G. Merola, cond. |
| Oct. 15 | San Francisco. *Bohème*. B. Sayão (Mi), M. Zubiri (Mu), F. Valentino (Ma), G. Cehanovsky (S), I. Tajo (C); K. Kritz, cond. |
| Oct. 25 | Ontario, CA. Recital (?). |
| Oct. 31 | Los Angeles (S. F. Opera). *Bohème*. As Oct. 12. |
| Nov. 5 | Houston. Recital. |
| Nov. 8 | Kansas City, MO. Recital (?). |
| Nov. 15 | New York, Rockefeller Center. "Telephone Hour," radio concert; D. Voorhees, cond. |
| Nov. 17 | Quincy, MA. Recital. |
| Nov. 20 | New York, Columbia University. Recital (?). |
| Nov. 22 | Scranton, PA. Recital (?). |
| Nov. 29 | New York, Madison Square Garden. "Star-Spangled Carnival," |

concert w. other soloists (benefit for Hospitalized Veterans Music Service).

| | |
|---|---|
| Dec. 3 | New York. *Trovatore*. As May 13 except F. Valentino (DL). |
| Dec. 16 | New York. *Bohème*. As Jan. 3. |
| Dec. 21 | Philadelphia (Met). *Trovatore*. As Dec. 3. |
| Dec. 25 | New York. *Bohème*. As Jan. 3 except F. Valentino (Ma), G. Cehanovsky (S). |
| Dec. 26 | New York, Met. AGMA Christmas party w. A.-L. Björling and other soloists. |

## 1949

| | |
|---|---|
| Jan. 3 | New York. *Trovatore*. S. Roman (L), C. Elmo (A), G. Valdengo (DL), J. Hines (F); E. Cooper, cond. |
| Jan. 8 | Lancaster, PA. Recital (?). (One of the first of about 40 recitals on this American tour.) |
| Jan. 11 | Washington, Constitution Hall. Recital. |
| Jan. 13 | York, PA. Recital (?). |
| Jan. 17 | East Lansing, MI. Recital (?). |
| Jan. 20 | Cincinnati. Recital (?). |
| Jan. 24 | Evanston, IL. Recital (?). |
| Jan. 26 | Evanston, IL. Recital (?). |
| Jan. 30 | Cleveland. Recital (?). |
| Feb. 2 | Larchmont, NY. Recital (?). |
| Feb. 6 | Chicago, Orchestra Hall. Recital. |
| Feb. 8 | Superior, WI. Recital (?). |
| Feb. 11 | Des Moines, IA. Recital. |
| Feb. 14 | Baton Rouge, LA. Recital. |
| Feb. 19 | San Antonio. *Bohème*. D. Kirsten (Mi), L. Hunt (Mu), M. Harrell (Ma), J. Tyers (S), L. Vichegonov (C); M. Reiter, cond. |
| Feb. 21 | Houston. Joint recital w. A.-L. Björling (benefit for Scandinavian Club). |
| Feb. 25 | Charlotte, NC. Recital (?). |
| Mar. 2 | Utica, NY. Recital. |
| Mar. 8 | San Francisco, Opera House. Recital. |
| Mar. 14 | Reading, PA. Recital (?). |
| Mar. 18 | Detroit, Art Institute. Recital. |
| Mar. 19 | Detroit, Art Institute. Recital. |
| Mar. 21 | Montreal. Recital (?). |
| Mar. 23 | Quebec. Recital (?). |
| Mar. 25 | Baltimore. Recital (?). |
| Mar. 29 | Boston (Met). *Trovatore*. As Jan. 3 except M. Harshaw (A), F. Valentino (DL). |
| Apr. 1 | Wheeling, WV. Recital (?). |
| Apr. 4 | New York, Rockefeller Center. "Telephone Hour," radio concert; D. Voorhees, cond. |
| Apr. 7 | Cleveland (Met). *Rigoletto*. L. Pons (G), T. Altman (Gv), M. Lipton (M), L. Warren (R), N. Moscona (S); P. Cimara, cond. |
| Apr. 11 | New York, Carnegie Hall. "Sweden in Music," gala concert w. other |

|  | soloists (benefit for Swedish Seamen's Welfare Fund). (One of the last performances on this American tour.) |
|---|---|
| June 16 | Stockholm, Gröna Lund. Recital. |
| June 19 | Stockholm, Skansen. Festival soiree (on Co-operative Movement Day); S. Waldimir, cond. |
| June 29 | Stockholm, Skansen. Recital. |
| July 6 | Copenhagen, Tivoli. Concert; S. C. Felumb, cond. |
| July 11 | Stockholm, Sports Exhibition. Joint recital w. A.-L. Björling. |
| July 13 | Stockholm, Skansen. Recital. |
| July 21 | Stockholm, Gröna Lund. Recital. |
| July 30 | Stockholm, Skansen. Joint recital w. A.-L. Björling. |
| July 31 | Furuvik. Recitals (2; the second joint w. A.-L. Björling). |
| Aug. 13 | Stockholm, Skansen. Joint recital w. A.-L. Björling. |
| Aug. 23 | Los Angeles, Hollywood Bowl. Joint concert w. A.-L. Björling; I. Solomon, cond. |
| Aug. 28 | San Rafael, CA. Joint recital w. A.-L. Björling. |
| Sep. 6 | Honolulu. Joint recital w. A.-L. Björling. |
| Sep. 20 | San Francisco. *Tosca* (S. F. season opening). E. Barbato (T), L. Tibbett (S), S. Baccaloni (Sa); F. Cleva, cond. |
| Sep. 25 | San Francisco. *Bohème*. L. Albanese (Mi), L. Hartzell (Mu), E. Mascherini (Ma), G. Cehanovsky (S), N. Moscona (C); K. Kritz, cond. |
| Oct. 2 | San Francisco. *Faust*. F. Quartararo (M), H. Glaz (S), E. Mascherini (V), N. Moscona (Mé); K. H. Adler, cond. |
| Oct. 7 | San Francisco. *Manon Lescaut*. L. Albanese (M), E. Mascherini (L), S. Baccaloni (G); F. Cleva, cond. |
| Oct. 13 | San Francisco. *Faust*. As Oct. 2. |
| Oct. 16 | San Francisco. *Manon Lescaut*. As Oct. 7 except F. Valentino (L). |
| Oct. 23 | San Francisco, Opera House. "Standard Hour," joint radio concert w. A.-L. Björling; G. Merola, cond. |
| Oct. 25 | Los Angeles (S. F. Opera). *Manon Lescaut*. As Oct. 7. |
| Oct. 28 | Lafayette, IN. Joint recital w. A.-L. Björling. |
| Oct. 29 | Lafayette, IN. Joint recital w. A.-L. Björling. |
| Nov. 1 | Peoria, IL. Recital. |
| Nov. 4 | Milwaukee, WI. Recital. |
| Nov. 7 | New York, Rockefeller Center. "Telephone Hour," radio concert; D. Voorhees, cond. |
| Nov. 13 | Ithaca, NY. Recital. |
| Nov. 19 | New York, Hunter College. Recital. |
| Nov. 23 | New York. *Manon Lescaut*. D. Kirsten (M), G. Valdengo (L), S. Baccaloni (G); G. Antonicelli, cond. |
| Nov. 26 | New York. *Tosca* (benefit for New York chapter of Hadassah). E. Barbato (T), A. Svéd (S), G. Pechner (Sa); G. Antonicelli, cond. |
| Nov. 29 | Philadelphia (Met). *Manon Lescaut*. As Nov. 23. |
| Dec. 5 | New York. *Tosca*. As Nov. 26. |
| Dec. 10 | New York. *Manon Lescaut*. As Nov. 23. |
| Dec. 15 | New York. *Tosca*. As Nov. 26 except L. Tibbett (S). (Last performance on this US tour.) |

**1950**

| | |
|---|---|
| Jan. 8 | Stockholm. *Roméo et Juliette*. H. Schymberg (J), K. Löfgren (S), C. Söderström (T), C.-A. Hallgren (M), L. Björker (L); N. Grevillius, cond. |
| Jan. 11 | Stockholm. *Bohème*. H. Görlin (Mi), H. Guermant (Mu), E. Larson (Ma), A. Wirén (S), F. Jonsson (C); N. Grevillius, cond. |
| Feb. 13 | San Francisco, Opera House. Recital. |
| Feb. 17 | Los Angeles, Philharmonic Auditorium. Recital. |
| Feb. 20 | Portland, OR. Joint concert w. A.-L. Björling; J. Sample, cond. |
| Feb. 22 | Victoria, British Columbia. Recital (?). |
| Feb. 24 | Vancouver. Recital (?). |
| Feb. 27 | Kansas City, MO. Recital (?). |
| Mar. 2 | Lexington, KY. Recital (?). |
| Mar. 4 | Louisville, KY. Recital. |
| Mar. 6 | New York, Rockefeller Center. "Voice of Firestone," joint radio and TV concert w. A.-L. Björling; H. Barlow, cond. |
| Mar. 11 | Chicago, Orchestra Hall. Recital w. Swedish Glee Club. |
| Mar. 16 | Oak Park, IL. Recital (?). |
| Mar. 19 | South Bend, IN. Concert; Hames, cond. |
| Mar. 21 | Oxford, OH. Recital (?). |
| Mar. 24 | Rochester, NY. Recital. |
| Mar. 28 | Washington. Recital. |
| Mar. 30 | Boston (Met). *Tosca*. L. Welitsch (T), P. Schöffler (S), G. Pechner (Sa); G. Antonicelli, cond. |
| Mar. 31 | New York, Carnegie Hall. "Night of Swedish Stars," joint recital w. A.-L. Björling and the Augustana Choir (benefit for Swedish Seamen's Welfare Fund). |
| Apr. 3 | Charleston, WV. Recital (?). |
| Apr. 8 | Toronto. Recital. |
| Apr. 10 | Toronto. Recital. |
| Apr. 12 | Johnstown, PA. Recital (?). |
| Apr. 15 | Cleveland (Met). *Manon Lescaut*. D. Kirsten (M), G. Valdengo (L), S. Baccaloni (G); G. Antonicelli, cond. |
| Apr. 17 | Miami. Recital (?). |
| Apr. 20 | New Orleans. *Ballo in maschera*. S. Morris (A), A. Schuh (O), M. Larrimore (U), M. Rothmüller (R), N. Treigle (S), J. Dabdoub (T); W. Herbert, cond. |
| Apr. 22 | New Orleans. *Ballo in maschera*. As Apr. 20. |
| Apr. 24 | Glen Ellyn, IL. Recital (?). |
| Apr. 27 | Winnipeg. Recital (?). |
| Apr. 28 | Calgary, Alberta. Recital. |
| May 2 | Pasadena, CA. Recital (?). |
| May 5 | Santa Barbara, CA. Recital (?). |
| May 8 | Chicago (Met). *Tosca*. As Mar. 30 except A. Svéd (S). |
| May 12 | Chicago (Met). *Rigoletto*. P. Munsel (G), T. Altman (Gv), J. Madeira (M), L. Warren (R), J. Hines (S); J. Perlea, cond. |
| May 21 | Stockholm, Skansen. Recital (at Djurgårdsmässan). |
| June 11 | Helsinki, Messuhalli (Mässhallen). Gala recital (Helsinki 400th anniversary). |

| | |
|---|---|
| July 6 | Stockholm, Gröna Lund. Recital. |
| July 12 | Gothenburg, Liseberg. Recitals (2). |
| July 18 | Malmö, Folkets Park. Recitals (2). |
| July 25 | Stockholm, Skansen. Recital. |
| Aug. 3 | Stockholm, Gröna Lund. Joint recital w. A.-L. Björling. |
| Aug. 12 | Stockholm, Skansen. Joint recital w. A.-L. Björling. |
| Sep. 2 | Copenhagen, Odd Fellow Palace. Recital. |
| Oct. 1 | Berlin. "Stars aus Europa," radio concert w. other soloists; K. Gaebel, cond. |
| Oct. 6 | Uppsala, Cathedral. Recital w. other soloists (benefit for opera artists' relief fund). |
| Oct. 13 | Stockholm, Concert Hall. Joint concert w. A.-L. Björling; N. Grevillius, cond. |
| Oct. 23 | New York, Rockefeller Center. "Telephone Hour," radio concert; D. Voorhees, cond. (One of the first of about 55 recitals and concerts on this American tour, 15 of them joint with A.-L. Björling.) |
| Nov. 6 | New York. *Don Carlo* (Met season opening). D. Rigal (El), L. Amara (V), F. Barbieri (Eb), R. Merrill (R), C. Siepi (F), J. Hines (I); F. Stiedry, cond. |
| Nov. 9 | New York, St. John's Cathedral. Memorial service for King Gustaf V of Sweden. |
| Nov. 11 | New York. *Don Carlo*. As Nov. 6. |
| Nov. 14 | New York. *Don Carlo*. As Nov. 6 except B. Thebom (Eb). |
| Nov. 16 | New York. *Don Carlo*. As Nov. 6 except H. Hotter (I). |
| Nov. 20 | New York, Rockefeller Center. "Voice of Firestone," radio and TV concert; H. Barlow, cond. |
| Nov. 24 | New York. *Don Carlo*. As Nov. 16. |
| Nov. 28 | Philadelphia (Met). *Don Carlo*. As Nov. 16. |
| Dec. 4 | New York. *Don Carlo*. As Nov. 14 except J. Hines (F), H. Hotter (I). |
| Dec. 12 | New York. *Faust*. D. Kirsten (M), A. Bollinger (S), F. Guarrera (V), J. Hines (Mé); F. Cleva, cond. |
| Dec. 19 | New York. *Faust*. As Dec. 12 except E. Steber (M), C. Siepi (Mé). |
| Dec. 23 | New York. *Faust*. As Dec. 12 except C. Siepi (Mé). |
| Dec. 25 | New York. *Don Carlo*. As Nov. 14 except P. Silveri (R), H. Hotter (I). |
| Dec. 29 | New York. *Faust*. As Dec. 12 except N. Conner (M), M. Roggero (S), R. Merrill (V). |

**1951**

| | |
|---|---|
| Jan. 1 | New York. *Faust*. E. Steber (M), A. Bollinger (S), L. Warren (V), C. Siepi (Mé); F. Cleva, cond. |
| Jan. 6 | New York. *Manon Lescaut*. D. Kirsten (M), G. Valdengo (L), L. Alvary (G); F. Cleva, cond. |
| Jan. 8 | New York, Rockefeller Center. "Telephone Hour," radio concert; D. Voorhees, cond. |
| Jan. 10 | New York. *Manon Lescaut*. As Jan. 6 except L. Albanese (M), H. Thompson (L). |
| Jan. 16 | Portland, ME. Joint recital w. A.-L. Björling (?). |
| Jan. 19 | Syracuse, NY. Recital (?). |
| Jan. 23 | Schenectady, NY. Recital (?). |

| | |
|---|---|
| Jan. 25 | Hartford (Connecticut Opera). *Bohème*. B. Sayão (Mi), E. Likova (Mu), A. Pilotto (Ma), E. Dunning (S), N. Scott (C); N. Rescigno, cond. |
| Jan. 31 | Quebec. Joint recital w. A.-L. Björling. |
| Feb. 2 | Montreal. Joint recital w. A.-L. Björling. |
| Feb. 9 | Detroit, Art Institute. Recital (?). |
| Feb. 12 | Denver. Joint recital w. A.-L. Björling. |
| Feb. 16 | New York, NBC studio. "We, the People," TV program. |
| Feb. 19 | Columbus, GA. Recital (?). |
| Feb. 22 | Urbana, IL. Joint recital w. A.-L. Björling (?). |
| Feb. 25 | Chicago, Orchestra Hall. Recital. |
| Feb. 27 | Buffalo, NY. Recital. |
| Mar. 3 | New York, Hunter College. Recital. |
| Mar. 6 | Toledo, OH. Joint recital w. A.-L. Björling (?). |
| Mar. 12 | New York, Carnegie Hall. "Telephone Hour," radio concert; D. Voorhees, cond. (Probably the last performance on this American tour.) |
| Apr. 2 | Stockholm, Concert Hall. Recital. |
| Apr. 8 | Stockholm. *Manon Lescaut*. E. Oldrup (M), C.-A. Hallgren (L), S. Nilsson (G); K. Bendix, cond. |
| Apr. 11 | Stockholm. *Manon Lescaut*. As Apr. 8 except H. Schymberg (M). |
| Apr. 19 | Stockholm. *Ballo in maschera*. H. Guermant (A), E. Prytz (O), M. Bergström (U), C.-A. Hallgren (R), E. Sundquist (S), P. Höglund (T); K. Bendix, cond. |
| Apr. 22 | Stockholm. *Ballo in maschera*. As Apr. 19. |
| Apr. 26 | Stockholm. *Faust* (benefit for H. Görlin). H. Görlin (M), B. Lemon-Brundin (S), E. Larson (V), J. Berglund (Mé); N. Grevillius, cond. |
| May 19 | Milan. *Ballo in maschera*. M. Caniglia (A), D. Gatta (O), C. Elmo (U), P. Silveri (R), S. Maionica (S), V. Susca (T); F. Capuana, cond. |
| May 22 | Milan. *Ballo in maschera*. As May 19. |
| May 27 | Milan. *Ballo in maschera*. As May 19 except L. Bonello (O), B. Ronchini Senni (U). |
| May 30 | Milan. *Ballo in maschera*. As May 27 except C. Elmo (U); A. Quadri, cond. |
| June 2 | Milan. *Ballo in maschera*. As May 30 except C. Araujo (A), C. Tagliabue (R). |
| June 6 | Milan. *Ballo in maschera*. As June 2. |
| June 20 | Helsinki, University. Sibelius concert; N.-E. Fougstedt, cond. |
| July 5 | Stockholm, Gröna Lund. Recital. |
| July 18 | Stockholm, Skansen. Recital. |
| July 25 | Gothenburg, Liseberg. Recital. |
| July 29 | London, Royal Albert Hall. Recital. |
| Aug. 10 | Stockholm, Gröna Lund. Recital. |
| Aug. 15 | Stockholm, Skansen. Recital. |
| Aug. 18 | Ljusterö. Recital (for charity). |
| Sep. 6 | Stockholm. *Tosca* (benefit for E. Larson). B. Hertzberg (T), E. Larson (S), S.-E. Jacobsson (Sa); N. Grevillius, cond. |
| Sep. 10 | Stockholm. *Manon Lescaut*. As Apr. 8 except N. Grevillius, cond. |
| Sep. 21 | San Francisco. *Roméo et Juliette*. B. Sayão (J), H. Glaz (S), J. Schwabacher (T), R. Herbert (M), N. Moscona (L); P. Breisach, cond. |

Sep. 27    San Francisco. *Roméo et Juliette*. As Sep. 21 except A.-L. Björling (J), L. Alvary (L).
Sep. 30    San Francisco, Opera House. "Standard Hour," joint radio concert w. B. Sayão; G. Merola, cond.
Oct. 8     San Francisco. *Bohème*. B. Sayão (Mi), U. Graf (Mu), G. Valdengo (Ma), G. Cehanovsky (S), N. Moscona (C); P. Breisach, cond.
Oct. 10    San Francisco, Civic Auditorium. "Fol de Rol" concert (w. other soloists).
Oct. 12    San Francisco. *Tosca*. D. Kirsten (T), R. Weede (S), S. Baccaloni (Sa); F. Cleva, cond.
Oct. 14    San Francisco. *Bohème*. As Oct. 8 except L. Hartzell (Mu), N. Rossi-Lemeni (C).
Oct. 20    San Francisco. *Rigoletto*. L. Pons (G), E. Baldwin (Gv), H. Glaz (M), R. Weede (R), L. Alvary (S); P. Cimara, cond.
Oct. 22    Fresno, CA (S. F. Opera). *Bohème*. As Oct. 8 except D. Kirsten (Mi), F. Valentino (Ma).
Oct. 26    Los Angeles (S. F. Opera). *Bohème*. As Oct. 14 except R. Herbert (Ma).
Oct. 29    Los Angeles (S. F. Opera). *Roméo et Juliette*. As Sep. 21 except G. Cehanovsky (M).
Nov. 3     Los Angeles (S. F. Opera). *Rigoletto*. As Oct. 20 except D. Ernster (S).
Nov. 5     San Francisco, Opera House. Recital.
Nov. 11    Los Angeles, CBS radio studio. "Edgar Bergen–Charlie McCarthy Show," radio program. Joint performance w. A.-L. Björling; R. Noble, cond.
Nov. 19    New York, Rockefeller Center. "Voice of Firestone," radio and TV concert; H. Barlow, cond.
Dec. 2     Los Angeles, CBS radio studio. "Edgar Bergen–Charlie McCarthy Show," radio program. Joint performance w. A.-L. Björling; R. Noble, cond.
Dec. 9     Chicago, Orchestra Hall. Recital. (Probably the last performance on this US tour.)

**1952**

Jan. 22    Stockholm, Concert Hall. Recital w. other soloists (benefit for Red Cross).
Mar. 10    New York, Rockefeller Center. "Voice of Firestone," radio and TV concert; H. Barlow, cond.
Mar. 21    New York. *Don Carlo*. D. Rigal (El), L. Amara (V), F. Barbieri (Eb), P. Silveri (R), C. Siepi (F), H. Hotter (I); F. Stiedry, cond.
Mar. 24    New York. *Don Carlo*. As Mar. 21.
Mar. 27    Trois-Rivières (Three Rivers), Quebec. Recital.
Apr. 1     Washington. Recital.
Apr. 2     Washington, Walter Reed Army Medical Center. Recital for wounded soldiers.
Apr. 4     Chattanooga, TN. Recital.
Apr. 7     Lexington, KY. Recital.

| | |
|---|---|
| Apr. 9 | New York. *Don Carlo*. E. Steber (El), L. Amara (V), R. Resnik (Eb), R. Merrill (R), J. Hines (F), N. Moscona (I); R. Cellini, cond. |
| Apr. 14 | Houston. Recital. |
| May 17 | Oslo, Jordal Amfi. Joint concert w. A. Brown (on Norwegian National Day); O. Grüner-Hegge, cond. (partly recital w. piano). |
| May 25 | Stockholm, Skansen. Recital (on TCO Day). |
| June 15 | London, Royal Albert Hall. Recital. |
| June 17 | Copenhagen, Tivoli. Concert; S. C. Felumb, cond., and separate recital w. piano. |
| June 26 | Stockholm, Gröna Lund. Recital. |
| July 2 | Stockholm, Skansen. Recital. |
| July 13 | Malmslätt. Recital (at JUF congress). |
| July 15 | Malmö, Folkets Park. Recitals (2). |
| July 17 | Stockholm, Gröna Lund. Recital. |
| July 20 | Gothenburg, Liseberg. Recitals (2). |
| July 25 | Helsinki, University. Recital (benefit for Red Cross). |
| July 27 | Helsinki, Linnanmäki (Borgbacken). Joint recital w. A.-L. Björling. |
| Aug. 10 | Furuvik. Recitals (2; the second joint w. A.-L. Björling). |
| Aug. 13 | Stockholm, Skansen. Recital. |
| Oct. 7 | Uppsala, University. Folket i Bild festival. |
| Oct. 9 | Malmö, Amiralen. Folket i Bild festival. |
| Oct. 12 | Vimmerby. Recital. |
| Oct. 26 | Stockholm, Concert Hall. Concert (benefit for Kungafonden); N. Grevillius, cond. |
| Nov. 6 | Reykjavik. Recital. |
| Nov. 10 | Reykjavik. Recital (benefit for Children's Hospital). |
| Nov. 14 | London, Royal Festival Hall. Recital. |
| Nov. 16 | Manchester. Recital. |
| Nov. 23 | London, Royal Albert Hall. Recital. |
| Nov. 26 | Glasgow. Recital (benefit for Glasgow Jewish Board of Guardians Auxiliary). |
| Nov. 29 | Dublin. Recital. |
| Dec. 4 | Stockholm, China Theater. "Stjärnnatt" (Star Night), gala evening w. A.-L. Björling and other artists (benefit for Höstsol, a home for retired artists). |
| Dec. 14 | Helsinki. *Bohème*. A.-L. Björling (Mi), M. Vilppula (Mu), E. Eirto (Ma), L. Lehtinen (S), L. Wager (C); L. Funtek, cond. |
| Dec. 16 | Helsinki, Messuhalli (Mässhallen). Recital. |
| Dec. 29 | Stockholm. *Bohème*. R. Moberg (Mi), K. Dellert (Mu), C.-A. Hallgren (Ma), A. Wirén (S), F. Jonsson (C); N. Grevillius, cond. |

**1953**

| | |
|---|---|
| Jan. 2 | Stockholm. *Rigoletto*. E. Prytz (G), K. Meyer (Gv), B. Wermine (M), H. Hasslo (R), S.-E. Jacobsson (S); L. Gardelli, cond. |
| Feb. 3 | New York. *Cavalleria rusticana*. F. Barbieri (S), M. Roggero (Lo), T. Votipka (Lu), F. Valentino (A); A. Erede, cond. |
| Feb. 7 | New York. *Rigoletto*. H. Güden (G), T. Votipka (Gv), M. Lipton (M), L. Warren (R), L. Vichegonov (S); A. Erede, cond. |

| | |
|---|---|
| Feb. 10 | New Haven, NY. Recital (?). |
| Feb. 22 | Stockholm, Concert Hall. Joint recital w. A.-L. Björling and other artists (benefit for victims of Dutch flooding). |
| Mar. 12 | Paris, Théâtre de Paris. Recital (press gala). |
| Mar. 17 | Glasgow. Recital. |
| Mar. 22 | London, Royal Albert Hall. Recital. |
| Apr. 29 | Gothenburg, Concert Hall. Recital. |
| May 5 | Örebro. Recital. |
| May 7 | Uppsala, University. Recital. |
| May 9 | Östersund. Recital. |
| May 15 | Sundsvall. Recital. |
| June 6 | Stockholm, Stadion. Swedish Flag Day ceremony. |
| June 8 | London, Royal Festival Hall. Recital. |
| June 10 | Swansea. Recital. |
| June 12 | Cardiff. Recital. |
| June 15 | London, Royal Festival Hall. Recital. |
| June 25 | Stockholm, Gröna Lund. Recital. |
| June 28 | Helsingborg. Recitals (2; at Öresundsmässan). |
| July 12 | Leksand. Recital (at rowing competition). |
| Aug. 6 | Stockholm, Gröna Lund. Recital. |
| Aug. 29 | Stockholm, Skansen. Recital (benefit for Barnens Dag). |
| Sep. 6 | Gothenburg, Liseberg. Recitals (2; benefit for Barnens Dag). |
| Sep. 11 | Stockholm, Kungsträdgården. Recital. |
| Sep. 13 | Stockholm, Skansen. Recital (on Sweden-America Day). |
| Sep. 25 | Stockholm. *Tosca*. B. Nilsson (T), S. Björling (S), S.-E. Jacobsson (Sa); S. Ehrling, cond. |
| Sep. 28 | Stockholm. *Bohème*. H. Schymberg (Mi), I. Quensel (Mu), C.-A. Hallgren (Ma), A. Wirén (S), F. Jonsson (C); S. Ehrling, cond. |
| Oct. 15 | Detroit, Masonic Auditorium. Recital. |
| Oct. 20 | Hartford (Connecticut Opera). *Tosca*. W. Spence (T), R. Weede (S), L. Davidson (Sa); P. Cimara, cond. |
| Oct. 31 | New York, Hunter College. Recital. |
| Nov. 16 | New York. *Faust* (Met season opening). V. de los Angeles (M), M. Miller (S), R. Merrill (V), N. Rossi-Lemeni (Mé); P. Monteux, cond. |
| Nov. 24 | New York. *Faust*. As Nov. 16. |
| Nov. 28 | New York. *Faust*. As Nov. 16 except F. Guarrera (V). |
| Dec. 2 | New York, United Nations. Joint recital (soiree) w. L. Albanese. (JB canceled part of his program owing to voice problems.) |
| Dec. 17 | New York. *Faust* (JB replaced by T. Hayward after act 1). As Nov. 16 except G. Valdengo (V). |

## 1954

| | |
|---|---|
| Jan. 27 | Milwaukee, WI. Recital. (First performance on this US tour.) |
| Feb. 1 | New York. *Bohème*. L. Albanese (Mi), J. Fenn (Mu), R. Merrill (Ma), G. Cehanovsky (S), C. Siepi (C); A. Erede, cond. |
| Feb. 27 | Miami Beach (Opera Guild of Greater Miami). *Trovatore*. A. Varnay (L), C. Turner (A), R. Weede (DL), E. Doe (F); E. Buckley, cond. |
| Apr. 21 | Copenhagen, Odd Fellow Palace. Recital. |

| | |
|---|---|
| Apr. 23 | Jönköping. Recital. |
| Apr. 25 | Borås. Recital. |
| Apr. 27 | Gothenburg. Recital. |
| May 2 | Stockholm. *Bohème*. H. Schymberg (Mi), K. Dellert (Mu), C.-A. Hallgren (Ma), A. Wirén (S), F. Jonsson (C); S. Ehrling, cond. |
| May 27 | Swansea. Recital. |
| May 30 | London, Royal Albert Hall. Recital. |
| June 4 | Stockholm. *Rigoletto*. H. Schymberg (G), K. Meyer (Gv), B. Wermine (M), H. Hasslo (R), S.-E. Jacobsson (S); L. Gardelli, cond. |
| June 6 | Stockholm, Skansen. Recital (on Swedish Flag Day). |
| June 9 | Bergen (Norway). Festival concert; C. Garaguly, cond. |
| June 15 | Stockholm, Concert Hall. "Nordisk samling," Nordic gala program; S. Westerberg, cond. |
| June 23 | Stockholm, Skansen. Recital. |
| July 4 | Stockholm, Skansen. Recital (on US Independence Day). |
| July 29 | Stockholm, Gröna Lund. Recital. |
| Aug. 4 | Stockholm, Skansen. Recital. |
| Aug. 15 | Johannesburg (South Africa). Recital. |
| Aug. 18 | Johannesburg. Recital. |
| Aug. 22 | Johannesburg. Recital. |
| Aug. 24 | Durban (South Africa). Recital. |
| Aug. 26 | Cape Town (South Africa). Recital. |
| Aug. 29 | Johannesburg. Radio concert; J. Schulman, cond. |
| Sep. 1 | Cape Town. Concert; F. Schuurman, cond. (partly recital w. piano). |
| Sep. 3 | Pretoria (South Africa). Recital. |
| Oct. 22 | Stockholm, Town Hall. Festival soiree (for Swedish Finland Associations). |
| Nov. 6 | Stuttgart (Germany). *Bohème*. L. Weissmann (Mi), F. Wachmann (Mu), E. Czubok (Ma), F. Sentpaul (S), W. Schirp (C); W. Seegelken, cond. |
| Nov. 11 | Belgrade. *Bohème*. V. Heybalova (Mi), N. Sterle (Mu), S. Janković (Ma), Z. Milosavljević (S), M. Čangalović (C); K. Baranović, cond. |
| Nov. 12 | Belgrade. Recital. |
| Nov. 15 | Zagreb (Yugoslavia). *Bohème*. B. Deman (Mi), V. Grozaj (Mu), I. Francl (Ma), M. Kučić (S), T. Neralić (C); D. Žebre, cond. |
| Nov. 24 | Gothenburg, Concert Hall. Recital. |
| Nov. 28 | Stockholm. *Rigoletto*. As June 4 except M. Sehlmark (Gv). |
| Dec. 1 | Stockholm. *Cavalleria rusticana*. A. Nordmo-Løvberg (S), E. Söderström (Lo), M. Sehlmark (Lu), A. Näslund (A); K. Bendix, cond. |
| Dec. 1 | Stockholm. *Pagliacci*. H. Schymberg (N), A. Ohlson (B), H. Hasslo (T), Å. Collett (S); L. Gardelli, cond. |
| Dec. 8 | Stockholm. *Cavalleria rusticana*. As Dec. 1 except B. Björling (Lo), G. Svedenbrant (A). |
| Dec. 8 | Stockholm. *Pagliacci*. R. Moberg (N), A. Ohlson (B), E. Sundquist (T), C.-A. Hallgren (S); L. Gardelli, cond. |
| Dec. 19 | Stockholm, Opera House. Svenska Dagbladet Christmas Concert (w. other soloists). |
| Dec. 20 | Stockholm, Söder Hospital. Recital for patients (to be broadcast on hospital radio). |

| | |
|---|---|
| Dec. 30 | Stockholm, Beckomberga Hospital. Recital for patients (joint w. E. Larson and E. Wohl, violin). |

**1955**

| | |
|---|---|
| Jan. 14 | Stockholm. *Tosca*. B. Nilsson (T), S. Björling (S), S.-E. Jacobsson (Sa); S. Westerberg, cond. |
| Jan. 18 | Helsinki, Messuhalli (Mässhallen). Recital. |
| Jan. 20 | Tampere (Tammerfors, Finland). Recital (benefit for war invalids). |
| Jan. 23 | Helsinki. *Tosca*. E. Pihlaja (T), L. Lehtinen (S), H. Heikkilä (Sa); J. Jalas, cond. |
| Jan. 27 | Stockholm. *Aida*. B. Nilsson (Ai), B. Björling (Amn), S. Björling (Amo), S. Nilsson (R), L. Björker (K); S. Ehrling, cond. |
| Jan. 29 | Sundsvall. Recital (for Skid- och Friluftsfrämjandet). |
| Feb. 3 | Stockholm. *Bohème*. H. Schymberg (Mi), K. Dellert (Mu), C.-A. Hallgren (Ma), A. Wirén (S), F. Jonsson (C); K. Bendix, cond. |
| Feb. 9 | Copenhagen, Odd Fellow Palace. Recital. |
| Feb. 11 | Helsingborg, Concert Hall. Recital. |
| Feb. 13 | Malmö, Municipal Theater. Recital. |
| Feb. 15 | Halmstad. Recital. |
| Feb. 18 | Lund, University. Recital. |
| Feb. 20 | Nässjö. Recital. |
| Mar. 10 | Helsinki. *Tosca* (benefit for new opera house). As Jan. 23. |
| Mar. 13 | Helsinki. *Rigoletto* (benefit for new opera house). S. Långholm (G), L. Rope (Gv), M. Kuusoja (M), L. Lehtinen (R), Y. Ikonen (S); J. Jalas, cond. |
| Mar. 15 | Helsinki, Messuhalli (Mässhallen). Recital. |
| Mar. 20 | London, Royal Albert Hall. Recital. |
| Apr. 22 | Stockholm, Concert Hall. Soiree (benefit for Barnens Dag). |
| Apr. 24 | Borås. Recital. |
| Apr. 26 | Turku (Åbo, Finland). Recital. |
| Apr. 28 | Eskilstuna. Recital. |
| May 5 | Stockholm. *Bohème*. As Feb. 3 except R. Moberg (Mi), A. Näslund (S). |
| May 8 | Stockholm, Skansen. Recital (on Red Cross Day). |
| May 9 | Stockholm. *Cavalleria rusticana*. A.-G. Söderholm (S), E. Söderström (Lo), K. Meyer (Lu), G. Svedenbrant (A); K. Bendix, cond. |
| May 9 | Stockholm. *Pagliacci*. H. Schymberg (N), A. Ohlson (B), H. Hasslo (T), C.-A. Hallgren (S); K. Bendix, cond. |
| May 20 | Gothenburg, Ullevi. Recital. |
| June 2 | Oslo, Jordal Amfi. Joint concert w. E. Schwarzkopf; D. Dixon, cond. |
| June 6 | Stockholm, Skansen. Recital (on Swedish Flag Day). |
| July 19 | Stockholm, Town Hall. KSSS (Royal Swedish Yacht Club) Festival Dinner. |
| July 31 | Furuvik. Recitals (2; on Dalarna Day). |
| Sep. 24 | New York, Carnegie Hall. Recital. (One of the first performances on this American tour, which included about 25 recitals.) |
| Oct. 6 | Saskatoon, Saskatchewan. Recital. |
| Oct. 20 | Seattle, Civic Auditorium. Concert. |

| | |
|---|---|
| Nov. 5 | Chicago. *Trovatore*. M. Callas (L), E. Stignani (A), E. Bastianini (DL), W. Wildermann (F); N. Rescigno, cond. |
| Nov. 8 | Chicago. *Trovatore*. As Nov. 5 except C. Turner (A), R. Weede (DL). |
| Nov. 12 | Chicago. *Rigoletto*. T. Stich-Randall (G), A. Krainik (Gv), M. Dunn (M), T. Gobbi (R), W. Wildermann (S); N. Rescigno, cond. |
| Nov. 15 | Chicago. *Faust*. R. Carteri (M), M. Dunn (S), R. Weede (V), N. Rossi-Lemeni (Mé); T. Serafin, cond. |
| Nov. 18 | Chicago. *Faust*. As Nov. 15. |
| Nov. 25 | Chicago. *Rigoletto*. As Nov. 12. |
| Nov. 29 | Chicago. *Ballo in maschera*. A. Cerquetti (A), P. Bonini (O), C. Turner (U), T. Gobbi (R), W. Wildermann (S), A. Foldi (T); N. Rescigno, cond. |
| Dec. 3 | Chicago. *Ballo in maschera*. As Nov. 29. |
| Dec. 8 | Atlanta. Recital. |
| Dec. 10 | Ruston, LA. Recital. |
| Dec. 12 | Ruston, LA. Recital. |
| Dec. 14 | New Orleans. Recital. |
| Dec. 20 | New York, Carnegie Hall. Joint concert w. R. Tebaldi; L. Bernstein, cond. (Last performance on this American tour.) |

## 1956

| | |
|---|---|
| Jan. 30 | New York, Rockefeller Center. "Producer's Showcase: Festival of Music," joint TV concert w. R. Tebaldi and other artists; M. Rudolf, cond. (Probably first appearance on this American tour.) |
| Feb. 1 | Pittsburgh. Recital. |
| Feb. 6 | Toronto. Recital. |
| Feb. 17 | New York. *Ballo in maschera*. Z. Milanov (A), L. Hurley (O), J. Madeira (U), R. Merrill (R), G. Tozzi (S), N. Scott (T); D. Mitropoulos, cond. |
| Feb. 24 | Milwaukee, WI. Recital. |
| Feb. 26 | Chicago, Orchestra Hall. Recital. |
| Feb. 29 | Pasadena, CA. Recital. |
| Mar. 10 | New York, Met. Gala concert (w. other soloists) for president of Italy; P. Cimara, cond. |
| Mar. 14 | Philadelphia, Academy of Music. Recital. |
| Mar. 31 | New York. *Manon Lescaut*. L. Albanese (M), F. Guarrera (L), F. Corena (G); D. Mitropoulos, cond. |
| Apr. 4 | New York. *Tosca*. Z. Milanov (T), W. Cassel (S), G. Pechner (Sa); D. Mitropoulos, cond. |
| Apr. 10 | Baltimore (Met). *Tosca*. As Apr. 4 except L. Warren (S). |
| Apr. 13 | New York. *Manon Lescaut*. As Mar. 31. |
| Apr. 14 | New York. *Fledermaus* gala; T. Kozma, cond. |
| Apr. 17 | Boston (Met). *Ballo in maschera*. H. Nelli (A), D. Wilson (O), M. Anderson (U), L. Warren (R), N. Moscona (S), N. Scott (T); T. Kozma, cond. |
| Apr. 24 | Cleveland (Met). *Ballo in maschera*. As Apr. 17 except Z. Milanov (A). |
| Apr. 27 | Cleveland (Met). *Rigoletto*. R. Peters (G), T. Votipka (Gv), R. Elias (M), L. Warren (R), G. Tozzi (S); F. Cleva, cond. |

441

| | |
|---|---|
| May 27 | London, Royal Albert Hall. Recital. |
| June 6 | Stockholm, Skansen. Recital (on Swedish Flag Day). |
| June 9 | Stockholm, Town Hall. Concert at luncheon given for Queen Elizabeth II of Britain; S. Ehrling, cond. |
| July 10 | Copenhagen, Tivoli. Concert; S. C. Felumb, cond., and separate recital w. piano. |
| July 19 | Stockholm, Gröna Lund. Recital. |
| July 22 | Furuvik. Recitals (2). |
| Aug. 1 | Gothenburg, Liseberg. Recital. |
| Aug. 9 | Stockholm, Skansen. Recital. |
| Aug. 19 | Östersund. Recital (on Sweden-America Day). |
| Aug. 27 | Stockholm. *Rigoletto*. H. Schymberg (G), B. Ericson (Gv), K. Meyer (M), H. Hasslo (R), S.-E. Jacobsson (S); K. Bendix, cond. |
| Aug. 31 | Stockholm. *Tosca*. A. Nordmo-Løvberg (T), S. Björling (S), S.-E. Jacobsson (Sa); S. Westerberg, cond. |
| Sep. 3 | Stockholm, Skansen. Recital. |
| Sep. 5 | Stockholm. *Tosca*. As Aug. 31. |
| Sep. 13 | San Francisco. *Manon Lescaut* (S. F. season opening). D. Kirsten (M), L. Quilico (L), L. Alvary (G); O. de Fabritiis, cond. |
| Sep. 16 | San Francisco. *Trovatore*. E. Farrell (L), O. Dominguez (A), A. Colzani (DL), N. Moscona (F); O. de Fabritiis, cond. |
| Sep. 20 | San Francisco. *Manon Lescaut*. As Sep. 13. |
| Sep. 23 | San Francisco. *Tosca*. R. Tebaldi (T), A. Colzani (S), G. Cehanovsky (Sa); G. Curiel, cond. |
| Sep. 30 | Sacramento (S. F. Opera). *Tosca*. As Sep. 23. |
| Oct. 3 | San Francisco, Civic Auditorium. "Fol de Rol" concert (w. other soloists). |
| Oct. 19 | Los Angeles (S. F. Opera). *Manon Lescaut*. As Sep. 13 except F. Guarrera (L). |
| Oct. 23 | Chicago. *Trovatore*. H. Nelli (L), C. Turner (A), E. Bastianini (DL), W. Wildermann (F); B. Bartoletti, cond. |
| Oct. 27 | Chicago. *Trovatore*. As Oct. 23 except G. Ribla (L). |
| Oct. 30 | Chicago. *Tosca*. R. Tebaldi (T), T. Gobbi (S), C. Badioli (Sa); B. Bartoletti, cond. |
| Nov. 2 | Chicago. *Tosca*. As Oct. 30 except L. Kopp, cond. |
| Nov. 5 | Chicago. *Tosca*. As Oct. 30. |
| Nov. 7 | Detroit (New York City Opera). *Rigoletto*. S. Stahlman (G), S. Winston (Gv), M. Dunn (M), C. MacNeil (R), R. Humphrey (S); E. Leinsdorf, cond. |
| Nov. 16 | Chicago. *Bohème*. R. Tebaldi (Mi), D. Wilson (Mu), E. Bastianini (Ma), H. Noel (S), M. Čangalović (C); B. Bartoletti, cond. |
| Nov. 24 | New York, Hunter College. Recital. |
| Dec. 11 | New York, Brooklyn Academy of Music. Recital. |

**1957**

| | |
|---|---|
| Jan. 3 | Stockholm. *Tosca*. B. Nilsson (T), S. Björling (S), S.-E. Jacobsson (Sa); S. Westerberg, cond. |

| | |
|---|---|
| Jan. 5 | Stockholm. *Rigoletto*. E. Prytz (G), B. Ericson (Gv), K. Meyer (M), E. Sundquist (R), S.-E. Jacobsson (S); K. Bendix, cond. |
| Jan. 11 | Stockholm. *Trovatore*. A. Nordmo-Løvberg (L), K. Meyer (A), H. Hasslo (DL), E. Saedén (F); K. Bendix, cond. |
| Jan. 15 | Stockholm. *Bohème*. E. Prytz (Mi), K. Dellert (Mu), H. Hasslo (Ma), A. Wirén (S), F. Jonsson (C); K. Bendix, cond. |
| Jan. 19 | Zurich. *Tosca*. B. Nilsson (T), S. Björling (S), G. Zeithammer (Sa); E. Hartogs, cond. |
| Jan. 26 | Stockholm. *Trovatore*. As Jan. 11 except M. Bergström (A); H. Sandberg, cond. |
| Jan. 29 | Stockholm. *Bohème*. As Jan. 15 except A. Näslund (S). |
| Feb. 4 | Copenhagen, Tivoli. Recital. |
| Feb. 6 | Gothenburg, Concert Hall. Recital. |
| Feb. 10 | Stockholm. *Aida*. A. Nordmo-Løvberg (Ai), H. Ekström (Amn), E. Sundquist (Amo), F. Jonsson (R), L. Björker (K); S. Ehrling, cond. |
| Feb. 17 | New York, CBS studio. "Ed Sullivan Show," TV program. W. H. Güden, T. Votipka; F. Cleva, cond. |
| Feb. 24 | Milwaukee, WI. Recital (?). |
| Feb. 26 | Chicago. Recital (?). |
| Feb. 27 | New York. *Tosca*. R. Tebaldi (T), L. Warren (S), S. Baccaloni (Sa); D. Mitropoulos, cond. |
| Mar. 3 | Washington. Recital (?). |
| Mar. 7 | Philadelphia, Academy of Music. Recital. |
| Mar. 16 | New York. *Don Carlo*. D. Rigal (El), E. Cundari (V), I. Dalis (Eb), E. Bastianini (R), C. Siepi (F), H. Uhde (I); F. Stiedry, cond. |
| Mar. 19 | Philadelphia (Met). *Trovatore*. A. Stella (L), I. Dalis (A), E. Bastianini (DL), N. Moscona (F); M. Rudolf, cond. |
| Mar. 29 | New York. *Don Carlo*. As Mar. 16 except A. Stella (El), R. Merrill (R), J. Hines (F), N. Moscona (I). |
| Apr. 4 | New York. *Don Carlo*. As Mar. 29 except H. Uhde (I). |
| June 4 | Stockholm. *Aida*. As Feb. 10 except M. Bergström (Amn), S. Björling (Amo), S. Nilsson (R). |
| June 6 | Stockholm, Skansen. Recital (on Swedish Flag Day). |
| June 8 | Stockholm. *Trovatore*. As Jan. 26 except K. Bendix, cond. |
| June 16 | Stockholm. *Bohème*. As Jan. 29. |
| June 19 | Stockholm. *Trovatore*. As June 8 except H. Schymberg (L), K. Meyer (A). |
| July 28 | Gothenburg, Liseberg. Recital. |
| Aug. 5 | Stockholm, Gröna Lund. Recital. |
| Sep. 29 | Malmö, Municipal Theater. Concert (Swedish-Italian Music Week); A. Tronchi, cond. |
| Sep. 30 | Malmö, Municipal Theater. *Bohème*. E. Mårtensson (Mi), A. Herseth (Mu), N. Bäckström (Ma), A. Hasselblad (S), B. v. Knorring (C); S.-Å. Axelson, cond. |
| Oct. 2 | Malmö, Municipal Theater. *Bohème*. As Sep. 30. |
| Oct. 7 | Stockholm. *Bohème*. As Jan. 15 except H. Schymberg (Mi); S. Ehrling, cond. |
| Oct. 16 | Chicago. *Bohème*. A. Moffo (Mi), E. Likova (Mu), A. Protti (Ma), H. Noel (S), K. Smith (C); G. Gavazzeni, cond. |

| | |
|---|---|
| Oct. 21 | Chicago. *Manon Lescaut.* R. Tebaldi (M), C. MacNeil (L), C. Badioli (G); T. Serafin, cond. |
| Oct. 24 | Portland. Recital (?). |
| Oct. 25 | Chicago. *Manon Lescaut.* As Oct. 21. |
| Nov. 4 | Chicago. *Bohème.* As Oct. 16. |
| Nov. 9 | Chicago. *Manon Lescaut.* As Oct. 21. |
| Nov. 15 | Chicago. *Ballo in maschera.* A. Cerquetti (A), S. Stahlman (O), C. Turner (U), A. Protti (R), W. Wildermann (S), A. Foldi (T); G. Solti, cond. |
| Nov. 18 | Chicago. *Ballo in maschera.* As Nov. 15. |
| Nov. 29 | Chicago. *Tosca.* E. Steber (T), T. Gobbi (S), C. Badioli (Sa); B. Bartoletti, cond. |
| Nov. 30 | Chicago. *Don Carlo.* A. Cerquetti (El), S. Stahlman (V), N. Rankin (Eb), T. Gobbi (R), B. Christoff (F), W. Wildermann (I); G. Solti, cond. |
| Dec. 4 | New Orleans. Recital (?). |
| Dec. 5 | Greensboro, NC. Recital (?). |
| Dec. 8 | New York, Carnegie Hall. Sibelius concert; M. Similä, cond. (Last performance on this US tour.) |

**1958**

| | |
|---|---|
| Feb. 8 | Stockholm, Cirkus. "Stora famnen" (A Big Hug), TV program. |
| Feb. 12 | Borås. Recital. |
| Feb. 17 | Stockholm. *Trovatore.* H. Schymberg (L), K. Meyer (A), E. Sundquist (DL), E. Saedén (F); B. Rigacci, cond. |
| Feb. 23 | Malmö, Municipal Theater. Recital. |
| Mar. 2 | New York, Carnegie Hall. Recital. |
| Mar. 6 | Toronto. Recital. |
| Mar. 9 | Cleveland. Recital. |
| Mar. 12 | Ottawa. Recital. |
| Mar. 16 | Chicago, Orchestra Hall. Recital. |
| Mar. 21 | Fort Lauderdale, FL. Recital. |
| May 20 | Stockholm. *Tosca* (JB replaced by E. Andersson after act 1). B. Nilsson (T), S. Björling (S), S.-E. Jacobsson (Sa); N. Grevillius, cond. |
| June 7 | Stockholm, Skansen. Recital. |
| June 26 | Stockholm, Gröna Lund. Recital. |
| June 29 | London, Royal Albert Hall. Recital. |
| July 8 | Copenhagen, Tivoli. Concert; S. Ehrling, cond. |
| July 18 | Stockholm, Concert Hall. Radio concert; G. L. Jochum, cond. |
| Aug. 11 | Ljusterö. Joint recital w. H. Theorell, violin (benefit for Ljusterö Community Center). |
| Aug. 13 | Gothenburg, Liseberg. Concert; M. Schönherr, cond., and separate recital w. piano. |
| Aug. 14 | Gothenburg, Götaplatsen. "Cabaret Götaplatsen." |
| Aug. 19 | Stockholm, Stadion. European Athletics Championship opening ceremony. |
| Aug. 24 | Åtvidaberg. Recital. |
| Aug. 28 | Helsingborg, Concert Hall. Recital (benefit for spastics). |

| | |
|---|---|
| Sep. 26 | San Francisco. *Trovatore*. L. Price (L), C. Turner (A), L. Quilico (DL), M. Elyn (F); G. Sebastian, cond. |
| Oct. 2 | San Francisco. *Bohème*. L. Della Casa (Mi), E. Ratti (Mu), R. Panerai (Ma), J. Gillaspy (S), G. Tozzi (C); J. Fournet, cond. |
| Oct. 5 | Sacramento (S. F. Opera). *Trovatore*. As Sep. 26 except L. Alvary (F). |
| Oct. 8 | San Francisco, Civic Auditorium. "Fol de Rol" concert (w. other soloists). |
| Oct. 11 | San Francisco. *Trovatore*. As Sep. 26 except I. Dalis (A). |
| Oct. 20 | Chicago. *Trovatore*. E. Ross (L), G. Simionato (A), E. Bastianini (DL), W. Wildermann (F); L. Schaenen, cond. |
| Oct. 24 | Chicago. *Trovatore*. As Oct. 20. |
| Oct. 29 | Chicago. *Trovatore*. As Oct. 20. |
| Nov. 2 | Los Angeles (S. F. Opera). *Trovatore*. As Oct. 11. |
| Nov. 4 | Los Angeles (S. F. Opera). *Don Carlo*. L. Gencer (El), R. Daniel (V), I. Dalis (Eb), F. Guarrera (R), G. Tozzi (F), G. Modesti (I); G. Sebastian, cond. |
| Nov. 8 | Los Angeles (S. F. Opera). *Rigoletto*. L. Gencer (G), K. Hilgenberg (Gv), C. Ward (M), R. Weede (R), L. Alvary (S); J. Fournet, cond. |
| Nov. 15 | Chicago. *Rigoletto*. A. Moffo (G), A. Krainik (Gv), S. Steffan (M), T. Gobbi (R), W. Wildermann (S); G. Sebastian, cond. |
| Nov. 19 | Chicago. *Rigoletto*. As Nov. 15 except C. MacNeil (R). |
| Nov. 24 | Chicago. *Aida*. L. Rysanek (Ai), G. Simionato (Amn), T. Gobbi (Amo), W. Wildermann (R), K. Smith (K); G. Sebastian, cond. |
| Nov. 26 | Chicago. *Aida*. As Nov. 24. |
| Nov. 29 | Chicago. *Aida*. As Nov. 24. |
| Dec. 6 | Stockholm, Cirkus. "För hela familjen" (For the Whole Family), TV program. |
| Dec. 14 | Malmö, Municipal Theater. Concert; S.-Å. Axelson, cond. (unfinished owing to voice problems). |
| Dec. 20 | Stockholm. *Manon Lescaut*. E. Söderström (M), H. Hasslo (L), S. Nilsson (G); N. Grevillius, cond. |
| Dec. 28 | Stockholm. *Manon Lescaut*. As Dec. 20 except A. Tyrén (G). |

**1959**

| | |
|---|---|
| Jan. 4 | London, Palladium. "Sunday Night at the Palladium," TV program. |
| Jan. 20 | Stockholm. *Manon Lescaut*. E. Söderström (M), H. Hasslo (L), S. Nilsson (G); N. Grevillius, cond. |
| Feb. 12 | Stockholm. *Tosca*. K. Dellert (T), A. Wirén (S), S.-E. Jacobsson (Sa); N. Grevillius, cond. |
| Feb. 15 | Stockholm. *Manon Lescaut*. As Jan. 20. |
| Feb. 24 | Ithaca, NY. Recital. (First performance on this US tour, which included about 20 recitals.) |
| Mar. 1 | State College, PA. Recital. |
| Mar. 4 | Boston, Symphony Hall. Recital. |
| Mar. 7 | New York, Hunter College. Recital. |
| Mar. 19 | Tulsa. *Trovatore*. E. Ross (L), J. Madeira (A), L. Warren (DL), N. Moscona (F); G. Bamboschek, cond. |

| | |
|---|---|
| Mar. 21 | Tulsa. *Trovatore*. As Mar. 19. |
| Mar. 24 | Charlotte, NC. Recital. |
| Mar. 28 | Corpus Christi, TX. Concert; J. Singer, cond. |
| Mar. 31 | Beaumont, TX. Recital. |
| Apr. 2 | Baton Rouge, LA. Recital. |
| Apr. 10 | Kansas City, MO. Recital. |
| Apr. 13 | Atlanta. Recital. |
| Apr. 17 | Baltimore. Recital (?). |
| Apr. 20 | San Francisco, Opera House. Recital. |
| Apr. 23 | Berkeley, CA. Recital. |
| Apr. 24 | Berkeley, CA. Recital. |
| Apr. 29 | New York, Carnegie Hall. Joint recital w. G. Johannesen, piano, and Upsala College Choir (benefit for Swedish Seamen's Welfare Fund). |
| May 3 | Stockholm, Engelbrekt Church. Service (Ann-Charlotte Björling's confirmation). |
| May 24 | Stockholm, Skansen. Recital (at Djurgårdsmässan). |
| May 26 | Oslo, University. Recital. |
| May 28 | Skien (Norway). Recital. |
| May 28 | Porsgrunn (Norway). Recital. |
| May 31 | London, Royal Albert Hall. Recital. |
| June 3 | Stockholm, Town Hall. Co-operative Movement Festival. |
| June 6 | Stockholm, Skansen. Recital (on Swedish Flag Day). |
| June 16 | Stockholm, Gröna Lund. Recital. |
| Aug. 20 | Stockholm, Gröna Lund. Recital. |
| Oct. 16 | Copenhagen, Falkonercentret. Recital. |
| Nov. 1 | Stockholm. *Manon Lescaut*. As Feb. 15 except H. Schymberg (M), A. Tyrén (G). |
| Nov. 16 | New York. *Cavalleria rusticana*. G. Simionato (S), R. Elias (Lo), T. Votipka (Lu), W. Cassel (A); N. Verchi, cond. |
| Nov. 21 | New York. *Tosca*. M. Curtis-Verna (T), C. MacNeil (S), L. Davidson (Sa); D. Mitropoulos, cond. |
| Nov. 27 | New York. *Cavalleria rusticana*. As Nov. 16 except Z. Milanov (S). |
| Dec. 8 | New York. *Faust*. E. Söderström (M), M. Miller (S), R. Merrill (V), C. Siepi (Mé); J. Morel, cond. |
| Dec. 11 | New York. *Tosca*. Z. Milanov (T), L. Warren (S), G. Pechner (Sa); D. Mitropoulos, cond. |
| Dec. 16 | New York. *Tosca*. As Nov. 21 except L. Albanese (T), L. Warren (S). |
| Dec. 19 | New York. *Faust*. As Dec. 8. |
| Dec. 22 | New York. *Cavalleria rusticana*. M. Curtis-Verna (S), H. Vanni (Lo), T. Votipka (Lu), C. Bardelli (A); D. Mitropoulos, cond. |
| Dec. 27 | New York, Hunter College. Recital. |

**1960**

| | |
|---|---|
| Mar. 6 | Stockholm. *Trovatore*. H. Schymberg (L), K. Meyer (A), H. Hasslo (DL), E. Saedén (F); H. Sandberg, cond. |
| Mar. 10 | London. *Bohème*. R. Carteri (Mi), M. Collier (Mu), J. Shaw (Ma), G. Evans (S), J. Rouleau (C); E. Downes, cond. |
| Mar. 12 | London. *Bohème*. As March 10. |

| | |
|---|---|
| Mar. 15 | London. *Bohème*. As March 10. |
| Mar. 18 | London. *Bohème*. As March 10. |
| Mar. 29 | San Francisco (Cosmopolitan Opera). *Trovatore*. M. Roberti (L), I. Kramarich (A), C. MacNeil (DL), V. Patacchi (F); C. Moresco, cond. |
| Apr. 1 | San Francisco (Cosmopolitan Opera). *Faust*. D. Warenskjold (M), M. MacKay (S), P. Lisitsian (V), N. Treigle (Mé); C. Moresco, cond. |
| Apr. 3 | San Francisco, Opera House. Recital. |
| Apr. 5 | Pasadena, CA. Recital. |
| Apr. 7 | Santa Monica, CA. Recital. |
| May 8 | Amsterdam. Joint concert w. M. Aarden, F. Giongo, and Amsterdam Opera Chorus; W. Lohoff, cond. |
| June 6 | Stockholm, Skansen. Recital (on Swedish Flag Day). |
| June 9 | Stockholm, Gröna Lund. Recital w. Royal Opera soloists. |
| July 4 | Rättvik. Recital (on US Independence Day). |
| July 28 | Stockholm, Gröna Lund. Recital. |
| Aug. 5 | Gothenburg, Concert Hall. Radio concert; N. Grevillius, cond. |
| Aug. 17 | Ljusterö. Joint recital w. H. Theorell, violin (benefit for Ljusterö Community Center). |
| Aug. 20 | Stockholm, Skansen. Recital. |

# INDEX

449